GREENPEACE

GREENPEACE

How a Group of Ecologists, Journalists and Visionaries Changed the World

REX WEYLER

RAINCOAST BOOKS
Vancouver

Raincoast Books acknowledges the ongoing financial support of the Government of Canada through The Canada Council for the Arts and the Book Publishing Industry Development Program (BPIDP); and the Government of British Columbia through the BC Arts Council.

Editor: Lynn Henry
Cover design: Paul Hodgson
Interior design: Sari Naworynski
Typesetting: Teresa Bubela

CANADIAN CATALOGUING IN PUBLICATION DATA

Weyler, Rex, 1947-
Greenpeace : the inside story / Rex Weyler.

Includes index.
ISBN 1-55192-529-X

1. Greenpeace Foundation--History. 2. Nature conservation.
I. Title.

QH75.W38 2004 333.72 C2004-901974-0

Raincoast Books
9050 Shaughnessy Street
Vancouver, British Columbia
Canada, V6P 6E5
www.raincoast.com

At Raincoast Books we are committed to protecting the environment and to the responsible use of natural resources. We are acting on this commitment by working with suppliers and printers to phase out our use of paper produced from ancient forests. This book is one step towards that goal. It is printed on 100% ancient-forest-free paper (100% post-consumer recycled), processed chlorine- and acid-free, and supplied by New Leaf paper. It is printed with vegetable-based inks. For further information, visit our website at www.raincoast.com. We are working with Markets Initiative (www.oldgrowthfree.com) on this project.

Printed in Canada by Friesens
10 9 8 7 6 5 4 3 2 1

To Lisa Gibbons

"Sail forth — steer for the deep waters only,
Reckless O soul, exploring, I with thee, and thou with me,
For we are bound where mariner has not yet dared to go,
And we will risk the ship, ourselves and all."

— Walt Whitman

CONTENTS

CHAPTER ZERO: WHO GOES THERE? 9

BOOK I: WAR & PEACE

CHAPTER ONE: THE BOMB STOPS HERE 17
CHAPTER TWO: DON'T MAKE A WAVE 55
CHAPTER THREE: ON AN OCEAN NAMED FOR PEACE 91
CHAPTER FOUR: LAW OF THE SEA 133

BOOK II: ALL SENTIENT BEINGS

CHAPTER FIVE: STOP AHAB 197
CHAPTER SIX: THE GREAT WHALE CONSPIRACY 236
CHAPTER SEVEN: MENDOCINO RIDGE 276
CHAPTER EIGHT: YEAR OF THE DRAGON 327

BOOK III: POLITICAL ECOLOGY

CHAPTER NINE: HOTEL PAPA 387
CHAPTER TEN: A NAME FOR WHAT IS NATURAL 438
CHAPTER ELEVEN: LAWYERS OF THE RAINBOW 489
CHAPTER TWELVE: THE SCEPTRE 527

CHAPTER ETERNITY: WERELDRAAD 565

APPENDICES

CAST OF CHARACTERS 576
NOTES & SOURCES 583
INDEX 613
ABOUT THE AUTHOR 623

CHAPTER ZERO

WHO GOES THERE?

"The past is no place to rest ... I never felt that we were making history."

— Harald Zindler

World changers, artists, and social misfits stumble upon history and make the best of it. Or they make a mess of it. In either case, they "touch the flesh of the matter," as Greenpeace strategist Ben Metcalfe once dreamed. Or they discover the soul that has no name and enter the eternal battle between spirit and matter. They're on spirit's side but in matter's grip. "Imagination is seizing power," proclaimed the Paris students in 1968. "Our tears prove we are connected to the suffering of others," said pacifist Joanna Macy. We shall not be moved. Blessed are the peacemakers. Let freedom ring.

World changers aren't planners. The planners come later, with critics and social philosophers to mop up and win awards. Bureaucrats arrive to invent systems. World changers are the mothers weary of seeing their children abused and fathers who have had enough of petty tyrants. Rosa Parks, the seamstress who refused to sit in the back of the bus. Jesus. Buddha.

History declines to wait for the world changers and creators to sort things out, but rather rolls over them with the same inevitable nonchalance with which it buries empires.

ON SPUI PLAZA

At dusk on November 18, 1979, coloured lights blinked on and reflected in the wet Amsterdam streets. A northerly breeze gusted from the east docks, along the canals, and swirled through Spui Plaza. Inside the Hoppe Bar, where the low corner of the wooden door had been kicked raw by a hundred years of beer-drinkers, four men listened to a dark-haired woman tell about the ice caves on Belle Isle, off the coast of Labrador. Susi Newborn, with an immense smile and dark eyes, conjured winds that carried away tents and recalled the crunch of ice pans breaking apart at night. Slender David Moodie, who had sailed his Baltic trader *Fri* into nuclear test zones, sat next to her, his face baked brown after eight years in the South Pacific.

I found them around an upturned cask. Listening intently and gripping glasses of beer sat Robert Hunter, Patrick Moore, and William Gannon, emissaries from the Greenpeace Foundation in Canada, who had come to Amsterdam to help launch the new Greenpeace International. Gannon, thirty-two — a short, dark-haired Irishman, a mathematics and music prodigy, and a Greenpeace accountant these last four years — half grinned with red cheeks. Moore, thirty-two, a stout, curly-headed Canadian, sat back, arms crossed. He had received the first ecology doctorate from the University of British Columbia, sailed on the first Greenpeace boat in 1971, and was the last president of the Greenpeace Foundation. Like Moore and Gannon, I was thirty-two years old. Seven years earlier, in 1972, I had arrived in Canada, a destitute Vietnam War draft resister from Colorado. I had fallen in with these ecological evangelists and sailed on ships with them.

Hunter, the elder at thirty-eight, with a wild frock of auburn hair, sipped his beer and stroked his face with lithe fingers. He had been a crucial journalist on the inaugural mission to Amchitka Island, had stumbled upon the "Warriors of the Rainbow" myth, and had served as president of Greenpeace for four years until he passed leadership on to Moore. He typically dominated pub conversations, but in this case, he leaned across the table, entranced by Newborn's stories.

She told how the crew of a converted Aberdeen trawler, now the *Rainbow Warrior*, had slipped from the clutches of the Spanish Navy after disrupting a clandestine whaling hunt in the Bay of Biscay. "They ordered the ship into the naval dock," she said, "but Bogey stalled. He said he had to sort out some engine problems first. That night, he wouldn't let the military police use our radio to receive instructions, so when they went ashore to talk to their officers, the crew just turned off the lights and slipped out of La Coruña."

When Newborn and Moodie left, Hunter ordered more beer. "We talk about history on the assumption the player's actions are in line with his or her awareness," said Hunter, "but that's wrong. It's the tension that is the interesting part. The warped things that ego made us do. Think how sad it was whenever we screwed up or our little band broke up, like losing a member of the family, and to have old comrades turn on you, betrayals, and the twisted things power did to each of us in different ways. It made us angry at the wrong people. At each other. The way we denied the facts to make ourselves look better. The clinging. It makes me cry," he said, "when I think back how agonized we were at every turn. There was no manual. We made it up."

Dissolving the Greenpeace Foundation was perhaps the most emotionally difficult thing any of us had ever done. Moore remained the most distraught. Hunter cajoled him. "Look, Pat, you get to be an ecologist now instead of an administrator. Isn't that better?"

"Yeah." He looked across the room. A stout, bearded man with tattoos and a tall woman in black leather sat next to us. Above the dark, wooden bar, a huge, twelve-foot painting rested on two stacks of Amstel beer coasters, the top few flared and bent under the great weight. The painting depicted a horse and rider departing a tavern, looked upon by admiring townspeople, particularly a hardy maid holding a large pewter flagon, the light falling on her face. The woman is not cowed by the rider's importance. She looks defiantly at him. I imagined her thinking, "We'll be here when you get back, hero." A white-haired man sat at the end of the bar, sipping bitters. I heard the high voice of a young girl.

"I can be a freelance mindbomber, now," said the spirited Hunter. "Maybe we're not the cutting edge anymore …"

"Maybe we never were."

"… True, but at least we have an eco-strikeforce, which is what we wanted."

"We're ecoholics," said Moore. "No one wants to get off the boat."

"Do everything once," said Gannon, quoting a trusted refrain.

"That was Metcalfe," said Hunter. "Go back to the costume shop. Reinvent yourself. And he was right, of course." Ben Metcalfe had been Hunter's media mentor during the Amchitka voyage. Hunter and Moore learned to be activists from seasoned campaigners like Dorothy and Irving Stowe and Marie and Jim Bohlen, in their fifties when we were in our twenties. "Mindpunks," Hunter had called us.

"Are the whales in good hands?" I asked.

"Sure," said Moore. "Spong, and Joanna, Sidney Holt, Jean-Paul," and he rolled his fingers imagining the legion of committed stalwarts.

"Plenty of hands," said Hunter.

As we drank beer in the Port of Amsterdam, we harboured contradictory grief and elation. Greenpeace represented an idea, as well as an organization, an idea with a role to play at the interface between nature and society. Wish it or not, we had become Gaia's advocates, heirs to St. Francis and Rachel Carson.

"Blood has been spilled," said Moore.

"And psyches," Hunter added.

"It's all accounted for," said Gannon waving his hand.

Later, outside the Hoppe Bar, the bronze street urchin, *Lieverdje*, glistened in the rain in Spui Plaza. History surrounded us. The Law of the Sea in the mind of a young Dutch boy. Anne Frank in her hiding. Only fifteen years earlier, in 1964, in this square, restless youth dubbed "Provos" for their provocative behaviour — staging "happenings," marching with all-white signs, and calling the police on themselves — danced around the statue. The little bronze street youth had been commissioned by a tobacco company, which the Provos taunted as a "Nico-dope syndicate," profiting from addicted youth. Each Saturday night at midnight, as the square filled with beer-drinkers and police, performance artist Robert Jasper Grootveld entered in costume to purge *Lieverdje* and the young audience of Nico-demons. In 1965 they circulated a newsletter, and two years later controlled the Amsterdam City Council. The Provos distributed free, white, community bicycles that became legendary in the city. Before their demise, they inspired street theatre groups in Europe and North America, such as the Diggers in San Francisco, and ultimately the idea of global electronic theatre, Hunter's "mindbomb."

The ironies and tension of history simultaneously provided the gift of history: that we got to live, to see the flourishing Earth, the flying fish, dolphins, caribou, seal pups, the raging sea, the blue light of morning, and the miracle and terror of survival all rolled into one; and that we were blessed with an opportunity to serve it.

FLAG SHIP

We ambled through the tiny streets after midnight. Gannon and I laughed at Hunter ahead of us, his long navy coat flapping in the wind, yapping as if he was a tour guide for Moore, shuffling his gumboots along the Nieuwmarkt canals. A light rain fell. Hunter stood with his hands out, face to the rain. I grabbed his arm and pushed on toward the train station where we could cut through to the docks and find bunks for the night on the *Rainbow Warrior*. His head fell on the damp wool jacket over my shoulder.

We found the central train terminal locked, spoiling our shortcut to the docks. I jiggled each door under the stone columns and the golden clock that read just after three in the morning. At last, we found a dark ramp into the terminal, but a sign read *Geen Ingang*, "No Entrance." We slipped past, up the forbidden ramp, and into the dark interior of the rail yard. In the pitch-blackness, we lumbered across the tracks. Hunter made whooping whale sounds that echoed in the shadows.

"*Wie gaat daar*?" When we heard the voice from deep in the train terminal, perhaps the call of a night watchman, we ran. In a dim light on the far side of the tracks, Hunter leapt and rolled over obstacles as if filming a scene from an action movie. At a vast chain-link fence that disappeared upward into the darkness, we saw no apparent exit.

Our little troupe walked away from the terminal, along the tracks, for twenty minutes, until we reached the end of the fence, and then back along the other side toward the pier. A thick fog had enveloped the ships. Harbour lights sent ghostly rays above us. Invisible vehicles intermittently passed through the fog before us. We did not know where we were and could not see through the mist.

In the damp air at the edge of the road, a gust of wind parted the haze. There, across the road, as the fog opened like a curtain, we saw the huge green bow of the *Rainbow Warrior* slicing into the swirling vapour. Multicoloured flags waved in the North Atlantic breeze. The great white dove of peace, with an olive branch in its beak, painted on the ship by Susi Newborn, flew from the rainbow on the bow. The Earth flag snapped in the wind, high on the mast. The vessel momentarily disappeared in a gust of fog and then reappeared like an apparition, as if it were blinking into mortal existence at this very moment. Hunter opened his arms, faced the wind, and caught the salt air on his face like Hamish Bruce on the bow of the *Phyllis Cormack* in 1975. His coat flapped in the wind. Moore clutched his own coat, peeked up and down the road, and then stepped out to cross. Bill followed. Again, I grabbed Bob's arm, and we crossed the asphalt like Ulysses' paltry crewmen, stumbling down the beach of *Æea*, returning to our ship after Circe had turned us into pigs for our voluptuousness — and all our other lapses and errors — and then, graciously, turned us back into sailors.

We were fragile pilgrims, not makers of history, but participants, lucky to have had the opportunity to meddle in the affairs of the world. The fog erased the waterfront again, except for the great bow of the flagship of the Eco Navy.

"Not *one* miracle, Uncle Bob," Gannon said, "Thousands."

On the far side of the road, we stepped over a cement embankment and stood under the majestic bow. Hunter put his hands together in a little *namasté* before the rainbow and the dove. Moore and Gannon made their way up the gangplank to the deck. Hunter and I followed. On board the ship, Bob Hunter took a Kwakiutl flag in his hand and rubbed it as if touching the magic one last time.

BOOK ONE

WAR AND PEACE

CHAPTER ONE

THE BOMB STOPS HERE

"The Zeitgeist of every age is like a sharp east wind which blows through everything. You can find traces of it in all that is done, thought and written, in music and painting, in the flourishing of this or that art: It leaves its mark on everything and everyone."

—Arthur Schopenhauer

We, the children of Celia Clinton Elementary School in Tulsa, Oklahoma, USA, enjoyed the air raid drills of 1954. We stood in lines on the playground and goofed off. We watched the bald-headed principal come out in his shiny grey suit and herd the teachers as they herded us. The classroom version of the drill had us under our desks, little seven-year-old fingers clasped behind our heads, elbows at the ears, like the fingers and elbows of thousands of other children in Moscow, Frankfurt, New York, and Winnipeg. An alternative strategy was to take the position under the windows. Not *away* from the windows, our teacher explained, but *under* them, so when the glass was blown out, it would sail harmlessly over our heads. I doubted the tactic. I wanted to be far away from any bomb that would blow out our windows and I resolved that when the real one came, I would escape and run home. Then, I thought about my older sister. I would pick her up in grade three. But where was that?

Although I had no sense of it during my childhood, between 1945 and 1965 the world was stitched together like a great quilt. The more obvious threads in that stitching were new technologies such as telecommunications, electronic media, and jet air travel. Less obvious threads were ideas such as human rights and images like the blue Earth turning in space. One thread remained invisible, yet it touched everyone, rich and poor, all creeds and races, touched people to the marrow of their bones and made them global siblings. That thread was strontium-90.

THE GADGET

In August 1939, Albert Einstein wrote a letter to President Franklin Roosevelt from his home on Long Island explaining how uranium fission might create a nuclear chain reaction that could unleash more energy than ever before contemplated. Einstein warned Roosevelt that this process was known in Nazi Germany and that uranium research was underway at the Kaiser-Wilhelm Institute in Berlin. The scientist told the president that the United States had poor uranium deposits and cited Canada, Czechoslovakia, and the Congo as the best-known sources. Germany, however, had stopped the sale of uranium from Czechoslovakia. The primary supply for the United States was in Canada. Einstein was morally distressed by the prospect of building a nuclear bomb, but he feared the horror that might result if Hitler achieved the weapon first.

On December 2, 1942, Einstein's colleagues, Hungarian Leo Szilard and Italian Enrico Fermi created the world's first controlled nuclear chain reaction on a volleyball court in Chicago. The work chilled the bones of many scientists. Szilard wrote to physicists around the world: "[I]t is within our power to construct atomic bombs. What the existence of these bombs will mean we all know." Had they not been confronted by the extraordinary malevolence of Hitler, the small community of nuclear physicists who knew what was about to happen might have convened a meeting with world leaders and dissuaded them. But fear of Hitler provoked the urgency to produce a nuclear bomb. In response to Einstein's letter, Roosevelt sought the advice of American businessman Alexander Sachs, who convinced the president that if a nuclear bomb was going to be built, America should be first.

Roosevelt gave the order: Build it.

After Hitler's demise in the spring of 1945, Polish physicist Joseph Rotblatt quit the US bomb project and became known as the first antinuclear "peacenik." But the momentum could not be stopped. By July, the physicists and technicians under the direction of J. Robert Oppenheimer had built the bomb. The first test went by the code-name Trinity, a reference to Christian theology that unsettled some insiders. The official schedule of events referred to the bomb as "the Sphere." The scientists themselves never referred to a bomb. They called their creation, "the gadget."

At 8:00 a.m. on the morning of July 14, technicians pulled a canvas tent from a 100-foot metal tower in the New Mexico desert on the western slope of the San Andres Mountains, and lifted the gadget to the top. Ukrainian engineer George Kistiakowsky inspected the detonators. At 17:00 the test was ready. The gadget sat poised for two days while the army made a sweep of the area.

US Army Col. Stafford Warren headed the Medical Section responsible for safety from radioactive fallout. The mild southerly breeze was considered ideal for dispersing the radioactivity. Local inhabitants were identified and catalogued by Col. Warren's troops. One family with a small child, the Raitliffs, lived in a canyon downwind from the site. They were considered most at risk from dangerous levels of radiation but were not notified. Troops stood by in case an evacuation was deemed necessary.

On Sunday, the day before the test, director Norris Bradbury suggested that everyone "Look for rabbits' feet and four-leafed clovers." He asked in a memo, "Should we have the chaplain down there?"

On the night before detonation, the scientists huddled and discussed the temperatures that might be generated and the neutrons that would be emitted. Although they had performed thousands of calculations, they did not know what the explosive yield would be. Most believed the explosion would be in the range of a thousand tons of TNT, similar to the 1917 munitions explosion that destroyed North Halifax, Nova Scotia. In Halifax harbour on December 6, 1917, the French ship *Mont Blanc*, carrying wartime cargo, collided with the Belgian freighter *Imo*. The hold of the *Mont Blanc* contained 225 tons of TNT, guncotton, benzol, picric acid, and thousands of ammunition rounds, approximately equivalent to 1,000 tons of pure TNT. The explosion caused complete destruction inside a mile radius, sent metal shrapnel flying four miles, and broke window glass sixty miles away. Two thousand people were killed, and North Halifax was destroyed. To calibrate their bets, the scientists used the Halifax explosion, the greatest known human-made explosion of the time, as a unit of measure. "One Halifax" was a one-kiloton explosion.

The bets came in: one Halifax, ten, fifteen. Whereas a traditional TNT explosion might yield temperatures of a few thousand degrees, the atomic scientists expected the gadget to yield temperatures as high as tens of millions of degrees. Neutrons with enough energy to kill a person might radiate over a mile. The human health effects depended on how the radioactivity would be dispersed by the wind. Edward Teller, leader of the Theory Group, bet Enrico Fermi that the bomb would exceed an equivalent of forty Halifaxes, or 40,000 tons of TNT.

There was a question about the free oxygen and hydrogen in the atmosphere exposed to the intense heat. Fermi was concerned that the atmosphere could ignite. If so, would it incinerate the entire test site? Would it burn up the atmosphere of the whole planet? Fermi took bets on whether or not the atmosphere would ignite, much to the annoyance of Lt. General Leslie Groves, Military Director of the project. Groves called the governor of New Mexico and alerted him to prepare for a possible evacuation of the state.

Just before midnight, troops took up positions along local roads intersecting the state highways into Almagordo and Albuquerque. Monitor teams stood by in San Antonio, Roswell, and Fort Sumner. The army placed 628 soldiers in trenches at various calibrated distances from ground zero, under the command of Brigadier General Thomas Farrell. These were the guinea pigs.

In the predawn of Monday, July 16, Fermi stood at his observation post at the Base Camp, 10 miles from ground zero. At 05:30 he turned away from the explosion site. He saw the flash of light race across the desert and felt the heat from the bomb on his exposed skin. The temperature at the centre of the explosion was four times greater than at the centre of the sun. The pressure was 100 billion times normal atmospheric pressure, strong enough to create a massive crater and fissure the rock below ground. Fermi turned back to look at the explosion, his face protected with dark welding glass. He saw an enormous flame that morphed into a pillar of smoke and expanded on the top, an image that he could only describe as a gigantic mushroom. The column rose beyond the clouds to a height of 30,000 feet. He counted off the seconds. The blast of air reached him 40 seconds after the light, and he quickly calculated the velocity of the wave at 900 miles/hour and estimated the force was equal to at least 10,000 tons of TNT, a 10-kiloton blast. Ten Halifaxes. Later calculations put the explosion closer to 20 kilotons. General Farrell, six miles south of ground zero, reported that soldiers were knocked flat by the blast of air. The flash was seen 150 miles away in Juarez, Mexico.

On July 27 monitoring data reached General Groves' office, showing that the Raitliff family, less than a mile from the test site, had received a 60-rem dose of radiation, enough to cause immediate nausea and later cancers or early death. General Groves was concerned and asked the army for permission to visit the family "to see how they feel." The army refused, and no one from the military ever visited the Raitliffs. The soldier guinea pigs received massive doses of radiation and some would later suffer from leukemia, thyroid cancer, and other ailments.

The day after the test, Fermi's colleague Leo Szilard drafted a petition to US president Truman, signed by 68 scientists, opposing the use of the bomb on moral grounds. The appeal was too late. The Hiroshima bomb was in the final stages of assembly. On Monday, August 6, exactly three weeks after the Trinity test, Hiroshima was destroyed. On August 7, Truman sent a message to Japan: "Surrender or be destroyed." He received no response. The US military urged a quick victory before the Soviets arrived in Japan. On August 9 Nagasaki was destroyed. Japan surrendered five days later.

World War II was over. Fifty million people had been killed, an average of 25,000 people per day for six years. The two nuclear fission bombs that ended the war dashed any hope that weaponry could protect humankind from itself. An estimated 200,000 citizens perished in Hiroshima and Nagasaki. Radiation sickness and cancer among the *hibakusha*, the survivors, claimed thousands more over the next two decades. The Hiroshima bomb was the equivalent of 12 Halifaxes, the new standard for human devastation. "Science has torn from nature a secret so vast in its potentialities that our minds cower from the terror it creates," American Bernard Baruch told the new United Nations Atomic Energy Commission. "... Adequate defense does not exist."

LUCKY DRAGON

First light was common starting time for a tuna fisherman on the *Fukuryu Maru*, but on the first day of March 1954, radio operator Aikichi Kuboyama rose in the pre-dawn and entered the galley at 03:40. Crewman Yoshio Misaki was already up and had tea water boiling. The *Fukuryu Maru*, the "*Lucky Dragon*," had followed the tuna 3,000 miles southeast from its homeport of Yaizu, south of Mount Fuji. The prevailing northeast trade winds had subsided, the morning breeze was westerly, and the air balmy in the tropical mid-Pacific. The 91-ton trawler drifted north of Rongelap Atoll, 85 miles east of Bikini Atoll, among the Marshall Islands. Aikichi saw the cabin window catch the yellow light. The sun is up, he thought.

But he was confused. It was too early, not yet 4:00 a.m., and — he cocked his head and peaked through the glass — that's west. *Am I turned around*? Aikichi stepped outside to get his bearings, and the sea lit up brighter than day. Yoshio followed him onto the deck. The light felt strange to Yoshio, heavy, as if it was pushing the *Lucky Dragon* down into the sea. Red, yellow, and white lights sparkled like jewels on the western horizon. *What peculiar light is this*? The fishermen looked across the decks to the east. The sun was not yet up. The yellow light faded and the western horizon turned a dull, pulsing red, like an iron ingot cooling in the air. The fishermen had watched the lights for seven minutes when they heard a low, rolling sound. Perhaps a volcano had erupted. They feared a tsunami, but no giant wave appeared.

Pikadon, said crewman Sanjiro Masuda, but no one took notice. By 7:30 a.m., as the fishermen worked with winches and nets, a fine, white ash drifted over them. The ash rained down for several hours, settling as a white dust on the deck. Aikichi Kuboyama left the radio room and felt the ash between his fingers. It was alien, mysterious. Crewmembers collected the ash in bags for souvenirs. By mid-afternoon, Aikichi had a headache and felt unusually tired. Some crewmembers felt nauseous. Yoshio's eyes were inflamed and painful. He wiped his face clean with his shirt but the itching got worse. By dusk, all hands were sick, most had lost their appetite, and some were vomiting.

The fishermen began to throw their souvenir dust back into the sea. They washed the ash from the deck and washed their faces with seawater.

Some climbed to the top of the wheelhouse to get free from the dust and breathe fresh air. Few slept well. Some could not sleep at all for the itching and nausea. The fishermen went to work the next day, but by the second evening, some men had developed open sores on their bodies. Within a few days, the men were jaundiced and their exposed skin had turned a dark brown. Many were half blinded. They cursed the dust from the sky and called it "death ash."

The crew could not work, and the captain turned the trawler northwest for Japan, seven days running if all went well. Two weeks after the morning that the sun rose in the west, the crew of the *Lucky Dragon* made landfall at the island of Mikura Jima, rounded the point of Iro Zaki into the bay of Surruga Wan under the watchful eye of the great volcano Fuji-san, and put in at the port of Yaizu. They were home. The families had been warned that the crew was ill, but they were not prepared for what they saw. Aikichi had lost most of his hair. Yoshio was nearly blind with swollen eyes. Faces were burned and open wounds had appeared on the blackened skin of the fishermen.

The medical examiners in Yaizu were overwhelmed. They sent the crew north to hospitals in Tokyo, where doctors recognized the sickness. They had seen it among the *hibakusha*, the survivors. Doctors from Hiroshima and Nagasaki arrived to inspect and treat the crew of the *Fukuryu Maru*. All twenty-three fishermen had radiation sickness. Their eyes were jaundiced from the failure of their swollen livers. They had low counts of blood cells and their bone marrow slowly deteriorated.

A reporter from the *Yomiuri Shinbun* caught wind of the story and poked around the hospital asking questions. On March 16, the newspaper announced what everyone close to the case suspected. Crewman Sanjiro's guess had been correct. *Pikadon*. Atomic bomb. The tuna fishermen of the *Lucky Dragon* were victims of radiation, the very molecules of their blood, bones, and flesh bombarded with billions of invisible missiles. The reports located the source of the radiation to the west of *Lucky Dragon's* position, most likely Bikini Atoll.

The US Atomic Energy Commission (AEC) had moved their nuclear testing station to Bikini Atoll two years earlier, after blowing up most of Enewetak Atoll 500 miles to the west. AEC chairman Lewis Strauss denied that "death ash" existed. The skin lesions reported by the fishermen in Tokyo, Strauss said, "are thought to be due to the chemical activity of the converted material in the coral rather than to radioactivity."

An analysis at Shizuoka University near Yaizu revealed that the *Lucky Dragon*'s eight tons of tuna and shark were contaminated. Other boats arrived on the coast of Japan with radioactive fish, but the fish were sold in four major cities before a warning went out. Engineers in lab coats walked into fish markets in Nagoya, saw the needles on their hand-held monitors rap against the little aluminum pegs, and discreetly vanished. Men in protective suits came back to clean up the contaminated markets. Some fifty tons of fish were confiscated and destroyed each month during the spring. Warnings and rumours spread, people stopped eating seafood, and the fishing industry of Japan collapsed.

Several weeks later, AEC chairman Strauss, under the weight of evidence, admitted that a nuclear test had been conducted at Bikini Atoll. He assured the American public that US citizens from the test station were okay, the local islanders were okay, and that the problems of the Japanese fishermen were "minor." Strauss reported that the *Lucky Dragon* was inside a US prohibited zone and had probably entered the area for purposes of espionage.

Strauss' comments were a ruse. The logbook of the *Lucky Dragon*, made available to the press, showed that the tuna trawler had been some 40 miles outside the US zone. Did the Americans know the fish boat was there? The Japanese government wanted to know. Surely the US military knew the direction of the wind and knew the islands downwind were populated. The Americans had relocated Bikini Islanders to Rongelap. Did they know what was going to happen? These questions were discussed in the hallways of the Tokyo hospitals. Were the islanders and the fishermen of the *Lucky Dragon*, like the American soldiers ten years earlier, used as guinea pigs?

TRITIUM BONUS

The nuclear test Castle-Bravo on March 1, 1954, had been no ordinary nuclear bomb. It was something special, designed by the US military in response to the Soviet Union's first nuclear test in 1951. The Castle tests were for a new, high-yield hydrogen fusion bomb, hundreds of times more destructive than the fission bombs that destroyed Hiroshima and Nagasaki. Fission bombs split heavy atoms like uranium, converting some of the matter into energy. Fusion bombs compress light atoms like hydrogen, also converting matter to energy.

The fusion bomb was trickier. American designers had been stumped by a problem of how to compress the fuel, liquid lithium and heavy hydrogen. The nuclei of atoms repel each other with tremendous electrostatic force; to fuse them together requires a temperature of millions of degrees. Edward Teller conceived the idea to create these unearthly temperatures inside a uranium fission reaction, to build a fusion bomb within a fission bomb. On paper, it worked.

The American generals knew the Soviets were working on a similar plan, and they were determined to reach the goal first. Once the theory problems were solved, the challenge was to acquire the rare lithium-6 needed for the calculated reaction. Teller's team learned how to convert common lithium-7 to lithium-6, by eliminating one neutron from the nucleus. They built a lithium enrichment plant, designed a prototype bomb, and tested it in 1952 at Enewetak Atoll near Bikini. The explosion, 500 times the power of the Hiroshima bomb, completely destroyed a small islet, leaving only a mile-wide crater.

The Soviet Union successfully tested a hydrogen fusion bomb in 1953, temporarily drawing even in the arms race. The American designers built a bigger bomb for the Castle-Bravo blast. They removed 170 residents from Bikini Atoll and sent them to Rongelap Atoll, telling them they were making a great contribution to science and to humankind. The thermonuclear bomb was detonated seven feet above the Bikini reef, on March 1, 1954, at 03:45, just as Yoshio Misaki made tea on board the *Lucky Dragon*. The physicists had predicted a "maximum possible yield" of 8-megatons, about 600 times the power of the Hiroshima bomb. Eight thousand Halifaxes.

The prevailing trade winds would have blown the fallout away from Rongelap, toward New Guinea. On the morning of the blast, however, the breeze blew from the northwest toward Rongelap and the other atolls of the Marshall Islands. The military did not evacuate or even warn the islanders. No warning went out to boats that might be in the area. Despite the wind, the military chose not to postpone the test. Too many important people, with busy schedules, were involved, and the Russians were on their heels. But there were more odious reasons. Military documents released thirty years later confirmed that the islanders were being used to test the effects of radiation.

When Castle-Bravo exploded, Edward Teller and the assembled physicists were astonished. The actual yield was twice their "maximum possible" yield of 8-megatons; a 17-megaton explosion, the largest in history. The high yield of the bomb was due to an unpredicted reaction of the more stable lithium-7. This common isotope was expected to be inert, but when high-energy neutrons from the fusion reaction collided with lithium-7 atoms, some of the atoms were fragmented into a helium atom and a tritium atom. This extra tritium fed the fusion process and increased the explosive yield. Teller later called this the "tritium bonus."

The explosion left a crater in the atoll reef well over a mile wide and 250 feet deep. The mushroom cloud rose 25 miles into the sky, with a stem five miles thick, and a 60-mile cap at the top. The wind direction, the unexpected yield, and failure to evacuate local islanders resulted in massive radioactive exposure to the people on Rongelap, Rongerik, Ailinginae, and Utirik atolls.

The exclusion zone around Bikini Atoll was immediately increased to a radius of 425 miles, encompassing 567,000 square miles of ocean. US personnel on Nan Island were trapped in a bunker by deadly radiation levels. Twenty-eight Americans were immediately evacuated to medical facilities. The local islanders were evacuated three days later, with symptoms similar to those of the fishermen of the *Lucky Dragon*, most notably skin lesions and hair loss.

The US military was thrilled with the test. New weapon designs were completed in July 1955, production began in December, and 275 new Mk-21 thermonuclear warheads were added to the US arsenal within the year.

In his hospital bed in Tokyo, *Lucky Dragon* radio operator Aikichi Kuboyama had trouble breathing and his liver failed. He was being poisoned by the radioactivity in his blood. His friend Yoshio suffered in a bed nearby, nauseous and jaundiced. Their skin lesions refused to heal. Treatment was complex guesswork. The doctors did not know how to address the problem of dosage from inside the body. Citing national security, the US military refused to reveal the contents of the fallout. Throughout the summer, as all twenty-three fishermen remained in Tokyo hospitals, the panic over contaminated seafood swept Japan, and fishermen were out of work. Japan petitioned the US for compensation for the gutted economy and medical costs, but the US denied responsibility.

Disarmament sentiment in Japan was aroused. A group of women from Tokyo collected 32 million signatures on a petition demanding an end to nuclear tests. The Science Council of Japan called for "the abolition of mass-destructive nuclear weapons." The *hibakusha* from Hiroshima and Nagasaki constructed peace parks and memorials so no one would ever forget the destruction caused by the atomic bombs.

By August, Aikichi could barely speak in a whisper. He told his doctors that he could not breathe but the doctors did not know how to help him. In September, just six months after he first felt the death ash between his fingers, Aikichi Kuboyama stopped breathing and died, the first human casualty of the hydrogen fusion bomb.

BEARING WITNESS

In the spring of 1954, common citizens around the world began to hear strange new words like "fallout" and "genetic mutation." The post-nuclear disarmament movement that started in Japan soon linked up with older pacifist traditions around the world. Two of the millions influenced by the nuclear bomb were Irving and Dorothy Strasmich (later "Stowe") in Providence, Rhode Island. In 1954 the young couple had been married for a year and Dorothy was pregnant with their first child. They were from middle-class, socially active Jewish immigrant families. Dorothy Anne Rabinowitz had been born in Providence in 1920. Her Russian mother was a Hebrew teacher, her Galician Polish father a jeweller and active Zionist. As a young woman, Dorothy was aware of the Holocaust in her family's homeland and met distinguished Jewish political activists, like the future first president of Israel, Chaim Weizmann, at their dinner table. She attended Pembroke College, majored in English, and pursued a career in social work.

Irving Strasmich was born in Providence in 1915, studied economics at Brown University and law at Yale. He studied social philosophy and read Marx and Engels, but was not attracted to Communism, which he felt had abandoned freedom for political power. He grew up believing in Franklin Roosevelt's New Deal, the egalitarian hope for working-class people within the structure of American capitalism. Out of law school, he helped draft anti-trust legislation, joined the Civil Air Patrol, earned his pilot's licence, and joined the Office of Strategic Services, the OSS, President Roosevelt's precursor to the CIA. Strasmich believed that America could successfully export democratic freedom around the world. He dedicated himself to this cause in Washington D.C. throughout World War II. However, he was so upset by the Hiroshima bomb that he broke down in tears in front of the White House and returned home to Rhode Island.

In Providence, Strasmich played the violin and tuba and hung out at the Celebrity Club, where he made recordings of Louis Armstrong and Duke Ellington. The black jazz musicians invited the Jewish lawyer into the National Association for the Advancement of Coloured People, the NAACP. In 1951, he met Dorothy Rabinowitz, and they were married in 1953, with a rabbi presiding and renowned British jazz pianist George Shearing as best man. The reception dinner was held at NAACP headquarters.

Inspired by its tradition of informed citizen action, Dorothy joined the Women's International League for Peace and Freedom. In the Providence Child Services office, she took initiative to mediate staff and management disputes and organized the first social workers chapter of the American Federation of State, County and Municipal Employees.

Irving worked as a tax lawyer and offered pro bono services to citizens called before Senator Joseph McCarthy's US House Un-American Activities Committee. He was particularly dismayed that pacifism was considered unpatriotic. An avid letter writer and early riser, he thought nothing of knocking off letters to President Eisenhower, Secretary of Defense Charles Wilson, and the editors of the *New York Times* or the *Washington Star,* all before breakfast.

Dorothy and Irving were unsettled by the militarism of the American and Soviet governments. They joined the Quaker Society of Friends, became committed pacifists, and joined protests against nuclear weapons. Irving and Dorothy were attracted to the Quaker idea of "bearing witness," which meant not only witnessing events, but also speaking out, bearing witness to others. The Quakers believed that a witness to atrocity becomes an agent of change.

SOLDIER PACIFIST

Canadian RAF pilot Eustace Bennett Metcalfe was twenty-five in 1945 when news of the bomb reached the Royal Air Force flight school at Wheaton Aston in Staffordshire, England. Metcalfe and the other pilots were "retreads," old soldiers in young men's bodies, who had already survived thirty or forty missions over Berlin. Metcalfe provided advanced training to younger pilots about to fly off into the teeth of the Pacific war. Their biggest nightmare was to end up in the South Pacific jungles fighting the Japanese. They had heard stories of brutality, suicide grenade bombers, crucified prisoners, and exotic tropical fevers. The terrified pilots celebrated on the night they heard about the bomb. It wasn't until two years later, when he was working as a journalist in Paris, that Metcalfe learned about fallout and the full devastation of Hiroshima. By this time he had overcome what he called the "soldier's mentality," and felt uneasy about nuclear bombs. He referred to the bomb as "a period in history." Not a period like the Romantic period, he explained to his friends, but a full stop, the dot at the end of a sentence.

Ben Metcalfe was born in Winnipeg, Manitoba, Canada, on October 31, 1919. His mother was true Cockney, born within the sound of the Bow Bells in East End London, his father a surveyor from Yorkshire. Emulating Tom Sawyer on the shores of the Assiniboine River, he supplied his family with fresh fish and partridge during the Depression. He idolized Charles Lindbergh, left home at fourteen, and made his way to England to join the Royal Air Force.

Metcalfe entered the RAF at sixteen and trained as an aerial gunner. In 1937, he boarded a troop ship to Karachi with the Number-2 India Wing, 39 Squadron. At nineteen, he gripped a Lewis machine gun in the rear of a two-seat, open cockpit Hawker Demon biplane, searching for rebel bands loyal to the Indian Congress Party that wanted to boot the British out of India. Rebels sat in the hills and sniped at the RAF planes, but the worst Metcalfe saw was a soldier who took a bullet in his buttocks.

When Congress Party lawyer Mohandas Gandhi refused to cooperate with the British war effort, Metcalfe found himself in the middle of a pacifist movement that made the British look like hypocrites. To avoid bombing Indian villages as instructed, Metcalfe and his Hawker Demon pilot dropped their bombs in fallow fields while villagers watched and waved. The airmen's defiance was probably an act of treason under British law, but Metcalfe and his pilot were on Gandhi's side.

In 1942 Metcalfe fought in the Battle of El-Alamein against German general Rommel's desert army. After witnessing the machine-gun death of a close friend, he walked alone in the foothills near his squadron barracks in Yemen. The wild flowers in bloom after a spring rain touched off a deep memory of wandering the prairies of Manitoba. He'd had enough of war. He wanted to be a writer.

After his discharge from the RAF, Metcalfe applied at newspapers in London, but had to settle for work at an ad agency on Bond Street. He wrote promotional copy and read Dickens and Ian Fleming novels. The British Foreign Office hired him at the age of twenty-seven, and he felt like James Bond escorting journalists through occupied Germany. From seasoned news correspondents he learned how to ask tough questions and uncover decisive stories. While visiting a community of 10,000 liberated Jews in Belsen, he noticed that the Jewish guards wore curious new uniforms. He poked around and discovered that Israel would soon be declared a nation. He passed the scoop on to grateful journalists, who broke the story in Europe. However, when he learned about the British sending Russian prisoners back to certain death under Stalin, no one seemed interested. "It's not the kind of story they're looking for, Ben," Canadian journalist Ross Munro told him. "They want stories about dismantling the German war machine and rebuilding Europe."

Metcalfe resigned from the Foreign Office and made for Paris with a glowing reference from an editor at the *Herald Tribune*. He stayed in the swank St. Petersburg Hotel, mixed with incognito royalty, and took drinks at the British officer's club, but was not able to land a newspaper job. At a British embassy party, he met a stunning, self-assured Belgian, Mademoiselle Baya de Frahan. He and Baya were soon married, moved to a hotel they could afford on Boulevard St. Germain, and Metcalfe began to work on a detective novel. With 90 quid to his name, he learned to nurse a cup of coffee with Jean-Paul Sartre and Simone de Beauvoir at Les Deux Magots café. Hemingway frequented the Café de Flore nearby. The existential movement unfolded around him, but the 90 quid melted away. He and Baya had a baby, Sophie, and he finally got a job as sports editor at the *Continental Daily Mail* in Paris. But Metcalfe wanted to cover the real news, like Molotov stonewalling the West at the Moscow Conference.

"I still haven't touched the flesh of the matter," he told his writer friends.

He sold a story to Reuters News Agency about Canadian uranium supplying the US nuclear bomb effort, but he and Baya remained desperately poor. He was entitled to the Canadian War Veteran's Grant but had to return home to receive it, so in 1950, Ben and Baya settled in Winnipeg. Metcalfe took a job at the *Winnipeg Tribune*, and the couple had a second daughter, Charlotte. However, Baya soon tired of the Canadian prairies and returned to Paris with the girls.

Winnipeg reporters traditionally gathered after work for bootleg Black Label scotch, and at one of these sessions Metcalfe met Dorothy Harris, a reporter for the *Winnipeg Tribune*. Harris had been born Dorothy Hrushka, to Ukrainian-Polish parents, but her father had changed the family name to fit into Canadian society. Ben and Dorothy shared a passion for good journalism. They departed for Europe in 1953 and filed stories for the North America Newspaper Alliance. Their daughter, Michelle, was born in London. Shortly thereafter, in 1954, the massive thermonuclear bomb test spread radioactive elements like strontium-90 around the globe. The Metcalfes, like Dorothy and Irving Strasmich in Providence, investigated the strange new threat of radiation.

They returned to Manitoba, where Ben Metcalfe found work as editor of the *Flin Flon Daily Reminder*. Ross Munro, whom he had met years earlier in Germany, recruited him to *The Province* newspaper in Vancouver. The young couple arrived on the west coast of Canada in 1956. Their son Michael was born that year and Christopher two years later. The *Province* assigned Metcalfe to a story about Axel Wennergren, a Swedish Nazi industrialist who had supported Hitler and was now engaged in hydroelectric deals with British Columbia Premier W.A.C. "Wacky" Bennett. Metcalfe discovered that a dam in northeastern British Columbia would flood the homeland of the impoverished Sekani Native nation. The story inspired in Metcalfe the two themes that would define his career: ecology and the duplicity of the ruling elite in protecting the status quo.

THE FUTURIST

In 1947, six-year-old Bob Hunter already knew about the destructive power of the bombs that could blow up anything. Hunter was born in St.

Boniface, Manitoba, the French district of Winnipeg, on October 13, 1941, the same year Rachel Carson wrote her first book, *Under the Sea*, and the United States entered World War II. Hunter's father was an instructor in the Commonwealth Air Training School; his mother was a devout French Catholic. When his father went away to the war, Bob and his mother moved to the Air Base in Aylmer, Ontario. His only sibling, a brother, Don, was born there in 1943. Young Bob Hunter spoke French at home and English with his playmates in Aylmer. After the war, his mother moved back to Winnipeg, to the English district of St. Vital. She took the two boys to the Church of St. Boniface in the French district, although the family now spoke English at home.

Hunter's father returned from the war and worked as a tanker-truck driver. Bob admired his father as a war hero, but his father cringed to talk about it. The war had changed him, made him dour and aloof. The boy rarely saw him. His father was either on the road or at the Legion pub with his soldier buddies. When Bob was six, his father took him on a road trip in the tanker. He sat on his father's lap as they drove across the prairies. Bob pretended to steer, while his father smoked a cigarette with one hand and held a beer in the other. "What's that?" asked Bob, pointing straight ahead.

"That's the horizon," his father said.

"How far to the horizon?" Bob wanted to know.

"It's a long way to the horizon, Bobby," his father told him. In the hotel room that night, the boy's father introduced an "Aunt" and Bob slept on the sofa. After that trip, Bob rarely saw his father, and then one day he was gone, out of their lives. His mother worked as a waitress to support the two boys. They were a close, affectionate family of three. Bob was quiet and thoughtful. He had learned to read well before he started school, and he devoured comic books and adventure stories. At twelve, he read science fiction novels and filled notebooks with his own handwritten stories. In school, he ignored his lessons while composing "novels." Most teachers lost patience with him, but he impressed his art and English teachers.

By the time he was a teenager, his shelves were crammed with well-worn books. By age fourteen, Hunter had filled ten notebooks with his own handwritten science fiction stories. His mother bought him an Underwood typewriter for his fifteenth birthday, which became his most treasured possession. With his new typewriter, he wrote a 75-page story called "The Long Twilight," in which a boy is kidnapped by a flying saucer and ends up alone in the universe. The young author designed and illustrated the covers of his books, and even contrived book review quotes. One hand-illustrated cover declares, "Bob Hunter's best book yet."

He learned about fallout and radiation. Talk of the bomb and the evil intentions of the Communists terrified the youth. He read the newspapers and picked up the idea of the "military-industrial complex" from American President Dwight Eisenhower. He read about US nuclear weapons arriving in West Germany. The Soviet Union had their own atomic bombs and the United States had vowed to build bigger bombs. US Army General James Gavin told the US Senate that a Soviet nuclear attack could leave vast regions of the United States uninhabitable, but that the US could do the same to Russia. Physicist Edward Teller assured the American Joint Chiefs that civilization could survive a global nuclear holocaust. This was little comfort to young Bob Hunter in Winnipeg.

The news stories inspired him to write "After the Bomb," a short, futurist novel about a post-nuclear-holocaust civilization. The book included illustrations of a city with an elevated road he called a "skyway." The eccentric student quit school in 1958, after Grade 11, but received an arts bursary to study painting at the University of Manitoba. Although he had not graduated, he went to his classmates' graduation ceremony and, with dramatic flair, burned his bursary letter on the steps of the school. His mother was horrified and cried. The teenager, however, had no interest in art school. He wanted to travel, and he knew he was going to be a writer.

STRONTIUM-90

In Providence, Rhode Island in 1955, Irving and Dorothy Strasmich had a son, Robert, and the following year a daughter, Barbara. Irving practised law and Dorothy became president of the Rhode Island public employees union. They attended Quaker meetings and followed the news of blacks boycotting the bus lines in segregated Montgomery, Alabama. From the example of Gandhi, Irving believed that citizens acting with integrity and courage could defeat powerful forces that would turn the world into their own private battleground. From the American Friends Society he adopted the idea of "Replacing the Death culture with a Life culture," a rally cry he would champion for the rest of his life.

The global fallout from the Bravo nuclear test the previous year had changed the balance of human emotion around the world. In London, Bertrand Russell had formed a union of international scientists opposed to nuclear bomb tests. On his deathbed, Albert Einstein drafted a disarmament Declaration with Linus Pauling, signed by fifty-two Nobel laureates. Soviet nuclear physicist Andrei Sakharov defied Soviet censorship and wrote about the health dangers of low-level radiation. A young Harvard biologist, Dr. Barry Commoner, collected deciduous teeth from children in St. Louis and documented the absorption of strontium-90, a radioactive by-product of nuclear explosions. Although no one had quite articulated it yet, the peace movement and the ecology movement began to merge.

In the summer of 1955, the Wenner-Gren Foundation for Anthropological Research held a symposium in Princeton, New Jersey, on the theme "Man's Role in Changing the Face of the Earth." Lewis Mumford, one of three chairmen, linked global problems to personal awareness when he declared: "We have not yet created the sort of self, freed from nationalistic and ideological obsessions, capable of acting within this global theatre." The UK Fellowship of Reconciliation circulated Mumford's speech to its 12,000 members around the world. Irving and Dorothy Strasmich were among the thousands who were stirred my Mumford's message: Civil defence was a fraud; drilling children to hide under their desks was ludicrous; the arms race was a waste of resources. And radiation kills.

In the US, federal civil defence drills were made compulsory, but on June 15, 1955, Dorothy Day of the *Catholic Worker* and Abraham Johannes Muste from the War Resisters League refused to take shelter in New York. "I refuse to prepare for nuclear war," said Dorothy Day. Twenty-eight people were arrested, but the protests spread to Boston, Philadelphia, and Chicago. In Providence, Irving and Dorothy took notice. Ben and Dorothy Metcalfe joined protests in Vancouver. And young Bob Hunter wrote his post-nuclear-war stories in Winnipeg.

Citizens became pacifists, and pacifists became activists. The usually apolitical *Scientific American* wrote that the hydrogen bomb had "become too big to be entrusted any longer to the executive sessions of rulers in Washington." The change in human attitude had been building for decades.

Gandhi had given the disenfranchised more than hope, he had given them a strategy. The change had been prepared at every level, but it needed a catalyst, a common theme, to give it form. Strontium-90 in baby's milk was just the sort of horrifying image that everyone on the planet could understand, and a threat to which they would respond.

Irving and Dorothy were among those nudged toward activism. Following the lead of Dorothy Day, Irving refused to participate in civil defence exercises in Providence, but to his disappointment he was not arrested. Providence had a long tradition of public activism. Before the Boston Tea Party, the citizens of Providence had launched the American Revolution when they torched the British schooner, M.M.S. *Gaspee* on June 9, 1772. Providence was the North American refuge of the Quakers, who were chased from England and then from Boston by the Puritans. The colony in Providence had been founded on religious freedom by Roger Williams, who wrote, "... The blood of so many hundred thousand souls of Protestants and Papists, spilt in the wars of present and former ages, for their respective consciences, was not required nor accepted by Jesus Christ the Prince of Peace."

A. J. Muste and other Quakers formed an activist wing of the American Friends Service Committee and launched *Liberation* magazine, which declared itself independent of right/left politics. In 1957, Muste's Committee for Nonviolent Action entered the Nevada nuclear site, where eleven pacifists were arrested, convicted, and served jail time. Irving Strasmich was inspired by the fact that the modern disarmament movement integrated class, religion, and cultural differences, and that business leaders and union leaders stood side by side at peace marches. In 1958, with three-year-old Robert and two-year-old Barbara in tow, Irving and Dorothy picketed President Dwight Eisenhower during a speech at Fort Adams, Rhode Island. Increasingly, Irving Strasmich spent more time on disarmament work and less time on his legal career. "Prepare for life, not for death," he insisted.

AN ICON BORN

In the United Kingdom, Bertrand Russell convened a public meeting at Central Hall in Westminster and convinced the peace groups to collaborate under a new name, the Campaign for Nuclear Disarmament (CND). They marched from London to the Aldermaston nuclear weapons plant in Berkshire over the Easter weekend, 1958. This march gave birth to an icon.

Russell asked artist Gerald Holtom, a graduate of the Royal College of Arts, to create a logo for CND. His first sketches used the Christian cross within a circle, but priests in the group objected. Holtom, a conscientious objector during World War II, created variations on the cross design and hit upon the idea of incorporating the naval semaphore code letters "N" and "D" for Nuclear Disarmament. A flag straight up and one straight down formed the "D." Two downward diagonal flags formed the "N." Holtom saw in the image that emerged a representation of himself in despair, with arms down and palms out. The idea reminded him of Goya's famous painting of a peasant with his hands held out before a firing squad, the image of the simple citizen resisting violence. He formalized the drawing with a serif swirl and drew a circle round it. The Campaign for Nuclear Disarmament had its logo, which the world later adopted as the peace symbol.

During the Easter march, protestors placed the new symbol on 1,500 round placards on sticks. Half the placards were black on white, and half were white on green. Just as the church's liturgical colours change over Easter, so the colours on the placards were changed, black and white on Good Friday and Saturday, and green and white on Easter Sunday: "From Winter to Spring, from Death to Life." American Bayard Rustin, an associate of Martin Luther King, marched with the pacifists to Aldermaston and carried the peace symbol back to the United States. Civil rights marchers adopted it and later anti-Vietnam War demonstrators picked it up. Some American servicemen put the peace sign on their helmets in Vietnam. The Campaign for Nuclear Disarmament did not copyright the image and explicitly offered it free for public use. Peace groups all over the world adopted the design. When Soviet tanks rolled into Prague in the spring of 1968, the icon greeted them on city walls. South Africa tried to ban it, American Christian fundamentalists claimed it was Satanic, but the image endured.

On May 2, 1958, former US Navy captain Albert Bigalow sailed his 32-foot ketch, the *Golden Rule,* from San Pedro, California, bound for Enewetak Island nuclear test site, bearing the peace symbol across the Pacific Ocean. The US Coast Guard intercepted the ship and arrested

Bigalow. In Honolulu, the American government charged him with "criminal conspiracy." Supporters in seven American cities, as well as in Montreal and London, staged demonstrations in support of Bigalow and the *Golden Rule*. The innovative campaign launched the era of seagoing protest.

THE ADVOCATE

In 1960, nineteen-year-old Bob Hunter left Winnipeg with a friend and his beloved typewriter to see the world. He had vowed to himself to "be at sea" by the time he was twenty-one. The boys headed for Australia, but lost their money playing blackjack in Las Vegas and arrived in Los Angeles broke. Hunter was awed to see the manifestation of his make-believe elevated "skyway" in the massive concrete freeways. With no money for passage to Australia, he took a bus to Vancouver, Canada, lived on hot dogs and water in a skid row hotel, and began a novel. He hung out in the library, discovered Jack Kerouac's *On the Road* and Marx's account of the London poor in *Das Kapital*. Destitute, he located an aunt and uncle, who took him in. Hunter passed the summer working in a bottle factory and writing. In the fall, he hitchhiked back to Winnipeg. His first world tour was over.

At the age of twenty, Hunter completed his novel while working in the Burns & Company Packing House, an abattoir. He could not wash the smell of blood from his body, and he quit in disgust. He was arrested for selling encyclopedias without a licence and spent a night in jail in Flin Flon, Manitoba. Finally, he showed his stack of manuscripts to the managing editor of the *Winnipeg Tribune* and was hired on. He bought a suit and showed up for his first day as a reporter, only to discover he was a copy boy. He spent a year covering municipal council meetings until he got his break.

When the editor asked, "Who wants a byline?" Hunter leapt from his desk, raced across the newsroom, and stood at attention. "Hunter," said the editor. "Of course." The assignment, a skydiving story, required that he leap from an airplane, which he did, but on landing he seriously injured his back. Decades later, the chronic back pain became a reminder of the karmic consequences of his ego. In the meantime, his name was in real printer's ink, which was like a shot of heroin for the writer.

In 1962, Hunter read enough of Rachel Carson's *Silent Spring* to understand that "in nature, nothing exists alone." Although chemical companies ridiculed Carson, newly elected US President John Kennedy established a Science Advisory Committee to study the impact of toxins in the environment. Hunter, however, had not yet embraced ecology or political protest. He was more interested in the work of Hemingway and Thomas Wolfe. He sported a goatee and wore a black turtleneck, like the beatniks. As his twenty-first birthday approached, he left Winnipeg to fulfill his vow of going to sea. He dreamed of the cafés of Paris, where he imagined communing with the existential literary crowd.

Through a travel agent friend he secured a $90.00 ship's passage from Florida to Genoa, Italy. In October, he made his way to Key West and boarded a rusting, black Yugoslav freighter, the *Vares*. Two days before his twenty-first birthday, he was at sea. As the ship headed south across the Straits of Florida, it suddenly changed course with no explanation. The last land slipped from sight and the ship bucked into a mid-ocean storm. No one among the Slavic crew spoke English, so Hunter had no idea where he was headed until he saw islands off the port bow and heard a crewman say "Azores." *What happened to Cuba*? Unwittingly, Hunter had run into the middle of the biggest news story on the planet. The freighter had sailed into the midst of the Cuban missile crisis, literally between two flotillas in a nuclear showdown. Hunter figured this out when he read a *Time* magazine at a café in Rome. "Hey," he told other American expatriates, "I was there."

After the crisis, the fear of nuclear war gripped the world, and civil defence drills resumed. Kennedy's negotiators had convinced the Soviets to turn their ships around, and war was averted, but the scare accelerated the peace movement. Anti-war songs like *Blowin' in the Wind* appeared on the Top-Twenty charts in America and Britain, supplanting teen hits like *It's My Party*. Western culture changed, almost imperceptibly, but inexorably.

Bob Hunter, the stylish beatnik, made it to Paris with his typewriter, rented a room on the Left Bank, and sat down to write his existential novel of a young man's life in Paris. The problem was, he had no life in Paris. He had only his little room and his walks to the market for cheese and wine. He ventured along the Boulevard St. Germain, but Sartre and Hemingway were long gone. He met a woman, an American writer, who claimed to be well known but would not reveal her name, for fear, she claimed, that he would use it in his novel. She invited him to move in with her, but Hunter got nervous about the arrangement and fled to London.

In London, he began what would be his first published novel, *Erebus*, a searing, dark farce about finding love while working at the abattoir in Winnipeg. The writer supported himself with work at a medical library, where he met a beautiful co-worker with long, auburn hair. Something about her air of confidence fascinated him, and he summoned the courage to talk to her. Zoe Rahim was a member of the Campaign for Nuclear Disarmament and had participated in marches to the Aldermaston nuclear weapons plant. She now took Hunter to disarmament rallies. At Speaker's Corner they listened to Bertrand Russell expound the philosophy of pacifism. Zoe moved in with Hunter, and he continued to write his novel, although his ideas had begun to shift away from bleak existentialism. Zoe became pregnant, they married, and took a short honeymoon in Wales. They joined in the 1963 peace march to Aldermaston, Hunter's first political protest.

The couple flew to Winnipeg, where their son, Conan, was born and Hunter returned to a reporter's job at the *Winnipeg Tribune*. He transformed himself from Beat generation literati to Vietnam-era social reformer. He became an advocate for native rights, single mothers, and struggling artists. He had an instinct for the scoop, a flair for personal drama, and his stories regularly made the front page. He completed *Erebus* and sent it to publisher McClelland and Stewart in Toronto, but he was already inspired by a new intellectual direction. He read Herbert Marcuse's *One-Dimensional Man*, a book that held the sort of sweeping worldview he appreciated. He began using Marcusean language like "repressive desublimation" to describe what he witnessed all around him, citizens distracted from social problems by entertainment and political posturing.

In 1965, Zoe became pregnant with their second child, and Hunter landed a reporter's job at the *Singapore Times*. He resigned from the *Tribune* and prepared to leave, but the job fell through at the last minute. Unemployed, they headed west to Vancouver, where Hunter got a job at *The Province* and started out again as a copy boy. However, when *Erebus* was published and earned a Governor General's Award nomination, he moved up in the newsroom pecking order to a reporter's job at the *Vancouver Sun*. When a popular columnist quit to enter politics, the editor held a contest for the columnist position. Hunter won, again leapfrogging past journalists who bristled at the precocious twenty-four-year-old with his published novel, literary acclaim, and now his own column.

Hunter used his column to distill and refine new ideas. He wrote about edgy psychologists like Carl Jung, was particularly enamoured by media guru Marshall McLuhan, and began writing about a new "global consciousness." He gleaned from Max Born that "… a measurable quantity is not a property of a thing, but a property of its relation to other things." This holistic view reiterated Rachel Carson's ecology. Hunter's column became one of the most popular features in the newspaper. Mingling with Vancouver intellectuals, he met Ben Metcalfe, now with a Canadian Broadcasting Corporation (CBC) radio show. When cultural heroes such as Allen Ginsberg or Theodore Roszak came to Vancouver, Hunter had a press pass to meet them and the intellectual capacity to engage them in serious conversation.

Bob and Zoe Hunter's daughter, Justine, was born in 1965. For their first real holiday, they packed up the two children in their Volkswagen van and drove to Mexico. Hunter had long hair and a beard. Mexican police, looking for *mordida*, a payoff, arrested him on five occasions. In Mazatlan, bandits stopped the family at a roadblock, but because they had no shoes, the bandits considered them poor, *los campesinos*, and let them go. On their way home from Mexico, they stopped in San Francisco and experienced the consciousness revolution in full bloom.

FULL-TIME PACIFISTS

In the spring of 1960, Irving and Dorothy Strasmich joined peace activists in Groton, Connecticut, where the Electric Boat Company was building the *USS Ethan Allen*, designed to carry sixteen Polaris nuclear ballistic missiles. Seventy-four-year-old perennial arrestee A. J. Muste had recently attracted media attention by scaling a fence at a ballistic missile plant near Omaha, Nebraska. His group, the Campaign for Nonviolent Action, had now targeted the Polaris submarine. A march from Boston to Groton passed through Providence where Irving and Dorothy hosted the marchers, distributed leaflets, and talked to the media. David Dellinger, a World War II pacifist, attempted to enter the docks but was rebuffed. Changing tactics, a small group paddled boats in front of launching submarines, swam to the vessels, and boarded them by climbing up ropes. They were arrested and received nineteen-month jail sentences. However, some workers offered to quit their jobs if the pacifists could find them alternative employment. Just as it had become possible to be a patriotic pacifist, workers believed they could be against war and still be loyal union members. A thin wedge of pacifism had entered the American psyche.

Ed Sanders, founder of the Peace Eye Bookstore in New York City, and lead singer for the irreverent rock band, Fugs, boarded one of the submarines at Groton and spent thirty days in jail. Sanders and other radicals brought cultural rebellion and street theatre to the peace movement. The Polaris campaign signalled a new era of media-savvy activism jazzed up with cheeky impertinence, celebration, music, and humour.

Irving and Dorothy could see that the Vietnam War was heating up, they did not want to pay taxes for war, and they wanted to raise their children in a country that was at peace, so they decided on New Zealand. In the spring of 1961 they flew to Auckland, never again to live in the United States. As a part of his changing worldview, Irving decided to change the family name. He identified more with Quaker pacifism than with his Jewish roots. He did not like the aggressiveness of the new Zionists in Israel against their Semitic cousins, the Palestinians. He took Lewis Mumford seriously, believing that what humanity needed were *fewer* "nationalistic and ideological obsessions." He and Dorothy came up with the name "Stowe." Harriet Beecher Stowe had been a Quaker and an advocate for women's rights and the abolition of slavery. It was an American name that rang of freedom. In New Zealand, Irving and Dorothy Strasmich became Irving and Dorothy Stowe and dedicated their lives to pacifism.

They joined a Quaker group in Auckland and met local pacifists who had launched a campaign to halt French nuclear weapons tests in Polynesia. The Stowes met other Americans in New Zealand who had fled the United States, some chased out by Senator McCarthy and others, like themselves, who left in protest of American militarism. One expatriate, Bob Stowell proposed the idea that the campaign against the French tests could include "sailboats, rafts, or even small aircraft placed in the testing area by private organizations."

Irving was concerned when he learned that one approved US strategic plan was a nuclear first-strike against the Soviet Union. He rose early most mornings to write letters to President John Kennedy and Secretary of Defense Robert McNamara. In November 1963, however, the assassination of Kennedy devastated him. Irving was skeptical of the Warren Commission investigation and not surprised to see the Vietnam War escalate within a few weeks. While young Robert and Barbara went to school and ran barefoot through the green hills of New Zealand, Irving wrote letters to his fourth president and staged demonstrations at the US Embassy in Auckland. However, when New Zealand and Australia sent troops to Vietnam in 1965, the Stowes turned their protests on the New Zealand government, accused them of being "lackeys of the Americans," and looked for a new home.

In April 1966, Irving stopped in Vancouver, British Columbia, on his way back to New Zealand from a visit to Rhode Island. The city was bathed in sun, the fruit trees were in bloom, and the blue water and snow-capped mountains soothed his heart. Canada was not sending troops to Vietnam and was quietly accepting American pacifists who were evading the military draft. Irving and Dorothy decided to move their family to Canada.

In the summer of 1966, Irving, Dorothy, eleven-year-old Bobby, and ten-year-old Barbara arrived in Vancouver. They took an apartment in the busy West End section of downtown. Young Barbara was horrified. She'd grown up barefoot in New Zealand and she accused her parents of taking her to New York. But the family soon settled across the water in the quiet neighborhood of Point Grey, near the University of British Columbia, surrounded by like-minded intellectual, peace-loving Canadians and more than a few expatriate Americans. They purchased a two-storey, wooden home on Courtenay Street, surrounded by cottonwood, maple, and oak trees, near acres of woods. From the large upper-storey deck off their kitchen, they could survey downtown Vancouver and the mountains on the northern shoreline of Burrard Inlet.

Irving, now fifty-one years old, with a receding hairline, told Dorothy that the time had come for him to be a full-time pacifist. Dorothy found a job in family services, and Irving registered as a private estate planner, but he would dedicate the rest of his life to stopping the bomb and bringing about peace. His morning letter-writing sessions started earlier than ever. Their quiet home on Courtenay Street would soon become a hub of monumental, global significance.

ENGINEER FARMER

By 1967 Vancouver was a haven for American draft evaders. That spring, Jim and Marie Bohlen and their draft-age sons, Lance Bohlen and Paul Nonnast, arrived in Vancouver from the United States. Jim Bohlen was born in the West Bronx in 1926 and grew up shuttling between the homes of his estranged parents. He studied diligently and avoided the street gangs. From his paternal grandfather, who lived on a New Jersey farm, he learned rudimentary mechanics and farming. After high school, he spent a year at New York University but dropped out and enlisted in the US Navy. On the deep-sea tug *USS Recovery*, he travelled around the Pacific Rim and cleared warships from Tokyo harbour and from the defeated Japanese garrison at Attu Island at the western end of the Aleutians.

After his navy service, Bohlen completed an engineering degree at New York University, married Anna Arndt, an art student from Pennsylvania, and became father to a son and a daughter. Bohlen tried his hand at farming in Pennsylvania, but lost money on a corn crop and gave up. The family toured Europe and returned to New York at the end of 1950. Bohlen was twenty-four and desperate for work when he found an engineering job with a defence contractor on Long Island. He met famed engineer R. Buckminster Fuller and helped build plastic geodesic domes, designed to protect US radar installations in the Arctic. He later started his own company, making fibreglass-reinforced plastic caskets, but the business failed. His marriage faltered and he separated from his wife and children. At a civil defence workshop in Florida, Bohlen saw pictures of the Hiroshima victims. The idea of a civil defence against such weapons seemed hopeless, and he wanted to do something to end the nuclear arms race.

In 1958, on the Easter weekend that the peace symbol was born in London, Bohlen marched with a group of Quakers from Doylestown, Pennsylvania, to Philadelphia City Hall. During the march he talked to Marie Nonnast, a woman he had known in high school. Marie was a nature illustrator, a member of the Sierra Club, and a committed pacifist. She was also the single mother of a ten-year-old son, Paul. She had vowed the day Paul was born that he would never go to war. Marie took Jim Bohlen to Society of Friends meetings and convinced him to join the Sierra Club. In 1964, they married.

Jim Bohlen found work at Hercules Power Company in New Jersey, but he struggled to reconcile a nagging contradiction with his ethics. His employer had received a military contract to design an anti-personnel, shoulder-fired rocket. The missiles were to be filled with small, razor-sharp metal blades, designed to maim victims, not necessarily kill them, thus taxing the enemy's battlefield medical resources. Bohlen could not bear the thought of contributing to such a sinister device, and he resigned from the company in the summer of 1965.

When Marie's son Paul became eligible for the military draft in 1967, Bohlen flew to Vancouver to investigate job opportunities. Within a few hours of submitting his resumé to the University of British Columbia forest products laboratory, he had a job. That summer, Jim, Marie, three children, and two dogs moved into their new home on West 19th Avenue, in the Dunbar neighbourhood, near the university and close to where the Stowes lived in Point Grey. The treed neighbourhoods of Kitsilano, Dunbar, and Point Grey are on a peninsula where the University of British Columbia (UBC) sits on the bluff at the extreme point. The Fraser River empties into the Gulf of Georgia to the south, and steep mountains rise up from Burrard Inlet to the north. Between the university and the mountains, linked by bridges over the inlets, is the city of Vancouver.

On a Saturday morning in the spring of 1968, Jim and Marie Bohlen travelled over the Burrard Bridge into the heart of the city for an anti-war demonstration on the lawn of the Provincial Court House. A coalition of church groups called End the Arms Race sponsored the event. The eclectic Vancouver crowd included the British Columbia Voice of Women, a leftist alliance called the Internationalists, street theatre groups like the Vancouver Diggers, American draft resisters, ecologists, hippies, wide-eyed students, and young radicals such as Paul Watson and Walrus Oakenbough. Anarchist Rod Marining and his Rocky Rococo street theatre company staged spontaneous comic performances with Town Fool Joachim Foikis. The counterculture's "provisional mayor," writer Stan Persky, read poetry. UBC undergraduate biologist Patrick Moore was there with his friend, filmmaker Fred Easton. UBC whale researcher, Dr. Paul Spong came with his wife, Linda, and their infant son, Yashi. Ben and Dorothy Metcalfe recorded speeches for his CBC broadcast. Bob Hunter interviewed participants for his *Vancouver Sun* column. Zoe Hunter clung to their toddlers, Conan and Justine. Bob Cummings, Dan McLeod, and Julie Palmer from the city's new radical tabloid, the *Georgia Straight*, sold newspapers for ten cents. Although most of these people did not yet know each other, they soon would.

The Bohlens knew almost no one, but they looked for the Quakers among the maze of protestors. Finally, from a distance, they spotted a Quaker banner and made their way through the crowd, past the jugglers and musicians. Holding the Quaker sign were Irving and Dorothy Stowe. Jim and Marie Bohlen approached and introduced themselves. The four elder pacifists spent the day together and soon became devoted friends.

THE SHIRE

Vancouver was a quiet backwater in global affairs, but by the mid-1960s, no city in Europe or North America stood immune from the cultural upheavals roused by the fear of nuclear bombs and the unsightly mess in Vietnam, and stimulated by electronic media. In Vancouver, long-haired hippies, artists, and revolutionaries mixed in the red brick coffee houses downtown and in the rainbow-painted organic juice bars on Fourth Avenue, the hippie row that ran from the downtown bridges to the university neighbourhood of Point Grey. Fourth Avenue, in the neighbourhood of Kitsilano, was lined with psychedelic shops, record stores, and scores of young people from the prairies, eastern Canada, and the Maritimes, who had found their way west in pursuit of rock music, marijuana, and sexual liberation. American draft dodgers slipped north into Vancouver. Québécois arrived from Montreal. There were Chinese and Japanese communities, Buddhist temples, Tibetan meditation centres, Quakers, Unitarians, a dock front community of boat-builders and fishermen, an underground beat poetry tradition, and a radical network of young back-to-the-land farmers and old-style conservationists who called themselves "ecologists."

A small city with a global citizenry, Vancouver could almost be forgotten in the burgeoning cultural clashes of the era. I was in Berkeley, California, by this time, where riot police tear-gassed anti-war demonstrators, military jeeps patrolled the streets, and barbed wire perimeters surrounded government buildings. Paris, Zurich, Amsterdam, Prague, Chicago, Newark, and hundreds of other cities were the sites of high-profile cultural revolution.

But even quiet Vancouver simmered with tension. Conservative mayor Tom Campbell clashed regularly with hippies in the parks. Four Vancouver "Diggers," fashioned after a San Francisco political theatre group, were arrested in front of the Vancouver Public Library in the middle of the day, for vagrancy. Such attempts to restrain the emerging youth culture only inspired more defiance.

In March, 1967, Vancouver's alternative community staged the first "Easter Be-in" at the city's magnificent Stanley Park. The Retinal Circus opened, featuring rock music, light shows, and psychedelic drugs. Young vagabonds brought copies of *Provo* from Amsterdam and *Guerilla* from Detroit's South End, newspapers that blended politics with humour, beat poetry, jazz, theatre, and rock music. Inspired by these publications, math student and aspiring poet Dan McLeod founded *The Georgia Straight*, named after the inside passage between Vancouver Island and the mainland. "Every weather forecast and gale warning in the Strait of Georgia will give us free publicity," McLeod reasoned.

The first issue of the irreverent tabloid appeared on May 5, 1967, carrying front-page stories about the vagrancy arrests, the Vietnam War Crimes Tribunal, and the Provo movement in Amsterdam. A week later, McLeod was arrested and jailed for "investigation of vagrancy." Mayor Tom Campbell, known to the hippies as "Tom Terrific," suspended the newspaper's business licence, but McLeod won a legal challenge and continued to publish. In his newspaper, McLeod ridiculed the mayor, flaunted free speech, and goaded the establishment. Within a year, weekly circulation reached 60,000, and *The Georgia Straight* became a voice for the emerging youth movement. Bob Hunter supported the newspaper in his *Vancouver Sun* column. Student radicals Paul Watson and Walrus Oakenbough became correspondents. Ben Metcalfe submitted articles.

Metcalfe's news story about the hydroelectric power reservoir that flooded Sekani First Nation families from their homeland shocked Vancouverites and inspired local businessman Jack Diamond to send food donations to the Sekani. Toronto newspapers picked up the story, Cabinet Minister Jack Pickersgill blurted out, "I'm not interested in sick Indians," and Metcalfe became a Canadian media celebrity.

Ben and Dorothy Metcalfe lived in an upscale West Vancouver neighbourhood, on the north shore of Burrard inlet. But Metcalfe participated in a government program to help juvenile offenders and there he met troubled teenager Bob Cummings. He liked the boy's spirit, mentored Cummings in journalism, and got him a job at *The Province*. Cummings later became a columnist at *The Georgia Straight*. In the summer of 1968, Cummings and McLeod were arrested and charged with criminal libel for awarding a Pontius Pilate Certificate to Judge Lawrence Eckhardt, who had convicted poet and "provisional mayor" Stan Persky on charges of loitering in a public park. The arrest made Cummings a local hero. Allen Ginsberg and folksinger Phil Ochs visited Vancouver to stage a benefit for Persky, McLeod, Cummings, and *The Georgia Straight*, which faced obscenity and libel charges. Radio host Jack Webster grilled Ginsberg about his support for the radicals. Ginsberg insisted the issues were "free speech, freedom to assemble, and freedom of the press." Webster cut him off. "I don't want to get bogged down in technicalities," he said. Ginsberg laughed. "Into the technicalities of sitting in the park and publishing a newspaper? It's not very technical, Jack."

In the fall of 1968, Persky invited American Yippie leader Jerry Rubin to Vancouver to support the embattled *Georgia Straight*. Although the mayor called Rubin an "outside agitator" and blamed him for stirring up trouble, he failed to grasp the global nature of the upheavals that were taking place. As Marshall McLuhan had revealed, we now lived in an electronic, yet still tribal, global village, connected but diverse. When Martin Luther King and Robert Kennedy were assassinated that year, American cities erupted in anger, but so did London and Paris. French students transcended traditional politics in their own way. On the walls of the Sorbonne students painted: "*l'imagination au pouvoir*." Imagination is seizing power. The French students did not advocate a political party seizing control of the culture. They glimpsed the deeper revolution of the human spirit.

Later that summer, the Yippies staged a Festival of Life at the Democratic National Convention in Chicago, but the affair turned bloody as police and demonstrators rioted. Rubin, now one of the most famous defendants in America, joined University of British Columbia students protesting the university's complicity in the Vietnam War. With Persky, Cummings, and renegade UBC researcher Paul Spong, the students burned dollar bills. Rod Marining performed with his Rocky Rococo political satirists.

Seventeen-year-old radical Paul Watson was there with his friends in the Vancouver Liberation Front. Bob Hunter recorded events for his newspaper column. The students claimed that members of the faculty, who professed to be against the war, had failed to support them, so the mob occupied the Faculty Club and demanded disclosure of UBC military research. The faculty refused to talk with them, police surrounded the building, some 200 people stayed for the night, and the numbers swelled the next day. Local musicians entertained the crowd, creating a Festival of Life North. Unlike in Chicago, however, in Vancouver the protest remained a festival. Police held back, at the request of the faculty. Marining was elected "non-leader" of the Northern Lunatic Fringe of Yippie. Persky, the "mayor" of the hippie community, negotiated with the administration and police. Persky, Rubin, and Rod Marining gave speeches. The protestors finally made a deal with the administration for future discussions about university military research, the university promised no prosecutions, and the students departed.

The little protest, however, had galvanized the Vancouver radicals and united the inner-city crowd with the university students. The university neighbourhoods of Point Grey and Kitsilano were known locally as The West Side. The downtown working-class neighbourhoods were the East Side. A central meeting point between these two subcultures was the Cecil Hotel Pub on Granville Street, just over the bridge from Kitsilano. The dark, smokey pub had no windows, and entrances were labeled "Ladies and Escorts" and "Gentlemen," vestiges of antiquated drinking laws. Pool balls cracked and the jukebox blasted out "Chain of Fools" by Aretha Franklin, "Dock of the Bay" by Otis Redding, and "Revolution" by the Beatles. Beer-stained terrycloth covered the small, round tables. Glasses of draft beer were 25 cents. McLeod, Cummings, and Hunter often sat in the intelligentsia corner and talked. Dr. Paul Spong would come in after work at the Vancouver Aquarium. On a particular afternoon following the UBC protest, Hunter and Cummings jousted over the merits of the so-called "establishment" media that Hunter represented and the "underground" *Georgia Straight.* Hunter believed that the alternative press forced the traditional press to become more open, but he also felt that Cummings and the *Georgia Straight* "indulged in too much leftist rhetoric and posturing." Cummings claimed that Hunter had it easy because he was "protected by the establishment."

Hunter was clearly an intellectual leader in the counterculture in Vancouver. He talked about "systems theory" and "old operational modes of thinking," and insisted that "to address systemic global problems, we need a large-scale change in human mentality." From Paul Sears Hunter had picked up the idea that ecology was subversive because it called into question the entire philosophical foundation of Western philosophy and civilization. "Ecology suggests that engineering solutions won't solve our problems," Hunter said. "The organic world has its own laws."

Hunter was working on his first non-fiction book, in which, he told his friends, he would "rough in the outlines of the greatest revolution in human history," a revolution that would involve electronic media, collective shifts in human consciousness, and ecology. He grew convinced that the next big change in society would not be a social or political revolution but an ecological revolution. He told his friends at the pub, "Ecology is the thing."

Compared to the upheavals in Paris, Chicago, or Prague, the cultural stirrings in Vancouver were mild. Vancouver — with its tree-lined streets, seaside parks, and gardens — was an idyllic paradise. Hunter saw his adopted city as a quiet refuge from the main stage of history. In his *Vancouver Sun* column, he referred to Vancouver as "the Shire," in reference to J. R. R. Tolkien's tranquil community of Hobbits, far from the centres of power and conflict.

STRANGE AND PROPHETIC DREAMS

In the summer of 1969, a rusted, red Chevy pick-up rattled up the driveway of Bob and Zoe Hunter's new farmhouse on the Fraser River, south of Vancouver. Bob Hunter's thrice-weekly column had made him a celebrity. He enjoyed the attention at the pub in town, but sought refuge on the farm, where he could write in peace. He had written a series of columns about chemical and biological weapons, the United States making anthrax, and Canada's clandestine participation. He described marijuana as "mild ... non-addictive," less of a problem than alcohol. He called Barry Commoner's *Environment* magazine, "the first major vehicle for organized resistance to pollution." It was expected that such ideas would appear in the underground press; to read them in an establishment newspaper was shocking.

Hunter sat on his front porch under the greengage tree, the yellow-green plums starting to ripen. Zoe worked inside, and the children toddled about the house. The writer squinted at the pick-up. *Who could this be*? He turned back to his book, *The Hidden Dimension*, Edward Hall's famous treatise on spatial perception in human culture. Hunter prided himself in keeping up with the visionary writers of the era. Jacques Ellul's *The Technological Society* and Paul Ehrlich's *The Population Bomb* sat in the stack of books beside him. He was working on his sweeping analysis of culture and ecology, *The Enemies of Anarchy*. The title of his book derived from his thesis that the "real anarchists" were the military nation-states that ran willy-nilly about the planet with a "me first" attitude, ignoring the laws of nature, blowing up Pacific atolls, and devastating environments. From Betty Friedan and the feminist writers, Hunter realized the new consciousness would be more sensual than intellectual, an idea that Hall's book emphasized.

But ecology was the thing. A massive oil well blow-out off the coast of Santa Barbara, California in January had been an example of what Hunter considered the cost of industrial anarchy. A Union Oil Company well, six miles off shore and 3,500 feet below the ocean floor erupted, created fissures in a fault line, and disgorged 200,000 gallons of crude oil into the ocean. The corpses of seabirds, seals, and dolphins had washed ashore. Such disasters, he thought, implied that society had a deadline. Humanity might not endure a slow evolution of perception. New technologies were too slow to save society from its myopia. Without a fundamental change of vision, Hunter believed, environmental disruption, climate change, and war over resources could foreclose options and destroy the culture before humanity woke up to create the technologies that were needed.

He suspected, however, that a social transformation was emerging. His book predicted a paradigm shift as dramatic as the Copernican shift four hundred years earlier. "Copernicus figured out that the earth wasn't at the centre of the universe," Hunter had often expounded in the pub. "Well, ecology teaches that humans aren't the centre of life on the planet." This realization, he thought, would change everything from psychology to politics.

He looked up from his book as the red pick-up approached. Mounted on the back was what looked to him like a Hobbit house, with a roof of cedar shakes, a crooked stovepipe, and a macramé God's-eye in the window. The truck stopped in a stir of dust, and a wild-looking hippie with a full blond beard and long hair stepped out of the cab. The visitor wore beaded moccasins and a brightly coloured skullcap. Hunter was used to odd people tracking him down. His column attracted people with progressive ideas. He had read Carl Jung and believed he should pay attention to synchronicity. He cocked his head and watched the smiling hippie walk toward him. "Hi," said the stranger. He carried a small book in his lithe fingers. "Hi," said Hunter, getting up, stepping from the porch, and shaking his hand. The visitor explained that he was a dulcimer-maker, an itinerant craftsman. He thrust forward the little book. "This is for you," he said. "It will reveal a path that will affect your life."

On the cover of the slim volume an Indian warrior sat below what appeared to be an eagle and a buffalo. The dulcimer-maker explained that these were animal spirits counselling a chief who had gone into the wilderness to fast and pray for spiritual guidance. Hunter looked at the title: *Warriors of the Rainbow, Strange and Prophetic Dreams of the Indian People*. He thumbed through the book as the visitor watched silently. There were references to peyote ceremonies and Buddhist teachings, quotes from the Bible, the Koran, and the Bhagavad-Gita. He read an underlined passage: "No mind is a powerful mind … unless it is a seeking mind." Pictures of the authors on the back cover revealed a smiling Aleut from Alaska and a biologist from Stanford University. "Yeah, okay," Hunter said to the stranger, "thanks."

The dulcimer-maker nodded. He did not attempt to engage Hunter in conversation, which was a surprise and relief to the writer, who wanted to return to his work. The visitor asked if he could take some old fence posts he had spotted out in the field, explaining that the wood might make excellent dulcimers. "Sure," Hunter said. The stranger thanked him and departed. Hunter watched the pick-up bump back down the gravel driveway. He thumbed the little volume as he walked into the house, read a few passages, and filed the book on his shelf with the other spiritual books in his library, *The Teachings of Don Juan*, the *I Ching*, and *The Tibetan Book of the Dead*. He went back to his reading and later scribbled in his notebook: "All human societies are transitional. The only thing certain about a status quo is that it will not endure."

LOOK IT UP

In later years it would be difficult to imagine, but the word "ecology" was not well known at the end of the 1960s. Few colleges offered ecology courses. High school students did not perform ecology experiments. But quietly, a shift in perspective had reverberated around the globe. In New York, four frustrated scientists formed the Environmental Defense Fund to bring environmental abuses before the courts. The recognition that we were our own biggest enemy had awakened a deeper, perhaps ancient, knowledge of who we really are. Before her death in 1964, Rachel Carson, in her unassuming manner, had pointed out, "The more clearly we can focus our attention on the wonders and realities of the universe about us, the less taste we shall have for destruction."

In Vancouver, Irving Stowe now worked full-time as a househusband, father, and activist. Although he viewed Canada as a liberal, democratic country, his New Zealand experience had made him skeptical. A little research revealed that Canadian companies mined uranium for American weapons and some forty Canadian universities provided military research to the war effort. At Suffield, Alberta, inside a 1,000-square-mile Defense Research Establishment, Canadian contractors devised chemical and biological weapons for export to the United States, including napalm and Agent Orange used in Vietnam.

Stowe learned that the United States had begun a series of nuclear tests on Amchitka Island in the Aleutians, the first one detonated in 1965 and another scheduled for the fall of 1969. *There's nowhere to run*, he realized. He vowed to make his stand against nuclear bombs right here, in Vancouver. He contacted the Canadian Committee for Nuclear Disarmament, founded in Edmonton in 1962, and began to build a network. He directed his letter-writing campaign toward newly elected Prime Minister Pierre Trudeau, urging Canada to dissociate from the American war in Vietnam. His letters were articulate and respectful, but he was relentless to the point of being pushy. He allowed no deflection of his questions and leveraged every answer into a larger question. He encouraged others to get involved. "He's a hard man to say 'No' to," Dorothy warned their new friends.

Irving and Dorothy Stowe found Vancouver culture refreshing. They soon found their natural allies among the environmentalists. They read

Hunter's columns in the *Vancouver Sun*, attended meetings at the Quaker House on Tenth Avenue, and led peace marches to the US Embassy. They met Deeno Birmingham from the BC Voice of Women and Lille d'Easum, who wrote about nuclear radiation. Some of the older pacifists considered the sexually explicit art of the *Georgia Straight* crude, but they embraced the libertarian politics and the free speech issues. Irving wrote his first article in the *Georgia Straight* in 1969. He was media savvy, and used Hunter, Metcalfe, and Cummings to publicize his causes. The Stowes and Bohlens socialized and talked about organizing the anti-war sentiment in Vancouver.

Ben Metcalfe introduced a CBC television show about the outdoors, *Klahanie*, and used it to launch a media campaign to halt the flooding of the nearby Skagit River Valley by the Seattle power company. An environmental movement began to take shape in Vancouver. One of the naturalists behind the Skagit campaign, civil engineer Ken Farquarson, discovered that a ski development in the North Shore mountains had violated its approved plan with an expanded logging operation. He and his friends formed the Cypress Bowl Committee and stopped the renegade clearcutting.

In the working-class neighbourhood of East Vancouver, twenty-two-year-old Bill Darnell joined a government-sponsored development program, the Company of Young Canadians, and organized an Ecology Caravan that toured the province. When the government proposed a highway through Vancouver and along the beach around Point Grey, Darnell helped organize the East Vancouver community to halt the project. Farquarson, Stowe, and other environmentalists joined the campaign. Rod Marining's street theatre company brought musicians to the public rallies. Ben Metcalfe and Bob Hunter publicized the cause. On the West Side, near UBC, a citizen's group — including the Stowes, Jim and Marie Bohlen, and Rod Marining — blockaded bulldozers at the popular public beaches at Spanish Banks. The highway was stopped. Years later, the highway campaign would be seen as a turning point in Vancouver history, preserving the seaside quality of the downtown core and the shoreline of English Bay. The environmentalists in Vancouver had discovered the greatest inspiration for any social visionary: They could win.

Within the quiet Shire, a critical alliance of committed social activists took shape, while their future *raison d'être* unfolded far away. In 1969, Ben Metcalfe went fishing for sea-run cutthroat trout in Howe Sound, near

Vancouver, and saw the Port Mellon pulp mill for the first time. His outing was blighted by the stench from the bellowing smokestacks. A few weeks later, he attended a Forestry Commission meeting, where a vice-president from Canadian Forest Products talked about the booming BC economy. Metcalfe asked the speaker what they planned to do about the foul air in Howe Sound. "We have to accept it," the executive told Metcalfe. On his own initiative, at a cost of $4,000, Metcalfe placed twelve billboards around the city. He created a logo to represent the environment, two waves joined together into a spiral maze. "If you can promote companies and products," he told his friends, "you can promote ideas." The billboards declared:

ECOLOGY?

LOOK IT UP! YOU'RE INVOLVED.

CHAPTER TWO

DON'T MAKE A WAVE

"Find out just what people will submit to and you have found out the exact amount of injustice and wrong that will be imposed upon them."

— Frederick Douglass

In August 1969, the United States announced a one-megaton nuclear bomb test, code name Milrow, scheduled for October on remote Amchitka Island, 4,000 miles northwest of Vancouver in the Aleutian Islands. Irving Stowe alerted his network. Deeno Birmingham at the British Columbia Voice of Women petitioned the Canadian government to protest. Bob Hunter researched the background of the US tests and took up the cause in his column.

In 1963, the US had signed a Test Ban Treaty with the Soviet Union, limiting atmospheric tests, while simultaneously initiating an era of underground nuclear blasts. The test site in the Nevada desert had aroused objections from Las Vegas locals, most notably from billionaire Howard Hughes, who drafted ecologist Barry Commoner to bolster his campaign. The US Department of Defense surveyed the distant Aleutians and drilled shafts into the granite rock of Amchitka Island, a registered National Wildlife Refuge. US military chiefs claimed the Soviet Union "cheated" by disguising underground tests as natural earthquakes. The tests on

Amchitka Island were meant to answer two strategic questions: Could the US detect Soviet underground tests with seismic sensors, and conversely, could the US hide their own tests from the Soviets?

In 1965, the Americans detonated an 80-kiloton bomb, six times the power of the Hiroshima bomb, in a hole under Amchitka. Roads fissured and stream banks crumbled a mile from Ground Zero. Mud geysers blew from lakes and granite crumbled from rock cliffs where seabirds had nested. Robert Jones, Manager of the Wildlife Refuge, raged that the sanctuary had been violated. The Department of Defense predicted the site would not leak radioactivity for hundreds of years, but tritium, iodine, and krypton were detected in freshwater ponds on the island. The blast caused seismic readings of 5.75 on the Richter scale. The next test would be fifteen times more powerful.

In his research, Bob Hunter discovered that on Good Friday, 1964, an earthquake registering Richter 8.3 had opened a 500-mile fissure through Alaska, killed 115 people, and launched a tsunami across the Pacific to Japan. In Port Alberni, on the west coast of Vancouver Island, the tsunami caused $1.5 million in damage. The huge wave provided Hunter with the image he needed to communicate the danger of the bomb. He phoned Robert Ellis at the University of British Columbia, who estimated the next bomb test would register 7.0. "Would the bomb cause another tidal wave?" he asked. No one knew, but in a four-column series, Hunter summarized the new geological science of plate tectonics and fault lines. On September 24, he wrote in the *Vancouver Sun*: "Beginning at midnight tonight, the United States will begin to play a game of Russian roulette with a nuclear pistol pressed against the head of the world." He quoted *Science* magazine, geophysicists, and AEC scientists. He outlined the risks of the bomb test: radiation, fallout, shockwaves, and earthquakes. "There is a distinct danger," he wrote, "that the tests might set in motion earthquakes and tidal waves which could sweep from one end of the Pacific to the other."

When ecologists Gwen and Derrick Mallard organized a demonstration at the US Consulate in downtown Vancouver, they called Bob Hunter for help. The Mallards had formed an ecology group and Hunter had suggested the name Society for the Prevention of Environmental Collapse, with the acronym SPEC. In the end, the group kept the acronym, but substituted the more awkward Society for Pollution and Environmental

Control. Hunter was slightly disappointed, but did not quibble. He was happy to see *any* environmental group emerge. Near the end of September, he met Gwen Mallard at the SPEC office in a small East Side house on Sixth Avenue, where they discussed strategy and made placards for the protest. Hunter conjured up slogans, playing on the earthquake and tidal wave theme. They painted IT'S YOUR FAULT IF OUR FAULT GOES onto signs, but the slogan seemed too long. Hunter wanted something snappy, and he came up with DON'T MAKE A WAVE. They made several of these placards.

The next day, at the US Consulate, the usual crowd — Bob and Zoe Hunter, their children, Irving Stowe, Bob Cummings, Lille d'Easum, Paul Watson, Ben Metcalfe, Rod Marining, Paul and Linda Spong, and others — gathered up the placards. The SPEC organizers avoided anti-American sentiment, insisting that the event be non-partisan. Someone showed up with a sign, AMERICA IS DEATH, and Mallard steered him aside. Knowing that Stowe had a decidedly anti-American edge to his rhetoric, the organizers asked him not to address the crowd. Thus began a long-running conflict between SPEC and Irving Stowe. The US Consul-General greeted the protestors on the street and promised to pass their message along to his bosses in Washington, D.C.

Local newspapers covered the event, and one of Hunter's colleagues chided him: "Hunter, are you reporting the news or making the news?"

"Both," he conceded. His transformation from literati to reformer was almost complete. Privately, Hunter struggled to balance his ecological advocacy with a journalist's objectivity, but his newspaper column was a halfway house where he was allowed to expound his subjective opinions. The ecology movement, he believed, was a natural outpouring from the public. "Loyalties were drifting like icebergs from the barren reaches of the social Arctic where live poets and rebels," Hunter mused in his column that evening, "down into the warm Sargasso Sea of suburbia, where dwell mothers and housewives."

As the day of the scheduled blast approached, SPEC and the UBC Alma Mater Society organized a demonstration at the US/Canada border south of Vancouver. On Wednesday, October 1, 1969, a dozen buses picked up students from the university for the half-hour ride. Several high schools shut down for the day as students left for the demonstration. Six thousand protestors milled about Peace Arch Park, under the towering monument to the friendship between Canada and the United States, the longest undefended border in the world. The Stowes held the Quaker banner. Protestors brandished DON'T MAKE A WAVE signs.

The British Columbia Attorney General had warned that "serious charges" could be laid against anyone blockading the road, but no Royal Canadian Mounted Police arrived to enforce the threat. The crowd closed in on the northbound traffic lane. A police siren wailed from the American side of the border, which stirred more of the throng onto the road. Rod Marining and his friends performed spontaneous theatrics. The Bohlens arrived with a Sierra Club group. The more radical elements — including Paul Watson and the Vancouver Liberation Front — were held in check by the SPEC organizers, but a high-school student burned an American flag. Gwen Mallard, Hunter, and others spoke from a raised podium. Hunter mentioned that not since the War of 1812 had the border between the two countries been closed. After an hour, UBC Alma Mater Society president Fraser Hodge announced that the point had been made and he urged the multitude to disperse from the road, which they did, peacefully. Irving Stowe was impressed with the exercise. He later told Dorothy that the crowd represented a robust political constituency.

"The … demonstration against the Amchitka Island A-bomb test has begun," Hunter wrote that night for his *Vancouver Sun* column. "Who are we? A collection, initially, of very proper and respectable and decently paid and serious and a bit less than illiterate citizens, some professors and some ministers and housewives involved in the Society for Pollution and Environmental Control."

He delivered his column to the newspaper the next morning, only to learn that the Milrow blast had just been detonated 4,000 feet below the surface of Amchitka Island. Ground zero heaved 14 feet into the air. Rock was pulverized 500 feet below the surface. Fish were blown from lakes as geysers soared to 50 feet. Two lakes were partially drained through fissures. House-size chunks of granite fell from bluffs into the sea. Gulls and Harlequin ducks, sunning themselves on the rocks, were found later, backs broken, legs driven up into their bodies. At Duck Cove, on the southwest coast, a mile from ground zero, the fault line was displaced by five inches. The shock wave killed fish and seals and split the eardrums of sea otters found floating dead on the surface of the frothing ocean.

The blast was detected in every ocean of the world. Seismologists at the University of Victoria recorded a Richter scale 6.9 shockwave. Gene Phillips, a seismologist in Barrow, Alaska, detected a series of aftershocks for thirty-seven hours. He wrote to Alaska Senator Mike Gravel and the AEC that future tests "could trigger earthquakes." Only a month later, however, in November, the United States Department of Defense announced their next test, five times more powerful, a 5-megaton thermonuclear fusion blast, code-named Cannikin, scheduled for Amchitka in the fall of 1971. The trial for the US Spartan anti-ballistic warhead would be the largest underground nuclear explosion in American history.

THE COMMITTEE

In one of his letters, Irving Stowe had demanded that Prime Minister Pierre Trudeau object to the test "on behalf of all Canadians." The Prime Minister's office replied that on September 19, Foreign Affairs Minister Mitchell Sharp had delivered a message to the White House stating Canada's concerns. Stowe wrote back insisting Sharp formally object. Dorothy Stowe wrote to the BC Association of Social Workers and asked them to wire the Prime Minister and support a boycott of US products until the test was cancelled. The Stowes drafted a petition and sent it to their friend Deeno Birmingham to circulate. Support poured in, and the Stowe home on Courtenay Street in quiet Point Grey became a hub of protest to stop the Amchitka nuclear blast.

Jim and Marie Bohlen visited the Stowes with Terry Simmons, a postgraduate geography student at Simon Fraser University, a new university east of Vancouver. Simmons had attended some of the SPEC meetings but had little interest in, or tolerance for, the Yippies, hippies, and the *Georgia Straight* crowd. He wanted environmentalism to be respectable and scientific. Simmons had come to Vancouver from the University of California, where he was a member of the Sierra Club. The Sierra Club had no Canadian chapters, so Simmons and Sierra Club member Katy Madsen had started a BC group. Irving and Dorothy Stowe joined, along with Jim and Marie Bohlen and Ken Farquarson from the Skagit River campaign. Irving Stowe and Jim Bohlen became directors along with Simmons, Madsen, and Bill Darnell, who had helped stop the highway through

Vancouver. Their first crusade was to preserve a small islet at the mouth of Nanaimo harbour in the Strait of Georgia. American installation artist Robert Smithson wanted to pave the islet with toffee-coloured glue and shards of broken glass. The BC Sierra Club sprang to the defence of the seabirds, garnered news coverage, and halted the art project.

Flushed with victory, they now wanted to stop the Amchitka Island bomb test, still two years away. Stowe proposed that in order to stop the Cannikin blast, they should harness the momentum from the border blockade. They struck a committee to develop the idea and Stowe suggested a name borrowed from the placards: The Don't Make A Wave Committee. Bohlen agreed to talk with the student organizers at UBC. Marie and Dorothy would work with BC Voice of Women on petitions and membership. Irving would liaise with the Quaker groups and other local activists and would be responsible for raising money.

Although their task was to contact student leaders, Jim Bohlen and Terry Simmons avoided the radicals who had occupied the Faculty Club at UBC. Simmons felt the hippies gave the disarmament movement a frivolous reputation. So Bohlen drafted Paul Cote, a student he had met at the border blockade. Cote had been studying at the Sorbonne during the 1968 riots in Paris, sitting innocently at a street café when he was mistaken for a protestor and whacked in the head by a French policeman. This blow had infuriated Cote, and on his return to UBC, he became active in the student movement against the Vietnam War. He was a smart, responsible young law student, the sort of scholar who appealed to Bohlen and Simmons.

Stowe, Bohlen, and Paul Cote assumed positions as directors of the Don't Make A Wave Committee. Lille d'Easum wrote a study of radiation effects, the BC Voice of Women joined the coalition, and labour groups and churches offered help. Stowe agreed with Bohlen that the disarmament movement should be respectable, but he did not want to exclude the radicals. Irving Stowe had an inclusive style. He admired the courage and pluck of the radical young *Georgia Straight* crowd, even if they smoked marijuana and taunted the establishment with sexually explicit artwork. He admired the offbeat writing of Bob Hunter, and he thought the creative pranks of the hippies added spirit to the movement. Stowe encouraged the radicals who met at the Cecil Pub, such as Hunter and Marining, to join their committee.

GREEN PANTHERS

Vancouver lawyer Hamish Bruce read Bob Hunter's columns about ecology and the bomb, phoned him at the newspaper office, and met him at the Cecil Pub. Hamish had an idea about organizing a group that he called the Green Panthers, the ecological equivalent of the Black Panthers in the United States. "Ecology," said Hamish, "is a sleeping giant. It's the big issue that is going to rock the world." On this, they could agree.

Hunter had just returned from a tour of California and Chicago and was writing about the counterculture revolution in America. "Hamish," he said, "there are probably a hundred environmental organizations in California. I counted twenty-four in Berkeley alone. A guy named Cliff Humphrey has a group called Ecology Action. He got sixty people together to smash a 1958 Dodge Rambler on a Berkeley street to protest smog. He predicts a mass uprising around ecology. He said: 'This thing has just begun.'"

Hunter told Hamish his theory that society was about to go through a "fundamental reorganization of the operating belief system." He told him that futurist John Platt had written an article for the *Bulletin of the Atomic Scientists* explaining how all natural systems — organisms and societies — go through periods of "self-structuring hierarchical growth." The interesting thing, Hunter said, is that "the coming change is almost invisible before it happens. The system seems to be in chaos, characterized by cognitive dissonance, and seemingly contradictory realities — like hippies and rednecks. Then the system suddenly restructures, jumping to a new level, like the quantum jump of an electron in an atom." Hunter told his new friend that the next paradigm shift "would be global, and its name is ecology."

Hunter and Bruce passed the afternoon talking and drinking beer. They strategized about the Green Panthers and how to do "ecology actions." Six months earlier, Hunter had participated in an all-night vigil with the SPEC group at Reichold Chemicals Company, which was dumping toxic effluent into Vancouver's Burrard Inlet. "We were on the wrong side of the building!" said Hunter. "We need a boat." The two friends came up with the idea to acquire a boat so they could cruise Burrard Inlet and expose polluters. Hamish said he would look around for something cheap.

In December 1969, Hunter reproduced in his column a symbol that he had received in the mail. It was designed and released into the public domain by Los Angeles Free Press cartoonist Ron Cobb. "I venture to predict," Hunter wrote, "that it will become as familiar as the peace symbol." Cobb had explained that his new ecology symbol combined the small "e" for ecology — signifying the yielding, feminine nature — and a small "o" for one, organic, and orgasm. The inner circle represented wholeness and harmony, and the outer ellipse represented the transcendent unity that pervades all dualities. "Anyone can be proud to wear it," Hunter wrote in the *Vancouver Sun*. He proposed an ecological index, like the consumer price index, to measure government environmental progress, and fines for "environmental crimes." In that same month, Marshall McLuhan, working for Toronto's Pollution Probe, said: "In the 1970s we will see a rampage of ecological prosecutions." I had just left college in Los Angeles, when Ron Cobb drew a cartoon in the *LA Free Press* showing a father and son sitting on the hood of their car in a rubbish heap sprawled to the horizon. "What's Ecology?" the boy asks his father. In 1969, probably no more than one college student in a hundred could give a credible answer, in spite of the popularity of the Sierra Club and proliferation of ecology groups.

In Vancouver, a vision of ecology was taking shape at SPEC, in Hunter's columns, Metcalfe's radio shows, and in the Stowes' many campaigns, but also in the research of young brain neurologist Dr. Paul Spong. Spong had been hired by the Vancouver Aquarium to perform the pioneer studies on a captured *Orcinus orca*, or killer whale, by the name of Skana. It would be four years before his ideas would influence Hunter and the others, but on December 11, 1969, when fishermen trapped four whales in Pender Harbour, 50 miles north of Vancouver, Paul and Linda Spong, with their one-year-old son Yashi, headed north to stop the capture. They felt somewhat alone at the time, but their passion for the whales would change the face of the environmental movement.

In the meantime, Hamish Bruce found a cheap, 32-foot double-ender fishing troller sitting up on blocks at the mouth of the Fraser River, south of Vancouver. He and Hunter bought the boat and hired a truck to deliver it to the dock where they launched it down the Fraser River and into the Strait of Georgia. This was to be their first run through Burrard Inlet to look for polluters. They managed to get the 1933 Chrysler Crown engine running, but the wooden planks of the hull had dried out in dry dock, and water poured into the bilge. On their swing around Point Grey into

Burrard Inlet, they got the bilge pump working to remove the water and went up to the wheelhouse. The little troller, named *Maddy*, had been painted robin's-egg blue with white trim. Hunter admired the wooden wheel and felt like a real seaman. The two friends talked about their "Green Panther" ideas, but Hunter was not so sure now about the name. He told Hamish a chilling story.

While in Chicago earlier that year, he had interviewed 21-year-old Black Panther leader Fred Hampton. "Fred was a local neighbourhood hero," Hunter recalled, "not at all like the media image of the violent radical. He got the street gangs to help provide a daily breakfast for school children in the ghetto, and they formed a 'Rainbow Coalition' of blacks, Latinos, and whites. Hampton was a responsible guy, although he talked tough. He told me the FBI and Chicago police had infiltrated his alliance, disrupted them, provoked violence, and arrested their leaders at every opportunity. He said, 'Here, take our phone number. Next time there's trouble down here you call us and find out what *really* happened.'"

Two months later, back in Vancouver, Hunter read that police in Chicago had shot Fred Hampton in an early morning raid on his home. Media stories reported "a gun battle." Hunter called the phone number Hampton had given him and learned from a woman in the Black Panther office that Hampton was shot while asleep in his bed at 4:00 a.m. There had been no warning. A woman eight months pregnant was beaten so badly she was taken to hospital.

Hunter confided to Hamish that absolute non-violence was the only way to approach social change. He wondered if the Green Panther name might be the wrong image. "Anything short of non-violence," Hunter said, thinking of the Black Panther experience, "only gives the police an excuse to eradicate you. Besides, violence is a cop-out," Hunter said, "because it is based on ego and revenge."

In California Hunter had been ordained as a minister in the Universal Life Church by the founder, Reverend Kirby Hensley. He now told Hamish, "Part of the change is going to be spiritual. God has been buried under industrialism. Ecology is, at its root, a spiritual movement because it returns sacredness to the Earth. The new spirituality is direct and available to anyone, without priests or churches. Here." Hunter reached across the wheelhouse and pointed a finger at Hamish Bruce's forehead. "Zap!" he exclaimed. "There. You're a member of the Universal Life Church."

Meanwhile, seawater poured through the dry hull faster than the bilge pump could send it back out, and the *Maddy* was sinking. By the time the budding ecology activists realized this, the water was only inches from the gunwales. By bailing water from the sinking boat, they limped through English Bay, under the Burrard Bridge, and tied up at Fisherman's Dock in the inner harbour. They spent several days caulking the planks, but the exercise was useless. *Maddy*, the first ecology protest boat of the Green Panthers, sank at dockside.

A PLAN

The spiritual ecology movement that Bob Hunter imagined was but half the critical mass in Vancouver. Hunter had not yet formally met Irving Stowe, who represented and championed the other half, the disarmament movement, although Stowe had sent frequent notices of events to Hunter at the newspaper.

In the first week of January, 1970, Stowe sent letters to Hunter and to Ben Metcalfe at the CBC, asking them to help publicize a campaign to stop oil and gas exploration in the Strait of Georgia. He signed his letter, "Director, Sierra Club." Metcalfe broadcast the item on his radio show and wrote back to Stowe advising that he had received a "wave of enquiries." Metcalfe suggested in his letter, "Perhaps we should meet soon."

As full-time activist, Stowe supported virtually every disarmament or ecological campaign in Vancouver. He belonged to the Quaker Friends Service Committee, the Sierra Club, the World Peace Council from Helsinki, the Skagit River group (ROSS), and the BC Environmental Coalition (BCEC). He helped Bill Darnell and Gwen Mallard plan a Festival of Survival for Vancouver's Stanley Park. With the Society to Advance Vancouver Environment (SAVE), he promoted a pedestrian mall for the downtown city core. He helped start the Take Back the Earth Committee (TBTEC) to foster urban ecology and the Stop Pollution from Oil Spills (SPOILS) to battle oil tanker traffic in the Strait of Georgia. However, the planned US nuclear bomb test occupied most of his time. The Don't Make A Wave Committee joined the Canadian Coalition to Stop the Amchitka Nuclear Blast (CCSANB). Dorothy kept track of the correspondence and replied to every offer of support. She not only earned their family income, she also acted as secretary for several groups. Her filing cabinet was a sea of acronyms.

Irving Stowe and SPEC continued to debate tactics stubbornly. Stowe complained that the Mallards did not support the Amchitka coalition, and they complained that Stowe was too inflammatory. Nevertheless, the Don't Make A Wave Committee and SPEC joined forces for a second demonstration at the US Consulate, while Rod Marining and his friends "liberated" Granville Street in downtown Vancouver. Musicians walked through the streets with bells, drums, and flutes, as revellers on bicycles circulated among the cars and handed out an ecology manifesto to the drivers.

In February, the World Peace Council held a Conference in Vancouver. Stowe and Jim Bohlen meet with Secretary-General Romesh Chandra and discussed a coordinated strategy to stop the US bomb testing. Inspired by this meeting, the Don't Make A Wave Committee met at the Stowes' home to plan their protest against the Amchitka test. Irving Stowe was articulate, intelligent, and well informed. In some cases, this worked against him. His complex analysis of the issues facing humankind would sometimes frustrate his associates. The committee's consensus process resulted in long, tedious debates and slow resolution. Jim Bohlen often got frustrated with the pace. The larger problem, however, was that the committee had no plan.

On Sunday morning, February 8, 1970, after one such meeting, Jim and Marie drank coffee in their kitchen. From the typically overcast winter sky, a diffused light filtered through the chestnut trees and into the large window. Marie, the nature illustrator, watched busy juncos and chickadees in the damp morning foliage. Jim told Marie he was frustrated with the Amchitka campaign, with the Sierra Club for its failure to take up the nuclear weapons issue, and with the Don't Make A Wave group for its inability to arrive at a strategy. Marie sipped her coffee and watched the birds. Jim seethed as he read the newspaper. He got a second cup of coffee. Finally, somewhat casually, Marie said, "Why not sail a boat up there and confront the bomb?"

The Bohlens, and most of the disarmament crowd, knew of the *Golden Rule*, the boat that had attempted to sail into the Enewetak test zone in 1958, the *Phoenix* that actually made it, and the *Everyman* that was arrested en route. Hunter and Hamish Bruce had endured the *Maddy* fiasco, but neither had yet attended a Don't Make A Wave Committee meeting. Marining and others in the group had discussed the idea of procuring a ship, but Marie's suggestion was pure inspiration, detached from the practicalities. It just seemed to her like the right thing to do.

Jim and Marie were contemplating this when the phone rang. A reporter from the *Vancouver Sun*, making a routine call and looking for a story, asked what campaigns the Sierra Club might be planning. The synchronicity of this phone call caught Bohlen off guard. Out of frustration, he took the plunge. "We hope to sail a boat to Amchitka to confront the bomb," he explained. To Bohlen, this may have been a hypothetical idea, but to the *Sun* reporter, it was a scoop. The journalist dug for more information, and before Bohlen knew it, he was describing how they would sail inside the 12-mile limit. "If the Americans want to go ahead with the test," he said, "they'll have to tow us out. Something must be done to stop the Americans from their insane ecological vandalism."

The *Sun* ran the story the next day. The headline pronounced: SIERRA CLUB PLANS N-BLAST BLOCKADE.

GREEN PEACE

The initial glitch was that the Sierra Club had approved no such campaign. This was a concern for Terry Simmons, who had set up the BC chapter with the blessings of the Seattle group but had not received official sanction from Sierra Club headquarters in San Francisco. What happened next would be later disputed in people's memories and clouded by myth, but over the next week a plan to sail a boat to Amchitka Island was adopted by the Don't Make A Wave Committee and the boat was given a name, although no such boat had been committed to the cause.

That week, in the Fireside Room of the Vancouver Unitarian Church on Oak Street, the Don't Make A Wave Committee held an emergency meeting. Light entered the unadorned room from two tall, thin windows in the west wall facing Oak Street. Wooden and grey metal chairs had been pulled out, facing a table where Irving Stowe presided between the windows. The throng pulsated with anticipation. Although Marie's idea and Jim's pronouncement to the media had bypassed the consensus process, no one opposed the plan for a boat. On the contrary, the idea had given the group some direction. Terry Simmons made it clear that the Sierra Club might have nothing at all to do with the plan. Although the Don't Make A Wave Committee had originally been a committee of the Sierra Club, it now assumed an ad hoc status. The group unanimously ratified the action, although they had neither a boat, nor the money to charter one, nor any legal standing other than the democratic right of citizens to assemble and challenge their governments.

As the meeting wound down, there was a great deal of discussion about what kind of boat they needed and who would find it. Some people drifted into the courtyard of the Unitarian Church grounds and others milled around inside and talked in small groups. When Irving Stowe left the meeting, he flashed the "V" sign, as was his custom, and said "Peace." Bill Darnell, the quiet activist who rarely spoke at the meetings, said modestly, in the same offhanded manner in which Marie Bohlen had suggested the boat, "Make it a *green* peace."

The assembly went silent for a moment. Darnell was not aware that anyone took notice, yet everyone heard the magic in the two words. Others in the group had discussed the confluence of disarmament and ecology, Hunter and Metcalfe had written about the idea, yet no one had quite articulated the fusion so succinctly. The indelible conjugate lodged in people's minds. A *green* peace. A few days later, Irving Stowe confided to Darnell that he could not stop thinking about the words. Bob Hunter believed the expression fused together the two most urgent movements in human affairs. Metcalfe said, "Yeah, well it fits better in a headline than The Don't Make A Wave Committee." Over the next few days, people talked about the hypothetical boat as if it already existed, and some called it "the *Green Peace*."

Back at home, at the kitchen table, on a sheet of lined paper, Jim Bohlen sketched a ship with the name "*Green Peace*" on the bow. He imagined a large ship, like the USS *Recovery* that had carried him around the Pacific Rim and past the Aleutians twenty-five years earlier. He scribbled a note about "300 to 500 people including press" on the voyage. He imagined a team of "natural scientists," who would perform "geological surveys to precisely assay possible damage" on Amchitka.

On February 15, the *Vancouver Sun* ran a second story about the intended voyage, including an appeal from the Don't Make A Wave Committee for volunteers "to sail on the *Greenpeace*," the first time the term appeared in print as a single word. Three days later, *The Georgia Straight* ran a story by Bob Cummings about the boat *Greenpeace*.

Marie Bohlen's son, Paul Nonnast, designed a one-inch button with green lettering on a yellow background, with the ecology symbol above, the peace symbol below, and in the middle, the single word: GREENPEACE.

OUT OF NOWHERE

The Associated Press wire service picked up the *Vancouver Sun* story and sent it around the United States. Sierra Club member Phil Berry read the story in California and phoned Simmons. "What's going on?" he asked. The Sierra Club was used to plans, budgets, approvals, and resolutions before media stories were released. The Board of Directors was miffed. There were trademark issues. The Sierra Club Board had not even endorsed the BC chapter. The California headquarters sent a letter to Simmons complaining about the "unauthorized use" of the trademark. In March, Simmons travelled to California to explain the plan and plead with the Sierra Club to embrace it.

The senior leadership of the Sierra Club included surgeon Edgar Wayburn, famed photographer-naturalist Ansel Adams, and executive director Michael McCloskey. These men were serious conservationists who left a legacy of parks in the United States, but they were not prepared to launch a seagoing protest against the American government. John Muir had had a radical idea for his time: nature for its own sake. He resisted the utilitarian "optimum use" philosophy of most conservationists at the end of the nineteenth century, and the Sierra Club was the legacy to his biocentric view. However, institutions often clash with the very ideas that inspired them. David Brower, who had been Sierra Club executive director since 1952, had been ousted only six months earlier in a conflict with the old guard. Brower, influenced by Buddhism and skeptical of the American military-industrial elite, had adopted activist tactics to defend the environment. He became too radical for the Sierra Club and had moved on to form the more activist Friends of the Earth, which would become both an ally and rival of Greenpeace in North America and Europe.

"It's not our issue," McCloskey told Simmons in San Francisco. "The Campaign for Nuclear Disarmament should sponsor it. It's important, but it's a distraction for us." Simmons figured this was fair enough. The Sierra Club could not be expected to take on every issue. Perhaps it was better this way. However, Sierra Club fundraiser and World War II conscientious objector Denny Wilcher supported the idea, and promised to help raise funds.

McCloskey would disclose later that he was "surprised by the sudden new forces" that exploded onto the ecology scene. He told an interviewer in 1989 that he had been "severely disoriented" to discover "new personalities emerging to lead something new, mainly people out of the youth rebellions of the 1960s who had all sorts of notions that just came out of nowhere." Of course these new ideas did not come out of nowhere. The new ecology movement moved the Sierra Club to publish *Ecotactics* in 1970, a "handbook for environment activists." The tactics included using the law and media, organizing teach-ins, lobbying, and using "guerrilla" theatre, already in use by groups like Ecology Action in Berkeley. In Vancouver, Ben Metcalfe hailed the *Ecotactics* handbook on his radio show and expressed hope that the book would "inspire and encourage the most meaningful revolution of the century."

When Simmons reported that the Sierra Club would not sponsor the campaign, the Don't Make A Wave Committee simply decided to incorporate as a non-profit society, raise the money, and launch the boat themselves.

On the inaugural Earth Day, April 22, 1970, an ecology group in Alaska published the small tabloid, *Conservation Scene*, including a report on the Amchitka Island nuclear test that revealed: "Rumor has it that some Canadian groups are planning a float-in around the island."

The Don't Make A Wave Committee published the first Greenpeace pamphlet in March 1970: *Nuclear Testing in the Aleutians*, written by seventy-one-year-old Lille d'Easum, an executive of the BC Voice of Women. Quoting AEC scientists, including Dr. Ernest Sternglass, and other scientists from Cal Tech, the Massachusetts Institute of Technology, and UBC, the eight-page booklet outlined the dangers of detonating a bomb near the Aleutian Thrust Fault.

ROOM FOR EVERYONE

Jim Bohlen and Paul Cote searched the Vancouver docks for a boat. In June, they found a 105-foot retired US Army tug, the *Northern Girl*, that could do 10 knots and sleep thirty-nine. The Don't Make A Wave Committee could acquire the ship by assuming the $25,000 mortgage, but the ship required mechanical and structural work. Stowe travelled across Canada, visited Quaker groups, and raised money. Volunteers sold buttons for 25 cents and placed small donation cans with the Greenpeace symbol on store counters throughout Vancouver. A cheque for $1.00 arrived made out to "Green Peas." In June 1970, Irving Stowe opened a bank account and deposited $556.

Stowe reckoned they would need about $45,000 for a boat, repairs, fuel, and provisions for the voyage. Twenty-five-cent buttons weren't going to do it. One Sunday morning in June, Irving Stowe turned excitedly to Dorothy and said, "We'll have a rock concert!" This was a shock to Dorothy Stowe, because Irving was more of a jazz fan. "Who will organize it?" Dorothy wanted to know. "I'll do it," Irving said. Some members of the Quaker group did not like the idea of a rock concert, but once again their tradition of tolerance paid off. The Quakers have an expression, "I won't stand in the way," meaning, "I don't agree with you, but I won't stand in your way if you believe it is right." Through his connections in the American disarmament community, he wrote to Joan Baez. She called Stowe at his home, with regrets that she could not perform at the event, but she recommended he call Joni Mitchell and Phil Ochs and gave Stowe their phone numbers. Baez later sent a cheque for $1,000. Stowe called Joni Mitchell's manager, who called back and said, "Yes, Joni would like to do it." A date was set for October 16.

Dan McLeod, publisher of *The Georgia Straight*, helped promote the concert. In June, Stowe launched a regular column in the underground newspaper, calling it "Green Peace is Beautiful," with the words still separated. The first *Georgia Straight* ad for the concert used the name as one word, but with the "P" capitalized: GreenPeace. The name was written and published in three forms over the next several months before it settled consistently into one word: "Greenpeace."

Ben Metcalfe now attended the Don't Make A Wave meetings, though he confessed to his wife, Dorothy, that he found them "a bit loose on both ends."

The Stowes second-level living room was the most common meeting place. Participants sat on sofas, on floor cushions, and on chairs at the dining room table. The Committee still had no formal standing. Membership was defined simply by those who attended: The Stowes, the Bohlens, the Metcalfes, the Hunters, Hamish Bruce, Rod Marining, Lille d'Easum, Bill Darnell, and new volunteers Lilly Jaffee, Lois Boyce, photographer and chemistry student Bob Keziere, Lou Hogan, and Dr. Lyle Thurston, a friend of Hunter's, who had volunteered for a free youth medical services project. Paul Watson, the radical among radicals, would show up occasionally wearing a Mao cap and an Army jacket with the North Vietnamese flag stitched to the sleeve. Watson seemed fearless, but his aggressive tactics made some of the pacifists nervous.

Although the committee ostensibly operated by consensus, Irving Stowe was clearly the leader, experienced at organizing and attracting talent. He was articulate and charismatic, but also opinionated. He became notorious for long speeches. At times, both Metcalfe and Hunter grew impatient with him because they felt he unnecessarily dominated the discussions. As well, some of the younger women felt that the predominantly male leadership was sexist. Dorothy Stowe and Marie Bohlen were both strong-willed and devoted, and whatever their complaints might be regarding puffed-up male egos that often clashed, they simply pushed forward and served the cause.

Stowe's battle with SPEC was aggravated when a SPEC volunteer accused him of being "a total fake," and of causing unnecessary confrontations. Jim Bohlen was uncomfortable with Stowe's anti-American rhetoric, but generally supported his leadership. Bohlen was far more skeptical of the psychedelic misfits like Hunter and Rod Marining.

Although Stowe and Hunter respected each other, Stowe objected to Hunter's smoking at meetings. "You call yourself an ecologist!" Stowe challenged Hunter. "Why do you pollute your own body with cigarettes?"

"Because I'm addicted," Hunter shrugged. He had attempted to quit four times but found himself hopelessly in nicotine's grip. Dorothy Stowe banished Hunter, "Doc" Thurston, and several others to the deck of the Stowe home for their smoke breaks during meetings. The Amchitka bomb test, however, kept the group unified, and the upcoming concert provided a common vision and inspiration. It also brought together the 1950s-style disarmament crowd with the 1960s ecology-minded counterculture.

Although they challenged each other and clashed over style and philosophy, Irving Stowe and Bob Hunter were allies who saw the advantage of keeping the disparate subcultures working together.

Inevitably, attitudes toward illicit drug taking became a conflict in the group. Both Metcalfe and Dr. Lyle Thurston had taken LSD as control subjects in clinical trials in the 1950s when the drug was still considered a miracle treatment for alcoholics. Metcalfe and Hunter had openly written about marijuana and LSD in the Vancouver media. Hunter considered marijuana far less addictive than tobacco and less dangerous than alcohol, which had claimed his own father. "How many traffic deaths could be attributed to LSD or marijuana?" Hunter would ask.

Stowe was a purist who did not smoke or drink, yet he tolerated, respectfully, the personal choices made by others. Acceptance of diversity was perhaps the most endearing quality that Stowe brought to the radical mix of ecologists. "Everyone is a channel for truth, and a channel for failure," Stowe would say, paraphrasing the Quakers. Dorothy and Irving Stowe brought a certain activist maturity to the mix, which saved it from disintegrating into partisan chaos. On Courtenay Street, tea and cookies were put out on the table while joints were passed around on the smoking deck.

BOTH SIDES NOW

On October 5, 1970, the Don't Make A Wave Committee was incorporated as a British Columbia non-profit society. The group had raised $8,000 from donations and button sales and had spent $1,600 running their campaign and preparing for the benefit concert.

On that same day, the *Front de libération du Québec* (FLQ) kidnapped British Trade Commissioner James Cross and demanded an independent Quebec. Prime Minister Pierre Trudeau invoked the Canadian War Measures Act, suspended civil liberties, and arrested suspects off the streets. The government later appeared justified when the FLQ kidnapped and murdered Quebec Labour Minister Pierre Laporte, but some Canadian police took advantage of the opportunity to round up hippies, writers, and political radicals with no connection to events in Quebec. Bob Hunter talked to colleagues who had found themselves under police interrogation and he joined protests against the excessive arrests. At one such demonstration at the Vancouver Court House, he ran into Irving Stowe. Although the two men knew each other from Don't Make A Wave meetings, standing on the protest line together facing a battalion of riot police sealed their alliance. After the demonstration, they walked the Vancouver streets and talked. It was a cool, fall evening. Stowe wore a long overcoat and Hunter a wool Navy seaman's coat. Irving Stowe, now fifty-five, sported a full beard and wore a hairpiece. Hunter was twenty-nine, two inches taller than Stowe, with auburn-brown hair down to his shoulders, a moustache and beard. Rather than carping at each other over Hunter's smoking and Stowe's long-winded speeches, they talked about the Amchitka campaign.

The elder Jewish Quaker shared with Hunter his belief in the power of bearing witness and taking personal responsibility for changing society. Hunter shared his theories of how to use the electronic media to communicate revolutionary ideas. Hunter called the tactic "mindbombs," using simple images, delivered by the media, that would "explode in people's minds" and create a new understanding of the world. The tidal wave image had been an example. Prior to this particular evening, Stowe had not known that Hunter had originated the "Don't Make A Wave" slogan, and he was impressed with the young journalist. The upcoming concert with Joni Mitchell, Stowe said, "could be the next mindbomb."

One-on-one, the two men could agree on most of the issues that faced the Don't Make A Wave Committee. This alliance between Stowe and Hunter — a meeting of America and Canada, a meeting of generations, a meeting of the full-time pacifist and the advocate journalist — would ultimately see Greenpeace beyond the single issue of the bomb. This cross-fertilization of ideas and cultures would breathe life into something entirely new. Hunter now began to actively promote Stowe's many campaigns: the oil spill protests, the downtown mall, the Amchitka campaign, and the imminent benefit concert, only a few days away.

The following night, as Irving, Dorothy, and their children, fourteen-year-old Barbara, and fifteen-year-old Robert, sat down to dinner, the phone rang. Irving answered, covered the receiver, and whispered to his family, "It's Joni Mitchell." The singer had just released her second album, *Clouds*, with popular songs like "Chelsea Morning" and "Both Sides Now." The teenagers gritted their teeth with excitement.

"Oh, yeah, okay," Irving murmured on the phone.

"What? What?" the kids wanted to know.

Irving covered the phone and whispered, "She wants to bring James Taylor. Who's James Taylor?" Dorothy and Robert shrugged. Barbara thought he meant James Brown. "He's that black blues singer!" she said.

Irving nodded. "Yeah, sure," he said to Joni Mitchell over the phone. "Bring him."

The next day, they drove down Fourth Avenue to a record store and discovered that James Taylor had just released his debut *Sweet Baby James*, which was already at the top of the charts. They bought the record album, brought it home, and swooned at the music. Folksinger and stalwart anti-war activist Phil Ochs had agreed to perform at the Amchitka benefit concert as well. The local concert producer added popular British Columbia band Chilliwack to the show and booked the Vancouver Coliseum, a hockey arena. The impending concert sent a buzz through the Shire. *The Georgia Straight* published a concert poster in a foldout, and thousands went up on lampposts and refrigerators. Hunter and Metcalfe announced the event in the mainstream media, billed as "Joni Mitchell, Chilliwack, Phil Ochs, 'GreenPeace' benefit concert. Presented by the Don't Make A Wave Committee." There was no public advance notice of the mystery guest, James Taylor. At school, Barbara Stowe found herself the centre of attention because she could verify rumours and feed the buzz. A boy she fancied, who had ignored her all year, now hit on her for the latest news. Greenpeace was cool.

The concert was a sellout, the biggest counterculture event of the year. Phil Ochs, the senior pacifist artist at 31, opened the show and spoke most directly to the raison d'etre of the evening with his "I Ain't Marchin' Anymore." Chilliwack got the crowd in a good rock and roll frenzy. James Taylor stunned the crowd with his cryptic "Carolina On My Mind" and "Fire and Rain." Joni Mitchell was visibly nervous, but her popular songs "Chelsea Morning" and "Big Yellow Taxi" brought shrieks of joy from the crowd. James Taylor joined her for an encore, singing Bob Dylan's "Mr. Tambourine Man." Irving Stowe, grinning and raising the peace sign, delivered flowers to Mitchell.

After all expenses were paid, the event netted just over $17,000. By the end of October, the Don't Make A Wave Committee had $23,467.02 in the bank. After the concert, the enthusiasm of the group took one of those order-of-magnitude leaps that Bob Hunter had written about. Attendance at the meetings swelled, and money poured in. No one seemed worried that they did not yet have a boat.

ALL SEASONS PARK

Bob and Zoe Hunter and their two children dressed up for a big night. Hunter's first non-fiction book, *The Enemies of Anarchy, A Gestalt Approach to Change*, was launched that fall on a houseboat in Vancouver's live-aboard community of False Creek. At the event, Hunter met Rod Marining, who had attended the party with the express intention of talking to Hunter. Marining had wild blond hair and a seemingly permanent smile. His most compelling physical attribute was that he possessed one blue eye and one green eye. The effect could be mesmerizing. Hunter and Marining had crossed paths at demonstrations and meetings, but had not yet conversed in depth. Marining now wanted Hunter's help.

In 1962, at the age of ten, Rod Marining's favourite place was a pond in East Vancouver where he played with frogs. When the pond disappeared under the blade of a bulldozer, to be replaced by a fast-food restaurant, young Marining took up a lifelong war against creeping urbanization. He left home at the age of seventeen and moved into a commune on Vancouver's North Shore. He and his friends received a federal-government sponsored Youth Initiatives Program grant to start their radical Rocky Rococo Theatre Company in the tradition of Julian Beck, Judith Malina, and the Living Theatre, but with a decidedly environmental motif.

Like Hunter, Marining harboured outrageous ideas about how masses of people could be moved, not just by media, but also by "happenings," performance art, and even — though he did not say this to everyone — by telepathic communication. Many of the Sierra Club members and older disarmament activists dismissed Marining as a loony, but Hunter appreciated his combined seriousness and self-mocking sense of humour. After the book party, the two ecologists sat on the quay, overlooking the harbour. Marining revealed that he wanted to stop the Four Seasons Hotel development at the entrance to Vancouver's magnificent Stanley Park.

The Four Seasons Hotel chain had announced a plan to raise six towers at the park entrance. Vancouver citizens treasured the view, opening onto a vast lagoon, where swans nested in the bulrushes. The site was private property, but had been used traditionally by the public. The park itself was one of the largest and most spectacular urban parks in the world, a point of pride in Vancouver. A construction firm had put a chain-link fence around the land, but Marining intended to occupy the site and demand it remain a park.

Hunter agreed to help and revealed his "mindbomb" theory to Marining. Having described in his book the revolution he foresaw taking place, he now wanted to show how activists could bring it about. "The holistic revolution won't be like storming the Bastille, or even a storming of cultural institutions," Hunter told Marining, "but a *storming of the mind*," which would be the title of his new book. Marshall McLuhan, Hunter said, had provided him with the central image to express his thesis. "The global media absorb information, interpret it, and package it for the public. This creates a sort of unified experience around the globe. The thing is," Hunter continued, "McLuhan says, to change public perception we have to move 'from the ivory tower into the control tower.' The communication network. So why not create a mass experience of ecology? The electronic media provide the delivery system. We provide the mindbombs."

Marining had taken a job at *The Province* newspaper, editing the Ships in Port column. He told Hunter he was frustrated with the editors because he saw important stories and photographs from the Vietnam War, which did not get used. He had also seen news and photographs from the People's Park showdown in Berkeley a year earlier. "Look," he told Hunter, "we can do the same thing, but without the riot police. I've already got a name for the new park: All Seasons Park. Your mindbomb, Bob, is going to be me camped out in there, in a tent."

"Great," said Hunter.

A few days later, in a light snowfall, Marining and his friends — Haida Natives, Québécois transients, hippies, and local homeless youth from the streets — set up a camp outside the fence. Paul Watson and David Garrick, both writers for the *Georgia Straight* and members of the radical Vancouver Liberation Front, joined them. Garrick, a serious young ecologist with links to the Native community, had a drooping moustache and was known to his friends as Walrus Oakenbough. Watson had just turned twenty. He was born in Toronto, to a French-Acadian father and a Danish mother. At sixteen, he hitched on trains to the West Coast and signed onto a Norwegian freighter as a deckhand. He was burly, strong, and seditious. Watson made no excuses for his anarchistic recalcitrance; he was a militant. He had a habit of mimicking John Wayne for dramatic effect, which got on some people's nerves, but on the other hand, his performance mocked his own bravado.

Police and television camera teams arrived at the site. Marining pitched his tent in the snow, as Watson and a small cadre of radicals charged the developer's fence and ripped down one section before they were arrested. The images made all the local media and more young people arrived at the park, but the battle with police was not the image Marining had prepared. He waited for a three-day weekend, when he knew the site would be abandoned. Nurseries throughout Vancouver had donated sod and shrubs. Marining borrowed a small bulldozer from a construction firm and a wheelbarrow from Irving Stowe. In one lightning move, 300 people arrived at the site, methodically removed all the bolts from the fence, and carefully stacked the sections on the ground. They laid sod over the construction roads, planted shrubs, erected tents, and put up signs proclaiming "All Seasons Park."

Technically, most of them were trespassing on private property, but Marining had carefully studied the maps and pitched his tent on a pile of dirt that covered a public road. He had advised Hunter, Ben Metcalfe, and other journalists about his camp-out. Metcalfe brought bottles of wine for the squatters. The story appeared in the local media before the work crews returned or the owners could respond, and attracted more street youth, who arrived with tents. Vancouver mayor Tom Campbell stormed the site with police and demanded the protestors leave the private property. Marining pulled out his maps, showing that his tent was on a public roadway, not on private property. The police refused to arrest him. The media recorded every word. The mayor went back to City Hall for maps and lawyers, while hundreds more people arrived. Marining demanded a public referendum. Hunter and Metcalfe conveyed the demand in the media. Rather than launch a messy assault on the camp, Vancouver City Council agreed to conduct a referendum. The citizens of Vancouver voted 56 percent in favour of keeping the park entrance, but the by-law required 60 percent for approval. Still, Marining refused to leave, claiming he was supported by a majority of the people in Vancouver. The defining media image, the mindbomb, was Marining's tent in the snow with the hand-painted "All Seasons Park" sign dangling over the door-flap.

The police refrained from arresting the 500 campers and after a four-week standoff, the wealthy father of a protestor offered to purchase the property for $4 million. The Coal Harbour entrance to Stanley Park was saved. The city dropped criminal charges against Watson for tearing down the fence, and Marining became a local hero, his one blue eye and one green eye blinking proudly in front of the television cameras.

Irving Stowe had embraced Marining as someone who could get things done, but during the park campaign, Marining had lost Stowe's wheelbarrow, and Stowe called him weekly looking for it. Marining felt the lost wheelbarrow was a small price for saving the entrance to Stanley Park, but Stowe considered this attitude irresponsible. "It's the principle," he chastised Marining. "If you borrow something, you return it." The lost wheelbarrow remained a sore point between them.

CAPTAIN JOHN CORMACK

Throughout January and February of 1971, Jim Bohlen and Paul Cote explored the docks around Vancouver, looking for a suitable boat. The ocean tug they had considered, *Northern Girl,* was deemed too expensive. Cote, a skilled sailor, worked his contacts on the Vancouver waterfront, but came up with nothing. Most skippers scoffed at the idea of risking their boats across the notorious Gulf of Alaska, only to end up hove to off the site of a nuclear explosion.

Cote paced a Fraser River dock in March, looking for a boat that had been recommended to him. When he failed to find the boat, he asked a stout fisherman in gumboots, who was washing his gear with a hose. The fisherman had never heard of the boat Cote was inquiring about, but he grilled the young student to find out why he wanted a boat. "Well," said the fisherman, "I have a boat."

Captain John Cormack, 60, owned and operated a 66-foot halibut seiner named after his wife, the *Phyllis Cormack*. Captain Cormack had suffered several years of poor fishing, and his vessel was in need of repairs. In the engine room, a four-by-four timber, wedged between the hull and the diesel engine, held the manifold in place. Cormack himself was covered in grease and oil. The captain was a huge man, and self-assured, but he had a modest bearing. He was missing two fingers on his left hand, missing most of his teeth, and had a rough grey stubble of a beard. He had forty years' experience fishing the West Coast, including the continental shelf off the coast of the Queen Charlotte Islands. The idea of taking his boat across the treacherous Gulf of Alaska did not faze him. And he needed the money.

Cote brought Bohlen to the dock to see the *Phyllis Cormack*, but the ex-Navy seaman was not entirely convinced that the halibut seiner was seaworthy. He asked UBC graduate student Patrick Moore to go to the Fraser River dock and assess the *Phyllis Cormack*. Moore had grown up in his father's logging camp at Winter Harbour, 200 miles north of Vancouver, around wood stoves, boats, and fishing gear. As a child, Moore rowed solo into the Pacific Ocean for cod and halibut, and he knew the forest trails through stands of giant Western red cedar and Sitka spruce. His mother had introduced him to the philosophy of Bertrand Russell as a teenager, and he'd boarded out at St. George's High School in Vancouver, where he graduated among the top in his class. In 1964 he enrolled at UBC, where he earned a science degree. His mentor, Dr. Ian McTaggart-Cowan, had established the first ecology department at a Canadian university, and Moore decided that his doctoral degree would be in the new field of interdisciplinary ecology. He studied forestry, oceanography, zoology, law, and regional planning. He was now writing his dissertation on the environmental impact of the Island Copper Mine on Rupert Inlet near his boyhood home. The Utah Mining Corporation had applied for a permit to dump tailings from the copper mine into the inlet. The company claimed the forty thousand tons of mine waste per day would be harmless to the ecology of the inlet. Moore's study showed this was not so.

He claimed that economic considerations should be limited and that "environmental considerations should be paramount in determining the constraints within which the development should take place." Mining companies in British Columbia were not used to upstart doctoral students standing in their way. Dr. McTaggart-Cowan told Moore that unnamed "industry leaders" had relayed a message through the Dean of the Faculty: "Persistence in this issue might make it difficult for you to land a job after graduation." The elder scholar took no side in the matter, but seemed amused at the honour of delivering the threat. Moore, however, was not intimidated. He agreed to represent the Pacific Salmon Society at a Pollution Control Board hearing about the mine-tailings and appeared on radio and television, talking about the issue. The Ph.D. committee, stacked with mining industry supporters, became deadlocked over Moore's dissertation, but would eventually, with the help of an independent adjudicator, award the candidate his degree. In the meantime, Moore had applied to sail on the Greenpeace ship to Amchitka Island. "I'm completely familiar with large fish boats," he had written to Bohlen, "and would be capable of operating the entire boat if the situation arose."

At the Fraser River dock, Moore climbed over the *Phyllis Cormack* with the captain. Moore found the wooden structure was sound enough, but the mechanical and electrical systems appeared suspicious. The four-stroke Star diesel required a steady diet of oil, and Moore was horrified to see that the bolts had been sheared from the manifold cover, which was held in place by the timber lodged against the hull. On closer inspection, however, he detected a workingman's ingenuity. Metal rods had been filed to use as hexagonal wrenches, wires ran safely through recycled conduits, and cables were tied off with simple copper wire rather than expensive split bolts. The circuits had been well identified. The entire engine room was haywired, but masterfully so, the work of a man who had more common sense and practical experience than money. Moore was impressed with the captain. The unassuming John Cormack was a legend among West Coast fishermen. There was no doubting his seamanship and nerve.

"Do you think," Moore asked the captain, "the boat could make it to Amchitka Island?"

"To Amchitka Island? Oh, yeah," Cormack said. "I can get ya to Amchitka Island all right. Ya just stay inside to Dixon Entrance and then over to Dutch Harbor."

The halibut and salmon fisheries were both closed on the coast. Cormack needed repairs and money and he had time on his hands. He agreed to a six-week charter for $12,000, plus fuel costs.

"She's a bit jury-rigged," Moore told Bob Hunter later, "but Captain Cormack knows his stuff."

ONE IDEA AT A TIME

In May, Bohlen and Moore flew to Anchorage for Atomic Energy Commission hearings about the 5-megaton Cannikin test scheduled for October. A month earlier, the Don't Make A Wave Committee had invited John Gofman — former director of the US Nuclear Lab at the University of California, Berkeley — to Vancouver. Gofman had told them about a 1963 study he had completed for the Atomic Energy Commission, which showed there was "no safe threshold of radiation for the human body," since a single energized particle could cause genetic or somatic damage. Subsequently, Gofman's AEC contract had not been renewed, and he became a public critic of the nuclear industry. "The production of cancer and leukemia by radiation is twenty to thirty times more severe than was thought by 'experts' less than a decade ago," he had told Bohlen and Moore.

The first blast on Amchitka Island, the 80-kiloton Long Shot in 1965, leaked radioactive tritium, iodine, and krypton-85 and caused seismic readings of 5.75 on the Richter scale. The 1969 test, Milrow, had registered 6.9 and triggered two days of aftershocks. The Cannikin test was going to be five times more powerful than Milrow. Amchitka Island, forty miles long and five miles wide, sits on a fault line in one of the most active earthquake zones on the planet. The island had been proclaimed a US Federal Wildlife Refuge in 1913, a haven for 131 species of sea birds, including the rare Emperor Goose and the Lapland longspur. The granite bluffs and headlands provided habitat for 28 nesting species including peregrine falcons and bald eagles.

Bohlen and Moore presented scientific briefs about radiation and the dangers of an earthquake. They charged the United States with violations of the very terms they had just proposed in the Strategic Arms Limitation Talks. Dr. Jeremy Stone, director of the Federation of American Scientists, told Moore that the Spartan Ballistic Missile system, for which the Amchitka bomb had been designed, "is redundant and irrelevant." Cannikin, he said, was a "bureaucratic oversight." Dr. Herbert York, chairman of the Federation of American Scientists, told the hearing that the Cannikin test "is a pointless experiment in search of an unnecessary weapon." The only voices supporting the test were the employees of the AEC. Alaskan Senator Mike Gravel said the deadly experiment "assumes there is some issue between Russia and the United States that the

American people are willing to massacre millions over."

Bohlen and Moore returned from Anchorage with fresh data for the coming information war. Former UBC chemistry student Robert Keziere condensed the material into a report for the media. Bob Hunter hammered the AEC in the *Vancouver Sun* and Ben Metcalfe filled the airwaves from his CBC studio. Bob Cummings and Lille d'Easum wrote for the underground press. Irving Stowe sent the Keziere and d'Easum reports to newspapers in the United States, and in June, *The Wall Street Journal* ran a story under the headline: "Blasting the Blast: Critics Fear Quakes, Waves, Harm to US-Soviet Ties." The US Senate withheld funds for the Cannikin test pending an ecological review and direct approval by President Nixon. When the case went to the US District Court, a *New York Times* editorial said, "The argument for postponing the test is persuasive." The little media mill in the Shire of Kitsilano was making global waves.

Some of these waves bounced back. In April, within days of signing his agreement with the Don't Make A Wave Committee, Captain John Cormack had received a letter from the Canadian Ministry of Fisheries, stating that his vessel insurance would not be renewed for the non-fishing charter. Cormack was furious. Law student Paul Cote complained by letter to Minister of Fisheries Jack Davis, who happened to be from West Vancouver. Davis wrote back, quoting the regulation that insured vessels must operate in the commercial fleet. Metcalfe and Hunter counterattacked with charges that Davis was supporting nuclear testing in cahoots with the Americans, a deathblow to any Canadian politician. The news stories stirred up a tsunami of angry letters and phone calls into Davis' constituency office.

Moore wrote the minister, citing his affiliation with the BC Environmental Council and the BC Federation of Labour, comprising 300,000 members. He pointed out that the regulations only stipulate that the vessel must be used "primarily" for fishing. Moore drew the minister's attention to the fact that the minister "did not cancel a fisherman's insurance if he took his family to Mexico in the off-season." Davis replied in June, declaring, "I am taking a closer look at our regulations." The flustered minister squeezed five equivocations into a single sentence: "It may, perhaps, be possible to continue the insurance on Mr. John Cormack's vessel for part, at least, of this trip."

Hunter and Metcalfe launched another media assault, demanding a decision. By the end of June, Davis wrote that his legal advisor had informed him: "My discretion in the matter is sufficient to enable me to continue coverage of the vessel during the proposed voyage." The ecologists in Kitsilano celebrated a victory in the first media skirmish with their own federal government. "We Greenpeaced 'em," said Metcalfe, turning the new word into a verb.

Ben and Dorothy Metcalfe brought a tough attitude to the mix. Canadians, Metcalfe said, were too polite about criticizing their government, not used to making *demands* on the government and fingering ministers personally. The Americans were more aggressive in this regard, but Americans attacking the Canadian government did not play well in the Canadian media. Ben and Dorothy Metcalfe, on the other hand, were Canadians who had experience in international journalism. They had learned from the best European journalists of the era that they could take industry and the government to task, name names, and demand a response. In one of his CBC broadcasts, Metcalfe had attacked Angus MacBean, a highly respected chief forester for MacMillan Bloedel logging company. MacBean had commented that "amateurs" should leave ecology to the "experts."

"It's really remarkable," declared Metcalfe on the CBC, "how many ordinary dumb citizens, trusting only their eyes, ears, nose, and throat, claim to know something about the environment — which, as every forestry engineer, chemist, and miner can tell you right away belongs to the experts ... It took real experts to kill Lake Erie, not a bunch of amateur fanatics. It took decades of mechanical genius to turn out enough internal combustion engines to get the fumes into the stratosphere. Mere faddists from some church group couldn't have done that."

At a Don't Make A Wave meeting, in the basement of the Unitarian Church in the summer of 1971, Metcalfe explained what he considered the "right attitude" for a citizen-critic. Metcalfe was a meticulous researcher, but he believed the research was not the message. "You don't have to explain and justify everything you feel. Sure, do your homework, bow to the facts, but forget arguing the science while the world burns. How many leukemia victims are acceptable? None! Don't count the dead with the bureaucrats. They're wrong! Nuclear bombs are insane. It's okay to just say 'No!' To launch this campaign, we need to reach escape velocity with a single idea. Don't confuse the public. That works against you. One idea at a time: No more nuclear bombs! Stop now!"

THE CRADLE OF STORMS

In July 1971 the US Coast Guard announced a three-mile security zone around Amchitka Island from August 31 to October 20, citing the Espionage Act of 1917. Violations, they warned, were punishable by seizure of the vessel, a $10,000 fine, and ten years in prison. The Atomic Energy Commission announced a 50-mile "warning zone," which extended into the international high seas. The Vancouver group asked, through Senator Gravel's office in Anchorage: "What would happen if a boat were five miles from Amchitka?" Dixon Stewart at the AEC office in Anchorage replied, "You'll get warned by the Coast Guard." Inquiries to Captain Warren Mitchell, Chief of Operations at the Coast Guard station in Juneau, revealed that he knew of no such 50-mile zone. In Vancouver, Captain Cormack was not intimidated.

"It's the high seas," he huffed. "They can't do nothin' to us."

Most alarming to some of the crew was the prospect of violent seas that could swallow the little fish boat. The Aleutian archipelago is known as the Cradle of Storms. In October and November the worst North Pacific storm fronts form in the low-pressure trough off the coast of Asia. The monster winds intensify along Kamchatka and sweep through the Aleutians into the Gulf of Alaska, pushed by cold, high-pressure Arctic air masses. Fluctuations in solar radiation can intensify the earth's electromagnetic field and cause sudden, severe cyclonic storms, heavy rains, and dense fog.

The tempests routinely kick up fierce 50-knot gales and 40-foot cresting waves streaked with foam and bullets of spray. In these conditions visibility can be reduced to a few yards and rogue waves can reach 100 feet in height. Such waves would tower over a tiny fish boat. Gusts of wind, known as williwaws, sweep down from the Arctic at over 100 knots, at greater speed and force than a hurricane. Conflicting currents and winds will set up standing columns of water called haystacks. A fisherman told Bohlen and Moore of a 140-foot crab boat torn in half in the Gulf of Alaska.

"Shit, Bob, this is crazy," Moore said to Hunter over a beer at the Cecil. "We're all gonna die!"

These perils, however, were in the open sea. The great circle route from Vancouver to Amchitka is 2,150 nautical miles. By hugging the coast north to Dixon Entrance, between the British Columbia and Alaska islands, the journey is about 2,400 nautical miles. When the crew of the *Greenpeace* reached the Aleutians and the Bering Sea, they would have to navigate rocks, currents, riptides, and notorious kelp beds thick enough to snap propeller shafts and stop boats dead in the water. A naïve mariner's view of the archipelago as independent islands is an illusion. Below the surface, they are a single mountain range of granite ledges, shoals, and reefs. The notorious Aleutian fog can reduce visibility to virtually zero. A helmsman might not be able to see the bow of his ship, much less the hazards. A small fish boat in these conditions, at the mercy of the wind, could be quickly shredded on the rocks.

When the Japanese Navy occupied Attu and Kiska during World War II, the United States sent submarines to Amchitka on a reconnaissance mission. US Sub S-27 was literally swept up by the currents off Amchitka, dashed upon a reef five miles off shore, and ripped open. The crew abandoned the sub and rowed ashore in rubber boats, where they remained until rescued a week later. On January 11, 1943, US Navy destroyer *Worden*, ripped by gale winds and coastal currents, foundered on the rocks of Amchitka's only natural anchorage, Constantine Harbor, where it sank. Fourteen sailors lost their lives in the frigid waters of the Bering Sea.

If and when the crew of the *Greenpeace* made it through all of this, they would face a nuclear blast 400 times more powerful than the bomb that destroyed Hiroshima. If the blast caused an earthquake, the sea swells could obliterate the boat in an instant. "Getting arrested by the US Navy," Hunter confided to Moore, "would be a relief."

A CREW

In spite of the danger, competition for the remaining crew spots was intense. The fishing boat could carry a crew of twelve. For the engineer position, Cormack selected Dave Birmingham, husband of Deeno Birmingham from the BC Voice of Women. Pat Moore and Jim Bohlen would be counted on to help operate the boat. Stowe wanted Hunter, Metcalfe, and Bob Cummings on board as media. Bohlen acquiesced regarding Hunter, but balked over Cummings. Stowe and Metcalfe, however, insisted that the "alternative media" should be represented since the readers of the *Georgia Straight* comprised a large segment of their supporters. Hunter's column and his news stories would be picked up by the wire services. Metcalfe would broadcast from the boat for the CBC, and these broadcasts would also be picked up by international news services.

Stowe could not go because of his proclivity for seasickness, due to an inner ear condition. This shocked Hunter, who had assumed that Stowe was the leader. "How can our leader not go?" Hunter grumbled. In spite of their conflicts, Hunter felt that Stowe's charismatic authority was needed. Without a dynamic leader on the boat, Hunter feared the crew would struggle over decisions. Bohlen represented the Don't Make A Wave Committee as purser for the voyage, but Hunter was not convinced that Bohlen possessed the spark to galvanize a crew of misfits and lead them across the Gulf of Alaska into the Cradle of Storms. Indeed, this question over campaign leadership would haunt the voyage.

Terry Simmons, the red-haired science student in thick, dark-rimmed glasses, represented the Sierra Club on the crew. Tall, dark, slender, and serene Robert Keziere was selected as the photographer. Keziere, one of the most promising young photographers in Vancouver, was also a chemist who understood radiation science. Easygoing Bill Darnell would be cook and second photographer to Keziere. Dr. Lyle Thurston would go along as medic. Marie Bohlen, whose idea had launched the campaign, would represent the Quakers and be responsible for provisions during the voyage. Lou Hogan and Rod Marining wanted to go, and were placed on the list as alternates.

Captain Cormack had said from the beginning that no unmarried women could be on the crew. The rule was sexist, which Hogan and others pointed out, but conformed to the traditions of the sea to which Cormack adhered. "There's reasons," he told Hunter. Cormack had a sincere, if dated, respect for women. He was gracious and never impertinent, never swore in a woman's presence, and berated Hunter like a father whenever Hunter did so. His wife Phyllis was equally charming, and even motherly toward the young radicals. Nevertheless, the idea of unmarried couples cohabitating on John's boat was just too much of a stretch for them. Marie Bohlen, Dorothy Stowe, and Dorothy Metcalfe did not accept disrespect from anyone, and none of the macho young men dared test them, but they put the campaign first and accepted the Captain's rule.

As these preparations were made, the Amchitka story percolated in the media. Canadian Minister of Foreign Affairs Mitchell Sharp formally protested to US Secretary of State William Rogers. Emperor Hirohito of Japan expressed opposition, and the Soviet newspaper *Izvestia* expressed its fear of a tsunami on the USSR's eastern coast. In London, *Peace News* published "Greenpeace Survival" about the fusion of the peace and ecology movements. The story was an amalgamation of Irving Stowe's "Green Peace is Beautiful" columns from *The Georgia Straight*.

When the US Senate approved the annual military procurement bill, they added a special amendment that required President Nixon's personal approval for any nuclear test on Amchitka Island, strapping the embattled president with the responsibility. A coalition of US environmental groups in Washington D.C., led by the Committee for Nuclear Responsibility, challenged the Cannikin test in US District Court before Judge George Hart. On August 30, 1971, Judge Hart stopped the hearings and ruled that the test complied with all treaties and laws. The environmental plaintiffs appealed to the US Supreme Court. The Aleut League, representing 3,500 residents of the Aleutian Islands, filed their own lawsuit to halt the test. The Alaska State Medical Association and the Federation of American Scientists passed resolutions critical of the test. Five US federal agencies — the Environmental Protection Agency, the President's Council on Environmental Quality, the State Department, the Office of Science and Technology, and the US Information Agency — recommended that the Cannikin test be cancelled or postponed. Nixon invoked an Executive Order to classify the objections and suppress further comments from these agencies. Nevertheless, Russell Train, chairman of the President's Council on Environmental Quality, broke ranks with the administration and publicly voiced concern. The decision now hung on a Supreme Court decision and President Nixon's approval. The AEC had set September 23 for the test, but now moved the date to October 2.

By mid-August, the Don't Make A Wave Committee had nearly $30,000 dollars in the bank and had already spent $10,000. Denny Wilcher from Sierra Club had raised $6,000 for the campaign, which he sent to Vancouver through the Eugene, Oregon Quaker group. The Eugene Quakers matched the $6,000 contribution, as did the Palo Alto, California, Quakers. By the end of the summer, $60,000 had been raised. Marie Bohlen, Zoe Hunter, and Dorothy Stowe provisioned the ship. Marie ordered bulk potatoes, carrots, chicken, turkey, onions, radishes, peanut butter, and tea. They bought life jackets, flashlights, and batteries. Dorothy Metcalfe's Ukrainian mother cleaned the boat, stem to stern, at the Fraser River dock. Bohlen, Moore, and Bill Darnell built bunks, storage boxes, and a workspace in the engine room. Engineer Dave Birmingham checked every circuit and switch, and replaced some of them. He and Captain Cormack cleaned and tuned the four-stroke diesel engine.

Dr. Lyle Thurston, the medic for the voyage, acquired painkillers, eye drops, Ringer's Lactate, Gentrum, tetracycline, dimenhydrinate tabs, and a hundred tablets of Valium. He brought a suture kit, gauze, and splints. Ben and Dorothy Metcalfe set up a radio communication post in their home in West Vancouver. Dorothy Metcalfe would manage their news service, broadcasting tapes while linked by phone to the marine radio on the *Phyllis Cormack*, standing by daily while the boat was at sea. Ben phoned from the dock to test the system.

THERE WE GO

On September 9, seven days before the boat was to depart, Marie Bohlen decided not to go. That meant there was no longer a woman on the crew. Lou Hogan felt she was entitled to go and was, in fact, the first name on the alternate list. Rod Marining was the second name on the list. Stowe, Metcalfe, and Hunter strongly favored Marining's presence on the crew, but would not preempt Lou Hogan, who had done as much work as anyone and deserved to go. The fifth name on the list was an academic from Juneau, Richard Fineberg, who had met Bohlen at the hearings in Alaska. Fineberg had discovered that the US military used the deep-sea channels near Amchitka as a toxic dump and had written a book on the subject, reporting that 1,000 tons of mustard gas were now in danger of being released by impact from the Cannikin blast. Bohlen wanted to give Fineberg the open crew spot, but that meant the American would leapfrog over four devoted volunteers who had already contributed a good portion of the past year to the campaign.

Captain Cormack's embargo of single women on board did not apply to Marie Bohlen, since she was married to Jim, and Lou Hogan felt that she should have the same status. She and Robert Keziere were a couple just as legitimately, in her mind, as the Bohlens. Why should non-married status exclude anyone? For that matter, why should being a *woman* exclude anyone?

Hunter commented months later, in a *Georgia Straight* interview, "The crew should have been half women," but that would be little consolation to Hogan. Dispute over the last crew spot now dominated the final meetings.

If Hogan could not go because of Cormack's rule, Metcalfe and Hunter believed Rod Marining should be on the crew, but Bohlen argued that he didn't have any real skills that were needed. "Not true," said Metcalfe. Marining had proven organizing talents and boundless energy. Irving Stowe had recruited him because of his enthusiasm and good nature, and had supported his place on the crew after his success at All Seasons Park. The incident with the lost wheelbarrow, however, gave Stowe some pause regarding the hippie. Consensus aside, Jim Bohlen and Irving Stowe retained the final word.

Cormack brought the boat around from the Fraser River and tied up in Burrard Inlet. On September 13, two days before the scheduled departure, Bohlen had a dockside quarrel with Ben and Dorothy Metcalfe, concerning Marining. Metcalfe suspected that Jim Bohlen might have used Marie to hold a spot, which he could fill at the last minute. Marie, on the other hand, said she had genuinely wanted to go, but felt she would be far more helpful on land helping the Stowes in Vancouver. Ben Metcalfe argued that Marining had taken on the most menial chores for months, had even painted the ecology and peace signs on the sail. "He deserves to go!" Metcalfe shouted at Bohlen on the dock. "Besides, we already agreed on Marining if Marie didn't go."

Fineberg, Bohlen believed, could help get media coverage in the United States. Ben and Dorothy rebutted that Fineberg had no meaningful media connections and that they were already getting media in the US and didn't need him. If not Marining, they should insist that Cormack accept Lou Hogan. Having a woman on the crew was important, they argued. But Bohlen was adamant. Marining was out, Lou Hogan was out, and Fineberg was in.

When she received the news, Hogan felt both disappointed and relieved. After discussions with Dorothy and Ben Metcalfe, she begrudgingly resigned herself to the decision. Hunter delivered the news to Marining, who took it stoically. "Well," he said, "if this guy can help us get American media, maybe he should go." Marining agreed to stay in Vancouver and help Dorothy Metcalfe with communications. However, he fixed Hunter with his green eye.

"Bob?"

"Yeah?"

"Don't worry about it. Before this is over, I'll be on the boat."

On the night before the departure, Hunter picked books from his shelves and crammed them into his duffle bag. The little volume from the mysterious dulcimer player, *Warriors of the Rainbow*, fell from the shelf to the floor. Hunter picked it up and looked at the cover. "Okay," he spoke to the book. "You want to come with me?" He stuffed it in his bag.

On the morning of September 15, 1971, the *Phyllis Cormack*, rechristened *Greenpeace* for the voyage, stood at a Vancouver dock. Cormack and Bohlen affixed a hand-painted sign on the flying bridge, below the wheelhouse that read, GREENPEACE. The crew assembled and prepared to depart at 4:00 p.m. They had food for six weeks. They expected the blast on October 2. They planned on four days to Dixon Entrance, seven days across the Gulf of Alaska, and perhaps three days along the Aleutians to Amchitka, which gave them four days' grace.

At 4:00 p.m., the final stores were loaded aboard, but the boat still had to take on fuel in Burrard Inlet, so the departure was delayed until after dark. To accommodate the television crews, the boat feigned a departure, with crew aboard and supporters waving, as they headed around the point to the fuel dock. Hunter, Moore, Thurston, and Marining took the opportunity to slip off for a final round at the pub.

In the pub they ordered two rounds of golden Molson's beer. When those were gone they ordered two more rounds. Moore pumped his arms and vowed they would bring down the American war-makers. Friends in the pub came by, shook their hands, and wished them luck. When the jukebox blared out The Doors' "Riders on the Storm," the ecologists sang along: "… into this life we're born!" As they sipped beer and celebrated, the 6:00 news came on featuring film from the departure of the *Greenpeace* to Amchitka Island to protest the US nuclear blast. "Hey, there we go," said Moore, shoving his chair back. Thurston grinned. Hunter raised his glass. "The Battle of Amchitka has begun," he declared. "You know that war of images thing? Well, the first mindbomb has been launched!"

CHAPTER THREE

ON AN OCEAN NAMED FOR PEACE

"One must think like a hero to behave like a merely decent human being."

— May Sarton

The *Phyllis Cormack* slipped quietly out of Burrard Inlet at dusk on September 15, 1971, past Point Atkinson and Bowen Island and into the gentle roll of the Strait of Georgia, the half moon high above the port stern. Captain Cormack and Dave Birmingham stood alert in the wheelhouse. Everyone else sat below, drinking wine or beer around the galley table.

Cormack gave the wheel to Birmingham and directed him northwest along the coast. They would cross the strait at the southern tip of Lasqueti Island and then head north-northwest toward Discovery Passage where the open water collapses into treacherous narrows.

Birmingham, a modest man in work clothes and wire-rim glasses, was a no-nonsense, capable, even brilliant, engineer. Cormack confided, "We'll shape up these hippy farmers and newspaper guys." The two men could stand for hours without speaking. Then Cormack might say, "Stay outside of White Island there, then ya just head north o' them lights."

"Yup," said Birmingham, and it was done.

Below, at the galley table, airtime was not so easy to come by. Metcalfe, with his booming, low-frequency radio voice, grasp of history, and worldly experience, dominated the banter. Hunter rivalled him by pouncing on any loose string of an idea. If there was a whiff of dead air, Moore or Bohlen might get in a salient scientific or political point. The rest were left to feed on the bones of time, interrupt, or sit silently and observe.

Underground journalist Bob Cummings, frustrated that no one listened to him, chafed his goatee. Terry Simmons, the rationalist, collected his thoughts and waited his chance. Dick Fineberg, a skinny young American intellectual, scribbled notes to himself. Lyle Thurston howled with laughter. Bob Keziere discreetly took photographs but remained silent. Bill Darnell, who had given the whole affair its name, calculated group dynamics from under the bill of his engineer's hat. Bohlen and Metcalfe, with grey streaks in their beards, shared World War II stories and clinked their coffee cups filled with wine.

"Picasso came up with the dove symbol in 1946," boomed Metcalfe, "after Churchill's Iron Curtain Speech, with Truman in Fulton, Missouri, which more or less started the Cold War. The Soviet Union was the new enemy."

When Metcalfe paused to sip his wine, Hunter jumped in. "The Commies, Black Power, all political revolutions ultimately fail, because they only address materialism. The real revolution will be ecology. People who were scared to death of Black Power will embrace Green Power."

"Hunter, you're —" Cummings tried to jump in, but Metcalfe was already in full voice.

"Marcuse figured out that the Communists were just as bad as the capitalists, or worse, at creating a boring, industrial culture, and he realized art was revolutionary because it preserved the cultural memory of a liberated way of being —"

"I need a liberated way of peeing," said Thurston.

"You guys are —"

"Let him out."

"Gandhi, you know, was inspired by the Quakers," Metcalfe went on, "and in turn inspired the disarmament groups after the war — Germany, Scandinavia, England — people started getting arrested at the War Office in London and called their thing Project Gandhi.

Metcalfe believed knowing history was vital. "To know what to do in this world," he insisted, "you have to figure out how we got here. As Roosevelt said, paraphrasing Disraeli, 'If it happened, you can bet it was planned by someone.'" The crew were all intelligent, but Metcalfe simply had more experience and had done more research, making him the Alpha Intellectual. Nevertheless, the camaraderie was as palpable as the competition. They drank, toasted, and shouted over each other.

Birmingham came down for a cup of coffee, looked over the galley table filled with wine bottles and cigarettes, shook his head, and muttered something about expecting the crew of the *Greenpeace* to be "men of religion." No one challenged him.

Shortly after midnight, Cormack entered the galley and asked, "Which of you fellas is gonna take the first watch?" Hunter and Cummings volunteered.

In the wheelhouse, Cormack gave Hunter a heading of north-northwest and stood back to watch. "The less ya turn the wheel," he said, "the straighter she goes." With this, he ducked into his quarters for a few hours' sleep.

THE GREENPEACING OF AMERICA

In the blue glow of morning, Hunter and Cummings saw Cape Mudge at the northern end of the Strait of Georgia. As they approached Discovery Passage, Cormack appeared from his cabin and surveyed the situation.

"Back 'er off there, Mr. Hunter."

"Sir?"

Without a word, Cormack stepped in beside Hunter, slid the throttle back, bumped him from the wheel, and took over.

"What are those lights, John?"

"That's Campbell River. Discovery Passage. Seymour Narrows ahead. Oh yeah, we'll show ya some places up here. Y'ever been in a whirlpool?"

Cummings, eyes red from glaring into the radar screen all night, stumbled down to the galley. Hunter watched through the window as the sun lit Victoria Peak on Vancouver Island and they passed the bellowing smokestacks of the pulp mill at Elk Falls. Cormack eyed Hunter discreetly as the journalist gazed about the cabin and wrote into his notebook. Above his head, the radio sizzled with static. Cormack reached up, switched the channel, and picked up terse communiqués among fishermen.

The 66-foot seiner *Phyllis Cormack* cut through the calm water, far more sound and stately than she may have appeared to Jim Bohlen a year earlier. Marine View Boat Works in Tacoma, Washington, built the fish boat in 1941, designed for stability and space — beamy, with massive oak timbers and fine, edge-grain gumwood planks fixed flush with each other against the oak ribs. She rested solidly in the water, not tossing about at each petty stirring of the sea. The wheelhouse and flying bridge stood forward with just enough room at the foredeck for a few coiled lines, two air-intake columns, and the anchor chain. The iron-plough anchor sat out on the bow where a forebrace rose over the wheelhouse to the single mast, rising 30 feet above the cabin, amidships. Metal stabilizing poles stood up from the gunwales on either side of the boat, to be lowered in heavy seas. Off the wheelhouse, outside on the flying bridge, was a second wheel — weathered wood, with eight spokes and knobs, looking to Hunter like the Buddhist eight-fold wheel of the Dharma.

The Greenpeace symbols — a peace sign and an ecology sign — appeared on a great, pale-green, triangular sail, fixed to the mast and to a boom that was lashed securely to the stern. The decks were rough, working decks, tortured by boots and salt, knives, chains, and fallen tools. A large square hatch-cover stood three feet above the afterdeck. Behind that, the deck rose to the stern, where aluminum rollers sat ready to feed seine nets to and from the sea. The boat was painted white and trimmed out in aqua-green, with PHYLLIS CORMACK in black letters at the bow.

The glum engine room and oily bilge notwithstanding, the *Phyllis Cormack* made for a proud vessel. As beamy and stately as she was, however, this was no pleasure boat. The cabins were small and the gangways tight. Six small, round portholes provided scant light in the confined forward crew cabin, where ten bunks had been crammed for this voyage, although a fishing crew would be smaller. Sleepers had the Northern single-sideband radio hissing above their heads and the diesel engine pounding below them. The captain's quarters opened from the wheelhouse.

Hunter relished steering and grew fond of both the boat and the skipper. That first morning, Cormack left Hunter at the wheel, found fresh coffee in the galley, stormed through the bunkroom cursing the sleeping crew, and returned to the wheelhouse. "Go ahead and get yerself some coffee," he said to Hunter, "and send a coupla them mattress-lovers up here."

Cormack stayed at the wheel all morning through the narrows. Twenty thousand years earlier, advancing glaciers had gouged these straits from the granite rock. Now, twice every day, some 100 billion cubic metres of

Pacific Ocean flowed in and ebbed out of this inland sea through Juan de Fuca Strait in the south and Queen Charlotte Strait in the north. The seawater brought a bounty of herring, halibut, salmon, sea lions, dolphins, and whales. Swift tidal currents rushed between the islands, making navigation tricky. The *Phyllis Cormack* passed red-barked arbutus, eagles feeding in the eddies, abandoned canneries, and boarded-up hovels swallowed by the forest. The hungover pacifists lounged in the sun on the hatch-cover, sipped coffee, and marvelled at the gnarly cedars growing from rocky bluffs. Moore identified the trees and sea birds, a cormorant on the wing and a merganser in the shallows. Hunter slept. Metcalfe sat alone in the galley, composing a radio report.

That afternoon, as they rounded Chatham Point into Johnstone Strait, Metcalfe raised the marine operator on the single-sideband radio. He placed a call to Dorothy, who had the tape recorder cued. Metcalfe's transmission would be broadcast across Canada on the CBC that evening:

"We Canadians started the Greenpeacing of America last night," he began. "We call our ship the *Greenpeace* because that's the best name we can think of to join the two great issues of our times, the survival of our environment and the peace of the world. Our goal is a very simple, clear, and direct one — to bring about a confrontation between the people of death and the people of life." The crew crowded around the door to listen. "We do not consider ourselves to be radicals. We are conservatives who insist upon conserving the environment for our children and future generations ... If there are radicals in this story, they are the fanatical technocrats who believe they have the power to play with this world like an infinitely fascinating toy of their own. We do not believe they will be content until they have smashed it like a toy. The message of the *Greenpeace* is simply this: The world is our place ... and we insist on our basic human right to occupy it without danger from any power group. This is not a rhetorical presumption on our part. It is a sense and idea that we share with every ordinary citizen of the world."

Metcalfe, in his wool Cowichan toque, gripped the transmitter firmly as he broadcast to the world. "While it may be true that it began as the idea of a few men and women in the city of Vancouver, it was not long before these men and women were joined by thousands of others, and now millions who have learned about it over the past few days. Indeed, the crew of the *Greenpeace* know today that they are part of a massive international protest against the insanity of the Amchitka test. They know too, of course, that they are confronting a power that has a certain experience in ignoring and opposing and even scorning protest ... But there is a certain feeling on board ... that a new and tougher situation has now developed for the nuclear people. That is what we call the Greenpeacing of America. It could work."

EYES OF FIRE

On the second day, the engine conked out. Birmingham spent the afternoon repairing it, and Metcalfe used the breakdown as an item in his broadcast. When Cormack heard the story on the CBC, he bristled that his noble vessel had been maligned for everyone in Canada to hear. "It's just a way of getting some news coverage," Metcalfe tried to explain, but Cormack could not be consoled.

"Buncha newspaper crap," the skipper bellowed. Metcalfe apologized, but he sank to the bottom of the captain's pecking order and did not dare come near the wheelhouse. The following day Metcalfe composed a story in praise of the gallant ship and this earned him some reprieve. When the Canadian Coast Guard vessel *Camsell* radioed the boat and described their voyage as a "courageous effort," Cormack recovered his pride. And when the CBC announced that Prime Minister Pierre Trudeau had attempted to contact the boat, Cormack forgave Metcalfe.

After witnessing the Metcalfe faux pas, Hunter made every effort to ingratiate himself to the skipper. Just before leaving on the voyage, Hunter had learned that his father, whom he had not seen since the age of six, had passed away. Hunter admired the tough captain. He studied his moods and steered around them carefully. He studied his desires and tried to please him. Cormack, for his part, appreciated the effort and more or less adopted Hunter. The young writer dubbed the captain, "Lord of the Piston Rings," and although the elder skipper didn't recognize the reference to Tolkien, he took it as a compliment.

Cormack, however, could turn ferocious when the crew made minor errors. Darnell opened a can of evaporated milk upside down in the galley, and when Cormack saw it, he shrieked. "Bloody idiots!" He hurled the can overboard and stomped back into the galley. "You damned perfessors don't know shit!" The captain grabbed his coffee and disappeared into the wheelhouse. The crew learned from Birmingham that opening cans upside down was considered bad luck, and obviously the captain took it seriously. There were more rules. Hanging cups open end out was also bad luck. Standing in a doorway could prove perilous as the captain might run you over as if you were invisible. When the skipper entered the galley, anyone sitting at the end of the table would be well advised to slide over and make room. Ignorance of these rules was no defence.

On the third day, the *Phyllis Cormack* passed through Johnstone Strait and approached the Kwakiutl Indian village at Alert Bay. Cormack informed the crew that they had been invited ashore for a blessing and a gift of salmon. Lucy and Daisy Sewid, the chief's daughters, met the crew at the dock and escorted them to a formal ceremony in the longhouse. Kwakiutl families came aboard and blessed the ship, and fishermen brought coho salmon. Daisy Sewid told Hunter that although the Kwakiutl supported *Greenpeace*, the ceremony was made possible because the fishing families from the village were devoted friends of John Cormack.

The following morning, Hunter filed a column with the *Vancouver Sun* by radiophone. He saw something disquieting in the closed canneries and abandoned fish boats along the coast. The Kwakiutl had lived from the bounty of the inland sea for thousands of years before the factory trawlers arrived in the 1960s with their massive drift nets. Catch levels in the North Pacific had reached all-time highs and then crashed. As the Pacific perch, herring, and yellowfin sole disappeared, Japanese and Soviet trawlers moved north after the Bering Sea pollock. By the fall of 1971, the pollock harvest had increased from 175,000 tons per year to almost two million tons per year, and then declined like the other commercial species. Crab and shrimp populations went into decline. Hunter saw in the depressed fishing economies a warning from the environment, a sign that humankind had reached some dangerous Rubicon.

After transmitting his column, Hunter dug into his duffle bag and found the *Warriors of the Rainbow*. Since the book had first been given to him, he had browsed the stories and even quoted from it in his new book, *The Storming of the Mind*. Now, he read with a fresh perspective. He paused at an excerpt from *The Ten Grandmothers*, by Alice Marriott.

"'Of course you don't know what it's about when I sing of the old days,' said the Grandmother. 'You're just calves. You don't remember. You were born inside the fence, like my own grandchildren.' " Hunter found himself weeping on the back deck.

A story called "Return of the Indian Spirit" told of a twelve-year-old boy who asked his great-grandmother, Eyes of Fire, "Why have such bad things happened to our people?" Hunter discovered in the story a confirmation of his feeling in Alert Bay, that the aboriginal people had something important to offer humanity. It impressed him that they didn't hate the race that had stolen their land. In the story, the old grandmother tells the boy that there are many good things in the religion of the White race, and that they were sent here to learn about other ways of being. She tells the boy of a prophecy that someday people from all the races of the world will join together to save the earth from destruction and that these people will be known as "Warriors of the Rainbow."

The *Phyllis Cormack* passed between Hope Island and Cape Caution, and into Queen Charlotte Sound. Long, lazy swells rolled in from the open ocean, and crewmembers had their first taste of what they would face in the North Pacific. Cormack tucked inside again through a patchwork of narrows, 100 miles north to the Kitasoo fishing village of Klemtu. Cheering Kitasoo children, who had seen the ship's departure on television, met them at the dock. They grabbed the hands of the crew of the *Greenpeace* and toured the boat. They fawned over the long-haired crewmembers wearing beads and bright colours — Hunter, Moore, and Thurston. They sang nursery rhymes, television theme songs, and national anthems to entertain their guests. Hunter could not stop the tears from welling in his eyes. *These people are counting on us*, he thought to himself. The crew gave the children Greenpeace buttons, and they gave headbands and plastic peace pins to the crew.

As the crew prepared to depart, the children sang to the tune of, "We Love You Conrad," from the musical *Bye Bye Birdie*, but they changed the words to "We Love you Greenpeace; oh yes, we do." They added the names, "We love you Uncle Bob," and "We love you Uncle Bill," for each crewmember. The children wanted to go with them, but the crew shooed them off the boat with promises to return.

TODAY'S THE DAY

On Saturday, September 18, the *Phyllis Cormack* made its way north through Hecate Strait, around Rose Point at the north end of Haida Gwaii — home of the Haida Nation, the boldest seagoing culture of the pre-Columbian West Coast — and headed west-northwest on a great circle route that would put them into the Aleutian archipelago at Dutch Harbor on Unalaska Island. The open ocean was calm on the first day, but the wind turned from the north, the swells rolled in abeam, and Darnell, Keziere, and Cummings grew seasick and disappeared to their bunks.

Metcalfe patched through to Dorothy, who told him they were in the news across Canada and in the United States. "It's a big story," Dorothy told Ben. "Nixon's under pressure from his own party. Russell Train is opposed. Gravel and Inouye in the Senate. Hirohito is going to meet with Nixon in Anchorage this month and *he's* not in favor of the bomb. No one wants to come out in favour of the bomb. It's going to come down to the Supreme Court."

"Roger," said Ben over the radio. "We've left the coast, Dorothy, and we're headed across the Gulf. Next stop: the Aleutian Islands." Dorothy was worried about the little fish boat, although she did not let on. Ben transmitted his radio show while staring out the window at the grey, impartial North Pacific.

Later, Metcalfe reported to the crew that Nixon and the Supreme Court were wrestling with the issue. "All *we* have to do," he said, "is keep up the pressure." Metcalfe, as was his habit, explained the political background. "You know," he said, "both Khrushchev and Eisenhower wanted to end the arms race in the fifties. Nixon was the hawk, even back then. Eisenhower had said, 'This world in arms is not spending money alone. It is spending the sweat of its laborers, the genius of its scientists, the hopes of its children.' "

Metcalfe explained, to those who would listen, that after the Bikini tests, US presidential candidate Adlai Stevenson took up disarmament. "Eisenhower was torn. He was a member of the military elite, but in his heart he believed nuclear weapons were a bad idea," said Metcalfe. "But he kept quiet about it while Nixon attacked Stevenson as 'unpatriotic.' Eisenhower and Nixon won the '56 election handily."

The Soviets experienced the most serious nuclear accident to date in 1957 at the Chelyabinsk-40 plutonium reactor on Lake Kyzyltash, approximately 900 miles east of Moscow. The explosion sent eighty tons of nuclear waste into a cloud that rained deadly fallout over a quarter-million people. "Khrushchev saw the inevitable," explained Metcalfe. "At the Albanian Embassy the Soviet leader made a famous plea for disarmament. 'We shall never take up arms to force the ideas of Communism upon anybody ... we are ready on mutually reasonable principles to disarm.'

"This was an astonishing statement," said Metcalfe, "intended to reach American ears. The problem," he said, "is that neither Eisenhower nor Khrushchev could allay the appetite of their own military elite. It's the same today. They feed off the fear of each other. Nixon is still at it. Remember Eisenhower's great comment. He said: 'The people want peace so much that one of these days governments had better get out of the way and let them have it.' Okay, then, today's the day."

A chipper Patrick Moore came into the galley to summon Hunter for his watch. "I saw a whale," he told them.

Cormack had sat down to drink his coffee. "It used to be," he said, "you could see whales from horizon to horizon in the Gulf of Alaska."

A GOOD JOINT

The crew was on four-hour shifts, but Cummings, Keziere, Darnell, and Fineberg were down with seasickness, so Thurston volunteered to join Hunter on his watch. He made his rounds through the bunkroom, handing out Gravol and making sure his ailing shipmates were not dehydrated. Seasickness is an alien, unrelenting discomfort. Sailors have found God in the horror of it, or thrown themselves into the sea to end the nausea. Cormack knew this, but there was little he could do. He checked on his charges by going from bunk to bunk with a tape measure. "Just measurin' these guys up for their coffins," he chuckled to Thurston, who grabbed his cassette player and joined Hunter in the wheelhouse.

Hunter had found that a cure for seasickness was a good joint. The crew of a boat can be divided along many lines of allegiance: workers and bosses, the religious and secular, the brave and the timid, the carefree and the calculating. This crew revealed most of these fault lines and a few new ones. There were the "mystics and the mechanics," as Hunter pointed out to Thurston, and there were those who smoked marijuana and those who didn't, namely Cormack, Birmingham, Bohlen, and Simmons. Bohlen believed the pot smoking endangered the campaign.

"Does wine endanger the campaign?" argued Hunter.

"Wine's not illegal."

"What we're contemplating doing at Amchitka Island is illegal."

Bohlen shrugged. Hunter contended that the "straight, industrial civilization is destroying the planet and building nuclear bombs. Prove to me," he challenged Bohlen, "that *not* smoking pot is better."

It was a stalemate. Bohlen was right about the danger of getting busted in some Alaskan port and blowing the entire campaign in a single drug headline, and Hunter knew this. When Hunter took to calling the crew "Captain Cormack's Lonely Hearts Club Band," and talking about guerrilla theatre, Bohlen responded that it was more like "a guerrilla musical comedy!" Bohlen and Hunter showed respect to each other, but they represented two irreconcilable camps among the crew.

In the wheelhouse with Thurston, Hunter checked the compass to confirm that he was on the west-northwest heading that Cormack had given him. He told Thurston his theory about marijuana as a treatment for seasickness.

"Yeah," said the doctor. "It gimbals your brain." He set the tape recorder on the console in front of them. "Beethoven or Moody Blues?"

"Moody Blues."

As a connoisseur of music, dance, and theater, Thurston normally shunned rock music, but he appreciated the Moody Blues. While "The Voyage" from *On the Threshold of a Dream* filled the cabin, the sea swells grew and the fish boat bucked directly into them. Like the Sorcerer's Apprentice, Thurston conducted the ocean swells to the music. Hunter squealed with delight as they topped a wave and descended.

He told Thurston about his reading of the *Warriors of the Rainbow*. "It's a prophecy. When the air is blackened, the rivers poisoned, the land tortured by human ignorance, citizens from all nations of the world will come together to save the Earth. Man, it's like we're helping to fulfill the prophecy. We're the Warriors of the Rainbow."

Thurston continued conducting as he nodded. “Uh-huh.” Pat Moore entered, saw there was a party underway, and stayed. Hunter told him about the Warriors of the Rainbow. “Cool,” Moore said.

As the Gravol took effect, Fineberg and Darnell found their way to the wheelhouse. Cummings arrived, slumped in the corner under the radarscope, and puffed his pipe. Keziere swayed gaily to the music as Thurston conducted the rise and fall of the great, unknowable sea.

Jim Bohlen looked in and called them the “Fabulous Fury Freak Brothers,” the underground comic hippies. He pointed out to Hunter and Thurston that the tape recorder next to the compass might throw off the magnetic reading, but the consensus in the wheelhouse was, *nah, it’s not a problem.* At the end of their watch, Thurston grabbed his cassette player and went below. Hunter sat in the galley and typed out a column for the *Sun.*

Bohlen, concerned about the tape recorder, took a loran reading, the common navigation system that uses radio signals from shore stations. He discovered that they were 90 miles off course and reported this to Cormack. The captain found Hunter in the galley and asked him what the hell he was doing on his watch. Hunter insisted he had stayed on course. “John, I kept my eye on the … Oh, wait.” He had to tell the skipper about the tape player. Cormack bonked his protegé on the head with a knuckle hard enough that he would remember it for years. Hunter confided to Doc Thurston, “Bohlen must have been right about the tape recorder.”

“You want the really bad news?” said Thurston. “Both tapes are completely erased! Beethoven and *On the Threshold of a Dream.* They’re history.” Word got around among the crew and Hunter stood humbled. Bohlen had scored a point in the debate about intoxicants. He could not have known that the debate was about to take a bizarre twist.

Five hundred miles to the north, at the Kodiak Air Station, the US military had lost track of the *Phyllis Cormack.* Massive C-130 Hercules planes sat on the runway awaiting orders. A directive went up on the airmen’s notice board: SEARCH CAN VES GREEN PEACE. “Find the Canadian vessel, the *Greenpeace* ship! They’ve either evaded us, or they’ve sunk.’

Scrambling the $10-million planes was a serious operation. The crew included two pilots, a navigator, a flight engineer, and a loadmaster. The C-130, with a 132-foot wingspan, was powered by four turboprop engines. The planes in Kodiak had extra fuel tanks to extend their range to nearly 2,000 miles. They could travel at 345 air-miles per hour at a cost of about $1,100 per hour in fuel. By veering 90 miles off course, the crew of the *Phyllis Cormack* had inadvertently eluded the US Navy and caused one of these Hercules planes to spend two 10-hour days searching for the boat. The mission burned $22,000 worth of fuel, required 100 crew-hours, and left bruised egos in Kodiak.

When the *Phyllis Cormack* crew saw the plane, they were not surprised that the US military kept an eye on them. The cargo/reconnaissance behemoth made several passes, and the boat crew could see a video camera in the open hatchway. Keziere, Darnell, and Moore took pictures of the plane. "The media war is on," yelped Hunter. Metcalfe raised the C-130 captain on the radio.

"Hello," the pilot answered. "How are you doin' down there? Over."

"We had a few rough days," said Metcalfe, "but we're okay. You know, we're pretty much amateurs down here, except for the skipper and the engineer."

"Yeah, well, looks like you should have a few days of good weather now."

"Thanks for the forecast."

"No problem."

When the crew heard the story of the search from Dorothy Metcalfe, who was in daily contact with the US Coast Guard, they laughed. Hunter declared around the galley table that the Moody Blues, the Great Spirit of the Warriors of the Rainbow, and impulsive spontaneity had contributed to their "victory in the first great naval engagement of the Battle of Amchitka."

"Moody Blues one, US Military zero," he insisted.

THE CIA

On September 20, the *Greenpeace* pushed through calm seas in the Gulf of Alaska. They expected the bomb to be detonated on October 2. Dorothy Metcalfe reported three new US border blockades in British Columbia and twenty crossings closed between Vancouver and Fredericton, New Brunswick. Canadian Members of Parliament made three separate motions urging the United States to cancel the test. The only dissenting vote came from a Conservative member from Saskatchewan. Dorothy blasted the prairie politician for siding with the American perpetrators of nuclear crimes. Irving Stowe staged a vigil in front of the US Embassy in Vancouver.

Dorothy Metcalfe called Prime Minister Trudeau's office to insist he go to Washington to confront the Americans. When she received no reply, she attacked Trudeau in the media with a message "from the wives and families of the men on board the *Greenpeace*. Our men are risking their lives … for the benefit of all mankind." She scolded Trudeau, "Your posture is cowardly." Some Canadian supporters thought she had gone too far, calling the Prime Minister a coward, but she never wavered. "This is a democracy," Dorothy Metcalfe insisted. "People have a responsibility to speak their minds."

In the BC coastal community of Kitimat, students at Mount Elizabeth Secondary School took the day off, marched to the telegraph office, and sent hundreds of telegrams to Pierre Trudeau and Richard Nixon. The scene was repeated across Canada. In Toronto, over 100,000 students skipped classes to protest the bomb. Even ultra-conservative premier of British Columbia W.A.C. Bennett joined the protest, citing the environmental dangers.

The US Supreme Court deliberated the ruling of Appeals Judge David Bazelon that the US "must consider … the adverse environmental consequences" of the test. William Ruckelshaus, head of the US Environmental Protection Agency, announced that he was "personally opposed," to the test.

A fundamental difference between the *Greenpeace* and earlier protest boats like the *Golden Rule* was the sophisticated media campaign. As Metcalfe said, "Whoever gets the best headlines and photographs wins." Hunter had long since worked out his "mindbomb" theory. The wire services picked up news stories from both journalists. "John Lennon had the right idea," said Metcalfe, "when he ran the 'War is over, if you want it' ads and staged the anti-war sleep-in with Yoko. Like Lennon said, Why not *sell* the idea of peace?"

Fineberg, on the other hand, argued for scientific logic. "The facts," he said, "speak for themselves. We don't need to create media stories. Exploding nuclear bombs in an earthquake zone is crazy. We can win this on the scientific facts."

"You're wrong," said Metcalfe. "Debating statistics with the US military just plays into their hands." Metcalfe had gone through this point with the Don't Make A Wave group before they departed. As far as he was concerned, they had a strategy. Fineberg had entered the mix later, and Metcalfe grew frustrated at having to cover these points again. "Look," he said, "we've done our research. We're not shooting in the dark. We have our scientific facts straight, but that's not how this will be won. Debating the science is a trap. The bombs are a threat to everyone on earth. It's time to say 'No!' Keep it simple. We've already gone over this. Our message is to place ourselves in harm's way as a demonstration of our concern. The bombs threaten humanity. Period."

Fineberg made the surprising suggestion that the *Greenpeace* crew shouldn't violate American law and even suggested they go back to port to rethink their strategy. Metcalfe grew suspicious of Fineberg. The American didn't seem to be a journalist as claimed, and he seemed too quick to take issue with the agreed-upon strategy. Meanwhile, Terry Simmons supported Fineberg. He believed in rigorous scientific evidence rather than dramatic news stories. Simmons felt the media message should be about the direct ecological impact of the blast, like the dead sea otters. As the debate over tactics spread, Metcalfe saw the crew being divided, and he blamed Fineberg.

Metcalfe found Hunter alone in the wheelhouse and revealed his distrust. "Fineberg makes me nervous," he told Hunter. "He never interviews anyone or files any stories. Is he CIA? He's no journalist."

"Yeah, but that doesn't mean he's from the CIA," said Hunter. "Maybe he just used the journalist thing to get onto the boat."

"He's dividing the crew. Simmons too. He picked up on Fineberg's complaints too quickly."

"You're paranoid," said Hunter.

"Even if Fineberg's not CIA," said Metcalfe, "he's not adding anything. He's confusing the focus of the campaign."

Over the next few days, Thurston and Cummings confided their own suspicions about Fineberg. "I'm beginning to think he's an agent for the CIA," Cummings told Hunter. Bohlen disagreed. He said he had lived in the United States long enough to spot a CIA agent. "Believe me," he told Hunter, "our boy Dick isn't the type."

Fineberg seethed that Metcalfe disputed his logic, although Simmons and Bohlen were sympathetic. Cormack and Birmingham ran the ship and didn't get involved. Thurston and Moore made jokes about CIA scenarios, even suggesting that if anyone might have CIA connections, it would be Metcalfe. "What were you doing in the British Foreign Service anyway?" Moore chided Metcalfe.

Complaints among the crew became petty. Cummings protested that Metcalfe and Hunter were paid journalists, while he, the underground journalist, delivered the message to the core supporters for free. A scandal erupted when crewmembers revealed that someone was stealing their chocolate. A chocolate thief on board? "Get some perspective," said Darnell, who rarely spoke up. He pointed out that squabbling was exactly what the CIA would want anyway, "So we're just doing their work for them." Darnell and Keziere rarely joined in the debates, and Metcalfe accused them of "competing for low profile."

Captain Cormack was the ultimate realist. "There's nothin' but an inch-and-a-half plank between you and the devil," he told everybody.

On September 21, a 25-knot wind quieted the bickering. As crewmembers fell to seasickness, those left standing took double four-hour shifts at the wheel. The sea heaped up in 15-foot swells, and white foam blew down the breaking waves in streaks. That night, with Metcalfe at the wheel, a 40-foot wave hit the boat, threw several crewmembers from their bunks, dropped Metcalfe to the floor of the wheelhouse, and spun the boat 180 degrees.

Hunter loved the fury of the sea and savoured his turn at the wheel. Through the worst weather, he took extra shifts. Quite suddenly, the sea calmed again and the weary seasick cases staggered to the galley. For two days the sea remained placid. Cormack remarked that he had never seen the North Pacific so calm this time of year. "You fellas are charmed," he told Thurston.

"It's karma," Thurston said.

"It's shithouse luck, is what it is."

"Okay, John," said Thurston, "shithouse karma."

On the eighth day out — Thursday, September 23, nine days before the scheduled test — Hunter, Darnell, and Moore chatted around the galley table, excited about being no more than a day's running from landfall in the Aleutians. Cormack entered, looking serious.

"Test's been delayed," he said in his matter-of-fact cadence.

"What? Till when?"

"Don't know. Just been delayed. Announced on the radio."

This tactic they hadn't counted on. The US military and the Atomic Energy Commission could likely wait them out indefinitely.

AKUTAN

The *Phyllis Cormack* now moved west of Kodiak and entered the Cradle of Storms, the sea of williwaws and haystacks, but the sea was at peace. With the test delayed, crewmembers wanted to know, "What are we gonna do now?"

"What's happening with the court thing?" Cummings asked.

"Supreme Court hasn't ruled yet," said Metcalfe. "But they'll approve it and hand it back to Nixon. It's Nixon's court," said the journalist. "Brennan, Douglas, and Marshall will vote against the test, but they'll lose. The Senate made certain the test won't proceed without presidential approval, so it will be back in Nixon's hands and he'll go with the military."

"We should push on for Amchitka," said Hunter. "We have them on the run. Keep up the pressure."

Bohlen wasn't so sure. He summarized their options. "We can return to Vancouver and wait for the announcement and then come back out, or we could go into Kodiak."

"Kodiak's two hard days running *back* from here," said Birmingham.

"If we go to Kodiak, we have two choices," Bohlen continued. "Wait there, or fly home and wait, then return when they announce the date. Otherwise, we can carry on toward Amchitka and find a place to rest and resupply in the Aleutians."

The idea of continuing toward Amchitka, not knowing the test date, would be foolhardy, Cormack suggested. "That sea ya had out there? That ain't nothin'. When yer fishing, ya wait for a break in the weather, like we're having now, and then ya run out and get back in." No one said anything. "You been charmed so far, but you don't wanna be lookin' for a place to get out of the weather when it blows up on ya."

Bohlen nodded. "I suggest we go into Kodiak and think about this. Nixon has to give seven days' notice."

Hunter pushed for seeking refuge southwest toward their goal, in the Aleutians, not going back, away from their goal. Cummings agreed, but Bohlen, Metcalfe, and the others preferred the safe harbour in Kodiak.

Unable to reach consensus, they voted. Cormack and Birmingham abstained. The result was 7-2 for Kodiak.

The skipper turned northeast, but Metcalfe talked to Dorothy that night and heard news of protests across Canada. "The momentum is building," Dorothy said. Metcalfe conferred with Bohlen and wondered if maybe Hunter wasn't right. "We don't want to see '*Greenpeace retreats*,' in a headline." Metcalfe and Bohlen directed Cormack to change course again, west into the Aleutians. Other than a few shrugs about the demise of democracy, everyone went along with the new plan.

On September 24, the thin black line of the Aleutian Islands appeared through the low clouds on the northwestern horizon. As the boat approached, the serrated contours took shape in the mist. The archipelago runs for 1,100 miles along the seam of two geologic plates, the Pacific "ring of fire," a locus of volcanoes that gave birth to these islands right up until the violent 1906 formation of the still-smouldering Bogoslof Island. Half of the archipelago's fifty-seven volcanoes had erupted within the past two centuries, creating black, gnarled coastlines. A rolling fog shrouded the jagged rocks. If the crew of the *Greenpeace* comprised the Fellowship of the Piston Rings from the Shire of Vancouver, their first look at the Aleutians fulfilled a vision of Mordor. They approached Unimack Pass that night, the spires of Pogromni Volcano rising over the starboard bow. Cormack took the wheel, bucking riptides between saw-toothed black cliffs. At 4:00 a.m. in the pitch-black night, they arrived in the Bering Sea.

Cormack did not attempt to sleep that night. At dawn, he dropped anchor north of Akutan Island. The skipper raised Coast Guard vessel *Balsam* on the radio and requested permission to put in at Dutch Harbor, a military base and Aleut village on Unalaska Island. The Coast Guard relayed the message to Commander Duke Schneider in Juneau, who had talked with Dorothy Metcalfe throughout the voyage. He relayed the request to the naval commanders. No one outside the US military knew how high the message ascended through the corridors of command, but when it came back through Schneider, the answer was "No." The navy, however, cleared the *Phyllis Cormack* to anchor off the Aleut Village of Akutan.

As the boat slipped into Akutan Bay, the Mordor image of the Aleutian Islands transformed into something more like the Elysian Fields, paradise of the heroes. To Moore, Akutan was a naturalist's dream. Seabirds nested in the rocks and patrolled the shoreline — red-necked grebes, loons, cormorants, and armies of wigeon in small coves. Curious seals and sea lions lolled in the surf. Over the objections of Cormack, Hunter, Moore, Bohlen, Simmons, Fineberg, and Darnell went ashore in the skiff. In the intertidal swirl they saw sculpin, giant sea anemone, and barnacles as big as fists. They landed on coarse black sand and followed a path through spongy tundra, among scattered salmonberries and blueberries. The summer wildflowers had wilted, but lupine and daisies endured. Further on, lush green slopes rose to a barren rock ridge.

The sea-going Aleuts had arrived among these islands 10,000 years earlier and built a great maritime nation, hunting and fishing in sealskin boats. They ate seabirds and their eggs, gathered spawning salmon, and harvested mollusks and seaweed from the shoreline. Russian sailors massacred the Aleuts and occupied their homeland after 1741. The invaders decimated the fish and fur-bearing marine mammals. In 1971, the 120 Aleuts in Akutan were among the remnants of that island nation, now working in crumbling crab canneries and running a tab at the company store. Each week a plane from Anchorage brought whiskey and a new movie.

The little band of ecologists walked past abandoned boats, through the graveyard, past a Russian Orthodox Church, and into the town. The fairy-tale vision from the bay now turned bleak again. Young men on the boardwalk scowled at the invaders, a response unlike the reception in Alert Bay and Klemtu. The party avoided the village, wandered up the hill, and bathed in the stream. Later, they walked back to the beach and made for the *Phyllis Cormack*. On board, Metcalfe informed them that their bath in the stream, which fed the village drinking water, had not been well received by the Aleuts. On top of that, the ship radio was useless inside the ring of hills that formed the bay. "There's a radiophone on the island," said Metcalf, "but it shares rationed time with Unalaska, and it's busy."

"And us white guys aren't too high up on the list," said Darnell.

Dang, thought Hunter. *We're blowing our Warriors of the Rainbow thing*.

"I'll be able to get through about once a day to Dorothy," said Metcalfe.

"What's our strategy now?" wondered Fineberg.

"Well, we didn't plan on this delay," said Bohlen. "We have no idea when they'll detonate the bomb."

"We're three days full-on to Amchitka," said Birmingham.

"They could hold off for months," said Thurston.

"But," said Cummings, "we get seven days notification?"

"Hum," Bohlen sighed. "Supposedly."

NIXON

In Washington, D.C., lawyers for Barry Commoner's Committee for Nuclear Responsibility, the Sierra Club, and other plaintiffs delivered testimony in the US Supreme Court about the dangers of the bomb. This information found its way into the newspapers and onto radio and television. The Amchitka test had become an embarrassment for the Nixon administration.

Nixon did not want to detonate the bomb prior to his September meeting with Emperor Hirohito in Anchorage. On the other hand, he was under pressure from the US military and hard-core anti-Communists to proceed with the test. In a taped discussion in Nixon's office, National Security Advisor Henry Kissinger suggested that the best way to announce the Amchitka test was to let the Supreme Court rule on it. Nixon had appointed the Chief Justice Warren Burger and the newest member, Harry Blackmun. Kissinger was certain they would win the vote, 4-3. Always the strategist, however, Kissinger advised Nixon to pre-approve the test, knowing that the media would not take notice of the matter still before the Court, and when the vote was finally taken, the media would report the test as a Supreme Court decision, not a presidential decision. "If, uh, the environmentalists —" Kissinger began, but Nixon cut him off.

"To hell with them," growled Nixon. "They've bled over every goddamn atomic test that's been made."

On board the *Phyllis Cormack*, Terry Simmons held out hope that the groundswell was too big to ignore. "The anti-Amchitka alliance stretches across Canada and into the US," he said. Support for the Don't Make A Wave Committee ranged from radicals like Ecology Action and the Vancouver Liberation Front to members of Nixon's own Cabinet. "We're winning," Simmons insisted.

Ben Metcalfe had learned from Dorothy that the United Church of Canada had sounded church bells across the country asking the United States to cancel the test. The *New York Times* came out against the test.

Prime Minister Trudeau was against it, and so was former US Secretary of State Dean Rusk.

What Metcalfe did not tell the crew, except Bohlen, was that another ship stood by in Vancouver. Back in July, Stowe had sent a budget for the second boat to Quaker groups and the Sierra Club. They needed $19,000 to launch a bigger, faster ship to Amchitka. Because of the media attention generated by the *Greenpeace* in the Aleutians, they had raised the money and located a Canadian minesweeper, The *Edgewater Fortune*. The six-week charter agreement with John Cormack terminated at the end of October, and the US military probably knew this. Nixon and Kissinger likely knew. The storm season would be at its peak in October and November. If Nixon delayed the test beyond the staying power of the *Phyllis Cormack*, the minesweeper stood ready.

In Vancouver, Irving and Dorothy Stowe, Marie Bohlen, Zoe Hunter, Dorothy Metcalfe, Rod Marining, Paul Watson and others prepared *The Edgewater Fortune,* renamed *Greenpeace II* (or *Greenpeace Too*), for a departure within weeks. The 152-foot minesweeper was capable of 20 knots. From Kodiak, the *Phyllis Cormack* would be five days from Amchitka. If the *Edgewater Fortune* reached Kodiak, they would be only *two* days from Amchitka. Although most of the crew on the *Phyllis Cormack* knew there had been talk of a second boat, they did not yet know it existed. Bohlen and Metcalfe decided to keep the secret. The crewmembers had risked their lives to get here. This was not the time to tell them they might be replaced.

GREENHAWKS

Akutan stood roughly halfway between Kodiak and Amchitka, so waiting there made sense to the crew. Metcalfe maintained good relations with the villagers and was able to use the radiophone daily. Birmingham discovered an abandoned whaling station across the bay and brought whalebones to the boat. Moore and Hunter rowed over for more whalebones and returned with several vertebrae and an inner ear bone the size of a fist.

Bohlen, Darnell, and Simmons organized a hike up the 1,700-foot peak of Akutan. Hunter, Moore, Thurston, and Keziere took a dose of peyote and went with them. Cummings joined in, all eight dressed in hooded green windbreakers purchased by the Don't Make A Wave Committee. The party walked up the lee side of the hill, but as they ascended, they became more exposed to the winds, and had to yell to be heard. A full gale howled from the Bering Strait. Sudden gusts snapped twigs from shrubs and whipped them over the rocks like bullets. Thirty-foot waves pounded the north side of the island. Hunter brought up the rear with Moore, who stopped to paw around in the sub-Arctic tundra, identifying exotic flora. Hunter stopped with him as the others moved ahead.

"Greenhawks," Hunter said.

"These little things have pollen in them," said Moore. He lifted the green mantle from a rock and followed the roots into the crevices. "Man, the real estate is in serious demand down here." He looked up at his new friend, the funny journalist. "Green *what*?"

"Greenhawks," said Hunter. He pointed up the slope to their six shipmates in green jackets. "Maybe we're the Greenhawks."

Moore shrugged. "Greenhawks?"

"The Blackhawks were superheroes. Comics."

"Like Spiderman?"

"Different. Whenever they jumped out at the bad guys they shouted, 'Hawkaaaa!'" Hunter demonstrated the crouch and martial-art hand positions. "That's it," he said, lost in his own thoughts. Neither Bohlen or Simmons had liked his earlier use of Green Panthers, claiming it had a violent connotation. In the end, Hunter had agreed. Maybe, he thought, Greenhawks was better.

Moore and Hunter caught up to the others below the summit, where they stopped to rest for the final ascent. Hunter called them all Greenhawks and cajoled Moore into helping him demonstrate how to do a proper *Hawkaaaa!* He bounded onto a rock, facing the wind, crouched and ready. Bohlen and Simmons joined in and took up the yell against the howling gale. *Hawkaaaa! Hawkaaaa!*

When a joint was passed, everyone but Simmons partook. Near the peak, the men built a stone cairn, making a peace sign and an ecology sign from rocks. Moore took up his investigations of the tundra. When the others joined him in probing the exotic flora, he delivered an ecology lecture. "There's no place where organic chemistry ends and life begins. Does the mineral compound become life when it enters the root, or the water that carried it there, or when it combines with a biopolymer?" said Moore.

"Plants, animals. Organic, inorganic. It's a continuum. We classify things so we can talk about them, but everything exists in relationship. Everything feeds from its environment, takes up water, minerals, air, food." Moore looked up, grinning. "That means: A flower is your brother."

To Hunter, Moore's catchphrase echoed the sentiment of Francis of Assisi — Brother Ant, Sister Moon, Sister Fire, and so forth — and perfectly captured the essence of his growing ecological-political vision. With a "Zap!" he ordained everyone into the Universal Life Church, but changed the name to the Whole Earth Church. And he added, "A flower is your brother! *Hawkaaaa!*"

"Climbing this mountain is more interesting and more important," shouted Cummings over the howling wind, "than going to the moon." Borrowing the "Eagle has landed" line from the Apollo moon mission, Cummings pronounced, "Eco has landed!"

At the summit, they could barely speak against the wailing wind. They leaned out against the tempest at 45 degrees to the mountainside and hung in the air.

"Greenhawks!"

"*Hawkaaa!*"

Moore told Hunter during the descent, "Humans have a political relationship with other creatures, with the Earth itself."

"I have to warn you, Pat."

"What?"

"I'm a journalist. Anything you say is on the record."

SEIZED

On September 24, Hunter wrote about the Greenhawks and the *Warriors of the Rainbow* for his *Sun* column the next day, filed by telephone from Akutan. That afternoon, the crew met in the galley and resolved to push west along the archipelago to Atka Island, just one day east of Amchitka. On the last day of September, six days after entering Akutan Bay, they prepared to depart, stowing food and making final phone calls. Moore placed a whale vertebra on the galley table. Darnell prepared supper. Cormack leaned over the chart table with Hunter, Metcalfe, and Bohlen. Through the window, the captain caught a glint of sun off a white bow at the mouth of the bay. "Coast Guard cutter's comin'," he said casually. Metcalfe and Bohlen pressed against the glass. Hunter ran out to the flying bridge. *Oh, jeez.*

In the bunkroom of the 210-foot US Coast Guard cutter *Confidence*, eighteen recruits — young men including Joe Grimes, James Pratt, Steven Todd, and others from different parts of the United States — hurriedly signed a crumpled piece of paper. One of the sailors folded the paper and stuffed it into his pocket. Then they dispersed.

Meanwhile, the *Phyllis Cormack* crew lined the deck to watch the tiny bow wave in the distance. Suddenly, they heard the whirring of the anchor winch and felt the diesel fire. Cormack bolted from the engine room to the wheelhouse. Bohlen tried to ask him what was going on, but Cormack said nothing.

"I guess we're making a run for it," Bohlen told the crew.

"Cool."

"Against a Coast Guard cutter?"

"*Hawkaaa!*"

Cormack moved half a mile down the bay, away from the village and dropped anchor. Birmingham later explained, "He just doesn't want to be arrested in front of everyone in the town." The *Greenpeace* crew was eating supper as the cutter came to rest and dropped anchor a few hundred yards away.

"Wadda ya think they're doin', John?" asked Cummings.

"They're gonna charge us."

"For what?"

"Customs. I told you nincompoops to stay on the boat." Cormack retreated to the bow and waited casually for what was coming. Birmingham scowled at the Nixon poster on the galley wall and the darts in the president's face. He ripped down the poster and handed it to Cummings. "Get rid of this thing."

Three Coast Guard crewmen in black toques and an officer in a cap approached the *Phyllis Cormack* in a motor launch, circled the boat, and came alongside. Commander Floyd Hunter of the *Confidence* introduced himself with a smile and requested permission to board. Bohlen offered a hand. Simmons stood by. The quiet shutter of Keziere's Leica clicked.

A rope called the "sissy line" ran across the deck and down the ladder of the *Phyllis Cormack*. As Commander Hunter climbed aboard, he tripped on this line and sprawled across the deck. The crew in the motor launch stifled their amusement. Bohlen leapt to the man's aid and apologized. The Coast Guard Commander took it in good humour, preserved his dignity with a self-deprecating nod, and asked to speak with the captain. Metcalfe and Bohlen escorted him to the bow. Cormack greeted the Commander and led him to the wheelhouse.

In the captain's quarters, Metcalfe turned on the tape recorder as Commander Hunter read the indictment. Because crewmembers had gone ashore, the US government charged Cormack with failing to make formal entry with customs within 48 hours of landing in Akutan, in violation of the Tariff Act of 1930. Commander Hunter instructed him to make formal entry by radio with customs in Anchorage within 24 hours. The penalty for the violation was a $1,000 fine. Failure to report in 24 hours was punishable by a $5,000 fine and forfeiture of the vessel. Commander Hunter handed the paperwork to Cormack.

"And that terminates my business with you," he said graciously.

Metcalfe left the Commander and the skipper alone to talk.

Below, on the deck, the three Coast Guard crew stood in the launch with cups of brandy given them by the *Greenpeace* crew, jabbering furiously with Bohlen, Simmons, Thurston, Hunter, and Cummings. Metcalfe switched on his tape recorder.

"It's far out what y'all are doin'."

"We're with you guys all the way."

"Everybody on the crew wanted to sign this thing, man," said one of the crewmen, pointing to a crumpled piece of paper that Hunter read then handed to Metcalfe. The note read:

DUE TO THE SITUATION WE ARE IN WE THE CREW OF THE CONFIDENCE FEEL THAT WHAT YOU ARE DOING IS FOR THE GOOD OF ALL MANKIND. IF OUR HANDS WEREN'T TIED BY THESE MILITARY BONDS, WE WOULD BE IN THE SAME POSITION YOU ARE IN IF IT WERE AT ALL POSSIBLE.

GOOD LUCK WE ARE BEHIND YOU 100%

Metcalfe counted eighteen signatures. He nodded at Bohlen and Hunter and looked at the sailors. "You don't mind if I mention this on the radio?" he asked.

"No, man," said one of the sailors, "we don't care."

"Everybody wants to be in the Coast Guard," one of the recruits explained, "so they don't have to be in Vietnam."

"Except for a few officers, we're all against the war."

"Shit, man, we heard about y'all three or four weeks ago, before you ever left. Everybody's talkin' about it, man."

Hunter placed his hand on the head of a friendly crewman and ordained him into the Whole Earth Church. He told the man he now had the authority to ordain others. "Being an ordained minister is one more way to avoid the draft," he said.

Commander Floyd Hunter and John Cormack entered the galley. Bohlen, Metcalfe, and Hunter went inside as the Commander explained the charges. The exchange was pleasant and respectful. To Bob Hunter, the scene felt like a meeting of generals in a medieval drama.

"Are we free to go then, once we clear customs?" Metcalfe asked.

"Well," Commander Hunter paused and chuckled. "I, uh, would hesitate to give you a curbstone ruling on something like that."

Outside, *Greenpeace* crewmembers handed gifts to the Coast Guard sailors — books, Canadian flags, cigarettes, peace buttons, and the Nixon poster along with the darts. "Tell yer buddies we really appreciate the support," said Thurston.

"This means a lot to us," said Darnell.

When Commander Hunter rose to leave the galley, Bob Hunter bolted for the door and warned the crewmen. They stuffed the presents into their pockets and jackets, passed back the cups, and shook hands all around. They stood at attention as their Commander appeared. The sissy line had been pulled clear of the deck. Commander Hunter climbed into the motor craft and pulled away. The crewmen flashed peace signs back to the *Phyllis Cormack* and Hunter and Cummings responded.

"My god! Do you realize what just happened!" said Cummings.

"Yeah, we just got arrested," said Simmons.

"This is incredible. They're on our bloody *side*!"

Cormack pulled out toward the mouth of the bay where they could use the radio. Metcalfe talked to Dorothy and relayed the story of the letter from the *Confidence* crew. Dorothy Metcalfe sent the story of the arrest and letter to the wire services. The Coast Guard sailors had risked the brig, perhaps treason charges, with their action. They had done something as brave as anything the *Greenpeace* crew had done, and in doing so, they raised the visibility of the story in the US media. By 11:00 that night, the crew of the *Greenpeace* heard the story of the sailors' letter on radio.

The following morning, Cormack called US customs in Anchorage as instructed, and was told the vessel must report to the closest Customs port, Sand Point, a full day back toward the mainland. He broke this news to the crew.

"We've been tricked," grumbled Simmons. The US Navy had given clearance to go into Akutan Bay, not to go ashore. The only person who had not gone ashore was the skipper. Now that the *Phyllis Cormack* had been charged with a violation, they were vulnerable to the whims of the US authorities. It was no surprise that they had been sent 180 degrees away from their goal.

Hunter eyed the skipper over a cup of coffee. Cormack had warned the crew about going ashore, but had not explained his reasoning or raised a hand to stop them. Did the wily seadog *let* them go ashore? Did he figure it would be better to get arrested than dashed to splinters on the Aleutian rocks? Cormack looked up at Hunter's stare. The journalist smiled, but could not crack the skipper's stoic veneer.

Simmons and Fineberg argued that the arrest was a disaster, but Metcalfe had a different view. "This is the best thing that could have happened," he insisted. "We're now a major story in the US media. We've been arrested and we have the support of Coast Guard sailors, US Senators, religious leaders, and everyone else. Everybody but Nixon and a few generals and rednecks are on our side. Well, that and four Supreme Court judges."

Cormack rose and slid his cup across the table. "You don't mind washin' my cup, there, do ya Mr. Hunter," he said on his way out.

KING CRAB

On October 1, icy winter winds bit down from the north as the crew of the *Phyllis Cormack* chugged 200 miles back along the Alaska Peninsula. By nightfall, they passed Sanak Island, and the following morning, October 2, the day the bomb had been first scheduled to explode, they reached Sand Point, a small fishing town on Popov Island. A broken sign on the wharf greeted them with this decree: PLEASE DO NOT.

On the wharf in front of the cannery, the crew found wooden bins filled with hundreds of live, clacking king crabs, shells cracked, pincers torn off, eyes and body parts floating about in the muck. "I have a bad feeling about this place," said Hunter to Doc Thurston.

The denizens of Sand Point — Aleut Native people, fishermen, crabbers, and cannery workers — knew all about the crew of the *Greenpeace* from newspaper and television reports, and they either revered them or despised them. Rough-looking labourers glared and spat. A man in a cowboy hat and mirror sunglasses nearly ran over Thurston in an Aleutian Airline truck. A drunk in the Sand Point Tavern called Moore and Cummings "Pinkos." However, fishermen bought them drinks, visited the boat, shook their hands and donated halibut, crab and shrimp.

Visiting fishermen told stories about the demise of the shellfish, salmon, halibut, and herring, blaming the huge factory trawlers. Like everywhere along the coast, catch levels were in steep decline. "The king crab ya see out there on the pier? That's nothin'. We used to catch those things nearly five feet across, big as a man," a fisherman told Hunter and Moore. "Used to call 'em spider crabs. They changed it to king crabs so's they could get a better price for 'em in New York. But they're gettin' smaller every year."

Bohlen posted a $1,000 bond with the Customs office, which left the crew nearly broke. Darnell bought 100 loaves of bread and a dozen apple turnovers from the Shumigan Bakery for $69.90. Meanwhile, Cummings, a former private security guard, solved the mystery of the chocolate thief. He'd discovered the most improbable alliance of Fineberg and the captain, sugar addicts in cahoots, picking off any candy left lying around. The skipper had an appetite for chocolate and his own stash of jellybeans. Hunter henceforth called Cormack "Captain Jellybean."

On October 12, still waiting for a decision from the Customs officials, the crew of the *Phyllis Cormack* gathered around the galley table to determine their strategy. Captain Cormack stood against the wall by the doorway. They faced a decision now to push on or go home. Workers at the cannery had given them a white paper hat with "Wakefield's Alaska King Crab" printed on the side. To keep order, one person at a time wore the king crab hat and commanded the floor.

"We're winning," said Metcalfe, wearing the white king-crab hat on top of his Cowichan wool toque. "We have overwhelming, non-partisan, interdenominational, intergenerational support. We've peaked. I think we've won. I don't see any sense in taunting death to prove how brave we are." Bohlen agreed, but both Bohlen and Metcalfe knew about the second boat.

"Push on to Amchitka!" Hunter argued. "Let's do what we said we were gonna do."

"In the beginning," declaimed Moore, "we accepted some risk of dying to make our point, and we made a commitment to go to Amchitka. We accepted a bit more risk than we accept every day. But now, we're just getting emotional. What we're trying to decide here are *tactics*. What's the best way to stop the bomb? Personally, I'm not willing to die for foolishness. To stop the bomb I'll accept some risk, but the desire to live, I have to admit, is strong."

"I'm not saying we're trying to die, Patrick, I'm —" Hunter cut in.

"Well, a death wish wouldn't be conscious, would it?" said Moore.

"One at a time."

"Eco has landed, or Ego has landed?" sniped Thurston.

"Pass the hat," Bohlen said, trying to keep order.

Metcalfe reached for the hat. "Give 'im the hat," said Cummings.

"Well, what are we trying to prove?" said Metcalfe. "Go All the Way? Sure, fine, but all the way where? Stopping the bomb was our goal. Floating around Amchitka Island and surviving williwaws is not our goal. If we can stop the bomb by going home and doing interviews on the CBC, then let's go home. Is this a practical protest to raise public opinion or is it a hero trip for the gratification of a few egos?"

"Hunter."

"Fine, it's a battle of icons," said Hunter. "Mindbombs. But I say the image we want to project is us sitting off the Coast of Amchitka Island risking our lives, not sitting in a fucking CBC —"

"But the image is already alive in millions of brains."

"So, keep it alive!"

"Terry."

"Give 'im the hat."

"This mission so far is a failure," said Simmons. "Sitting around here talking about whether to go home or not makes it a failure."

"We're in every newspaper in North America, so —"

"One at a time!"

"Gimme that," said Fineberg. "We have a responsibility to go to Amchitka," he insisted, reversing his earlier position.

"We have a responsibility to stop the test," said Moore. "No one cares how we do it."

"Hat."

"King crab!"

Hunter surveyed the table and realized he was now in an alliance with Fineberg and Simmons. Metcalfe grabbed the hat again. "You guys are acting like some kinda psychedelic kamikaze squad. Fear is a strange seduction. I've seen it. It's a big adrenaline -rush, war-hero thing. Only at the end of the movie you might not be kissing Lana Turner, you might be on the bottom of the fucking Bering Sea."

"Crab bait."

"Lyle?"

Thurston put on the king crab hat and paused for a moment, his normal sense of humour extinguished. "Look!" he snapped at Hunter and Metcalfe, "I'm getting sick and bloody tired of the fighting between … you! And … you!"

"I'm not fighting, Lyle, I'm just —"

"Shut up."

"Is this a strategy session or a tea-group? You're fighting," said Thurston. "Snide remarks. Innuendo. The Kamikaze element isn't just with these guys. It draws on all of us. We all want to be out there risking our lives to stop this test. We've *already* risked our lives to stop this test. Who bloody cares? If this nit-picking bullshit is the best we can do, then they should just blow off the bombs and get rid of the whole lot of us."

"If we go back now," said Fineberg, "Nixon will just blow that thing off. If we look like we're giving up, they'll just —"

"We're not giving up. We're choosing where to fight," insisted Metcalfe.

"We can make it to Amchitka," said Fineberg.

"Maybe."

"John? Give the hat to John."

"I don't need no hat," said the Captain, stepping away from the wall. "Yeah, sure, we can make it to Amchitka. But let me remind you boys, you ain't seen any real weather yet. You *think* you have. We can make it, sure. This is the finest sea boat on the West Coast, and she's been out in a lot worse than any a' you 'ave ever seen. Yer darn right we can get to Amchitka."

Cormack let his message sink in. "It's gettin' on the middle of October. You can expect serious weather out there now. You chartered me to take you to Amchitka. And that's what I'll do. October. November. Don't matter. But …"

He paused again and the room was silent.

"You'd be darn crazy to try it."

Bohlen reached for the hat. "Our charter deal with John is over at the end of the month. John might be willing to extend it, but I agree with Ben. We're winning. We've kept our commitment."

Metcalf took the hat from Bohlen. "We've generated a mass movement across North America. When we started out, the facts were with us. Now the facts are against us continuing to Amchitka. Nixon could delay the test until December. Winter storms are coming. Our charter is up. We have them on the run! We'll be more powerful in Vancouver than we are out here. We'll get on the radio, TV, in the newspapers."

"Fine for you," said Fineberg. "You have a job to go back to —"

"Hat, hat!"

"I'm not done," said Metcalfe. "Let's get serious. We're not going to reach consensus here. You go to Amchitka or you don't go to Amchitka. There's no compromise."

"We could go back to Akutan," said Thurston.

"If we can't reach consensus," said Metcalfe, "it's the responsibility of the executive to make a decision."

"What does that mean?" said Hunter. "You and Jim decide?"

"We're not gonna get a consensus," said Moore. "We should just vote."

Again, Cormack and Birmingham abstained. They had made it clear that their job was to take the boat wherever they were instructed within the terms of the charter. Hunter, Darnell, Fineberg, and Simmons voted for pushing on for Amchitka, but they lost. Bohlen, Metcalfe, Moore, Thurston, Cummings, and Keziere voted to return to Vancouver and to carry on the media campaign. They won the vote 6–4.

The next morning, October 13, Fineberg made arrangements to fly home. Bob Hunter turned thirty that day, and Keziere and Thurston took him on a walk along the beach to cool him down. "Cowardliness is next to godliness," said Thurston, but Hunter remained silent, steaming over the decision to return.

They came across an abandoned fish boat, half buried in sand, named the *Lou*. "Lou?" said Keziere. They thought of Lou Hogan, who hadn't made the crew list. "We shoulda had Lou," said Hunter. The three spent an afternoon in the cabin of the abandoned gillnetter. They smoked cigarettes and joints and cried and talked and finally Hunter laughed at the absurdity of their Quixotic protest. "Greenhawks?" he snarled. "Warriors of the Rainbow?"

"Systematize your delusions," said Thurston.

"Huh?"

"Whatever you think you're doing, at any give time, that's what you're doing. Doesn't matter how crazy your ideas are. If you think you are manifesting them, you are. When you don't think you're doing it any longer, then you're not."

In a final act of ecological insurrection, Hunter and Thurston decided to free the king crabs on the wharf. The night before they were to leave, they crept along the pier, but found they couldn't pry open the bars of the crab containers. Hunter decided that if he couldn't save all the crabs, he might at least save one. Reaching into the morass of snapping pincers, he gripped one crab by the back legs and inched it toward the bars. After several minutes of careful manoeuvring, he freed the crab, held it by the back legs, and ran for the edge of the wharf, where he let it go.

The crab fell 20 feet to the water and hit the surface with a smack. Legs and shell fragments flew off in every direction. Hunter stared over the edge of the wharf.

"This Rainbow Warrior thing?" he said without looking at Thurston.

"Yeah?"

Hunter shook his head. Thurston patted him on the shoulder and escorted him back to the *Phyllis Cormack*. That night, Hunter could not sleep. He lay awake listening to the incessant clicking of the crabs on the wharf. When he did sleep, he told Thurston later, hordes of doomed crustaceans invaded his dreams.

HAVE A BLAST

Meanwhile, in Vancouver, sixteen-year-old Bobby Stowe and his friends organized a student walkout from high schools throughout the city to stage a protest at the US Consulate. When the school board refused to allow students the day off, the news stories incited more students to enlist. On October 6, 12,000 high school students, teachers, and parents marched to the consulate, where Irving Stowe delivered a rousing discourse on nuclear weapons and social action.

Dorothy Stowe returned home on October 8 to find a note from Bobby, explaining that he had left for Ottawa with his friend Peter Lando, "to talk to the Prime Minister." The boys had received money from the UBC Alma Mater Society and the BC Voice of Women, and Lando's mother had given them her credit card. In Ottawa, the two students appeared on CBC television and met with Trudeau's assistant, David Thompson, and with Paul St. Pierre, secretary to the Minister of External Affairs. They presented demands that the Canadian government withdraw from defence agreements with the United States and call an emergency meeting of the United Nations Security Council. The politicians promised to advise the prime minister and referred them to the Canadian UN delegation in New York, where the representative to the Strategic Arms Limitation Talks assured them that Canada was petitioning the US to stop the test.

On October 15, the Parliament of Canada passed a unanimous motion against the bomb test with wording that included "all nuclear powers," to make it clear that they were not anti-American. Jack Davis, the Member of Parliament (MP) who had previously attempted to cancel the insurance for the boat, now suggested the blast could violate the 1963 test ban treaty, due to leakage of radioactive elements.

The *Vancouver Sun* ran a spread of Robert Keziere's photographs from the *Greenpeace*. The quiet, serious Keziere was an accomplished photojournalist, and the wire services picked up the photographs and reproduced them around the world. In London, the *Peace News* printed a story about the Amchitka campaign, quoted Metcalfe and Cummings, and reproduced the Greenpeace button in their tabloid. On October 17, five US Navy sailors in Honolulu protested the Amchitka test by refusing to sail with their ship.

On October 23, during Soviet Premier Alexei Kosygin's visit to Vancouver, the Stowes, Rod Marining, and others protested Soviet nuclear tests, partially in riposte to those who had accused Greenpeace of being anti-American.

Throughout the first weeks of October, on the Fraser River near Vancouver skipper Hank Johansen and his crew prepared the minesweeper

Edgewater Fortune. Johansen, who had not yet taken the vessel beyond coastal waters, relied on his more experienced First Mate, Bill Smith, to help run the ship, now called *Greenpeace II*.

Rod Marining had intended to ship out on the *Edgewater Fortune*, but after Fineberg left the *Phyllis Cormack*, he packed a duffle bag, flew to Anchorage, Alaska, and hitched to Kodiak to claim Fineberg's spot on the crew. He distributed flyers and petitions, rallied the media, and prepared a welcome for the protest boat.

The *Phyllis Cormack* left Sand Point, hugged the coastline, and arrived in the port of Kodiak, where a small flotilla greeted them with signs: THANK YOU GREENPEACE, and WELCOME TO ALASKA, YOU'LL HAVE A BLAST. Metcalfe covered the retreat of the protest boat by filing a story about Hunter turning thirty. "Editors love birthdays," he told Hunter. The media campaign did not slow down, and Metcalfe's theory that they were winning gained credibility. In Kodiak, children swarmed the boat. The mayor presented them with the Alaska flag and held a banquet with the chief of police and city councillors in attendance. The media clogged the dock and interviewed everyone on the crew. Even Cormack and Birmingham took their bows, lauded as the two men who had kept this crew of misfits alive.

To Marining, no stranger to craziness, the crewmembers appeared like ghostly wards from a maritime sanatorium. "Spooky," he told Bob Hunter. Marining, Hunter, and Thurston drank beer with a gang of Coast Guard sailors, who told them that the crewmen of the *Confidence* were now famous. Each crewman who had signed the letter supporting Greenpeace had been reprimanded and given a $100 fine, but the Alaskan Mothers Against Cannikin donated the money to pay the fines. Two of the junior officers were busted down, but when replacements refused the commissions, their ranks were reinstated.

"They got off scot-free," said Hunter.

"Exactly."

LOSING THE EGO

The *Phyllis Cormack*, with Marining now aboard, kept to the coast, and made for the inside waters at Glacier Bay. The furies of the North Pacific visited them one last time as they rounded Cape St. Elias. A full gale drove spray over the bow of the fish boat. While most of the original crew spent long hours in their bunks, Marining danced about the boat with headphones on, listening to Grateful Dead tapes, straddling the boom to ride the waves. Cormack called him "the Spaceman." Hunter trained Marining into the crew's watch procedures. "Basically," he told Marining, "listen to the captain."

During the storm, Cormack left the wheelhouse only for quick tours of the bilge and the engine room. No one else on the crew could hang onto the wheel for long. He warned Hunter that waves can merge into giants that can come upon a boat with little warning. "Watch fer the freak ones," he told Hunter.

"How do we watch for the freak ones when it gets dark, John?" Hunter wanted to know.

"Waaall," said the captain, "that's the thing, ya see."

Cormack took 15-minute naps through the night. When the swells became too dangerous to head into, he swung around west again, back across the Gulf of Alaska. Now, rather than bashing into walls of water, the boat glided before the swells. "Gotta watch this kinda thing," Cormack told Hunter. "With a following sea like this, you can get caught nappin'. If them swells get to be the length of the boat, then that's somethin' else."

Marining believed fate had conspired to drive them toward Amchitka after all, but when the storm blew out that evening, Cormack turned the boat back around and they made for the coast. After two days, they arrived in Juneau to another rousing welcome by citizens, although Alaska Governor William Egan cancelled his appearance with Greenpeace, allegedly because he heard disparaging reports about the pacifists from friends in Kodiak. On the way south to Ketchikan, they passed a pod of whales, migrants returning south to the winter calving bays in Mexico or Hawaii. No one on board was familiar enough with whale species to identify them. Marining convinced Hunter, Moore, Thurston, and Keziere to gather on the bow and call the whales to the boat with telepathic messages. Sure enough, one of the whales withdrew from the pod, surfaced for a breath just 200 feet from the boat, dove under, and came up on the other side. The massive cetacean lifted their spirits. Moore's whale vertebra sat on the galley table.

On October 24, the crew attended a disarmament rally in Ketchikan. The next day, they passed into Canadian waters, and stopped at Prince

Rupert, where snow fell and ice covered the docks. Canadian television crews interviewed the crew. The *Phyllis Cormack* retraced its route, back through Hecate Strait, between Hope Island and Point Caution, to Alert Bay. Forty Kwakiutl Native people greeted them and paraded them to the longhouse for a ceremony. Inside the longhouse, massive cedar pillars supported an enormous roof. Totems of thunderbird, eagle, beaver, and bear fixed the crew with grave eyes. A fire burned, several men beat a long, wooden, hollow log drum, and women in beaded totem blankets danced.

Captain Cormack stepped against the wall with the elder men. Families and children sat in a circle. The crewmembers stood in their gumboots on the soil floor, in work shirts and rain slicks, hands folded and heads instinctively bowed. They smelled sage and felt the flap of eagle feathers about their heads. Their hosts anointed them with water, placed beaded hats on their heads, draped blankets over their shoulders, and made them brothers of the Kwakiutl.

The women performed a dance of stepping away from selfishness, losing the ego. In the dim light and smoke, they twirled and the red blankets flared. A second dance celebrated a successful voyage at sea and a safe return home. The women then led the crew out to join a third dance, the dance for peace. Crewmembers wept openly. The psychedelic Greenhawks and the scientists, the mediasmiths and the engineers, even the captain, danced, celebrated, and gave thanks.

IS THAT ON OUR SIDE?

On October 27, as the boat headed back through Discovery Passage, Nixon set a test deadline of November 4, a week away, but the Supreme Court still had not ruled. Metcalfe chose this moment to reveal to the crew that a second boat was prepared to take up the protest. Captain Johansen's crew were prepared to depart within 24 hours of Nixon's announcement. When Cummings heard about the second boat, he raged at Metcalfe, "You deceived us!," but he calmed down when he learned that, if he desired, he could join the minesweeper crew.

In Vancouver, Will Jones, expatriate American and former navigator on the *USS Iowa*, heard about the impending departure of the *Greenpeace II* on the evening news. He had been working for IBM in San Francisco when he and his wife, Ann, decided to move to Canada to keep their two teenage sons out of the Vietnam War. He landed a job at Simon Fraser University (SFU) and moved to Vancouver with his sons while his wife stayed in California to sell their home. When he heard about the *Greenpeace II*, he sensed the organization could use his help. "I'm going," he told his boys. He phoned his wife and asked her to call his boss at SFU to explain. He left the boys some money, packed his seabag, and went to the dock. Captain Johansen talked to Jones for five minutes and introduced him as "our navigator" to First Mate Bill Smith. The following morning, on October 28, young radical Paul Watson let go the lines from the ship, and they headed north.

Johansen made radio contact with the *Phyllis Cormack* and arranged for the two boats to meet near Union Bay, a day out of Vancouver. The *Phyllis Cormack* crew lined the gunwales as the military ship approached in the morning fog. The *Edgewater Fortune* was one of twenty Bay Class Canadian minesweepers built after the war, with wooden hull and aluminum framing, displacing 390 tons of water, 152 feet long, 28 feet across the beam. It had been commissioned in 1954 as the *Fortune*, sold a decade later as a workboat, and picked up by Johansen. Two 1,200-horsepower Lancaster diesel engines pushed the sleek, white hull through the water. The spacious wheelhouse stood amidships and surveyed the vast forward deck. The galley and bunkrooms accommodated a crew of thirty-eight. The ship had once carried mechanical minesweeping equipment and a 40-mm gun. The array of sonar, radar, and radio antennae gave the ship a serious martial look.

"Is that on *our* side?" muttered Cummings.

Moore smiled broadly. He had wavered on the vote to return, but had been swayed by Metcalfe's theory that they were winning and could be more effective in Vancouver. "This makes it real," he said to Hunter. "We're not defeated. We're reinforced."

The two crews shouted, hugged and shook hands as the boats pulled abeam of each other. The *Phyllis Cormack* crew offered warnings and tales from the Cradle of Storms and the Eco-cairn of Akutan. Bohlen handed the Greenpeace flag from the *Phyllis Cormack* to Don't Make A Wave stalwart Christian Bergthorson on the *Edgewater Fortune*. Cummings, Marining, Simmons, and engineer Birmingham joined the minesweeper, and the ship headed north, with a week to reach Amchitka before the blast deadline of November 4.

WE'RE OKAY

In Vancouver, Irving and Dorothy Stowe, Zoe Hunter, Dorothy Metcalfe, Lou Hogan, and the ecology community that had stopped the highway through Vancouver and saved the Skagit River Valley greeted and toasted the sailors from the *Phyllis Cormack*, who had faced down the US nuclear behemoth. The next morning, Hunter and Metcalfe went to work writing and broadcasting stories about the minesweeper, *Greenpeace II*.

Once the *Edgewater Fortune* left the protection of the inside passage, the winter storms that Cormack had forecast lashed down from the north and beat against the minesweeper. One by one, the crew fell into their bunks, some unable to keep even water in their tortured stomachs. Johansen, Will Jones, Bill Smith, and Paul Watson operated the vessel. The ship carried a CBC film crew, *Vancouver Sun* reporter Jim McCandlish, and news photographer Gerry Deiter. Few of these volunteers, however, appeared on deck.

The violent wind and waves smashed the radar dish, ripped antennae from the mast, and bent the aluminum framing on the flying bridge. Bucking into the storm burned a hundred gallons of fuel per hour, and although the twin diesels could push the minesweeper at 20 knots, they were slowed by the wind and sea to less than 10 knots. In some gusts and against the larger waves, Johansen saw bubbles from the props surfacing in *front* of the ship, meaning they were being driven backwards. Will Jones modestly assumed command in the wheelhouse. "We're okay," he assured his skipper.

Most of the crew simply endured each breath, one at a time, in their bunks. After two days, Dr. Joseph Stipec grew alarmed about the ability of one crewman to actually survive the dehydration. The fuel tanks were being drained and the ship battered. Three days out, Jones, Smith, and Johansen finally had no choice but to come about and submit to the sea, which drove them back toward the coast.

As his dream of reaching Amchitka Island faded, Bob Cummings broke down emotionally, unable to write stories or successfully communicate whatever private purgatory he had fallen into. Rod Marining stayed active on deck and got to see the infamous haystacks, huge columns of water several storeys high, much taller than the radio antennae on the mast of the minesweeper.

Greenpeace II ducked into Juneau on November 2, billeted the seasick cases with local supporters, refuelled, and headed back out for Amchitka Island, only to meet a storm more furious and stubborn than the last. They fled back into Juneau, refuelled again, and then made a final push across the Gulf. This time, however, the sea indulged them. The Gulf of Alaska turned calm and they struck west at over 400 nautical miles per day.

On November 3, one day before Nixon's deadline, with the Supreme Court convened in a special session, Marining made radio contact with Ben and Dorothy Metcalfe in Vancouver and told them, "We're on our way to Amchitka."

FUN FOR THE KIDS

On November 2, British Columbia Unions representing over 150,000 workers went on a half-hour work stoppage in support of the protestors. "For the first time in North America," said B.C. labour leader Ray Haynes, "workers are downing tools not over wages, not over working hours, and not over working conditions, but because of a danger to all mankind." In Vancouver, workers in hard hats marched on the US Consulate carrying peace signs.

"Does US need reminding that it doesn't own the world?" blared a headline in the *Toronto Star*. The *Washington Post* published an open letter signed by prominent Canadians, including Burrard First Nations Chief Dan George and former Canadian Prime Minister Lester Pearson, urging the United States to stop the nuclear bomb test. The *New York Times* declared that the thermonuclear test represented "the folly of a species that burns and poisons and blows up its own home."

Canadian authors Pierre Berton and Charles Templeton drafted a petition to President Nixon demanding that he "immediately cancel" the test. "As your neighbours, we consider your action in approving this test incomprehensible ... You are playing Russian roulette next door to where we live. We ask you in the name of sanity and common sense, to stop it now." Radio station CKEY in Toronto collected 60,000 names on the petition. Across Canada, church leaders, labour leaders, and Native leaders signed the petition. Nobel laureate Linus Pauling, Jean-Paul Sartre, and Simone de Beauvoir signed.

On November 4, Nixon's deadline, Berton delivered the petition, with 177,000 signatures, to the White House. US Senator Mike Gravel turned his office over to the Canadian, and two Washington radio stations gave Berton free airtime to appeal for support. At the White House, Berton demanded to see Nixon, but presidential counsel John Dean accepted the petition on Nixon's behalf. On that same day, protestors closed US-Canadian border crossings and stormed US Consulates across Canada. The Ambassador Bridge between Windsor, Ontario, and Detroit, Michigan, was jammed with 5,000 protestors. Thousands more protested in Sarnia, Thunder Bay, Niagara Falls, Cornwall, and in Fredericton, New Brunswick. Eight thousand people surrounded the US Consulate in Toronto.

The *Greenpeace II* pushed toward Amchitka, racing the deadline, but the bomb remained silent.

On November 5, thirty US Senators, headed by Republican Edward Brooke from Massachusetts, submitted a statement to Nixon, saying, "to proceed with the test is to endanger national security and world peace, not to further it." The governor of Minnesota pleaded with Chairman James Schlesinger of the Atomic Energy Commission to halt the test. Schlesinger, however, announced he would fly with his family to Amchitka to show the world how safe this test was. "It's fun for the kids, and my wife is delighted to get away from the house for a while," he told reporters at the Washington airport, as he posed for a photograph with his smiling teenage daughter and visibly nervous wife.

At 1:00 on Saturday afternoon, November 6, US Supreme Court Chief Justice Warren Berger announced the 4-3 vote, to allow the test to proceed, exactly as both Metcalfe and Henry Kissinger had predicted. Justice William O. Douglas, appointed to the court by Franklin Roosevelt in 1939, wrote the dissenting opinion, stating that the AEC had not met legal requirements under the National Environmental Policy Act.

Five hours later, at 6:00 p.m. Washington, D.C. time, 11:00 a.m. local time, the Atomic Energy Commission detonated a 5.2-megaton hydrogen bomb 5,875 feet below the surface of Amchitka Island. The blast created a molten cavern inside the rock, fissured the volcanic substrate, and blew a mile-wide crater on the surface that filled with water, later named Cannikin Lake. Radioactive krypton gas leaked from the fissured rock. Military buildings and trailers crumpled, roads collapsed, and the fault line lifted three feet across 14 acres of tundra. Six natural lakes drained dry. Forty thousand cubic metres of granite crumbled from shoreline cliffs. The shock wave registered 7.2 on the Richter scale, the largest human-made earth tremor in history. As with earlier blasts, the shock instantly killed seabirds on the rocks and split the skulls of thousands of sea otters.

James Schlesinger's jetlagged family felt the tremor as they sipped coffee and hot chocolate in a concrete bunker at the naval base on the north end of the island, 40 miles from the test site.

When the bomb detonated, the *Greenpeace II* was south of Sand Point, 700 nautical miles from Amchitka Island. Marining sat at the bow of the *Greenpeace II*, listening to his cassette tapes, waiting for the tidal wave that never came.

On the way home, the minesweeper ran before a fresh breeze. On November 9, as the *Greenpeace II* approached Dixon Entrance, crewmember and jazz musician Joe Breton sat on the deck, leaning against the bulwark, playing his saxophone. Marining sat beside him in the sun. Breton stopped playing for a moment and told Marining that he had never felt so inspired as a musician. Something about the decision to take a stand against the bomb had unlocked his creativity. They talked about the fact that the Soviet Union and France both tested nuclear weapons. Marining mentioned that the French had refused to sign the Limited Test Ban Treaty and continued to explode nuclear bombs in the atmosphere over the South Pacific.

Breton thought about this, then went back to playing music. After 10 minutes, he turned again to Marining. "We should just keep going," he said casually. "We should go to Polynesia and take on the French." He leaned back against the wheelhouse bulwark, took up his saxophone, and played.

A BRIDGE OF GREEN

Because they had failed to stop the bomb on Amchitka, the crews of the *Phyllis Cormack* and the *Edgewater Fortune* arrived home thinking their effort futile. However, the opinion among disarmament activists from law offices in Washington, D.C. to coffee bars in Kitsilano was that the

Amchitka debate had been won. Opposition was so massive, campaigners believed, that the United States might not attempt to complete the scheduled series of tests.

Time magazine reported "Seldom, if ever, had so many Canadians felt so deep a sense of resentment and anger over a single US action. For once, the cries of protest were not confined to the radical Left, but came from a broad spectrum of Canadian society." The magazine, however, only reported this in the Canadian edition; American readers were spared this revelation. University of Toronto political professor James Eayers wrote in the *Vancouver Sun,* "Hundreds of thousands of citizens around the … Pacific Rim have been radicalized by Amchitka."

"All along," Hunter wrote in his column, "I have believed that ecology is a bridge of green, spanning not only the generation gap but the gap between workers and students, left and right, rich and poor." Hunter pointed out that labour unions, churches, women's groups, and high school students had all contributed to the Amchitka success. He took this as proof of his thesis that ecology could unite humanity. During the voyage, his new book, *Storming of the Mind*, had been published, setting out his media and social change theories. He now gave radio and press interviews about nuclear weapons, ecology, and the influence of global media. Television, Hunter said, had become "a great mirror, reflecting images and ideas back onto society from every corner of the world. Knowledge has been democratized." He insisted that small, once-powerless communities everywhere could use the media combined with civil protest to resist the headstrong advance of pollution and war. The notion may have sounded naïve, but the little *Greenpeace* boat with a marine radio had proven that it was true.

In February 1972, the US Atomic Energy Commission announced that the Amchitka Island test site would be abandoned "for political and other reasons." The military returned the remote Aleutian island to its status as a wildlife refuge, albeit with three radioactive caverns in the granite below. The fish boat from Vancouver had been the most visible symbol of public outrage. The Stowes and Bohlens cheered. Ben and Dorothy Metcalfe uncorked champagne. Hunter proclaimed victory in his newspaper column. Hundreds of glasses clinked in Vancouver pubs. The upstarts from the Shire had brought the Lord of Mordor to account for his treacheries. Or so it seemed for a moment in time.

CHAPTER FOUR

LAW OF THE SEA

"In our century of almost universal violence of humans against fellow humans, and against our natural and cultural commonwealth, hypocrisy has been inescapable because our opposition to violence has been selective or merely fashionable."

— Wendell Berry

When Rod Marining returned from the *Greenpeace II* voyage, he met with Dorothy and Ben Metcalfe to discuss Joe Breton's idea of continuing on to Polynesia with the minesweeper and confronting the French atmospheric nuclear tests. "Not a good idea to just charge off with a boat," Ben Metcalfe cautioned. "Let's think about this thing." The spectre of French thermonuclear bombs haunted the South Pacific. France intended to detonate a nuclear bomb on Moruroa Atoll in June 1972. The *Vancouver Sun* published a letter from UBC Professor Ole Holsti, chiding Greenpeace for being "hypocrites" for not protesting the French tests. Marining, the Metcalfes, Bob and Zoe Hunter, Lyle Thurston, Will and Ann Jones, Patrick Moore, and others met informally, in various configurations at the Metcalfe home or the Cecil Pub, and talked about how to stop the French tests. Hunter took up the issue in his column, Metcalfe on the CBC.

French General Charles de Gaulle had been a hero among the South Pacific Islanders when he promised them independence after World War II. By the 1960s, however, he had lost his hero status as France clung to its Polynesian colonies and then irradiated them with nuclear fallout. In May 1958 when he became President of the French Fifth Republic, de Gaulle backed the military vision of an independent *force de frappe*, a French nuclear strike force. He established the Commissariat à l'Énergie Atomique (CEA), consigned to design and build a ballistic submarine fleet armed with nuclear warheads.

The French selected the Reggane oasis, approximately 600 miles southeast of Casablanca, for their first nuclear test, Gerboise Bleue, in 1960. The 70-kiloton blast lit up the Algerian desert as if the sun had exploded from the sand. France conducted three more atmospheric tests at Reggane, but on April 25, 1961, they scuttled the last Reggane test to prevent the warhead from falling into the hands of the Algerian liberation army. Algeria gained independence in 1962, but France continued their nuclear testing at an underground site below the Ahaggar foothills, in southern Algeria, near the Niger border, where they detonated fourteen nuclear bombs until forced out in 1966.

The French moved their bomb program to the South Pacific. De Gaulle sent 18,000 French troops to Tahiti and established the Centre d'Expérimentation du Pacifique on the twin atolls of Moruroa and Fangataufa, 800 nautical miles southeast of Tahiti. An officer misspelled the local name Moruroa and French authorities have since called the atoll "Mururoa." Thirty members of the Polynesian Territorial Assembly objected to the nuclear tests, but on July 2, 1966, the French exploded a plutonium fission bomb on a barge in Moruroa lagoon, sucking all the water from the lagoon and raining dead fish and mollusks down on the atoll.

This, however, represented mere preparation for the *ouverture grande* in September 1966. President de Gaulle arrived for the occasion on the French battle cruiser *De Grasse*, fitted with iron shields and sprinklers for washing away radioactive dust. Southeast trade winds blew toward Tahiti, Rarotonga, and Pago Pago, but to accommodate de Gaulle's busy schedule, the French detonated a 120-kiloton plutonium bomb. Monitor stations detected radioactive contamination throughout the Cook Islands and on Samoa, 2,000 miles to the west. Iodine-131 turned up in cows' milk in

New Zealand. A painful rheumatic skin condition appeared within months among the islanders, which they called "*la contamine*."

In 1968, new French President Georges Pompidou wanted to deliver the promise of de Gaulle's *force de frappe*. He deployed French ballistic missiles armed with 120-kiloton fission warheads, but Pompidou and his generals wanted a thermonuclear fusion bomb like the United States and the Soviet Union had. On August 24, 1968, the Commissariat à l'Energie Atomique detonated the 2.6-megaton thermonuclear Canopus, which irradiated the entire planet with fallout. Fijians recorded a five-fold increase in radioactivity in their rainwater, and doctors diagnosed the first known case of leukemia in Polynesia. Fangataufa Atoll became so heavily contaminated that the French did not return to the site for six years. Rather, they moved their test site to Moruroa Atoll.

THE FOUNDATION

On November 1, 1971, Jim Bohlen, Irving Stowe, and Paul Cote met to wrap up the Don't Make A Wave Committee. They agreed to cover John Cormack's expenses to fight his customs violation, and Stowe undertook a final accounting. The Stowes led or supported a dozen such committees, and held to a policy after a campaign to dissolve the committee and move on. They discussed Bob Hunter's proposal to keep the organization alive and rename it the Greenpeace Foundation, but the idea raised controversy.

While on their way into Vancouver on the *Phyllis Cormack*, Metcalfe, Moore, Hunter, and Bohlen had talked about what they should do next. "Greenpeace is more than the name of a boat," Hunter had said to Bohlen. "Potentially, it's the movement the world needs." Metcalfe and Moore agreed. Hunter suggested renaming the organization the Greenpeace Foundation. The term "Foundation" he borrowed from Isaac Asimov's *Foundation Trilogy*, in which a corrupt and brutal Galactic Empire is in decay. A rebel group sets up two Foundations — one public, one secret — to overthrow the tyrants. When an infiltrator creates chaos, the secret Second Foundation turns out to be a brilliant pre-emptive strategy. Hunter believed this story served as a metaphor for the new "ecology age." He imagined an "ecological strike force" that would fulfill the vision they had shared on Akutan, to fuse the ecology and disarmament movements. The Greenhawks. A flower is your brother.

Bohlen, however, did not want to associate with the counterculture crowd, Hunter's radical lifestyle, science fiction references, and Native Indian prophecies. At the meeting on November 1, he and Stowe decided that the new ecology group should be set up separately and have nothing to do with the Don't Make A Wave Committee. In the meeting notes, Bohlen wrote: "Greenpeace Foundation / Hunter set up himself."

But this isn't what happened. The Don't Make A Wave Committee had legal standing and a surplus of funds, so on reflection, it seemed counterproductive to start over, and Metcalfe brokered a compromise. Metcalfe, every bit as extreme in his thinking as Hunter, had not adopted the trappings of the hippies. He wore dashing suits and ties, spoke with civility and authority, and commanded the respect of journalists and business executives. Bohlen and Stowe believed that Metcalfe would make a better leader than Hunter, so they stayed involved and steered developments in that direction.

In January, 1972, Metcalfe organized a protest against two of his most powerful antagonists: Canadian Fisheries Minister Jack Davis, who had stalled the boat insurance for the *Phyllis Cormack*, and Canadian Minister of External Affairs Mitchell Sharp, who Metcalfe felt had been too lenient with Nixon over the bomb test. Davis returned to British Columbia from Ottawa to host the eminent federal minister at the Capilano Gardens restaurant not far from the Metcalfe home in West Vancouver. "The event almost demands our presence," Metcalfe told Marining. Davis had mocked Greenpeace for being "sensationalists," but Metcalfe had more than revenge on his mind. Sharp and Davis would represent Canada at the United Nations Conference on the Human Environment in Stockholm that summer. Metcalfe had pressured Sharp to put nuclear testing on the agenda of the conference, and to pressure France to halt their tests, but Sharp had not responded. "Of course, he'd rather avoid the issue," said Metcalfe. "Let's Greenpeace 'em."

Demonstrations in the street, Metcalfe claimed, weren't enough. The situation required an act of civil disobedience that would "expose the perpetrators." Although Canada did not officially support the war in Vietnam or nuclear testing, the country contributed to both, Metcalfe said, as "a resource colony for everything from uranium to napalm." The Metcalfes,

Stowes, Bohlens, Hunter, Thurston, Moore, and Keziere went to the sumptuous Liberal Party brunch at the Capilano Gardens with the denizens of one of the wealthiest suburbs in Canada. After the polite speeches, Metcalfe rose during the question period. "Is there any reason," he asked Mitchell Sharp, "that you won't put atmospheric nuclear testing on the Stockholm agenda?" When the minister fumbled, Metcalfe said, "Do you consider radioactive fallout an environmental issue?" Davis rose to defend his guest, but the protestors goaded Davis for supporting the American military against Canadian citizens. The Liberal faithful of West Vancouver looked on in dismay. Jack Davis' face turned flaming red. After the event, the little gang of troublemakers returned to the Metcalfes' home and proclaimed themselves The World Greenpeace Foundation, with Ben Metcalfe as chairman.

On January 21, the Don't Make A Wave Committee resolved to change its name to the Greenpeace Foundation. The Metcalfes, the Hunters, Patrick Moore, Rod Marining, and others remained active. The Stowes and Bohlens withdrew but stayed in contact with the Metcalfes. Stowe's closing financial statement showed that between June 1970 and December 31, 1971, the Don't Make A Wave Committee raised $62,703, and spent $53,025 on the Amchitka campaign. Stowe turned over $9,678 to Dorothy and Ben Metcalfe.

On May 4, 1972, the Provincial Societies office in Victoria, British Columbia registered the name "Greenpeace Foundation."

THE LAST DRAFT RESISTER

I arrived in Vancouver in June 1972, a draft resister with the FBI on my trail, intimidating my family to give me up. I faced twenty-five years in prison for five separate breaches of Selective Service laws. My wife of six months, Glenn, and I slept next to a furnace, in the cellar of a shelter provided by the Committee to Aid War Objectors, founded by sixty-six-year-old Unitarian Amy Dalgleish and others, including Jim and Marie Bohlen. Through Unitarian minister Mac Elrod and his wife Norma, Glenn and I found jobs and rented an upstairs flat on First Avenue in the heart of Kitsilano.

Like everyone else in the post-World War II generation, I grew up with bomb mythologies. At eleven I dug a hole in an empty lot where I could hide from the Communists if they invaded Tulsa, Oklahoma. At fourteen, in Denver, Colorado, my neighbour and schoolmate told me, "We're at war," after he had seen the Cuban missile showdown on television. In a Midland, Texas, high school, as the mood of the United States almost seemed to be turning toward peace, girls wept and some boys laughed when we heard that President Kennedy had been shot. In the fall of 1966, I drove my first car, the notorious Chevrolet Corvair, to Los Angeles to study mathematics and physics at Occidental College. We spent a week running through Einstein's calculations from electromagnetic theory to end up at $E= mc^2$. To an impressionable young mathematician, this experience is like seeing God. I worked the next summer as an apprentice engineer for Lockheed Aerospace, south of San Francisco, and during a weekend in the city I stumbled upon the Summer of Love, Janis Joplin and the Grateful Dead playing for free to gathering tribes of Diggers and hippies in Golden Gate Park.

Back at school, I followed the music, listened to Miles Davis at Shelly's Mann Hole jazz club in Los Angeles, and heard the Doors at the Cheetah rock club. In June of 1968 I arrived in Paris and marched with students in the courtyards of the Sorbonne. Seeing images of burnt children and body bags in Vietnam, I ripped up my draft card and sprinkled it through an Austrian forest. I held a student draft deferment and my physics education fell under the "national interest," according to the US Army Memorandum on Channeling. But in the spring of 1969 I blockaded military recruiters on our campus with forty-six other students, the college suspended us, and my informal academic career began.

I took mescaline on the beach at Big Sur, spent a few months at Joan Baez's Institute for the Study of Non-Violence, witnessed the demise of the Love Generation as Hell's Angels assaulted hippies and blacks at the tragic Altamont Rolling Stones concert in December of 1969, and then headed for India to learn about meditation. I ran out of money by the time I reached Istanbul, so I backtracked to Amsterdam to find work. A magnanimous young Dutch student, Albert Hendricks, gave me a sleeping room on his boat in the Amstel River. I found work in a chocolate factory and settled in for the winter. Hendricks and his girlfriend Francine Jonathans, ex-Provo "white theatre" activists, took me to their hometown of Nijmegen, where I meet Francine's sister, Glenn. I fell in love, but grew so stunned and shy that I said nothing. In the spring of 1971, I headed for

India on my own. A year later, I returned, Glenn and I married in Nijmegen, and we settled in 1972 in Palo Alto, California.

On June 9, 1972, two FBI agents showed up at the home of my sister and her husband in Los Angeles with a warrant for my arrest, implying they could be charged with a crime if they failed to reveal my whereabouts. My sister sent the agents away and phoned me in Palo Alto. Two days later, aided by a disarmament group in Seattle, Glenn and I crossed the border into Vancouver. Over one million draft evaders and deserters fled the United States during the Vietnam War. I crossed the border to join some 150,000 in Canada, the largest single political exodus in US history.

From our upstairs flat on First Avenue, Glenn and I could watch the sun rise over the mountains directly behind the city skyline that seemed, from our view, to float in the bay. I had dreams of being a photojournalist and found a second job in a photography studio. The first Greenpeace member I met, photographer Robert Keziere, lived a block away. I discovered Bob Hunter's columns in the *Vancouver Sun*, heard Metcalfe on the CBC, and in a photography course at UBC, met filmmaker Ron Precious. It would be a year before Precious and I got involved with the Greenpeace crowd, but he introduced me to the Cecil Pub and pool hall where I met *Georgia Straight* publisher Dan McLeod, writer Bob Cummings, some wild-eyed poets, and later, Paul and Linda Spong. At the Cecil I first heard talk of the French nuclear tests in the South Pacific and a boat that would sail for Moruroa.

MURUROA MON AMOUR

Earlier that spring of 1972, Ben Metcalfe had vacillated over the timing and strategy for a South Pacific campaign. The Amchitka voyage had been two years in preparation, but if Greenpeace intended to confront the French that summer, Metcalfe would have only three months to launch a boat. When columnist Lorne Parton at *The Province* taunted Greenpeace for not addressing the French bombs, saying, "I bet they don't go," Metcalfe paced the house, seething. He awoke at 3:00 a.m. and lay in the dark thinking about it. Greenpeace had $9,000 in the bank and no boat. Never mind, he thought, we *have* to do it. He roused Dorothy and told her, "We're going."

Metcalfe abhorred long meetings and consensus politics, the antithesis of Irving Stowe in this regard. "Committees don't have visions," Metcalfe would say, "people do." He believed that the Don't Make A Wave Committee had been naïve to reveal their plans about the Amchitka campaign and had thereby given their adversaries too much information. He devised a strategy on his own, with Dorothy, and in private sessions with Hunter, Moore, Thurston, and Marining. He called the Stowes and Bohlens with updates. Otherwise, he avoided meetings. He believed that if he developed the right strategy, people would come forth to carry it out. "They'll come if they dig it," he told Marining. "It's like jazz improvisation. Like the way the high school kids just walked out of class during the Amchitka voyage. You can't plan those things, you have to create the context for them to happen spontaneously."

The campaign would be an international, multi-front assault on the French nuclear establishment. Initially, Metcalfe launched a letter-writing campaign directed at President Pompidou of France, calling on his prominent friends worldwide to participate. He planned a public demonstration at Notre Dame Cathedral in Paris to bolster and provoke French pacifists. Ben and Dorothy would then go to Stockholm in June to get atmospheric nuclear testing on the agenda of the UN Conference on the Human Environment.

During the Amchitka campaign, Dorothy Metcalfe had solicited support from the Pope. Others had doubted she would ever reach the Catholic pontiff, but in March 1972, she received a reply from the Archdiocese of Montreal. Pope Paul VI would see them at the Vatican in June. The Pope's blessing could have tremendous influence in Catholic France. Dorothy also contrived the name of the campaign. To raise funds, she screened Alain Resnais' 1959 film classic *Hiroshima Mon Amour*, a cryptic love story set against the Hiroshima holocaust. She called the event "Mururoa Mon Amour," and later printed the slogan on buttons, posters, and T-shirts. (During the early years of its campaign, Greenpeace used the French misspelling "Mururoa," which had persisted on most maps.)

Ben Metcalfe planned to launch *two* boats to Moruroa Atoll, one from New Zealand and a clandestine boat from Peru. He told no one except Dorothy, and intended to spring the Peruvian boat on the unsuspecting French at the last moment. "Make the right noise at the right time. Deliver punctuated, planned messages," was Metcalfe's theory. "If we flood the system with too many similar images, we just become background noise. Timing is everything."

Regardless of Metcalfe's surreptitious style, Greenpeace meetings convened throughout the spring of 1972, usually in Fisherman's Hall near the East Side commercial waterfront. Metcalfe employed a technique he called "running the meeting backwards." He would devise a strategy, talk it up privately, and then conduct the meeting so his plan would be the outcome. It was elitist, but effective. Time, he believed, did not allow for the cumbersome meeting style of the Don't Make A Wave Committee.

Finally, Metcalfe imagined that if he announced the campaign locally, the story would die. The Vancouver media had grown jaded with Greenpeace stories and the French tests would take place far away, without obvious impact on Canadian citizens. He phoned his contacts at the *Wellington Post* in New Zealand and told the journalists that he had a scoop for them. He gave his friends a few hours head start on the story, then wired Reuters in New Zealand and Australia that Greenpeace would sail a boat into the French test zone, and he included background information on the Amchitka voyage and radiation. Like a flared-up pufferfish, Metcalfe made the meager Greenpeace resources sound robust: "Our people are in France, New Zealand, Australia, Japan, Peru, the United States and several other countries." He claimed the demonstration in Paris "will arouse in the French people a sense of horror and disgust." And he left room for a sequel: The mysterious Greenpeace operatives, he announced, "will make themselves known at the appropriate time." He added that the Greenpeace Foundation sought a boat and a skipper willing to sail to Moruroa Atoll.

The story of a Canadian protest boat challenging French hegemony in the South Pacific proved to be big news in Wellington, Auckland, Melbourne, Sydney, and throughout the Polynesian Islands. Within hours, Reuters sent the story to London, where American and Canadian Press services picked it up. The following day, the story hit the Vancouver media as a full-fledged international feature. Miffed local reporters called Metcalfe wondering why they had not been informed earlier, but he placated them with tidbits he had held back. "Have you heard about the Pope?"

In Hamilton, New Zealand, 70 miles south of Auckland, one-armed retired logger Gene Horne read the story on the front page of the *New Zealand Herald*. Horne took special notice that the announcement came from Vancouver. His nineteen-year-old daughter, Ann-Marie, lived with a thirty-nine-year-old sailor from Vancouver. Horne asked his daughter's boyfriend, David McTaggart, "Who's the Greenpeace Foundation?" McTaggart had never heard of them.

McTaggart had never before given a thought to nuclear bombs, radioactive fallout, or social causes of any kind. He had already lived a lifetime of adventure as a championship athlete and a successful, then bankrupt, entrepreneur. After a few seasons on the Western South Pacific, the handsome, hard-drinking Argonaut had become an accomplished sailor. His boat, the *Vega*, needed repairs, and he wondered if the charter to Moruroa involved a fee. "Moruroa Atoll?" He peeled open an atlas and found the coral reef at 139° west, 22° south of the equator, among the Gambier Islands, between Tahiti and Pitcairn, a stretch of sea he had sailed a year earlier. The French had scheduled the test for sometime after June 1, seven weeks away.

In a direct line, Moruroa lay 3,000 nautical miles east of New Zealand. McTaggart traced out a route along the southern Pacific currents, then running north to Moruroa on the trade winds, which added about a thousand miles. Even with the most auspicious weather, the voyage required four weeks hard sailing, and more likely five or six weeks. "Impossible," he told the elder Horne, "accounting for time to make the *Vega* ready and find a crew." However, when McTaggart visited Ann-Marie that evening in the hospital, where she had undergone minor surgery, she encouraged him to consider the voyage. Walking the street that night, he found a Campaign for Nuclear Disarmament (CND) poster about Moruroa in a store window and copied down the phone number.

The next morning, he phoned seventy-year-old New Zealand CND leader Mabel Hetherington and asked her what the protest against France was all about. The matron of New Zealand disarmament gave the young sailor the phone number of Ben Metcalfe in North Vancouver. Thus began one of the most bizarre relationships in Greenpeace history, one of its most successful campaigns, and the remaking of David McTaggart into an environmental activist.

ENTREPRENEUR

In the genteel Vancouver neighbourhood of Kerrisdale, near the Fraser River, south of Point Grey, David McTaggart was born on June 24, 1932.

He spent boyhood summers at his family's cabin on Buccaneer Bay, 40 miles north of Vancouver, where he listened to stories from a retired mariner and dreamt of going to sea as captain of his own ship.

As a student he cut classes and received mediocre grades, but no one doubted his intelligence or willpower. At fifteen, he won five of six championship cups at the Vancouver Under-16 Badminton Tournament. Following an argument with a teacher during a rugby game, his high school expelled him and his Scots father, George, enrolled him in the private St. George's boarding school. At eighteen, he inadvertently hit a youth with his 1932 Essex roadster and fractured the boy's skull. George McTaggart paid an $18,500 settlement, enough money in 1950 to cost the family their home. David quit school, went to work to repay his father, and ascended quickly through the ranks of the construction trade.

He won the Canadian junior and senior badminton championships, although he openly drank, smoked, and caroused in bars. In 1955, he overwhelmed the US champion, and two years later, beat the French champion in Paris. At twenty-five, ranked second in the world, he married his first wife, Shirley. He left her and their nine-month-old daughter in 1959 to coach racquet sports for the Venezuelan military. When the junta arrested his army colonel patron, McTaggart fled Caracas for San Francisco, where he returned to the construction business. He made money, drove a silver Mercedes 280SL, and married his second wife, Dorsey. They had two daughters, but McTaggart continued his affairs and his second family broke apart.

His Scottish ancestors might have called McTaggart a chancer, but he earned a reputation in the business world as a person who got things done. In 1965 he formed Bear Valley Development Corporation in the Sierra Mountains east of San Francisco with rancher Bruce Orvis. Orvis provided the money and property and McTaggart built a 400-acre ski resort that opened in December 1967. He married the stunning, blonde Betty Huberty, whose family owned choice real estate at Lake Alpine. He took a photograph of his new wife in the buff, wearing only ski boots, which became a marketing classic "Ski Bear" wall poster. He and Betty flew to Tahiti for a honeymoon, where McTaggart got a taste of South Pacific sailing, his boyhood dream.

The dashing promoter converted another Sierra lodge into a ski resort specifically for young singles. He borrowed from the bank and from his mother-in-law to purchase a hotel and open a nightclub he called MegaBear. In the winter of 1969, a few days before the opening of his new lodge, his maintenance man reported the smell of propane. McTaggart insisted the installation had been inspected and the resort would open on schedule. The following day, the propane tank exploded in a fireball. The entrepreneur clambered through the snow toward the smoke and falling debris until he found the maintenance man pinned under a roof timber, in agony. The severely burned man lost a leg. A cook injured in the explosion suffered a permanently mangled arm. McTaggart had not purchased adequate insurance and the disaster bankrupted him. His mother-in-law lost her investment.

He sued the propane company in California and worked for a real estate consortium in Colorado, but his renegade style earned him enemies. He lost his job, lost the lawsuit, and Betty Huberty divorced him. He left behind $125,000 in debt, three ex-wives and three daughters, gathered his meagre resources, and flew to Tahiti with enough cash to buy a boat and fulfill the dream of a ten-year-old boy in Buccaneer Bay: he went to sea.

McTaggart bought the 38-foot, hand-built, kauri pine ketch, *Vega*, in the bay of Picton, on New Zealand's South Island, restored it, and roamed the South Pacific, sometimes giving his name as "David Fraser." He sailed over 8,000 nautical miles from New Zealand, east to Tahiti, southeast to Pitcairn, and back. He lived by his wits and traded in petty cargo. When the American dollar slid during 1971, McTaggart exchanged his dollars in Fiji for 150 duty-free Seiko watches, cargo that he could conceal on the boat and sell at a profit. In January 1972 he met student and waitress Ann-Marie Horne in New Zealand's Bay of Islands. When McTaggart first heard about the Greenpeace request for a boat to Moruroa, he thought it might be a way to make enough cash so he and Ann-Marie could sail to the Mediterranean.

A CREW

In Vancouver, Metcalfe received calls and cables from a hundred prospects offering to take a boat from Australia or New Zealand to Moruroa. Only a handful seemed qualified. Metcalfe wanted an experienced sailor with an indomitable attitude, not a romantic, but a scrapper who could survive the physical and political storms to come. The call from expatriate Canadian McTaggart seemed promising. McTaggart had sailed the South Pacific, had a boat in Auckland, and spoke persuasively. A Canadian citizen at the helm would keep pressure on Mitchell Sharp and the Department of Foreign Affairs. Metcalfe realized McTaggart was not an activist or ecologist any more than John Cormack had been, but he possessed an assertive attitude. Most callers hedged, but McTaggart said flatly that he could reach Moruroa in five weeks sailing, and Metcalfe believed him.

Initially, McTaggart felt skeptical of the ecology group. Metcalfe told him about their broad-based support from people like Linus Pauling, Jacques Cousteau, and Simone de Beauvoir. McTaggart had heard of Jacques Cousteau, but was not convinced. He insisted that Greenpeace pay up front for provisions, fuel, and a new radio, and agree to pay for any medical costs or damages to the *Vega*. He asked for a $25,000 advance to provision the ship.

"Well," said Metcalfe, "we've got $9,000 in the bank now, and I can send you $8,000. We'll fund the voyage. No promises beyond that. I'll be on board to run the media." McTaggart said he would consider the deal.

From Mabel Hetherington, McTaggart learned about the disarmament movement and the French tests at Moruroa. He sympathized with the pacifists, but expressed outrage that France dared to claim authority over 100,000 square miles of the high seas. He knew the cordon violated international law, and he decided to challenge the French audacity.

McTaggart phoned a sailing buddy, twenty-four-year-old Wellington and Oxford graduate Nigel Ingram. Ingram had spent five years as a Royal Navy navigator and had served as crewman on the English national sailing team. He knew all about radiation, nuclear bombs, and the Law of the Sea. He told McTaggart he would cancel a Caribbean boat delivery to join him for the Moruroa voyage.

The next day, McTaggart phoned Metcalfe and agreed to a fee of $8,000, which he received two days later by wire. He wrote a letter to Metcalfe, formally applying for the position and describing his history. He acknowledged that he had "never been involved in demonstrations," but asserted his eagerness to sail to Moruroa. "Amusing, when you think," he wrote, "*Vega* is constructed entirely by hand — no power tools. Setting out against all the computers, machines, equipment and nuclear power. Old girl welcomes new name, *Greenpeace III*."

If McTaggart seemed like an odd choice to skipper a pacifist and ecology boat, he represented the sort of alliance that would shape Greenpeace into something unique. Ecologists, one would think, could appreciate the value of diversity. McTaggart brought his championship athlete's will to win and his entrepreneur's tenacity to the festival of ideas that shaped Greenpeace. In Auckland, he selected for the crew local Campaign for Nuclear Disarmament volunteer Roger Haddleton, a devoted pacifist with six years experience in the Royal Navy. Haddleton — tall, strong, and capable — set to work on the diesel engine, removed the fuel injectors and oil filters, cleaned and replaced parts, and fit a new propeller. The fifth and final crew spot would go to Ann-Marie Horne's father, Gene Horne, an experienced mechanic and decent sailor. One member of the crew McTaggart wasn't so sure about was the unproven wildcard, Ben Metcalfe.

CUSTOMS INSPECTOR

McTaggart, Ann-Marie Horne, Nigel Ingram, and Ingram's friend Mary Lornie provisioned the boat with rigging wire, nylon warps, safety flares, and survival gear. McTaggart bought a 12-volt generator, bilge pump, barometer, a spare sextant, binoculars, cameras, film, and a tape recorder. He bought a new Swan-500CX single-sideband radio, with a high frequency transceiver. He did not install the radio immediately, as there was still much to be done in preparing for the voyage.

The Campaign for Nuclear Disarmament provided an office, a phone, student volunteers, and money for supplies. Richard Northey, a young law professor at the University of Auckland, drafted a legal brief outlining the rights of sailors on the high seas. Volunteers talked excitedly in the bars and coffee houses and offered to join the crew. Since the 1950s, New Zealanders had opposed US atmospheric tests, and now the French tests. Recently, however, France had retaliated by threatening New Zealand lamb and dairy exports, and Prime Minister John Marshall had conceded to the pressure by rescinding official opposition to the tests. The Labour Party made the French bombs an election issue and proposed New Zealand send her own Navy ships to Moruroa to protest. "We're in the middle of something big," McTaggart told twenty-six-year-old volunteer Grant Davidson.

From West Vancouver, Dorothy and Ben Metcalfe fed story updates to New Zealand about the French nuclear program and the effects of radiation. Meanwhile, the Peace Media Research Project at Victoria University in Wellington provided data and news features. When journalists appeared at the boat, however, McTaggart ducked them. He did not trust reporters, and he protected his privacy. Nevertheless, he mentioned to Ingram and Haddleton that this could be "an historic voyage." The entrepreneur, well schooled in recognizing the back end of a deal, imagined interest in the story rights, perhaps from *Der Stern* or *Esquire*, maybe a Hollywood film. He consulted with journalist David Axel, a former in-law working in Auckland television. "I'm not a protester in the usual sense," he told Axel. "My reasons are personal." Axel warned that challenging France's authority in its Polynesian territories would meet stiff resistance. "You will have powerful enemies," he told McTaggart.

On the morning of April 18, New Zealand police arrived at Westhaven marina, boarded the *Vega*, tossed the cabin, and found a revolver and seven watches. The revolver was registered and considered routine among sailors in the South Pacific, but the Seiko watches, with their guarantees still attached to the straps, posed a problem for McTaggart. The police charged him with smuggling and ordered him to the Customs office the following day.

By the time McTaggart arrived, the Auckland Customs inspector had traced the watches and knew that McTaggart had purchased 150 of them in Fiji. The pallid, frail bureaucrat did not look up when the sailor entered.

"McTaggart?"

"Yes."

"Sit down." The sailor surveyed the musty office, with pale green walls, tiny windows, metal cabinets, and bad lighting from a central bulb. The inspector lingered, shuffling items about his desk. "Where are the rest of the watches?" he asked, without laying eyes on his victim.

McTaggart had deposited 120 watches in a safety deposit box in an Auckland bank, but rather than disclose this, he challenged the inspector to charge him for the seven watches that sat on his desk. The functionary tapped on an overturned single piece of paper and revealed his amusement in a wry smile. "No watches, no Mururoa," he said. But when he finally looked up, he saw no fear in McTaggart's eyes. He fidgeted in his chair and pressed his fingers together in front of his lips. The calculator was now the calculated. McTaggart sensed that he could gain no advantage by arguing, but he guessed he might gain an advantage by pouncing on the petty tyrant's moment of insecurity. He rose, walked to the door, and ignoring the inspector's objections, walked out.

Mary Lornie introduced McTaggart to Mr. Pleasant, a gentle, white-haired lawyer, who invited McTaggart to sit in a deep-burgundy leather chair in his library-office. "If you're going to Mururoa," the lawyer advised, "you're going to have to turn the watches over to them. We can try to get an agreement to let you off if you surrender the watches." McTaggart acquiesced, and the two of them returned to see the inspector. The stung mandarin agreed to recommend to the magistrate that McTaggart be released if he produced the 120 watches.

"We have your word?" Mr. Pleasant asked.

"Yes," scoffed the inspector. Two Customs officers escorted McTaggart and the lawyer to the bank, returned with the watches, and the inspector counted them. He stamped and signed papers and handed them to Mr. Pleasant. The government indicted McTaggart for smuggling and for making a false customs declaration, and demanded he appear before the magistrate five days hence, on the twenty-fourth of April.

The departure for Moruroa could not be put off much beyond this date if they were to arrive by the first of June. The boat still had to be slipped, and the hull coated with anti-fouling paint. The *Vega*'s sails — the mizzen, the Yankee, and two genoas — had been beaten threadbare. McTaggart had counted on money from the sale of watches to replace them. "These sails will have to do," he told Nigel Ingram.

McTaggart sent a telegram to Pierre Trudeau, informing the Canadian prime minister that he was a Canadian citizen setting sail for Moruroa in international waters. He appealed for Canada's support should there be a conflict with the French. He called Metcalfe in Vancouver and set April 27 as the deadline for departure, giving them a slim five weeks to cover 4,000 miles of ocean.

"That's a five-knot push, around the clock for thirty-five days," said navigator Ingram. "It can be done."

GREEN ROBES

In Vancouver, Ben Metcalfe prepared to leave for Auckland. Dorothy would meet him in Paris before attending the Papal blessing at the Vatican in June. Rod Marining, Lyle Thurston, Patrick Moore, and Moore's new wife, Diane, would meet them in Paris as well. "Like the apostles," Metcalfe explained his strategy. "Spread ecological awareness. Like Jesuits. Act like couriers, go where you can go, find out who's on side, make allies, seek help. Find ways to make noise when the time is right." He called his band of ecology apostles the Green Robes.

The boat out of New Zealand would be the central story of the campaign, arriving at the test site by June 1, but Metcalfe now revealed to his inner circle, that there would be a second boat leaving for Moruroa from Lima, Peru. In 1968, Metcalfe had travelled to Lima for the CBC to interview General Juan Velasco Alvarado, recently installed as president by the Peruvian military junta. Metcalfe had maintained a friendship with lawyer and translator Roberto Lett, involved in a popular movement to restore civilian government. President Alvarado had opposed the French tests, but France offered him 60 million US dollars in monetary credits, which Metcalfe suspected would quell Alvarado's protests. The French, Metcalfe assumed, would do anything to stop boats from reaching Moruroa, so he drafted Lett to organize a boat from Lima. The intention, Metcalfe explained, was not to make it to Moruroa, but to become a media story in South America, ignite local opposition to the tests, and distract France, splitting their intelligence and naval forces. "Once at sea," Metcalfe had instructed Lett, "strike your colours, raise the Greenpeace flag, and make lots of radio announcements about a voyage to Moruroa. However," Metcalfe had warned, "do not announce what you're doing until you are beyond Peruvian territorial waters."

With $1,000 in his pocket, a passport, Greenpeace brochures, and "Mururoa Mon Amour" buttons, Metcalfe departed for Auckland.

Pat and Diane Moore flew with Jim and Marie Bohlen to New York City to lobby Pacific Rim countries prior to the UN Conference on the Human Environment in Stockholm. The French, Americans, and Chinese claimed that nuclear tests were not an environmental issue, but Moore and the Bohlens talked to delegates from Mexico, Guatemala, Ecuador,

Peru, Chile, New Zealand, and Australia. They argued that radiation and the destruction of the Pacific coral atolls were indeed environmental issues, and they won allies. From New York, the Bohlens returned to Vancouver and the Moores flew to Paris.

Before leaving for Europe, Lyle Thurston invited Bob Hunter to his home in North Vancouver, where he introduced his former shipmate to Bobbi and Myron MacDonald, lawyer Davie Gibbons, and others. This was not the pub crowd. Thurston's friends had careers, connections, and money to support the cause. They admired Hunter for his columns and wanted to help bring about the ecological revolution that he advocated. Meanwhile, with Zoe, Marining, and his Green Panther friend Hamish Bruce, Hunter formalized the Greenpeace Whole Earth Church. He drafted a certificate of "Credentials" using the peace and ecology signs and Moore's adage from Akutan, "A flower is your brother."

"We believe that the Earth is One," Hunter wrote in his manifesto. "When the land is degraded, so is the air and water … So are the insects. So are the crustaceans … So are the people … Any form of life which goes against the natural laws of inter-relatedness and inter-dependency has fallen from the State of Grace known as ecological harmony… The Whole Earth Church believes that all forms of life possess some degree of consciousness … Members of the Whole Earth Church are asked only to assume their rightful role as Custodians of the Earth. The Whole Earth Church has no hierarchy. Only ministers. Every member is a minister. Every minister is a Custodian of the Earth. With absolute responsibility for its preservation." Hunter regularly zapped new members with a finger to the middle of the forehead, thereby ordaining them. On the surface, his antics mimicked Merry Prankster theatrics, but his flippant humour masked a deep and genuine seriousness, Hunter's version of Metcalfe's Green Robes.

CLOAKS AND ALIASES

In mid-April, Marining headed for Paris with a backpack, a hundred dollars, and the authority to ordain activists into the Whole Earth Church. He carried a press card from *The Province* and had arranged to act as a news stringer for the *Auckland Star* and the *Canterbury News*. He flew to London and met pacifists from the Campaign for Nuclear Disarmament and *Peace News*, a group that had already assumed the Greenpeace name after the Amchitka voyage. Marining made allies and distributed pamphlets about the French tests to editors and journalists. He took the ferry from Dover to Calais and hitchhiked to Paris.

French science had played a role in the development of the bomb, through the pioneering work of Madame Marie Curie and her son-in-law Jean Frédéric Joliot, but Joliot had had a change of heart and joined Bertrand Russell in a disarmament statement. The French nuclear program dismissed Joliot, but he became Chair of Nuclear Physics at the Sorbonne, President of the World Peace Council, and, before his death in 1958, set in motion a French pacifist movement. In the 1960s, Trappist monk Thomas Merton claimed pacifism and respect for nature as tenets of Christian spirituality. When the anti-war students revolted in 1968, young workers, the Blousons noirs, broke ranks with their unions and joined them, giving rise to a new French opposition. Rod Marining arrived in Paris in 1971 and met the vestiges of this movement, recently bolstered by *les écologistes*.

Quaker anti-nuclear activists in Paris took Marining to a peace conference, where he met Jean-Paul Sartre. He slept on floors and attended lunches with plenty of wine and political talk. Student pacifists took him to a Grateful Dead concert in Lille, where he met a tall woman in a black cloak who ushered him back to an underground warehouse in Paris, lined with bunks and crammed with political activists. The tall mystery woman would not reveal her name but she escorted Marining to a party where he met Joni Mitchell. He gave the singer a "Mururoa Mon Amour" button and told her about the success of the Amchitka voyages, which her concert in Vancouver had helped finance.

The cloaked woman invited Marining to give a speech at a peace gathering a few days later. She led the Canadian through a dungeon-like labyrinth below a Left Bank building to a windowless room. The woman introduced Marining on a small speaker's platform that stood before an audience of workers, farmers, hard-core Communists, and young intellectuals. He could not deliver the sort of political analysis that Metcalfe or Hunter might have dispensed, but he told his personal story about growing up in the semi-wilderness and his love of nature. Leftist ideas, he said, had never been part of his experience. He described his meetings with Native Indians, his crusade to save All Seasons Park, the voyage to Amchitka, and the campaign against the French bomb. He told the assembly that "green politics is the wave of the future." The crowd listened intently to his twist on politics, and applauded whenever Marining disparaged the French government. He had discovered a nascent French political alliance of workers, students, and environmentalists, not unlike his community in Vancouver.

After the speech, he met three politically active environmentalists, Les Amis de la Terre members Nicholas Desplats, Brice Lalonde, and Janine Bensasson. They talked excitedly about his Green Politics idea, and Bensasson offered to work as Marining's translator in Paris. Still, the gathering gave Marining a spooky feeling. None of the hard-core leftists revealed their names. They used aliases, nicknames, or cryptic single names. He soon learned why.

Janine and an older Jewish man with white hair and a cane, known only as Nico, escorted Marining to the Quaker centre and to surreptitious meetings around Paris. Nico claimed to be sleeping with an Admiral's wife and therefore had access to information about the French Navy. His claim gained credibility when he told Marining details about the French payoff to Peru and mentioned that the French "know about the Peruvian Greenpeace boat." *What*? Marining was astonished that *anyone* knew about the Lett boat.

"You don't want to get arrested in Paris," Nico warned him. "People disappear in France." Nico explained to Marining about the notorious "Ninth Bureau" of French security police. "You don't want to meet the Ninth Bureau," he said. He introduced Marining to Herbert Marcuse, who was speaking at the Sorbonne on "ecology and revolution." Marining held a press conference with Marcuse about Moruroa and nuclear politics. *Le Monde* ran the story under the headline "Mururoa Mon Amour." Later, Marining tried to contact the journalist who wrote the story, but the writer did not resurface. Once-friendly editors no longer returned calls. "Word has come down from the bosses," said Nico.

"Forget the French media," said Bensasson. "They won't be our allies now."

MOUNT EDEN

Ben Metcalfe arrived in Auckland on April 21, but his luggage had been lost and Customs officials searched him thoroughly. McTaggart, Ingram, and Haddleton met him at the airport and waited until his luggage appeared, albeit dishevelled from an apparent search. Metcalfe checked into a hotel and went out with McTaggart to discuss the campaign over a beer. McTaggart revealed the Customs bust for the watches, but Metcalfe, unperturbed, said, "It'll make a good news story." This shocked McTaggart, who remained skeptical about media exposure. "We shouldn't talk to the media about what we're doing until we've done it," he said. "Too late for that," Metcalfe told him. He explained that media was a key weapon for Greenpeace, and he revealed the plans for Paris, Rome, and Stockholm. He did not, however, reveal the existence of the second boat from Lima.

McTaggart grew suspicious of Metcalfe's motives. From the moment they met, the sagacious journalist and the entrepreneurial sailor clashed. Metcalfe — World War II veteran, seasoned political advocate, and chairman of Greenpeace — assumed an air of authority. McTaggart — thirteen years younger, a post-war athlete, entrepreneur, and playboy sailor — assumed that, as skipper of the boat, he was in charge. He confided to Metcalfe that their story might be sold to *Life* magazine, to a book publisher, or film studio. Metcalfe sensed the tension and tried not to offend the younger man. "Don't worry," he said. "When this is all over I can get you a book contract."

On the first Greenpeace campaign, everyone on the boat, except Fineberg, had been an insider. Cormack had been initiated into the group over several months. Personal loyalties were at work. Cormack had signed a charter agreement and remained faithful to it. Now, Metcalfe realized, his skipper challenged his leadership. From his side of the table, McTaggart also saw problems. His concern was to get the *Vega* off the dock before April 27, and he didn't want the media attention to interfere. Furthermore, he saw financial value in the story of the voyage and was not eager to share that with Metcalfe.

Back at dockside, McTaggart reigned as undisputed captain. He introduced Metcalfe to the crew and the shore team and they each bent into the work. To Metcalfe, Ann-Marie and Mary Lornie appeared bright and devoted to the cause. The quiet and industrious Nigel Ingram stood out as an accomplished sailor. Roger Haddleton shook hands with Metcalfe, spoke as a genuine pacifist, and worked diligently. Volunteer Grant Davidson talked with Metcalfe at length, revealing vulnerabilities of the Australian and New Zealand prime ministers.

As they talked at dockside that afternoon, McTaggart broke into their conversation, sent Davidson to the bilge with Haddleton, put Metcalfe in charge of installing the marine radio, and said very little to him thereafter. Metcalfe did not intend to spend his time installing a radio, a technical job better suited to an engineer. He wanted to visit the Auckland media and, as an avid fly fisherman, investigate one of New Zealand's famous trout streams, but he did not want to upset the prickly skipper. He asked Davidson if he would unpack the radio and take a look at it, which Davidson agreed to do.

On Monday, April 24, McTaggart headed to his court appearance, promising the crew he would return for a farewell dinner that evening. A dozen journalists sat in the courtroom. McTaggart pled guilty to the smuggling charges. Mr. Pleasant explained that his client had only attempted to mitigate the monetary crisis and had not attempted to sell the watches in New Zealand. The magistrate fined McTaggart $800 and ordered him held in prison until the fine was paid. The prosecutor spoke up for his colleague Mr. Pleasant and informed the judge that the Customs Department did not intend for the accused to be held in jail, honouring the Customs inspector's word. The judge, unmoved, ordered the bailiffs to take McTaggart away. At Mount Eden, New Zealand's largest, most secure prison, an officer led the prisoner through metal doors and dank corridors to a windowless cell, where his cellmate looked at him, turned away, and said nothing. When the door clanged shut, McTaggart believed he would never reach Moruroa.

Metcalfe, Ingram, Davidson, Haddleton, Horne, and Lornie waited for McTaggart at the restaurant. Mr. Pleasant arrived, told them McTaggart was in jail, and asked Metcalfe for $1,000 to get him out. The $1,000 Metcalfe carried was all he had for the voyage, but what else could he do? Without McTaggart, the campaign stalled. Metcalfe shrugged and gave the lawyer the $1,000. Technically, McTaggart could not be released until the next day. Mr. Pleasant paid the fine and placed phone calls to friends in the justice system.

At Mount Eden, the cell door opened a few hours after it had clanged shut. "David McTaggart!" He followed the guard back through the corridors and metal doors, into a room, where he met one of Mr. Pleasant's assistants. The guard smiled and told McTaggart they had bent the rules to release him before morning.

"We got you out," the guard told him. "Go get 'em, and good luck."

DEPARTURE

Back at the boat, McTaggart felt he had lost face by being arrested, and his temper flared, especially at Metcalfe over the fact that the radio had not been installed. Metcalfe shrugged it off. The man's gone to jail for the cause, he thought. Let him rage. Bob Hunter sent a telegram to Metcalfe, in care of the *Vega* at Westhaven Yacht Harbour. "Zap. Stop. The crew of the *Greenpeace III* are now all ministers of the Universal Life Church. Stop. Bless you brothers. Stop." Signed, "Pope Uncle Bob and Queen Zoe." Metcalfe showed the telegram to Davidson, but didn't think the others would appreciate the humour.

Meanwhile, a technician helped Metcalfe set up the Swan-500CX radio with his tape recorder installed so he could record transmissions as he had done on the first voyage. The technician mentioned that the radio had not been designed for the *Vega*'s power system, a common mistake among yachters. "It's a great radio," said the installer, "sideband rejection, better ALC than the old ones, but I don't know." The radio jargon lost Metcalfe, but he understood that the 500-watt transceiver might draw too much power. However, he raised a marine operator, talked to Dorothy in Vancouver, and felt satisfied.

The next day, the crew and volunteers attended a press conference at the University of Auckland. Reporters knew about the smuggled watches, but most suspected the charges amounted to political harassment and laughed about it with McTaggart. The skipper announced that his boat would leave in two days, at 11:00 in the morning. Metcalfe had not wanted to reveal this until the last minute, and he took the lead during the press conference. "We're not quibbling about radiation doses with the French military. We're saying, 'No.' The people of the world are saying: 'No.' No more preparing for war. No more of this insanity." A scientist from the University of Auckland told McTaggart and Ingram about the nuclear test procedures. "If you see the balloon," he warned, "you're too close."

When the crew returned to the dock, a Marine Department agent, a Mr. Turner, confronted McTaggart about changing the name of the boat. Volunteers had stitched GREENPEACE III on the main sail, and Ingram had painted the name at the bow. "You realize you cannot do that," the Marine Department agent said. McTaggart escorted him to the stern of the boat and showed him the name *Vega* properly displayed. "*Greenpeace III* is not the yacht's name," he said. "It's the name of our voyage and identifies us with the Greenpeace Foundation in Canada." Then the agent insisted the *Vega* undergo a marine survey and ordered him to appear at the office the next day.

On April 26, McTaggart arrived at the Marine Department office with his sailing mentor, Harry Pope, with whom he had survived nine days of 50-knot winds in the Tasman Sea. Pope asserted that the Marine Department could not force a vessel survey on a Canadian citizen. McTaggart returned to his boat within the hour.

The crew prepared to sail the next morning, but that afternoon another New Zealand policeman arrived at the jetty and ordered McTaggart to the police captain's office the next day at 11:00, to complete paperwork regarding his revolver. McTaggart told the cop he would be there, but secretly he moved the departure time forward to 5:00 p.m. that evening. At the last minute, Ann-Marie's father, Gene Horne, learned the Immigration Department would not issue him a passport because other applicants stood ahead of him. Twenty-six-year-old Grant Davidson, with New Zealand and Australian dual citizenship, had been helpful around the boat, so McTaggart invited him onto the crew.

The last food stores came aboard — fresh fruit and mutton — and the bonded stores, the wine, cognac, and cigarettes. A final check on the 500-watt radio indicated problems, and the radio technician returned to make adjustments. The crew left the boat, ostensibly locked it up for the night, and met an hour later in a nearby pub. After the meal and beer, McTaggart phoned a Customs clerk and requested an officer at the harbour to clear the vessel.

The sun set behind the upland as they let go the lines, slipped out of Westhaven Yacht Harbour, and made for Matia Bay, where they anchored for the night and slept. The next morning, April 27, they sailed out through the Gulf of Hauraki. Ben Metcalfe patched through to Dorothy and went live on the Jack Webster talk show in Vancouver as the boat rounded Cape Coville, past Great Barrier Island, and set sail for Moruroa. On board the *Vega* (now *Greenpeace III*), the crew included skipper McTaggart, navigator Nigel Ingram, Metcalfe, seaman Roger Haddleton, and cook and anti-war activist Grant Davidson. They had thirty-five days to cover 4,000 miles to Moruroa before the bomb detonated on June 1.

That afternoon, Metcalfe tried again to raise Dorothy, but the radio would not respond. McTaggart fiddled with the power supply and got it to work, and Metcalfe filed a report for the CBC. McTaggart, however, grumbled that the journalist didn't know what he was doing with the radio. The tension between the skipper and the Greenpeace chairman troubled Davidson, not a good sign at the beginning of a long sea voyage.

The *Vega* clipped east-southeast, and the crew expected to make five or six knots around the clock, taking two-hour watches at the tiller. They made 335 miles in the first two days, a steady seven-knot pace. By April 30, they reached 40 degrees south of the equator. April signals the coming of winter in the southern oceans, the skies turned overcast, and the 15-knot breeze carried a biting chill.

LAW OF THE SEA

By the time the *Vega* sailed for Moruroa, France had conducted twenty-seven atmospheric nuclear tests on Moruroa and Fangataufa. The Pacific coral atolls thrive in the warm, upper 20 metres of water, and range across 6,000 miles of ocean, from the mid-Pacific to the Philippine Sea. Charles Darwin investigated the atolls aboard the Beagle in 1835 and correctly guessed that they were the remains of volcanoes that had risen above the ocean surface during the Eocene, some 60 million years ago. As the volcanic rock eroded away, coral reefs accumulated and created the atolls. Calcified organic debris formed the beaches and shallow lagoons. The atolls, as Darwin noticed, provide habitat for millions of plants, sponges, sea fans, anemones, mollusks, moray eels, green turtles, sea urchins, shrimp, lobster, and tropical fish.

A thousand nautical miles east of New Zealand, over the Southwest Pacific Basin, Nigel Ingram minded the tiller of the *Vega*, navigating the southern current and westerly winds toward Moruroa. Below, around the galley table, Metcalfe, plied with brandy, told stories about the first Greenpeace voyage and the support of cultural celebrities such as Joan Baez, Linus Pauling, and Jean-Paul Sartre. "Fair dinkum," said Grant Davidson, whose agile Aussie wit kept the elder journalist laughing.

McTaggart, too, had hair-raising stories, like his survival in the Tasman Sea. McTaggart insisted, "My beef with France is the 100,000-square-mile cordon around Moruroa. It's an insult to any self-respecting sailor." Technically, the cordon was illegal, just as the American zone around

Bikini Island had been two decades earlier. McTaggart thumbed the legal brief prepared by Richard Northey in Auckland. The *Vega's* arrival at Moruroa would challenge French authority over the South Pacific under the International Law of the Sea, a code honored by mariners for three hundred years.

At the close of Europe's bloody sixteenth century, a bright twelve-year-old Dutch boy, studying at the University of Leiden, discovered a book, *On the Law of War*, by Italian writer Alberico Gentili, proffering a radical idea that nations at war agree to protect unarmed civilians, safeguard children, and outlaw torture. The boy, Huig de Groot, developed those ideas, and in 1605, at the age of twenty-two, wrote *The Free Sea*, declaring that no nation could claim the open seas as its own. He cited "natural law," to which the affairs of human culture must defer. He later fled political persecution in Holland, served the Swedish throne in Paris as Hugo Grotius, and died in Germany in 1645, frustrated, believing no one cared about his ideas. However, his belief that the high seas do not belong to any state survived, a principle accepted by all nations of the world and known to mariners as the Law of the Sea.

The *Vega* crew carried a second copy of their legal brief, outlining these rights, to give to the French Navy should they be confronted. After a week at sea, however, the crew had their own internal disputes over other, unspoken, laws of the sea. It became clear to everyone on board that McTaggart and Metcalfe clashed over leadership of the voyage. McTaggart scoffed at Metcalfe's lack of sailing knowledge and Metcalfe at the skipper's political naïveté. After leaving his journal on the galley table, Metcalfe noticed McTaggart reading it, but did not say anything. Instead, he planted messages to McTaggart in the journal. The skipper stopped snooping but found ways to catch up his rival. He accused Metcalfe of incompetence because the radio repeatedly failed.

Metcalfe insisted that as president of the organization funding the campaign, he was in charge not only of the political message, but also of campaign strategy. However, McTaggart insisted that as the captain of the *Vega*, he held final authority. Whereas captains John Cormack and Hank Johansen had been willing to follow the strategies of their clients, McTaggart took orders from no one. Ingram remained loyal to the skipper, Grant Davidson sympathized with Metcalfe, and Haddleton grew frustrated with McTaggart's domineering and erratic style. Metcalfe and

McTaggart shared moments of camaraderie and made an effort to overcome their aversion for the sake of the campaign, but something had to give.

Alone at the wheel one night, Metcalfe bristled when McTaggart came up to talk. They chatted idly. Metcalfe explained the 1963 Test Ban Treaty and the resistance of France and China to add atmospheric tests to the agenda of the UN Conference. McTaggart wanted to talk about the book deal and the movie. Metcalfe assured him again that he would help arrange a book contract, but McTaggart slipped in the point that he owned the rights to his own story. He told Metcalfe that he accepted Greenpeace and CND support, but that this was *his* boat, *his* campaign.

"David," Metcalfe said, hand on the tiller, "you answered an ad for a skipper and boat. You accepted $8,000 from me. You have *Greenpeace III* stitched to the sail."

"Yeah, yeah, don't worry. It's all right." McTaggart dropped the conversation and disappeared below.

BLOOD IN PARADISE

On the night of May 7, the skipper pulled the crew together and rolled the chart out on the galley table. They had stayed south of the 40th parallel, covering 145 miles per day. McTaggart had planned to turn northward at longitude 140, another week's sailing, and use the southeast trade winds to approach Moruroa. But now he announced they would turn north and head for Rarotonga, in the Cook Islands, 1,400 miles west of Moruroa.

"We're all tired," he explained. "We can resupply and maybe we can find a way to get the radio working properly." The new route would later require bucking the trade winds eastward from Rarotonga to Moruroa, but they had gained two days on their schedule, and Ingram, by far the most accomplished seaman among them, said, "We can still make Moruroa by June 1." Metcalfe did not object.

That night, Ingram and McTaggart brought the *Vega* about, and ran north. They pushed against warm currents and a northerly breeze, but after the first day, they picked up the southeasterlies and made good time. When a gale hit, McTaggart stood on the deck in 40-knot winds as the lines whistled and the sheets snapped taut. With Ingram at the helm, they made eight and nine knots, spray whipping past their faces, the bow of the boat slicing into 20-foot swells. The two sailors grew ever more exhilarated, and their rapture proved contagious.

As they sailed toward the equator, a nasty tropical fever struck all five. Haddleton, the sickest, could not keep fluids in his stomach and became dangerously dehydrated. A cut on McTaggart's finger festered; he dragged it in the saltwater, but it did not heal. Metcalfe and the skipper rarely spoke.

On Saturday, May 13, Ingram spied landfall to the north. Soon they saw white surf against the rocks of Rarotonga and then the lush green of the hillsides. They approached the southern flank of the weathered volcano, tacked around the western shoreline, and put into Avarua on the north coast. Mynah birds screeched in the gardens of the harbour town. The island, a weathered four-by-six-mile oval cone with no appreciable bays, offered scant refuge from the ravages of the sea. A fresh gale pounded the island, hammering the hull of the *Vega* against the dock and chafing the lines. McTaggart and Ingram fixed eleven lines and three anchors to save the ketch from ruin. McTaggart wanted to get back to sea, but if they attempted to buck the surf through the coral reef, they would be crushed like the empty cigarette pack that he twisted in his fist. Haddleton spent the first night in a delirium in his bunk. The next day, he and McTaggart went to a clinic for penicillin.

Metcalfe took a hotel room in Rarotonga and called Vancouver and Auckland from the local radio station. Dorothy reported that international interest in the story of Moruroa had swelled after the *Vega*'s departure, the New Zealand Federation of Labour had refused to service French vessels, and France had attempted to influence New Zealand, as they did Peru, with a loan of 75 million French Francs, some $12 million US. "Good," said Metcalfe.

Dorothy had more. In the port of Lima, Peru, President Alvarado's security forces had uncovered Roberto Lett's plan to sail for Moruroa and had seized his boat before it could depart. The story broke in South America and was picked up in Europe. Furthermore, the French had announced the *Greenpeace III* would not be allowed into the test zone "out of concern for people's lives." Some journalists had claimed the boat would never get to Moruroa, already tagging the campaign as an "abortive mission."

"That's fine," said Metcalfe, "but they haven't met this skipper."

Meanwhile, in New Zealand, Ann-Marie and Mary Lornie heard a radio story about the Lima boat and the decoy plot. They relayed the news to Ingram, who told McTaggart. Metcalfe heard from Grant Davidson that the skipper was upset that he had not been apprised, so he went to the boat to see him. He explained that the Lima boat had been a valuable news story for South America and a decoy to confuse France, and that it had to be kept secret. The explanation did not calm McTaggart's fury. He believed the news reports were a disaster, that the attempt by France to bribe New Zealand and the attacks on Greenpeace in the media were bad news.

"There's no such thing as bad press," Metcalfe repeated the axiom. "The story is Moruroa, not Greenpeace. If they're ridiculing us, we're winning."

McTaggart waved his arm. "You're supposed to be running the media," he shouted, "and you've got the media turned against us." McTaggart accused the journalist of setting up the *Vega* to be a decoy. He screamed at Metcalfe on the deck of the boat, smashed a beer glass, cut his hand, and spilled blood all over the cockpit of the *Vega*. This only further enraged the skipper. "I don't know what you intend to do, Metcalfe, but this boat is going to Moruroa."

"I know," said the Greenpeace chairman. Metcalfe invited the crew to his hotel room for a beer and announced that he would fly from Rarotonga to Paris. The skipper nodded. Nigel Ingram seemed relieved. Roger Haddleton, still severely sick, announced that the Campaign for Nuclear Disarmament in Auckland would send fare to fly him home. Metcalfe put a positive spin on the next phase of the campaign — the boat, Notre Dame, the Vatican, the UN — and he said to Ingram, McTaggart, and Davidson, "I have no doubt you three can make it to Moruroa."

In Rarotonga, Metcalfe met supportive Maoris and Pukapukan leaders, although the Cook Islands prime minister had threatened to deport foreigners who supported Greenpeace. Metcalfe met a New Zealand Customs officer in Avarua, privy to government radio transmissions, who agreed to pass information to Metcalfe in Europe.

Before leaving Rarotonga, David McTaggart phoned his brother, Drew, in Vancouver and asked him to investigate the Greenpeace people. He reported to Davidson and Ingram that his brother said they were a bunch of Communists. "Jean-Paul Sartre is a Communist!" he raged. " I don't want to have anything to do with these people." McTaggart told the others that he was going to take the *Greenpeace III* name off the sail, but he didn't do it.

On May 15, the crew prepared to depart Rarotonga. Grant Davidson, who remained carefree and upbeat, promised to send his photographs to Metcalfe in Vancouver, but McTaggart caught wind of this and told Davidson that all photographs belonged to the boat, and that if he could not go along with those terms, he was off the crew. Davidson conferred with Metcalfe. "Don't worry," said Metcalfe. "But send me copies of the photographs." At dockside, Ingram shook Metcalfe's hand. "It's been an honour to sail with you," he said. McTaggart and Metcalfe shook hands and said goodbye, the last time they ever saw each other.

Ben Metcalfe flew to Fiji, Samoa, and Tahiti, where he met supporters and left behind pamphlets and "Mururoa Mon Amour" buttons. On his way to Vancouver before going to Paris, he stopped in Mexico City and called Roberto Lett in Peru. Lett's boat had been impounded, but he was free. The affair had blown over, and Lett had become a hero among his friends in Lima. "Thanks," said Metcalfe, touched by the lawyer's courage. He had risked his life at the hands of the junta to support the cause. "It helped," Metcalfe said.

ADMIRAL CLAVERIE

As the gale subsided in Rarotonga, the three remaining crew set out for Moruroa, McTaggart now the undisputed master of his boat. They had thirteen days to cover 1,500 nautical miles. This would be fine, but they now headed into the southeasterly trade winds, which pushed them north toward Tahiti and required a deep tack that could turn the voyage into well over 2,000 miles. Each two-hour watch, heeled over from the wind and fighting the tiller, left the men tired and sore, with only four hours to catch sleep before doing it again. After four days of this, the *Vega* remained north of the 20th parallel, driven inexorably toward Tahiti where the French fleet waited at Papeete, delivering them into the arms of their adversary. They broadcast false positions, assuming correctly that the French monitored their radio, but they had no idea how closely the French Navy tracked them.

The French had amassed destroyers, cruisers, minesweepers, and support vessels in Papeete, presided over by Admiral Christian Claverie aboard the battle cruiser *De Grasse*, the ship that had carried Charles de Gaulle to watch the bomb explode on Moruroa in 1966. The fleet included three Canadian minesweepers identical to the *Edgewater Fortune* that had served Greenpeace. These ships — *La Dunkerquoise*, *La Bayonnaise*, and *La Paimpolaise* — had been assigned to shadow the *Vega* once it entered the cordon around Moruroa.

Later court testimony and leaks from the French Navy would reveal that on May 20, Admiral Claverie assembled his captains for a special briefing. He informed the officers that the *Greenpeace III* was attempting to reach Moruroa, but had been blown north. He showed them the *Vega*'s exact position on a chart, west of Papeete. The politicians in Paris had insisted they could not detonate the bomb if there was a chance of injuring the crew of this boat. Should the *Greenpeace III* arrive inside the cordon, the Admiral explained, they would track the boat with radar from *La Bayonnaise* and *La Paimpolaise*. "Why don't we just run them down at night?" one of the French captains suggested. "No one will know." A second captain thought this was a good idea and volunteered for the assignment, but Admiral Claverie quieted them.

"No," Claverie said. He explained that the skipper of the sailing vessel was a Canadian, the navigator was British, and the crewman had dual Australian and New Zealand citizenship, all countries with which France had reason to maintain good relations. "Even if they make it to Mururoa, I don't think they will be able to last too long, hove-to around the atoll," the admiral said. "If they unknowingly drift into our 12-mile limit, they will be boarded and taken away. The weather is their worst enemy and the long-range forecast is poor. That should take care of them. If not," Admiral Claverie assured his officers, "we have a contingency plan."

LES DÉPORTÉS

Ben and Dorothy Metcalfe and their secretary Madeleine Reid arrived in Paris at the end of May. They made their way along the Seine to meet Moore and Marining for a planned protest against French nuclear testing at Notre Dame Cathedral. At Quai St. Michel, French security agents disguised as hippies surrounded them, demanded their passports, and placed the three Canadians in a decrepit-looking Citroen. Exotic communications gear had been built into the car and the dashboard looked like the cockpit of a jet airplane. Metcalfe told Dorothy he suspected the French police had been tipped off by Canada, "probably by Jack Davis."

Inside a windowless room at the Securité National headquarters, an agent told them they would be deported back to Canada.

"*Non*!" said Dorothy Metcalfe defiantly. "You can't."

"*Pourquoi*?"

Dorothy reached into her handbag and produced the Vatican cable. "We have an audience with the Pope," she insisted. The agent grabbed the cable. There followed a great deal of stomping back and forth from the adjoining room, voices on the telephone, and finally the officer in charge said, "Fine, we're deporting you to Italy."

"We have to get our luggage," Dorothy insisted. The officer said he would arrange to collect their things from the hotel, but Dorothy refused the offer. "It's personal." More stomping and phone calls. Reluctantly, the agents allowed Dorothy and Madeleine to return to their hotel to retrieve their own luggage, but they held Ben Metcalfe in custody. As Dorothy left, her eyes met her husband's and a faint smile crossed her face.

On their way to the Left Bank hotel, Dorothy and Madeleine stopped at the Reuters office, reported their arrest and deportation, and left information about the Moruroa campaign. At the hotel, Dorothy called Lyle Thurston in Rome and told him they would meet him on the Spanish Steps the following day. The two women returned to the Securité National office, where a young agent, assigned to escort them to Rome, ushered them into a cab. He carried a thin briefcase and appeared nervous in his new trench coat.

In the cab, Metcalfe spoke in French with the agent, which seemed to relax him. When they arrived at Gare de Lyon, a Reuters photographer waited at the train platform. The agent threw up his hands. "*Non*! *Non*!" he protested, but it was too late. The photographer weaved and crouched, clicking his shutter. A crowd gathered to see the celebrities. The Canadians waved and smiled. The agent attempted to hustle them onto the train, but Dorothy and Madeleine took their time and chatted with the crowd. "Madame. Madame," the agent pleaded. "*S'il vous plaît*. Please."

Once aboard, Metcalfe opened the window and waved as the train pulled out. The UPI photographer took more pictures. A photograph of Metcalfe hanging from the window went out on the wire services with the story. Metcalfe, Dorothy, and Madeleine looked like international jewel thieves, well dressed, suave, but in custody. The flustered agent appeared to be on his first big assignment, discreetly whispering to the conductors.

A youthful waiter in the dining car heard they were from Greenpeace and shook their hands. The agent rolled his eyes. The waiter returned with a free round of cognac for the four travellers. The agent enjoyed his cognac, so Metcalfe bought another round. Then the agent felt compelled to buy a round. His confidence bolstered, he now appeared pleased to be escorting such famous villains.

The drinking continued through Dijon, the Alps, and into Torino. Ben and Dorothy kept the agent entertained with stories of Canada and World War II. The young man shared stories of his boyhood in the French countryside. Metcalfe kept ordering cognac. Madeleine pasted a Greenpeace "Mururoa Mon Amour" sticker onto the agent's briefcase. Ben Metcalfe explained to him the horror of nuclear weapons and radiation. The young man defended France's right to protect itself, but Metcalfe, the aerial gunner who had helped rout Rommel at El-Alamein, soon had the Frenchman agreeing that nuclear bombs might not be the best solution to world problems. The agent fought off sleep as they roared south toward Rome.

When they arrived at the Rome terminal, sixteen hours from Paris, the story of their deportation had appeared in the international newspapers. The French agent stepped gingerly along the platform, pale and appearing queasy. Madeleine and the Metcalfes headed off to see the Pope and left him in the train station with the "Mururoa Mon Amour" sticker still on his briefcase.

A PAPAL BLESSING

In Rome, Patrick and Diane Moore, the Metcalfes, and Lyle Thurston met at the Spanish Steps, walked through the grounds of Villa Borghese to the Pincio terrace, and gazed past the Piazza del Popolo to the dome of St. Peter's in the haze beyond. The Vatican: the seat of Christ's vicar, the Pope, "the infallible dispenser of spiritual graces" and "protector of the oppressed." The Green Robes drank coffee and beer in a café near the Pincio and prepared for their audience the next day at the throne of the wealthiest religious fraternity in the world. Lyle Thurston drained his beer and ordered another round. "I don't know why we're doing this," he said. "We're all atheists."

"Agnostics," said Moore.

"It doesn't matter what we believe," said Dorothy Metcalfe, "France is Catholic."

The delegation passed a pleasant afternoon swapping stories. Moore told them about Rod Marining's encounters with French dissidents. Lyle told them about running into people in London with Greenpeace buttons. Ben Metcalfe described the progress of the *Vega* and the tenacity of the new Greenpeace skipper, McTaggart. "If anyone can make it to Mururoa, he can, but I wouldn't count on him being particularly loyal to Greenpeace. He thinks we're a bunch of Communists."

The next day, they arrived at the Vatican for what they had thought would be a private audience with the Pope. Under his coat, Thurston carried the Greenpeace flag that had flown on the *Phyllis Cormack* and on the *Edgewater Fortune*, and had been blessed by the Kwakiutl. At the fence that ringed St. Peter's Basilica, Dorothy presented their documentation to a security guard, and they soon discovered that their audience was not private. An usher escorted them into an auditorium with 2,000 other pilgrims, including children from Latin America, converts from Africa, and visiting priests and nuns. In the front row sat a group that had walked from Spain. The Greenpeace party sat behind them, slightly disappointed. However, the Pope welcomed "the Canadian group, Greenpeace" and used the occasion to deliver a short address on nature and peace in Catholic doctrine. "You young people are doing a good thing," he said. As the Pope blessed the multitude, Thurston and Moore held up the flag to catch the consecration.

"I guess that counts," shrugged Moore. Pope Paul VI continued with a long sermon on Christian faith. Thurston grew restless and craved a cigarette. He slipped the flag back under his jacket and eased from the gallery toward a door that opened onto a courtyard. A few heads turned to see who in the world was walking out on the pontiff of the Catholic Church. Ben and Dorothy Metcalfe cringed. When Thurston reached the door, a security guard stopped him and whispered. "Where are you going?"

"Out."

"You can't. No one leaves until it is over."

"I have to go outside."

"If you leave, you can't come back in."

"Okay," Thurston said. "I need to go outside. Thank you. *Grazie*."

The security guard let Thurston into the courtyard. The doctor lit a cigarette and sat on a rock wall, listening to the birds in the garden. Twenty minutes later, the Pope, surrounded by acolytes and security guards, emerged from the basilica into the courtyard. Thurston followed the pontiff, nudged through the guards, and held up the flag. The Pope stopped. Meanwhile, Moore and the Metcalfes arrived in the courtyard and saw Thurston with the Papal entourage. Pope Paul VI waved Thurston forward, raised his hand, and blessed the Greenpeace flag. Then he turned and disappeared with his retinue.

The satisfied Green Robes found their way out onto the Piazza in front of St. Peter's. "Good," said Metcalfe, "we just gained 700 million new members."

I'M A GREEN

The Metcalfes suspected they would be arrested again if they attempted to enter France, so they took a train directly to Stockholm. The Moores and Doc Thurston, however, drove back to Paris, where they met Marining, Bensasson, and environmentalists Nicholas Desplats and Brice Lalonde at Notre Dame. They spent a day handing out buttons and leaflets to visitors. Bensasson and Lalonde explained the mission to tourists. Marining struggled to explain "*le petit bateau*," to patient French visitors. "*Uh, pour Moruroa. Protest le bombe.*"

Near closing time at the cathedral, a reporter from *Le Monde* arrived. Security guards appeared at the doorways. Desplats and Lalonde stood back. A priest asked the protestors — Moore, Thurston, Marining, and Bensasson — to leave. They refused. An older priest arrived and explained in English that they must leave. They told him they had come to protest the French nuclear tests, that the Pope had blessed their flag, and they sought refuge in the sanctuary of the church. A civilian security guard stepped in and explained that they could not take refuge because Notre Dame was not, technically, a church. It was a French national monument. The protestors had miscalculated, and now found themselves inside government property.

Bensasson argued with the guards, but French police arrived in no mood for a discussion. After a bit of shouting between Bensasson and the police, she told Marining, Thurston, and Moore that they had two choices: "Get your heads cracked, get dragged out of here and thrown in jail, *or* we leave now on our own. But if we avoid arrest, we must be out of Paris within twenty-four hours."

"Well, maybe we've made our point," said Thurston.

The group departed, and a story appeared in *Le Monde* the next day. Marining issued a press release saying, "France is behaving like invaders from Mars, shooting nuclear missiles at Spaceship Earth!"

The Green Robes dispersed. The Moores drove to Stockholm, Thurston returned to London, and Marining remained underground in Paris. Meanwhile, the Metcalfes travelled casually by train through Germany to Hamburg, into Denmark, then on to Stockholm, where the UN conference would start on the fifth of June.

Marining, frustrated at the lack of news coverage in Paris, returned to Notre Dame and chained himself inside. Police arrested him and took him to a dark, underground jail cell, where he was interrogated at a wooden table with a lamp in his face. The officers insisted on speaking French, although Marining understood very little. He told them the only French he knew was "Mururoa mon amour." Finally, an officer asked him in English what he was doing in France. "Stopping nuclear war in Europe," he said cheerfully, and they laughed. They left him in his cell for a few hours and then released him.

The next day, however, when Marining walked out the front door of the Quaker centre, two plainclothes French agents grabbed him, twisted his arm behind his back, and shoved him into a car. The agents said nothing as they drove Marining some distance outside the centre of Paris. They stopped in an abandoned lane, dragged the Canadian from the car, shoved him to his knees, and commenced kicking and slapping him. Marining pleaded and covered his head, but they continued the beating. The taller of the two agents hauled him up against a fence and demanded to know who he was.

"Pacifist, pacifist," said Marining. "Canadian. Moruroa. No bombs. *Le bombe*?"

"Who have you talked to in Paris?"

"Environmentalists. Pacifists."

"Communist!" the man screamed at him.

"No."

"You're a Red!"

"No."

"*Batard rouge.*" The agent slapped him. "You're a Red."

"No." Finally Marining blurted, "I'm a Green!"

The agents thought he was mocking them, and they beat him again. "I'm a Green! Environment! A Green!"

They took his wallet and discovered his *Province* press card. "Journalist?"

"Yes, oui," said Marining. "Oui, journalist." The bigger man hit Marining in the stomach. He desperately sucked for air as they threw him into the back of the car and drove away. After about five minutes, the door of the car opened, and the big agent flung Marining into the street. Bruised and holding a bloody lip, he made his way back to the Quaker centre where Bensasson and Nico attended to him.

"I think I met the Ninth Bureau," he told Nico.

"No," Nico laughed, "you haven't met the Ninth Bureau."

"How do you know?"

"Because you're still here and you're not dead," said Nico. "But you have to leave Paris. They *will* kill you."

Marining — the first Greenpeace protest casualty — nursed his wounds at Bensasson's flat. A few days later, Nico showed him a report from the newspaper about a union leader at the Renault plant found beaten to death. "See?" said Nico. "These people are ruthless." Marining took a train to Brussels.

MORUROA

By May 25, David McTaggart, Nigel Ingram, and Grant Davidson nursed sore arms and backs in the sweltering heat. The *Vega* had covered 700 miles from Rarotonga, still pushed north by 25-knot winds. They faced another 800 miles to Moruroa with the strong breeze right on their nose. At midday, they prepared for a long tack, south-southeast, back across the wind.

They slipped south of Tahiti, just catching a glimpse of the dark spire of Mount Roniu on the peninsula of Taiarapu. On the night of May 28, a 45-knot gale kicked up waves that broke over the bow as they maintained their course south of the Gloucester Atolls. Should the *Vega* be blown into these atolls, the ketch would be shredded. Ingram checked their position with the sextant whenever possible, but getting a sightline in the fierce seas proved difficult. He attempted to make contact with someone by radio, but the Swan-500 failed to get through to a marine operator. Ingram tried the smaller marine radio on the all-ships frequency but did not raise a single reply.

They tacked across the storm for two days and nights until, on May 31, the day before the announced test, they reached 200 miles northwest of the cordon. The following day, the wind settled into a strong breeze. They passed to the south of Tematagi Atoll, and at 22:45 on the night of June 1, 1972, intersected the boundary of the French cordon. Reaching this goal represented a feat of extraordinary nautical skill and toughness. The three mariners slouched in the cockpit as McTaggart held the tiller for two hours, savouring the achievement. Finally, he turned into the wind, dropped the sheets, and they hove to in the darkness. Below decks, the crew opened a bottle of champagne and toasted their triumph.

The three sailors now wondered: Had the bomb gone off? Will we hear it? Will we see it? What was that about a balloon? Davidson took the first night watch as Ingram and McTaggart fell to their bunks and slept.

In fact, the bomb had not yet been detonated. Admiral Claverie aboard *De Grasse* sent the minesweeper *La Bayonnaise* to shadow the Greenpeace boat, with orders to keep the vessel on radar and report on its progress toward Moruroa.

The wind calmed the next morning, and the *Vega* prepared to take a position 20 miles northwest of Moruroa, leaving them eight miles of leeway between their position and France's legal territorial limit around the atoll. As they busied themselves in the cabin they heard a deafening roar, climbed to the deck, and saw a French plane dropping toward them like a dive-bomber. Davidson thought his eardrums had shattered as the plane roared in low, banked around, buzzed them again, and departed over the horizon to the northwest.

The crew of the *Vega* raised the main sail — with the ecology symbol, the peace symbol below, and GREENPEACE III stitched between — and set out for the far side of Moruroa Atoll. In the heart of the Tuamotu Archipelago, coral reef deathtraps lay in every direction. A position northeast of Moruroa provided options for escape should the wind change and push them toward one of the atolls. Maintaining one's position among these reefs required precision and vigilance. Warm currents flowed west from the coast of South America through the atolls, and local currents eddied back around in every direction. The winds could turn and gust and turn again, and the only points of reference for the *Vega* — without loran capabilities — were the heavenly bodies above. Should the boat drift into the 12-mile limit of any French atoll, they would be boarded and arrested.

Ingram had taken responsibility for knowing their position. To do so, as the boat pitched in the waves, he would site along his sextant to determine the angle between the horizon and some celestial body — the sun, the moon, or a star — by turning a radial arm mounted with a half mirror until the object's reflection coincided with the horizon. The angular distance of the sun or star above the horizon could then be read from the arc of the sextant, and the exact time of day noted. From this information, Ingram drew a line across the chart. To determine the position of the vessel, a second line had to be calculated with a second celestial object. But to plot these lines precisely, a navigator must account for the "dip," the angle of his eye to the horizon, and for the refraction angle of the light through the atmosphere, which made the heavenly bodies appear slightly higher near the horizon. Assuming all of this was done accurately, the point on the chart where the two lines intersected showed the position of the boat. Since their vessel and their lives depended on these readings, Ingram devoted a great deal of time to the problem. Between readings he estimated their drift from wind and currents.

When he determined they were in position, 20 miles northeast of Moruroa, they hove to, dropped a sea anchor, and balanced the rudder and sail to maintain the position. The following morning, they saw the minesweeper *La Bayonnaise*. Ingram raised the jib and main. As they started to move, black smoke bellowed from the French ship. Davidson managed to tune in a BBC broadcast and heard news of the Stockholm Conference and labour groups in New Zealand and Australia boycotting French ships. The three sailors sensed, correctly, that their little sailboat bobbed at the centre of a massive political storm.

The next evening, with *La Bayonnaise* shadowing them, they moved close enough to the atoll to see the lights of the French encampment. Then, on June 7, a gale hit the Tuamotus from the west. Hurricane force gusts drove the *Vega* 60 miles eastward toward six atolls known as Îles Actéon. An eight-foot shark circled the boat, and a land bird appeared, indicating they had drifted near a reef. As the gale blew out, they fought their way back west and hove to again off Moruroa.

McTaggart sent a radio call to all ships on the emergency frequency, and received a faint reply. What he did not know was that the reply he raised came from the *De Grasse* radio room masquerading as a Belgian vessel, the *Astrid.* He confirmed their position with the phantom ship, explained their mission, and announced that they had provisions to hold out for at least five weeks. He asked the *Astrid* to forward their message to the news services, but then lost contact. Later, Davidson picked up an Australian news broadcast and learned about a resolution at the UN meeting to ban atmospheric nuclear tests, but the *Vega* crew had no idea if anyone other than the crew of the *Astrid* knew their location.

On Friday evening, June 16, still east of Moruroa in a westerly breeze, McTaggart saw an odd bulbous object in the clouds above the atoll. He and Ingram looked through the binoculars. "What is it?" Davidson asked.

"It's a balloon," said Ingram. The warning of the professor from the University of Auckland came back to them: If they could see the balloon they were too close.

"My God," whispered McTaggart, "they're really going to do it."

SEX AND URANIUM

In June, the Metcalfes arrived in Stockholm along with 1,200 delegates and their entourages from 113 nations and 400 international agencies attending the UN Conference on the Human Environment. Banners hung in the streets and music played through the long summer twilight. Borrowing an idea from the Provos of Amsterdam, Stockholm provided white bicycles to help visitors get around the city. Canadian Maurice Strong had been selected Secretary-General of the Conference; Mitchell Sharp and Jack Davis led the Canadian delegation. The Green evangelists from Vancouver — the Metcalfes and Moores — mixed with thousands of environmentalists at an encampment in the Skarpnäks grasslands south of Stockholm. They had no official non-governmental status. To get the nuclear debate on the agenda, these citizens would have to lobby their national delegates. At the Grand Hotel in Stockholm, Metcalfe found Jack Davis, his North Vancouver nemesis. Davis smiled broadly and shook Metcalfe's hand. "How was Paris, Ben?"

"Paris is burning, Jack," said Metcalfe. He told Davis he wanted the Canadian delegation to sign off on his media pass. Davis said he would get him the pass if Metcalfe agreed not to quote him in any Greenpeace story. Metcalfe agreed, received the credentials, and thereafter had access to all the committee meetings. He lobbied Davis to put the nuclear issue on the agenda, but Davis flatly refused.

"No, Ben!" said Davis. "And that's the end of it."

"I doubt it's the end of it, Jack. How's the uranium business?"

"Has nothing to do with it," said the politician, but Metcalfe knew that it did. Canadian newspapers had revealed that the federal government subsidized the uranium industry and had agreed to "take a more active role in trying to push export sales." Two months earlier, in Paris, the Western nuclear powers — France, Britain, and the United States — had established a cartel and fixed prices with the producing nations — the Congo, Ghana, Australia, and Canada. Over the next three years, the new cartel would push the price of uranium from $9 per pound to over $40 per pound. France had invested in Canadian mining through Seru Nucléaire in Quebec, to secure a source of uranium.

At the time of the Stockholm meeting, Canada promoted new uranium customers by selling reactors to India, Taiwan, South Korea, and Argentina. Four years later, an auditor general's inquiry would reveal that millions of dollars in bribe payments had moved from Canada — through Intercontinental General Trading Establishment in Liechtenstein and United Development Inc. of Tel Aviv — to these clients. Ostensibly, Canada now banned uranium exports for military purposes, but politicians understood the plutonium product from reactors could and would be used in weapons. India had used plutonium from its Canadian reactor to build an atomic bomb, which they would test two years later.

Metcalfe did not expect support from Canada, so he hosted other delegations in his hotel room. Australian delegates told him that Prime Minister William McMahon had received 5,000 letters condemning the tests and had been influenced by the trade union boycotts in Melbourne. When France retaliated with threats of embargoes against Australia, the International Confederation of Free Trade Unions, representing 50 million workers around the world, threw support behind the South Pacific unions, and France backed off. Meanwhile, Chile, Peru, and Japan formally condemned the French tests.

The Metcalfes had become minor celebrities at the conference, since the story of their Paris arrest had appeared in *Le Figaro* and *Le Monde*.

In the Grand Hotel bar, a reporter from *Le Figaro* advanced the theory that Metcalfe had returned to Europe to take revenge against the man who stole his first wife, Baya. "What?" Metcalfe asked. The reporter informed Metcalfe that Baya had married Henri Messiah, chief of security for the French Atomic Energy Commission. The reporter presumed that Metcalfe now sought revenge on Messiah. "The French always get sex into it," Metcalfe laughed. "It's a juicy bit of investigative reporting, though. Go ahead and use it." He even suggested the headline: "Nuclear cuckold returns."

EXIT FRANCE

In Stockholm, Patrick Moore participated in his first anti-whaling protest. W. J. Hickel, former US Secretary of the Interior, advanced the plight of the world's whales at a Skarpnäks camp rally: "Whales are a symbol of life, and their extinction is an omen." Moore joined a parade into the centre of Stockholm, led by Hickel, Joan McIntyre from Project Jonah in California, political clown Wavy Gravy carrying a large papier-mâché whale, and crusaders from the World Wildlife Fund and Friends of the Earth. The Japanese delegation attempted to keep the whale issue off the agenda, but in the end, the conference adopted a resolution for a moratorium on commercial whaling that would be presented to the International Whaling Commission the following summer.

Sweden had initiated the Stockholm Conference on the Human Environment in response to acid rain from industrial Europe, but the meeting swelled into the world's first intergovernmental political forum designed to act on global environmental problems. Moore met with environmental scientists and attended what became an historic debate between Paul Ehrlich and Barry Commoner on the issue of human population. Most environmentalists agreed that human population growth was an environmental issue — cities choking on smog, wars over land, food, and fuel — but Commoner argued that consumption by the industrial nations was the bigger problem. Nevertheless, Ehrlich argued, the entire planet and all nations would be better off if governments addressed human population with birth control strategies. This debate exemplified the complexity of ecology within the context of politics, class rivalries, economic theories, and cultural orthodoxies.

Margaret Mead emphasized that the problems comprised a single pattern and demanded integrated global solutions. Other delegates warned of the inherent danger of ecology managed by a "global elite" of large corporations and powerful nations. None of these ideas — ecology, whole systems theory, social ecology — were new, but there now existed a linked international community to talk about the ideas and act on them. The idea of "sustainable development" emerged from the conference, and the word "environment" entered the common lexicon after this meeting.

New Zealand took up the campaign to get bomb tests on the agenda. The French delegation counterattacked with their own meetings, but the prevailing sentiment in Stockholm favoured disarmament and a nuclear test ban. Attending scientists understood unequivocally that nuclear bomb tests should be on the global docket of environmental concerns. On June 14, the plenary assembly approved a New Zealand and Peruvian motion: "To condemn nuclear weapons tests, especially those carried out in the atmosphere."

The enraged French delegation voted "No," and walked out. China also voted "No," Canada and the United States abstained, but the resolution carried, 48-2. France boycotted the rest of the meeting and declared, "Our country cannot in any way whatever be bound" by the resolution.

The final plenary assembly on June 16 included in its List of Principles: "Man and his environment must be spared the effects of nuclear weapons and all other means of mass destruction."

"So locked are we within our tribal units, so possessive over national rights," wrote Barbara Ward and René Dubois in *Only One Earth*, based on the conference, "we may fail to sense the need for dedicated and committed action over the whole field of planetary necessities." Ecology had changed the nature of global politics and pushed humankind into a "wider allegiance," they wrote, a "loyalty to our single, beautiful and vulnerable Planet Earth."

The Green Robes believed they had played a valuable role with the other ecology advocates. Collectively, without official status, they had influenced the highest levels of international diplomacy, forcing the nuclear powers to face the opinion of the global community.

Meanwhile, the French government issued false reports that the *Greenpeace III* had left the test site in the South Pacific, but Metcalfe phoned the New Zealand Customs officer on Rarotonga and confirmed that the *Vega* was still there. Although he had no radio contact with the boat, he knew the skipper, and he assured the assembled delegates and media in Stockholm, "*Greenpeace III* is in sight of Moruroa."

WARSHIPS

On the morning of June 17, still in sight of the balloon, Nigel Ingram's sextant reading placed the *Vega* at 21°41´ south of the equator, 138°21´ west of Greenwich, a position east-northeast and downwind from the atoll, just outside France's territorial limit. Through the binoculars, they made out a smaller object below the balloon, possibly the bomb itself. They set out wooden plugs to be hammered into the boat's vents should the bomb go off, and they threw overboard a five-gallon can of gasoline for fear it could ignite.

The following day, they heard on the radio that the government of Australia had expressed concern about Australian citizen Grant Davidson on the Greenpeace vessel inside the test zone. The French Foreign Ministry had replied that they would take "all necessary measures to protect anyone" within the cordon.

The French minesweeper *La Bayonnaise* continued to shadow them, but that afternoon they saw another, larger military ship off their port beam on the horizon. They approached the ship, and using the long lens on his camera, McTaggart identified the new vessel as the USS *Wheeling*, a 455-foot missile and satellite tracker. US Congressman Jonathan Bingham would later confirm to McTaggart that the US military, and the *Wheeling* specifically, had assisted the French nuclear testing program in violation of the Test Ban Treaty that the United States had signed.

On June 21, a loudspeaker awoke the *Vega* crew, calling, "*Greenpeace III*! *Greenpeace III*!" They scurried onto the deck to find their constant shadow, *La Bayonnaise*, towering above them. Two French sailors and an officer came alongside the *Vega* in an inflatable. Ingram accepted the line, and an officer handed McTaggart a brown envelope, nodded, took the line from

Ingram, and departed. McTaggart opened the envelope on deck. "URGENT: *Reférence avis aux navigateurs ... expérimentations nucléaires ...*" A second page read in English:

"Mariners are warned that nuclear experiments will be conducted in the South Central Pacific area from the 20 June at 0001 TU. The following area has been declared dangerous: A circular area radius one hundred and twenty nautical miles centered on MURUROA ... Mariners are instantly requested to keep off the above area from June 20 at 0001 TU and till further notice."

Ingram hoisted the main, and the *Vega* moved toward Moruroa in defiance as McTaggart composed a reply. Davidson hoisted the "K" pennant announcing they wished to communicate with *La Bayonnaise*. Four French sailors returned to pick up the message from McTaggart and handed another envelope to him.

Back on board *La Bayonnaise,* the captain opened the letter addressed to him.

"Sir: We thank you for your message this morning, requesting us to leave this area. We have enclosed a copy of a document prepared for us by the legal department of the University of Auckland, New Zealand, stating our rights to sail in these international waters and we intend to remain, as long as we are able to maintain these rights."

The letter was signed: "D. F. McTaggart, N. S. Ingram, and G. J. Davidson."

On board the *Vega*, McTaggart opened the new letter from the French vessel.

FROM: ADMIRAL COMMANDING NUCLEAR TESTS FORCE

TO: GREENPEACE III

YOU ARE STILL IN THE AREA DEFINED IN THE NOTICE TO MARINERS YOU RECEIVED THIS MORNING — STOP — YOU ARE REQUESTED TO KEEP OFF THE ABOVE AREA OR AT LEAST SAIL IMMEDIATELY AND JOIN POSITION 15 (FIFTEEN) NAUTICAL MILES WEST (270) OFF TURÉIA WHERE I WILL INSURE YOUR SAFETY AGAINST NUCLEAR EFFECTS.

The position between Turéia and Vanavana atolls would be difficult to achieve without drifting into the 12-mile territory of one atoll or the other. Ingram, McTaggart, and Davidson ignored the notice and dropped the sea anchor.

The next day, the flagship *De Grasse* arrived with Admiral Claverie fuming on the bridge. The 581-foot, 7,600-ton battle cruiser, with 600 officers and men, carried a battery of 60 guns and four 22-inch torpedo tubes. An anti-submarine warfare helicopter sat on the quarterdeck. The flagship bore down on the *Vega* at well over 20 knots, followed by *La Bayonnaise* and another ship, a deep-sea tug, *Hippopotame*. The *Vega* crew had now seen one US and three French warships. The admiral's flagship charged past the *Vega* at 50 yards. McTaggart took the helm, Ingram fired up the engine, and they barely avoided a collision. Sailors on the deck of *De Grasse* looked directly down on them as Ingram and Davidson raised the jenny and came about.

The minesweeper and the sea tug now came along either side, pincered the *Vega*, and seemed to be ushering it toward Moruroa, perhaps attempting to push the ketch inside the 12-mile limit. Ingram hoisted the "can't-manoeuvre" pennant as they fought to avoid a collision. He attempted a sun sight to determine their position, but the tug *Hippopotame* blocked his view. Ingram snarled at the insolence, but when the sea tug drifted, he grabbed a quick reading and determined they remained safely outside the 12-mile limit.

That night, phantom aircraft buzzed overhead and searchlights swept across the deck of the *Vega*. On Sunday morning, June 25, the harassment commenced again. *La Bayonnaise* and *Hippopotame* pincered in close and revved their engines, while a twin-engine aircraft flew tight figure eights overhead, so loud that the crew could not hear each other speak.

During this bizarre assault, the French set off their first test, a nuclear triggering device like the one that would be used to detonate the bigger bomb. The racket around the *Vega* prevented the crew from hearing the explosion.

INVOLVED IN AN EXPLOSION

Back in Vancouver, the Metcalfes read a Canadian Press wire stating, "Reports from Paris say the first blast of the test series was held Sunday, June 25, four days after the last sighting of *Greenpeace III*. French government informs the Canadian Government that the *Greenpeace III* has left the test site." Ben Metcalfe, however, suspected that the *Vega* remained inside the cordon around Moruroa.

Earlier, on June 19, Ontario Member of Parliament Heath Macquarrie had questioned Minister of Foreign Affairs Mitchell Sharp about the French tests and the whereabouts of the Canadian vessel. Sharp claimed the *Greenpeace III* was not registered in Canada and "did not carry our flag." As he spoke these words, the red Canadian maple leaf snapped in a 25-knot breeze 15 miles off Moruroa. "There is a Canadian aboard," Sharp said, "and of course I do hope the ship is not going to get involved in the explosion and that necessary steps will be taken to see it is removed from the area."

Metcalfe called ex-Vancouver journalist and Member of Parliament Paul St. Pierre, who served as an assistant to the foreign affairs minister. "How do you get 'involved' in an explosion?" Metcalfe berated St. Pierre. "The boat is on the high seas! Was the minister suggesting that Canadian citizens be 'removed' from the high seas?"

St. Pierre told Metcalfe, "You can't just harangue us like this!"

"Yes we can," Metcalfe insisted.

The next day, Heath Macquarrie rose again in parliament and asked Mitchell Sharp "whether it was the view of the government of Canada that the government of France has the right to arrest ships on the high seas?" The House Speaker ruled that the "question raises a legal interpretation and is out of order."

On June 23, MP Mark Rose, from British Columbia, goaded Sharp about "appalling external affairs timidity that would embarrass the president of a banana republic." Sharp claimed that Canada had made "very strong protests to the French government against nuclear weapons testing of all kinds." When asked about the nature of these protests the next day, Sharp snapped: "... If they wish to place themselves in special hazard in this way," he fumbled in frustration, "there is nothing that I can do."

"Yes, there is," fumed Ben Metcalfe over the radio in Vancouver. "You can defend the rights of your citizens to sail on the high seas."

COLLISION COURSE

Aboard the *Greenpeace III*, Ingram, McTaggart, and Davidson rationed food and water. They had been at sea for five weeks since departing Rarotonga. Their flesh had softened from the humidity and lack of vitamins, and open sores festered in the tropical heat. Each time the winds blew them away from the atoll, they returned. After twenty-six days off Moruroa, McTaggart pulled out his last bottle of champagne and toasted their "world record for being hove-to in a nuclear test zone."

On June 27, the protesters heard a Radio Australia report of the trigger test and realized it had taken place while the airplane buzzed them two days earlier. They heard on a New Zealand broadcast that Prime Minister Marshall had repeated the French ruse that, "the Canadian peace vessel *Greenpeace III* sailed away from the Pacific nuclear test area on June 21 and has not been seen since." The *Vega* crew could not counter these stories because of their on-board radio problems and the fact that the French Navy had jammed any radio transmissions they had been able to send.

At 08:30 on the morning of July 1, 1972, the *Vega* crew heard a distant thunder. After five seconds, they felt the tremor. The French bomb had been detonated. The breeze blew 25 knots out of the northeast, dispersing the radioactive cloud south, away from them.

A second minesweeper, *La Paimpolaise*, the fifth warship they had seen, joined the *Vega*'s shadowy escort as they made a course toward Moruroa. *La Paimpolaise* flew the ensign "MY2," warning them, "Do not continue present course." The *Vega* remained under full sail at seven knots. *La Paimpolaise* cut dangerously across the bow of the *Vega* and slipped aft of the sailboat. Ingram held the tiller and McTaggart and Davidson took photographs as the minesweeper moved dangerously close. French officers on the bridge glared down upon them. Ingram attempted to come about into the wind, but the bow wave of the minesweeper lifted the little ketch, and the *Vega* faltered. The metal bow of the warship rose above the sailboat and sliced down through the portside gunwale, snapping lines, splintering the railings, and cracking planks and ribs. The impact knocked all three sailors to their knees on the deck. *La Paimpolaise* reversed with its bow still caught in the rigging of the *Vega*, and the sailboat heeled over dangerously. Ingram cut the nylon topping lift, and the *Vega* recoiled upright. McTaggart screamed at the French officers. The collision had damaged the bowsprit, bobstay, and masthead fittings. The starboard hull had been stove in, and the sailboat took on water.

The crew reefed the sails, sent off two hand flares, and raised the "F" pennant announcing, "I am disabled." The crew of *La Paimpolaise* lowered an inflatable, and the captain and a sailor came alongside the crippled ketch. Rarely does a captain leave his vessel at sea, but McTaggart found himself giving the French captain a hand to board the *Vega*. The tall, strapping officer had crewcut black hair and heavy black eyebrows. McTaggart had expected a cold-hearted military man, but Captain Patrick de la Rochebrochard had a look of deep concern.

"*Je regrette*. I'm sorry, sorry," Captain de la Rochebrochard pleaded as he shook McTaggart's hand. "*Oh Dieu! Oh Dieu*," the captain mumbled as he surveyed the damage to the *Vega*. "*Oh, lamentable*!" The captain spoke in English: "I was ordered to stop you. I didn't mean to hit you. You turned sideways on me."

"That's bullshit!" McTaggart shouted. He demanded the French captain report the collision and their exact position to the governments of all the crewmembers. "I want confirmation that this has been done," shrieked McTaggart. "I want to hear it broadcast on New Zealand and Australian radio. And I want you to escort me to port for repairs."

Captain de la Rochebrochard returned to his vessel, conferred with Admiral Claverie, and brought back a document for McTaggart to sign, stating that McTaggart requested help from the French Navy. He refused to sign. "I'm not asking for help!" he shouted, "I'm asking for reparations for being rammed on the high seas!" McTaggart demanded to speak to the admiral. The French officer shrugged and invited McTaggart to join him on *La Paimpolaise*.

McTaggart sensed his opportunity. The French captain looked worried. He had not only broken maritime law, he had violated the code of sailors, and his own crew had witnessed the transgression. Aboard the French minesweeper, McTaggart sent a message to the admiral on the *De Grasse*, repeating his demands. Captain de la Rochebrochard offered McTaggart lunch and revealed to him that some officers had favoured running the *Vega* down in the dead of night. Over sandwiches, he confirmed that the sound they had heard that morning was the bomb. A reply arrived from Admiral Claverie, who refused to allow a message to be sent regarding the *Vega*'s position, but promised to repair the sailboat at his expense on Moruroa. McTaggart believed this offer amounted to an admission of guilt, and he demanded it in writing. With the *Vega* taking on water, he had little choice. On the morning after the collision, the French warship towed them to Moruroa.

ADMIRAL'S LUNCHEON

The lagoon at Moruroa looked like a theatre of war, ringed with a squadron of cruisers, destroyers, escort carriers, minesweepers, frigates, and service vessels, each mounted with armaments and sophisticated communications antennae. Helicopters buzzed about like giant, dark mosquitoes. Small boats escorted the *Vega* into the dock. Curious seamen and officers lined the decks of the ships, snapped pictures, and waved. On the dock, in private, beyond the eyes of their officers, sailors shook hands with the *Vega* crew, patted them on the back, and congratulated them on their seamanship.

McTaggart gave Captain de la Rochebrochard a letter for the admiral, demanding that he report the incident and their presence on Moruroa. He said his crew refused to leave the atoll until he received confirmation that the report had been received. The captain crossed the lagoon, boarded *De Grasse*, and disappeared inside.

At a dock next to the maintenance ship *Garonne*, some twenty carpenters and technicians inspected the damage to the *Vega* and set to work. De la Rochebrochard returned with a lunch invitation from the admiral and a place to shower. The captain revealed to McTaggart that decisions about the affair had issued from sources much higher than the Admiral, meaning from the Minister of Defence or from President Pompidou himself.

Admiral Christian Claverie — a short, strong, white-haired patriarch — greeted his guests for lunch under the palm trees. He wore wire-rim sunglasses and three gold stars on the shoulders of his finely pressed, but otherwise unadorned, khaki uniform. De la Rochebrochard wore dress whites and acted as translator. A junior officer sat McTaggart on the admiral's right, Ingram on his left, and Davidson next to McTaggart. Other young officers served the guests wine. After the entrée, they brought Camembert cheese, liqueurs, coffee, and cigars. The admiral drank very little, cut his wine with mineral water, and entertained them with stories in faltering English of sailing these islands in his youth. When confronted with the illegal cordon and the ramming of their vessel, the admiral responded, "I must put human life above human rights."

"I believe them to be the same thing," McTaggart countered, "where atomic fallout is concerned."

"But you do not have Russia at your doorstep," said the admiral. "There has to be a third nuclear power. I would never hurt anyone. I'm a Catholic."

"The bomb was designed to *destroy* human life."

"Yes," said the admiral and he pondered this. "Things could have been different and I could easily be sitting in your seat."

McTaggart huffed. After lunch, in private, he repeated his demand that the admiral report they were safe on Moruroa.

"I will ask Paris," Claverie promised.

The next day, McTaggart, de la Rochebrochard, and Admiral Claverie met again. Claverie told McTaggart he would advise Radio Tahiti that the Greenpeace crew was safe. That evening, with the repairs completed, the *Vega* crew ate dinner with the officers of *Garonne*. The following morning at 06:00, a tug towed them from the lagoon. The decks of the French ships filled with sailors who whistled and applauded. A bugle salute lifted from *De Grasse*. As they rounded the mouth of the reef, the grand flag ship pulled past them with the crew jammed at the railings, fists raised to their chests. *La Paimpolaise* passed, sailors cheering.

For ten days, the three sailors struggled toward Rarotonga, sails tattered and damaged planks taking on water, but sailing briskly before the prevailing southeasterlies. They heard on Radio Australia that they were safe and on their way to Rarotonga. The admiral had kept his word, but the French launched a little mindbomb of their own. They had photographed the lunch meeting on Moruroa, and sent the pictures to the French newspapers. According to the reports out of Paris, the French had rescued the mariners after a reckless manoeuvre by the *Vega*, repaired the boat, and then hosted the grateful crew at a lavish luncheon. International news services repeated the story around the world.

WHERE ARE THE PHOTOGRAPHS?

In Rarotonga, McTaggart called Ann-Marie Horne. She told him the Campaign for Nuclear Disarmament volunteers had seen the luncheon pictures, and were upset. Ann-Marie believed McTaggart's story but told him Auckland activists had laughed at them. The three sailors had just accomplished a monumental feat, but the French government had run a more clever media campaign. Ann-Marie told McTaggart that a 50-foot trawler, the *Boy Roel*, sponsored by Peace Media, had left Auckland for Moruroa. McTaggart, Ingram, and Davidson sat on the dock in Avarua, 2,000 miles from Auckland, nearly broke, with a leaky boat. There was no money coming from New Zealand. And they had no watches to sell.

McTaggart called Ben Metcalfe in Vancouver and told him he needed $1,500 for repairs and provisions to get back to Auckland. Metcalfe said he would try to wire some money but that Greenpeace did not have $1,500. Fundraising had virtually stopped during the summer while the Greenpeace team travelled Europe. Metcalfe said the photographs would help and he asked McTaggart if he would please send copies. McTaggart sounded evasive, unsure about what he might have captured on film. "Whatever you have," said Metcalfe, "send pictures to me."

In Rarotonga, desperate for money, McTaggart's entrepreneurial instincts kicked in. Bankrupt? Cut the frills, marshal your assets, and leverage yourself back into a positive cash flow. The resources at hand included the *Vega*, his story, and a potential claim against the French. He sold the 500-watt radio for $700 and bought a plane ticket to Vancouver. He intended to find out who these Greenpeace people really were, sell the photographs to a magazine or land a book deal, and use the money to repair the *Vega*. Then, he vowed, he would make a legal claim against the French for ramming his boat on the high seas.

He gave some money to Ingram, who agreed to stay with the boat and begin repairs. Davidson called the Campaign for Nuclear Disarmament in Auckland and received passage home. McTaggart insisted that Davidson turn over his eleven rolls of film, and the Australian did so on the promise that McTaggart would keep the commitment to send copies to Metcalfe. McTaggart also promised to return copies to Davidson within two weeks.

McTaggart ducked the local media on Rarotonga, but a New Zealand reporter tracked him down. The French luncheon trick had made McTaggart look bad, and the reporter wanted his side of the story. McTaggart could have countered the French deception, then and there, by telling his story and releasing the photographs, but he refused to even talk with the reporter. He did not yet wield the sort of media instincts that had become second nature to the Metcalfes, the Stowes, and Bob Hunter. He did not know about Marshall McLuhan, Provos, or mindbombs, and he didn't care. He was a master mariner, a tough competitor, and a flamboyant entrepreneur, but he missed the moment to win this battle of icons.

The spurned journalist filed his story with information from Grant Davidson and Nigel Ingram, but he had no pictures and he put a resentful spin on it. "The yacht proved a source of irritation to the French," he wrote, "but it seems just a trifle disappointing that a preoccupation with financial rewards should have clouded the success."

David McTaggart shrugged off the story and flew to Vancouver. He had a long-term plan that made sense to him. It would be tough, but possible. On the plane, overlooking the vast Pacific, he studied the Law of the Sea document prepared by the University of Auckland. He had international law on his side, and 300 years of nautical tradition. He asked for a beer and drank to his companions. Nigel. Grant. He sipped his beer. Good lads. Ann-Marie. Roger. Even Metcalfe, damn him. He thought of the admiral and the customs inspector. "They're not going to get away with it," he muttered to himself. He wrapped the Law of the Sea under his arm and slept.

(Left): 1. Irving and Dorothy Stowe, 1966, on their way to Canada. (Right): 2. Ben Metcalfe, 1958: the reporter.

3. Ben Metcalf's "Ecology" billboard, Vancouver, 1969.

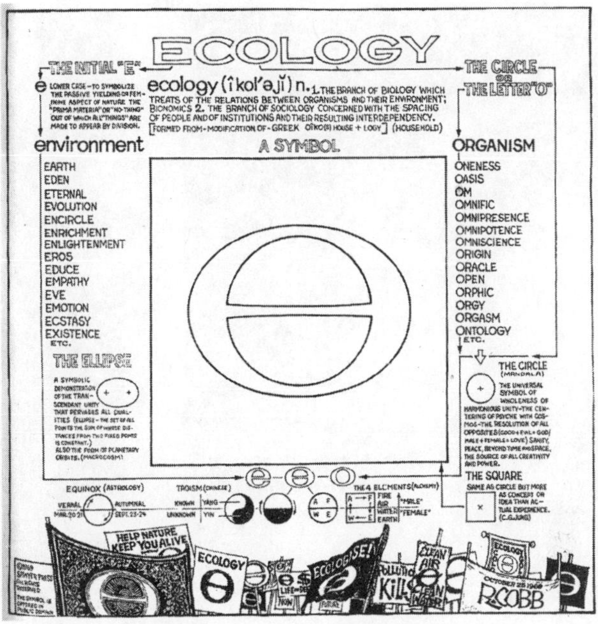

4. Ecology symbol, developed by Ron Cobb in 1969.

(Left): 5. Irving Stowe, 1971. (Right): 6. Jim and Marie Bohlen, 2002.

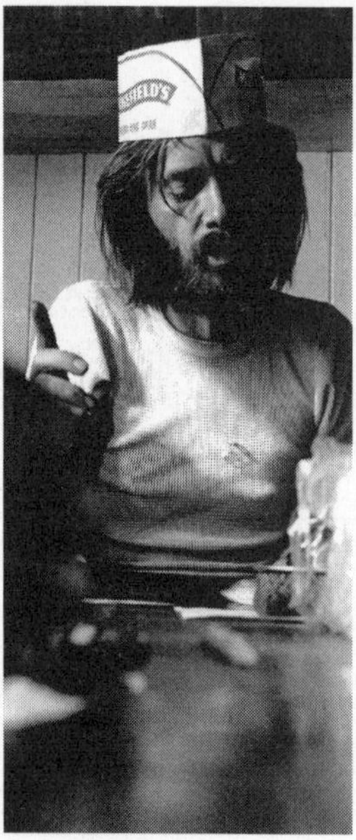

(Left): 7. James Taylor and Joni Mitchell at the Don't Make A Wave Committee Fundraiser, Vancouver Coliseum, October 1970. (Right): 8. Bob Hunter, with the King Crab hat.

9. Breakfast on *The Greenpeace*, 1971: Terry Simmons, Jim Bohlen, Dr. Lyle Thurston, David Birmingham, Richard Finberg, Bill Darnell, Robert Hunter, Patrick Moore, Captain John Cormack.

(Left): 10. The *Phyllis Cormack* at sea. (Right): 12. "La Paix!" *Zoe II* confronts the French battleship *Jeanne d'Arc*, Vancouver Harbour, 1973.

11. *Edgewater Fortune, Greenpeace II.*

13. The crew of *Vega*, *Greenpeace III*, in Rarotonga: Nigel Ingram, David McTaggart, Ben Metcalfe, Roger Haddleton and Grant Davidson, May 1972.

14. Moruroa, Cook Islands: *La Paimpolaise* approaches *Greenpeace III* just prior to ramming it, July 1972.

(Left): 15. Dr. Paul Spong and Skana. (Right): 16. Allen Ginsberg, early advisor and mentor of Greenpeace, reads his "Plutonian Ode" at a disarmament rally.

17. The first Greenpeace public office, Fourth Avenue in Vancouver, 1975. Around the table: Neil Hunter, Henry Payne, Leigh Wilkes, Rod Marining, Kurt Musgrove (hidden) and Bob Hunter. Standing at the door: Al Clapp; leaning against the map (right): Bree Drummond.

(Left): 22. Soviet harpoon ship and a dead sperm whale, Mendocino Ridge, California, 1975. (Right): 23. Cameraman Fred Easton, Mendocino Ridge, June 1975.

18. Glenn Jonathans, Patrick Moore, Eileen Chivers.

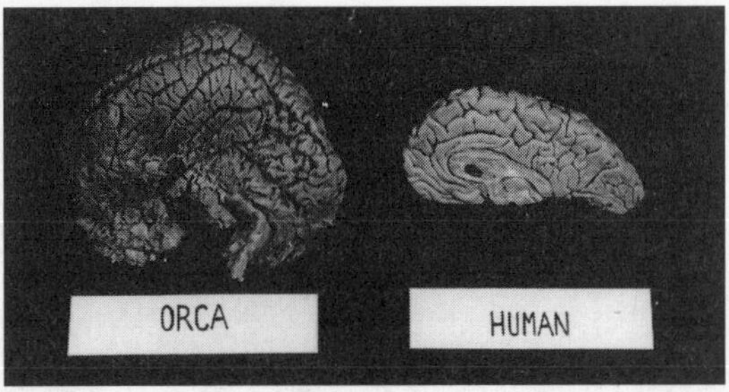

19. The brains of *Orcinus orca* and *Homo sapiens*.

20. Media centre: Don Franks, Bob Hunter and Walrus (David Garrick) type out news stories.

21. Radio failure: Hunter in the radio room of the *Phyllis Cormack* with the skipper, June 1975.

25. Sperm whale flukes lashed to side of a harpoon boat.

24. Whaling crew on the Soviet factory ship *Dalnyi Vostok*, 1975.

26. Patrick Moore, Rex Weyler and Bob Hunter returning to Vancouver, July 1975.

BOOK TWO

ALL SENTIENT BEINGS

CHAPTER FIVE

STOP AHAB

"The 'control of nature' is a phrase conceived in arrogance, born of the Neanderthal age of biology."

— Rachel Carson

On July 19, 1972, David McTaggart arrived in Vancouver, the hometown he had not seen since 1957. He made no attempt to find Ben Metcalfe, but he poked around town asking about Greenpeace. He saw "Mururoa Mon Amour" posters on storefronts and tiny donation cans on grocery shelves, but he found no public Greenpeace office. One day in a grocery store, he saw a woman wearing a Greenpeace pin, approached her, and met Dorothy Stowe. She took his phone number and arranged a quick meeting with her husband Irving, along with Jim and Marie Bohlen, and Ann and Will Jones — the elder, expatriate Americans of the group.

They had heard Metcalfe's critique of McTaggart, knew about his ex-wives and real estate dealings, and felt skeptical of McTaggart's motives. Still, they wanted to hear about the voyage and give the man a fair chance to speak for himself. He impressed the group with his stories and tough attitude, in spite of his limited knowledge about nuclear issues. McTaggart told them he wanted Greenpeace to support a court case against France. They encouraged him, but Irving confirmed that Greenpeace could not likely finance a protracted court battle with France. In any case, Irving Stowe told McTaggart, "The Metcalfes are in charge now."

McTaggart did not seek out the Metcalfes and did not yet know the Hunters, Marining, or the others. During the last half of 1972 and early 1973, Greenpeace would fragment into factions: the disarmament wing, the ecology wing, and McTaggart more or less on his own. Intermittent Greenpeace meetings convened at the Fisherman's Hall on the East Side. Leftist college students showed up and challenged Metcalfe's leadership, demanded democracy, and turned some of the meetings into tedious discussions of revolutionary theory. "Greenpeace is not interested in materialist politics," Metcalfe responded. "We're opposed to war and we champion ecology. That's it. We're not attempting to gain political power."

Hunter added, "Greenpeace is about changing the way humans think about their world. Consciousness is the citadel that must be stormed." The leftists eventually gave up.

At Greenpeace gatherings, people asked Metcalfe about David McTaggart, but he had no idea where the mysterious *Greenpeace III* skipper might be. In September, he received a letter from Grant Davidson, who revealed the confrontation with the journalist in Rarotonga and told Metcalfe that McTaggart had taken his photographs and that he had not seen them. Meanwhile, no one other than the Stowe group had heard from McTaggart directly. The French stuck to their story about the *Greenpeace III* colliding with their boat. The newspapers told nothing of the boat being rammed, and Vancouver journalists remained skeptical. To Hunter, Metcalfe complained that they had no pictures. "We're taking a big hit here," he fumed.

David McTaggart's brother Drew, a Vancouver psychiatrist, knew about the leftists at the Fishermen's Hall meetings and also knew that Irving Stowe had recently travelled to China, which only fueled his opinion that Irving Stowe, Jim Bohlen, and others in Greenpeace were Communists. Stowe had indeed travelled to China in June of 1972 with twenty University of Toronto educators, and had met with Chinese academics and environmentalists. The Stowes and Bohlens held liberal views and criticized American militarism, but Drew McTaggart's perceptions missed the mark and influenced his brother. David McTaggart called Metcalfe and yelled at him. "You're all a bunch of Communists! Your guys went to China!"

"Well, David," said Metcalfe, "Pierre Trudeau went to China. That doesn't make him a Communist." The two men argued and finally hung up. Later,

McTaggart phoned back — a style that would become familiar over the years — apologized, and told Metcalfe he was just trying to get support to carry on the fight against the French. "We have a case," he claimed. "We can take them on in their own courts." McTaggart said he needed $13,000 for *Vega* repairs, and $10,000 to begin the legal work. Metcalfe agreed to help, but emphasized that the group did not have much money. "We have about a thousand dollars in the bank," said Metcalfe. "We'll have to get busy with fundraising. Why don't you come over? Let's talk about it. Bring the photographs from the voyage."

"Yeah, yeah," said McTaggart. "I'll try to come by."

PRIME MINISTER

But McTaggart never visited Metcalfe. Instead, in August, he retreated to his boyhood summer home at Buccaneer Bay with his notes, log books, and photographs from the voyage. He intended to write his book and prepare a legal case. A few days after he arrived, a white yacht entered the bay. McTaggart learned from local children that Pierre and Margaret Trudeau, the prime minister of Canada and his bride of one year, were on board. Bob Hunter might have called it Jungian synchronicity, but to McTaggart it was simply an opportunity not to be missed. He endeared himself to two young women from the yacht and convinced them to deliver a message to Trudeau. He then paddled out to the yacht in a canoe and approached within 20 yards when Pierre and Margaret Trudeau stepped out on deck accompanied by two solemn security officers.

"Yes, Mr. McTaggart," said the prime minister, "what can I do for you?"

McTaggart paddled forward, clutched the ladder of the yacht, and told his story quickly: the voyage to Moruroa, the Law of the Sea, and the ramming by the French.

"I'm not very sympathetic to the Greenpeace Foundation," said the prime minister frankly.

"I'm a Canadian citizen whose boat was rammed by the French Navy in international waters," pleaded McTaggart. "All I'm requesting is the defence of my rights."

They talked for forty minutes, McTaggart clinging to the ladder, sitting barefoot in his skiff, the prime minister towering above him with powerful blue eyes and an air of supreme confidence. Margaret said nothing, but watched McTaggart throughout. Trudeau explained the legal complications of Canada taking another nation, particularly France, to court. The politician was smooth and noncommittal, but appeared keenly interested.

"Is the Canadian government going to help me or not?" McTaggart finally wanted to know.

"Mr. McTaggart, do you expect us to go to war over your boat?"

"No," said McTaggart. "I just want the government to stand up for me because I'm a Canadian citizen."

The prime minister shrugged, and the chat was over.

A few weeks later, near the end of August, McTaggart received a telegram from Minister of Foreign Affairs Mitchell Sharp telling him, "The French authorities have not reacted in any way to your account of the incident," and "there is little the government can legally do to assist you."

McTaggart felt caught between two worlds. His old, conservative friends thought he was on a fool's errand. On the other hand, he did not quite fit in with the radical disarmament crowd. And his government seemed to have abandoned him. Lawyer Francis Auburn advised McTaggart that his best hope would be to get the Government of Canada to espouse his legal action, but in October he met lawyer Jack Cunningham, who believed the sailor had a good case and helped him prepare a lawsuit against the French Navy. McTaggart travelled to Toronto to tape a national television show and plead his case for government support. The day before he arrived, however, the Department of External Affairs called the station to inform them that the government would take up the cause with France. Mitchell Sharp sent a hurried telegram to McTaggart. "I have asked my officials to give careful consideration to your case," he promised, "to determine if some form of assistance might be possible." McTaggart couldn't help but notice that a little media attention might not be so bad. He returned to Buccaneer Bay, where Ann-Marie Horne joined him in November, and together they worked on the book manuscript.

That fall, McTaggart read *Greenpeace*, the story of the voyage to Amchitka Island written by Bob Hunter with photographs by Robert Keziere. McTaggart realized that Hunter had fought with Metcalfe during the voyage and figured Hunter might be an ally in getting Greenpeace to support his court case against France. On a typically wet, dreary night in East Vancouver, McTaggart arrived at the home of Bob and Zoe Hunter.

They drank beer and talked late into the night. McTaggart carefully dropped into the conversation his aversion to Ben Metcalfe and his general distrust of Greenpeace. Bob and Zoe Hunter were sympathetic, but Bob Hunter defended Metcalfe's prowess as a journalist. "And we're not Communists," he said. Hunter explained to McTaggart his own larger ecological vision, and the extended circle of Greenpeace supporters. He mentioned that France planned a megaton-range hydrogen bomb test for Moruroa the following summer. "Maybe," suggested Hunter, "we should go back to Moruroa." McTaggart, however, felt his litigation against France was the right direction for Greenpeace. The Hunters offered encouragement but warned McTaggart that there wasn't much money to go around. McTaggart retreated to Buccaneer Bay, but he liked Bob and Zoe Hunter, and from this evening on, the three became close friends.

MUSHROOMS FOR JEANNE D'ARC

Rod Marining had returned from Europe, accompanied by Janine Bensasson, and with the Metcalfes organized a boycott of French wines in Canada. Marining and Bensasson picketed liquor stores and organized rallies at the French Consulate. When the Vancouver Greenpeace members learned that Grant Davidson had been hospitalized for suspected radiation sickness, Bob Hunter lashed out against France in his column and Metcalfe blasted them on the CBC.

In January 1973, a small item in the Vancouver newspapers announced that a French Navy ship, helicopter carrier *Jeanne d'Arc*, would visit Vancouver. Marining wanted to take action, but Ben Metcalfe had left to teach journalism for one semester in Penticton, 250 miles east of Vancouver. Marining huddled with Bensasson, Hunter, and Hamish Bruce. On Tuesday, February 13, as the 10,000-ton French carrier *Jeanne d'Arc* rounded Point Grey from the Strait of Georgia, Marining and his friends walked across the Lion's Gate Bridge, the gateway to the harbour in Vancouver. They carried rope and a folded piece of canvas.

Jeanne d'Arc approached the bridge, arrayed with electronic tracking equipment and wartime armaments, including six Exocet missile launchers and four 100-millimetre guns. During peacetime, the vessel served as a training ship for *Ecole d'Application des Officiers de Marine*, the French

Naval Academy. One hundred and fifty young cadets stood among the 600 officers and crew lining the flight deck fore and aft. As *Jeanne d'Arc* entered the narrows, Marining and his crew unfurled a 30-foot banner from the bridge inscribed: MURUROA MON AMOUR.

They lowered the banner far enough to cause the warship — rising seven storeys above the waterline with another 60 feet of communications gear — to change course. As *Jeanne d'Arc* dodged the banner and passed under the bridge, Marining and the others dropped mushrooms and marshmallows onto the deck. The cadets and officers in dress uniform below had no idea what rained down on them. They broke rank and ducked for cover as the media boats waited in the harbour.

Among the welcoming flotilla, a tiny, 24-foot, 1930s wooden gillnetter, the *Zoe Too*, piloted by Bob Hunter, pushed out from the other boats and made for the 600-foot French vessel. The crew of protestors — Zoe Hunter, their children Conan and Justine, Kimiko and Hamish Bruce, Janine Bensasson, Lyle Thurston, Paul Watson, Paul Spong, and new SPEC president Gary Gallon — waved "Mururoa Mon Amour" signs. A three-by-five-foot piece of plywood sheeting rested against the cabin of the gillnetter, painted yellow with green letters:

GREEN

PEACE

Hunter handed the wheel to Paul Watson, who steered toward the French warship, as he joined the protestors in chanting, "*La paix, la paix.*" They flashed the peace sign and held up their placards below the huge grey hull and ominous guns of the *Jeanne d'Arc*. Bensasson spoke to the French sailors with the aid of a microphone and loudspeakers.

"*Arrêtez le bombe à Mururoa. L'amour, ne pas la guerre. Les opinions publiques sont en faveur de la paix. Canadiens. Français. Tout le monde. Nous sommes pour l'abolition de toutes les armes nucléaires. La paix est possible.*"

"*La paix. La paix,*" the crew of the *Zoe Too* chanted.

High above, on the Lion's Gate Bridge, police arrested Marining and questioned him in the back seat of a police cruiser. "What were you throwing from the bridge?"

"Mushrooms and marshmallows," said Marining. He showed the police officers mushrooms from his pocket and handed them an empty marshmallow bag. He told them about Moruroa and radiation and his encounters with undercover police in Paris. "It's okay if you want to arrest me," Marining said. The officers shook their heads in slight amusement and released him. The next day, the newspapers carried a photo of the little Greenpeace boat under the guns of the warship.

After the *Jeanne d'Arc* incident in early 1973, Hamish and Kimiko Bruce hosted Greenpeace meetings at their home in Kitsilano. Hunter brought McTaggart to one of these meetings, where he petitioned the group to support his court case. There had been talk of a peace flotilla descending on Moruroa from all over the Pacific Rim, and the consensus at the meetings favoured sending a Greenpeace boat to join them. McTaggart was willing, but he wanted to fight the lawsuit as well. Others had concerns. "Who is going to raise the money?" people wanted to know. Some members, including Hunter, felt frustrated that McTaggart had not made the photographs from his voyage available. The photographs would help prove French transgressions and would help to raise money. Greenpeace, the group felt, did not have the resources to repair the *Vega*, fund a voyage, *and* fund a lawsuit in Paris.

Hunter also brought Dr. Paul Spong and Linda Spong to Greenpeace meetings in early 1973. Most people knew Spong from his celebrated split with the Vancouver Aquarium and his public statements that the whales at the aquarium wanted to be set free. He had been interviewed in *The Georgia Straight*, saying, "The whale's number one on this planet ... the highest creature ... I'll prove it to you one of these days ... excuse me ... the whale will prove it." At Greenpeace meetings he talked discreetly about the plight of the whales and the need to protect them. McTaggart took exception to the idea and told Hunter, "It will only suck money away from the nuclear thing." But Hunter assumed the role that Stowe had once served: the includer, the peacemaker among factions. Spong gained allies and began to form an idea that would soon shake up this little coterie of pacifists and ecologists.

SKANA

In the fall of 1969, while Hunter contemplated ecology and the Stowes organized the disarmament forces in Vancouver, Spong had performed the pioneer studies on the world's first live, captured *Orcinus orca*, or killer whale, at the Vancouver Aquarium. Spong was short and lean, with long hair falling over his shoulders from under a wool toque. He had grown up in Whakatane, on the northeast coast of New Zealand, and studied law at the University of Canterbury in Christchurch. In 1963, he entered a graduate program in psychology at the Brain Research Institute at the University of California in Los Angeles (UCLA), where he analyzed brain wave patterns in humans and tracked information pathways. He lived with art student and musician Linda Hidalgo; together they provided a home for an Afghan puppy and three cats adopted from a lab experiment. He wrote his doctoral dissertation on sensory stimulation, perception, and human consciousness. In 1967, the head of the UCLA lab recommended Dr. Paul Spong for a unique opportunity to work with a captured whale.

In 1964, Dr. Murray Newman at the Vancouver Aquarium had organized the capture of an orca whale as a model for a sculpture. An aquarium crew harpooned a male orca, shot it with a rifle, and towed it, still alive, across the Strait of Georgia into English Bay. They mistook the whale for a female and named him "Moby Doll." The tormented orca survived for 86 days. The neurological lab at UBC preserved the whale's brain.

Newman, however, wanted a live whale and offered a good price. No one had yet captured a live whale. In the 1940s, the Royal Canadian Air Force and the United States Air Force used pods of orcas as training targets for bombing crews. In 1958, the Canadian Department of Fisheries — facing a decline in the salmon fishery — attempted to eradicate orcas with bazookas mounted on speedboats and a machine gun mounted on the rocks overlooking Johnstone Strait, at the north end of Vancouver Island. After the hit movie *Flipper* in 1963, dolphins became a popular public attraction. Dolphin-hunters in the Florida Keys killed half the dolphins they attempted to capture. When entertainment entrepreneurs set their sights on orcas, a crew from Marineland near Los Angeles captured a young, 4,000-pound female in Newport Harbor. The whale crashed repeatedly into the walls of the tank and died the next day. On February 15, 1967, fishermen surrounded a pod of fifteen orcas in Yukon Harbor near Seattle. The whales thrashed against the net barrier. Three whales died during capture, seven were released, one died in the Seattle Aquarium, and three were shipped to Sea World in Florida and California, where they died in captivity. The final whale — a young, adolescent female, 13 feet long, weighing about 2,500 pounds, one-third of her adult weight — was sold to

The Pacific Northwest Boat Show. She was named "Walter," and exhibited in a tank not much bigger than she was. When the Boat Show visited Vancouver, Newman bought "Walter" for $25,000. The aquarium staff learned she was a female and launched a contest to rename her. The young female became "Skana," a Haida name for the orca, meaning "Supernatural one."

Newman needed a whale scientist and Dr. Patrick McGeer, head of the Neurological Lab at UBC, agreed to help find a candidate. In the spring of 1967, Dr. Paul Spong arrived in Vancouver to interview for the job. His previous work had been with human neurology, so he read background material on *Orcinus orca*, a member of the Delphinidae family of toothed cetaceans. He had discovered Dr. John Lilly's work, which showed cetaceans possessed brains as complex as human brains. Dr. Ken Norris, a cetologist at UCLA, had explained cetacean hearing to Spong. In 1959 Norris had found the jawbone of a bottlenose dolphin in Mexico and surmised correctly that the oil-filled chamber in the bone — which Norris named the "acoustic window" — collected audio information and transmitted it to the inner ear. He suggested to Spong that cetacean vision needed research and Spong had prepared a proposal for McGeer and Newman.

He arrived on the University of British Columbia campus in April, almost simultaneously with Jim Bohlen. The seaside city reminded Spong of his boyhood home in Whakatane. Dr. McGeer gave him a tour of the labs and drove him over the bridge to the aquarium in Stanley Park, where Dr. Newman escorted him to see the whale. Skana swam in slow, silent circles. "She's docile," aquarium curator Vince Penfold told Spong. She was the largest animal Paul Spong had ever seen.

McGeer offered Spong the job two days later. In Los Angeles, Paul and Linda loaded their belongings and their pets into a van and headed north. In Vancouver, they married and found a house on Third Avenue in Kitsilano, halfway between UBC and the aquarium in Stanley Park. A year later, their son Yasha was born.

Spong devoted himself to learning about the whale. To test the resolution of her sight, he taught Skana to distinguish between a single line and two lines on a card lowered into the water. He rewarded her for success with a herring fillet. Once she caught on, Skana consistently signalled "two lines" by touching a lever with her nose. Over time, he narrowed the gap between the two lines, starting at four inches, then reducing the gap to one inch, half an inch, and so on, to determine at what point she could no longer distinguish two lines from one. Performing 72 trials per day, over a period of two months, Spong reduced the gap down to one-thirty-second of an inch, at which point Skana had difficulty distinguishing the two lines.

Spong returned to a one-sixteenth inch gap, for which Skana had previously scored over 90 percent correct responses. When he rang the bell to start the test, the young whale swam lethargically. Skana had performed the procedure some 2,400 times, and her enthusiasm had waned. On the first trial, the whale signaled the wrong answer, but on the second trial she signalled correctly and received her half a herring reward. However, on the next two trials she signalled wrong answers. The whale vocalized loudly above the water before and after each answer. Skana signalled incorrectly on the next 68 trials. Even if she had been guessing, she would have scored 50 percent, yet she scored almost zero where she had previously scored better than 90 percent. Spong found himself on the threshold of his own private paradigm shift.

The data did not make sense, so he brought a lab assistant to witness the test. Skana scored zero again, and vocalized loudly before and after each response. Spong changed the gap between the lines to a quarter inch and then to two inches, but it made no difference. Skana flunked every test. Spong had never before witnessed anything like this. He feared the contradictory data rendered his entire experiment a flop. "She's toying with me," he confided to Linda later.

"She's probably bored," Linda said.

The scientist pondered his results. Was the lab animal rebelling? Unless the whale's eyesight had suddenly faltered, the experiment revealed something rarely documented: a lab animal in open revolt. Spong thumbed through John Lilly's books and papers. Dolphins and whales have large brains and a complex communication system that human scientists don't yet understand. They might be as intelligent as humans. Spong thought about the vocalizations. "She's trying to communicate," he told Linda. "What if ..." Spong paused. The idea he contemplated was not something scientists were trained to consider. "What if she's giving wrong answers on purpose?"

GOING CRAZY

In April 1968 when fishermen working for the aquarium captured eight orcas behind nets in Pender Harbour, 50 miles north of Vancouver, Spong travelled to see the whales. He recorded vocalizations between free family members outside the nets and the captured whales inside. He took particular interest in a mother and young male who swam side by side and rose to breathe in unison. The captors fed fish to the whales. The young male, named Hyak by the team, got annoyed at the seagulls stealing the fish. Spong observed the whale as he grabbed a gull by the legs, towed it under, and then let it go. The startled gull gasped for air at the surface and flew away. On another occasion Hyak grabbed a gull by the head but released it without harming the bird. This seemed like unusually compassionate behaviour from the so-called "killer" whales. Why would they not simply crush the gulls between their six-inch teeth? To study whales properly, Spong thought, he would need a research station where the whales could be observed in the wild.

When bungling staff accidentally killed the mother whale, they brought the young male to the Vancouver Aquarium but kept him separated from Skana. Spong watched over the orphaned Hyak, who seemed to sink into a deep depression. He conducted experiments with the whale using sound as a reward, and Hyak recovered from his lethargy. The result confirmed his belief in the importance of acoustics for orcas. When the staff put Skana with Hyak to clean her pool, she swam with the young whale, vocalized with him, and he began to respond.

John Lilly had theorized that humans could communicate with cetaceans, so Spong began arriving at the aquarium early in the morning, when no one else was around. He had learned enough flute technique from Linda that he could sit by the pool and play for Skana and Hyak. Their reaction indicated to him that they enjoyed the sessions.

Early one morning, as he sat on the training platform dangling his bare feet in the water, Skana approached slowly, opened her jaws, and abruptly raked her teeth across the tops and soles of his feet. Spong jerked his feet from the water and could feel his heart racing. He gingerly put his feet back into the water. Again, Skana bared her teeth, as if taunting him, then brushed her teeth across his feet, as he instinctively jerked them from the pool. Skana repeated the routine eleven times, and eleven times Spong pulled his feet from the water. On the twelfth time, after Skana brushed her teeth across his feet, the scientist controlled the urge to flinch. Skana stopped the game, circled into the middle of the pool, raised her head, and gave out a high, modulating call.

"I became the subject and she became the experimenter," he told Linda. By daring him to leave his feet in the water, Spong believed, Skana had consciously deconditioned his fear of her. "When I stopped reacting with fear, she ended the exercise," Spong told his friends at the pub. Nothing in his scientific training had prepared him to accept that an animal could consciously tutor *him*. "This is extraordinary," he said. "She taught me to not be afraid of her."

Spong began to swim freely with Skana and Hyak. He invited local musicians to the aquarium at night to play for the whales and learned that the whales appreciated classical music, particularly flute and violin music. Hyak and Skana would sometimes mimic the human music. Hyak recovered his vitality from the attention of Skana and Spong.

In the fall of 1968, Spong delivered a lecture at the University of British Columbia. He described the odd, spontaneous reversal of Skana's response, and his hypothesis about her intention. Hyak and Skana had come from different family groups with different vocal dialects. Spong guessed that Hyak, from a northern BC pod, was learning Skana's southern dialect, a hypothesis later confirmed. He described whales as "highly intelligent, social animals" and suggested they should not be held in captivity. The tanks, he said, amounted to "a sensory depravation environment" for the acoustic animals. "In isolation they become depressed," he said. "It might be better to study the whales in their natural habitat." Spong proposed moving his whale study to Pender Harbour in a semi-wild environment, then releasing the whales after a time in captivity. He mentioned that it might be possible some day to actually communicate with whales. His comments were published in the daily newspapers, and radio host Jack Webster called to schedule an interview. However, Dr. Newman at the Vancouver Aquarium scolded Spong for suggesting the whales should be freed. He suspended the research project and told Spong to submit a new proposal.

At UBC, the acting head of the lab gave Spong some hope that the university might support wild whale research, but then he sent Spong to the office of Dr. James Tyhurst, the head of the Department of Psychiatry. Spong had been working long hours. His hair had grown wild, and his eyes were red from lack of sleep. Tyhurst told Spong that his references to communicating with whales were detrimental to the reputation of the Department of Psychiatry. "Paul," he said, "you are a little bit out of control. We're going to ask you to check in downstairs."

Downstairs was the university hospital's psychiatric ward. Spong explained that he just needed a rest. "You can check in voluntarily or not," Tyhurst declared. Spong agreed to check in. After three days of rest in the psych ward, he announced he was ready to go home, but Tyhurst refused to release him. Spong panicked and became agitated, which only reinforced the opinion that he was out of control. Tyhurst told him that his job at the aquarium had been terminated. A rumour reached the media that Spong had mental problems. Jack Webster cancelled his radio interview.

Once out of the psych ward, he spoke with Stan Persky at *The Georgia Straight*. Spong quoted the *I Ching*, admitted taking mescaline during some of his sessions with Skana, and chanted, "Let the whales go."

At the Cecil Pub, the intelligentsia crowd toasted the diminutive scientist as a visionary. From a stranger in the pub Spong learned about Alert Bay on Cormorant Island, home of the Nimpkish band of the Kwakiutl Indians, approximately 150 miles north of Vancouver, in prime orca whale habitat. As part of Spong's separation package from the university, he received a $4,000 research grant for his remote orca observation project. With this money, the Spongs formed the Killer Whale (*Orcinus Orca*) Foundation, known affectionately as "KWOOF." They sold their Volkswagen, bought a Land Rover, and prepared to travel north in search of orcas.

On December 11, 1969, fishermen trapped twelve more whales in Pender Harbour. Shortly after the Spongs arrived, one of the captured female orcas gave birth in the harbour, which may have been the reason they were there. The captors freed the mother and newborn, and six whales escaped. Of the remaining five whales, one was shipped to Marineland in France and four were sold to aquaria in California. Four of these whales died within two years, but one female, named Corky, endured in captivity. Spong would spend three decades attempting to free her, and in the meantime, vowed to stop whale captures in British Columbia.

KILLERS

In the summer of 1972, as David McTaggart sailed to Moruroa, the Spongs built a laboratory and home on a quiet bay on remote Hanson Island, 200 miles northeast of Vancouver. Here, *Orcinus orcas* make their summer home, feed on the abundant salmon, give birth, and scratch their backs on the pebbly shallows of Robson Bight. From the lab, Spong could observe the whales and record their vocalizations. The alien communications seemed complex, beyond his ability to decipher, but he faithfully catalogued the recordings and attempted to transcribe the ethereal modulations in his notebooks.

Whaaaaaa-eeeee-aaaaa-eeeee-aaaaa-uup!

The Spongs received financial support from the Point Foundation in California, organized by publisher Stuart Brand to distribute surplus cash when the company that published the *Whole Earth Catalogue* closed. They shared research results with Russian scientist A. G. Tomlin, who had studied the humpback whales in the Sea of Okhotsk and discussed that cetacean brains allow for extremely fast neural processing of acoustic information. Tomlin's work, like that of John Lilly and Gregory Bateson, supported Spong's notion that whales live in a rich acoustic world. In Blackfish Sound near their home, the Spongs kayaked freely among the whales and played flutes to curious orcas, which never once acted aggressively. The Spongs learned to recognize family groups and even gave the orcas names: "Nicola" for a female with a nick in her dorsal fin, and "Wavy" for a male with a distinctive wave in his fin. The extended whale families remained together season after season.

That summer, a Canadian National Film Board crew documented Spong's work with whales and recorded jazz flutist Paul Horn playing for captive orcas at Sealand Aquarium, a male, Haida, and an albino female, Chimo. Chimo had refused food in captivity and only began eating when Haida brought her salmon. Paul Horn's music, however, appeared to lift Chimo's spirits. Within a few months, Haida and Chimo mated, and the aquarium hoped to achieve the world's first live, captive birth. The resulting film, *We Call Them Killers*, became the first film to depict whales as intelligent, sensitive creatures.

In 1972, author Farley Mowat toured Canada to promote his new book, *A Whale for the Killing*, documenting the tragic death of a stranded fin whale in Newfoundland. An elderly fisherman had told Mowat that a second whale remained outside the cove and breathed in unison with the trapped whale until she died. As a boy, when Mowat was lost at sea for a week off Nova Scotia with his father, they heard the voice of a whale through the fog. They followed the whale to gain safe passage through the reefs toward anchorage in Halifax. The whale, he believed, had saved his life, and he now wanted to repay the debt. His speaking tour had turned into a crusade for saving the last whales.

In December of 1972, Mowat's tour reached Vancouver. Paul Spong attended his reception party and struck up a friendship with the writer. A month earlier, Chimo, the albino female at Seaworld in Victoria, had died. Spong and Mowat took a ferry to Victoria and visited Chimo's surviving mate, Haida. The lonely whale appeared depressed, and Spong called Paul Horn, who agreed to visit the aquarium regularly to play the flute to help cheer him up.

Although Spong had grown to love the whales, and knew they were hunted, Mowat revealed to him the extent of the carnage caused by floating factory ships and exploding harpoons. He explained that the whaling companies controlled the International Whaling Commission (IWC). After the UN Conference on the Human Environment voted 52-0 to recommend a 10-year whaling moratorium, the United States proposed the ban at the Whaling Commission meeting in London. The United Kingdom, Argentina, and Mexico supported the moratorium, but Japan, the Soviet Union, Norway, Iceland, Australia, and Brazil opposed it. "We lost, 6-4," Mowat said, "and Canada shamefully abstained, essentially supporting the whalers." Sir Peter Scott, cofounder of World Wildlife Fund (WWF) accused the abstaining nations of selling out the whales for minor trade deals. "If we cannot save the whales from extinction," said Scott, "we have little chance of saving mankind." In Bolinas, California, Joan McIntyre had organized Project Jonah, and marched that summer on the streets of Stockholm with Patrick Moore and others from around the world. Mowat had affiliated a Canadian chapter of Project Jonah and now asked Spong to open a West Coast office.

"Listen, Paul," Mowat told him, "there are only a few people who have seen what you've seen, who've had the experience. Most of the world still gets its ideas about whales from lingering images of Moby Dick. The factory ships are wiping out the whales as fast as they can. What do they care?

It's all for a few dollars. When the whales are gone, the whalers will transfer their assets to another business. They make dog food and lipstick out of the whales. The Russians lubricate their nuclear missiles with whale oil. So do the Yankees. It's a disgrace."

PERSEVERANCE FURTHERS

At their winter home in Vancouver — a squatters' community built on the North Shore mudflats of Burrard Inlet — Spong read a column by Bob Hunter about the protests in Moruroa. He brooded over the image of intercontinental missiles, lubricated with whale oil, delivering nuclear annihilation to human civilization. "I've got to talk to that Bob Hunter guy," he told Linda.

While Ben Metcalfe had been teaching journalism for a semester in the BC interior, Hunter had assumed the title of Greenpeace "president," although Metcalfe had not resigned as chairman. Metcalfe first learned of his "resignation" in Hunter's column. At a birthday party for Lyle Thurston, he confronted Hunter.

"Bob, I see you've announced my resignation."

"Uh, yeah, well," said Hunter, "you want the job back?"

"No, no, it's okay." But the mentor added one final bit of counsel for his protegé. "Fear success," he whispered. Hunter would puzzle over this for two years before circumstances would reveal that the elder journalist possessed uncanny foresight.

At Greenpeace meetings Hunter touted Charles Reich's "Green revolution," and invoked "all sentient beings." In the spring of 1973, when Paul Spong called and talked about saving whales, Hunter invited him for a cruise aboard the *Zoe Too*. As they chugged out into English Bay, Spong told about families of orcas lulling about his kayak and eyeing him. He told Hunter about the Bio-Sonar Conference at Stanford University in Palo Alto, California, where he had gleaned from his old mentor Dr. Ken Norris that cetaceans have one voice for social communication and a separate voice for sonic navigation. "Whales, particularly the toothed whales like the orcas, literally see with sound," Spong told Hunter. "They send out clicks that rebound from objects in the water, and from the echo they are able to interpret size, shape, texture, speed, and location of the objects around them. I've recorded the clicks from Hanson Island. I'll bet the audio image in the brain of a whale is every bit as rich as the visual image created in a human brain. The problem is, Bob, just as we're getting to know the whales, we're wiping them out. Get this: The military lubricates its bloody nuclear missiles with whale oil!"

Hunter shook his head in half-mocking despair and steered the *Zoe Too* past anchored freighters toward Point Grey in the distance. Spong drank from his beer bottle and continued. "The Whaling Commission scientists are whaling company lackeys. They opposed the whaling moratorium on the grounds that more research is necessary. It's bullshit, Bob, and time is running out for the whales."

"Okay, I'm with ya, Paul," said Hunter, "so what do you suggest?"

"Well, that's just it," said Spong. "We'll do the Greenpeace thing. We'll take a boat out there and confront the whalers."

Hunter and Spong drank beer, drifted in Burrard Inlet, and talked about saving the whales. "Greenpeace doesn't have much money, Paul. We're trying to get McTaggart's boat back out to Moruroa. Boats are expensive. There are already competing factions in Greenpeace. And even if we *had* the money, how do we find the whalers? It's not like going to an island. They're moving all over the ocean."

"Just think about it, Bob," said Spong. "We don't have to figure it all out right here. Let's see what the oracle says." Spong pulled out his Wilhelm/Baynes translation of the ancient Chinese *I Ching*, the Book of Changes. He set his beer down, shook three Chinese coins in his hand and cast them upon his notebook. He repeated the process six times while scratching lines onto the open page. Spong was a self-taught *I Ching* scholar. He took one look at the six yin and yang lines forming the hexagram and said, "Wind over water. Dispersion." He scanned and paraphrased the text. "When our vital energy is blocked, gentleness and humility will break the impasse. Aggression won't work. It furthers one to cross the great water."

Hunter nodded. "Sounds good."

"Perseverance furthers," Spong continued. "Spiritual force will overcome the egos that divide people. Sacred music and ceremony will awaken in people the consciousness of the common origin of all beings. When the boat is crossing the water, all hands must unite. But only those who are free of selfish motives can dissolve the barriers of egoism. A warm breeze in spring melts the ice."

"Okay," said Bob. "I guess we wait and stay humble."

"There's a changing line," said Paul. "The second line changes to a yin line. It means you hurry to that which supports you. It's not a time to be passive. A leader contemplates heaven and sets a lofty example to the people. When the wind blows over the earth, it disperses far and wide. We have to travel, learn what's going on, and see how we can influence events."

"Yeah, okay."

Hunter and Spong clinked their beer bottles, drank, and opened two more. A steady breeze blew across the bay and a light choppy sea rapped against the hull of the *Zoe Too*.

OH, MY GOD!

That winter, Spong met George Dyson, a bright young naturalist and son of a famous American physicist. Dyson lived 90 feet high in a fir tree and built Aleutian kayaks, "baidarkas," on a stretch of Indian Arm, the northerly arm of Burrard Inlet east of Vancouver. Dyson paddled a baidarka to Hanson Island the next summer, and in Blackfish Sound, he and Spong observed whales herding salmon. The orcas split into small groups, corralled the fish in a ring, and took turns feeding. Spong asked Dyson about using kayaks to blockade whalers. "Hmm, I don't know," Dyson remarked.

Department of Fisheries and Oceans marine mammalogist Dr. Michael Bigg asked Spong to help compile a Canadian orca census. Bigg estimated that 300 *Orcinus orcas* lived in three groups along the West Coast. The whales Spong knew around Hanson Island comprised the northern resident community; southern families gathered in the Strait of Georgia and Puget Sound. Both groups left for the deep sea during the winter, and a third group migrated along the West Coast and occasionally entered the Inside Passage. This community of orcas would prove to be larger and more diverse than Spong and Bigg first guessed, but their work confirmed that orcas live in tight, matrilineal family units. The smallest family unit, a "pod" might consist of three to twelve whales related to an elder female. These families would gather into larger groups to feed or lull in the shallows at Robson Bight.

Spong observed whales breathing in unison while resting, something he had watched Skana and Hyak do in the aquarium pool. Perhaps, he thought, this was another form of coöperation. Whereas land mammals breathe automatically, even while asleep, whales remain semi-conscious to avoid drowning. Spong hypothesized that breathing in unison might aid survival and kindle a heightened sensitivity for communication.

Joan McIntyre in California asked Spong to contribute an account of his observations to an anthology of whale essays to be called *Mind in the Waters*. Mowat and Spong kept up the pressure for the Canadian government to support the whaling moratorium at the upcoming 1973 IWC meeting. Paul and Linda Spong became full-time whale advocates, printing flyers on a hand-operated Gestetner mimeograph machine that they bought at a secondhand shop for $50. They circulated the flyers at shopping malls in an effort to raise public awareness about whales.

"Wales!" one elderly woman exclaimed in front of a supermarket. "Oh, my God! What's happening in Wales?"

"Save the whales?" another shopper asked Spong. "Save them for what? What are they good for?"

Spong sent petitions and whaling data to the Canadian Minister of Fisheries and Oceans. At the Whaling Commission meeting that summer of 1973, the United States again proposed a 10-year moratorium, citing data that showed whales had been decimated from populations of some four or five million, down to a few hundred thousand. The blue whale and the humpback whale had been reduced to about a thousand individuals, the right whale to a few hundred, and the Atlantic gray whale to extinction. The whaling nations claimed that the species currently being hunted — fin, sperm, and sei whales — remained numerous enough to survive, even at five percent of their pre-whaling populations. To enact the moratorium, the US motion required a three-quarters majority. The UK, Argentina, Mexico, Canada, France, Panama, and Australia voted in favour. Japan, the Soviet Union, Norway, Iceland, and South Africa — all active whaling nations — voted against. The 8-5 vote did not achieve the three-quarters majority, and the ban failed.

The Commission defeated a Japanese attempt to raise quotas on minke whales, but the achievement masked business as usual. The Whaling Commission set most quotas higher than the previous year's catches. The annual North Pacific sperm whale catch had plummeted by half in only four years, to about 8,500 whales, and yet the commission set the quota at 10,000. The Scientific Committee of the Whaling Commission remained a closed and guarded cabal, run by Japan. When environmentalists learned that Japanese whalers operated pirate whaling ships out of Peru, a nation that did not belong to the Whaling Commission, Cleveland Amory of the Fund for Animals called for a boycott of Japanese goods until the sham stopped.

That fall, the Canadian government announced an official end to Canada's obsolete whaling industry. Farley Mowat called Spong to celebrate the minor victory. "Next," said Spong, "the world!"

UPRISING IN THE PACIFIC

Thus, throughout 1973, Hunter hosted Spong at Greenpeace meetings, where he pressed his case for a whale campaign. Marining, Hamish Bruce, and others supported the idea. Hunter attempted to unify the developing schism between the disarmament wing and the ecology wing, which had become known as the "whale group." Money remained scarce, and the French nuclear campaign took precedence. Greenpeace sent $1,000 to Nigel Ingram in Auckland to prepare the *Vega* for a return to Moruroa. McTaggart received a $1,500 advance from a publisher for his book, *Outrage!*, including the never-before-seen pictures. He sent half the money to Nigel, and then joined him in New Zealand. Through June and July, Greenpeace sent $6,890 to McTaggart to provision the *Vega*, primarily because of Hunter's insistence. The ecology group SPEC and the Sierra Club each loaned $500 to Greenpeace to support the campaign. Greenpeace paid $1,000 to McTaggart's lawyer, Jack Cunningham, to prepare the Law of the Sea court case. Marining succeeded in getting $200 to the support group in Paris, to prepare a Greenpeace presence during the summer. No money remained to finance a whale campaign, so Spong undertook his own fundraising.

The French had scheduled five bomb tests for the summer, the largest, a hydrogen bomb test, was slated for August. In one year, however, nuclear politics had changed. Soviet leader Leonid Brezhnev and US president Richard Nixon signed a nuclear non-aggression pact, freezing current nuclear arsenals and, ostensibly, limiting the proliferation of nuclear weapons. France and China were now the only countries still testing nuclear weapons in the atmosphere. In Australia and New Zealand, since the previous summer, Labour Party leaders Gough Whitlam and Norman Kirk had used the disarmament issue to win national elections. The two leaders teamed up to launch proceedings against France in the International Court of Justice at The Hague, charging France with endangering their citizens. In June, the court ruled that France should halt the testing in the Pacific, but the Pompidou government ignored the order. In response, the Pacific Island nations and territories sent up an outcry, groups around the world boycotted French goods, the United Nations General Assembly voted 106-4 in favour of a ban on atmospheric nuclear tests, and the International Confederation of Free Trade Unions voted again to boycott French airlines and shipping lines. Scientists released data about the expected number of leukemia cases and birth defects from the radioactive fallout, but Pompidou disregarded the uproar and proceeded to test France's new thermonuclear fusion weapons.

Citizens launched an international flotilla throughout Polynesia. Native people set out in canoes from Fiji and Samoa. The Australian government sent its navy ship, *Supply*, and the New Zealand government sent the military cruiser *Otago*. Boats departed from Brisbane, Christchurch, Lima, Hawaii, and Tahiti. More than thirty vessels headed for Moruroa, though few actually made it to the remote atoll. US authorities stopped a boat out of Honolulu, but most simply failed to navigate the unpredictable South Pacific Ocean. The yacht *Spirit of Peace* did make it into the test site with a crew of Campaign for Nuclear Disarmament pacifists, including Kurt Horn, who had been aboard the *Greenpeace II*. The crew did not confront the French directly and received scant media coverage. The crew of the Baltic trader *Fri*, however, did unnerve French authorities.

In March, the *Fri* departed Whangarei, New Zealand, and sailed for Moruroa, supported by the CND and Peace Media. American skipper David Moodie, his wife Emma Moodie, Dutch sailors Rien Achterberg and Martini Gotjé and their crew sailed the southern route to Pitcairn Island and northwest on the trade winds to Moruroa. They arrived at the test zone on May 25 and rendezvoused with the 40-foot sloop *Spirit of Peace*. Thereafter, David Moodie wore a Greenpeace T-shirt given to him by Kurt Horn. On July 15, the 48-foot yawl *Arwen* arrived from Rarotonga to resupply both ships. On board the *Arwen*, Brice Lalonde — president of Les Amis de la Terre, who had met Rod Marining a year earlier in Paris — watched the *Fri* approach. With Lalonde stood General Jacques Paris de Bolladiére, a French war hero who had objected to French brutality in Algeria, become a pacifist, and formed Bataillon de la Paix, the *Arwen*'s sponsor. Also on board were Catholic priest Jean Toulat, author of *La Bombe ou La Vie?* and French philosophy professor Jean-Marie Muller. These four pacifists transferred to the crew of the *Fri*.

Two days later, inside the cordon, French warships surrounded the *Fri*, and saliors abord *La Dunkerquoise* threw grappling hooks over the railings. Achterberg and Gotjé cut the lines as Moodie held his course. In pure high-seas piracy, French commandos leapt aboard the *Fri* with truncheons and knives. The pacifists screamed at their assailants and Moodie ordered them off his boat, but they did not fight back. In Gandhian tradition, they submitted to the attackers, who forced the crew to the decks, bound them, and seized the vessel.

The French Navy towed the *Fri* into Moruroa and took the crew to the atoll of Hao, 300 miles to the north. The protestors launched a hunger strike, demanding the return of their boat. After eight days without food, their captors took them to the hospital on Papeete, where they continued to refuse food until they won the release of the *Fri*. They sailed for the Marshall Islands, where the communities who had been irradiated by the 1954 Bikini blast welcomed them. At Majuro, Bikini, and Rongelap atolls, US authorities begrudgingly gave Moodie and the crew permission to go ashore at the request of the islanders. From Rongelap, their host, Chief Nelson Anjain, joined the *Fri* on a world tour to explain what had happened to his people as a result of the 1954 radiation.

In Auckland, McTaggart, Nigel Ingram, Ann-Marie Horne, and Mary Lornie raced to provision and prepare the *Vega* to join the protests.

In London, a group of pacifists who had met Rod Marining and Lyle Thurston the previous summer had begun to call themselves "Greenpeace London." They joined Quakers, protestors from War Resisters International, and radical activists from *Peace News* in a procession to Paris. Some of the protestors wore Greenpeace buttons printed by the *Peace News* office, and they carried a Greenpeace banner. Several hundred protestors from Lille met them at the Belgian/French border. When French riot police stopped the march at the border, hundreds of marchers slipped across at night, made their way into Paris, and joined French pacifists in a massive demonstration at the Eiffel Tower. They raised the original Campaign for Nuclear Disarmament peace symbol and unfurled the Greenpeace banner.

Police moved in, swinging clubs, arresting demonstrators, and sending many to the hospital. Protestors chained themselves to pillars inside Nortre Dame Cathedral and were arrested. A week later, thousands of French citizens converged on the Eiffel Tower to protest the French nuclear bomb. Among them marched Janine Bensasson, who had returned to Paris from Vancouver.

In Bonn, West Germany, pacifists and environmentalists adopted the Greenpeace name, painted a banner with the peace and ecology symbols, and marched on the French Embassy. The French government found itself under siege around the world.

TRUNCHEONS

David McTaggart's lawyer, Jack Cunningham, petitioned the Canadian government to act on McTaggart's behalf against the French government. Finally, Minister of Foreign Affairs Mitchell Sharp forwarded a damage claim to Paris, which goaded the French government into responding. René de Saint-Legier, diplomatic counsellor in Canada for President Georges Pompidou, replied on behalf of *Quasi D'Orsay*, the French Foreign Ministry.

"I beg to inform you," he wrote, "that the inquiry which I ordered into the matter allows one to conclude that the said collision was caused by a faulty maneuver on the part of skipper McTaggart." The French lawyer claimed *La Paimpolaise* had approached "very cautiously," and that the *Vega* "fully altered course to throw herself under the minesweeper's bow." The French government concluded, "Taking into account the errors on the part of the 'Green Peace' in causing the collision and … the repairs made free of charge to the sailing ship at Mr. McTaggart's request, to enable him to sail away safely, the Government deems that the damage claim which you submitted to me in your above-mentioned letter is without foundation."

Although the evasive language, "allows one to conclude," rendered the statement not technically a lie, the French government made no serious attempt to disguise the deception. The letter seemed to McTaggart like a transparent sneer from the highest ranks of the French ruling elite.

However, since McTaggart had not released the photographs from the previous year, there was no public proof that France had lied. As McTaggart prepared to depart Auckland, Ben Metcalfe and Bob Hunter released the news in Vancouver, Ottawa, London, and Paris that the *Greenpeace III* was returning to Moruroa. This news flushed another response from the French government. Through Mitchell Sharp, Paris backtracked on its previous statement and agreed to pay McTaggart $5,000 for damages to the *Vega*, but only on the condition that he not sail again into the test zone.

McTaggart interpreted the offer as a sign of France's vulnerability. He refused the French offer and assembled his crew. In June, McTaggart received a letter from Prime Minister Pierre Trudeau. "The Canadian government," said the prime minister, "is fully in accord with you on the question of principle involved in your personal protest against these tests last year."

"What about *this* year?" McTaggart scoffed to his navigator, Nigel Ingram.

The 38-foot ketch *Vega* departed Auckland on July 11 with McTaggart, Nigel Ingram, Ann-Marie Horne, and Mary Lornie on board, but a gale pinned them in Hauraki Bay for twelve days. They heard news on July 21 that the New Zealand ship *Otago* remained just outside the 12-mile limit around Moruroa when the first French bomb of the summer detonated. Two days later, the gale subsided and the *Vega* slipped around Great Barrier Island and made for Moruroa.

The *Vega*'s radio capabilities were no better than the previous summer, but McTaggart had devised a communication system using Morse code letters that could be clicked out on the radio transmitter: "A" for "sighted the French," "B" for "being boarded," and other letters for "being harassed," or "rammed," "bomb exploded," and so forth. Greenpeace had a copy of the code in Vancouver, and radio stations in Rarotonga and Auckland had a copy. The crew carried two 35-mm cameras and a video camera.

On August 2, 1973, with the *Vega* halfway to Moruroa, the crew heard news of a second French blast and the presence of a second New Zealand navy ship, *Canterbury*, near the test zone. The megaton thermonuclear blast was still to come, sometime in August. On August 9, after seventeen days at sea, the *Vega* ran into massive sea swells rolling up from the Antarctic Circle. Atop one of these giant swells, in 20-knot winds, the crew could see the next crest some two miles away. In the trough, dark and eerie like a canyon, there was no wind at all, and the little *Vega*, under its sagging *Greenpeace III* sail, seemed almost lost.

On August 12 they made radio contact with the *Fri* and crossed into the French cordon. By sunrise, they were 35 miles from Moruroa. The other protest boats had left the area or been driven off by the French warships. The next day, a French Navy Lockheed Neptune patrol plane buzzed them. On Wednesday, August 15, the *Vega* cruised 14 miles from Moruroa, shadowed by the minesweeper *La Dunkerquoise*, and the crew saw the balloon above the atoll. A small navy vedette — a sleek, white, 40-foot patrol boat, faster and more manoeuvrable than the warships — arrived with the tug *Hippopotame*. "I think we're going to be boarded," Ingram told McTaggart. Ann-Marie Horne stood ready with a camera.

The three ships closed in around the *Vega*. The speedy vedette pulled along the *Vega*'s starboard beam, towing a small rubber inflatable — a 12-foot, grey, French-made "Zodiac," mounted with an outboard engine. Seven tough-looking French sailors in the Zodiac watched the sailboat, let go from the vedette and moved effortlessly over the waves toward the *Vega*. Ingram ran below and sent out a Morse code SOS on the international distress frequency. McTaggart attempted to outrun the inflatable under diesel power, but the Zodiac proved too fast. They pulled alongside, grabbed the railing, and boarded the *Vega* at the stern. McTaggart let go the tiller and moved to intercept the invaders. He saw knives in scabbards at the sailors' waists and black truncheons in their hands. Unlike the crew of the *Fri*, McTaggart had no background in non-violent resistance. As far as he was concerned, pirates were boarding his vessel and he had every right to defend himself. Ann-Marie snapped photographs and fought off panic. Mary Lornie screamed as she aimed the video camera.

French sailors grabbed McTaggart, beat him on head and body with truncheons, and tossed him like a corpse into the Zodiac. The French sailors in the inflatable pinned McTaggart to the wooden transom and savagely attacked him with their truncheons. They jerked him upright, and McTaggart was only half conscious when he felt a vicious blow to his right eye. He passed out and slumped at the feet of his attackers. When Ingram reappeared on deck, the sailors seized him, beat him unconscious, and left him facedown in the cockpit. Horne captured the assault on film and hurried below. Mary Lornie lowered the video camera and shrieked as the thugs seized hold of her, ripped the camera from her hands, and threw it into the sea.

Below, Ann-Marie placed the second 35-mm camera in the galley, partially hidden, as a decoy. She crawled into the forward cabin with the camera containing the evidence and locked the louvered door. The assailants' boots stomped down the companionway and she heard their sneering voices as they looked for her. They rattled the louvered door as she thrust the camera through a hole in the wall planks and concealed it in the hollow of the boat. The French sailors ripped open the door, dragged her screaming from the cabin, and shoved her up on deck where Ingram lay bleeding from the face. Mary Lornie screamed at her attackers. One Frenchman threw up over the side of the *Vega*. Another emerged from below waving the decoy camera. The French sailors hauled McTaggart away in the inflatable and confined Ann-Marie and Mary on deck. They dragged Ingram below, tossed him into a bunk, and then towed the *Vega* toward Moruroa.

On board *La Dunkerquoise*, a paramedic examined McTaggart's bloodied eye and made hurried arrangements to transport him to the hospital at Papeete, on Tahiti. McTaggart could hardly see. He screamed at the French medics, demanding to speak to Admiral Claverie, see his crew, and call Canada. He sensed that the French officers were worried and spared them no respite from his wrath. At the dock on Moruroa, paramedics transferred McTaggart to an ambulance. An officer promised him a phone call in Papeete, and allowed Horne and Ingram to see him before the ambulance departed for the airfield. Ann-Marie Horne, in tears, said nothing to McTaggart about the hidden camera since French officers surrounded them. The nervous paramedic and a French civilian policeman rushed McTaggart onto a flight to Tahiti.

That night, Ingram, Horne, and Lornie slept on the *Vega* under armed guard. In the morning, aching from his wounds and bruises, Ingram discreetly hid all the charts and logs deep within the structure of the boat. The next morning, a French officer informed the crew they would be flown to Hao Atoll. They demanded to call their respective governments, but were denied. Before leaving the *Vega* under guard, Ann-Marie Horne retrieved the camera, unloaded the film, and concealed the plastic cartridge within her vagina. During her painful walk to the plane, under the glare of French military police, she leaned on Ingram and held her head high.

At the hospital in Papeete, doctors rushed McTaggart into an operating room, but he refused medical care until he was allowed to phone Canada. The chief doctor pleaded, then insisted, and then screamed at him, but

McTaggart pushed him aside and refused the injection of anesthetic. Two military police guarded the door. The hospital authorities, civilian police, and military police discussed the matter under obvious strain. McTaggart knew they were concerned, and the civilian doctors finally prevailed. At 7:00 a.m., fourteen hours after the beating, McTaggart was allowed a phone call. He spoke to his brother, Drew, in Vancouver, told him the story, and dictated a telegram to be sent to Prime Minister Trudeau. Exhausted, he submitted to the doctors. They wheeled him back into the operating room and went to work on his damaged eye.

THE CAMERA IS MIGHTIER

In Vancouver, Drew McTaggart called eye specialist Dr. Robert McCreery, then Bob Hunter. The Greenpeace bank account had been drained, but privately, among the group, they raised $1,000, enough to buy an airplane ticket and provide expense money for Dr. McCreery to travel to Tahiti and look after McTaggart.

On the remote atoll of Hao, the French military headquarters of the Tuamotus Archipelago, legionnaires kept watch over Ingram, Horne, and Lornie for two days. They gave Horne and Lornie plane tickets to Auckland and intended to escort Ingram to London. Before she departed, Ann-Marie Horne gave the critical roll of film to Ingram. While changing planes in the Los Angeles airport, Ingram slipped away from the French officers and traded the remainder of his London ticket for a flight to Vancouver. Once in Vancouver, he looked up Drew McTaggart and gave him the film with instructions not to release the images until he received direction from his injured brother.

France, believing they had confiscated all the cameras, circulated the story that McTaggart hurt his eye by falling onto a cleat while attempting to "throw our sailors back into the sea." The French claimed, "Our men boarded his vessel unarmed and without striking a single blow."

In Vancouver, Hunter learned that Drew McTaggart had the film, and he visited him with Jim Bohlen. Drew balked at handing over the film, which he considered to be his brother's property and perhaps his only asset for recovering his medical expenses. David, he said, wanted to sell the pictures to *Life* magazine. But Hunter and Bohlen insisted. The Moruroa voyages were a Greenpeace campaign, financed with Greenpeace funds. Using the news media was Greenpeace's fundamental tactic. "The photographs," said Hunter, "might prove the French are lying." He explained that France had been able to lie the previous year because the photographs of the voyage had never been released.

They persuaded Drew McTaggart, and Hunter drove the film to Robert Keziere's home, where Keziere developed it and made prints. Hunter watched in the darkroom as the images emerged in a tray of developer. He saw an image of French sailors approaching the *Vega* in the small inflatable. He saw truncheons and McTaggart bent over, under assault. The next morning, Hunter delivered the photographs to the newspapers.

The *Vancouver Sun* ran the pictures under the headline, "Film Shows France Told Outright Lie." The wire services picked up the photographs and sent them to Europe. The images showed the warships, French sailors boarding the sailboat with knives, and the brutal beatings of McTaggart and Ingram. The French lies unravelled around the world, except in France, where the government censored the photographs from the media. However, the damage had been done. The Canadian Bar Association voted unanimously to urge Canada to seek reparations. Minister of Foreign Affairs Mitchell Sharp protested to French Foreign Minister Michel Jobert in New York. Nevertheless, France stuck to its story that no beating had occurred. *Time* magazine reported that the incident "sunk Franco-Canadian relations to the lowest point since Charles de Gaulle dropped his '*Vive le Québec Libre*' clanger in 1967."

On August 28 McTaggart returned to Vancouver, a hero. He walked from the plane with a black eye-patch and spoke to journalists. His brother drove him to a Vancouver hospital for extended care. At the hospital, McTaggart confided to Drew and Hunter that the decision to release the photographs was the right move. Hunter reaffirmed his support for McTaggart and left him with his family.

Meanwhile, in the South Pacific, France detonated two more bombs, one of them in the face of a heavy wind that blew fallout 2,000 miles west, past Tahiti and Rarotonga, to Samoa. French defence minister Robert Galley announced, "France will never undertake to stop testing in the atmosphere." But this was pure bravado. By November, under international pressure, the French ambassador to the UN General Assembly announced they would cease atmospheric nuclear tests after 1974 and conduct all future tests below ground. Greenpeace celebrated the half victory. Atmospheric nuclear testing had been driven from the entire Pacific Ocean.

Throughout the fall of 1973, McTaggart pressed the Canadian government to espouse his case against France. The foreign office made public statements of support, but nothing came of their efforts. Lawyer Jack Cunningham accused the Canadian government of "exhibiting a lack of concern for the rule of law in the world." After much prodding, France agreed to return the *Vega* and the Canadian government agreed to ship the ketch to Canada. McTaggart flew to Tahiti. At dusk on December 11, the French troop carrier *Medoc* pulled into Papeete harbour with the *Vega* lashed to the foredeck. McTaggart took possession of his boat the next day, shipped it to Vancouver by freighter, and followed two days later.

ZODIACS

In Vancouver, the whale faction within Greenpeace, which had received no financial backing, split off into a quasi-separate group. Bob Hunter presided over the Stop Ahab Committee meetings. In November 1973, as the Moruroa story lingered in the media, Bob Hunter phoned Paul Spong and told him he had exciting news. They met at the Cecil Pub. "This whole thing," said Hunter, "about how to blockade the whalers?"

"Yeah?"

"I've got it."

"What?"

"Zodiacs."

"Zodiacs? Like kayaks?"

"No. Kayaks are too slow. Inflatables. With outboards. The French had 'em.

"Like Jacques Cousteau uses."

"Yeah. Will Jones knows where to get 'em. There's a company that makes 'em. They're called Zodiacs. The guys who beat up McTaggart," explained Hunter, "they had Zodiacs. That's how they boarded the *Vega*. It was choppy out there, but no problem for the inflatables. Right across the waves. They're fast and manoeuvrable. When I saw the pictures at Keziere's house, I knew this was it. Check it out. I guarantee you this is what we're looking for."

The idea about using Zodiacs spread through the Shire. I heard about them from Rod Marining. Glenn and I had settled into a new life in Vancouver. Glenn taught at the government-funded City School for alienated teens and prepared Indonesian dishes at Isadora's cooperative restaurant. I had found a job as reporter and photographer for a community advertising circular, the *North Shore Shopper*. Publisher Peter Speck wanted to transform his weekly shopping guide into a real newspaper, and he changed the name to the *North Shore News*. He allowed me a free hand as long as I came up with decent stories and pictures. I monitored the police scanner and chased fire trucks, but I also covered ecology stories wherever I could find them. At the corner of First Street and Lonsdale, the main avenue, near the waterfront, I met a woman attempting to save a stand of cottonwood trees from city work crews by camping out in one. The woman, Bree Drummond, lived with Rod Marining in North Vancouver, in a crumbling shack heated by a wood stove. For two weeks, I covered the cottonwood tree story, but one night Drummond took a night off from her perch, and the city crews dropped the trees at dawn and bucked them up like cordwood. Bree wept on her back porch as if a friend had died. Through Drummond and Marining, I met Paul Spong and Bob Hunter. "Could you take photographs from a Zodiac?" Marining asked me.

"I don't see why not," I said.

On occasion, I now attended Greenpeace meetings, which seemed disjointed as factions jockeyed for funds. Marining temporarily became the chairman of what we called the "Greenpeace Collective," with a changing membership that included Will and Ann Jones, Paul and Linda Spong, the Stowes, and others. Everyone was a volunteer. The entire organization operated from kitchen tables and phone booths in Kitsilano and North Vancouver. The bookkeeping was impeccable, following the standard set by Irving Stowe, but no financial plan existed. The group made decisions about money over beer at the Cecil Pub and on the sidewalk on Fourth Avenue. Competition for funds between the disarmament faction and the Stop Ahab Committee dominated debates. To some of the hard-core pacifists, including Stowe, the whale issue seemed irrelevant when humankind faced nuclear holocaust. Hunter championed a strategy for integrating ecology, disarmament, and social justice, but the various factions had not yet embraced the idea.

Participants came and went. Paul Watson and Walrus Oakenbough travelled to South Dakota to join the Lakota Nation traditional leaders in the occupation of Wounded Knee, and returned with harrowing stories of US Army units and SWAT teams. Pat and Diane Moore had divorced and Pat Moore took up residence in Fowler's Rest Home in Kitsilano, a crash-pad for hippies, fishermen and rock musicians. There he met Eileen Chivers, who had just separated from her husband. They went to Mexico and returned the night before Moore defended his doctoral thesis at UBC. Two days later Moore and Chivers headed north to Winter Harbour, where he worked in his father's logging camp, and they began building a house. Pat Moore and Eileen Chivers both liked hard work, wild fun, and each other. They would have only peripheral contact with Greenpeace over the next year.

Paul and Linda Spong organized a whale celebration in Stanley Park. Rod Marining distributed whale information handouts to the media. Bree Drummond made an enormous blue whale balloon filled with helium and carried aloft by the crowd. The Hunters, Hamish and Kimiko, Myron and Bobbi Macdonald, and others joined a parade with local musicians, walking through the park and past the aquarium where Skana remained confined. Spong gave a speech about whales and called for Skana's release.

THE GREENS

I met with Hunter at the Press Club on Granville Street, a sparse beer parlour with a tinted window looking out above the traffic. An orange light filled the room. Hunter lifted his large leather bag from his shoulder, heaved it onto the table, and pulled out his oversized black notebook, in which he incessantly took notes. His deep-set eyes darted about the room. He wore a full beard and an auburn mane flowed over his shoulders.

For three years I had felt that, although the Vietnam War continued, the anti-war movement had won. The US military had commenced its long, messy withdrawal from Southeast Asia, and the time had come to move on. Hunter felt the same way about the disarmament issue. "The US has turned Amchitka Island back into a bird sanctuary, the French have been driven underground, and the Arms Limitation Treaty is going to get signed. There's not much more we can do to enlighten the public. But ecology? Whales? The tragedy of the commons? There's lots to do."

Hunter recounted Marining's plea to the security police in Paris: "I'm a Green."

"It's the future," Hunter said, "but I'm not interested in replacing one human police state with another. This is about shifting mythologies. We're trying to live out this 5,000-year-old mythology and it isn't working. The countermovement, all over the planet, is ecology."

I had read about a group of Himalayan villagers who stopped loggers from cutting down a stand of hornbeam trees by joining hands and hugging ("*chipko*") the trees. Thus emerged the "Chipko Movement" in India — the original "tree-huggers." Three years earlier, philosopher Arne Naess and a group of farmers had saved the Laxá ("salmon") River in Norway from a dam that would have flooded their farms. The Stockholm Conference and the first Earth Day had advanced new ideas about "limits of growth" and "spaceship Earth." From Ecology Action in California to Friends of the Earth, a new ecological ethic had emerged.

"Scientists are coming at the same thing from the data anyway," said Hunter as he flipped to a page in his notebook and read a quote he'd scribbled down about quantum mechanics: "'The world is an indivisible unit,' bla, bla, here, 'at the quantum level of accuracy, an object does not have any intrinsic properties belonging to itself alone. Instead, it shares all its properties mutually and indivisibly with the systems with which it interacts.' There you have it. Cybernetics. Ecology. We live inside interlocking feedback loops. It's the new spirituality. Talking to Ginsberg just put it all together for me like that."

Allen Ginsberg had returned to Vancouver for a poetry reading, and Hunter had arranged to meet him. The two discussed social transformation, ecology, and mysticism. "Giving yourself up for all sentient beings is classical Buddhism," Ginsberg told Hunter. "The old scientific logic is looking like a dead end. It's as if the culture is returning to Gnostic consciousness, accepting direct knowledge of the world around them."

"Ginsberg saw it," Hunter told me. "He thinks the combined influence of television, alienated youth culture, Third World politics, and ecological destruction has shifted human consciousness toward a holistic mode, the Gnostic idea: We live inside the miracle all the time!"

At three in the afternoon, we were alone, but for the bartender. We drank our amber beer in the dim, warm light. I told Hunter about my travels through Europe and India and he told me about his adventures in Paris and London and meeting Black Panthers in Chicago.

"Violence multiplies violence," said Hunter. "Gandhi got this right. So if you want to change society, you're stuck. You can jump on the cycle of violence and it's just the whole *Animal Farm* thing, or you have to stick it out like Gandhi and Martin Luther King, and if you're effective, they'll probably try to kill you anyway. But Gandhi understood media. It wasn't just non-violence, it was non-violence with communication savvy. He understood a clear message, a good image, and a well-timed leak to the newspapers."

"So what's the deal with the whale committee plan?" I asked him.

"To most people," said Hunter, "whaling is all nineteenth century stuff. Brave men in little boats. They have no idea about huge floating slaughterhouses, steel-hulled chaser boats with sonar to stalk whales, and harpoons fired from cannons. We have to bring back photographs that will turn the whole thing around, show people that the whales are *small* compared to the technology of industrial whaling. And we have to show people that whales are intelligent beings living in sophisticated societies." By this time I had read *The Storming of the Mind* and knew about his mindbomb idea, which seemed simple, like most profound ideas. The picture of the earth from space had demonstrated how a single image could stimulate mass changes of consciousness. He wanted to do something similar for the whales.

When we discussed the internal squabbles between the disarmament and ecology factions of Greenpeace, Hunter sighed for a moment, and declared, "Assume everyone is growing."

THE ESSENCE

"We are wiping out the largest minds on the planet before we even get to know them," Spong pleaded at a Greenpeace meeting at Hamish Bruce's home. Hunter had handed the presidency of Greenpeace over to Hamish when he formed the Stop Ahab Committee with Spong. Hunter had supported McTaggart faithfully, but he believed Greenpeace should adopt the whale campaign. "It puts the Green in Greenpeace. Besides," he said, "it's an ecological atrocity." Rod Marining, Bree Drummond, Hamish and others supported Spong's idea.

McTaggart, still suffering from his beating, lobbied for litigation in the French courts. "The legal case is an extension of the campaign," he said. "We could win in France and it would show governments everywhere that they can't just attack private citizens who have every right to protest." Furthermore, he revealed, a supporter at the University of British Columbia Law Faculty had written a letter on his behalf to *L'Express* editor Jean-Jacques Servan-Schreiber in Paris, an eminent liberal intellectual, who in turn had agreed to help find a lawyer who would take the case against the French government.

Irving Stowe, the group's elder at fifty-eight, now experienced frequent stomach pains, and could only attend meetings with considerable effort. Two years earlier, he had written a touching lament, "After the Whales are Gone, What Dreams May Come?" in *The Georgia Straight*. The tolerant Quaker appreciated both sides of the debate, but now he felt Greenpeace's limited resources should remain focused. "In spite of all the success we've had," he said, "and in spite of all the test ban treaties, there is still an average of one nuclear bomb blast going off every week. The United States, Great Britain, France, the Soviet Union, and China are all building up their nuclear arsenals. They sign treaties, but they keep building more bombs. It's insanity. We should be in every test zone, above ground, below ground, anywhere, until this insanity stops."

"No one's saying that stopping nuclear bombs isn't important," said Hunter, "but we have to shift the human-centred perspective. From a very real point of view, saving whales is as important as saving humans. We shift from the sacredness of human life to the sacredness of all life."

Spong speculated that the whale campaign "will bring in *more* support."

These debates endured all summer, and in the fall of 1973, Spong proposed a way to avoid the impasse. To raise money for the whale campaign, he would stage a "Whale Show" in Vancouver, invite musicians, show films and pictures of whales, and educate people about the issue. "We can raise enough money to launch a worldwide tour, and I'll take the Whale Show on the road and raise the rest of the money. We'll do the first one at Christmas. A family thing. Kids, whale balloons, music." But there was a catch. Spong needed money to set it up and he wanted Greenpeace to finance the first show. Predictably, the disarmament wing of Greenpeace opposed the idea. What if the Whale Show lost money? McTaggart lobbied for the Paris litigation, but the disarmament wing developed its own schism when some people felt the money should go to the new Greenpeace group in Melbourne, Australia, which wanted to launch a third mission to Moruroa in the summer of 1974.

This plan frustrated both Spong *and* McTaggart. After a while, McTaggart refused to attend Greenpeace meetings and would only talk to Hunter. He opened a "Greenpeace" bank account in his name in West Vancouver and raised money for his court case. Hunter and Spong opened their own bank account for the Stop Ahab Committee, and began raising their own money. Suddenly, three separate Greenpeace campaigns and three bank accounts existed simultaneously. The Greenpeace Foundation, under the direction of Hamish Bruce, sent $3,000 to Greenpeace Pacific in Melbourne to provision a new boat that would sail to Moruroa the following summer.

McTaggart called it "a waste." Hunter proposed Greenpeace portion its funds to all three initiatives: the whale campaign, disarmament, and McTaggart's court case. "We're being tight-fisted, unimaginative, and petty," he lamented.

Hamish, a defence lawyer and committed Green Panther, had become the tacit spiritual leader of the group. As president, he said very little in the meetings, but when he spoke, he summarized debates fairly, often reminding everyone of the higher purpose. His moral authority served as the balance of power and emotion between the disarmament and ecology factions. Hamish finally rose to quell the schism.

"The essence is being lost in the particular," he said. He paused, and his compatriots listened intently to hear what he was on about. *The essence*? *The particular*? "Look," he said, "all of these projects are worth supporting. There's no point in fighting over whether or not saving the whales is more important than stopping nuclear war, or if launching a boat is more important than fighting France in the courts. These are the particulars of our larger mission. They're all important and there is probably enough money out there to pay for it all and more. But not if we divide ourselves over these things. The culture of conflict is taking the whole world down a dangerous path. Don't let Greenpeace disintegrate into the same sort of conflict. If we're ecologists, then let's rise above our particular issues to see the bigger pattern. If we do that, the support we need will come. Okay?"

What could anyone say? Hamish was right.

This little speech had a lasting effect. Whenever people found themselves bickering, someone would say, "Keep to the essence. Keep to the essence." It became a mantra through the fall and winter of 1973. Instead of competing for funds, the factions started believing that it all could happen. The psychic logjam loosened.

"Change can happen at the speed of thought," Spong began to say, in the face of any impasse.

Hunter travelled to Victoria and convinced newly elected provincial Premier Dave Barrett to help save the whales. Barrett had led the socialist New Democratic Party to power after thirty years in opposition, in part by appealing to environmentalists. Hunter had supported him and now wanted him to follow through on his commitment to the environment. "Whales?" said the Premier. "No harm in that." He told Hunter that he had considered having a Ministry of the Environment, a fresh idea at the time, and that he would ask his Minister of Lands, Forests, and Resources to look into the prospects of outlawing the capture of orcas in British Columbia. Subsequent legislation created the world's first orca sanctuary.

"Everything is ready for the change," Hunter said in the pub. "The momentum is turning our way." The US Marine Mammal Protection Act and the amended Endangered Species Act had closed the American market for whale products. The UK had banned certain whale products. Canada had ceased whaling and supported the moratorium. Botanists revealed that jojoba bean oil could replace whale oil as a highly viscous lubricant, resistant to temperature change. "It just needs a push to bring pressure on Japan and Russia," said Hunter.

Spong resolved the conflict over financing the Whale Show by signing a guarantee to cover any losses. He felt he needed $10,000 to launch his tour across Canada to Europe and Japan. Paul Hovan, a local music producer who had raised money for the Moruroa campaign, helped Spong produce the Whale Show at Vancouver's elegant Queen Elizabeth Theatre. "If you want to convert street support into financial support, you have to have a coherent identity," Hovan said. "What's your message?"

"We're going to save the whales," said Spong.

The Greenpeace Whale Show opened in Vancouver on December 28, 1973. I attended with my wife and Ron and Dorothy Precious. Canadian folksinger Valdy and jazz flutist Paul Horn provided music. Paul Spong showed films and slides of orcas. Linda and Yasha sold T-shirts and whale buttons. The theatre filled, but the show would net only about $3,000. As Spong contemplated how he'd get the balance of the money, an usher approached and directed him to a telephone. Canadian folksinger Gordon Lightfoot was on the line. Hovan had asked him to play, but he had had a commitment in eastern Canada.

"Sorry I can't be there tonight," said Lightfoot, "but I'm gonna go five for you."

"Five?" Spong did not understand.

"Five thousand. I'm gonna write you a cheque for $5,000."

Spong shared the news with Linda and Hunter. "Perseverance furthers," the journalist said.

MEET THE COMMANDER

In February of 1974, writer James Wilde arrived in Vancouver to interview Spong about whales for *Time* magazine. Spong and Hunter decided to use the opportunity to announce the whale campaign. Spong wanted to see Skana before he left for Japan, but he was now *persona non grata* at the Vancouver Aquarium. "She started it all," he told Hunter. "In case you wondered, we're working for Skana. We're her ambassadors. She wants out, and she wants her people to be free."

"Don't tell the guy from *Time* that," replied Hunter. He and Spong hatched a plan to hold a press conference at the aquarium. They knew that if Aquarium boss Dr. Newman knew that Spong had requested the venue, he would refuse. But if James Wilde, *Time* magazine reporter, requested a photo session, Newman would have to say yes. "We'll announce the whole campaign there," said Hunter. "We'll tell Wilde ahead of time. The Travelling Whale Show, the Japan mission, Stop Ahab, the whole thing. We'll say we have a plan. We'll lay the Zodiac thing on 'em later."

Wilde asked to witness Spong and the whale together, so Dr. Newman agreed to host the event on the proviso that Spong not say anything about Skana's release. Spong agreed. Hunter would attend in his role as columnist for the *Vancouver Sun*. The aquarium administrators did not know that Hunter and Spong intended to make an announcement about a whale campaign.

"When I introduce you to Skana," Spong told Hunter a few days before the event, "she will test you. She'll test your level of fear. If there's no fear, she'll love you."

But as the day approached, Hunter did feel fear, not of Skana, but of his colleagues. He would soon tell the whole world that he had a plan to save the whales, but he had no real plan at all. "Zodiacs. Fine," he agonized to his friend Lyle Thurston. "We don't even have a boat. Would Cormack do it? His boat is probably too slow. How are we gonna find the whalers anyway? Everyone thinks we're crazy. Who's gonna go out on a boat with Spong and me? Jeez. What am I doing?"

Hunter told me in the tiny Press Club lounge that he was tired of writing his column for the newspaper, but was afraid to give up his livelihood. Like Stowe before him, he wanted to be a full-time activist. He had grown bored with advocating change; he wanted to make it happen himself. But he feared failure. He said he looked up to other men — tough, confident men like Stowe and McTaggart and Metcalfe. "I always wanted to be tough like those guys. What's it going to look like if I try to pull off this whale thing and it's a big flop?"

Following Spong's example, Hunter regularly consulted the *I Ching* and strove to follow the advice of the Taoist masters. "Marshal your armies against yourself. Discipline your own ego. Cast from yourself what is inferior and degrading." The fragments of wisdom provided some direction and courage. "Do not expend your powers before the time is ripe. Seek happiness for yourself and others in only one way, by perseverance in what is right. Success will come from the primal depths of the universe."

On the day of the event at the aquarium, Spong led Hunter onto the whale platform. I watched from the gallery of journalists and photographers. The whales, Skana and Hyak, swam to Spong and fawned over him like two old friends. The scientist nuzzled the whales and played his flute as cameras whirred and clicked. Finally, Spong motioned Hunter closer. Skana let Hunter stroke her massive jaw and she rubbed her head against his. The whale's balance and dexterity in the water astounded the nervous journalist. She opened her powerful jaws, revealing rows of six-inch teeth, and she gently stroked him with her lip behind his ear. Hunter's head was half inside her mouth. The media throng pressed forward. "She'll test your fear." Hunter recalled Spong's warning. He felt Skana's power, yet she seemed so tender and completely alert to his every move. She sank back into the water, and Hunter remained motionless, head bowed, still stunned. "Well," he thought, "that wasn't so bad."

Then Skana rose again and took Hunter's entire head inside her mouth. He was alone with her and completely at her mercy. She caressed his scalp with her teeth, gently, like a mother might when her child isn't feeling well. Fear reverberated through his entire body and he felt himself start to weep, but he endured and breathed. As his body relaxed, the whale released his head and slipped backward into the water.

Hunter felt too shaken to look anyone in the eye. He avoided the stares and gasps of his friends and media colleagues. As the journalists moved outside the aquarium, Hunter left Spong to talk about the whale campaign, and wandered off through the park.

Spong found himself alone in front of the media, all of whom were eager to hear the plan. "I'm going to Japan," he disclosed, "where we will explain the whaling issue to the Japanese people. We believe that the key to ending whaling is to convince the Japanese people to accept the moratorium that the United Nations has recommended. If that doesn't work, we are prepared to blockade the whalers, using small boats launched from a ship."

Meanwhile, Hunter walked alone through a grove of giant red cedars, and sat down to catch his breath. The experience with Skana had rattled him. Fear? Yes, Skana had exposed all his fear, but something else even more profound had taken place. Skana seemed to have looked inside him. She seemed to have seen him as no one had ever seen him before. He could not impress Skana with wit, charms, or plans. She had exposed the emptiness of his ego.

"There's no choice, really," Hunter told us later in the pub. "We have to go through with the plan." It didn't matter that it seemed insane to others. It was more insane to stand by and let humans slaughter these exquisite beings. "We're going. Greenpeace, Greenhawks, Stop Ahab Committee. I don't care what we call it, we're going."

CHAPTER SIX

THE GREAT WHALE CONSPIRACY

"Anyone who proposes to cure the environmental crisis undertakes thereby to change the course of history."

— Barry Commoner

From the open sea, just above 50 degrees north latitude, Quatsino Sound runs 24 miles across Vancouver Island, then splits into three inlets extending east, south, and northwest. Fishermen have ducked into this natural harbour to save their lives for generations. Kwakiutl adventurers came in here to avoid the Haida or the raging Pacific Ocean. Spring tides can run 13 feet or more. On a typical tide, some two billion cubic metres of seawater rush through Quatsino Sound, bringing nutrients and sea life, and then recede, leaving behind salt grass flats, lagoons, and mudflats. A fourth arm, the smaller Forward Inlet, runs north off the main channel and provides safe anchorage. Europeans established a trading depot here, and the site became known as Winter Harbour.

By the spring of 1974, Patrick Moore's father had operated a logging camp here for thirty years. Moore spent his childhood in Winter Harbour. In the eastern extreme of Quatsino, Rupert Inlet, Island Copper Mine had intended to dump tailings containing lime, phosphates, and sodium cyanide, a plan Moore had challenged in his 1972 doctoral dissertation. Now, Moore and his new partner Eileen Chivers built a home on the shoreline of Winter Harbour.

Over the Easter weekend, Bob and Zoe Hunter drove 300 miles from Vancouver to Winter Harbour for a family holiday. Bob and Zoe had struggled in their marriage and hoped the break would give them time with their children Conan, eleven, and Justine, nine, and with each other.

Twelve hours in the car, in ferry line-ups, and on logging roads did not advance their cause. The children grew restless and the parents squabbled. Furthermore, Hunter had a second motive for the trip. To pull off a whale campaign, he would have to gather allies, raise money, find a vessel, and navigate the Pacific Ocean in search of a moving target. Desperate for assistance, he sought the advice of Patrick Moore, who knew about boats and marine biology. Moore and Chivers greeted them and hosted a birthday party for Conan, but Chivers observed the tension and noticed that Zoe fought off despair.

Hunter discovered the whale vertebra from Akutan that Moore had placed on a windowsill, turned it over in his hand, and recalled Cormack's comment about once seeing whales "from horizon to horizon." He took Moore aside and told him, "I need a reality check." They sat on a dock overlooking the harbour.

"Am I completely insane," he asked Moore, "to be taking direction from a mad scientist, who is taking direction from a whale?" Moore shrugged. When Spong had claimed that Skana told him to free her, some, even within the Greenpeace group, cringed. Now, Hunter felt that Skana had communicated with *him* in some realm beyond mere language. There were legions of doubters, but Hunter took comfort in the notion of psychologist R. D. Laing that schizophrenia might be a natural response to an insane world. The person in the family who acts crazy is not necessarily the sick one.

"Is it possible that a research animal would try to communicate with its captors?" he asked.

"Sure."

"Is Skana saying she wants to be released?"

"Probably. Wouldn't you? Look Bob, whales have sophisticated communication, but I don't think anyone knows what they are actually communicating. Are they enlightened beings, as Spong says? Who knows? Big brains don't evolve without a reason." In Stockholm, Moore had garnered a basic understanding of declining whale populations. "There used to be whaling stations all along this coast. I think the last one was here in Quatsino

Sound. It closed ten years ago. From a scientific point of view, with the whales reduced to less than ten percent of their peak populations, species near extinction, yes, it makes sense to stop killing them."

Hunter nodded, and finally Moore assured him, "You're not crazy."

On Easter Sunday, Moore and Chivers took the Hunter family out into Quatsino Sound in a 21-foot plywood workboat. They headed out of Winter Harbour and rounded Hazard Point into Forward Inlet. The day started out overcast and rainy, but sun broke through and they could see grebe and loon in the water where the inlet met the main channel. Moore turned south and made for the Kains Island gap opening into the wild North Pacific Ocean. As they approached the gap, they saw nesting cormorants in the high rock cliffs and surf scooters in the shoals. It was nesting season, and Hunter delivered an impromptu invocation to spring, the Christian resurrection, and the pagan spirit of nature's rebirth. He stood up in the boat, arms spread. "This," he declared "is what we're doing this for."

Zoe sat near the diesel engine in the middle of the boat to guard the excitable children from burning themselves on the exhaust pipes. The workboat beat against the sea swells, and Moore saw whitecaps breaking beyond the rocks. "We can peek around Kains there and see what kind of seas are running," said Moore. As they motored out, tucked in behind Kains Island, a sinewy, dark shape, like a sea serpent, emerged and slid back into the spirited, blue-grey sea.

What was that? Hunter thought, not sure if he'd really seen anything unusual. Eileen Chivers pointed, and the others leaned over the portside gunwale. "Whale," said Chivers. Conan and Justine shrieked. The rippling dorsals of two gray whales rose again. Moore followed the pair of gray whales toward the gap. Hunter leapt to the bow of the boat. Conan and Justine clutched Zoe and stared, wide-eyed. The whales surfaced 30 feet in front of the boat. During his twenty-seven years in Winter Harbour, Moore had never before seen a whale in the sound.

The migration of the Pacific gray whale, from the Siberian Arctic to Mexico, is the longest of any mammal on earth, up to 11,000 miles. They give birth and mate in the shoals of Baja, California, in the winter and begin moving northward in February. The two whales in Quatsino Sound might have been the first of the year's migration, or among the few gray whales who had taken up year-round residence along the west coast of

Vancouver Island. What Moore and the others didn't know at the time was that they were witnessing the Pacific gray's recovery from the edge of extinction. The mothers and their calves in the enclosed tropical shallows had been easy targets for whalers, and the Atlantic gray whale had been wiped out to the last whale a hundred years earlier. The Pacific species had been nearly decimated when Norwegian factory ships invaded the calving grounds in Baja's Magdalena Bay at the turn of the century. In 1925, only 100 gray whales could be found and killed, and by 1929, only two. This is why Moore had never before seen a gray whale in Quatsino Sound. The Mexican government had established a sanctuary for whales in 1972.

The whales made their way through the gap, and Moore trailed behind. Hunter waved him forward, but where the breach opened into the ocean, the breaking sea swells beat back the little plywood boat. They could not follow. Moore stood with Hunter and watched the flukes of the whales disappear below the churning sea. A swell lifted the boat and slammed it down with a thud. The two friends had crossed the Gulf of Alaska together. They knew what the Pacific Ocean could be like, but this vision provided a sobering reminder.

"We're going out there?" Hunter muttered.

They turned back and stopped for a picnic in a cove sheltered from the wind. Eileen talked with Zoe, attempting to lift her sagging spirits. Moore showed the children goose barnacles and sea anemones. Hunter wandered off into the sun-warmed rainforest and sat by a stream. *The whales were a sign*, he thought. As he sat alone, he beheld the wild forest surrounding him. *Miracles are real*, he thought. Miracles aren't hidden from mortals. Look, he said to himself, the miracle of nature unfolds without anyone making it happen. Nature will be on our side if I commit to this. We'll begin the voyage right where we stopped, at the entrance to the Pacific. We'll just bring a boat up here to Winter Harbour and head west, in the direction the whales were moving. Have courage, he told himself. All we have to do is take the first step and trust in the universe to guide us.

On the way back into Winter Harbour, he asked Moore, "Are there whale hunting grounds?" Moore knew about boats and ecology, but he didn't have any idea how to find whalers. "I'm sure there are whale hunting grounds," he surmised. "That can't be too hard to find out."

SAMURAI

In Vancouver, Hunter searched for a ship's crew and volunteers who could raise money and prepare to depart in a year's time. Some Greenpeace members still considered the idea quixotic, but the throng of whale advocates grew, particularly after *Time* magazine published the story about Paul Spong with pictures of him and Skana. Then, in March, Irving Stowe was diagnosed with stomach cancer, and it became apparent why he had been sick and absent from Greenpeace meetings. When he did attend meetings, he spoke on behalf of maintaining the disarmament focus. "He only has so much energy," Dorothy Stowe told friends as Irving retreated from the environmental front lines. Meanwhile, Jim and Marie Bohlen, had left Vancouver to start an organic farm on Denman Island, off the northeast coast of Vancouver Island, where Jim wrote his principles of ecological homesteading in *The New Pioneer's Handbook*.

Month by month, Hamish Bruce, still the president, looked less lawyerly and more like a mystic prophet. At Greenpeace meetings, he leaned against the wall, wrapped in a Mexican serape, tanned, with a beatific grin, long blond hair rolling over his shoulders. "Ecology is like the cosmos," he said when I first met him and we spoke at length. "It's there whether anyone understands it or not."

Although the Easter weekend had inspired Hunter to pursue the whale campaign, it had not helped his troubled marriage. Bob and Zoe Hunter separated a few weeks later. A dramatic increase in divorce had become a malady of the era, fallout from the so-called sexual revolution. Within weeks of returning from Winter Harbour, Hunter invited Bobbi Innes, who had separated from Myron MacDonald, to Buccaneer Bay, where they played darts in the local pub with David McTaggart and Ann-Marie Horne. Hunter told McTaggart about the whale campaign and promised to lobby the Greenpeace group to support the court case in France. Innes pledged to help with fundraising.

Bobbi Innes had been a popular student at Port Moody High School, east of Vancouver, before she attended the University of British Columbia for two years, then spent 1969 in Europe with friends. They visited museums and castles by day and nightclubs at night, from London to Rome. She married medical intern Myron MacDonald. Lyle Thurston, the MacDonalds, and Dave and Caroline Gibbons had represented the young professional wing of Greenpeace for three years, supporting Greenpeace with professional services and emergency cash donations. Innes and MacDonald had separated amicably, and Hunter and MacDonald, rather than become rivals, developed a friendship. The doctor agreed to go along on the whale campaign as medic.

Bobbi Innes helped organize the disjointed Greenpeace group. By day, she worked as a project manager for the local cable company, tracking hundreds of technicians in their workflow. For Greenpeace, she tracked all correspondence, a job once held by Dorothy Stowe, acted as logistical organizer, and helped volunteer Katerina Halm keep the books.

Greenpeace had three international campaigns underway: Spong's Stop Ahab crusade, which Hunter now called "The Great Whale Conspiracy," McTaggart's court case, and a new boat destined for Moruroa out of Melbourne, sponsored by Greenpeace Australia. McTaggart no longer came to Greenpeace meetings, but prepared for his court battle.

Hunter poked around the docks, looking for a boat and a skipper who would go out after the whalers, and a crew that would go to sea with him. In April, he called radical activist Paul Watson. Hunter and Watson met at the East Side, working-class Alcazar Pub. Watson had made a name for himself in Vancouver, leading an assault across the US border in Blaine, Washington, during the Amchitka protests, sailing on the Greenpeace II, and getting arrested at the All Seasons Park demonstrations. He had some experience on boats as a deck boy on a Norwegian freighter. Hunter described to Watson the exploding harpoons that were shot from cannons on the whaling ships and the plan to disrupt the whalers. "We're going to start from Winter Harbour," he said. "What I want to know, Paul, is whether or not you'd be willing to pilot a Zodiac in front of a whaling boat and its exploding harpoons."

"Sure," said Watson.

FOX ON ICE

In March, 1974, Paul and Linda Spong flew to Tokyo with their son, interpreters Maya Koizumi and Michiko Sakata, and their Whale Show — pictures, slides, recordings, and research documents about whales and whaling. In Japan they met with journalists and told stories of their encounters with orcas. To cover expenses, they sold "Let Them Live" T-shirts, "Stop Ahab" bumper stickers, and Greenpeace buttons. The Japan Wildlife Club welcomed the whale troupe and threw a birthday party for six-year-old Yasha. School children cheered the whale pictures and recordings, and scientists showed an interest in Spong's research, but the *Suisan Neizai* fisheries newspaper accused Spong of "brainwashing" the children and being part of "a conspiracy of the United States." The newspaper called the whale campaign a "lunatic and unnatural movement."

Koizumi and Sakata helped Spong reach out to local supporters and Japanese scientists who might be sympathetic. Swiss cetacean brain scientist Giorgio Pilleri had recently published three papers comparing cetacean and primate brains. He and his colleagues had shown that the vast "association" area, or cerebral cortex, of the whale brain is similar in structure to primate and human brains. The patterns of neurons, synapses, and dendritic fields of the whale brain are every bit as complex as in humans. Spong, Lilly, and others were discovering that cetacean communication and social behaviour might also be equally complex. At the Research Institute of the Far Seas in Tokyo, Professor Hiroshi Omura welcomed Spong as a peer and discussed his ideas.

At Taiyo Fisheries, the largest Japanese whaling company, the public relations officer told Spong, "The moratorium is inevitable," but claimed, in the meantime, the whaling company had every right to kill whales. He insisted the IWC Scientific Committee already protected the whale stocks. The data, however, showed otherwise, and Spong's analysis of the declining whale populations won over some scientists. The Whale Show ignited debate throughout Japan, and Spong experienced first-hand the influence he could wield with pictures, stories, and research — as well as the opposition he would face. He knew the Japanese whaling companies would not be convinced by the polemics of science. They would need a dramatic push.

On the flight home, over the North Pacific, he confided to Linda that he did not know how they would ever find the whaling fleets. It occurred to him, however, that the whaling companies must have records of their annual routes. There had to be a way, he thought, to find that information. An *I Ching* reading during the flight warned, "The task is great and full of responsibility. It is nothing less than that of leading the world out of confusion. But it is a task that promises success. Move warily, like an old fox walking over ice."

CANADIAN DIPLOMACY

In May, David McTaggart flew to Paris, entering France as a tourist. At the office of *L'Express*, editor Jean-Jacques Servan-Schreiber's secretary directed him to a friendly law office and provided him with the names of local pacifist and environmental groups. At Les Amis de la Terre, McTaggart met Brice Lalonde, who had met Rod Marining two years earlier and had sailed on the *Arwen* and the *Fri* to Moruroa. Lalonde became McTaggart's companion and translator. They met with young lawyer Thierry Garby-Lacrouts, who reviewed McTaggart's papers and took the case. McTaggart rented a small apartment near Boulevard St. Germain, for $90 per month. Garby-Lacrouts filed a writ claiming $21,000 damages for the ramming and boarding of the *Vega*. His apartment was just two blocks from the house where Dutch statesman Hugo Grotius, author of the Law of the Sea, had lived in the seventeenth century. The case of the *Greenpeace III* would be the first legal test of that law by a private citizen against a national government in 300 years.

A fierce general election raged in France at this time, pitting right-wing Gaullist Valéry Giscard d'Estaing against socialist François Mitterand. Mitterand had been lagging behind in the polls when he seized upon the issue of French nuclear testing, claiming the tests hurt France's reputation, and promising to stop them if elected. When Giscard d'Estaing stood solidly behind the French nuclear arsenal, the issue lifted Mitterand into contention. He lost a close election in May, but like the social reformers in British Columbia, he had discovered the new political prowess of the disarmament and ecology constituency, a discovery that would later boost him into power in France.

In a surprising move, pacifist editor Jean-Jacques Servan-Schreiber supported the Gaullists, and was rewarded by being named Minister of Administrative Reforms for Giscard d'Estaing. Brice Lalonde and other environmentalists attacked the famous journalist for his defection, but Servan-Schreiber told them he would be a stronger voice for disarmament inside the government. Lalonde tested his sincerity by asking him to endorse letters to the new president, the prime minister, and the minister of defence, explaining McTaggart's case. Servan-Schreiber agreed and was unceremoniously fired for supporting a foreigner against the French government.

With Garby-Lacrouts preparing the legal case, McTaggart returned to Vancouver to raise money. He appeared at the Cecil Pub and charmed us with stories of high seas adventure and his litigation in Paris. But McTaggart remained aloof, didn't attend Greenpeace meetings, and lobbied Hunter privately for money. Hunter promised support, and Greenpeace continued to help fund his case, but he needed more. To raise cash, McTaggart made a painful sacrifice: he sold the *Vega*, his beloved ketch.

Hunter claimed in his column, "[Prime Minister] Trudeau has reneged" on his promise to espouse the McTaggart case. He counselled McTaggart on media tactics and convinced him that not all reporters were scoundrels. McTaggart told local journalists, "I'm getting no help from the Canadian government. I received a letter from Prime Minister Trudeau's office. He doesn't have the guts to write to me personally because he knows he lied to me. I was told I would have the help and backing of the Canadian government, that they would 'espouse my case.' They've done absolutely nothing for me. They broke their promise. I want Canada to say to France: 'You were wrong. In international waters you rammed a Canadian ship, boarded a Canadian ship, beat up the citizens of that ship, and detained a Canadian ship. It's wrong. It's illegal, and we object.' I want my government to have some backbone."

The media reports flushed a response from Mitchell Sharp, who replied, "If attempts to get a settlement fail, we'll step in." The Canadian government, however, had no intention of helping McTaggart. The Province of Quebec was selling France enriched uranium, material that could be used for nuclear weapons. However, Canada's collusion ran deeper than a uranium contract. Testimony in the Paris court would later reveal that Admiral Claviere, the man who had given the orders to board *Greenpeace III* and beat McTaggart, had transmitted a confidential letter to General Christian, Officer-in-Charge of the French Air Base in Tahiti, stating: "I want to remind you that I received confirmation from you that the Canadian government would not retaliate by stopping the flights of Air France into Montreal, at which time I ordered the boarding of *Greenpeace III*."

The Canadian government, McTaggart learned, had lent its approval to the boarding that had nearly left him blind in one eye. The promise not to retaliate when France boarded McTaggart's boat on the high seas could only have come from the highest levels of the government. The *Toronto Star* ran the story under the headline, "Ottawa sold out Greenpeace."

LA FLOR

In the summer of 1974, at St. Kilda pier in Melbourne, Australia, writer and children's book illustrator Rolf Heimann stood on the deck of his 30-foot ketch, *La Flor*, provisioned for a voyage to Moruroa. Heimann read from an open letter to the people of France. "In past years," he said, "your navy has harassed vessels navigating in international waters. They have seriously injured crewmen and have beaten them unconscious. This year, we will sail my boat, *La Flor*, into these waters. We are prepared to meet the same fate; we are even prepared to die. Remember: our death will not be suicide. It will be murder." Greenpeace had a new boat and a new skipper ready to take on the French bomb. *La Flor* departed Melbourne, under the banner of *Greenpeace IV*, and crossed the Tasman Sea toward New Zealand.

In New Zealand, Peace Media had changed its name to Greenpeace New Zealand and sponsored the *Fri* on a tour of all the nations still testing nuclear weapons. Former New York journalist Jim Boyack became the ad hoc director with Tahitian independence leader Francis Sanford, Peter Hayes from the Greenpeace London group, and Naomi Petersen, a former cook on the *Fri*. "Greenpeace was such a good name," Petersen later told Michael Szabo, who would write a Greenpeace New Zealand history. "It summed up what we were about." In Vancouver, Greenpeace members toasted the new group, but had no comprehension of the upheavals that would soon result from the proliferation of the name. In the meantime, Hamish Bruce resigned as Greenpeace Foundation president and the disarmament wing installed Lyle Thurston's friend, schoolteacher Neil Hunter (no relation to Bob) as the new president. Greenpeace temporarily halted funding to McTaggart and the Stop Ahab Committee, and focused on the voyage of *La Flor* to Moruroa. The campaign drew support from Australia, New Zealand, the Campaign for Nuclear Disarmament, and Brice Lalonde's Les Amis de la Terre in Paris.

Rolf Heimann sailed *La Flor* into Whangarei, New Zealand, to meet up with the *Fri*. Heimann was born in Dresden in 1940 and had barely escaped incineration when Allied western forces firebombed the city in World War II. As a teenager, he dodged the German military, fled his homeland, and ended up in Australia in 1959. Since first hearing about the peace ships to Moruroa, he had wanted to sign on. In Whangarei, Heimann found his crew in two men from the protest ship *Fri*: Richard Hudson, a sailor from New Zealand, and Rien Achterberg, the Dutch cook and seaman who had sailed to Moruroa with David Moodie the previous summer. On August 12, they headed east for Moruroa.

Hudson, Achterberg, and Heimann made amiable, steady progress toward the test site. They stopped at Rapa and Pitcairn for repairs and collected marine specimens along the way, which Heimann had promised to send back to scientists at the University of Melbourne. The French had detonated six bombs that summer by the time *La Flor* left Pitcairn and a seventh — the megaton explosion — in September when *La Flor* was 300 miles southeast of Moruroa. *La Flor* crossed into the French cordon on October 8, and caught sight of Moruroa the next day, but it was too late. The French tests were over for the year, and although *Greenpeace IV* got a visit from the minesweepers and a helicopter, the French otherwise left them alone. So did the media.

The crew of *La Flor* remained near Moruroa for several days, took plankton samples downwind from the tests, and then headed to Tahiti to post the specimens to the University of Melbourne. The specimens never arrived, and Heimann had good reason to assume French authorities had stolen them. French agents followed the crew everywhere. A scruffy, bearded Frenchman, who gave his name as "Maurice," befriended Heimann and stayed on *La Flor*, but Heimann soon learned that "Maurice" had once been in the French Navy and that other pacifists had suspected him of being an infiltrator. Hudson and Achterberg left the boat in Rarotonga and eventually Heimann made his way solo, east to Fiji and New Caledonia, and finally home to Melbourne.

Heimann's voyage seemed like an anticlimax to some, but he had been as courageous as any protestor before him and had put himself in harm's way for the benefit of all humankind. In fact, the voyage of *La Flor* served a function at a critical time. *Greenpeace IV* had been a nuisance and expense for the French officials; they had sent agents to follow Heimann and tied up naval vessels to track him. More importantly, the voyage of the *Greenpeace IV* distracted the French government from events in Paris, where David McTaggart, Brice Lalonde, and Thierry Garby-Lacrouts plotted the government's downfall in the courts.

After the summer of 1974, France moved its testing program underground to Fangataufa Atoll, 20 miles due south of Moruroa. Giscard d'Estaing vowed to deliver *la force de frappe*, but this stand would spell his defeat.

NEIGHBORHOOD HOUSE

In Vancouver, the disarmament wing of Greenpeace had failed to generate much public interest in the voyage of *La Flor*, and Hamish Bruce reclaimed the leadership of Greenpeace from Neil Hunter. We sent small amounts of money, a few hundred dollars at a time, to McTaggart in France, but the Stop Ahab Committee meetings swelled, and this group became the new core of Greenpeace. By September 1974, Greenpeace meetings had grown too big for private homes, and Bobbi Innes arranged for a meeting room at the Kitsilano Neighbourhood House on West Seventh Avenue.

The group adopted the Great Whale Conspiracy as an official campaign. Scores of new volunteers attended these meetings. Cameraman Ron Precious introduced me to his friends from film school, Michael Chechik and Fred Easton, who intended to document the voyage. Bob Hunter told me he had been sitting in his newspaper office, contemplating a way to get a film crew interested, when Chechik had phoned him and volunteered. "Synchronicity," explained the mystic journalist.

Hunter presided at the Greenpeace meetings and gave everyone an opportunity to speak. If someone raised a new question, like doing tours of the high schools, Hunter put them in charge. A young man inquired about the state of the mailing list. "Okay, Murray," said Hunter, scribbling in his book. "You're the mailing list coordinator." A public radio technician reported on a possible telepathic connection between whales and aliens from the Pleiades star cluster. Hunter listened respectfully. "Okay, Gary, I guess you're intergalactic communications coordinator." Gary attended every meeting, and played tapes of alleged transmissions from the Pleiades, which sounded eerily like whale songs. Will Jones and Elizabeth Dunn headed a crew selection committee for the whale campaign.

Strategy sessions convened in private homes, on Hunter's boat, the *Astral*, docked in False Creek, or at the Cecil Pub. In October, Hunter sat in the pub with Marining and discussed the fact that Spong would not be on the boat, since he would be in London at the International Whaling Commission. "We need someone who can communicate with whales,"

Hunter said. As they discussed this, street musician Mel Gregory appeared with his guitar. Hunter had known Mel from a story he had written about the musician being beaten by police years earlier.

"Do you like animals?" Hunter asked him.

"I talk to them," Mel said. He had three dogs, two cats, and an iguana named Fido. He claimed he could communicate with bees and spiders.

"Do you think you could communicate with a whale?" Hunter asked.

"Oh, sure," Mel said. The best coincidence of all was his name, Melville Gregory. Hunter was now hyper-receptive to miracles and synchronicity. "Melville! As in Herman Melville? Moby Dick! Melville Gregory! Didn't Gregory Peck play Ahab in the movie?"

To most rational observers, Melville Gregory's name would be no more than an amusing coincidence, but Hunter was thoroughly enamoured by Carl Jung's idea of synchronicity. Every situation is comprised of events that evolved together. If one can read the pattern of a moment, it is possible to discover insights that might be lost to rational cause and effect. Primal symbols like the cross or archetypes like the goddess or the warrior can influence states of mind and thus action. Synchronicity, according to Jung, lends power to prayer and to oracles such as the *I Ching*. Such tools of the occult may reveal one's own subconscious and perhaps even a collective unconscious. So the name Melville Gregory might be an amusing coincidence to some, but Hunter saw magic in it.

I met Mel a few weeks later, when Marining, Drummond, Hunter, and I sat in the corner of the pub at round tables crowded with beer glasses. Tough, skinny boys in torn Levi jeans and red plaid logger shirts played pool. Heavy-set, big-armed men with tattoos played darts. The jukebox buzzed with Lou Reed's "Walk On the Wild Side" and Maria Muldaur's "Midnight at the Oasis."

Mel walked up, grinning. He was short, with a round, red face and a full beard. If Vancouver was the Shire, Mel was Bilbo, the perfect Hobbit. Hunter introduced him as the campaign's "animal affinity expert." Mel set his guitar against the wall, emptied a fistful of change onto the table, and took up a glass of beer. He told us he'd written an anthem for the whale voyage. "We're gonna need a sound system," he said, "and underwater speakers and microphones."

"Okay," said Hunter. "Well, you're in charge of musical equipment. See if you can scrounge it up, or talk to Bobbi if you need money."

Bree Drummond pulled out a plastic bag the size of a soccer ball, full of change collected from the donation cans. Later, I gave Mel Gregory, Rod Marining, and Bree Drummond a ride over to Halm's suite in Kitsilano. Mel sang his new Whale Anthem while we sat on the floor and rolled quarters, dimes, and nickels into bank rolls. Ahab may not have trembled yet at the sight of these hippies, but the Great Whale Conspiracy was gaining momentum.

MOBY DOLL'S BRAIN

A week later, Hunter called me at home. He needed a photograph taken.

"Of what?"

"We'll come over. I've got Spong with me," he said.

Glenn and I lived in an upstairs suite in Kitsilano on West First Avenue. We had converted the bedroom into a darkroom and office, and slept in the living room with a view over rooftops to English Bay. At Vancouver's City School, Glenn befriended teenagers on the edge and took in strays. She had recently taken in the three children of a single father who lived in East Vancouver. In a quiet way, she was compassion in action. We had talked about me joining the whale voyage as photographer, and she supported the idea, although it would cost us my newspaper salary.

Hunter and Spong arrived well after 10:00 p.m. Hunter wore sandals and a hand-embroidered gold shirt, and had his long hair in a ponytail. Spong carried a bulging satchel and wore his customary grey toque. He smiled mischievously and cradled a cardboard box in both arms. Glenn set the teakettle on the stove, and Spong set the cardboard box on the kitchen table. He reached both hands into the box, pulled out a human brain, and placed it on a newspaper on the table. The damp, grey organ glistened. I looked at Hunter. "Wait," he said. From out of the box Spong lifted a much larger brain, at least twice the size of the human brain, also grey with a reddish-brown tint in the crevices. The surfaces looked like hardened gel, moist and rubbery.

"This is Moby Doll's brain," Spong said. "I want to have a slide of these for the whale show. People need to see this to understand what I'm talking about." Moby Doll was the whale harpooned by a Vancouver Aquarium crew ten years earlier and kept in a pen for three months before he died. Spong had claimed both brains from the neurological lab at UBC. He said the image of the two brains would help dispel the anthropocentric prejudice of humans. I asked him about the size of the whale brain in relation to body size. He turned the brain on its side and pointed to the stem. A milky liquid dribbled over the paper. "The motor functions of the body are driven by this part of the brain," he said, "the reptilian brain. It's about the same size in a whale, a human, and a dog. A dinosaur didn't need any more than this to function. A crow is probably smarter than a dinosaur. The point is: brain size is not necessarily proportional to body size; it's proportional to mental activity. The significant part of the human brain and the whale brain is here," he said, pointing to the frontal lobe. "This is the cortex and the neocortex, where we process information, form images, create, communicate, learn, and make associations. Not only is the orca cerebral cortex larger than the human, there are more convolutions, so more surface area." Spong ran his finger along one of the deep creases in the whale brain. "More connections, more complexity."

I set up a backdrop and lights. Glenn served tea. "Nothing in nature evolves without a reason," Spong said. "There's no doubt that whales are intelligent, but it seems like a different kind of intelligence. The primates, including humans, have an opposable thumb. We used our brains to manipulate the environment. We created agriculture, tools, and buildings. Nuclear bombs. Whales never developed technologies because they had no thumbs and because they had no reason. They have abundant food in the oceans, fairly constant temperatures, and no serious predators. They didn't face the same sort of environmental stress that the primates faced. Still, their brains were around 700 cubic centimetres thirty million years ago. Humans didn't have brains that size until about a million years ago, with *Homo erectus*. The whale brain had a survival value or it wouldn't have evolved. I suspect they developed these brains through sophisticated communication and social relationships. Whales have families and culture."

I made two small signboards, "HUMAN" and "ORCA," and placed them in front of the brains. I took light readings and began making colour slides.

"The whales have songs, and language," Spong continued. "I don't know what they are doing with their intelligence, but they are organized. It's possible they communicate with whole sonic pictures, like holograms. I have recordings of their vocalizations in the wild. Roger Payne has recorded humpback whales. They create new songs every year and repeat them, note for note, like a whale hit parade."

While I took photographs, Spong sipped his tea and talked. "When Skana flipped on me during the visual acuity tests, I was confused. How could she suddenly get every answer wrong? Even if she was guessing, she would get half of them right. She had to be getting wrong answers on purpose. She was messing with me. A dead herring wasn't enough of a reward. She was telling me, 'I'm bored, this is stupid, let's do something else.' Something like that. She was consciously sending me a message. From that point on, I began to enter into a more personal relationship with her, and, well, she's incredibly smart and sensitive."

Spong had stopped using the term "killer whale," and insisted on using "orca."

"It would make more sense to call humans 'killer apes,' " said Hunter.

I stared through the viewfinder. Spong was right. The image told the story better than any explanation. He believed, as did Hunter, that there is a consciousness in wild nature that is not unique to humans. I now looked at the most obvious evidence, the single most astonishing anatomy lesson of my life. Maybe humans aren't the paragon of animal. Maybe evolution has bigger plans and even greater potential than human culture. What if there is an equal or greater intelligence right here on our earth? I felt as if I had entered a secret lab doing an autopsy of a space invader.

I told Spong I would do the story with the pictures in the *North Shore News*. Hunter slid next to me and said, "Umm, the best timing would be just before the Whale Show in December. We'll announce the details of the voyage."

THE SHAMAN

In October 1974, the Greenpeace group reeled when Irving Stowe died from stomach cancer. Many of the whale crowd had hardly known Irving, but he had become legendary in Vancouver. His columns in *The Georgia Straight* had been an ardent environmental rant for years. Irving had been the hub around which the Don't Make A Wave Committee had formed. He made the phone calls. He recruited. He was both picky and broad-minded.

He liked people who knew how to do something, but he had a generous view of what constituted help. He got academics such as Terry Simmons and the Bohlens into the same room with the radicals such as Marining and Lille d'Easum. He attracted bright, mature couples like Ann and Will Jones, who had remained involved after Will spontaneously lent his naval experience to the *Greenpeace II*. Stowe made room for student extremists like Paul Watson and inspired his own children to lead high school students out in a mass demonstration. Dorothy Stowe, the Metcalfes, the Bohlens, and others had been elders, but Irving had been the leader to whom everyone could look for guidance. He loved music. He embodied Quaker tolerance, and he was pure: He remained a vegetarian and refused to wear leather. His friends, who may have grown impatient with his speeches at times, would now have given anything to hear one more seething tirade from Irving Stowe. His passing gave the group pause and reminded people: This mission is serious.

Volunteers packed into the Kitsilano Neighborhood House every Wednesday night for the weekly Greenpeace meeting. Former president Neil Hunter became regional coordinator and kept in contact with Greenpeace groups in Montreal, Victoria, Paris, London, Auckland, and Melbourne. The affiliations remained informal, generally based on some individual having stepped forward and taken an interest. Greenpeace America was established as an adjunct to Joan McIntyre's Project Jonah in Bolinas, north of San Francisco. Representatives from these regions occasionally passed through Vancouver and reported on the activities of the burgeoning Greenpeace. Peter Hyde, president of the Animal Defense League of Canada, arrived from Ottawa in November and proposed that the Greenpeace Foundation endorse an "Animal Bill of Rights," which included an end to trophy hunting and lab animal abuse.

Animal rights seemed as revolutionary in 1974 as the Bill of Rights might have seemed to King William III and Queen Mary in 1689, but Hyde cited a tradition dating from the Buddha to Aboriginal people of the twentieth century. Greek scholar Pythagoras and the Christian monk St. Francis of Assisi had believed in the sacredness of all living creatures, Hyde reminded us. In the eighteenth century, Rene Descartes postulated that animals were machines, void of understanding and feelings, but Voltaire scoffed at his "poverty of mind." German philosopher Arthur Schopenhauer had said, "The assumption that animals are without rights and the illusion that our treatment of them has no moral significance is a positively outrageous example of Western crudity and barbarity." In the twentieth century, Gandhi, Ruth Harrison, Albert Schweitzer, and countless others had supported the extension of rights to non-human animals. In 1973, Australian Peter Singer wrote in the *New York Review of Books*, "The tyranny of human over nonhuman animals is a struggle as important as any of the moral and social issues that have been fought over in recent years." Norwegian Arne Naess had introduced the idea of "deep ecology" in his journal *Inquiry*, urging environmentalists to address the philosophical and social roots of ecological problems. Patrick Corbett at Sussex University in the UK had recently written, "Let animal slavery join human slavery in the graveyard of the past." Peter Hyde attended two Kitsilano meetings, and we supported his Animal Bill of Rights.

In December, I published the Spong story and brain pictures in the *North Shore News*, and Hunter announced the whale campaign at the Second Annual Greenpeace Christmas Whale Show. But if we were to influence the IWC, Greenpeace had to solve some tangible problems. We needed a boat and we needed, Innes estimated, forty or fifty thousand dollars to pay for a charter and supplies. Innes took over fundraising and stepped up the sale of T-shirts and whale buttons. The Greenpeace Stop Ahab Committee had a Vancouver postal box that collected a few hundred dollars a month in donations. Innes and Katerina Halm watched over every single coin, but it clearly wasn't going to be enough. "We need to do something big," Innes said.

At a meeting in December, fifty volunteers crowded the room, young people sat on the floor, and an older couple sat on the one sofa with Mel Gregory squeezed against the armrest. Next to this couple sat an elderly man, whom I had not seen before. He wore a beaded headband around his long, grey hair. On the lapel of his tweed jacket he had Greenpeace buttons, dolphin buttons, and a small tree pin. He held a beaded eagle feather. When Hunter recognized the stranger's turn to speak, he rose, blessed the circle with his feather, and introduced himself as Henry Payne. He recited lines from a poem he had written: "I am the I of eternal I-am, of every creeping crawling thing, of every winged creature of the air, every finned creature of the sea ..." The assembly grew slightly restless, but after his poem, he announced that he had five acres of land to donate to help pay for a boat.

The meeting fell silent. I looked at Ron Precious, and he shrugged. Hunter, who knew this was coming, stepped in and explained that yes, Henry Payne had offered to give Greenpeace five acres of land to support the whale campaign. The meeting broke up as people crowded around the eccentric Payne. He acknowledged the gratitude with a modest nod, waved everyone away, and performed an impromptu ceremony and more chants.

The next day, Hunter and Innes confirmed with lawyer Davie Gibbons that Payne owned the land, five acres, in Langley, east of Vancouver. Word spread through Kitsilano, and Payne became a regular at the meetings. My wife Glenn agreed to let him stay with us when he was in town.

ECOLOGY'S SKIPPER

Hunter had scoured the Vancouver docks looking for a boat to charter. He wanted to find a vessel that could keep pace with the harpoon ships, reportedly 18–20 knots. Most boat owners and fishermen scoffed at the idea of heading into the Pacific to look for whalers. "You'll never find them," mariners told Hunter. "If you did find them, they'd just run away from you. Forget it."

Meanwhile, John Cormack heard through his friends at the BC Packers fish plant that Hunter was looking for another charter. Word around the docks indicated the salmon runs would be down in the spring. Cormack called Hunter. Most fishermen had little time for the Greenpeace crowd, but Cormack had endured six weeks in the Gulf of Alaska with Hunter, trusted him, and was willing to take a chance. The *Phyllis Cormack* was available.

In January 1975, as snow fell in Kitsilano, Hunter and Innes picked me up in their van for a drive to the Fraser River to visit Cormack and take photographs for the newspapers. Immense flakes fell as we drove over the north arm of the river and across the delta flats toward Finn Slough and Steveston. Innes revealed a plan she had hatched to transform the five acres of land, worth about $20,000, into "three times that much." Instead of selling the land, Innes had decided to hold a raffle, with the land as a prize. "We'll print 30,000 lottery tickets," she said as she rubbed her hands over the heater in the Volkswagen van and looked out at the snow.

"We'll sell 'em for $2 each. Sixty thousand."

Hunter, at the wheel, said he had hesitated to take Cormack up on his offer because of the fish boat's limited speed of 10 knots. "But," he said, "out of respect, I took Bobbi to Cormack's house for dinner." Bobbi chuckled as Hunter told me the story: When he introduced Innes to John and Phyllis Cormack, the skipper's wife recognized Bobbi's last name. "You're not related to Laura Innes, are you?" she asked. Bobbi's father, Bill Innes, had been born to Laura and Bob Innes, who had divorced. Laura, Bobbi's grandmother, had then married John Cormack. They divorced, and Cormack married his current wife, Phyllis. Hunter listened to this with amusement. The sea captain is Bobbi Innes' father's stepfather? His own father had died just before the Amchitka voyage, and the old skipper, who had no children of his own, had tacitly adopted Hunter. "I felt like I was sleeping with my sister," Hunter said as we pulled off Dyke Road by the Fraser River and stopped.

We walked down the frozen dock, and I caught my first glimpse of the sea captain. Cormack, an ex-wrestler, was a massive man. He had an enormous neck and arms and a powerful grip, even with two fingers missing. We followed him around the *Phyllis Cormack* and he showed off the refurbished engine room and new Caterpillar diesel engine. The old fish boat's 10-knot speed no longer concerned Hunter. The phone call from John, and the family coincidence, had reinforced his belief that if the group committed to this mission, the right people would come forward, and forces greater than ourselves would guide us. Cormack needed the charter. We needed a boat. Hunter and the skipper shook hands. The Lord of the Piston Rings would be our captain.

Generous flakes of snow drifted down like little parachutes as we stood on the deck of the *Phyllis Cormack*. "Where do think we'll find the whalers, John?" Hunter asked.

"Oh yeah, well, they'd probably be on the seamounts."

"Seamounts?"

"Yeah, where the whales would come to feed, I s'pose," said the old skipper, relying on a fisherman's logic and nothing more.

"Where are the seamounts?"

"Oh, well, they're all over. There's the Cobb seamount just south a'here, and Dellwood Knolls up north. They're all over."

"Oh," said Hunter, "okay. Would it make sense to go up to Winter Harbour and head out from there?"

"Oh, yeah. Don't make no difference."

THE BRAHMAN

In January 1975, the Kitsilano Neighbourhood House burned down. For those who followed the signs, this seemed decidedly inauspicious — and gave pause. "You know what it means, Mel?" asked Innes.

"No," said the musician.

"It means we need a new meeting place." Innes arranged to rent two rooms from SPEC, and Greenpeace established its first public office at 2007 West Fourth Avenue in the heart of Kitsilano.

The underground days ended suddenly. The public could now walk in off the street and find Greenpeace. We soon had a dedicated phone line and a message machine. A wooden table served as central depot and meeting place. Gary Gallon, the SPEC president, gave us a section of tiny plywood cubicles we used as workstations. We now had overhead but we had a clubhouse and, as loose as it was, a plan. The boat would leave in April from Winter Harbour and we'd search the seamounts for whalers. "All we need now are a couple of miracles and $40,000," Hunter said cheerfully.

When the Cecil Pub converted into a strip bar, Hunter took that as another dubious sign, but within weeks, a neighbourhood pub, Bimini's, opened right across the street from the new Greenpeace office, and the balance of nature seemed restored. The second-floor Greenpeace office looked out over the street and directly into the window seats at the pub. This arrangement proved useful, as Bobbi screamed phone messages from an open window across Fourth Avenue and various volunteers bolted in and out of both establishments on missions of import.

I did not ever make the conscious decision to go on the boat; it just seemed obvious that I would. I had already told my publisher, Peter Speck, that I would be away from April to July. He gave me a generous leave and promised to run stories and photographs from the voyage. I often left the newspaper by late afternoon, arrived at the Greenpeace office on Fourth Avenue or the "main office" across the street by 4:00 p.m., and remained until late at night.

Upstairs at the pub window, Rod Marining told me about his recurring dreams. He would dream of herds of stampeding buffalo or flocks of birds turning together as if directed by an invisible hand. One day, watching a marine science show on television, he saw a school of fish do the same thing. "I wondered," he said, "What's this all about?" He got his answer from a young Hindu Sadhu from India, Kannon, who had moved in next door in North Vancouver. "Kannon says that's natural telepathy," Marining told me. "Animals do it all the time. Humans can do it too, but most humans have lost the sensitivity. But in these dreams I keep seeing herds of animals all turning together and I think humans can do the same thing. We can turn away from the cliff."

Marining, already considered by some to be capricious, added telepathy to his psychic arsenal for changing the world. Under Kannon's tutelage, Marining developed his powers. He sat silently in meetings, attempting to beam his thoughts and images into everyone else's head. He confided — to those who would not think him completely psychotic — that we could save the whales by radiating the image of whales to the world. Many wanted to believe it, and some did.

In this milieu, Kannon found a place for his own brand of spiritual delirium. He claimed to be a Brahman, a holy man, and he convinced Marining that it was no accident that he had moved next door. Indeed, according to Kannon, he had followed his own inner voice to North America, and now knew why. His mission was to lead Greenpeace in its quest to save all sentient beings. Kannon wore an ascetic's linen robes, walked barefoot, and chanted Hindu mantras. He played the flute in a roughly pentatonic, minimalist style. When he couldn't pay his rent, he moved in with Marining and Drummond. He didn't eat meals but rather snacked occasionally on vegetables. He was so thin, he looked like he might pass out, yet he possessed surprising energy. Almost everything amused him. He chuckled and played practical jokes. He would wear other people's sandals, and you couldn't tell if he was stealing them, if he was just absent-minded, or if he intended a lesson about letting go of material possessions.

One afternoon on Marining's back porch I laughed during the wrong part of a story and Kannon soured quickly. I apologized, and he graciously patted me on the arm. He never came to Greenpeace meetings, but he hung on the fringes. The hard-core mystics, as they were known — Marining,

Kannon, and Hamish — organized a telepathic "call in" for whales at the beach. Kannon led them knee-deep into the bay, where they sent out telekinetic messages. Marining told the whales, "We'll speak for you. We'll help you." They called the whales into the harbour. No whales showed, but on the beach at sunset, the true believers danced to Mel Gregory's "Whale Anthem":

> Fifty tons of blubber, spouting rainbows to the sun
> We just love to go on cruising, making love, and having fun …

Henry Payne gained stature with the success of the lottery. The cash flow had leapt from a few hundred dollars per month to several thousand dollars per month. Payne attended every meeting or gathering, blessed everyone with his eagle feather, and chanted. He announced that he was a shaman and would be our spiritual guide. That was fine, but now we had two spiritual guides, Kannon and Payne. Hunter decided that the two gurus, known as the "Shaman and the Brahman," should meet, so he and Marining coaxed Kannon into a car and drove the 30 miles east to Langley, where Payne lived in a small cabin in the woods. Payne welcomed his visitors with ceremony and poetry, but Kannon acted aloof. He wandered from the cabin, through the snow, in his bare feet, chanting his own mantras. Payne complained to Hunter about the Brahman's insolence. Hunter enticed Kannon back to Payne's cabin for a talk. Payne tried to engage the Indian mystic in the subtleties of the shamanic arts, but Kannon tested the older Payne mercilessly with flippant jokes and antics. Payne responded with shouts of anger.

"Show respect! Don't point your finger at me!" he bellowed.

Kannon rose to his feet. "You're no shaman!" he said. "You're just a poet." With that, the meeting of the spiritual advisors was over. Kannon stomped from the cabin and made his way through the snow, toward the car. Marining attended to Kannon and Hunter apologized to Payne. On the drive back to Vancouver, Hunter scoffed to Marining, loud enough for Kannon to hear, "So much for higher beings." Kannon ignored him, staring out the window, humming softly to himself.

Thereafter, Payne grew more demanding. He insisted on leading long ceremonies at each meeting, and he complained to Glenn and me that no one in Greenpeace appreciated what he was doing for the cause. Glenn assured Payne that everyone appreciated him. She fed him, let him sleep on our floor, and we drove out to his cabin to pay our respects. Nevertheless, Payne's mood had soured.

NO FRATERNIZIN'

The editors of *Audubon* magazine dedicated the January 1975 issue to whales, with an article about the "Vanishing Giants." At the same time, Farley Mowat's book *A Whale for the Killing* reached bestseller status in Canada; Jacques Cousteau's *The Whale: Mighty Monarch of the Sea* was translated into English; William Schevill had edited *The Whale Problem: A Status Report*; and George Small wrote *The Blue Whale*. Joan McIntyre's *Mind in the Waters* appeared, including Paul Spong's reflections on living among wild orcas. Tamar Griggs published a collection of children's paintings and poems about whales, *There's a Sound in the Sea*. Schoolchildren flocked to whale shows around Vancouver. Even the AFL-CIO supported the whaling moratorium, urging Japan, "Abide by world opinion."

During the previous summer, 32,000 whales had been killed by IWC nations, most of those by Japan and the Soviet Union. The pirate whalers, operating outside IWC scrutiny, took thousands more. With the large baleen whales decimated, whalers sought the sperm whales, primarily for oil. The valuable spermaceti is a waxy oil that fills most of a whale's head. At the turn of the twentieth century, sperm-whale oil, which is odourless and burns cleanly, was a popular lamp fuel. The fine, pure oil still served to make candles, polish, detergents, dyes, and cosmetics. Sperm-whale oil maintains its viscosity over a wide range of temperatures, making it ideal to lubricate aircraft engines and ballistic missiles. For the trivial uses, like soap and cosmetics, there were substitutes, but it was believed that there were no good substitutes for sperm oil to lubricate missiles. However, American botanists had recently discovered that jojoba oil — from a shrub growing wild in the Sonora Desert of Mexico — had all the qualities of sperm-whale oil and represented the perfect replacement.

Georgia Straight writer David Garrick, alias Walrus Oakenbough, had researched the jojoba story and brought Greenpeace the information. Walrus was a keen naturalist and horticulturist and knew where to find psilocybin mushrooms in and around Vancouver. He signed onto the crew as news correspondent and cook.

Shy, eccentric electrician Al Hewitt owned an electronics shop on Fourth Avenue, near the Greenpeace office, a jumble of wires, gauges, boxes of resisters, capacitors, and projects in progress. In his shop, Hewitt built a Radio Directional Finder that might allow us to pick up Japanese or Soviet signals and locate their ships. He built underwater speakers and microphones for Mel. In the end, he signed on as the ship's engineer.

The campaign would need to translate radio transmissions and converse with the whalers if we did meet them. Myron Macdonald introduced us to thirty-three-year-old Czechoslovakian George Korotva, who learned Russian in a Soviet prison camp. In Prague, in 1962, Korotva told us, he had been dragged from his bed in the middle of the night by two KGB agents. They produced a picture of him at an anti-Soviet demonstration and hauled him off to a coal mine in some dark corner of the Gulag. He escaped, fled over frozen lakes into Finland, worked with the Czechoslovakian underground in Europe, and made his way to Canada, where he now worked as a deckhand in Tofino, on the west coast of Vancouver Island. He was strong, helpful, and good-humoured. He could pilot a Zodiac and was thrilled about the prospect of confronting Soviet whalers. "Dem foking Russians," he snarled. Korotva signed on.

Taeko Miwa, a student and environmentalist from Japan, agreed to be the Japanese translator. Her deceptively serene nature veiled a bright mind. She told us about mercury poisoning in Minamata Bay in Japan that had devastated a fishing community. In Tokyo, she had fought against air pollution and had protested the construction of a new airport that devastated a neighbourhood. Taeko joined the crew and helped Walrus provision the boat.

Carlie Trueman, a diver from Victoria, loaned the campaign a Zodiac and agreed to come aboard to maintain the inflatables. She was a no-nonsense, dynamic young woman with freckles and pigtails. She knew more about operating the inflatable boats than anyone in our crew. In March, a month before we were scheduled to depart, Trueman convened the crew at English Bay for Zodiac practice. Korotva and Watson sped around attempting to out-perform each other. Ron Precious and I took rides to see what it would be like to photograph from the speeding Zodiacs. Even with a small ripple in the bay, we were bounced around unmercifully.

"This isn't going to be easy," Precious whispered to me.

Dr. Myron MacDonald had agreed to be medic on board during May, and Leigh Wilkes, a nurse and secretary at the Greenpeace meetings, would take over in June. Hamish Bruce and Paul Watson would be on board, and Pat Moore would join the boat in Winter Harbour. I was going along as photographer and correspondent. Singer Ann Mortifee and jazz musicians Paul Horn and Paul Winter agreed to come aboard at times to make music for the whales. The crew broke down into what Hunter had called on the Amchitka voyage the "mystics and the mechanics." Al Hewitt, George Korotva, Carlie Trueman, and the captain were the mechanics. The rest of us, although some attempted to live in both camps, were the mystics. Cormack relaxed his rule prohibiting single women on the boat, although he told Hunter, "There won't be no fraternizin' on board." Hunter agreed, and the crew was in place.

ESPIONAGE

Hunter told Paul Spong about Cormack's guess that whales could be found at the seamounts, where the ocean bottom rises near the surface. Spong said he suspected the whaling companies would have records of their routes, and perhaps the IWC Scientific Committee would have the data. It might be possible, Spong thought, to convince Canadian fisheries agents to help him obtain the information.

In January 1975, Paul, Linda, and Yasha Spong crossed Canada on their way to London for the IWC meetings in June, staging Whale Shows along the way. The real goal of their tour was to find someone who would help locate the whaling fleet records for the previous summer. Neither Hunter nor Spong told anyone else in Greenpeace about the planned espionage, for fear of leaks. The campaign hinged on finding the whalers and confronting them before, or during, the meetings in London.

The Spongs arrived in Canada's capital city, Ottawa, in February 1975. Canadian delegates to the IWC refused to meet with Spong, and bureaucrats in the Department of Fisheries and Oceans could offer no help, so Spong called the embassies of other IWC nations. The Honorary Consul General of Iceland invited the Spongs into her home. On one wall, Spong noticed a painting of a water scene he recognized from near his orca lab on Hanson Island, and the painting provided a natural segue. He told the elderly stateswoman about his research with wild orcas, and he mentioned casually that he was looking for whaling fleet records, so he could observe sperm whales in their natural habitat. "Well," the woman told him, "you might find what you're looking for at the Marine Institute in Reykjavík." She gave Spong a letter of reference for scientists in Iceland.

The Spongs took the Whale Show across Canada to St. John's, Newfoundland, and flew via New York to Iceland. An impromptu Whale Show in Reykjavík yielded over fifty volunteers, who started a local Greenpeace group. Spong found no whaling ship records at the Marine Institute, but a scientist gave him the name of Dr. A. Jonsgard, the leading whale scientist in Norway, who had documented the few remaining blue whales in 1955. Two days later, the Spong family arrived in Oslo, where Dr. Jonsgard met them and invited Spong to lecture at the University of Oslo on orca behaviour. At the lecture, in the spirit of rigorous academic review, Jonsgard challenged some of Spong's conclusions, punctuating his points with a Narwhal tusk that he wielded like a sword. Jonsgard did not have the sperm whale data but suggested Spong might find the information at the Bureau of International Whaling Statistics in Sandefjord Harbour, 60 miles south of Oslo. He phoned bureau director Mr. E. Vangstein and arranged a meeting.

Sandefjord was one of the world's oldest whaling ports. Modern commercial whaling began there in 1870 with the invention of the exploding harpoon. At that time, whalers with small, open boats and hand harpoons had already devastated the right whales. The exploding harpoons, shot from cannons on swifter boats, allowed whalers to pursue the faster, deep-sea whales — the blue, fin, and humpback. In 1883 sixteen whaling companies in Norway enjoyed a profitable business. By 1904, they had devastated the whale populations along the coast of Norway, and the government banned whaling in Norwegian waters. The whaling ships moved south after blue whales, the largest animals ever to live on earth, four times the size of the largest dinosaurs. In 1931, over 30,000 blue whales were killed. By 1956, the blue whale was near extinction. The jaws of a blue whale formed an archway leading into Vangstein's office overlooking the harbour.

The administrator reported each year to the IWC Scientific Committee on the previous year's catch, with data supplied by the whaling ships.

The elder Norwegian gentleman took great pleasure in showing young Yasha whalebones and old photographs of whaling boats. Spong explained his orca research and asked if the bureau had records to indicate where sperm whales could be found. Vangstein said he couldn't release the whaling ship logs to Spong without permission from the IWC. Spong replied that he wanted to observe sperm whales in the wild and that he only had a few days in Norway. "We've travelled so far," he pleaded. The kind-hearted Vangstein took pity on the young scientist and his charming family. Maybe, he said, it wouldn't do any harm, and he led Spong to a back room filled with file cabinets. While Vangstein entertained Yasha and Linda, Paul Spong searched files. He felt his heart race when he saw the name *Kyukuyo Maru*, a Japanese factory ship, on a file tab. Behind it, he could see *Nisshin Maru*, and the Soviet factory ships *Dalnyi Vostok* and *Vladivostok*. He pulled the files and copied the ships' logs into his own notebook, filling thirteen pages.

From their hotel room in Oslo, celebrating with a bottle of champagne, Spong phoned Hunter and told him he had whaling fleet coordinates for the previous year. If they followed a similar timetable, Spong revealed, the Japanese ships would be in the North Pacific, west of Hawaii, over the Suiko and Yuryaku seamounts, probably beyond the fuel range of the *Phyllis Cormack*. But, said Spong, the Soviet ships, the *Dalnyi Vostok* and *Vladivostok*, would likely be over Mendocino Ridge, a rise extending 600 miles out to sea from the coast of California.

"Paul," Hunter gasped, "this is fantastic." The campaign now had a real target at which to aim: Mendocino Ridge, late June. His belief in miracles was working. The little spy from the Shire had penetrated the lair of the whalers, and Cormack had been right, not surprisingly, about seamounts. "Go to London," Hunter said to Spong. "Leak it out slowly, to the right people, that we're going to confront the whalers. Stay in touch with the boat through Bobbi and Rod in Vancouver. I promise you a six-column, front-page headline in the *London Times* during the IWC meeting."

JERICHO

The Great Whale Conspiracy now faced a new problem. The best chance we had of finding the whalers would be in late June, but the departure date had been set for April 27, and it was too late to postpone it. Cormack had prepared the boat and cancelled his fishing crew, provisions were ready, our crew had made plans, people were flying in from San Francisco, and a film crew had been assembled. Hunter had learned from his mentor Ben Metcalfe how to build a news story. Perhaps, he thought, we could turn the delay to our advantage, use a month at sea to train the crew, and generate news about whales. By the time we found the Soviet whalers, the story that we were hunting for them would be established. "Many in the media doubt us already," Hunter told Spong later, by phone to London, "but that's okay, maybe good. We'll build it up toward June. It's perfect."

Hunter revealed to Cormack and Innes the target date on Mendocino Ridge, but dared not tell anyone else. The public story — that we were looking for the whalers — would not be as interesting if we already knew where to find them. Furthermore, Hunter was afraid the collective energy of the crew could collapse if everyone thought we were killing time.

Retired Vancouver law professor Jacques Longini, who had bought the *Vega* from McTaggart, hung around Greenpeace meetings, and offered to take the *Vega* on the whale campaign. The *Phyllis Cormack* would be rechristened *Greenpeace V*, and the *Vega* would be *Greenpeace VI*. Innes made a payment to Cormack for the charter and we purchased a new Zodiac with the money coming in from the lottery.

That spring, Tibetan Buddhist teacher Chogyam Trungpa and author Theodore Roszak came to Vancouver for a discussion on East/West Integration. Hunter and I both attended. Having witnessed the clash of the gurus in our own circle, we remained guarded. Roszak talked about an "emerging culture … based on spirituality and nature," which he called "organicism." Trungpa talked about "spiritual materialism," or spiritual pride, the tendency to use spirituality as a means of bolstering the ego and escaping reality. Real spirituality, he said, does not ignore society, family, or one's relationship to the earth, a refreshing message. Hunter bought Trungpa's book, *Cutting Through Spiritual Materialism*; it would become a popular volume during the whale voyage.

Vancouver promoter Alan Clapp offered to produce the send-off event. Clapp had his own motives: Vancouver had been selected as the site for the United Nations Conference on the Human Habitat during the following summer. Clapp wanted to build an authentic rural village in the heart of Vancouver and stage an alternative "people's" conference he would call

Habitat Forum. The preferred location was an abandoned World War II naval base that included four wooden aircraft hangars, sitting idle behind a chain-link fence on Jericho Beach, west of Kitsilano. The Greenpeace send-off was his way of getting his foot in the door with Vancouver City Council. The plan worked, and the council gave Clapp permission to stage the launch at Jericho.

Departing from Jericho, the mystics in Greenpeace believed, confirmed the sacredness of The Great Whale Conspiracy. The historical Jericho was one of the oldest cities on the planet, one where humanity had made the transition from a migrant gathering culture to an agrarian one. Jericho represented one of humankind's earliest experiments in manipulating the environment and building defensive walls. Vancouver's Jericho Beach provided Greenpeace with another strong mythic image. We envisioned the walls of human myopia tumbling down. Furthermore, the Coast Salish — including the Sun'ahk village, whose Chief Khahtsahlano had inspired the neighbourhood's name — had used the site for potlatch gatherings. So Jericho Beach, a sacred Aboriginal meeting place, seemed a perfect site for the Rainbow Warriors to launch a campaign for the protection of all sentient beings. Alan Clapp's crew of artisans set out to transform the military wasteland into a festival of ecology.

Hunter decided that the Great Whale Conspiracy press conference, announcing the launch date, should be held at the Jericho site. To enter the hangars past the military sentries with German shepherd guard dogs, we used a password, "Greenpeace." Inside the aircraft hangars, caverns with broken windows and caked in dirt and salt air, we swept glass and dust from the floor and set up a table and rows of chairs. Reporters arrived, looking slightly spooked.

Hunter announced that the *Phyllis Cormack* and the *Vega* would depart from Jericho on April 27. We would find whales and conduct "interspecies communication experiments." Legendary whale scientist Dr. John Lilly and author Farley Mowat would join the crew for part of the voyage. We had inflatables with outboard engines. We would find the factory ships and the harpoon boats, and would disrupt the whale hunt. "The campaign will cost $40,000," Hunter emphasized. "The public can help by purchasing a lottery ticket for the five acres of land."

He said nothing about the whalers' secret coordinates or Mendocino Ridge.

IMPRISONED LEADER

By mid-April, with two boats to provision, the Greenpeace office on Fourth Avenue filled with equipment and supplies: outboard motors, boxes of food, Al Hewitt's Radio Directional Finders, a complete sound system, and underwater speakers and microphones for the whale communication experiments. Diving equipment accumulated in one corner, Mel's guitar rested in another. Scraps of paper bearing notes filled the message board. Cardboard boxes bore labels: "Boat," "Leigh," "Bobbi," "Bob," and "Lost and Found."

Strategy sessions continued in Bimini's Pub across the street. Gary, the intergalactic communications coordinator, pointed out that Bimini Island in the Bahamas was known for its friendly dolphins, near the spot that Edgar Cayce had named as the site of Atlantis. As a sign, it was a stretch, but no one cared. There were so many auspicious signs that Hunter insisted on at least "three miracles in a row" before he would entertain any change of course.

On the dock at Jericho, Mel's friend, artist Kurt Musgrove, painted the Kwakiutl orca design, "Skana," onto the sail, and incorporated the peace and ecology symbols and the name, GREENPEACE.

On Friday, April 25, two days before the launch, Mel and Canadian actor Don Franks organized a farewell serenade for Skana at the Vancouver Aquarium. The boat crew and friends attended. Franks had lived with Cree Indians in Alberta, where he had been given the name Iron Buffalo. He hung a Cree blanket over the railing by the whale pool and played flute while Mel improvised on his amplified guitar. Skana circled the pool, surfaced in front of the musicians, and listened. She dove, resurfaced, and vocalized. If nothing else, the show bolstered the commitment of the crew, exhausted from weeks of frantic work.

I had been to the aquarium before with Spong, but on this day I sensed the full tragedy of Skana's captivity. Her dorsal fin had flopped over after years of swimming around in circles in the tiny pool. Spong had been correct: for a whale, the aquarium was a prison. Wild orcas are almost always in tight family groups, on the move, and vocalizing among themselves. Putting a highly intelligent, social, and auditory animal in a small pool like this amounted to torture, no different than solitary confinement in a human prison. Skana had spent eight years here, and Spong felt that she had communicated to him, unambiguously, that she wanted out. As I left, I looked back to see her making lazy, gloomy circles in the pool. Maybe the idea that Skana was our leader wasn't so far-fetched. Why should we not hear the earth's call from one of its most magnificent creatures?

Outside the aquarium, Hunter, Katerina Halm, and Carlie Trueman sat on the sidewalk. Katerina held the Greenpeace cheque book open in front of her. Hunter had a fistful of invoices for supplies and equipment. Halm wrote cheques, then held up her hand. "That's it," she said. Hunter handed her the remaining invoices. "You and Bobbi can figure it out," he said, and Katerina stuffed the invoices into her bag with the cheque book.

Although the Great Whale Conspiracy was broke, Paul and Linda Spong were positioned in London to confront the whaling nations of the world, and now two Greenpeace boats prepared to sail out into the Pacific to find the whaling fleets. It did seem, at least for a moment, like a miracle.

I picked up film, batteries, a journal, duffle bag, and a wet suit. I found a watertight ammunition container at the Army Surplus shop, for storing film and lenses in the Zodiacs. I bought a large piece of foam that would fit into a trunk and cut holes for my camera gear. I packed a Leica, two 35-mm Pentax cameras, and a large-format 6" X 7" Pentax. Glenn and I drove downtown that night to the Commodore Ballroom, the most popular dance hall in Vancouver, where singer Ann Mortifee and the rock band Cement City Cowboys played a benefit concert for the whale voyage. Mel sang the "Whale Anthem," and Henry Payne brandished his eagle feather and praised the crew.

GALE WARNINGS

On Saturday, the day before our departure, Cormack moved the *Phyllis Cormack* around from the Fraser River to Vancouver's inner harbour. Crew and volunteers raced between the office and Centennial Pier, delivering provisions.

Watson, Innes, and a team of volunteers had given the hull a coat of white paint, and the boat glistened in the sun. The sail had been fixed to the mast and boom. Walrus and Taeko stowed food. Volunteers lifted sacks of cornmeal, flour, beans, onions, and potatoes down the ladder and onto the deck of the boat. Al Hewitt roamed about with pieces of gear in his hands. Henry Payne watched over the proceedings. Hunter, Cormack, and Korotva raised the yellow and green GREENPEACE signboard in place and nailed it to the flying bridge.

Paul Watson brought a five-gallon glass jar of formaldehyde on board to preserve specimens of tissue from harpooned whales, for later analysis. A volunteer kicked over and broke the jar in the bunkroom, soaking the floor and sending caustic vapours throughout the boat. Gasping volunteers clambered on deck and the enraged captain scolded Watson. A retching, weeping stowaway stumbled from inside the aluminum mantle around the smokestack. Nurse Leigh Wilkes helped flush his eyes and throat with water. Hunter volunteered to help Watson clean up the mess. They wore diving masks and breathed through wet towels, but could spend no more than a few minutes in the bunkroom. Hunter bolted from the cabin and gagged over the side. Equipment and stores accumulated on the pier as preparations for departure were suspended. Cormack went about his work scowling. "Good thing it broke now," observed Dr. Myron MacDonald, making the best of it, "and not in the middle of the night at sea." He mentioned that formaldehyde fumes could be fatal.

At Jericho Beach, Clapp's army of artists and carpenters completed the festival site, built booths for environmental groups, hung banners and tapestries, strung flags, and built a stage in a clearing among the trees. As the crews worked, a wind blew up across English Bay and clouds rolled in over Vancouver Island. That afternoon, the marine weather station issued gale warnings for the Strait of Georgia.

Glenn invited Henry Payne and Leigh Wilkes for dinner and prepared an Indonesian feast. The gale howled to 45 knots, winds whipped around Burrard Inlet, and large branches snapped loose from trees. The four of us ate dinner as twigs rapped against the roof and windows. After dinner, Payne gave a final blessing for the voyage. "Don't be afraid," he said. "You are the body of spirit-breath. You are a child of God." He launched into his long poem that he'd been reciting for four months, "I am the I of the eternal I-am, of every winged creature ..."

After midnight, Glenn and I fell asleep with the wind shrieking, windows rattling, and the light of the full moon on the windowsill.

Across town, at the False Creek dock, Hunter huddled against the wind at a pay phone near his boat. He called Captain Cormack to ask if the gale would stop us from departing.

"We can go no matter what she blows," the captain said, "but we're not pokin' outside in this. Don't matter what yer Ching Ching says. Not with this bunch of farmers. We'll go all right, so them TV guys can get their pictures, but we'll tuck into Gossip Cove."

Hunter hung up and packed. He looked at the record of whaling fleet routes that Paul Spong had sent to him from Norway. He read down the columns of longitudes, latitudes, and dates, and then he stuffed the paper into an envelope and shoved it to the bottom of his duffle bag.

The gale rocked the *Astral* in the harbour as he fell asleep.

HOIST ANCHOR

The next morning, toppled power poles lay across roads, sailboats sat battered at Jericho marina, and the roof of a nearby boating shed had been ripped off by the storm. Between my home and the beach at Jericho, Glenn and I dodged tree branches and debris. The gale had blown out, but a strong, 20-knot breeze gusted in from the water. Bands played and 25,000 people gathered at the Jericho send-off party. I met up with Ron Precious and the film crew as they stood along the railing of the pier filming the *Phyllis Cormack* and *Vega* in English Bay.

From the beach, as the scheduled departure time neared, Korotva, Dr. Myron MacDonald, Paul Watson, Taeko Miwa, Mel Gregory, and California musician Will Jackson rowed Cormack's dory out to the Greenpeace boat. I stayed back to help Hunter round up the stragglers, but the dory failed to return as arranged. He had promised his friends at the newspapers that the boat would leave by 4:00 p.m. On the shoreline, he clicked the speaker of a walkie-talkie, but was unable to reach the boat. "Shit," he howled. Hamish arrived under the pier and walked into the surf up to his ankles, held his arms out and lifted his eyes to the sky. "We need a boat," fumed Hunter to no one in particular, and a few moments later, a steel-hulled World War II landing craft appeared around the corner of the pier and nosed toward the beach. "I figured you'd need some help," said the cheerful skipper, who introduced himself as Dennis Feroce. Walrus climbed in, tied the Greenpeace flag to an oar, and held it aloft. Hamish, Hunter, and I climbed in. Photographer Matt Herron, who had arrived from California to join the *Vega*, leapt aboard. Feroce dropped Herron at the sailboat and delivered the rest of us to the *Phyllis Cormack.* We climbed up onto the deck at 4:00 p.m.

The flags on the mast of the *Phyllis Cormack* snapped like whips in the breeze. Captain John Cormack stood on the flying bridge and surveyed his unconventional deckhands with a fatherly tolerance.

"Sir?" said Bob Hunter, looking up from the deck.

"Yeah, we're ready," Cormack yelled down. Hunter gripped the gunwale with one hand and clutched his notebook to his chest with the other. His reedy thirty-four-year-old frame stretched as he held his notebook aloft in a clinched-fist salute across the whitecaps of English Bay to the crowd on the pier at Jericho.

Taeko Miwa stood beside Hunter. She held her hair out of her face with one hand and clung to one of the stabilizer poles. When the sun broke through the clouds, Taeko wrapped her arm around her face to block the light from her eyes. She appeared to be the calmest person on the boat. Over Taeko's head rose the triangular white mainsail with an orca painted at the peak, the ecology and peace symbols, and the Kwakiutl emblem of an orca below. Above the sail, a flag of the Earth, the United Nations flag, Tibetan prayer flags, and the Canadian maple leaf beat in the wind.

The haze of the city was gone with the gale, the sky bright blue. White cumulus clouds sailed overhead like ghost ships. "She's just a little breeze now," said Cormack. The *Vega* bobbed in the waves downwind of us. At the bow of the *Phyllis Cormack*, massive Czechoslovakian George Korotva stood at the anchor winch with a "Let Them Live" T-shirt stretched over his blue work shirt.

Hamish Bruce braced himself at the stern, feet apart, hands clasped behind his back, as the boat dipped and rose in the swells. He looked toward the crowd on the shoreline, but his wry smile was not of this world, as if he watched his dream of a Green Navy turning real before his eyes and did not want to disturb a thing for fear the entire facade might shatter. The Warriors of the Rainbow were at last putting to sea, not simply on behalf of human concerns, but for all sentient beings. His rough, red cheeks glowed in quiet satisfaction.

I didn't know the difference between the fog locker and the halyard I hung on to, yet I was about to sail into the middle of the Pacific Ocean with these people to find the whaling fleets. A small, black Leica and a large format Pentax camera hung about my neck. The rest of my gear was stored in the bunkroom, in my trunk and military ammo case with a whale sticker on the lid.

As Hunter raised his fist, the crowd roared on the pier at Jericho. He twisted and looked up to the bridge. "Okay, John."

"Hoist anchor," Cormack said, and Korotva started the winch. The anchor chain clanked onto the deck. Captain Cormack sounded the horn, and the crowd on the beach cheered again. The *Vega*, with peace and ecology symbols on the mainsail, flew past us through the whitecaps, west out of English Bay. The *Phyllis Cormack* followed, surrounded by a flotilla of pleasure boats.

Paul Watson coiled rope and barked orders. "Whose gear is this?" He smiled as if it was a theatrical production and he had landed the role of first mate. The fumes from Watson's broken bottle of formaldehyde still rendered the bunkroom almost unbearable. With grumbling about this among the crew, Watson made himself useful at every opportunity. As we rounded Point Grey into the Strait of Georgia, the full force of the northerly hit. "She's honkin' out here," hollered Watson.

Hamish had moved to the bow, where he stood in the breeze like the ancient mariner himself. I stood with him, silently attempting to show solidarity, hoping to let him know that, whatever private world he was in, I was with him in spirit. We turned southwest with the wind behind us. After months of work, thousands of phone calls, many a pint around the pub tables, late night meetings, and fundraising events, we were moving at last.

The *Vega* tacked northward across the wind. It would sail the inside channel, 300 nautical miles around Cape Scott to Winter Harbour. The *Phyllis Cormack* would take the slightly shorter route to Winter Harbour, along the Pacific coastline of Vancouver Island. From the northern harbour, where Hunter and Moore had seen grey whales, we would head for the Dellwood Knolls and Cobb Seamounts looking for whalers.

DO THE MATH

We were three hours across the Strait of Georgia in a following sea, the winds gusting to 30 knots and kicking up whitecaps atop six-foot swells. Half the crew was already sick, and engineer Al Hewitt had disappeared into the trailer that he had rigged behind the hatch cover on the back deck. The two musicians, Mel Gregory and Will Jackson, were nowhere to be seen. Taeko was in her cabin, which opened off the captain's quarters. "Where she'll be safe from you lot," said Cormack.

Cormack did not adhere to formal mariner language. He rarely used terms like "aft deck." He would send a deckhand to the "back of the boat." He would say: "This goes at the back a' the boat, there, by the roller," not "stow this astern, with the starboard tackle." He would say "four o'clock" even if he meant the afternoon, not "sixteen hundred," although he would write "16:00" in his logbook. When I first met Cormack, I assumed this was for the benefit of the "farmers," as he called his amateur crew, but I learned the captain did not pander to the crew or to anyone else. His language was his own.

Cormack stood in the wheelhouse at attention, Watson and Korotva beside him. Walrus Oakenbough, the cook, whistled as he stowed his goods in the galley. Hunter sat at the galley table and smoked a joint with Dr. MacDonald. I came in, perhaps looking a bit pale. Hunter laughed. "Here, this'll help," he said, handing me the joint. MacDonald nodded as if implying his medical approval.

Hamish was the only crewmember still on deck, standing like a sentry at the bow. "I'm a little worried about him," said Hunter. "You think he's okay?" We couldn't tell if Hamish's unusual behaviour represented spiritual inspiration or psychotic breakdown. MacDonald went out, checked on Hamish, and returned shaking his head. "He's all right," he shrugged. "He's pretty far out there, but he's okay."

The sun went down before we reached Active Pass between the Gulf Islands of Galiano and Mayne. A 5-knot tidal current ran through the passage in the darkness. The wind gusted and the boat lurched. Captain Cormack remained unruffled but watchful.

As evening fell, Hunter performed a casual head count. To his horror, he realized we had left the film crew behind. They had been filming the departure from the pier at Jericho and missed the shuttle. "Great," said Hunter, "we just spent a year plotting the greatest ecological media event in the history of the planet, and we leave the film crew on the dock." He got on the marine radio, tracked down the crew in Vancouver, and made arrangements for them to meet us in Tofino on the west coast of Vancouver Island.

Once through Active Pass, at 22:00, we tucked into a small cove on Salt Spring Island. Watson and Korotva dropped two anchors. The wind did not let up, but the sheltered anchorage remained relatively calm. Mel finally emerged, a red bandana around his head with a Tibetan button on the front. He sat at the galley table, rolled a cigarette, and played guitar. Hamish came in from the bow, sat silently for a while, and then disappeared. The Great Whale Conspiracy was at sea.

Sort of at sea. We rolled out a large chart of the Pacific on the galley table. The scale of what we contemplated sank in. We had crossed the Strait of Georgia, a thin white line on the large chart. The vast Pacific lay before us. Watson pointed out the seamounts. To the north, Campbell, Faris, Patton, Surveyor, Dellwood Knolls. To the south, Cobb, Mendocino, Jasper, California. These seamounts ranged over 4,000 miles of ocean — two weeks of solid running from one end to the other. The whalers could be on any one of them, anywhere within 1500 miles of the coast. I did the math in my head. Jeeze. "This is six million square miles of open ocean," I offered to the crew.

"Here," said Hunter, reaching across the table. "This'll help."

Later, I walked out onto the deck to check on Hamish. He was nowhere in sight.

BEHIND THE WHEELHOUSE

We departed Salt Spring Island at first light and made our way south through Juan de Fuca Strait to the open ocean. Cormack had not slept. I learned later that he never slept at anchor. "People die sleeping at anchor." The gentle sea swells drove Will Jackson to his bunk. I felt queasy, but Dr. Macdonald advised staying on my feet, and Hunter's "joint theory," if not proven, was at least rigorously researched. I wandered the boat, along every deck, learning all the ladder routes and shortcuts. Keeping the body in motion with the relentless rhythm of the sea eased the nausea.

After breakfast, Hunter gathered the crew on the quarterdeck, or as Cormack would say, "behind the wheelhouse, there." Hamish stood by and Will Jackson dragged himself up the ladder with determination in his ravaged eyes. Hunter wore a gaily dyed Peruvian wool cap with flaps turned up forming pastel rainbows above his ears. He set out a bottle of rum and nailed a whalebone to the mast. He recreated Captain Ahab's performance on the quarterdeck of the *Pequod* before Ishmael, Starbuck, and the other sailors. Ahab had served rum and nailed a gold Spanish doubloon to the mast. Reversing Ahab's vow, "Whosoever of ye raises me a white-headed whale with a wrinkled brow and a crooked jaw, he shall have this gold ounce," Hunter declared that whoever saw the whalers first would have the whalebone as a prize. Whereas the sailors of the *Pequod* drank to the death of Moby Dick from the sockets of their harpoons, we sipped rum from cups as Hunter thrust his sinewy fist to the sky and shouted, "Let them Live!"

"Let them Live," we chanted back.

"Greenhawks."

"Hawkaaaa!"

"For the protection of all sentient beings."

"Mitakuye oyasin."

"Cheers."

Al Hewitt leaned against the wheelhouse wall, still on watch, drinking from a cup but not joining the chant. He looked as if he might be contemplating Starbuck's quiet supplication, "God keep me! — keep us all!"

After the ceremony, Hamish returned to the bow in his white rain slicks. For five hours, as we made our way north, he stood facing the wind. At the galley table, Hunter set out his Underwood typewriter, the one his mother had given him on his fifteenth birthday, and he pecked away in his speedy two-finger style.

We arrived at the fishing town of Tofino in Clayoquot Sound at five in the evening. The camera crew stood on the dock, filming our approach. Native Nootka (Nuu-cha-nulth) children climbed onto the boat. Mel told them his name was "Captain Melo," gave tours, and played the "Whale Anthem" for the children.

I phoned Glenn and picked up the Vancouver newspaper. The April 28 edition showed us departing English Bay on the front page, but the five-column headline across the top was from another story: "Cong pierce Saigon defense." It turned out that we had launched our crusade on the last day of the bloody Vietnam War. I pinned the clipping to the galley wall. "Tough competition," said Hunter.

That evening, the crew went to the pub. Cormack joined us for one beer, then returned to the boat. Hunter, now wearing a handmade vest with a peace symbol on the right shoulder and the ecology symbol on the left, phoned in the first news story from the voyage: "Project Ahab is at sea. We are heading for Winter Harbour. From there we will begin our search for the whalers."

On May 1, heading north for Winter Harbour, Hamish resumed his station at the bow, silent, with the wind in his hair. By the time we reached Brooks Peninsula above the 50th parallel, the wind had turned directly into us from the north, and the *Phyllis Cormack* beat against the waves. Hamish stood unmoved, his hair blown straight back, matted with sea salt. His face was white from the salt but his eyes glowed.

We rounded Kwakiutl Point where gnarly, wind-swept cedars hung over the surf, and entered Quatsino Sound. Hunter pointed out the gap at Kains Island, where he had seen the two grey whales a year earlier. "There," he said. "We'll start right there."

We slid through Forward Inlet and entered Winter Harbour, where Patrick Moore stood on the dock in his seaman's cap. He took our line and tied the *Phyllis Cormack* to a cleat. I walked to the general store and phoned a story in to the *North Shore News*. We heard from Rod Marining that a journalist from the *New York Times*, Charles Flowers, was on his way to Winter Harbour by floatplane. We drank wine that night and toasted our good fortune. We would test the Zodiacs and sound equipment in the inlet while we waited for the *Vega* to arrive; then we would head west to the seamounts.

CHAPTER SEVEN

MENDOCINO RIDGE

"We must allow, when we consider the future, for the possibility of miracles ..."

— Lewis Mumford

In May, stories of our planned confrontation with the whalers reached Japanese newspapers, and whaling company officials attacked Greenpeace in the media for "regrettable" and "foolish" actions. This set off a week of news stories.

From Winter Harbour, Hunter responded with information about the decline of whale populations. A public relations firm hired by the six largest Japanese whaling companies retaliated. "They're fanatics," a spokesman said. "Their movement is like a religion. It's not normal."

We cheered at hearing this. "*Like* a religion?" scoffed Hunter. "Wait till they find out we *are* a religion." From Vancouver, Marining sent out a press release reporting that Greenpeace had been supported by the Pope, Kwakiutl chiefs, and the Buddhist Gyalwa Karmapa. He reminded Japanese leaders that Shinto and Zen traditions taught compassion for "all sentient beings." Whaling company officials ordered their fleets to "hide their positions to avoid detection," and to "shift to other locations if found."

This kafuffle escalated when Canadian Fisheries Minister Romeo LeBlanc came out in support of the whalers. The United Fishermen and Allied

Workers Union challenged the minister and pledged support for Greenpeace. "We deplore Canada's failure to speak out against whaling," barked union leader Jack Nichols. "The UFAW lends its full support to the actions by the Greenpeace Foundation to interfere with the Pacific whaling expeditions of both Japan and the Soviet Union. The wasteful slaughter of these magnificent animals must stop and the efforts of the Greenpeace crews to harass whale killers deserve nothing but praise and solid support from everyone."

"This is historical," Hunter declared at dockside in Winter Harbour. When the unions came out against nuclear bombs, he recalled, it signalled an important shift in public awareness. "But this? It's epic. A workers' union speaking out for whales over an issue that will impact the livelihoods of workers on whaling boats? The campaign is already working." To the media, Hunter proclaimed, "We are completely dismayed by the decision of the Canadian government to hand the surviving whales over on a platter to a handful of nations now bent on destroying them."

In Vancouver, Marining called for the dismissal of LeBlanc and the head of Canada's Whaling Commission delegation, Dr. Robert Martin. Marining quoted the head of the US delegation, Dr. Robert White, who told Greenpeace that Canada's support of the whalers had weakened the American position so badly that "the whole issue is going to be swept under the rug this year."

Taking the side of the Americans against Canadians was almost unheard of in Canada, but the whale campaign turned convention on its head. Even China weighed into the debate on the side of Greenpeace, albeit for their own political purposes, stating in the *People's Daily* in Beijing that China approved of the "Canadian attempt to challenge the hegemony of Soviet revisionism in the North Pacific."

In the meantime, *New York Times* reporter Charles Flowers arrived in Winter Harbour wearing brand new overalls and carrying a fine Hassleblad camera. We sat in the galley of the *Phyllis Cormack* and chatted with him. "Well, roughly speaking," said Hunter, "it looks like China, the United States, the Fishermen's Union, and Greenpeace are aligned against Russia, Japan, the whalers, and the Canadian government. I'd call that a new political gestalt."

Journalist Flowers scribbled this down. "The irony," Flowers said, "is that American whalers were once as ruthless and guilty as anyone for decimating the whales. Now they're the champions of the whales. And you know why, don't you?"

We sat in silence.

"The 200-mile limit," said Flowers. "The Law of the Sea Conference is going on in Geneva right now, as we speak. The US," Flowers said, "wants to increase their territorial fishing limit from 12 miles to 200 miles. The small countries like Sri Lanka and so forth don't want the superpowers to unilaterally take over large coastal regions, but the US wants control of the continental shelf. And it's not just about fish or whales." He paused for dramatic effect. We waited. "It's about oil. They want the mineral rights."

"They're supporting the whales to get the deep-sea oil rights?"

"Yeah," said Flowers, "and you guys are right in the middle of it. Welcome to global politics."

THE PARSEE PROPHET

In Flowers we had a smart media ally who would follow the campaign throughout the coming months, but we were concerned about his reaction to Hamish's increasingly peculiar behaviour. Technically, Hamish was the Greenpeace president, and we didn't want the *New York Times* story to conclude that we were psychotics. When Hamish arrived for breakfast one morning with his face painted green, Dr. Macdonald concluded, "It would be dangerous to take him out to sea again." At the same time, Hamish seemed to possess a metaphysical poise that made the rest of us feel almost petty and earthbound in his presence. The crew took turns hanging out with him, not just to protect our friend, but to bathe in his remarkable serenity. In the forest one afternoon, he said to me, responding perhaps to my look of concern, "Don't worry. Nothing can stop us now."

Macdonald called Dr. Lyle Thurston in Vancouver and arranged for him to fly to Winter Harbour with sedatives. The job fell to Macdonald, Hunter, and George Korotva to confront Hamish with the news that he would have to leave the boat, but the mystic rose up like a Titan, stormed across the deck, slipped down the ladder into the hold, and then snapped the ladder in two with a single twist.

"Hmm," said Hunter. "That didn't go very well." Journalist Flowers patrolled the boardwalk. Hunter wondered if maybe we should just ride it out. There had been a pagan prophet, the Parsee Fedallah, in the hold of the *Pequod*. Maybe it was our fate too.

Dr. Thurston arrived by floatplane, carrying the common sedative stelazine, and in case that didn't work, the horse tranquilizer phenothiazine. Korotva lowered a ladder into the hold, and he and Hunter went below to reason with Hamish. Twenty minutes passed, then Thurston climbed down into the hold to talk to Hamish himself. Dr. Macdonald crushed tranquilizer tablets into a cheese sandwich and a beer and passed the snack to Korotva. "It's got stelazine in it," Macdonald whispered to the Czechoslovakian. "Give this to Hamish."

Korotva, however, had no idea what stelazine was, and did not understand its significance. He offered the snack to Hamish, but when he declined, Korotva, Thurston, and Hunter shared the sandwich and beer. Suddenly, all three felt faint. Korotva and Hunter clambered up from the hold and passed out in their bunks. Thurston recognized what had happened and confronted Macdonald on the deck.

"You put the stelazine in the sandwich?" he asked.

"Yeah, and the beer. I told George to give it to Hamish."

Thurston drank coffee while Dr. MacDonald prepared an injection of the sedative. Doc Thurston returned to the hold to confront Hamish. "Look, Hamish," he said, "I have to give you a shot."

"Fine," said Hamish, perhaps feeling invincible. Thurston administered the injection, and in ten minutes, Hamish fell asleep. The crew hoisted our president from the hold on a logger's stretcher, wrapped him in a sleeping bag, and put him onto the floatplane with Thurston.

The next day, Thurston phoned Winter Harbour from Vancouver to assure us Hamish was okay. "He's got the Lions Gate Hospital psych ward in the palm of his hand," Thurston said. "He's telling stories about whales and how Greenpeace is going to change the world. He's hilarious. Everybody loves him."

Hamish remained our mystic leader in abstentia.

TRIANGLE ISLAND

The next day, Paul Watson developed appendicitis and he too was flown out of Winter Harbour. We had not only lost our Parsee prophet, we'd lost our Zodiac pilot. Mel threw the *I Ching* coins on the hatch cover. "Darkening of the Light," he reported, "the opposite of progress. The light has been wounded." Mel put the oracle under his arm. "It's time to protect your inner light," he said.

On May 6, the *Vega* arrived in Winter Harbour with skipper Jacques Longini and his crew: photographer Matt Herron, young American doctor John Cotter, and crewman Ramon Falkowski, who had sailed on the *Fri* into the Moruroa nuclear test zone the previous summer. Matt Herron wore two weathered Nikon cameras around his neck. He had covered the Civil Rights Movement in Mississippi, Jim Garrison's JFK assassination case in New Orleans, and the Polaris nuclear submarine demonstrations in Connecticut, during which Irving and Dorothy Stowe joined the Committee for Non-violent Action years earlier. He was also the most experienced sailor on the *Vega*.

At the same time, Carlie Trueman flew from Vancouver with two Zodiacs. Trueman, feisty and smart, was a diver, a Zodiac expert, and an able deckhand. Nicholas Desplats, a friend of David McTaggart's and a member of Les Amis de la Terre, arrived from France. Desplats, with his dark hair, scruffy moustache, and enduring grin, charmed everyone. We now had an international crew: Desplats from France, Taeko Miwa from Japan, Korotva from Czechoslovakia, two Americans, and eight Canadians. George Korotva, in his Czechoslovakian accent, had the habit of tacking "the" onto everyone's name. "Where's d'Bob," he'd say, or "Give this to d'Carlie." The Czech, therefore, became known as "The George."

On the morning of May 8, we departed Winter Harbour and passed through the mouth of Quatsino Sound for our first real strike into the Pacific. Taeko took the wheel and Mel flew a kite from the stern. We searched the reefs of Brooks Bay, and anchored that evening in Klaskish Inlet, where cedar trees grew over boulders at the water's edge. The George kept first anchor watch and woke me at 04:00 to relieve him.

At dawn, we headed west, explored over seamounts, and turned north toward the Scott Islands, off the northwest tip of Vancouver Island. Two albatross followed us all day. We saw seals, but no whales. We reached the Scott Islands at sundown. The chart warned of "Dangerous Tides, Rips, and Overfalls." At the tip of the archipelago, 35 miles northwest of Cape Scott, Triangle Island provides three protected bays, one on each face of the triangle, allowing some respite for fishing boats during a storm from any direction. With a near gale blowing from the southeast, we tucked into the northern bay for the night and dropped two anchors. Taeko, Walrus, and Nicholas Desplats prepared a meal of oysters and pasta. After dinner we lounged about the deck, watching the stars. A small light on the mast lit the sail and the Kwakiutl whale emblem.

Suddenly, we heard a strange, high-pitched hooting. Then the hoots became a constant screech and we heard dull thuds on the sail, a crashing on the deck, and squawking noises. Hundreds of storm petrels had flown from the darkness into the sail. We picked up the stunned birds and sent them back into the air, but more petrels hit the deck as fast as we could free them.

"Turn off the mast light," screamed Moore. Mel carried a bird into the galley. As our animal affinity expert, Mel took it upon himself to commune with the startled petrel. The bird was eight inches long, black, with white patches on its forked tail: *Oceanodroma leucorhoa*, Leach's Storm Petrel, known to land on boats during squalls. On deck we heard a frantic flapping of wings near the stern, where a large, tufted puffin nipped menacingly with a hefty orange beak. The puffin was twice the size of the petrels and much more fierce. Like petrels, puffins fly home each night to their burrows on the remote sea islands. Korotva tried to grab the bird, but it warned him off with vicious jabs of its beak. Mel came out on deck, let his petrel go, and offered to save the puffin. He sat in front of the bird and talked to it in an effort to calm it down. Indeed, the puffin seemed to relax. Mel reached out, took the bird in his hands, and stood up to carry it to the railing. The alarmed puffin attacked Mel's exposed hands with ferocious bites. By the time he released it over the side of the boat, his hands dripped blood across the deck.

In the galley, Dr. Macdonald patched up Mel, and life on board returned to normal. But I could not shake the feeling that we had intruded into this marine wilderness.

ZODIAC PHOTOGRAPHER

The next morning we explored Queen Charlotte Sound, north of the archipelago. Walrus climbed high in the rigging and surveyed the horizon for several hours, but again we saw no whales. Finally, we put into

Fisherman Bay on the north end of Vancouver Island, where Moore, Hunter, Al Hewitt, film cameraman Fred Easton, and I went ashore. Al Hewitt spent an hour salvaging bits of rope, latches, and electronic components from a capsized troller half buried in the sand. The next day, we ran 60 miles northwest.

That afternoon, we stopped to test our photographers and confrontation crews in the Zodiacs. Carlie Trueman and The George mounted Mercury outboard engines on the three 15-foot inflatables. The wooden transom, or floorboard, of each Zodiac fit together in three pieces. "You have to watch the transom," Carlie warned. "If it buckles going over a wave, the whole frame of the Zodiac can fall apart."

We dressed in wetsuits. Hunter, wearing his brightly coloured Peruvian wool cap, crouched in a Zodiac with Pat Moore piloting. Will Jackson went with Mel Gregory, and I rode in the bow of the third Zodiac with Korotva. I lashed the ammunition case, holding my film and lenses, to the inside of the Zodiac and attempted to take photographs as we bounded across the waves. To test the manoeuvrability of the inflatables, we roared in front of the *Phyllis Cormack* as if it were a whaling ship. Even in a light chop, this proved difficult. The two cameras about my neck flew into the air and pounded against my chest as I clung to the ropes on the side of the Zodiac. I tried to hold on with one hand and manipulate a camera with the other. Focusing proved difficult; taking photographs from a Zodiac in these conditions seemed preposterous. I put one camera into the ammunition case. The best I could do was to kneel in the bow for short periods of time, travelling at relatively slow speed, aim, and release the shutter before I was bounced off balance. After an hour manoeuvring through the choppy sea, I was exhausted.

With almost nothing to show for my efforts, I secured the camera inside my wetsuit, and postponed the attempt to take photographs from a speeding Zodiac. Hunter, Will Jackson, and Mel took turns leaping from the moving inflatables so we could practice retrieving riders who might accidentally fall out. The manoeuvre proved challenging in the rough seas. Even *seeing* a person overboard among the sea swells was difficult.

"This isn't going to be easy," I told Hunter.

"We have time to practise," he said cheerfully. That evening, we returned to Winter Harbour, yet to see our first whale.

WHALES

On May 13, we headed south for Wickaninnish Bay, where we knew gray whales gathered each summer. Desplats, who had suffered terrible seasickness, stayed behind in Winter Harbour and Gary Zimmerman, from the Oceanic Society in San Francisco, joined the crew. Hunter temporarily joined the *Vega* crew and headed northwest for an extended search to the edge of the continental shelf, where they would monitor the marine radio frequencies for Soviet or Japanese whaling fleets.

On our way south, under a bright sun, we came upon Dall's porpoises off Nootka Sound. Some thirty porpoises took turns riding on our bow wave as the crew hung over the anchor. Mel played a penny whistle, and Will Jackson improvised from the upper deck on his electronic synthesizer. The porpoises seemed in perfect control, with no purpose other than to amuse themselves.

Dall's porpoises had been reduced by accidental deaths in deep-sea nets and from being hunted by Japanese fishermen for a commercial market. They are the largest of the family Phocoenidea, cousins to the orca. The mammalian order Cetacea is made up of two distinct groups, the toothed whales like the sperm whale, orca, and porpoises, and the baleen whales like the humpback and gray whales. The Dall's porpoises grow to seven feet and 400 pounds, and can swim at 15 knots. The *Phyllis Cormack* cruised at about 9 knots, so the porpoises easily sliced in front of the bow, turned on their sides, and flipped belly-up in the bow wave. They are devoted parents and, like the orcas, remain together in large extended families. This group stayed with us for an hour, and then, as if on cue, departed west into the deeper ocean.

The next day, May 14, we found gray whales feeding in the sandy shoals of Wickaninnish Bay, where they sifted through the seabed for mud shrimp, worms, shellfish, and other sediment creatures. Rippling grey shapes emerged and disappeared among the gray sea swells. Glaucous-winged gulls and black-headed Bonaparte's gulls flew against the silver clouds over the pewter-grey bay, as if the entire scene had been sketched in charcoal. Hewitt hung hydrophones and speakers from the side of the boat, and Will Jackson played synthesizer music. We listened for a response but heard nothing. Eventually, Mel and I took a Zodiac out and drifted as Mel played his flute. Whales surfaced around us, gazed at us, and sank away. Whether or not the whales were attracted by the music, they were unafraid and did not protest our presence.

The grays, like other baleen whales, are among the largest creatures ever to live on the earth. By comparison, the largest Brachiosaurus dinosaur reached 85 feet long. The largest known baleens — the blue whales — reach 95 feet. Whereas Brachiosaurus' length was mostly neck and tail, the blue whale is solid bulk, weighing up to 175 tons, four times the weight of the largest dinosaur. The blue whale heart weighs 1,000 pounds, and a human could easily crawl through its arteries. Greek sailors called them *Mysticetes* for their "moustache," the bristles of baleen that protrude from their gums. The whales fill their mouths with water, then push the water out through the baleen to screen out zooplankton and krill. A typical blue whale will eat up to 9,000 pounds of plankton and krill per day during its summer feeding season.

The 40-ton adult gray whales in Wickaninnish Bay could as easily have flipped a rubber inflatable with outboard engine and two people as we might flip a soccer ball, but they did not once bother us, and we felt safe among them.

On May 15, in Wickaninnish Bay, Paul Watson returned from his surgery. Patrick Moore, who had assumed leadership on board in Hunter's absence, insisted there were no spots on the crew until we returned to Winter Harbour. Watson, not to be denied, swam from the beach to the *Phyllis Cormack*, tearing his stitches in the process. Moore bristled, but Watson ignored him. Their quarrel would ripen into one of the group's long-standing conflicts.

That same day, renowned saxophone player Paul Winter arrived on board. After signing with Columbia Records in 1961, Winter had toured Latin America and integrated Afro-Latin sounds and syncopations into his music. He'd played in the White House for the Kennedys, and his first album, *Jazz Meets the Bossa Nova*, became an underground hit. However, when Winter heard recorded humpback whales in 1968, he began to fashion a new music based on the natural voices of the whales, wolves, and other creatures. "Rhythm and harmony," he told us, "are fundamental to life. The songs of the humpback whale, recorded by Roger Payne, are as important in our musical heritage as Bach or Charlie Parker."

Mel, Winter, and I launched a Zodiac and once again we drifted among the whales of Wickaninnish Bay. Winter rested the curve of his saxophone on the wooden transom of the Zodiac and used it as a soundboard. He improvised freely in the quiet bay. Almost instantly, a gray whale surfaced beside us. *Whoosh*! Then another. And another. Four whales rose in succession, blew great mists of breath into the air, and sank again below the swells, leaving mirror-like circles in the water. Paul Winter played on. A whale would occasionally roll its huge head from the water and fix us with one six-inch-diameter eye. For two hours we drifted among the whales while Winter played his saxophone.

Later that afternoon, Carlie Trueman, Gary Zimmerman, and I took a Zodiac out in the light rain. We saw whale spouts at a distance, and I played on Mel's flute, resting it on the transom as Winter had done. Trueman fired up the engine and moved slowly ahead. At that moment, a whale surfaced directly in front of us and gently rapped the underside of the boat with its fluke, lifting us slightly out of the water. Was it a signal? Were the whales disturbed by the engine sounds? We could only speculate, but clearly the whale had made itself known to us.

In the galley that night Zimmerman told us about a study of gray whales conducted by two US fish and wildlife scientists, Dale Rice and Allen Wolman. "It was published a few years ago," he said. "*The Life History and Ecology of the Gray Whale*. It's the definitive study, as far as mammalogists are concerned. The thing is, they killed 316 gray whales to write the study."

"The death history," said Walrus.

"What we're learning out here," said Zimmerman, "you won't find in the book."

WAIT FOR IT

Far to the north, Bob Hunter and the crew of the *Vega* had arrived at an entirely different state of mind: tired and disheartened, hove to on the edge of the continental shelf, listening for whalers.

Two hundred miles off the coast of Haida Gwaii, east of the Campbell seamounts, unrelenting winds beat against the sailboat. Everyone but the photographer Herron was seasick and popping Gravol pills. Herron had sailed across the Atlantic Ocean with his family and was a more knowledgeable sailor than skipper Longini, but this led to problems. Herron would often be the first to notice weather changes and adjustments that might ease the motion of the boat. His suggestions led to clashes with Longini, and the tension became palpable to Hunter.

Longini — lean, tanned, and weathered — combed his greying blond hair back from his balding forehead. His blond sideburns, moustache, goatee, and bushy eyebrows gave him a swashbuckling look, like a character in an Ian Fleming novel. He told stories of the French Foreign Office after World War II, flying Madame Chiang Kai-shek's furniture and imperial art treasures out of Beijing to Taipei. He could be friendly and charming one minute, irascible the next. His mood swings led Hunter to call him "Captain Flapjack."

For eight days, the crew of the *Vega* listened for Russian or Japanese radio broadcasts. The wind blew cold and the sky grew dark with thunderclouds. The doctor, John Cotter, who had never been to sea, remained incapacitated with nausea and passed out from the effects of the Gravol pills. Falkowski and Herron crewed the boat.

On May 19, sitting in the galley of the *Vega*, rocking in the six-foot swells, the gimballed table swinging back and forth with their glasses of wine, Hunter, Herron, Falkowski, and Longini sat up late and monitored the radio. They heard Russian voices but, since no one aboard spoke Russian, they could not tell if they were hearing whalers, trawlers, or perhaps a tanker crew. Still, Hunter attempted to make radio contact with the *Phyllis Cormack* to relay the news. When this didn't work he tried the marine operators on shore, but could raise no one. When Herron attempted to get a fix on the Russian radio broadcast the needle of the Radio Directional Finder (RDF) swung wildly through 200 degrees of ocean. "Forget it," he told Hunter. "Either the signal isn't strong enough or the RDF is useless."

Waves bashed against the *Vega*. "Well," said Hunter, "Great. We have no idea where the Soviet ships are, we can't translate what they are saying, and we can't communicate with anyone anyway. As a spy ship, we're kind of a flop."

Hunter reached for his wine glass just as the gimballed table swung away from him and he nearly tumbled forward onto the floor. He sat up, and Longini grinned. "It's timing, Bob. Wait for it," he said. As the table swung back, Hunter took up his glass and raised it.

"Yeah. Wait for it. Good policy, sir. Cheers."

HIDDEN DRAGON

On May 22 the *Phyllis Cormack* rendezvoused with the *Vega* in Winter Harbour. There were more crew changes as Taeko Miwa, Michael Chechik, and Myron MacDonald returned to Vancouver and nurse Leigh Wilkes and camera operator Fred Easton signed on. Since the *Vega*'s reconnaissance had not been promising, and since it cost money to be out on the water, Hunter wondered if we wouldn't be better off practicing Zodiac skills in Winter Harbour.

Six months earlier, Hunter had met the grand lama of Tibetan Buddhists, the Sixteenth Gyalwa Karmapa, who had blessed the whale voyage and given him a red cloth, which he wore faithfully in a leather pouch around his neck, an amulet of divine protection. He massaged the bag between his fingers at the galley table. Finally, he took up the *I Ching* coins to see what wisdom the oracle might impart. He got six strong Yang lines: symbol of the Creative, the primal power of the spirit. This seemed auspicious, but a changing line warned of a "hidden dragon. Do not Act."

"The *I Ching* kind of says we should stay put," Hunter told me, "but the crew's restless." Furthermore, newspapers that carried stories of our encounters with whales would soon lose interest if we didn't actually find evidence of whalers. The next morning, Friday, May 23, both boats struck out for the Dellwood Knolls seamounts.

An hour out, a full rainbow appeared before us like a gateway to the North Pacific. Hunter placed his copy of *Warriors of the Rainbow* on the galley table for new crewmembers. The mystically inclined — Mel, Will Jackson, Walrus, and I — had long ago accepted that we were at least *helping* to fulfill the prophecy that people from all nations would unite to speak for the earth. Some of the "mechanics" — Hewitt, oceanographer Gary Zimmerman, and Zodiac expert Carlie Trueman — remained skeptical, though not adverse to the idea that the voyage was, at its root, a spiritual mission. Even our skipper donned a bandana and eagle feather.

At midmorning, Cormack announced, "There's a storm'll be here in about an hour. We're gonna be buckin' right into it. Stow yer gear." With this, he disappeared into the engine room below. Sure enough, an hour later, the sail wafted in the breeze, and within minutes we were running into 40-knot winds, taking waves over the bow. Gear flew across the galley and bunkroom. Will Jackson and Carlie Trueman lashed down the

Zodiacs. I joined the captain on deck to lower the stabilizer poles. Waves broke in spindrift, and the spray blew like bits of gravel into our faces. Jackson and I stayed on deck in the shelter of the cabin, pumped with adrenaline. "Yer at sea now, boys," laughed the skipper.

The gale quieted to 20 knots by the time we reached Triangle Island shortly after midday. Cormack tucked into the southern bay for the night. Caught up in all the excitement, Hunter, Will Jackson, Fred Easton, and Trueman ventured ashore. Easton took his 16-mm Bolex camera to film the nesting eagles. However, even on the lee side of the island, the surf swelled up onto the rocks, making it almost impossible to land. Trueman piloted the Zodiac in close and yelled at the others to jump. Easton made it safely to the rocks with his camera, but Hunter and Jackson landed in the surf. They pushed on the Zodiac to free it from the rocks, but the next wave lifted them across the barnacles, and then dragged them out into the deep water. Hunter's rubber gumboots filled with water and pulled him under. Jackson grasped the Zodiac rope with one hand and Hunter with the other. The swells hurled them toward the rocks again, then back out to sea. On the next wave, Carlie gunned the engine and carried Hunter and Jackson to the rocks, where they clambered up and out of the surf.

Bruised, cut, soaked, and shaking uncontrollably in the frigid wind, Hunter and Jackson huddled on the rocks, waiting to be rescued. The eagles, protecting their nests, swooped and hissed at the intruders. Carlie sped back to the *Phyllis Cormack*, picked up Zimmerman, and returned to rescue our stranded shipmates. It took them another hour to find an opening among the rocks and the right conditions to allow them onto the island. The sun set and darkness fell before Hunter and Jackson limped, shivering and blue from the cold, onto the deck of the *Phyllis Cormack*. "That'll teach ya," said the captain.

Musician Will Jackson, also a gifted cartoonist, had quietly drawn all the characters on the boat into a series of caricatures — Hunter in his Peruvian cap, Korotva the Slavic sailor, the skipper bursting from his khaki work shirt, Mel the lovable hippie musician, Watson the stout seaman, Walrus the lithe mystic, Moore the frizzy-haired ecologist, Hewitt the mad scientist, the film crews with our cameras ready, and Carlie with her pigtails flapping in the breeze at the controls of a Zodiac — and had posted them on the galley wall. Now, Jackson patched his wounds, cleaned up, and went to work on the cartoon version of the stranded sailors dodging eagles as Carlie attempted to rescue them.

Wrapped in a blanket in the corner of the galley, Hunter massaged his sacred pouch, confessed that he had ignored the *I Ching* warning about the hidden dragon, and remarked, "Won't do that again."

BATTLE OF THE TITANS

The next day, May 24, we reached the Dellwood Knolls, 60 miles west of Triangle Island, in the open Pacific. The knolls are part of a seamount cordillera that stretches from the Aleutian Trench to California, formed by volcanoes 600,000 years ago. The tallest of these seamounts rise within 100 feet of the ocean surface and bear scars from the wind and waves that carved their shorelines during past ice ages. Nutrient-rich water wells up from the trenches and through the gullies to form eddies that funnel organic matter to the surface. Sunlight filters through the ocean water to the slopes, where red and brown algae grow on the terraces. These light-eating plants are the nutrient store for an ecosystem as large as the entire western half of North America. Salp and prowfish live in the gorges and dells. Mussels and barnacles cling to the ridges of rock, where snow crab graze. Rockfish, halibut, cod, and sole feed in the slopes. Shark, octopus, and squid stalk the crab and fish. The giant squid hunts them all. And the sperm whale hunts the squid. Human whalers hunt the sperm whale, and here, over the Dellwood Knolls, we hunted the whalers.

On the evening of May 25, the sea turned dead calm, the sky filled with stars, and the nearly full moon lit up the ocean and the decks of the boat. In this environment, we imagined the first mariners who navigated by the heavenly bodies. In the rocking of the sea, we felt the slow twist of time. With the stars reflected in the mirror-like sea, the horizon vanished and we appeared to float free in space.

Marining called from Vancouver, explaining that some of our former media allies were growing skeptical. Knowing the slim chance we had of finding the whalers in the vast North Pacific, Hunter deliberated how to keep our story alive. "We're fading," he confided to me. "We need a grabber."

Hunter moved his Underwood typewriter from the galley table into the oily engine room. He worked under a single light bulb, beside the black water hoses and electric lines, with the syncopated pounding of the engine, in triplets, *pa-pa-boom, pa-pa-boom*, four feet behind his head. Invoking the full moon, the squid, and the sperm whales, Hunter came up with a story he called "The Battle of the Deep Sea Titans." The story was consistent with ocean ecology, but highly speculative. Quoting Dr. Patrick Moore, Hunter noted that phytoplankton rise to the surface to absorb moonlight. The entire food chain, including the squid and the sperm whales, might follow to the surface. Citing accounts of sailors who had witnessed such a thing during the full moon, Hunter wrote, "We hope to film and record the gathering of the sperms, and if we are extremely lucky, to document an encounter between a sperm whale and a giant squid."

Hunter ripped the story from his typewriter triumphantly and showed it to me. "Fantastic, Bob," I said. Hunter carried the press release up to the galley and posted it on the wall, as was his custom. Soon, the "Battle of the Titans" story had created a furor among the crew.

"Is this the best we can come up with?" jeered Trueman. "This is complete crap. Do you really think we're going to see a sperm whale fighting a giant squid?" Hunter shrugged.

"Technically," said Zimmerman, "I suppose something like this could happen, but this is really pushing the edge of credibility, Bob. It makes us look ridiculous."

"We *are* ridiculous," countered Hunter. "We may never see another whale out here and we may never find the whalers at all! That's not the point. It's a story. Every story that appears puts pressure on Japan and Russia. If it's technically possible, that's all I'm saying. I'm trying to get a bloody story of whales into the newspapers."

"We should be writing stories about whales then," argued Carlie Trueman. "We should be trying to educate people, not give them this drivel."

"Drivel?! Look, Carlie, you do your job, and I'll do mine," Hunter ranted. "The media is not interested in whale statistics. 'Fin whale hunt peaked in 1971' is not a headline, Carlie. Newspapers want action. If we provide a story, we can *perhaps* squeeze in a paragraph about the whale stocks."

"It's sensationalism, Bob," scoffed Carlie.

"It's media, Carlie! I don't make the rules."

"The media should print what's important not what's, what's —"

"Fritz Perls would call that a 'shouldism.' Do you want to tell the media how they *should* react? Fine. Will you have the global media machine retrained in time to save the whales?"

That evening, Will Jackson documented the row in a cartoon and began calling Trueman and Zimmerman the "Truth Squad." The name stuck. When tempers cooled the following day, Carlie Trueman proudly accepted the mantle of leader of the Truth Squad.

Meanwhile, Hunter transmitted his story by marine radio to Marining in Vancouver. The next afternoon, Marining called the boat. "They love it," said Marining. "The *Sun* is going to run it as their Page Six feature, and the wire services have picked it up along with the photographs from Wickaninnish Bay."

An Australian headline announced, "Man lands on giant squid-whale ground."

The full-page *Vancouver Sun* piece declared, "Greenpeace ships sail to see 'awesome' battle of Pacific giants."

True to his word, Hunter had tagged on data about the disappearing whales and the Japanese and Soviet whalers. Even Carlie, as leader of the Truth Squad, congratulated Hunter. "Okay," she said, patting him on the shoulder, "I have to give you this one. But it's still sensationalism."

The night of the full moon came and went. An albatross stayed with the boat, and we saw flying fish, but no giant squid and no whales.

ROSE HARBOUR

We sat over the Dellwood Knolls for a week. One full month had passed since we'd left Vancouver. Our worst fear was that we wouldn't find the whalers at all, and the mission would be a complete flop. I had been reading Hunter's copy of *Cutting Through Spiritual Materialism*, by Tibetan lama Trungpa Rinpoche. The book discussed the futility of attempting to *achieve* spirituality and warned of "false heroism." Real heroism, the book advised, involved more than sacrifice; it required that one "give up trying to be something special."

"That may be easier than we thought," said Hunter, sitting wearily at the stern, watching the albatross follow us. He revealed to me, trusting

I could keep a secret, that Spong's information indicated the whalers would be over the Mendocino Ridge seamounts, far to the south, in mid-June. We had two weeks, and did not want to show our hand, so on the first day of June we headed north and sent radio messages that we were "looking for the whalers."

On June 2, a Canadian Air Force Argus maritime patrol plane, equipped with sophisticated electronic surveillance gear, buzzed our little fish boat. "Ha!" laughed Hunter. "The Canadians are in cahoots with the Japanese and Russians. They're going to report that we're going the wrong way!" We were a thousand miles north of Mendocino Ridge, heading farther north. Hunter's unorthodox shrewdness was not something he had learned at a military academy, but a more primal impulse. He carried the burden of pulling off this campaign and agonized over it, but on this day savoured a private glee, imagining that the upstart Warriors of the Rainbow may have just deceived the combined intelligence services of Canada, Japan, and the Soviet Union.

Hunter often played the fool, and some observers interpreted his zany charisma for a big ego, but he was actually shy and self-conscious. To deflect attention in his media releases, he engaged his shipmates in conversation, and later quoted "Dr. Moore," or "oceanographer Gary Zimmerman," or "Japanese ecologist Taeko Miwa," rather than credit ideas to himself. Although he mocked his own mysticism, he remained deeply sincere. "Ecology needs a mythology," he said one night on the bow, "so people who live in a human-designed world can identify with it. As much as people love cuddly animals or exotic animals, few really grok ecology."

That afternoon, we practised Zodiac manoeuvres, and I learned that I could stand up in the Zodiac by holding onto the bowline. By bending my knees like shock absorbers, I could hold a camera in one hand and take photographs. Long lenses were almost useless in the Zodiac, because of the motion. Cameraman Ron Precious came to the same conclusions.

At dusk, we approached Cape St. James, the southern tip of Haida Gwaii, known on Canadian charts as the Queen Charlotte Islands. Haida Gwaii included Kunghit Island in the south, Graham and Moresby to the north, and countless smaller islands. On Kunghit, we stopped at Rose Harbour, once a thriving whaling station. We anchored in the bay at sunset, went ashore, and poked through the remnants of the abandoned whale slaughterhouse.

The Aleut, Tlingit, Tsimshian, Kwakiutl, Haida, Nuu-cha-nulth, and Salish, had hunted whales in the North Pacific before the Europeans. When the British ceded sovereignty of the North Pacific to Spain in 1790, they retained the whaling rights and sent British whalers into Nootka Sound. The French, Russian, and Yankee whaling schooners followed, stalking the abundant blue, fin, sperm, humpback, and right whales. By 1846 there were over 300 whaling ships in the North Pacific, most species had been decimated, and the right whale was nearly extinct.

Two years later, red-bearded American captain Thomas Roys discovered an abundance of oil-rich bowhead whales in the Bering Sea. Over 200 ships scoured the Bering grounds and the slow-moving bowhead were virtually wiped out within a few seasons. Roys employed the Norwegian exploding harpoon and added the refinement of firing the harpoon from a British cannon. He inadvertently blew his left hand off, but perfected the technology and used it to hasten the slaughter of the great whales. Ironically, he also wrote longingly of the disappearing whales and feared their extinction. Still, he sought new whaling grounds. In 1868 he discovered humpbacks in the Strait of Georgia and hunted them until he died of yellow fever a few years later.

In 1907, the Pacific Whaling Company took up humpback whaling in the Strait of Georgia, but met with opposition from J. A. Cates, manager of the Vancouver Terminal Steamship Company. Cates had founded the world's first whale-watching tours, taking customers from Vancouver to see the humpback whales, and he argued that the region would benefit more by keeping the whales alive. Pacific Whaling Company ignored him and decimated the remaining humpbacks in a single year.

Meanwhile, Japan and Russia entered the North Pacific whaling grounds with larger schooners that could process whales on the high seas, the first factory ships. As the whale populations declined, the pelagic fleets gave way to small shore stations along the British Columbia coast. The Consolidated Whaling Corporation established the shore station at Rose Harbour in 1911. Steel-hulled ships under steam and diesel power scoured the seamounts to the west for the remaining whales. A common technique among these whalers was to wound young whales to attract the adults. The shore stations processed all species including the much smaller fin and sei whales. As these species disappeared, the shore stations shut down. Rose Harbour closed in 1943, and the last station on the west coast of Canada, at Coal Harbour in Quatsino Sound, near Winter Harbour, in 1967, when fin and sei whales were too scarce to be hunted profitably.

At Rose Harbour we found rusted boilers with trees growing up through the metal vats and rust-red shards from broken winches, flensing knives, and engine parts mixed in among the beach rock. We found whalebone and teeth glazed red from the decaying iron. Thirty-two years after the last whale was processed here, the eerie feeling of death haunted the bay. The dismal story of the whales felt, indeed, like a portent for the ecological and spiritual bankruptcy of human civilization. How could our race be so short-sighted? Walrus stood in the lapping surf and played a long, soft requiem on his bamboo flute. Carlie had tears in her eyes. Hunter stood silent, as if in shock.

Collectively, our determination fused in Rose Harbour. We knew that one day, the factory ships that now hunted the last of the sperm whales would be rusting hulks like these forgotten machines. We swore that this day would come soon, and when it did, there would be whales left alive in the ocean.

HALLELUJAH, I'M A BUM!

I came to view the campaign as a delicate balance between the practical and the spiritual, Hunter's "mystics and mechanics," and imagined we each carried both qualities within us. The mystically inclined, or those who had read Carl Jung, believed that synchronicity was at work and that the forces of nature would help us succeed. On the other hand, our campaign required attention to the corporeal details. The *Phyllis Cormack* burned about 16-18 gallons of diesel fuel per hour, cruising at 9 knots, making our range 500 miles out from the coast before returning for fuel. We needed to double this capability if we had any real hope of investigating the seamounts to the south. Korotva, Pat Moore, and Mel Gregory had stayed behind in Winter Harbour to arrange for extra fuel tanks for the boat. Assuming we could acquire the tanks, we still had to raise $3,000 to pay for them and for the diesel fuel we needed.

We hatched a plan to stage whale shows at the coastal towns as we headed north. Innes sent raffle tickets and T-shirts to sell from the boat, and actor and entertainer Don Franks, who would be our master of ceremonies, joined us. There was one other element to our plan: fishermen along the coast knew things about shipping traffic. We had heard rumours of whaling ships. Perhaps we would stumble upon solid information among the coastal fishing towns. North of Rose Harbour we stopped at the community of Tasu, on the west coast of Moresby Island, site of an open-pit copper mine that supported a hundred families.

Oddly, in this remote island mining town, 500 miles northwest of Vancouver, two western Buddhist monks arrived on the dock and handed Hunter a flag that had been carried from Tibet by the lama Trungpa Rinpoche. The flag was adorned with animal figures and a blessing in Tibetan "for the emancipation of all sentient beings from the cycle of suffering." This seemed auspicious enough, but trundling behind the monks, along the dock, a fragile old man carefully made his way toward the boat. "This is someone you know," one of the monks told Hunter. Indeed, the old man was his father's long-lost brother, Hunter's beloved Uncle Ernie, whom he had not seen since childhood. Ernie was the camp's handyman. Hunter fell into his arms, sobbing. At the mining camp bunkhouse, Ernie told Bob stories of his father and Hunter told Ernie about whales and the Warriors of the Rainbow. As they talked, one of the monks returned, tapped on the window, and urged Hunter outside. "Look," he said grinning. A bright double rainbow arched through the bay and landed on the *Phyllis Cormack*. At that very moment I stood high on the hill above, where I took a photograph of the modest blessing from nature.

That night, at the Union Hall, Hunter delivered a spirited homily to the sacredness of life. This was followed by Don Franks and the Whale Band, which consisted of Will Jackson and me on guitars. Franks, a.k.a. "Iron Buffalo," wore a beaded headband and long braids that fell over each shoulder. He played autoharp and commanded the stage with jokes, stories of whales, and songs that we had rehearsed on the boat. The mine workers danced to rousing sea shanties, but the hit of the evening was the Depression-era hobo song, "Hallelujah, I'm a Bum." Franks had discovered that Cormack liked this song, and we had sung it on the boat to the great pleasure of the captain. The mineworkers knew the chorus, and we performed a 20-minute version, with Will Jackson delivering stinging guitar leads. We stumbled down to the boat with the last of the locals at about 3:00 a.m. with over $500 from raffle tickets and T-shirts. A few hours later, Hunter, Will Jackson, and I let the ropes go from the dock and we slipped away in the silent dawn.

In Skidegate and Alliford Bay, we repeated what Franks now called The Migrating Whale Medicine Show. Children gathered around the boat, and Franks held them spellbound with songs and monologues about whales. "How long does a mother whale carry her baby?" The children raised their hands and shouted answers. "Why does she bring it to the surface?"

"To breathe!"

"To see people!"

A lawyer in the town of Prince Rupert tipped us off that the Canadian Navy was tracking the *Phyllis Cormack* from the Naval Radio Base in Masset, at the northern tip of Haida Gwaii and just south of Alaska. Hunter wanted to visit the base and reinforce the misconception that we had no idea what we were doing. "We'll ask around about the whaling boats, as if we're desperate, and imply that we're on our way north," Hunter plotted. "If they *are* reporting to the Japanese and Russians, they'll tell 'em we're way off track." We arrived in Masset on Tuesday, June 10. A friend of the lawyer in Prince Rupert introduced us to three young officers. Hunter appealed for their help, but they either didn't know, or didn't say, where the whalers might be. Hunter let it slip that we would head north looking for the Japanese over the Patton and Faris seamounts.

We now provisioned the boat for a push south toward Mendocino Ridge.

ORCAS

On June 12, we slipped southward through Grenville Channel, a narrow fissure between granite cliffs, to avoid detection in the open ocean. Hunter sat in the engine room and hammered out a press release. The Scientific Committee of the IWC had just convened its preliminary meetings in London. Quoting Moore, he attacked the IWC scientists for ignoring the evidence about whales in favour of the whalers, and he vowed the Greenpeace boat would find the whaling fleets. We stopped at the abandoned fishing village of Butedale, where Hunter sent the press release from a radiophone at the home of the lone caretaker.

Further south, off Napiere Point near the town of Bella Bella, we came upon a pod of orcas with two babies swimming close to their mothers. Watson — now fully healed and officially back on the crew — thought he saw two orcas fighting, but what first looked like blood was in fact a long, pink orca phallus as two orcas made cetacean love off our forward bow. "What's that pink thing?" said Ron Precious. "It's the universe unfolding," said Hunter. "Keep filming." The entwined whales spun in the water, taking turns breathing, drifting in the current through the passage, the grandest demonstration of nature's miracle that any of us had ever witnessed. Trueman, Don Franks, and I ventured among the orcas in a Zodiac, cut our engine, and drifted as Franks played his flute. The curious orcas approached. A mother and her calf swam by, the baby no bigger than a small porpoise. We stayed with the whales for forty minutes through Lama Passage, then, like the Dall's porpoises we had seen off the west coast of Vancouver Island, they all simultaneously departed.

On June 14, we put into Winter Harbour for the last time, and made preparations for our final strike south. Bobbi Innes, Pat and Eileen Moore, Mel Gregory, George Korotva, and Rod Marining met us with eight 250-gallon fuel tanks. We had collected about $1,500 from our tour. Innes had paid for the fuel tanks with donations from Vancouver.

Our six-week shakedown had sharpened the Greenpeace team. The boat crew for the final leg of the campaign was comprised of Mel Gregory, Patrick Moore, Will Jackson, Al Hewitt, Bob Hunter, George Korotva, Paul Watson, Carlie Trueman, Walrus, and the camera crew — Fred Easton, Ron Precious, and me — plus Captain John Cormack.

The *Vega* would remain among the northern seamounts. Gary Zimmerman returned to California to find an airplane pilot who would fly reconnaissance missions over the whaling grounds. Bobbi Innes, Eileen Chivers, Rod Marining, and Leigh Wilkes returned to Vancouver to run the office and link us with the media. Paul and Linda Spong organized support in London at the IWC meeting.

Hunter now revealed to the entire team that we possessed the previous summer's coordinates of the Soviet whaling fleets. Moore spread the North Pacific chart out on the hatch cover and found Mendocino Ridge, running west from California at the 40th parallel, 1,000 miles to the south. The International Whaling Commission meetings in London would end on June 27. This was our deadline.

At first light, on Wednesday, June 18, we let go from the dock at Winter Harbour and slipped quietly from Quatsino Sound. The whalebone remained nailed to the mast of the *Phyllis Cormack*, the prize for whoever first saw the whalers.

RUSSIAN VOICES

We traced a route that would carry us southwest over the Cobb seamounts, then due south to Mendocino Ridge. Al Hewitt, the quiet engineer, became the centre of attention. We relied on his Radio Directional Finder to locate Soviet radio transmissions. Hewitt tested the RDF on random ship signals and incessantly fiddled with resisters and copper coils. I noticed that he used components he had salvaged from the beach at Fisherman's Bay a month earlier.

Camera operators Ron Precious and Fred Easton checked and rechecked their gear. They had limited reserves of film, and used it sparingly. Trueman fretted over the Zodiacs. Pat Moore and The George tore apart the outboard engines, tuned, cleaned, and reassembled them on the back deck. Paul Watson took the wheel. Mel and Will Jackson tinkered with the sound equipment and played music. Walrus ran the galley and wrote in his journal.

Mel, Walrus, Will Jackson, and I began a "whale watch" schedule of two-hour shifts up the mast. From the deck of the boat, we could see whales about three miles to the horizon, but 20 feet up the mast, we could see five miles to the horizon. Dall's porpoises and Pacific white-sided dolphins visited the boat and took rides on the bow. Once again, a lone albatross followed us, invoking Coleridge's "Ancient Mariner" and the bird of good omen.

On the second day out, a storm from the west forced us to lower the stabilizer poles to run across the wind. Swells coming in abeam rocked the vessel severely, but our schedule required that we stay the course southwest and absorb the sea swells. During the storm, diesel fuel leaked from one of the new tanks and spoiled our food stores. We unpacked the hold and Walrus salvaged what he could, cutting contaminated chunks from blocks of cheese, washing the fruit, and repackaging the good, or marginal, flour. In the end, our food stores were cut in half and some of what we had left remained tinged with a diesel smell.

When the sea quieted, we conducted Zodiac tests. Trueman timed the launch to see how quickly we could put three Zodiacs and crew on the water. Moore, Watson, and Korotva piloted the Zodiacs. Easton, Hunter, and I rode in the bows. We pounded across the waves and swerved in front of the *Phyllis Cormack*. Standing up in the bow of the Zodiac, holding on the bowline, it occurred to me to wrap the line around my waist and free up both hands. I had not been much of a Boy Scout, but at age twelve I did learn how to tie a bowline knot with one hand. Now, sixteen years later, this little manoeuvre proved helpful. With the line around my waist, I could lean back and use both hands to take photographs. Ron Precious and Fred Easton also adopted this method.

At 21:30 on the evening of June 20, Hewitt poked his head into the galley and asked, "Where's The George?" He had picked up what he thought were Russian voices. Korotva climbed to the radio room and listened. "Yawp," he said, "dere Russians." Korotva, however, could not tell if they were whalers or fishing fleets. He heard the name of a boat that sounded like "Voshtok." *Dalnyi Vostok* was on Spong's list of Soviet whalers. Hewitt got an RDF fix on the signal, to the south, and we headed for it.

The next day, we heard the Russians again. The plenary IWC meetings were to open the following day, and Hunter felt desperate to get into the news. He raised Rod Marining in Vancouver, and announced, "We're in the midst of Soviets." Moore and Trueman argued that this was a bit premature. "Kind of eliminates the element of surprise, Bob," argued Moore.

"I know. It's a calculated risk," admitted Hunter. "Rod says Spong is going nuts in London. He's promised the whale supporters a confrontation. We need to generate some news for London. If it turns out that we're nowhere near the whalers, fine. They'll think we still have no idea where to find them."

"Okay," shrugged Moore. The split between the mystics and the mechanics became prevalent, but it was a good-natured schism. Even with our charts, espionage, and electronics, we relied on providence and faith. That night, Cormack decided to test Hunter and the *I Ching*. He wedged himself in at the galley table, across from the journalist. "Mr. Hunter," he asked, "do you really believe in that hocus-pocus diddily-ocus book?"

"Yes, sir," said Hunter, "I do."

"Okay," said the skipper, "I want to ask: Are we gonna find these here Russians?" The entire crew, except for Hewitt on the wheel, crowded around. The skipper picked up Mel's Chinese coins and shook them in his huge hands with the two stubble fingers.

"All three coins," Walrus said. "Six times." Mel counted the values and recorded two strong yang lines followed by four broken yin lines, hexagram 19, *Approach*.

"Hmm," said the skipper.

Mel opened the book. "Approach" in the *I Ching* signifies a returning of the light. The strong lines at bottom approach a moment of influence. The strong approaches the weak. Mel interpreted this as the "righteousness of the mission approaching the weakness of the old mentality."

"I don't want your opinion," the skipper said, "I want to know what the book says. Are we gonna find these Russian whalers or not?"

Mel read the commentary. "Success is certain. But we must work with determination and perseverance to make full use of the propitiousness of the time." Then he paraphrased: "Says here, the superior person is inexhaustible, just as the earth is boundless in its tolerance and caring for all creatures."

"Hmm," the skipper shook his head.

"Well," said Hunter, "the book does say 'Success is certain,' so I guess the answer to your question is: Yes, we're going to find them."

"The *I Ching* isn't a fortune teller," said Mel. "It gives advice."

"Well if you want my advice," said the skipper, "you better keep listenin' on that radio."

That night, we arrived at the Cobb seamounts, the shallowest seamount in the North Pacific, rising to within five fathoms, 30 feet, of the surface. We heard Russian, Japanese, and Korean voices in every direction, so we hove-to under a gibbous moon, and waited for the morning light.

OVER THE HORIZON

On June 22, summer solstice, above the seamounts, we saw flashes of mysterious fish, sea turtles, and a lone blue shark. The albatross stayed with us. A shearwater flew by looking for refuse and then disappeared. In London, the IWC plenary meetings opened. We had five days to find the Soviet whalers.

Hewitt had devised simple radar reflectors for the Zodiacs so we could track the crews if they disappeared over the horizon during a confrontation with the whaling ships. Hunter, Mel Gregory, and I volunteered to take a Zodiac out to test the reflector. The truth is, all three of us wanted to experience floating in the middle of the ocean, beyond the sight of any other vessel.

We travelled southeast from the *Phyllis Cormack*, toward the morning sun, until the last trace of the boat's mast disappeared. I carried a compass, which I checked and then placed in the ammo case with my camera. After floating about in the open ocean for twenty minutes, fantasizing about being lost in a life raft, Hunter and I decided to take the experiment one step farther and go for a swim. We dove into the blue ocean, leaving Mel with the Zodiac. Having seen the shark earlier, I repeatedly dove below and looked through the sparkling ocean into the obscure depths, imagining that only thirty feet below me rose the peak of a mountain. As I surfaced from one of these dives, I saw Mel's head floating in the water beside me.

"Mel!" I screamed at him, "what are you doing?"

"Swimming," the musician replied. I saw Hunter surface, then I spun around and saw the empty inflatable, drifting with the light westerly breeze. I cursed Mel and swam off toward the Zodiac. Even in the light breeze, it moved briskly across the water. I submerged my head, pumped my arms, and focused my attention on pushing through the water. I turned to breathe every few strokes and stopped once to looked forward and gauge my progress. When I reached the inflatable, I swam alongside to measure its speed. Had the wind been blowing much faster we would have been stranded. I pulled myself in and rowed back toward Mel and Bob.

"That was dumb," I chastised Mel when I pulled him into the Zodiac. He shrugged. In this trio, I felt like the mechanic. We had been out of sight of the *Phyllis Cormack* for forty minutes. I checked the compass and we headed back northwest. I pondered whether the light Zodiac or the large boat would have drifted more with the wind and felt relieved once I could pick out the mast and sail.

On board, Hewitt located Russian voices to the south, so we headed in that direction. Hewitt wired a speaker into the galley, and once again we heard the name "Vostok," now to the southwest. We guessed the whaling fleet was moving eastward, toward the coast, so we travelled all night, running south under the full moon to intercept them over the Mendocino Ridge.

That night, Watson and Will Jackson argued. Watson claimed China had created an egalitarian society, and Jackson claimed that Mao Tse-tung was a mass murderer on the scale of Hitler. Korotva chimed in that he'd been in a Soviet prison camp. "Da Russians are foking devils," he said.

"Well, George," said Walrus, "you're biased. The Russian people themselves are no more devils than you or I."

Korotva feared that during a confrontation with the Soviets, our Zodiacs could be seized. If he were to be hauled aboard a Soviet ship, technically back in Soviet territory, he faced consequences that the rest of us could not contemplate. "You guys don't know shit about da Russians," he assured us.

Late that night, Hunter and Mel sat at the bow, a place of peace and quiet, where one could be alone with the sea. Anyone who spent long hours at the bow became known as a "bow case." Hamish had been the first. I sat down with them under the full moon. For a brief moment, earlier in the day, we had been shipmates lost at sea, and on the Zodiac I had felt like the captain, responsible to preserve their lives.

Walrus, Ron Precious, and Will Jackson arrived. Mel began to howl, then Jackson and the rest of us, indulging in sweet lunacy, invoking some ineffable force to intervene on our behalf. The months of strategy, espionage, fundraising, and the mechanics of running a boat seemed exhausted. We needed a miracle.

IONIC DISTURBANCE

On June 23, we were 300 nautical miles west of Coos Bay, Oregon. Walrus, Fred Easton and I worried about our leader, Hunter. He took liver pills for his health and Quaaludes to stay calm. He was short of cigarettes, not eating much, and rarely slept. Around the crew, he rallied his energy, made jokes, and tried to keep spirits up, but privately he deteriorated. Walrus had made him herbal tea and encouraged him to eat. But Hunter could not be comforted: If the Great Whale Conspiracy proved unsuccessful, the failure would be on him. Hamish, his Green Panther collaborator, had already flamed out. Would he be the next bow case?

That evening we reached Rod Marining on the radio, but he could barely hear us. Intermittently, we had experienced difficulties with the Northern sideband radio, and Al Hewitt had replaced the dynamometer. Once out of range of the coastal VHF radio, we relied on the sideband for communications. "We believe we're closing in on the Soviet fleet," Hunter reported to Marining.

"You're breaking up, Bob," Marining replied. "Can you repeat that?"

"We are *near* the *Russian ... fleet*," said Hunter, enunciating meticulously. "We believe we are near the factory ship, *Vostok*. Over." We waited.

"Are you talking about the Russian fleet? Are you with them?" We could hear Marining perfectly well. "Listen, Bob," he said, "If you can hear me: The Russians announced today that one of their whaling fleets will be dismantled next year. They said this was due to pressure from conservation groups. Do you copy that? Due to pressure from conservation groups! That's us. It's probably bullshit, of course, but it sounds like they are trying to diffuse the issue. Over."

"Roger, Rod, I can hear you. That's great. We think we are near the whalers now. Over."

Bobbi Innes came on the phone. "Bob, can you hear us?"

"Yes, I can hear you. Bobbi, can you take a press release? Over."

"Bob, I can barely hear you. Please repeat. Over."

Hunter keyed the handset with resolve, as if he could will the transmission to get through. "Bobbi, I can hear you fine, but if you can't hear me, we'll have to try again later." We heard no response. Bob spoke slowly and loudly. "Bobbi, Rod, I'll have to sign off. Radio is too poor for report. Call the *Sun*. Tell them I'll try again tomorrow. Copy that? Try tomorrow."

"I didn't get any of that," said Innes. "Did you say, tomorrow? We can't really hear you, Bob."

"I love you. We're signing off. *Phyllis Cormack* out."

Hunter hung his head in despair. Cormack and Hewitt stood by helplessly.

"The Russians could be jamming us," offered Walrus from the door of the radio room.

"It's atmospheric interference," said Hewitt. "It happens. Their signal gets through to us, but ours is whacked by electromagnetic disturbances in the ionosphere. It comes and goes."

None of this cheered up Hunter. The IWC was at the end of its second day of meetings. We had only occasional Russian voices to show for all our trouble, and now we could not even communicate with our own home office. "Shit," cursed Hunter and he dropped his head in his arms in front of the radio.

Later that night, I stood at the wheel on the flying bridge, with Carlie Trueman, when a mist settled around the boat. Hunter, Jackson, Walrus,

Mel, and Korotva gathered at the bow. Sometime after 01:00 on June 24, the sky glowed in the west, off our starboard beam. The strange radiance intensified, and we could see what looked like a long arching ray of light.

"What the heck is that?" asked Hunter.

Moore came out onto the bridge. Carlie pointed to the west. "A moon rainbow."

I stared in complete wonder. Moore said he had never seen the phenomenon before, but knew of no reason that moonlight couldn't generate a rainbow. The eerie light formed a small arc, but in shades of grey and silver. "That *has* to be auspicious," said Hunter. The mysterious light pulsated, growing weaker and stronger for about fifteen minutes, and then faded away entirely. We stood speechless at the gunwale, the decks awash in moonlight, and the yellow beam stretching out before us. "Okay," said Hunter. "Okay." He grabbed Will Jackson around the neck and rested his head on the musician's stout shoulder.

WOLVES GUARDING THE SHEEP

In Vancouver, Bobbi Innes and Rod Marining called marine operators attempting to reach the *Phyllis Cormack* and its crew. "What's wrong?" Innes asked, but the marine operators had no idea why the boat did not respond. Innes told inquiring reporters and worried families that the *Greenpeace V* was "somewhere on the whaling grounds."

Paul Spong called Marining from London, looking for news. "I think they're with the Russians," said Marining, "or close to them. That's all I know. The last radio contact was useless."

In London, Paul and Linda Spong, Joanna Gordon Clark from Friends of the Earth, and other environmentalists lobbied the delegates. The US, UK, Argentina, and Mexico again favoured a moratorium, but Japan, the Soviet Union, Norway, Iceland, Australia, Canada and new member Brazil backed the scientific committee claim that they were "managing the stocks responsibly." Spong pointed out to journalists that this was not true and handed out statistics showing the decline in the annual catch. The sperm whale catch in the North Pacific had dropped from some 15,000 whales to about 8,000 in five years.

Spong sought observer status at the scientific meetings, but IWC officers refused his request. At the Riverside House in southeast London, delegates and observers entered the security checkpoint with red and blue badges. Nearby, IWC delegates packed into the Anchor Pub for lunch. Spong sat with filmmaker Michael Chechik from Vancouver, producer of the documentary that Ron Precious and Fred Easton were filming on the Greenpeace boat. Chechik held a media pass, and had just interviewed Canadian commissioner Robert Martin about why Canada supported the whalers. "When I asked him if he thought whales might be intelligent," Chechik told Spong, "he refused to talk to me."

After lunch, when the delegates returned to the afternoon session, Spong sat dejected, plotting how he might get into the meetings. When he pulled his chair back, a flash of red on the floor caught his eye. Someone had lost a delegate's badge. Without hesitation, Spong put it on, walked to the Riverside House, and entered the meeting. There, the scientists carved up the remnants of the whales while two Japanese delegates napped through the entire proceeding. Although the shrinking quotas had not been reached in four years, the Scientific Committee approved a quota for 8,300 sperm whales to be taken from the North Pacific, and another 10,740 from the Southern Hemisphere.

"The whaling companies are clearly prepared to scour the oceans for the last of the whales," Spong complained to the media. "The wolves are guarding the sheep."

On June 24, Paul and Linda staged a Whale Show at the Lansdowne Club, an 18th-century townhouse near Piccadilly. Commission delegates, observers, environmentalists, and journalists attended. They had come from Japan, the Soviet Union, Spain, Canada, the United States, Argentina, Mexico, and Britain. Spong showed his films and slides. He recounted his observations of Skana in the aquarium and wild orcas in Blackfish Sound. "I moved from data collector and behaviour manipulator to participant and observer," he told the audience. "I interacted closely with the whales, to show them something of myself and my kind while I was learning about them. I came to respect the whales more and more. Eventually, my respect verged on awe. *Orcinus orca* is a powerful and capable creature, exquisitely self-controlled and aware of the world around it, a being possessed of a zest for life, a healthy sense of humour, and a remarkable fondness for, and interest in, humans. It is a tragedy that just as we are getting to know these creatures, we are wiping them out."

"Where's the boat?" guests wanted to know.

"Is there going to be a confrontation?"

"Have they found the whalers?"

"The Greenpeace boat is on the whaling grounds, near the whaling fleets," Spong reported. "Yes, they'll find the whalers and they will disrupt the hunt."

GHOST NETS

On the day of Spong's whale show, the *Phyllis Cormack*, just north of Mendocino Ridge, came upon a group of fin whales, with their telltale slick, black backs and small dorsal fins. These were among the last few fin whales in the North Pacific. The fins can reach 80 feet in length, but the populations had been decimated, and these adults were half that size. We saw a smaller whale that appeared to be a juvenile swimming with its mother. In the Zodiacs, we approached slowly from the side of the mother. The fin whales have an unusual asymmetrical colouring around their lower jaws, blue-grey on the left side and white on the right side, one of nature's mysterious anomalies.

Fred Easton and I now used the method of standing in the bow of the inflatable, with the bowline around our waists, hands free for the cameras. As we approached, the mother surfaced close to us, Korotva lurched the zodiac to a stop, and I tumbled over the bow with two cameras. Hunter attempted to pull me back into the boat, but he too fell out. Korotva hauled us both into the Zodiac. "Damn!" I cursed at having just doused a Leica and a Pentax in salt water. On board the *Phyllis Cormack* I tore the cameras apart and soaked the parts in fresh water, hoping to slow the corrosion from the salt, but in the end it was useless. The cameras and lenses were ruined. I was now down to two cameras and a few lenses, but Easton, Ron Precious, and I had discovered a final refinement of our technique: we extended the bowlines so we could lean back far enough that if we fell, we could slump into the boat.

The RDF readings indicated Russian transmissions to the southwest. Our own transmissions to Vancouver remained garbled. Hunter squeezed the transmitter until the veins on the back of his hand looked as if they would burst. Finally, he shrugged. Nature, it seemed, now conspired against us. As we headed toward the Russian signals, we reached Mendocino Ridge and observed garbage, plastic bottles, pieces of rope, and other gear. Near midday, we saw large boats on the horizon, raced into action, but soon discovered they were deep-sea trawlers, not whalers. We came upon the Soviet trawler *Armeniya*, the Polish *Taurus*, and two Korean ships, all rusting, 160-foot stern trawlers, rigged with drift nets. The floating factories bellowed smoke and left a trail of oil and rubbish.

Among these ships, a small American troller, the *Tilko*, fished for salmon with baited hooks. We launched a Zodiac, and the American skipper invited us aboard. He had not heard of Greenpeace and knew nothing of the whaling fleets, but he let us use his radio. Hunter broadcast a press release to Marining announcing, "We are in the midst of the whaling fleet. They are avoiding us. We have heard the killer boat *Charadinsky* and the factory ship *Vostok*, but now they are calling each other by number." Marining told us the IWC had declared that "Greenpeace is not an official non-governmental organization and will not be recognized by the Whaling Commission." We learned that Canada had voted with the Soviets and Japan to increase whale quotas. "The media in London are skeptical about Greenpeace," Marining said. "There are only two more days for the IWC."

"Yeah, we know, Rod," said Hunter.

The American fisherman told us, waving at the trawlers, "It's a bloody crime. We throw back the shakers and these guys strip mine everything that lives." By law, the trollers had to release any Chinook salmon under 26 inches while the huge trawlers hauled up everything. "They take seabirds, turtles, anything, and just dump it dead over the side." The factory trawlers used nylon nets up to 40 miles long and ensnared dolphins, porpoises, migrating seals, and whales. Although no exact figures had been compiled, it was estimated that some 100,000 marine mammals died each year in North Pacific fishing nets.

"They intercept the salmon on their way into the spawning streams," the fisherman told us. "All the trollers say their hauls are declining. We've raised bloody hell, but nothing happens. We're pushing for the 200-mile limit." The outcry from American fishermen supported the US government's desire for a 200-mile limit. The factory trawlers knew this and were taking everything they could from the continental shelf before the laws changed. Like the whalers, they had worked their way through preferred species, sent them into decline, turned to rockfish and flounder until those populations collapsed, and then went after pollock to grind up as generic seafood paste for fish sticks and imitation crab.

The fisherman told us that the huge drift nets sometimes broke loose and glided through the ocean. "They're called ghost nets. Our gear gets caught in them and so do the fish and dolphins." Hundreds of miles of net broke free every year, invisible death traps that drifted aimlessly until the weight of dead fish and mammals sank them to the bottom. "It's a disaster," lamented the fisherman, gazing at the rusting monsters. "When you guys get done with them whalers you should come and take care of these bastards."

"Yeah, all right," Hunter said. "We will." We didn't know what else to tell him, he looked so forlorn, trolling his lines through the water, pulling out one salmon at a time.

Back on the *Phyllis Cormack*, Paul Watson wanted to interfere with the factory trawlers right then and there, but we pushed west along Mendocino Ridge. Al Hewitt brought out his private stash of moonshine that night, and we drank the biting whisky as we listened to the radio and talked about ghost nets and trapped dolphins. "I get the feeling we're about thirty years too late," said Hunter, slouched in the corner of the galley.

"I don't think so," said Will Jackson. "The *Warriors of the Rainbow* prophecy says this wouldn't happen until the Earth was crying out. Maybe it takes the disaster before humans wake up."

"Yeah, 'spose so," mumbled Hunter.

We heard the Russians again at midnight, and Hewitt located the signal to the southwest. Mel took the wheel at 02:00. The skipper set the heading and went to his quarters for a nap.

THIS IS IT

That night, given our southwest heading, the moon, three days past full, was directly before us. Mel steered down the silver path of moonlight. All night, he followed the moonbeam. However, as every sailor knows, or should know, the moon moves. As the moon arched across the sky to the west, Mel inadvertently veered the boat westward. When the skipper awoke at 05:00 he noticed the sky growing light to the stern and glanced at the compass. "What the hell are you doing?" he asked Mel.

"Just finishing up my shift, Captain," said the musician cheerfully.

"You're 90 degrees off course."

"Huh?"

"Hippie farmer!" Cormack bellowed. He grabbed Mel by the hair and the back of the shirt and threw him out of the wheelhouse.

"Skipper's in a crotchety mood," Mel announced in the galley, and then went to his bunk to sleep.

The wind intensified and the sea heaped up into whitecaps. It was Thursday, June 26. In 48 hours the Whaling Commission meetings would be over. When Hewitt heard about the steering error, he dialed through the frequencies until he heard the Russian voices, and locked onto them. The transmissions now came from the *north*west, as if the Russians had slipped past us. "Maybe Mel was onto something," muttered Will Jackson. We turned northwest, roughly the direction Mel had been heading by following the setting moon.

We could raise no one on the radio all day. Hunter was out of cigarettes and Will Jackson was down to the last dusty bits of rolling tobacco. Walrus made pancakes with the remnants of the flour, but they had a distinct diesel taste. Hunter had taken off his Peruvian cap and was too depressed to consult the *I Ching*, so after breakfast, I took up the coins, hoping some auspicious counsel might cheer everyone up. Mel flipped open his journal to record the hexagram.

Chien. Wind over the Mountain.

"The mountains are the seamounts," said Mel, "and the wind —"

"Shut up," said Will Jackson. "Read it, Rex."

According to the book, the trigram "Wind" indicates "the gentle" and "wood," thus the image of a tree on a mountain. Although a tree develops slowly on a mountain, it stands firmly. Tranquility and gentleness on the inside, was the message, but firmness and perseverance on the outside. "The work of influencing people can only be gradual," the oracle warned. "No sudden influence or awakening is of lasting effect." We lodged this humbling thought. Perhaps we *weren't* going to find the whaling fleets. Maybe we should brace for a battle over years.

We sat quietly and rocked in the mounting breeze. The skipper came into the galley and surveyed his crew. "Storm," he said. "Will. George." He turned and walked out onto the deck trailed by Will Jackson and

Korotva. I followed. Watson and Carlie Trueman stood ready on the deck. We lowered the stabilizer poles as the wind whipped up spray. We were 100 miles from the coast, over the top of Mendocino Ridge, heading northwest. The storm intensified to a full gale, blowing dense foam across the deck and limiting visibility. Walrus climbed high in the rigging. We heard a loud crack, like a gun going off, as one of the stabilizer poles snapped in a squall and flopped over in the waves.

The broken piece now flew wildly, still attached, slamming into the hull. Korotva climbed out on the pole in the shrieking wind, grabbed a line to the broken piece, and crawled back on deck so we could retrieve it. His daring act had the effect of snapping us out of our gloom. With the pole safely on deck, Walrus brought out the last rum that he had stashed in the galley, and we toasted The George and his bravery. Will Jackson, inspired by The George, swung out over the raging sea from a line attached to the mast. Hunter took a turn swinging out over the water, then Watson. The George, Will, and Pat Moore broke into an a cappella rendition of the Whale Anthem. The mood shifted. The game was not lost. We had a radio read on the whalers and the *Phyllis Cormack* plunged on, though rocking mercilessly without the stabilizer. Walrus clung like a warrior to the mast. Hunter tried the radio again, but when it didn't work, he shrugged and ambled back to the wheelhouse.

As the sun went down, Russian voices indicated they were now to the northeast, behind us. Cormack and Hewitt huddled over the RDF. Hewitt switched it off and back on. The needle leapt back to the northeast and stayed there. "Northeast," said Hewitt.

Carlie Trueman stood at the wheel as the skipper entered. "Swing 'er round, there, Carlie,"

"Huh?"

"East-northeast," said Cormack.

"What's up, John?" Carlie asked.

"They're behind us."

I took my usual wheel duties at 04:00 and watched the sun come up at 04:40, June 27, the last day of the IWC meeting in London. The gale had blown through, the sky grew clear, and the ocean quieted. We got a strong RDF signal at about 10:00, still east-northeast, then the Russian broadcasts stopped. Cormack took another short nap, Mel spotted a rainbow to the southeast, took the wheel from Ron Precious, and he turned toward the sign on the horizon. After about twenty minutes, Moore arrived in the wheelhouse and looked at the compass. "Who changed the heading?" he grilled the musician.

Mel shrugged. Moore shoved him from the wheel, and put us back on a heading northeast, slightly north to make up for Mel's digression. At midday, Walrus climbed back up the mast. I stood on the flying bridge with Mel, Trueman, Easton, Precious, and Will Jackson.

Black dots appeared in the distance. We squinted and shielded our eyes. Eight small dots and one larger smudge sat like pencil marks on the silvery eastern horizon. Moore went into the captain's quarters and lifted the skipper's binoculars from a hook. John got up and came out to the bridge. "Draggers," he said.

"It's the whalers," said Mel.

Moore peered through the binoculars. "Holy shit," he said, and we turned to him. "There's one big boat and a bunch of small ones. On the smaller boats I can see the catwalk from the bridge to the bow." The catwalk was the harpooner's access to the cannon mount at the bow. "Those are whaling ships," said Moore. "That's a factory ship. This is it."

LEVIATHAN SUBJUGATED

Below, I put on my wetsuit and gathered camera gear. Fred Easton checked his power pack and 16-mm Bolex. Ron Precious loaded film into his sound-synch Éclair. Fred confided to me that they were almost out of film stock. The entire documentary budget, $15,000, had been used for film stock and equipment, but Easton was down to eight 100-foot rolls of film. "I've got about twenty minutes left," he said.

On the bridge, through my long lens, I could see the telltale catwalk and the harpoon guns mounted over the bow. Carlie Trueman hoisted the UN flag, to fly with the Canadian Maple Leaf, the Earth flag, the Buddhist prayer flags, the green-on-yellow Greenpeace flag, and the Kwakiutl emblem on the sail. She then went to the stern with The George and prepared the Zodiacs and outboard engines. Walrus searched the horizon with binoculars. Mel Gregory set up the sound equipment on the quarterdeck.

Captain Cormack stood at the radio. "They're hunting whales," he said, pointing out that the ships frequently changed direction. Hunter,

Moore, and Watson wore wetsuits on the flying bridge. Hunter spoke into the microphone of his tape recorder, the Peruvian hat back on his head. "June 27, 1975. The *Greenpeace V* is 40 miles west of California over Mendocino Ridge. We see what we believe is a Soviet factory ship and eight killer boats."

From our vantage on the flying bridge, the boats near the horizon were about three or four miles away. At nine knots, nine nautical miles per hour, we could close that distance in twenty minutes, but the fleet moved the same direction, northeast, and we could not tell how fast they travelled. After half an hour, we could make out the smokestack, windows, and other features of the nearest harpoon boat, perhaps two miles away.

Then we felt the boat turn. From the wheelhouse, Cormack pointed off the bow, where we could just make out a tiny red flag in the water. As we approached, we could see what looked like an antenna or light beacon. Little waves broke over a rippling grey form. "A whale," called out Watson.

We saw the underslung lower jaw, gaping open in the surf, exposing the pink tongue. "Sperm whale," said Moore. It had been sixty days since we left Jericho Beach. We had viewed over 250,000 square miles of ocean and this was the first sperm whale we had seen. Blood poured from a wound in the whale's flaccid skin and from its mouth. But this was no 70-foot giant. The whale looked no bigger than a small orca. "It's a baby," said Carlie.

"It's undersized, for sure," said Watson. The IWC had established a 30-foot minimum size for sperm whales taken by the whalers. This, the first dead whale we saw, looked to be in violation of that restriction.

Watson offered to crawl out onto the whale so we could gauge its length against his body. I scrambled into a Zodiac with Watson, The George, and Fred Easton. We pulled alongside the carcass, and Watson climbed on. Cormack steered the *Phyllis Cormack* behind Watson, to get into the picture. Over his wetsuit, Watson wore a Greenpeace T-shirt with the Kwakiutl whale image on the front. He hunched in bare feet and rubbed the whale with his hand. "It's still warm," he shouted. I took photographs. A fluke stuck up through the water, and we could make out the entire length to the submerged head. Watson was just under six feet tall. The whale was no more than four times this, 24 feet long, clearly under the IWC limit. We knew Japanese observers accompanied the Russian boats, but they didn't appear to be enforcing the rules. We had been certain that the IWC Scientific Committee was a travesty; here was the proof.

"Get back in the Zodiac," Hunter yelled from the *Phyllis Cormack*. Hunter and Trueman pointed to a harpoon boat, a mile away, smoke bellowing from the stack as it charged toward us. Watson balked, prepared to stand his ground, but Hunter and the others screamed at him. "Watson!" Hunter yelled again. "Get back in the Zodiac." Within a few minutes, the harpoon boat had closed on us. A severe-looking man stood at the bow, beside the harpoon gun, with a large hose, apparently ready to blast Watson from the whale and perhaps to strike the Zodiac. We pulled up beside Watson, hauled him in, and made for the *Phyllis Cormack*. "It's not time yet, Paul," Hunter explained. "Wait for it."

"Perseverance furthers," said Carlie Trueman.

The harpoon boat swung menacingly across our bow. We had no way of knowing how much these sailors knew about us, or what they thought. The officers on the bridge glared with naked malice, but below, on the decks, workers smiled, joked among themselves, and even risked waving. The officers probably knew exactly who we were. The working stiffs looked more like us: scruffy, young, and curious.

As the whalers pulled up to the carcass, I took photographs from the *Phyllis Cormack*. The whale rolled over in the water, showing its flukes and fins, just as the steel bow of the harpoon boat rose above it. Through my lens, I saw a picture we had had in our minds for a year or more: the harpoon gun, poised like a deadly missile above the whale carcass. I made three quick exposures. I looked up and saw Hunter staring at me. I nodded and he clinched his fist, a look of determination on his face. The whalers lashed the whale to the metal gunwales by its flukes, turned, and roared off toward the factory ship in the distance. We followed.

On the bridge of the *Phyllis Cormack*, Carlie Trueman's face grew red with outrage and mourning. "This isn't right," she muttered, fingers gripping the wheel.

"The mystics are gaining allies," Hunter whispered to me.

VOSTOK

Printed on the bow of the 160-foot steel harpoon boat, we could read the name, СВЕРНЛЫЙ, but Korotva shrugged when we asked him what it meant. The registration number on the side read ЛК-2052. The hull appeared to be a rusting hulk like the trawlers. The Soviets clearly avoided spending resources on superficial maintenance. The harpoon boat pulled away at close to twice our speed. Other harpoon boats moved about us in every direction, but we stayed with our escort toward the factory ship, the den mother for this brood of hunting dogs that ranged above the seamounts.

The monster factory ship dwarfed the harpoon boats. The *Vostok* rose some 40 feet above the waterline to a main deck, then another 20 feet to two upper decks. Laundry hung to dry from windows, and workers milled about and stared from open metal doors. Above the top deck rose smokestacks, radar antennae, satellite dishes, and an array of electronic gear. The ship skulked steadily forward at about four knots.

Astern of the *Vostok*, we launched two Zodiacs. Fred Easton, with his camera, rode with Pat Moore. I rode with Watson and Korotva. The Zodiacs were capable of 20 knots, but we approached cautiously, at half throttle. The ocean remained as calm as we had yet seen it. Hardly a light air passed over the ripples. Easton stood in the bow of the inflatable before me, bowline around his waist, camera at his eye.

Easton loaded a 100-foot roll of film, normally representing two-and-a-half minutes of filming time, but since he was shooting in slow motion, the roll only gave him 75 seconds. To conserve film, he had to wait for decisive moments. The scene we now approached was far more surreal and haunting than anything we had, or could have, imagined.

The industrial slaughter of the great cetaceans loomed before us. Two harpoon boats flanked the towering *Vostok*, off-loading dead sperm whales. Reddish-purple rivulets of blood trailed behind the ships. Shark fins cut through the burgundy water. A dark cavern opened at the stern of the factory ship and rose to the flencing deck. Two grey sperm whale carcasses were simultaneously hauled up this slip by their flukes, heads flopping and jaws gaping open. Above the slipway, Cyrillic script spelled out *Dalnyi Vostok*. Our escort, ЛК-2052, transferred the undersized whale to the factory ship, where it looked like a rubbery toy jerked ingloriously into the cavern.

On board the second harpoon boat, ЛК-2035, sailors waved. A small crowd of workers gathered. "Where you from?" a sailor called in English. "Canadinksi," said Korotva. Brawny sailors rolled cigarettes, laughed among themselves, pointed at us, and furtively glanced over their shoulders toward the bridge. They, of course, saw an image that was the absolute reversal of what we saw. To them, the *Phyllis Cormack* — painted white and aqua-blue, with red eyes on the flying bridge, and colourful flags arrayed in the rigging — looked like a psychedelic carnival, complete with rock musicians and barefoot jugglers.

We, on the other hand, rode over entrails and blood, through the stench and discharged offal of a floating slaughterhouse. Watson pulled around a harpoon boat and raced along the beam of the giant *Dalniy Vostok*. Idle workers and sailors stared. A volleyball game on the upper deck ceased as the players leaned against the netting to watch. Working women among the crew took pictures and waved. On the flencing deck, huge cranes ripped enormous strips of pink meat and sallow blubber from the whales. About two feet above the waterline a stream of blood poured from a six-inch pipe into the sea. I gagged from the stench.

We returned to the *Phyllis Cormack* as it pulled alongside the *Vostok*. Hoots and waves issued from the Russian crew. Fred Easton reloaded his camera. Mel Gregory and Will Jackson launched into a new song Mel had written about searching the empty seas for the last of the whales.

I declare,
We've been searching, but there's no one there …

The ballad segued into an upbeat refrain that Mel had written to sound like a Cossack folk dance with lots of shouting "Oh! Hey!" and balalaika-like guitar riffs.

Oh! Say! Just what are you doing
Killing the whales? Hey!
Does your mom know what you're doing
Killing the whales? Hey!
Does your child know what you're doing
If they did, you know, you'd
Hear them sing this song. Hey!

Whether or not it sounded like Russian music to our pelagic audience, they lined the railings of the *Vostok* to listen. Men and women danced almost involuntarily. A shy woman in a white head-wrap and what looked like a white food service uniform waved demurely from a rusting metal doorway. "Paul!" said Korotva. "I think she's flirting with you."

"Who?" said Watson, spinning his head.

Mel's song changed into eerie whale sounds created by Will Jackson on the synthesizer. The portside railings on every deck on the *Vostok* were jammed with Russians: common labourers, officers, and the Japanese observer watching discreetly from the rear. The bosses behind the glass in the wheelhouse wore long coats and fur hats with brass badges, but the moilers, machinists, flencers, and packers wore khaki work shirts, oily sweaters, and scruffy caps.

Mel ended his song and played tapes of the humpback whales. There could have been little doubt, even to the Russian workers who had never heard such a thing, what they were hearing. While the haunting whale sounds filled the Pacific air, George Korotva delivered a brief message. The George was visibly nervous about this. He held up a sheet of paper with his lines written out. In Russian, he told them: "We are Greenpeace. We are Canadians! We represent people from all over the world who want you to stop killing the whales." This last line, "stop killing the whales," he repeated several times in his faltering Russian. Several of the gruff-looking types on the afterdeck began to jeer, possibly as much at the Slovakian accent as the message.

George shrugged. "I told them to stop killing d' whales," he said. "They told me to get fokked."

"You did fine, George," Hunter said.

Mel and Will Jackson struck up a fresh improvisation. A harpoon boat, *Vlasny*, completed off-loading whales and headed back out for more. We followed with guitar and synthesizer blaring.

THE VLASNY

The *Vlasny*, boat number ЛК-2007, travelled at about 15 knots. Two miles ahead of us, the harpoon boat abruptly turned, and two other harpoon boats moved in unison. "They're lookin' fer whales," Cormack said. The harpoon boats possessed powerful sonar, allowing them to follow whales hundreds of fathoms below. When the whales surfaced to breathe,

the harpoon boats would be on top of them. Usually, a sperm whale breathes every fifteen minutes and stays on the surface for about ten to fifteen breaths. This pattern is based on the needs of the young whales. Long ago, whalers learned a rule of thumb, that for every foot of its length, a sperm whale breathes about once at the surface and spends about one minute underwater between dives. Therefore, a 15-foot infant will generally breathe about fifteen times and stay under for fifteen minutes. The adults simply accommodate the young whales, although they can, if they choose, remain below for hours.

However, frantic whales chased by harpoon boats dive immediately after breathing and eventually become exhausted. At this point in the chase — with the whales trapped on the surface, infants in the middle, flanked by females and then by the larger males — the whalers open fire with impunity. Like the shore whalers of old, they sometimes harpoon an infant to incite the adults. Males often turn to defend wounded females. These tactics allow the whalers to then pick off the protectors with ease. They attach beacons to the dead whales, like the first whale we saw, and move after the others.

Captain Cormack followed the *Vlasny* as it zigzagged before us. The Zodiac crews stood ready. Easton cleaned his camera as best he could. Eight weeks of salt air had eaten away at the delicate gears and electronic connections. Intermittently, the camera had failed to respond to the trigger. Hunter slipped out of sight, behind Al Hewitt's trailer on the aft deck, to meditate. There, alone, just to cover all spiritual possibilities, he prayed. On his knees, Hunter summoned a reservoir of supplications from his childhood catechism at the Church of St. Boniface in Winnipeg. "Dear Lord," he beseeched the Catholic deity, "whoever, whatever you are, if we are worthy, please help us."

By six o'clock, the sea had picked up a light chop from a southerly breeze. Walrus shrieked and pointed from the mast. Whale blows rose from the water in front of the *Vlasny* two miles ahead. With the harpooner over top of them, the whales dove again. To our surprise and elation, the harpoon boat turned back, toward us. Presumably, the frantic sperm whales had turned underwater and now led the whalers right at us. When they were about a half mile away, Hunter said, "Okay, this is it. Zodiacs."

Captain Cormack slowed the *Greenpeace V* to a crawl. Hunter and Watson, whose job it was to get between the harpooner and the whale, took off in the first Zodiac. Hunter stood in the bow in his Peruvian cap, with the red cloth from the Gyalwa Karmapa safely in the leather pouch around his neck. Watson, in his Kwakiutl T-shirt, gunned the throttle. Around his head he wore a white bandana, with the loose ends snapping in the wind.

Patrick Moore and Fred Easton followed. Easton had loaded a fresh roll, and was now down to ten minutes of film. He tested the camera and it failed. Then he tried the trigger again and it worked. "Shit," he mumbled to himself.

Korotva and I climbed into the third Zodiac. We pushed away, but the outboard engine knocked and coughed. Korotva paddled back toward the *Phyllis Cormack* and stood at the ladder shouting for the spare engine. Will Jackson jumped into the hold and single-handedly hoisted the 200-pound engine through the hatch. Carlie and Mel hauled it onto the deck. Korotva, in the meantime, had removed the faulty engine from the inflatable and handed it up to Al Hewitt. Jackson and Trueman lifted the spare engine down to Korotva. He locked it in place, hooked up the fuel line, started it with one pull, and sped after the others.

Hunter and Watson pulled abeam of the *Vlasny* as the frantic, exhausted whales rose before the gun. The harpooner sighted down the barrel and swung the green steel cannon from side to side, the explosive harpoon trained on his prey. Easton and I stood in our respective Zodiacs, as we beat against the waves. Easton tucked his camera inside his coat to keep off the salt spray.

Abruptly, Watson lunged his Zodiac in front of the *Vlasny*. Hunter stood and gripped the bowline in his hand. Watson held open the throttle as Hunter bounced into the air then slumped to his knees in the Zodiac. Looking past Watson's shoulder, Hunter saw the eyes of the harpooner. Then, the steel bow rose and slashed down behind them. Watson struggled in the bow wave, attempting to get closer to the fleeing whales.

The ocean churned as the great grey backs of the whales rose and their large, square heads breached for air. A strange characteristic of the sperm whale is that, unlike any other whale, the blowhole is skewed to the left side of the head, giving it an awkward look as it gasps for breath. The smaller, young whales pressed toward the middle of the group. They beat the surface, attempting to catch enough breath to dive from the threat, but they were helpless. Little rainbows appeared in the mist of each whale's breath.

Korotva and Moore throttled forward to keep up with the chase, but I could see that Easton was in trouble. The Bolex had finally seized from weeks of exposure to the salt air. Easton cursed and jiggled the electrical connections to the battery pack.

Hunter, from his crouched position, watched the harpooner. An officer on the *Vlasny* ran from the bridge to the harpoon mount, spoke some hurried words to the harpooner, and scrambled back up the metal catwalk. The harpooner stepped away from his weapon. My god, I thought, he's been ordered not to fire. We've stopped them.

Then Watson's Zodiac faltered and the bow of the harpoon boat sliced toward them. I expected them to be crushed, but the bow wave pushed the Zodiac aside. Watson tore at the starter rope. Hunter screamed for us to come toward them. The whales sounded with a flash of ten or twelve flukes, and disappeared. For a moment, all was still.

BULL'S EYE

Korotva and Moore steered in beside Watson's crippled boat, and Hunter leapt into our Zodiac. "Damn, Hunter," Easton shrieked, waving his camera. "I'm not running. Fucking thing is dead."

"Doesn't work at all?" Hunter said, his face dropping.

"It's intermittent, Bob, I can't rely on it. Something's wrong with the battery pack."

"Rex?" said Hunter.

"I'm fine," I said.

"Rex," said Hunter, "get in with Pat. Fred, you stay with Watson. See if you can get your camera going while Paul figures out this engine."

We assumed the exhausted whales would not be down long. Korotva and Hunter took off toward the harpoon boat. When the whales surfaced, the harpoon boat cruised above them once again. Hunter and Korotva raced in front of the harpooner, shielding the whales. Hunter looked at the fleeing whales then back up at the harpooner. He tried to stand, but was bounced again to his knees.

Moore kept pace to the side, closer to the whales, from where I trained my camera on Korotva and Hunter. In the meantime, Watson discovered that the fuel tank had bounced onto the rubber fuel line. He freed the line and the engine started, but Easton's camera still would not work. They returned to the *Phyllis Cormack*, Easton switched battery packs, and they rejoined the pursuit. Easton stood in the bow and aimed his camera at Hunter and Korotva.

Even from a short distance away, it proved extremely difficult to hold Korotva's bouncing Zodiac, the whales, and the harpoon boat in the frame of the camera. Easton and I were attempting to film three moving targets from a moving platform, with the sea tossing us around indiscriminately. We had been in the Zodiacs for almost an hour, but did not notice our own exhaustion, pumped as we were with adrenaline.

The officer who had previously instructed the harpooner returned down the catwalk, this time walking leisurely. He talked to the gunner and returned to the bridge. The harpooner swung the cannon around toward the whales. From Hunter's vantage in the Zodiac, he could see the man's eyes. "George," he screamed above the engines, "get ready." Korotva looked forward to where the whales churned the water. The Zodiac rose up on the crest of a wave, and Korotva could clearly see the whales ahead of them. As they dropped into the trough of the wave, Korotva saw Hunter's face turn ashen.

In the Zodiac with Watson, Easton squeezed the trigger of the Bolex and, miraculously, the gears hummed and the film fed through. "Yes," he said to himself. Through the eyepiece, he could see the *Vlasny* but the Zodiac had disappeared.

The explosion of the harpoon cannon was so loud and startling that I jerked my hand and banged the camera into my forehead. Moore shouted. Korotva, whose back was to the harpooner, instinctively ducked. Hunter froze. Easton held his camera steady, and panned forward to the whales.

The harpoon hit a small female sperm whale and exploded in her back. The cable slashed down through the air, just missing Hunter and Korotva. The wounded whale lunged and the harpoon cable sprung taut from the water, again just missing the Zodiac. Korotva gunned the outboard engine, turned, and carried himself and Hunter away from the slashing cable. Blood and froth spewed from the ocean. Massive flukes whipped up waves.

On board the *Vlasny*, a winch turned, drawing the doomed female toward the steel hull of the killer boat. True to the whalers' expectation, a bull turned, charged, and snapped desperately at the bow. The gunner stood ready and fired a second harpoon into the enraged bull's head. More blood and spray issued from the churning sea.

"Bastards!" shrieked Hunter. He turned to Easton and shouted, "What did you get?"

"I think I got it," the fatigued cameraman said, almost emotionless.

"Let's get outta here," Hunter screamed to Moore and Watson. "Back to the boat! Back to the *Phyllis Cormack*! Everybody."

Watson wanted to go back into the fray, but the dying bull sperm whale heaved in a fury of blood and foam in front of the *Vlasny*.

"No, Paul," urged Hunter. "That's it. Back. Take Fred back."

Korotva and Hunter headed to the *Phyllis Cormack*, but Watson turned toward the *Vlasny*. "Wait," I said to Moore, and we stayed. Easton instinctively raised the camera to his eye. A harpoon was imbedded in the bull, but with no cable attached. The bull turned and struggled toward the tiny Zodiac. Although it had viciously attacked the harpoon boat, the wounded whale did not threaten the Zodiac. The bull came alongside, close enough for Easton to touch it. A stream of purple-red blood spread out into the blue water. Although a sperm whale eye is relatively small among whales, it looked huge to Easton as the dying bull lifted a lid and looked at him.

Korotva came back for us alone. "Captain's orders," he said. "Back to the boat."

GLOBAL VILLAGE

On the deck of the *Phyllis Cormack*, the crew traded versions of the story. Hunter, usually the most eloquent raconteur, remained silent, listening to Fred Easton and Ron Precious talk.

"I think I got it," said Fred.

"Did the camera come on?" said Ron. "Could you hear it?"

"I think so," said Fred

"They turned and came right at us," Moore said. "The whales!"

"They knew," said Mel.

"That bull didn't even snap at us," said Watson.

The usually quiet Fred Easton turned from his conversation with Ron Precious and Hunter. "He didn't attack us," said the cameraman. "He swam to us like a wounded puppy. He just lay there. How did he know we weren't whalers? His eye was as big as my head. I swear. He just looked at me."

"Fucking bastards," said Carlie Trueman.

Easton turned back to Ron Precious and Hunter, "Eighty feet of film ran through the camera, Bob. It's hard to know exactly what we got. I definitely had the camera running on you and panned to the whales. But you kept coming in and out from behind the waves. I think I was running when the harpoon went off. The camera had not run for half an hour. I changed the battery. It came on, Bob. I think I got it."

"Skipper, will you try the radio?"

"Yup." Cormack disappeared into the wheelhouse.

Hunter retrieved his typewriter from the engine room and typed his story at the galley table. Walrus related how, from the mast, he had watched eight whales get away. The *Vlasny* killed two, but they lashed them to the boat right away and made for the *Vostok*.

"Yeah, I counted them too," said Mel. "We saved eight whales, Bob."

Hunter wrote it down.

Above us, from the radio room, we heard the skipper's voice. "Hello Vancouver. Hello Vancouver. gzcegzcegzcegzcegzcegzce. Vancouver. gzce. Vancouver, this is the *Phyllis Cormack*."

Hunter cocked his head. From above, the skipper thumped the floor with his boot. Boom. Boom. Hewitt appeared in the galley door.

"He's through," Hewitt said.

Hunter ripped his work in progress from the typewriter and bolted outside, up to the wheelhouse, and into the radio room. We crowded in. Bobbi Innes was on the line as clearly as if she were standing before us. Another miracle. We could hear Marining with her. Hunter took the transmitter and read, "Mendocino Ridge, 40 miles off the coast of California, Friday, July 27, 1975: We're on the *Phyllis Cormack*. We call the boat *Greenpeace V*. Today we saved eight whales. Are you picking this up, Bobbi? Over."

"Yeah, Bob, we hear you."

"Go ahead, Bob," Marining yelled in the background as he taped the conversation

"We saved *eight* whales. The soviet whalers fired an exploding harpoon over the heads of two Greenpeace protestors, Czechoslovakian seaman George Korotva and journalist Robert Hunter. They killed two whales. Eight escaped. In London today, the Japanese and Soviet whalers are plotting to hunt the last of the great whales. The first sperm whale we saw, after two months at sea, was dead. Significantly, it was under the legal limit set by the International Whaling Commission." Hunter dropped his yellow sheet of paper, which wafted to the floor. He recounted the rest of the story, the whales swimming toward us, the death of the female and the bull, the blood, and the frenzied whales.

"My god, Bob," said Bobbi Innes. "Is everyone okay?"

"Physically? Yeah."

After they signed off, Marining sent the story to the wire services in Vancouver, and Innes phoned Paul Spong in London. "The Russians shot a harpoon over Bob and George," she told him. "Nearly killed them. Eight whales got away. They have evidence of at least one, probably two undersized whales killed. They are with the factory ship *Vostok*."

Spong looked at his list. "Which *Vostok*?"

"I don't know, they… "

"The *Vladivostok* or the *Dalnyi Vostok*?"

"Oh, the *Dalnyi Vostok*."

After talking to Innes and Marining, Spong phoned the media in London. The next morning, June 28, the London newspapers carried headlines and stories about the confrontation. Journalists swarmed the Japanese and Soviet IWC delegates in their hotel lobbies. Paul and Linda held a press conference and attacked the ignominy of the IWC Scientific Committee presiding over the slaughter of the last whales and looking the other way when their own rules were violated.

International correspondents recorded everything they said on portable tape machines and in wildly flipped notebooks. The correspondents ran to pay phones. Editors in Hong Kong, Sydney, Auckland, San Francisco, and Madrid searched the wires for news and sent marked-up copy to typesetters. News cycled back through Vancouver, where Innes and Marining gave telephone interviews to international reporters. Charles Flowers, the *New York Times* reporter we had met in Winter Harbour, called Marining looking for photographs.

"You've done it now," Flowers bellowed. "You're heroes."

Amy Ephron, a film agent at Artist Entertainment Complex in Manhattan, received a call from her boss, high-profile producer Martin Bregman. "Find out who these people are," Bregman told her. "Find out where they are, and when they're coming in. Meet them when they get into port."

It did not take Ephron long to track down Rod Marining in Vancouver, where he, Bobbi Innes, and Eileen Chivers made arrangements to head for San Francisco to meet the boat.

HALF MOON BAY

Through the night and into the morning of June 28, the *Phyllis Cormack* followed the whaling fleet south. As the sun rose, near the end of my watch, the clouds to the east, over the coast, formed an uncanny image of a great white sperm whale head, with eye, lower jaw, and fins. Walrus and I stared at it from the wheelhouse door. It rose up from the clouds as if it were leaping from the water. A trail of smoke bellowed from the whale and the horizon below burned a fiery red.

The harpoon boats followed the factory ship, none of them hunting whales. We pulled abeam of the *Vostok*, travelling at about 6 knots, but the Russian crew had turned surly. The few who waved were aloof. Harpoon boats came and went from the stern of the factory ship, but transferred no whales. Whenever we followed the harpoon boats, they returned to the *Vostok*. On the *Phyllis Cormack*, the mood remained somber. Ron Precious and Fred Easton talked between themselves, anxious about what they might have captured on film. I assured Hunter that I had images of the dead whale under the harpoon gun and one of the Zodiac in front of the *Vlasny*. "We've got pictures for the wires," I promised him. Hunter took some comfort in this, though his expression remained strained.

Late in the afternoon, we came upon a dead whale with a beacon attached. Hunter vowed to sit on the whale when the whalers returned to collect it. "They'll either have to dump me in the water, or take me prisoner," he swore. We sat on the hatch cover and waited. Hunter fingered his leather pouch.

By dark, the Soviet whalers had not returned for the whale. Hewitt still had the fleet on the RDF. "They're moving southeast," he said.

"We should destroy the radio beacon on the whale," Watson suggested.

"That's destruction of property," said Cormack.

"Render unto Caesar," said Hunter, and that was the end of it. We left the dead whale and proceeded south after the factory ship.

Caught up in the previous day's events, we had forgotten about the whalebone that Hunter had nailed to the mast on the quarterdeck two months earlier. Korotva gave Hunter an enormous Cuban cigar, which he in turn presented to Moore in a ceremony as the award for sighting the Soviet fleet. Mel whispered to me that *he* had been the first one, but he didn't press his case. No one remembered the whalebone, as if the symbol of our resolve had itself fused with the vessel. In Herman Melville's story, Ahab remarked that to each member of the crew the gold coin "but mirrors back his own mysterious self." The whalebone remained on the mast above the quarter-deck, just as the doubloon had remained unclaimed on the *Pequod.*

By dawn we were three miles behind the whaling fleet on the southern horizon. At midday, the *Vostok* accelerated to about 12 knots, just enough to steadily pull away from us. Mel set up the sound system and we performed a concert for ourselves. We sang Mel's whale songs, the Beatles' "Don't Pass Me By" and Bob Dylan's "I Shall Be Released." Mel led a medley of bluegrass tunes that segued into sea shanties.

Ooo-ray, and up she rises
Early in the morning.

By dusk, we were 150 miles south of Mendocino Ridge. We had just enough fuel to make San Francisco, so we turned northwest, and by nightfall the Soviet vessels' lights passed out of sight. Walrus had stashed some food, and he surprised us with shepherd's pie and blueberry pie. Before daybreak, we could see the glow of San Francisco.

The radio reception remained clear, and I talked to my wife, Glenn, and to a Canadian Press photographer in Vancouver, who put me in contact with his UPI affiliate in San Francisco. Hunter got on the radio with Gary Zimmerman at the Oceanic Society and made arrangements to arrive at Pier 23 in San Francisco the following morning at 11:00. "You'll call all the media?" Hunter asked.

"Don't worry, Bob, they'll be there."

That evening, we reached landfall at Pescadero, saw a spotted harbour seal, and made our way north to Half Moon Bay, where Cormack was familiar with the anchorage. Word about the encounter had gone out among the fishermen, and as we moved slowly among the boats, fishermen on the decks cheered and raised their fists in the air. The reception caught us by surprise. It was all we could do to wave back. We had not cleared Customs, so we could not go ashore or board the other boats. However, once we anchored, fishermen motored by and greeted us. They knew all about our visit on the troller *Tilko* and our promise to go after the deep-sea draggers. They complained of the coho salmon disappearing and the need for a 200-mile fishing limit. Cormack stood at the gunwales and talked with his peers, the hero of Half Moon Bay that night.

As always, Cormack stayed awake at anchor. At dawn on July 1, we slipped from behind the breakwater, rounded Pillar Point, and moved north along the coast. The sun rose golden over the Montara Mountains and bathed us in warm light as we reached the seal rocks off Point Lobos and turned east through the Golden Gates of San Francisco. The crew cleaned up as best we could, and the skipper wore a fresh, pressed green khaki shirt and slacks.

We had once dreamed of changing the world, yet now we could not fully understand the changes in our own hearts. What we had witnessed remained a fog in our thoughts, yet it had already touched every cell in our bodies. It had also touched the world. We stood oblivious to the flurry that now unfolded on Pier 23, and to the fact that our private worlds would soon be torn apart and reassembled in a manner we could not remotely imagine.

CHAPTER EIGHT

YEAR OF THE DRAGON

"A lot of people are waiting for Martin Luther King Jr. or Mahatma Gandhi to come back, but they are gone. We are it."
— Marian Wright Edelman

At 10:00 a.m. on July 1, 1975, the *Phyllis Cormack* chugged into San Francisco Bay. As we passed under the Golden Gate Bridge, I sat with Paul Watson and Walrus Oakenbough in the skiff at the stern as they talked about harp seals breeding in the Arctic and what sort of survival gear they'd need on Labrador ice flows. Watson said something about green dye but before he could explain, Korotva interrupted us. Our halibut seiner, dressed out in all her colours, was easing past Alcatraz Island toward San Francisco's embarcadero.

A throng of television camera crews and reporters with microphones pressed forward on Pier 23 as the boat approached. Rod Marining, Bobbi Innes, Eileen Chivers, Phyllis Cormack, and Taeko Miwa from Vancouver waited among the crowd. Innes beamed with a relieved grin. Gary Zimmerman from the Oceanic Society waved. I saw my aunt and grandmother in the crowd. Paul Watson threw a rope to Zimmerman and we tied up.

We could not disembark until we cleared Customs and Immigration, so journalists leaned forward and interviewed crewmembers over the gunwale.

Walrus, Watson, Hunter, Carlie Trueman, Mel Gregory, Will Jackson, and Captain Cormack spoke into the microphones.

I leaned over the dock and kissed my grandmother, who had supported my anti-war stance three years earlier. Cameras flashed. I now entered the United States for the first time since leaving for Canada. My military draft case had been dropped, for "lack of prosecutive merit." Once I cleared Customs, I followed the UPI photo representative, Jack Holpert, to a waiting cab. The story of the Russian whalers had been in every Bay Area newspaper and on every radio and television station for two days. I processed the film myself in the UPI darkroom. Holpert held the wet negatives up to the window and eyeballed them. "Yep, yep, uh-huh," he mumbled as he checked several with a photographer's loupe. "This one, this one, and this one," he said to his darkroom assistant. Holpert had selected a photograph of Moore and Easton approaching the *Vostok*, Korotva in a Zodiac beside the harpoon boat *Vlasny*, and the dead whale under the Russian harpoon. We wrote captions, and he transmitted the three images on the UPI wire ten minutes later.

In the meantime, Fred Easton and Ron Precious took their 16-mm film to a local lab accompanied by representatives from the American television networks and the CBC. Hunter, Moore, Watson, Korotva, Innes, and Chivers toured radio and television stations. That afternoon, we met back at the Pier 23 Café, a whitewashed, converted fish shack on the bay with an aroma of fresh crab and steamed clams. We ordered beer and sat where we could see the television. Carlie Trueman told Rod Marining and Gary Zimmerman details of the encounter. Mel leaned his guitar against the wall and rolled a cigarette. Paul Watson and Walrus sat near the back and continued their discussion of harp seals and Norwegian sealing ships. At a table against the wall, Hunter clung to Innes, exhausted.

The local news at five o'clock showed the *Phyllis Cormack* arriving just outside the café. The bar staff served us a complimentary round of drinks and clientele toasted us. At 6:00 p.m., the bartender switched to CBS for the evening news with legendary anchorman Walter Cronkite. Making this broadcast was a litmus test for any self-respecting news story in America. We saw a clip of dictator Idi Amin in Uganda and the Khmer Rouge in Cambodia, and then the Soviet whaling boats and blue Pacific flickered on the screen. We cheered and sat forward in our chairs.

Easton's shot panned from the whales to the Zodiac, caught Hunter and Korotva on top of a wave, then moved to the harpoon as the cannon exploded. The Greenpeace Zodiac disappeared in a trough, then rose again as the cable snapped taut and the ocean erupted in spray and blood. Bar patrons cheered. Cronkite spoke of a "Canadian ecology ship" confronting the Russians. At this, there were more free drinks; the Americans applauded the fact that we had stood up to the Russians. Carlie Trueman waved a Canadian flag. Hunter beamed. After the whaling segment, the newscast went on to report that scientists had discovered a new asteroid and singer Cher had married rock star Greg Allman. "And that's the way it is," said Cronkite, "July first, 1975."

That night, the Oceanic Society hosted a party in their office at nearby Fort Mason. Local whale groups and environmentalists arrived, and Jim Roberts, from Project Jonah in Bolinas, performed a song he had written about the whales. The crowd instinctively hummed the alluring melody:

There's a song in the waters, a singing in the silence of the deep.
There's a song in the waters, I've heard it in the deepness of my sleep.

Mel accompanied Roberts on guitar and a throng joined the chorus:

Listen to the whales, stop the whaling slaughter
in the water, there's a high mind in the sea …

Mel sang the "Whale Anthem" and his Cossack folk-dance style song "I Declare," and the party raged on into the night. Bob Hunter, weak from stress, drink, and sheer exhaustion, slipped off to the San Francisco Motel with Innes, Moore, and Chivers. Later, I followed Will Jackson home and slept on his sofa.

The next morning, I went out to find a newspaper and coffee. At a *San Francisco Chronicle* newspaper box, I saw the bow of a Russian harpoon boat on the front page, and the headline "The Whale War." I read the paper in a coffee shop. Below the fold, the dead sperm whale floated under the steel hull of the harpoon ship, the menacing harpoon poised above. I sipped my coffee, peaceful and self-satisfied, watching other patrons read the story. In retrospect, I realized the odds of finding the whalers and getting those pictures had been overwhelming. But it had happened. We had planned this mindbomb for two years, yet we had relied on miracles to achieve it. I felt sanctified by something much greater than me.

Although we did not fully appreciate the fact at the time, the broadcast on the US evening news, and the subsequent media frenzy about whales, began the transformation of Greenpeace from an effective, but decidedly underground, international heckler into a global cultural celebrity. Already, however, the teeth of public scrutiny were grinding.

FEAR SUCCESS

On Wednesday, July 2, local visitors swarmed over the *Phyllis Cormack.* Among them we met rock and roll insider Hank Harrison and his ten-year-old daughter Love Michelle. Harrison was a fast-talking impresario who claimed to be a former manager of the Grateful Dead. On the way to lunch, his daughter sang songs with Mel in the cab and told him she had changed her name to "Courtney." Over Mexican food and Dos Equis, Harrison told us, "You guys have no idea what's going on. You've shown up the American government. You exposed the Russians right under their noses. Walter Cronkite must have flipped out when he saw those pictures. How come it isn't our American boys out there fighting the Russians?" The precocious Love Michelle slurped her straw.

"Hank," I said, "we have no axe to grind with the Russians. We're just trying to stop the whale hunt and talk about ecology."

"You don't get it," he insisted. "America just lost its first war. America is licking its wounds. You guys landed in the middle of cold war détente. Americans are about to orbit the earth with the Russians, and here comes this little halibut boat with wild-eyed ecologists battling the dark empire. It's mythological, man. You're shakin' their paradigm."

Harrison, full of ideas and radical bravado, told us he could help set up benefit concerts and later took us to meet Ron Turner, publisher of the *Last Gasp* underground comics. Turner tendered the idea of a comic book about our voyage and about ecology in general. Sure, we said. For days, Harrison escorted us about the city and introduced us to his radical friends. Meanwhile, from makeshift headquarters at the Oceanic Society, I supplied photographs to newspapers and magazines. Hunter and Moore toured the radio stations. Innes brought money from Vancouver, but told us, "We've got serious bills to pay. We have enough to refuel the boat but that's it."

"So," I said to Harrison, "Let's talk to some bands and organize a benefit."

"Patience," he told me. "You have to meet people first."

We attended parties every night, mixing university professors and cocktail circuit environmentalists with anti-war activists and hard-living rock and rollers. Mel, Jim Roberts, and the musicians formed impromptu bands. I selected sixty colour slides for a party in a large warehouse, where Hunter narrated the story of the campaign. "We're just doing what Martin Luther King or Gandhi did, but for something bigger than humans," Hunter said. "For all sentient beings. To Saint Francis!" He gestured toward the city that had honoured the humble friar. Hunter knew that our San Francisco friends were used to visionaries with big ideas. "It's nothing special," he said, and toasted everyone.

Marine ecologists we met discussed the 200-mile limit, oil exploration on the continental shelf, and the International Whaling Commission. It appeared that everyone knew that the IWC was a sham. We heard talk of a pirate whaling ship called the *Sierra*, operating outside IWC scrutiny, owned by the Norwegians and Japanese. We also learned about the Pelly Amendment to the US Fishermen's Protection Act, allowing the US to embargo fish and wildlife imports from nations violating international conservation agreements. Since Japan and Russia were exceeding quotas and killing undersized whales, the US had threatened to invoke this law.

We now had photographic proof of actual violations, so environmentalists asked me to send the photographs to a consortium of environmental groups, called Monitor, in Washington, D.C. Monitor's director, Craig van Note, had been a primary source of pressure on the American IWC delegation. California Congressman Paul McCloskey and Washington State Senator Warren Magnusson, both peace advocates during the Vietnam War, supported the environmentalists.

"There's trouble ahead," said one environmentalist, "from the bowhead hunt in Alaska. The Inuit subsistence hunters are taking bowhead whales, but there are probably less than 2,000 bowheads left. The US will look like a hypocrite when this comes out."

"Maybe the Inuit should be exempt since it's a cultural issue," Pat Moore jumped in, "but the problem is, the Japanese can say the same thing.

They can say they have a whale-hunting heritage and they have a lot more people, so they should be allowed to kill more whales. The moratorium has to be for everyone. It's not the Inuit's fault that the bowhead is nearly extinct, and it's not really the Japanese people's fault that the pelagic whales are decimated, but from an ecological point of view, certainly from the whales' point of view, there should be a moratorium."

We had talked about our policies on the boat. We had agreed that "we speak for the whales," a position that would pit us against many interests in the years to come. Even here, among environmentalists, not everyone supported our policies or strategies. Joan McIntyre from Project Jonah said that the important thing was to teach people to love and celebrate the whale. Some ecologists insisted the real work was in the political trenches, in Washington, D.C. and at the IWC. Hunter defended our contribution, the mindbomb approach: "Deliver the images that will turn public opinion in favour of the whales. Let the political chips fall. Win the public mind," he said.

Nick Wilson, a photographer with a group from Mendocino, warned me that some people who had been working on the whale issue for years saw us as latecomers, grabbing headlines for ourselves. "Look," he said, "don't worry about it. The whale movement's been around for years. It's talk, talk, talk." We soon began to get the first indications that our encounter with the Russians had ruffled some local environmentalists. Joan McIntyre, someone we looked up to as a pioneer of the whale movement, got into a mildly heated discussion with Hunter. She called the Greenpeace tactics, "macho." From her point of view, she was right. Greenpeace *was* macho. Men had thus far dominated Greenpeace crews and governance, and the tactics had been aggressive. Carlie Trueman and Bobbi Innes defended both the confrontations and the role of women in the ranks of Greenpeace. Hunter remained unapologetic. "Perhaps a little aggression is what the environmental movement needs," he said. Although McIntyre had every right to critique the tactics, Hunter felt offended. He saw Greenpeace as part of a global shift beyond politics and beyond the realm of the purely human.

"Joan," he pleaded, "isn't this what we wanted? To win some publicity for the whales?"

"I want to save the whales," McIntyre said, "but not *that* way."

Hunter slumped. He had just risked his life for the whales. "Fear success," he whispered later in a small crowd, repeating the admonition Ben Metcalfe had delivered two years earlier. "The problem is," said Hunter, "we planned to find the whalers, but we didn't plan what to do after that."

VISITATION

By Friday, July 4, the crew had grown restless. Hunter felt nauseous and was not eating. Fifteen people slept in the two Greenpeace rooms at the San Francisco Motel. To raise money to feed the crew, Innes handed out T-shirts and lottery tickets to sell on the dock to the Independence Day crowds. A friendly cab driver gave us free rides around town. Into this mayhem, Amy Ephron arrived from New York, sophisticated and smart, with a deal for us. She talked about "Marty" Bregman as someone we should know as the producer of Al Pacino films. We didn't, but we believed her. "Marty," she said, "will buy an option on your story for $25,000." To do the deal, however, she needed character releases from everyone on the boat. Hunter thought we should do it — sign our characters over to the film for Greenpeace and for the whales. Pat Moore, George Korotva, Cormack, and most of us agreed to sign on. But naturally, Ephron's charms did not work on everyone. Some crewmembers assumed we were being swindled by the New Yorkers. Walrus and Watson refused to sign.

Innes explained that we faced at least $25,000 in debts in Vancouver. We needed the money. Hunter, drained and disenchanted, made one last speech under the eucalyptus trees on the green grass of the Presidio overlooking the bay, proclaiming we should give up ego and personal gain and surrender ourselves to this opportunity. "It's a chance to create a major hit for the whales," he pleaded with the crew. "Forget yourselves. Do this for the whales." A good agent might have negotiated us a favourable contract, with or without everyone signing on, but we had no agent.

Hunter gave up and Moore took over negotiations with Ephron, but Walrus and Watson would not relent. Mel threw the *I Ching*, but whatever advice he got, he kept to himself. Hank Harrison told us he could get us a much better film deal. The friendly cab driver brought a bag of marijuana to the boat. Rumours circulated of cocaine around the hotel and Innes threw several visitors out of the rooms. Finally, Moore agreed with Ephron that Greenpeace and Bregman's Artist Entertainment Complex would discuss the film later and that Greenpeace would not sign any deals with anyone else in the meantime.

"Let's get out of here," Hunter said.

Will Jackson, Paul Watson, and Mel Gregory had decided to stay in San Francisco. Rod Marining, Gary Zimmerman, and photographer Matt Herron joined the boat crew. Jack Richardson, a reporter from the *New York Review of Books*, climbed aboard at the last minute. On July 6, we cast off the ropes just before noon, slipped out through the Golden Gates, rounded the Marin headlands, and made northwest for the Jackson seamounts. Within two hours, we heard Russian voices on the radio and saw a double rainbow in the west, so huge it seemed almost staged. Hunter shrugged and invoked the "three miracles" rule.

Mercifully, we were back at sea, where life was simple. Mel had left his flute and *I Ching* on the galley table. Now, Trueman took up the flute and Moore rattled the Chinese coins. Around the boat, a thin mist closed in like the sheerest satin veil. The horizon blinked in and out of the strange haze, then disappeared. The sky glowed, and just off the starboard beam, the shimmering light formed a tiny silver rainbow, like the moon rainbow we'd seen a month earlier, but so close to the boat that we could reach out and almost pass our fingers through it. Cormack shut the engines down, climbed to the back deck, and stood at the railing looking at the mysterious silver arc.

"Never seen nothin' like that," he said.

The little rainbow hung and pulsated in the air. Hunter reached his fingers for it. From my view on the hatch cover, his fingers glowed a warm silver tone. I took a picture of Hunter and the captain staring at the peculiar light. Then Hunter stripped naked and plunged from the deck, through the luminous visitation, into the sea. Walrus and Marining joined him, and their bodies glowed golden in the water. As Hunter climbed back onto the deck and the strange light faded, he admonished himself for being flippant about the first rainbow. "Sorry," he said to the heavens, palms pressed together.

In the galley, Walrus and Fred Easton prepared supper. Jack Richardson leaned in the galley door. The worldly journalist, good humoured and bright, had chronicled the exploits of cultural innovators like Lenny

Bruce, Gabriel García Márquez, and Jack Kerouac. "What now?" he asked Hunter.

"I don't know," said our leader, shivering at the galley table, "but it seems clear Planet Earth isn't going to let us off the hook."

POLITICS OF EVOLUTION

The next day a pod of twelve orcas kept pace off our port beam for half an hour. "There's yer third miracle, Bob," said Walrus casually. On July 9, we tied up among the fish boats in Eureka. Fishermen flashed peace signs, the Customs inspector put on a Greenpeace button, news crews arrived, and townspeople brought champagne. The next morning, we headed for the Cobb seamounts, listening for whalers, but picked up no sign of them. "Best case," Hunter said to Richardson, "we've driven them out of their Pacific hunting grounds."

Later, Richardson opened wine for our spaghetti dinner and asked each of us why we had joined the cause. Then Richardson said what some of us felt. "Well, there's no reason for you to find them again, anyway, is there?"

"Other than to actually save whales," said Walrus.

"True," said the journalist, "but finding them again won't really change the political impact of what you've already done."

"Not much," said Hunter.

Richardson's interrogations were not cynical. He seemed to appreciate the spiritual quirkiness of the campaign as much as the ecological philosophy. At the galley table he cajoled and probed our motives. "Some Americans will use this as a dig at the Russians," he suggested.

"Of course," said Moore. "When we took on atomic tests, people thought we were anti-American or anti-French. But the whales get a deeper response. We don't have to convince people with scientific arguments. It's enough that an intelligent and beautiful species is being turned into fertilizer and lubricating oil."

"What about animals that *don't* have big brains?" asked Richardson.

"The whales are a way to open people to the natural world," said Marining. "Ultimately, the message is that every creature has its own value and right to survival. When that survival is threatened, *we* have a right to step in. We're giving a political voice to the non-human world."

"Whether the perpetrators are Canadians or Russians or Americans?"

"Sure," said Hunter. "This isn't partisan. Everybody around the human table has to slide over to make room for the rest of nature. Everybody."

"Too bad it was the Russians," said Marining, "because that made it easy for Americans to cast them as the bad guys, which misses the point. Had we found the Japanese, they would have accused us of being racist."

"There's no escaping the human politics," said Hunter.

"But it changes politics," said Richardson.

"Yeah," said Hunter. "The politics of evolution. That's a much bigger deal."

"Declaration of Interdependence," said Moore.

Richardson scribbled in his notebook. He thought for a moment, became solemn, and looked up, around the table. "Not everyone is going to be nice to you."

"We know *that*," said Hunter.

On July 11, Walrus' birthday, Moore made a cake, and we celebrated into the night. The next day, we arrived south of the Cobb seamounts, 400 miles west of the Washington coast. We had not heard Russian voices since our first day out of San Francisco. The time had come to head home. On July 15, we made landfall at Cape Beale on Vancouver Island and entered Alberni Inlet. Matt Herron and Jack Richardson left the boat and made their way back to California. Two days later, we arrived in Winter Harbour in the full glory of summer. We spent a day there cleaning up, then rounded the north end of Vancouver Island, and headed south through Queen Charlotte Strait. We stopped at Alert Bay, lowered the wind-tattered Kwakiutl flag from the mast, and returned it to the Kwakiutl Nation in a ceremony at the longhouse. Men played drums and the women pulled us into their dance for "all our relations," all the creatures of the world.

In Alert Bay, Linda Spong, eight-year-old Yasha Spong, and their friend Bruce Logan joined the crew. We moved south through the Strait of Georgia, and a flotilla of sailboats escorted the *Phyllis Cormack* into English Bay, in the heart of Vancouver. The *Vega*, displaying the *Greenpeace* sail, met us in the middle of the bay. We could see supporters gathered along the shoreline with flags and horns. Music roared from a makeshift stage.

We came ashore in the Zodiacs as our friends splashed through the surf. On the stage, Paul Spong told the crowd that the campaign had changed the political landscape at the International Whaling Commission. "Japan and Russia are nervous now," he said. "They know the world is watching."

"We saved eight whales," added Hunter, "maybe more. We may have driven the whalers out of the North Pacific entirely. The point is, the whales have a voice. *Your* voice."

Over the next few weeks, we fielded calls from journalists looking for quotes and photographs, and from citizens offering help. The images of whales, and of people throwing themselves between leviathan and the harpoons, resonated with something fundamental in people, perhaps a fear of what we had done to the earth and a hope that we, humanity, could change. We would spend the next four years coming to grips with this.

EXCEPTIONAL CASE

While we had been on the whale campaign, David McTaggart's case against the French Navy for high seas piracy had come before a Paris court. Photographs documented the French warship *La Paimpolaise* ramming the *Vega* and French sailors beating McTaggart and Nigel Ingram. "The evidence is indisputable," lawyer Thierry Garby-Lacrouts told McTaggart. At 2:00 p.m.on April 8, 1975, at the Palais de Justice near Notre Dame, McTaggart and Garby-Lacrouts sat before the Tribunal de Grande Instance, consisting of three French judges. A government procurer, Jacques Simon, observing from his own high bench to the right of the judges, consigned to advise the court on the opinion of the French government.

International journalists listened from the gallery with curious French lawyers and Greenpeace supporters such as Brice Lalonde. Garby-Lacrouts rose before the court. Under French law, the lawyer had only one chance to present his case; there would be no cross examination of the government's defense. He told the story of the two voyages in 1972 and 1973 and emphasized the long tradition of free mariners on the high seas. Garby-Lacrouts perspired from the heat and tension as he detailed the events of the ramming, the boarding, and the beating. The judges listened, visibly moved by the savagery of the tale. The government's procurer scowled from his bench. Garby-Lacrouts brought forward the photographs. One of the judges acted uninterested, but two of the judges leaned forward to study the photographs. The lawyer pointed out the truncheons. The procurer rose from his bench to see the photographs.

The government's defence lawyer, Jean Gallot, a paunchy man in his late fifties, strolled to the bench, peeked at the photographs, and tossed his head. "*Je ne peux rien voir*," he scoffed. "I cannot see anything."

McTaggart's lawyer produced a black truncheon like the ones in the pictures. The apathetic judge perked up and claimed, "Military authorities use white truncheons, not black!"

"Yes, but this was not their usual activity," Garby-Lacrouts shot back. After an hour and a half of argument, he cited the Law of the Sea. "In peacetime," said Garby-Lacrouts, "it is illegal for a warship of any country to interfere with a foreign vessel on the high seas. The issue in this case," he concluded, "is whether the seas are free." He thanked the judges and sat down next to McTaggart.

Gallot, the defence attorney, stood, nodded to the judges and the procurer, and smirked at Garby-Lacrouts. He chided the novice lawyer for taking so long to present his case and proffered the excuse that he was "so young." He mocked Garby-Lacrouts's idealism and ridiculed McTaggart as an aging hippie agitator, living off the graces of society, and amusing himself by attacking the French government. The lawyer rambled and fumbled, claiming that the French Navy had been concerned about the safety of the crew aboard the *Vega*. As it turned out, he was ill-prepared, hardly grasped the rudiments of the case, and knew almost nothing about maritime navigation or law. When he claimed that the *Vega* had rammed the French minesweeper *La Paimpolaise*, the audience in the gallery laughed and one of the judges admonished him. "A yacht cannot sail backwards," the judge said dryly.

Gallot's only point of defence was that both the ramming of the *Vega* in 1972 and the beatings in 1973 were "exceptional cases," military acts required by national security, and therefore not subject to French civil law. He claimed that the Tribunal de Grande Instance, therefore, had no jurisdiction to hear the case, a point that clearly annoyed two of the judges. Gallot cited precedents for this opinion from the French-Algerian War, and with this, the government's lawyer sat down.

It was now the procurer's opportunity to give the government's opinion. He rose, shuffled over to the three judges, and whispered to them. The presiding judge announced that the procurer requested a postponement to prepare his opinion. The case was remanded to May 13, the judge banged his gavel, and the first court session came to a close. Garby-Lacrouts told McTaggart that the precedents from the French-Algerian War, cited by the government, had never before been invoked in peacetime and were likely irrelevant. "If they go along with that, they're opening the door for the military to do whatever they want, whenever they want. I think we have them cornered."

Five weeks later, McTaggart returned to the Palais de Justice to hear the opinion of the government. The procurer merely restated the defence lawyer's argument that the alleged violations were "exceptional cases" of national security, and that the Tribunal had no jurisdiction to rule. The government's opinion was that the entire case should simply be tossed.

On June 17, McTaggart and Garby-Lacrouts appeared again before the Tribunal to hear its decision. The somber presiding judge announced that, in the case of the ramming, the French Navy was guilty of "creating a dangerous situation," and of "deliberately ramming" the *Greenpeace III*. He ordered the government to pay for an independent marine survey of the boat to determine the damages due to McTaggart. On the charge of piracy, stemming from the boarding and beating in 1973, the Tribunal judges dodged the prickly implications and allowed that the piracy charge was an "exceptional case," upon which they had no jurisdiction to rule.

While Thierry Garby-Lacrouts, Brice Lalonde, and other pacifists in Paris celebrated the partial victory, almost unheard of in France, McTaggart raged that the government had eluded the piracy charge. His lawyer launched an appeal that was heard in January 1976. The appeal judges ruled in favour of the government and the case was closed. The procurer did add an odd disclaimer, however: "It should not be denied," he said, "that McTaggart may have helped to persuade the French government to decide to choose underground tests in place of atmospheric tests."

The French government refused to pay the court-ordered 2,000 francs for the marine survey, but Garby-Lacrouts hounded the government's lawyer until Jean Gallot himself paid for the survey. A government-appointed marine surveyor took the money but never looked at the boat. When McTaggart presented him with a marine survey performed after the ramming, the bureaucrat dismissed virtually all the damages. In the end, the French government paid nothing to McTaggart in reparation.

Later, during the summer of 1976, France would conduct its first underground nuclear bomb test on the island of Fangataufa near Moruroa. They deployed their first thermonuclear weapon, the one-megaton TN-60, on ballistic missiles mounted on five Redoubtable class submarines. France had its force de frappe. But the battle at Moruroa, already four years old, was far from over. In the corridors of influence within the French military, there was talk of revenge. The feud with McTaggart would lead, a decade later, to the first tragic death of a Greenpeace activist.

MONEY FOLLOWS

Meanwhile, in Vancouver in the fall of 1975, Greenpeace again moved in three separate campaign trajectories. Most of us worked on the complex whale campaign, liaising with colleagues in Washington, D.C., Tokyo, Ottawa, and London while Korotva looked for a bigger, faster boat for the next summer. We sent $1,000 to McTaggart in Paris, and Paul Watson and Walrus Oakenbough launched a third front: the Canadian harp seal hunt.

In the fall, pregnant mother seals head south from the Arctic to their nursery on the ice floes of Labrador and the Gulf of St. Lawrence, where the pups are born. When infants reach three days old, in early March, their fur will turn pure white. Then, the sealing ships from Halifax and Norway arrive. The pelts are taken when the seal pups, called whitecoats, are between three days and two weeks old. Watson and Walrus intended to stop the sealers by applying a green dye to the whitecoats, thereby rendering the pelts useless to the fashion fur industry.

On July 29, Bob Hunter wrote his "Farewell Column," announcing his resignation from the *Vancouver Sun* and his new full-time role as president of the Greenpeace Foundation. "My beliefs have been turned inside out," he wrote. "I no longer feel afraid or helpless … The generation that grew up in the wake of Hiroshima has come of age … Thanks to the atomic bomb, we know that humanity now has full responsibility for the salvation or destruction of the world … And thanks to the whales, we are now able to see ourselves as shepherds rather than unrestrained predators. Our true function in this world is becoming clear. We are here to be the handmaidens and interns of evolution … Beyond the whales, there is much to be done. The sooner we get on with it, the better."

The Greenpeace Foundation now had an office at 2007 West Fourth Avenue, a full-time president, and a reputation for doing what it said it would do. Unfortunately, we had no money to pay our president or our rent. Bobbi Innes juggled the cash against the demands of campaigns, debts, and the needs of new offices around the world for letterhead, photographs, and fundraising brochures. She tallied our debt at just over $40,000, mostly to local suppliers and to John Cormack. As a gesture of goodwill, Korotva, Watson, and others helped Cormack overhaul his seiner for the fishing season. The lottery for the five acres of land had been a success, but the whale campaign had cost some $80,000 and the lottery revenues only covered half of this. Our local creditors were supportive, but many of them were small businesses trying to survive themselves. The debts caused tension within the group over who would be paid when money did come in. We fielded calls from new Greenpeace offices, from the *New York Times*, ABC News, and the *Yomiuri* newspaper in Japan — all asking for photographs that we could not afford to print. A local photo lab printed the photographs at cost and invoiced us $54, knowing they would not soon get paid. Even so, when I brought the invoice into the office, the volunteer bookkeeper chastised me. "Bobbi's not going to like this," he said.

"I'll talk to her," I promised. I met with Bob Hunter and Bobbi Innes at the Bimini Pub across the street from the office and told them I knew someone who might help. I was back at work at the *North Shore News*. The accountant there, Bill Gannon, had been moonlighting from his regular job as the chief accountant for one of the largest commercial developers in the city. At the newspaper, we had formed a band that played each Thursday night, and Gannon was the best musician in the group. He was also the most interesting accountant I'd ever met.

Bill Gannon was born in Dublin in 1947. His father was a pianist and leader of a jazz band. The family immigrated to Canada when Bill was nine and settled in Winnipeg. Music filled their home, and Gannon and his siblings grew up as talented musicians. Gannon played bass in a 1960s Winnipeg band, Donny and the Footprints, which rivalled Neil Young's Squires as a top Winnipeg band of the era. After high school, he intended to follow his older brother, Oliver, to the Berklee School of Music in Boston, but the night before he was to leave, he became violently ill with meningitis. By the time he recovered, he had missed the opening semester.

He took a bookkeeping job with a national electrical contractor and two years later married his high school sweetheart, Mary.

Besides being a musician, Gannon had a natural talent with numbers, and he worked his way up to the position of branch accountant in Winnipeg. He was transferred to Vancouver in the spring of 1970, and the Gannons soon had two daughters, Maureen and Patrice. In 1974, he went to work for Daon Corporation. At the age of twenty-six, he was the commercial real estate developer's chief accountant, overseeing dozens of older colleagues. He had a special flair for financial planning, and his massive, handwritten cash-flow spreadsheets became legendary. He met publisher Peter Speck in the fall of 1974 and helped him create a financial plan for the *North Shore News*. I met him at the newspaper and we started our Thursday night band.

Gannon also had an enduring sense of righteousness that he had inherited from his family's lineage of Irish patriots. He was just what Greenpeace needed: a tough, city-hall-fighting, visionary accountant. On top of that, we needed a bass player in Mel's Migrating Whale Medicine Band. In the fall of 1975, I met with Gannon, Hunter, Bobbi Innes, and Peter Speck at the *North Shore News* office. "Don't worry about the debt," said Gannon. "What do you guys want to do?"

We told him all the plans: get a bigger, faster boat to chase the Soviet and Japanese whalers; launch a seal crusade in eastern Canada, a campaign that would require helicopters and ice crews; support McTaggart's legal case and office in Paris; be prepared to launch a boat to any nuclear test site anywhere; set up a film and photography division; pay office staff; rent our own, bigger office; start an American Greenpeace office; and so forth.

"Yep, yep," said Gannon, scribbling wildly on huge lined spreadsheets, "what do you need to do that? When do you need it? How big an office? How much for a boat?" Nothing we dreamed up daunted Gannon. "Money follows energy," he said. "But energy isn't enough. Money has its rules. You all know you have to account for where you've been, but here's the real secret: plan ahead for where you're going. Now, what else do you need?"

We came up with $200,000 in projects and overhead costs. "Okay," said Gannon, "how do you raise money?" Innes told him about the lottery, T-shirts, buttons, donation cans, and benefit concerts. Gannon scribbled it all down. "What else?" He coaxed out more ideas. Hunter mentioned the film offer. Innes mentioned new merchandise. "Okay, look," Gannon said, "your creditors are friendly. This is good. Ask 'em to hold on. Don't spend money on debts yet. Look for the new office and plan your campaigns. Make it a priority to computerize the names and addresses on the lottery tickets. Pay Bob whatever you can to keep him going. Keep the publicity happening. If you need film or photographs, get them. You're going to need capital to get the fundraising rolling. Don't worry about it. Leave this with me. Let's meet in a few weeks. This is all doable." Gannon looked at Innes, who carried the burden of the debts. "Don't worry," he said with confidence.

Greenpeace had found the right person at the right time, just as it had when Irving Stowe enlisted Hunter and the Metcalfes, when Captain Cormack offered his boat, when Metcalfe recruited McTaggart, or when Hunter met Paul and Linda Spong. Bill Gannon met with Bobbi Innes and worked out details of overhead and fundraising plans. He met with Hunter to flesh out the campaigns. Always, he carried the spreadsheets, scribbling, adding up numbers, erasing, re-adding.

"It's some kind of financial *jiu-jitsu*," said Hunter.

"You have something most companies *wish* they had," Gannon told us. "Public recognition and support. That's worth a lot. Just do the project. Money follows energy."

Okay, we repeated to ourselves. *Do the project. Money follows energy.*

POINTS OF GREEN LIGHT

In August, we learned that Soviet supply vessels used the port of Vancouver to supply their dragger fleet from Baja, California to British Columbia. "We promised to help the trollers," Hunter said at a meeting. "Here's our chance." On August 12, when the Russian vessel *Kurilsk* entered the port, thirty Greenpeace activists lined the dock. When longshoremen refused to cross our picket line, the loading of the Soviet ship halted. Journalists assembled at the waterfront. The harbour police arrived, and the officer in charge chatted with Hunter. They agreed amicably that six protestors would be arrested. Hunter, Patrick Moore, Melville Gregory, Bree Drummond, and student Janet Cook walked peacefully to the police wagon. Paul Watson refused to cooperate and was carried by the police.

The next day, the officer in charge showed up at Hunter's boat, the *Astral*, in Vancouver's False Creek Marina. The harbour cop was despondent. "I'm fed up with what's happening in the world," he told Hunter. "I'm afraid there won't be much left for my own children." Hunter made coffee and sat on the *Astral* with his melancholy visitor. "Sometimes," the policeman said, "I want to tear off my badge and join you." When the case came to trial, the officer booked off sick for the day. The prosecutor waved his arms in frustration, the judge dismissed the case, and all six Greenpeace defendants walked away free.

Our friend Paul Winter played a mind-bending jazz concert for Greenpeace in Vancouver's historic St. Andrews Church, drawing together music fans and environmentalists. Winter used the calls of wolves, eagles, and whales to create his distinctive music. The pieces would later appear on his *Earthdance* and *Common Ground* recordings.

Then on August 16, Bob Wright from Sealand Aquarium in Victoria had six orcas captured in Pedder Bay, in Juan de Fuca Strait. Spong and Mel Gregory rushed to the site the next day. Security was tight, but a platoon of whale advocates had arrived, including members of the local Metchosin Nation of the Coast Salish people. Police arrested a diver for attempting to cut the holding nets. Mel snuck into the bay at night and recorded the whales in the pen and their family members waiting outside the nets. Spong took these recordings to radio stations. A cry rose up across BC to free the whales, but Wright quickly lifted a young female from the pen and trucked her to the aquarium in Victoria. He named her Nootka III to replace the dead Nootka II, who had lived for nine months under his care. Nootka III died nine months later.

The day after Nootka III was shipped, Greenpeace convinced BC Ferries and Air Canada to refuse to transport whales, but Wright still managed to send a whale to New York by private charter. Hunter and I met Spong in Victoria, parliamentary seat of BC Premier Dave Barrett, who had promised two years earlier to "review the prospects" of outlawing the capture of orcas in British Columbia. We arranged a meeting with the premier. Spong explained that over the last twelve years, twenty-five orcas from BC had died in aquarium pools and twelve more during botched captures. "It's a crime," he said. "It's murder." The premier knew that a majority of the citizens would favour a ban on orca captures. "I'll take care of it," he said. On September 12, 1975, the new law passed in the legislature. No more orcas would be captured in the waterways of British

Columbia. Six months later, Washington State passed similar legislation protecting the whales in Puget Sound. The new orca sanctuary spanned over a thousand miles of coastline from the Columbia River to Alaska.

In the tiny Greenpeace office in Vancouver, the ecology agenda swelled. Taeko Miwa and Walrus brought reports from the Grassy Narrows Indian Reserve in Ontario, showing that the people suffered from mercury poisoning, similar to the poisoning that had devastated a fishing community in Minamata, Japan. Don Franks introduced us to music industry designer Barry Lavender, who created new T-shirt and poster art, and designed a new Greenpeace logo with the peace symbol embedded inside the ecology symbol. In October, the new logo appeared on the cover of the first issue of the *Greenpeace Chronicles*, assembled at *The Georgia Straight* newspaper office. The front page announced the orca capture ban and featured a photograph of the *Phyllis Cormack* and the *Vega*. Mel Gregory wrote about whale music. Walrus wrote a report about the mercury poisoning among the Ojibwa people in Ontario. Pat Moore described the long-term dangers of plutonium and Fred Easton wrote about the Trident nuclear submarine base at Bangor, Washington. We announced that the newspaper would not focus on Greenpeace, but would be dedicated to ecology and the "eco-fronts" opening everywhere. We published reports on the peace ship *Fri* in New Zealand, bloodsport saboteurs in London, and Native American land claims. The inaugural *Greenpeace Chronicles* promoted the work of the Coalition for Nuclear Responsibility, the Natural Resources Defense Council in California, Project Jonah, the Coalition for a Safe Environment in Seattle, and other groups.

Hunter compiled an account of Greenpeace campaigns to date. "No Greenpeace expedition has ever succeeded in achieving its goal by a single mission," he wrote. "Amchitka took two voyages. Moruroa took three." Hunter promised a "larger, faster vessel" to chase the whalers in the summer of 1976. Meanwhile, Paul Watson and Walrus Oakenbough announced the harp seal campaign. Watson had formed his own ad hoc group known as "Lifeseal," with himself and Walrus as directors, to raise independent funding. He contemplated splitting off and leading his own organization, as competition for money intensified, but in the end kept his affiliation. "Greenpeace intends to send an expedition to the Gulf of St. Lawrence next year," he wrote in the *Greenpeace Chronicles*. "In February, arctic-equipped protestors will set out in kayaks for the ice floes. Upon the floes these people will assume the role of nature's shepherds." Watson revealed that Greenpeace crews might mark the infant whitecoats with an indelible green dye. He quoted Newfoundland sealer Eric Nielson who said, "It's a miserable, tragic business. I don't like it at all. I think it's the most perverted trade that I have ever been in. I need the money they pay me, but they cannot make me like what I am doing."

Nielson worked among the "swilers," young fishermen who made a few hundred dollars each spring by braving the Labrador ice floes to kill and skin infant harp seals for the Norwegian merchants. Brokers sold the pelts to the fashion-fur industry in Europe, and the sparkling white harp-seal coats sold for hundreds of thousands of dollars in boutiques in Hampstead and along the Côte d'Azur. We established a Greenpeace policy to focus on the Norwegian ships and not lay blame for the seal hunt on the Newfoundland swilers. Still, we knew that we faced a cultural clash in Canada over the fate of the seals. To make it worse, Newfoundlanders considered Canadian mainlanders to be outsiders with no business telling them what to do. We suspected that bringing ecological protest home to Canada would test our resolve.

MONEY CHANGES EVERYTHING

Throughout the fall of 1975, Greenpeace met regularly in the upstairs office on Fourth Avenue in Vancouver. Bill Gannon joined the Greenpeace Foundation board of directors that included Bob Hunter, John Cormack, Bobbi Innes, Pat Moore, Eileen Chivers, Linda Spong, Paul Spong, Paul Watson, Michael Chechik, me, and SPEC president Gary Gallon. In nuclear campaigns of the past, unequivocal focus had contributed to Greenpeace's success. Now, however, Greenpeace was inescapably diverse.

In November, Hunter and Innes travelled across Canada with a slide presentation, selling T-shirts and whale buttons to raise money. Paul Spong attended the National Whale Symposium at the University of Indiana, where he discussed whale dialects with Dr. Roger Payne, who had recorded the humpbacks. Spong also met Japanese biologist Dr. Miwa, who demonstrated that oil from the jojoba plant could replace all known uses for sperm-whale oil. Whale lobbyists from Washington, D.C.

told Spong they could help track the whaling fleets the following year, through supporters in the US government.

Watson and Walrus attended the same symposium with their own purposes. They recruited schoolteacher Dan Willens to raise money for the seal campaign. They made alliances with Brian Davies of the International Fund for Animal Welfare and with Cleveland Amory, who had founded The Fund for Animals. Davies had flown journalists to Labrador to witness the seal hunt and now offered a helicopter to support Greenpeace. Cleveland Amory had helped stop the aerial slaughter of wolves in Alaska and had recommended 175 species, including the grizzly bear and African elephant, for an endangered list. "We speak for those who can't," declared Amory.

Meanwhile, Greenpeace offices sprouted around the world. In the UK, the ad hoc Greenpeace group seeded by Rod Marining in 1972 opened an office on Great Portland Street in West London. There were offices in Reykjavik, Iceland; Carlton, Australia; Auckland, New Zealand; as well as Portland, San Francisco, Boston, and Seattle. Canadian offices opened in Victoria, Toronto, Ottawa, Montreal, Saskatoon, Calgary, Prince George, Edmonton, and in Inuvik in the Northwest Territories. Three activists carrying a Greenpeace banner were arrested at the Southampton nuclear reactor in Ontario. Most of these groups operated semi-autonomously. We sent them buttons, logos, and photographs, and they raised and spent their own money. Bill Gannon attempted to account for the consolidated Greenpeace revenues and expenses, but few of the new offices kept, or reported, accurate records. Greenpeace subsisted in organizational limbo. The Board of Directors in Vancouver trusted the good intentions of these offices and in most cases the trust was warranted, but in some regions clashes over turf had already broken out.

In the San Francisco Bay area the growth rate of Greenpeace taxed the organization. In December, Hunter and I toured colleges and universities in San Francisco with the whale slide show, where students had set up Greenpeace offices on campuses. Meanwhile, Will Jackson and Gary Zimmerman had rented an office at 860 Second Street in the Mission district and hired administrator Marian Yesinski. *Realist* editor Paul Krassner, a member of Ken Kesey's Merry Pranksters and a founder of the Yippies, sat on the local board of directors with Stan Minasian from Save the Dolphins and Virginia Handley from Brian Davies' International Fund for

Animal Welfare. Young lawyer David Tussman filed the paperwork with the State and applied for federal non-profit tax status. Hank Harrison hung around the office with promises of benefit concerts. Clashes of style — similar to the early clashes in Vancouver — soon emerged, but without the element of Quaker tolerance. Harrison openly smoked marijuana in the office and offered joints to visitors. Marian Yesinski kicked him out, but according to Yesinski, Harrison distributed his own press releases, and directed donations to his private postal box in the East Bay.

Hunter and I talked to Harrison, who seemed to be hurt by the feud. He took me to Fantasy Records in Berkeley, ostensibly to meet Country Joe McDonald's manager after the musician had offered support. In the busy office, we migrated from cubicle to cubicle, but I could not figure out what we were doing there. "Patchin' in," said Harrison. He promised to introduce us to the Grateful Dead, but the meeting never materialized.

"He's nice to you guys," Yesinski told us. "He wines and dines anyone above him in the hierarchy, but he treats everyone else like peons and he hustles every young woman in the office. I don't want him in here." Until that moment, we had not realized we had a hierarchy, but in fact, we did. The days of everyone in Greenpeace sitting in a single room were gone forever. Lines of authority had to be established. Hunter told Harrison that he could not raise funds through his own postal box and he must clear media releases with Zimmerman. Harrison responded, "This will have negative repercussions in the rock and roll community."

Board member Krassner, stoic and droll about the clash, said, "Money changes everything." Krassner had been a cultural pioneer since the 1950s and had witnessed power struggles before. "You've only just glimpsed the dark side of your little Greenpeace empire," he remarked. "There is fame and fortune to be had. Even people who mean well can do a lot of damage. Get ready for it."

FIRE DRAGON

On January 31, 1976, the night of the second full moon after the winter solstice, dragons wound through bursting pyrotechnics in Vancouver's Chinese neighborhood, opening night of the Year of the Fire Dragon, the 4,675th year of the Chinese calendar. A fire dragon year comes around once every sixty years, a time of action and divinity. Chinese dragons breathe the celestial breath, *sheng chi*, and command the wind, rain, thunder, and lightning. They embody the power of nature, the ultimate divine force on earth. The fire dragon is the most intrepid, able to arouse massive popular support. This is a time to be outspoken and idealistic, but there is a danger of making errors in such an influential time, so one is advised to beware of becoming too stubborn or willful. To effect lasting change in the year of the fire dragon, one is advised to master humility and communication; it is a time to be bold, not impetuous.

In the first week of February, Bill Gannon presented the Greenpeace board with a one-year budget and cash-flow projection based on all the campaign ideas. The budget detailed $300,000 in campaign and overhead expenses, and an equal amount in income to pay for it. However, to make the plan work, we needed cash up front to launch the fundraising activities, so Gannon had prepared a financing proposal. From a plastic garbage bag in the office, volunteers had retrieved ticket stubs from the first lottery and transposed these into a mailing list of 20,000 names. With this, Gannon and Bobbi Innes prepared a mailing and calculated a response. They planned a second lottery, with a prize of two airline tickets to "Anywhere in the World." Mel and I conceived of a benefit concert to coincide with the launch of the hypothetical faster boat. Watson and Walrus raised money on behalf of the seal campaign. Gannon presented these fundraising plans in the proposal, along with financial statements and a history of activities.

With this in hand, he visited the loans officer, Lorene Vickberg, at our local branch of the Royal Bank of Canada. Vickberg phoned Gannon a week later and announced that the loan could be approved if secured by future Greenpeace income and personal guarantors. "My kids are really impressed that I have the Greenpeace account," she told Gannon.

To secure the loan, nine of us documented our modest net worth, and signed on as a guarantors. My meager assets included cameras, two guitars, and a Volkswagen beetle. Hunter had a typewriter, a Volkswagon van, and his tiny live-aboard boat. However, Hunter recruited the more established professionals with houses and bank accounts, like doctors Lyle Thurston and Myron Macdonald and lawyer Davie Gibbons. Bobbi Innes' father, Bill Innes, put his family's home on the line as security. Cormack, Gannon, and Michael Chechik signed on, and we had enough guarantors to make the bank feel secure. Gannon took us to meet the senior manager at the Royal Bank in Vancouver. Up the elevator we went, to a vast office overlooking Burrard Inlet and the North Shore mountains. Hunter charmed the bank manager with stories of adventure and visions of a global environmental movement. Innes talked about a new office, paid staff, and financial controls. The banker had reviewed the financial plan and asked us pointed questions about our fundraising proposals. "I've never approved a loan like this before," he said.

A week later, the Royal Bank of Canada advanced Greenpeace a $75,000 line of credit. We moved into a new office, a block west, at 2108 West Fourth Avenue, in the same block as the new *Georgia Straight* newspaper office. We now had our own telephones, a telex machine, and a copy machine. Lawyer Marvin Storrow and publisher Peter Speck joined the board of directors, and Innes hired a young bookkeeper, Starlet Lum. Conflicts among the factions surfaced almost immediately. The streetwise radicals such as Watson, Walrus, and Taeko had deep ties to what they considered the grassroots ecology movement and they remained skeptical of Hollywood deals and corporate accountants. The entrepreneurial faction, led by Bill Gannon and Bobbi Innes, administered an increasingly complex array of agreements and accounts. The new financial controls made fresh demands on the mystics and revolutionaries. Alliances formed in myriad directions and occupied an increasing portion of everyone's time. Hunter struggled to lead the fragile mosaic of grassroots activists, Native Nations, union leaders, rank-and-file fishermen, liberal ecologists, university professors, students, vegetarian hippies, biologists, rock and roll stars, and now legions of whale-lovers. Keeping everyone happy became impossible.

John and Phyllis Cormack provided a calming influence, since we respected them as clear-minded elders. Lessons to stay humble had been thoroughly drummed into our heads from the *I Ching*, the Chinese calendar, and mentors like Don Franks. Most of the rank and file — Eileen Chivers, Bree Drummond, Barry Lavender, George Korotva, Linda Spong, Ron Precious, Fred Easton, and the "hard-core mystics" like Mel and Rod Marining — continued to work quietly and transcend the fray of politics.

For the more conservative types, there was still too much dope-smoking, beer-drinking, and counterculture antics. On the other hand, the late night parties and rousing music sessions led by Mel Gregory, with Bill Gannon on bass and Linda Spong on fiddle, helped fuse the radical goofiness with the corporate earnestness. Bobbi Innes, a relentless business manager, would be one of the last standing when the band played "Please Mr. Spaceman," at two o'clock in the morning.

New board members such as Peter Speck complained that Hunter's open-handed organizational style was idealistic, yet Hunter held the factions together with the force of his zany charisma. Politically, he was a pushover for tough advocates like Watson, McTaggart, or Moore, who could convince him of the merits of almost any plan. Hunter supported everyone, a strength and simultaneously a vulnerability. The various spokes of the Greenpeace wheel did not always turn together. He covered this weakness with humour and moments of brilliance, by keeping up morale, by attracting smart people to the cause, and by inspiring them to work. On most afternoons, we moved from the office to the pub. Strategizing at the beer parlour had become a ritual. "The reason I do my crazy act," Hunter told me in the Bimini Pub one night, "is because if I acted as pious as I feel, it would make people sick."

Hunter's biggest challenge at this time was to broker a compromise between Patrick Moore and Paul Watson. Their clash had begun during the whale campaign, and now Watson did not want Moore on the newly minted seal crew, but Hunter insisted Moore be there as our scientific spokesman. Most in the group admired Watson's seditious bravado, but he irritated some people, and he thoroughly riled Moore, a smart ecologist with a steel-trap mind for scientific detail. Watson was an intuitive radical. They represented natural extremes of the environmental movement, and they made Greenpeace a stronger force, but working together in one organization grated on both of them.

In February, Byrd Baker of the group Mendocino Whale War asked Greenpeace to help his group find a boat so they could take their own crew out along Mendocino Ridge the following summer. This fit with our plans to go deeper into the Pacific after the Japanese fleets. We introduced Baker to John Cormack and helped negotiate a charter of the *Phyllis Cormack* to explore the coastal seamounts for the Russian fleets. This alliance might also, we thought, demonstrate to the California groups that we weren't trying to hog headlines for ourselves. "Remember the dragon thing," said Hunter. "Stay humble."

In March, we received a call from Washington, D.C. about a confrontation between loggers in Brazil and the peasant rubber tappers led by

Chico Mendez. The American group wanted us to send our Greenpeace boat to the Amazon, but we had no boat. Walrus suggested we send someone to Brazil to liaison, but Gannon convinced Hunter that the secret to managing a budget was to stick to it. Those with houses on the line at the bank were naturally more cautious, but once again, tension over money escalated among the factions.

Meanwhile, news arrived about a disastrous chemical spill in Seveso, Italy. An explosion at the Givaudan chemical plant had contaminated workers with dioxin. I dug into the story and found that in 1949, an explosion at a Monsanto plant in West Virginia had led researchers to suspect dioxins were a "potent carcinogen." As well, Dow chemical workers had been contaminated with dioxins and other organochlorines from herbicides in the 1930s. Dow had used the more toxic varieties to create the defoliant Agent Orange, 11 million gallons of which the US military had dumped on Vietnam. I heard stories of American veterans complaining of organ failures and nervous system disorders. The file on toxic chemicals swelled.

That spring, the oil tanker *Urquiola* spilled 9 million gallons of crude oil in the Spanish harbour of La Coruña. At the same time, news began to leak out about a chemical waste disaster in Love Canal, near Niagara Falls, New York State, where children had come down with unusual health problems and fish died in local ponds. "Maybe it's just selective perception," surmised Hunter, "but the ecological crisis seems to be expanding on an exponential trajectory."

"Bob," I implored, "we should be printing an ecology magazine every month."

"I know," said Hunter. "Work it out." I talked with Gannon about the idea, and we drafted a budget for a monthly ecology magazine.

So many ecological fronts had opened, even in our small office, that we could no longer keep pace with them. Rather than join the seal team, I stayed in Vancouver to work with Marining on media. Moore doubled as ecologist and photographer. He took his own camera, and I loaned him one of mine. Ron Precious and Michael Chechik comprised the film crew. Innes stayed in Vancouver to keep her job at the cable company and to oversee the Greenpeace office. We held a harp seal campaign benefit at the Commodore Ballroom in Vancouver, and on March 2, 1976, Walrus, Watson, and most of their crew departed by train across Canada to Halifax, Nova Scotia.

When the Greenpeace seal campaign was announced in Vancouver, the media in France — Gamma Photo Agency, TV5 International television, and editors at *Le Monde* and *L'Express* — phoned the little Paris Greenpeace office. David McTaggart and Brice Lalonde had been building allies among the supporters of François Mitterand, who had narrowly lost the French presidency to Valéry Giscard d'Estaing in 1974. The progressive opposition in France dreamed of forming the government that they had thought was theirs during the student riots of 1968. Mitterand courted feminists, pacifists, and environmentalists to pad his strong union support.

Almost overnight, and by default, McTaggart became an advocate for Canadian harp seal pups. The little whitecoats won the hearts of millions of French voters across all political boundaries, giving Greenpeace fresh political muscle in Paris. Student political lobbyist Rémi Parmentier offered to help McTaggart navigate French politics. Suddenly the Greenpeace name, almost anywhere in the world, conferred instant media presence and political power. As the fire dragon had warned, however, it was a time to be aware of the impetuous ego.

A NEWFIE WELCOME

Across the Prairies roared the crew of the first Greenpeace harp seal campaign, flags decorating the rail car, backpacks stashed overhead, and a makeshift kitchen between the seats. Twenty-five-year-old Paul Watson served as campaign leader. Henrietta Nielsen, a twenty-year-old student, represented Greenpeace Norway. Dan Willens, twenty-seven, a naturalist and music teacher from Indiana, had raised a substantial portion of the money for the campaign. Bonnie MacLeod, twenty-four, a bank teller from Richmond, BC, had answered an ad that Watson had placed in *The Georgia Straight*. Paul "Pablo" Morse was a twenty-two-year-old master seaman from the Maritimes. Marilyn Kaga from Vancouver came from a Hiroshima family with samurai ancestry. Al "Jet" Johnson, a commercial pilot living in San Francisco, had received Arctic survival training in the Royal Canadian Air Force. Walrus and Johnson, squad leaders, would guide teams over the ice.

At the railway station in North Sydney, Cape Breton Island, Walrus drove the UN flag, the Earth flag, and a new Kwakiutl-Greenpeace flag into the Maritime turf, proclaiming the first Greenpeace campaign on the Atlantic Coast.

The herds of Labrador harp seals had once numbered 30 million animals, when Basque and Cape Breton sealers first hunted them in 1534. Wooden schooners arrived in 1780, and from there the story of the seals unfolded much like the demise of marine mammals in the Pacific. The Labrador harp seals were reduced to 10 million by 1900. Steamships from Norway reduced the herd to four million by 1950, and modern diesel ships further diminished the herd to one million by the spring of 1976. Fifty million harp seal pelts had been harvested from the Labrador Sea, and although the hunt was a tattered remnant of its heyday, in Newfoundland it remained a tradition.

Cameraman Ron Precious, Pat Moore, Eileen Chivers, and Greenpeace president Bob Hunter flew to Halifax and met the others in North Sydney. They rented a van and crossed icy Cabot Strait by ferry to Channel-Port-aux-Basques on the southwest coast of Newfoundland. The party of twelve, their packs, and their ice floe survival gear could not fit into the van, so Hunter, Moore, Chivers, and Ron Precious took a bus 150 miles north to Corner Brook, as Watson and his crew eased along the frozen road in the van.

The Rainbow Warriors gawked at the alien landscape through flurries of ice and snow. The Great Northern Peninsula of Newfoundland is an extension of the Appalachian Mountains, formed by billion-year-old granite pushed up from ancient Cambrian seabeds. At Gros Morne, a 30-square-mile slab of the Earth's mantle is thrust up into a massive form the locals call the "Tablelands." Geologists say the area more closely resembles the surface of the moon than the rest of the Earth. The fjords along the coast, which must be crossed by ferry, feature 2,000-foot granite cliffs. In March, the straits and bays of northern Newfoundland are solid ice and the sea is a patchwork of ice floes.

In Corner Brook, they rented a second van and continued up the peninsula toward the tiny fishing harbour of St. Anthony, on the frozen Labrador Sea. The narrow road disappeared before them. The snow became deeper and thicker by the hour. Both vans slipped on the ice, plowed into snow-banks, and finally dropped off the road. The Greenpeace seal crew found themselves waist deep in snow, at night, with a gale blowing in from the Gulf of St. Lawrence. They pushed their rented vans back onto the icy road but abandoned their plan to drive through the night, and pulled into a roadside motel near Ingornachoix Bay. The motel lobby looked like a country inn, with fireplace, bar, and wooden tables. When the company of seal savers walked in, pool balls clicked to a stop and conversations faded.

Aware that local politicians and newspaper columnists had called for their heads, the protestors had removed their conspicuous Greenpeace flags and pins, but radio stations had broadcast their progress and they were easily recognized. Popular Newfoundland sentiment stood unanimously hostile to the "meddlesome mainlanders," and "big-city do-gooders." St. John's, Newfoundland radio pundit Rex Murphy called Greenpeace "conscience hustlers" and "noxious twits" who "fiddle around with nuclear testing, women's liberation, Native rights, the environment, pollution, and black studies." The Greenpeace anti-nuclear antics, wrote Murphy, "consisted of nothing more skillful than parking some scow as close as possible to the site of a blast." Now, Murphy ridiculed Greenpeace for fawning over dead baby seals.

The bar patrons in Ingornachoix Bay were rugged survivors in a stingy environment. For a few months each summer, Newfoundland blossoms into a maritime paradise, but for the rest of the year, the environment is merciless. The young "swilers" risked their lives each spring to make a few hundred dollars collecting seal pelts, but they ardently protected their way of life. They believed the fisheries officers who told them harp seals were responsible for the decline of the herring and capelin fisheries. Pat Moore had countered this argument on the radio and in national newspapers. "Seals aren't black holes!" he said. "They don't remove nutrients from the sea when they eat fish, like humans do. Tens of millions of seals coexisted with abundant fish for thousands of years. So blaming the seals for depleted fish stocks is bad science." Moore's logic, however, had not penetrated the fishing communities of Newfoundland.

At the motel, Chivers and Walrus talked to the manager and rented five rooms. Once inside their rooms, they turned on the televisions and saw film of an irate mob of fishermen blocking the road into St. Anthony. The fishermen and townspeople waved signs: MAINLANDERS GO HOME and PROTECT BC DRUG ADDICTS NOT OUR SEALS.

"Those Greenpeacers won't dare show up here," said a scarred swiler with icicles hanging from his beard.

Walrus sat on the bed next to Hunter. "We're in enemy territory now," he said. The crew discussed strategies for the next day, but there was not much they could do but drive north and meet their fate. Ron Precious, it was agreed, would hang back like a news cameraman and film whatever happened at the roadblock. Hunter awoke in the middle of the night as wind rattled the window. He trembled in the darkness at the thought of facing a pack of angry Newfoundlanders.

The next morning the Greenpeace crew slipped out of the motel and headed north. They heard on the radio that the mob had been blocking the road into St. Anthony since dawn. In the mid-afternoon they approached the harbour town on the northeast coast of the peninsula. Two hundred townspeople met them and blocked the road with pick-up trucks, cars, and snowmobiles for a mile behind the crowd. Moore drove the lead van with Watson beside him and Hunter and Chivers in the back seat.

This was a new experience for the Warriors of the Rainbow. Greenpeace had been heroes in Canada for standing up to the American and French war machines and the Soviet whalers, but now we stepped on Canadian toes, and worse, on the toes of Newfoundlanders, who didn't particularly like or trust mainland Canadians. Newfoundland had its own culture, dating from sixteenth-century Basque, Scottish, Irish, and Norwegian settlers. The inhabitants had their own way of doing things, including their own time zone divided from the rest of the world on the half-hour. Newfoundlanders remained fiercely independent.

Swilers and fishermen had come from outlying communities — Onion Bay, Goose Cove, Patyville — to join the blockade. The crowd hooted and shook signs, the curt, GREENPEACE OUT! and the poetic:

GO DYE YOUR SOCKEYE
AND YOUR BC PINE
HANDS OFF OUR SEALS
OR PAY THE NEWFI FINE

When the vans stopped, the throng surged forward. The toughest young swilers in front swung a hangman's noose at the window and rocked the two vans.

"This must be the place," said Moore.

Moore and Watson climbed from the same side of the van and faced the mob. They wore bright orange arctic survival suits, which contrasted sharply with the dark, weathered coats of the locals. Swilers screamed at them. Moore noticed men swigging from mickeys of whisky. Watson tried to speak but was drowned out by howling swilers.

When Eileen Chivers climbed from the van and stood beside Moore, the young men dangling a noose in Moore's face backed away. Murmurs grew and the taunting rose up again, but at a distance. A whisky bottle flew through the air above the van.

Hunter climbed from the back seat, on the far side of the van. He slouched toward the van behind and casually slipped into the crowd. With his dark navy coat, grubby jeans, gumboots, beard, and dark toque, he blended with the locals. He clomped up a snowbank and stood among a group of judicious observers. From this vantage, he saw a police car parked well behind the mob, but the two officers inside looked as if they had no interest in getting out into the cold. Among the crowd, Hunter spied a group of men directing the demonstration, and at the centre of this group a stout middle-aged man in glasses, with a green tie underneath his snowmobile jumpsuit. Hunter squeezed through the crowd, walked up to the man, and extended his hand. The Newfoundlander shook Hunter's hand with a curious twist on his lips. "Roy Pilgrim," he said.

"Bob Hunter."

Pilgrim peered out through thick glasses. The former town councillor headed the Concerned Citizens Committee of St. Anthony Against Greenpeace. "Yeah?" He squinted at Hunter.

"Can we arrange a meeting?" Hunter asked.

"'S already been arranged, b'ye," said Pilgrim. The townsfolk, Pilgrim explained, would gather at the elementary school auditorium at nine that night. There, they would present their grievances to the Greenpeace members.

"Okay. Good," Hunter said. The screaming at Watson and Moore continued for half an hour before Pilgrim quieted the crowd and announced the meeting. A convoy of trucks, snowmobiles, and whooping swilers escorted the Greenpeace team like captured outlaws through the icy streets of St. Anthony. The procession pulled up outside Decker's Boarding House, on the shoreline of the harbour, a white cottage trimmed in pale blue. Ice and snow covered the home and outlying buildings.

In front of the cottage, the throng closed in again. Moore and Watson appealed to them but were shouted down. Walrus Oakenbough, who had been silent throughout, strode forward and looked into the eyes of the toughest young fisherman waving his fist and dangling a noose. "Look," he said, "This isn't about you and me. This is about Mother Earth. I haven't heard one of you guys say one word about Mother Earth. The seals, the whales, the birds, everything belongs to Mother Earth. You think you own it? You don't. Those seals are as much mine as yours. We're here to save them and you're not going to stop us. It's Mother Earth's will. So get out of the way. Step aside."

The swiler stepped back.

Chivers, who had made the arrangements at the boarding house, stepped up beside Walrus. The crowd parted, and Walrus and Chivers led the company of Warriors of the Rainbow down the snowy path to Decker's Boarding House. Chivers doubted they would be welcomed now, with the angry mob following them, but kind, grandmotherly Emily Decker met them at the door. "A deal's a deal, dear," she said. "Just bring your things inside."

GREENPEACE SURRENDERS

Reporters from the CBC, NBC News, *The Washington Post*, the CBC, *Der Stern*, and other international agencies arrived in St. Anthony, or "S'n Ant'ny," as the mainlanders soon learned. The media teams stayed at the Vinland Hotel and the beer parlour of the Vinland became the ad hoc media centre. "Vinland" had been the Viking name for the island 500 years before English mariner John Cabot named it "New Founde Isle" on behalf of his sovereign, King Henry VII.

As the Greenpeace crew settled into Emily and Nat Decker's boarding house, Hunter paced and stewed over what to do. He asked "Ma" Decker for a phone book, found Roy Pilgrim's name, and called him. "Mr. Pilgrim," he said, "I think we should talk privately." The Newfoundlander agreed and Hunter slipped quietly from the boarding house and walked one block through the snow to Roy Pilgrim's waiting car. They talked with the windows rolled up and the heater on.

Moore had discovered a non-toxic green dye used by Department of Fisheries biologists, which Watson and Walrus planned to apply to the pelts of the infant whitecoats. Hunter learned from Pilgrim that the dye had become the object of scorn among the denizens of St. Anthony. He had the entire population of Newfoundland and the Department of Fisheries on his side, as well as the fuming multitude in St. Anthony. But the world media glared down on them. Pilgrim did not want to see Newfoundlanders portrayed as a lynch mob and Hunter did not want to see Greenpeace pitted against the common people of Newfoundland. Neither of them wanted violence.

"Look," Hunter told Pilgrim, "we need to focus on the commercial fleets. But to do that, we have to get our helicopters out to the ice floes. Roy, there're about a million seals left out of some 30 million. Same thing that's happening to the cod and everything else, and it isn't the fault of the coastal fishermen *or* the seals. It's the factory ships. It's the same on the West Coast. How long do you think this will last if you don't get rid of the Norwegian boats?" Hunter lowered his voice to a whisper. "And exposing them," he said, "will help make the case for a 200-mile fishing limit."

Pilgrim looked out the window. Newfoundland fishermen had been advocating the 200-mile limit for years. "Yeah, okay," he said. "Leave the landsmen alone and forget about spraying seals." In exchange, he agreed that the townspeople would not interfere with the Greenpeace helicopters getting to the ice floes. Hunter agreed to abandon the green dye that had infuriated the locals. They shook hands. Pilgrim drove off through the snow and Hunter trundled back to Decker's to sell the deal to his compatriots.

Meanwhile, Greenpeace lawyer Marvin Storrow, his wife Colette Storrow, and filmmaker Michael Chechik had arrived with the two Greenpeace helicopters and their pilots. Hunter conferred with Storrow, Watson, Moore, Walrus, and Chivers. Watson hesitated to give up the dye, but knew that forging an alliance with the people of Newfoundland against the Norwegian sealing industry was the right move. The green dye had already tipped the hand of the Canadian government by inducing the Liberal cabinet to pass a makeshift Order-in-Council outlawing the spraying of seals, although their own scientists did so regularly. The dye had roused Maritime pundits to tirades and acted as a lightning rod for Newfoundland fury. Greenpeace had gained full value for the green dye idea. The sensible strategy now was to target the Norwegian ships. Watson consented to the deal with Pilgrim.

That evening, 600 citizens of St. Anthony jammed into the school auditorium, filled the seats and crowded into the corners. Film crews set up cameras to the side of a small stage. High-spirited swilers jeered at the Greenpeace contingent, but the mood had shifted from that of a lynch mob to something more akin to a slapstick theatre troupe. Some in the crowd offered discreet nods and even polite smiles. Hunter noticed that one group of young men seemed stung by the commanding strength and beauty of the four women — Eileen Chivers, Marilyn Kaga, Bonnie MacLeod, and Henrietta Nielson. Likewise, a few young women peeked discreetly through the crowd at Walrus, Watson, Paul Morse, and Al Johnson. The tension of these emotions was held in suspension by a ruddy-cheeked Roy Pilgrim in his black horn-rimmed glasses. He sat at a table before the assembly with Hunter, Watson, Moore, and Chivers. He extolled the courage of the Newfoundland swilers, and the crowd roared. "Our guests understand," Pilgrim said, "dey can't come in here 'n tell S'n Ant'ny folks nothin' about how t' live." More cheers rose. "Anyway, I'll let dese b'ys speak fer demselves."

Watson took the mike. "The harp seal hunt peaked a hundred years ago," he began. The Newfies heckled him. "In 1972, Dr. Allen from the Canadian Department of Fisheries recommended that the hunt be phased out." Boos and whistles drowned him out.

Chivers made silent eye contact with each woman in the room. Moore spoke to more guffaws and heckles. "Politicians are telling you the seals are stealing your herring and capelin," he said, "to cover up bad fisheries management."

When Hunter took the microphone, he gave an ironic shrug. "We were impressed by your roadblock," he said. "It's obvious to us that Newfoundlanders know how to stand up for what they believe in." Cheers rose and the swilers raised their fists. "But Greenpeacers are rugged, independent people too." The auditorium quieted. Hunter told the people of St. Anthony about hard-working fisherman John Cormack and the maritime feats and bravery of David McTaggart. He told them about Carlie Trueman and Ann-Marie Horne. He told them what he had witnessed: Russian whalers and Korean draggers, West Coast trollers chasing declining fish stocks, disappearing king crab, and scarce halibut. The coastal families in the auditorium knew the story all too well.

"So," said Hunter, "out of respect for the serious economic hardships experienced by the people of Newfoundland, the Greenpeace Foundation will drop its plans to spray the seal pups with green dye."

The auditorium erupted in cheers. Swilers danced and chanted. Later, Hunter spoke privately with the assembled journalists and explained the deal. Back at Decker's Boarding House, he phoned Rod Marining in Vancouver and filed a news story, quoting Roy Pilgrim and explaining that Newfoundlanders would join Greenpeace on the ice floes to confront the Norwegian ships.

"Greenpeace Surrenders!" screamed the headlines in Newfoundland the next morning. "Greenpeace converted to sealers' side!" The victory of the Concerned Citizens Committee of St. Anthony Against Greenpeace rang across the frozen Maritimes.

In Toronto and Vancouver, however, the headlines trumpeted a different story: The alliance between Greenpeace and Newfoundlanders against the Norwegian sealers. "Greenpeace, Nflders unite in seal pact," proclaimed the *Province* newspaper in Vancouver. "Greenpeacers and Newfoundlanders," the report declared, "in an agreement worked out Tuesday, will go out on the ice together and place their bodies between the seals and Norwegian hunters."

Dan Willen phoned his home in Bloomington, Indiana, and found that his friends had seen St. Anthony footage on their local news channels. Halfway around the world, wide-eyed seal pups appeared in magazines at newsstands in London and in hotel lobbies in Davos, Switzerland.

Meanwhile, a theatre group in Corner Brook founded the Codpeace Foundation, whose primary purpose was to mock Greenpeacers and other high-minded mainlanders. They achieved national coverage and local fame.

UNION BOSS

One Greenpeace crewmember, wild-eyed Carl Rising-Moore, had been left behind in New Brunswick when he lost his pack on the train. He had recovered his lost gear, and now hitchhiked north along the icy road toward St. Anthony. In Corner Brook, he ducked into a pub to dry out and thaw his freezing fingers. He sat in a corner and ordered a bowl of soup. A television above the bar showed pictures of the roadblock in St. Anthony. A group of fishermen and serious men in suits sat at a table nearby.

The men were members and executives of the Newfoundland Fishermen, Food, and Allied Workers Union, the NFFAW. Among them sat union president Richard Cashin, a greying, red-headed lawyer and politician from St. John's, Newfoundland, a former Member of Parliament and former secretary to the federal Minister of Fisheries. He had been turned out by the voters in 1968 but wanted back into federal politics. The squabble in St. Anthony was the sort of populist uprising that could catapult him onto the Commission for the Northwest Atlantic Fisheries. "Damn Greenpeace assholes!" Cashin said loud enough for the long-haired mainlander to hear.

Rising-Moore wore a blue UN insignia on his parka. He walked across the room and introduced himself to Cashin and the fishermen. Since he was not with the Greenpeace crew, he led the men to believe he was a UN observer. Rising-Moore talked with Cashin about a common cause that he and his union might share with the environmentalists. "They're pushing for the 200-mile limit," said Rising-Moore. "Wouldn't that help your fishermen?" The next morning, Cashin was on a chartered plane for St. Anthony.

In St. Anthony, on March 10, Eileen Chivers worked with Ma Decker to prepare a meal while keeping in line the sixteen protestors, impatient journalists, visiting Royal Canadian Mounted Police officers (Mounties), and meddling federal fisheries officers. Chivers, friendly but firm, dispensed cash, guarded food supplies, and directed visitors to hang up their coats. Medic Marilyn Kaga packed and checked safety gear for the base camp team. She swept out the water and mud, and shook the doormats for Ma Decker. She had the ability to work briskly, pass out on the bed for an hour, then awaken and start up where she'd left off. Dan Willens, Henrietta Nielson, and Bonnie MacLeod stored the gear and made supply runs. This was the first Greenpeace campaign on land, but even so, communications and supply lines were no less fragile than they would have been on a boat. The phone at Decker's Boarding House stayed as busy as the prime minister's.

That morning, five days before the official hunt, as newborn seal pups first opened their eyes on the ice floes, Hunter and Watson handed the green dye to Roy Pilgrim in a flashy ceremony in front of the world media. Pilgrim clutched the bags of dye triumphantly. The crowd took possession of the compressed-air sprayers. Hunter and Watson handed out Greenpeace pins and seal pins to rejoicing Newfoundlanders, and cameras whirred. Later, Hunter told Moore and Chivers, "The sight of Henrietta Nielson, a

Viking goddess, and Marilyn Kaga, a daughter of the samurai, standing before the men and women of St. Anthony as Warriors of the Rainbow, nearly made me weep."

By mid-morning, union boss Richard Cashin had flown into town and met with Roy Pilgrim. He phoned Decker's Boarding House and invited Hunter to a meeting with his NFFAW union executives. Hunter, Moore, and Watson met with Cashin, and from this meeting, the Newfoundland union and Greenpeace issued a joint statement, agreeing on an "overall need for conservation and resource management." Cashin read the statement to the assembled world media outside the Vinland Hotel. "... Both organizations urge the Canadian government to make a formal commitment to unilaterally declare a 200-mile fishing management zone." He paused. "We are jointly planning a blockade of the ports of St. John's and Vancouver to all foreign trawlers and draggers by June 1, 1976, if Canada has not yet taken the action we have recommended."

To the south, Carl Rising-Moore, still masquerading as a UN observer and hitching scarce rides through snow flurries, found that the Newfoundlanders had grown pleasant and conciliatory toward Greenpeace. "Dem Greenpeace b'ys's okay," a driver on his way north to St. Lunaire told him. "Ya think we don't care about de'seals?"

BELLE ISLE

On March 10, Department of Fisheries information officer Charles Friend advanced the opening of the hunt by two days, to March 13. Steel-hulled sealing ships pushed toward the front. Greenpeace prepared to establish a base camp on Belle Isle, 30 miles north, close to the Labrador front where the seal hunt would commence. Two helicopters stood ready.

Helicopter pilot Jack Wallace — "Captain Jack," a Royal Canadian Air Force veteran, bald and fit, in his fifties — maintained a neat, pressed, blue uniform with a silver helicopter on his pocket. His colleague, Bernd Firnung — thirty-seven, cheerful, and almost indistinguishable from the protestors at Decker's — had trained in the German Air Force and served with NATO in Europe. Firnung and Captain Jack flew one-ton Bell Jet Ranger-II helicopters that could travel at 120 miles per hour. Short of breaking the law, and within the limits of reasonable safety, Wallace and

Firnung were prepared to fly the Greenpeace crews anywhere they wanted to go, ecology's first non-violent, confrontational airforce.

However, the campaign had two Achilles' heels: weather and fuel.

At the Imperial Oil station, federal fisheries officers visited the dealer and threatened that he might be subject to criminal charges if he sold fuel to anyone who had intentions of breaking government regulations. The manager, thoroughly intimidated, denied fuel to the Greenpeace pilots.

When Marvin Storrow heard this, he phoned the local RCMP detachment and told the corporal in charge that an attempted extortion had taken place. The Mounties headed to Decker's to meet with Storrow. Before they arrived, he phoned the Department of Fisheries office in St. John's, talked to the boss, informed him that his agents in St. Anthony had overstepped their jurisdiction and broken the law, and that the RCMP were on their way to sort it out. Then he hung up on the frantic bureaucrat. Two RCMP officers arrived at Decker's, and Storrow cited the Criminal Code of Canada regarding extortion. In the meantime, Hunter walked to the Vinland Hotel pub and informed the assembled journalists of the charges. The two Mounties left Decker's, visited the Imperial Oil dealer, and within an hour, the helicopters took on fuel, while Charles Friend and his mandarins in Ottawa fielded phone calls from the CBC and *Der Stern*.

The choppers carried 63 gallons of fuel, good for three hours' flying. Captain Jack suggested they ferry fuel to the base camp on Belle Isle to save time and extend their range. At the Imperial Oil dock, they filled four 36-gallon fuel drums. By nightfall, the advance team had packed. Captain Jack and Pa Decker sat in the kitchen by the barometer and talked weather.

That evening, CBC television aired a half-hour documentary on Greenpeace. The director had cut footage from St. Anthony with footage from the whale campaign and still photographs from the anti-nuclear voyages of the *Phyllis Cormack* and *Vega*. Virtually every family in St. Anthony watched the show. The next morning, March 11, patrons of the Vinland beer parlour nodded approvingly and even accepted a round of beer from Moore and Storrow. Still, a great deal of neighbourly fun was poked at the mainlanders.

At the boarding house, on March 11, Pa Decker and Captain Jack consulted again over the barometer and decided the choppers could make Belle Isle, 30 miles north. Jack recommended taking only two passengers in each helicopter so they could ferry fuel drums. Paul Watson, Walrus Oakenbough, Al "Jet" Johnson, and Patrick Moore departed with the gear to assemble the base camp.

The helicopters beat against swirling winds for half an hour, in and out of fog banks, until they reached Belle Isle in the white Labrador Sea. Ice covered the nine-mile-long island, except for a few exposed granite cliffs and outcrops. Captain Jack found a flat site to land, and the team climbed out onto solid ice, polished by the wind. The thermometer read 35 degrees Fahrenheit below zero. The crew stored the fuel drums a quarter mile from the campsite and the helicopters roared back to St. Anthony. In the ice, in front of his tent, Walrus planted a blue United Nations flag.

In the late afternoon, Moore walked over the ice sheet, heard icebergs crumbling far out at sea, and made his way to a bluff of exposed granite. The only life he could find on the island was lichen clinging to the rock. In the Strait of Belle Isle, red sandstone and orange limestone, once the bed of a Cambrian sea, had been driven to the surface by the collisions of tectonic plates. The stone was flecked with feldspar crystals and white calcite from ocean reefs of long-extinct archeocyathids. Moore found ice caves, chipped quartz from the ancient stone, and returned to the camp at sunset.

To the northeast, on the ice floes of the Labrador front, 100,000 harp seal pups suckled and slept. Within three days, their golden-yellow pelts would turn pure white. Further to the east, Norwegian and Canadian ice-cutters — the *Martin Karlsen*, the *Melshorn*, the *Theron* and the *Arctic Endeavor* — broke through pans of ice approaching the nursery.

Night fell across Labrador and the four Warriors of the Rainbow huddled in their sleeping bags, in blackness, listening to the wind and cracking ice.

VINLAND

Fresh media teams from New York and Paris arrived at the Vinland Hotel, and they all wanted access to the action, but Greenpeace had the only two helicopters not claimed by fisheries officers. Assertive NBC producers, homespun CBC teams, and gung-ho German photographers wanted rides out to Belle Isle. So did the Greenpeace camera team of Michael Chechik and Ron Precious, and so did the rest of the Greenpeace activists. Hunter and Chivers attempted to sort out the demands for rides. Each trip to Belle Isle with two helicopters cost $900 in time and fuel. Each Jet Ranger had five seats, one for the pilot, one for fuel drums, and three for passengers.

On Tuesday, March 12, Hunter negotiated with media teams in the Vinland Hotel. He asked them to pay for fuel for rides to Belle Isle, and some were willing, but others saw this as a breach of objective journalism. Hunter understood the reporter's ethic, but paying to travel to a remote site seemed reasonable to him. In any case, Greenpeace could not afford to operate a free shuttle. The NBC team flatly refused to pay. "You're dead in New York," the irate producer told Hunter.

As the weary Greenpeace president stewed over this in the Vinland, two young Newfies pulled up to his table and toasted him. Art Elliot, an experienced landsman, volunteered to guide Greenpeace over the ice floes. Doug Pilgrim, Roy's younger brother, offered to go out on the ice and to start a local Greenpeace chapter. Hunter had promised a Newfoundland presence on the ice and added them to the swelling list that now included fifteen from the Greenpeace team, five Newfies, and twenty-two journalists. To fly everyone out to Belle Isle once would cost $6,300.

As Hunter thought the campaign was spinning out of control, the chaos accelerated. Through the door of the Vinland Hotel burst a smiling David McTaggart, fresh from Paris with a French television crew and Gamma Agency photographer Jean-Claude Francolon, who had flown to St. Anthony from the war zone in Beirut. Hunter experienced space-time distortion as McTaggart pumped his hand and pounded him on the back. They drank beer, and McTaggart told Hunter that the seal campaign was big news in Paris. He easily persuaded Hunter that his friends should get bumped to the front of the line for a ride to Belle Isle. "This will *make* Greenpeace in Paris, Bob," McTaggart insisted. "And if I win these guys' support, it will help our appeal case." McTaggart had risked his life to stop nuclear weapons and nearly lost an eye for his troubles. Hunter was not about to refuse him now.

However, back at Decker's, Hunter met resistance to pushing photographer Francolon to the front of the crew list. It did not help that Francolon's brand new sealskin boots, picked up on the way to Newfoundland, became objects of scorn among the hard-core seal lovers like Henrietta Neilson and Bonnie MacLeod. But Francolon, a deceptively frail, slightly disembodied marquis, remained unflappable, and Hunter added him to the list.

On March 12, the Greenpeace camera teams shuttled to Belle Isle to get footage of the camp. Pablo Morse, Marilyn Kaga, Eileen Chivers, Hunter, and Ron Precious prepared to join the Belle Isle camp, but on March 13, a fresh blizzard hit Northern Newfoundland. The Labrador front was a whiteout. Captain Jack and Bernd Firnung tied down the choppers with heavy rope.

A full gale ripped at the Belle Isle tents. Sixty-knot gusts lifted everything not tied down and carried it off into boundless white space. Walrus barely saved the UN flag. The tape recorders and walkie-talkies sat frozen and useless. Two of the four stoves failed. Skin exposed to the wind turned rock hard in seconds. Walrus, Watson, Moore, and Jet Johnson finally had no choice but to move their camp away from the helicopter landing area, into the lee of a granite outcrop. Walrus planted the U.N. flag back in front of the tents, and they waited for their comrades to find them.

That afternoon, the skies opened over St. Anthony. Captain Jack and Pa Decker conferred. The helicopters lifted off during the respite, battled flurries and gusts north to Belle Isle, and found the new camp. Upon landing, Marilyn Kaga treated the advance crew for windburn, frozen fingers, cuts and burns from the stoves. Chivers moved into a tent with Walrus and Pat Moore; Pablo Morse and Ron Precious moved in with Jet Johnson; and Marilyn Kaga and Paul Watson shared the third tent. They offloaded supplies, and the pilots flew back to St. Anthony.

For the next two days, the storm over the Northwest Atlantic grounded the helicopters, halted the Norwegian ice-cutters and pinned the tiny forward platoon of Rainbow Warriors in their tents. Jet Johnson was the only one who could light the frozen camp stoves. To conserve stove fuel, they used the heaters sparingly and did not use the Coleman lanterns at all. To light the quirky stoves, Johnson would build a small fire with paper in a fry pan, set the stoves in the blaze, and stand back as they ignited in a burst of flame and black smoke. The team dubbed Johnson's sooty hovel the "black lung tent." They melted ice for water, but steam condensed on the walls of the tents, froze, and fell on them like guillotine blades as they slept at night.

The base camp crew expected a supply run of food and fuel on March 14, but the storm had isolated them. In Labrador, the weather is lord of all. While the Canadian government had pushed the hunt opening forward two days, no swilers were yet on the ice. What the government could legislate, the dragon gods of wind could steal away. Aboard the sealing ships, stopped dead in the ice, young swilers huddled around their own meager stoves and waited for the blizzard to pass.

THE FRONT

On March 15, the storm blew into the Atlantic and the Labrador front was clear. The pilots awoke before dawn. Ma Decker had the coffee on and the helicopters sat ready to lift off by 5:45. McTaggart, staying at the Vinland with the French photographers, arrived at the boarding house with Jean-Claude Francolon, ready for action.

On Belle Isle, Moore, Walrus and Chivers awoke as the eastern sky grew light. They watched the sun rise over the vast, mute whiteness. Walrus threw the *I Ching* coins in his tent and drew the hexagram *Chin*, fire over earth, the rising sun that emerges from darkness to spread its light. The commentary promised that a prince, loyal to an enlightened leader, would be granted an audience "three times ... in a single day." To Walrus, his enlightened sovereign was Mother Earth. He prepared himself.

The thick rhythm of helicopter blades broke the stillness at 6:45 a.m. Captain Jack and Bernd Firnung arrived with Bob Hunter, lawyer Marvin Storrow, Newfie guide Art Elliot, photographer Francolon, and two drums of fuel. They discussed which direction would lead to the ships. North? Northeast? Southeast? "Due east," said Walrus. Pablo and Jet Johnson unloaded the fuel at the depot, and the first team to the front — Watson, Walrus, Jet Johnson, Moore and Ron Precious with cameras, and guide Art Elliot — lifted off over the ice pans, heading into the rising sun.

Twenty minutes later, ships appeared as tiny black dots in the distant ice floes. Captain Jack and Firnung swung low, abeam of the ships. They saw swilers on deck and read the vessel names. The Norwegian *Martin Karlsen* and *Theron* cleaved through loose pans and slob ice. Captain Jack pushed ahead of the ships and found the rest of the fleet, eight more ships. Looking down, Paul Watson saw long red streaks across the white ice. "Blood," he yelled to Walrus over the shrieking helicopter engines.

"Yeah," yelled Walrus. "Look." He pointed ahead to where the streaks of blood merged like spokes at a dark mounded hub. The two Rainbow

Warriors stared down upon swilers dragging fresh pelts to a pile to be picked up by the ships. Captain Jack recorded his compass reading. The federal Seal Protection Act had made it a crime to land within a quarter mile of a sealing ship, working sealers, or living seals. The pilot swung around and found a legal spot to land. When the helicopter touched down, Watson flung himself from the machine and charged across the ice in the direction of the ships and sealers. Art Elliot stayed right behind him, followed by Walrus. Moore and Ron Precious followed with the camera gear. Moore had expected a strategy session and was miffed that Watson had bolted, leaving his crew behind.

Walrus, Johnson, and Art Elliot caught Watson and kept pace over crushed, car-sized blocks heaped up by the shifting ice pans. They stopped when they found themselves in the harp seal nursing grounds, surrounded by infant whitecoats. The pups looked at the intruders, the first humans they had ever seen, with big, dark eyes.

In the distance, from atop a block of ice, Watson saw ships and swilers. Blood and seal carcasses streaked the ice floes. The swilers carried hakapiks, long poles with a steel knob and sharp claw at the head. The swiler's job is to knock out the baby seal, skin it quickly on the ice, and pile the pelts. Other sealers drag the small piles of pelts to the central piles along the path of the icebreakers.

Jet Johnson ran toward the first swiler he met, hakapik raised over a wide-eyed seal pup. He leapt over the ice and covered the pup. He looked into the eyes of the swiler, hakapik stilled in the air over his head. The swiler sneered at the protestor and turned after other prey. Jet Johnson followed.

Watson and Walrus picked out swilers and stuck close to them, pressing between men and the seal pups. The swilers, smeared in blood, had 12-inch, razor-sharp knives on their hips. They cursed and threatened the protesters but held back pummelling the intruders with their hakapiks. A foreman screamed at the protestors. Moore and Ron Precious caught up and recorded the fracas on film. Swilers wiped more blood across their faces, taunting the Greenpeace crews. As the day wore on, the winds picked up and icy gusts blew over the bloodied nursery.

Watson moved toward the sealing ship *Melshorn* as the ship sliced a path through the ice. Moore and Precious followed with cameras. Frantic mother seals dove into the water before the steel bow of the *Melshorn* as it broke through the ice and crushed infant whitecoats it its path. Watson stormed in front of the advancing ship and lifted a seal pup from the ice. Even at a few days old the pup weighed nearly fifty pounds. It fought furiously in Watson's arms and bit his cheek. Watson, surprised by the strength and weight of the seal, stumbled across the ice. The white ground ruptured before the bow of the ship. Watson carried the seal 20 yards over fresh fissures, just out of the path of the icebreaker, and dropped to the ground. A swiler approached, but Watson clung to the seal, which now became docile in his arms, like a puppy.

Two fisheries officers in beaver caps with bronze badges watched Watson. The Seal Protection Act made it illegal for anyone other than a registered sealer to touch a seal pup. Swilers and protestors jockeyed on the ice floes. The ship's captain screamed Norwegian obscenities from the bridge of the *Melshorn*. The first day of the 1976 Canadian seal hunt turned to chaos.

Back at the helicopter, Captain Jack had kept an eye on the mounting wind. As the sky turned ominous, he sent Firnung across the ice after the Greenpeacers. Firnung came upon the scene of swilers and shouted to the protestors, "Time to go." The Greenpeace seal team stumbled back to the helicopters, lips quivering and eyes wide. Captain Jack ushered them aboard and lifted off, followed by Firnung.

"Bastards," cursed Watson, as they circled over the bloody carnage on the deck of the *Melshorn*.

SUPPLY LINES

In the fading light, Watson, Walrus, Moore, and Johnson flew a supply run back to St. Anthony with the pilots. The supply team loaded provisions in the helicopters as Dan Willens sped off to the store for stove fuel. The four seal shepherds took fast showers, told their tales, warmed their fingers and toes, and literally licked their wounds around the Decker kitchen table. Small bits of gear sat on the table, drying. Walrus had fire in his eyes as he cleaned a pocketknife with emery paper. Watson, in a righteous fury, related how seals had been crushed under the steel hulls of ships. Jet Johnson sat speechless. Moore stacked film cassettes in a row on the wooden table as Pablo Morse prepared to take Moore's place on the ice. He checked his gear, his matches, and a fresh cook stove.

Pa Decker gnawed away at Captain Jack. "Better get 'im goin'."

"Yep," said Captain Jack.

Firnung turned into the kitchen. "Is that camp fuel here?" he asked.

"Coming, coming," Henrietta said.

"I'm startin' 'er up in five minutes," Firnung said. Twenty-knot gusts whipped through St. Anthony from the northwest. Bonnie and Henrietta packed the available provisions: cereals, fruit, soup packets, matches, paper, rags, and dry gloves. They loaded these onto the helicopters. Firnung fired the 160-pound Allison gas turbine engine. After five minutes, the engine lit up with a roar, followed by the wail of the power turbine.

"Are the supplies in?" Captain Jack screamed.

"Willens is coming with the stove fuel."

"Gotta go. Three minutes." Watson, Walrus, Johnson, and Pablo Morse climbed into the helicopter with their gear. Henrietta screamed at Walrus from the door of the howling machine. "We packed what we had. Not everything's here. You've got matches and gloves."

Walrus gave her a thumbs up. "Tomorrow," he screamed. Henrietta returned two thumbs up, backed away, and threw them all kisses with her mittens in the frozen air. The shaft shrieked at 50, 80, 100 revolutions per second, and the chopper lifted off. The winds gusted to 35 knots over the Strait of Belle Isle, near the limits for safe navigation. Firnung remained transfixed on the weather conditions and on his instruments. He touched down for no more than two minutes on Belle Isle to unload crew and provisions and take on Hunter, Storrow, and Art Elliot. The pilot beat back toward St. Anthony before the squalls, hugging the ice and ducking into the lee of granite cliffs.

Once back at Decker's, Hunter slouched in the parlour. "Facing your death regularly," he whispered to Storrow, "is strong therapy."

Henrietta held Firnung by the arm and pointed to a box. "This *has* to go tomorrow," she said. "It's the rest of the food and the stove fuel."

On Belle Isle, the sun set into a whiteout. Squalls swept down from Labrador over the ice. The next morning, however, broke clear over Belle Isle. Watson and Marilyn Kaga woke up in a tent frozen solid, sides like plates of steel. Johnson had a fire going in the black-lung tent while Pablo and Ron Precious took a walk under the brilliant blue sky. Their cheeks froze hard in minutes. In Walrus' "medicine tent," Chivers made soup and Jean-Claude Francolon gripped his sleeping bag around ears and lips.

Once Chivers served him some soup, Francolon sat up and cleaned his camera gear. He did not participate in survival chores, but as a professional, when the time came, he would be prepared to bring back pictures for the glossy magazine pages throughout Europe. By good fortune, he had been assigned to the medicine tent under the gracious care of Walrus and Chivers.

In the black-lung tent, Jet Johnson used the last of the stove fuel. He went through the boxes of supplies, but found no more. Walrus had none. Watson had none. "There wasn't much food in that box, either," said Walrus. "They'll be here soon."

But the helicopters from St. Anthony did not arrive. At noon, with the sun high, sky blue, and the day relatively warm for a moment, the base crew walked through the crystalline wonderland. As the afternoon wore on, Walrus and Chivers felt confused. The helicopters should have been to Belle Isle and back twice by now in this weather.

They didn't know that over St. Anthony, 30 miles south, the blizzard had not let up at all. Snow swirled around Decker's Boarding House and the choppers remained tied down. "Not having a radio at the base camp is a problem," Moore said. Captain Jack lifted his eyebrows over his coffee cup.

As evening approached on Belle Isle, Johnson, desperate to solve the stove fuel problem, constructed a funnel from paper, soaked it in water, and left it outside to freeze. He, Pablo, and Watson marched the quarter mile to the fuel depot, hoisted one drum up onto another, and tipped helicopter fuel through the funnel into small containers. Sloshing gasoline soaked into Johnson's survival suit. "Won't burn as clean as the stove fuel," he remarked as he set up his fry pan fire outside the tent, ready to set the stoves into the blaze. *Whoosh!* The first stove ignited, a flame shot straight up, and black smoke rose over the camp. "There's one," said Johnson. He got three camp stoves going as the sun set.

The next day, Belle Isle remained clear in the morning, but no helicopter arrived. By the afternoon, the skies had socked in with fog and snow. Johnson lit the stoves for soup and the base crew huddled in for another night on the frozen rock.

In St. Anthony, Pat Moore asked Department of Fisheries pilots if they could reach Belle Isle, but their helicopters were no more able to negotiate the storm and low visibility than the Greenpeace helicopters. "No one's going anywhere," said a fisheries officer, "until this storm clears." At Decker's, Captain Jack and Pa Decker sat in the kitchen, watched the barometer, and discussed atmospheric pressure. "Not today," said Pa Decker. The blizzard had shut down everything east of Montreal.

At midnight, Pa Decker still sat at the barometer, with the radio on. Weather reports predicted the storm would last another two days. Captain Jack stood nearby. "Trough comin'," Pa Decker told the pilot. "First light. You might have a coupla hours."

The Captain looked at the instrument. "Yeah, okay."

Before dawn on March 18, Captain Jack and Firnung fired up the helicopters. As Pa Decker had predicted, only a light breeze blew. "Beeline to Belle Isle and straight back," Pa Decker said. "You'll make it, b'ye. No foolin' 'round, mind."

The pilots lifted off with the first light on the snow. Ninety minutes later, they returned. The base camp crew staggered into Decker's, hacking black phlegm and nursing frozen fingers. An hour later, the Gulf of St. Lawrence and the Labrador front were hit by a full gale, 60-knot winds and zero visibility. Heavy objects flew wildly through the air. The sealing ships hung dead still in the ice.

The infant seals were now a week old, halfway through their whitecoat phase. Once they started moulting, at twelve to fifteen days, they became "ragged jackets," less valuable to the fashion-fur industry.

ARCTIC ENDEAVOUR

When the Greenpeace crew returned to Belle Isle on the clear morning of March 19, the base camp had been obliterated and swept over the cliff by the storm. Only the fuel tanks and two tent pegs remained. The sealing ships moved through the ice and swilers returned to work. Hunter, Watson, Pat Moore, Eileen Chivers, Ron Precious, Michael Chechik, Jean-Claude Francolon, and Newfie guide Doug Pilgrim rushed to the seal nursery. Hunter had conferred with the *I Ching*, had his red cloth from the Buddhist Karmapa in the pouch around his neck, wore a Kwakiutl/Greenpeace

T-shirt underneath his survival suit, and prayed to St. Francis as he pushed across the ice behind Watson and Walrus. Even so, he fell between two ice pans, soaked his legs, and filled his boots with water.

When they came upon seal pups, Francolon fell to his knees to take close-ups. After an hour across the ice, they saw the first streaks of blood. They followed these to great avenues of blood, and soon they were upon the swilers. Among the carnage of pelts, Doug Pilgrim and Paul Watson talked to the young seal hunters, who had blood under their eyes and knives in hand. Moore and Hunter talked to fisheries officers. Chivers wandered away, on the verge of nausea. She followed a swiler and saw him lurch after a young pup. The whitecoat snapped at the swiler with hakapik raised. Chivers ran for the seal, slipped, and watched from her knees as the hakapick came down on the seal's head. The swiler had it skinned in less than a minute. He hauled the pelt away, leaving the dark-eyed carcass in the snow.

Chivers chased another swiler, was brushed aside, fell to the ice, and watched another seal die. She got up and threw herself in front of another sealer, who pushed her away. Francolon, the man she had kept alive with soup and tea on Belle Isle, followed her every move and recorded every encounter. Twelve times Chivers blocked a swiler and twelve times she was thrown aside. Francolon, suddenly agile and swift, leapt over blocks of ice and dropped to the ice for the best angles, changing lenses, focusing, releasing the shutter.

The Halifax sealing ship *Arctic Endeavour*, a hundred yards away, steamed slowly toward a mound of seal pelts. Watson and Hunter conferred with the camera team and then made for the bow of the ice cutter. As the ship backed up to make a lunge forward into the ice, Hunter and Watson took up a position directly in the ship's path. They turned their backs on the heavy, red steel bow. "Ya better move, b'yes," a crewman hauling pelts yelled. "The old man ain't one ta tink twice 'bout runnin' ya into the ice." The "old man" was Captain Jim Gillett, a tough, experienced sealing captain.

"Tell the old bastard to do what he wants," Hunter yelled back, only half turning. "We're not moving." Hunter closed his eyes and meditated on the Clear Light, the Buddhist tradition of absorption into complete non-attachment. The smokestack bellowed and the 900-ton steel ship lunged forward. Hunter felt the ice pan quiver. Watson turned his head slightly to peek at what was coming. Great shards of blue-white ice thrust up before the bow of the Halifax sealer. Fissures opened in the ice pan.

"Stop 'er Cap," someone yelled from the bow. "Stupid asses ain't movin'." The *Arctic Endeavour* halted and the ice groaned. Sailors shouted Norwegian and English curses from the bow of the sealing ship. The vessel backed up and plunged forward again.

"Crummy way to die," Watson said to his friend.

"Just don't look back, Paul," Hunter whispered.

Ron Precious squeezed the trigger on his film camera. The *Arctic Endeavour* roared forward, and the ice burst, but once again the lookout on the bow screamed at Captain Gillett to stop. Screams of outrage descended from the bow, directed at the two men who stood immobile on the ice.

The fisheries officers took photographs and discussed what sections of the new regulations the protestors might be violating. Francolon snapped photographs. He caught Doug Pilgrim standing among a large group of swilers who had stopped to watch, Eileen Chivers sitting near an infant whitecoat, and Hunter and Watson obstructing the path of the ship. For half an hour, the *Arctic Endeavour* sat stymied, before Bernd Firnung advised Hunter that it was time to make for the helicopters.

Swilers jeered as the company of Rainbow Warriors filed back across the ice. Darkness fell over the ice floes. Frantic mother harp seals sniffed along the blood trails for their missing pups. That night, aboard the sealing ships, sailors and swilers talked about the showdown with the *Arctic Endeavour*. The men in their cold steel galleys knew that word had come down from their bosses in Halifax, Oslo, and Ottawa that they were not to intentionally harm the protestors, certainly not in sight of any fisheries officer. They laughed at the "publicity hounds," and the "idiots" who stood in front of the ship.

From Decker's Boarding House, Chechik made arrangements to fly out with his film to the CBC lab in Toronto. Hunter phoned me and Marining in Vancouver and his media allies across Canada. At the Vinland Hotel, he assured the NBC producer that the film would be made available to his New York office. The blustery producer bought him a beer. "Does this mean I'm alive again?" asked Hunter.

"If the film's any good."

"Cheers."

Upstairs in his room, Jean-Claude Francolon packed his gear and prepared to fly out the next morning, knowing that his editors would be euphoric when they saw the images. David McTaggart flew back to Paris with Francolon. Eileen Chivers wept silently and privately in the embrace of Patrick Moore, unable to exorcise the images of infant seals skinned alive on the ice.

Walrus, Watson, Marilyn Kaga, and Pablo prepared to go back out the next day. But on March 20, as soon as the helicopters landed on the ice floes, fisheries officers charged Captain Jack and Bernd Firnung with violating Section 12 (5) (b) of the Seal Protection Act, for allegedly landing within a quarter mile of a seal. The pilots, now under arrest, flew the Greenpeace team back to St. Anthony.

The RCMP came by Decker's, seized the helicopters, and erected a rope fence around them. The government demanded a $20,000 bond to release the two Jet Rangers. Storrow arranged for the bond by way of personal guarantees, and the helicopters were returned to Captain Jack. Fisheries Minister Romeo LeBlanc and his spokesman Charles Friend ridiculed Greenpeace in the media and promised to control the "circus" in Newfoundland the following year.

Hunter, Dan Willens, and Carl Rising-Moore drove 20 miles across the peninsula to Raleigh, where they met with seventy volunteers who wanted to start a Greenpeace group in Newfoundland. Hunter gave them copies of the *Greenpeace Chronicles* and a handful of pins.

On March 22, the 1976 Greenpeace seal campaign crew cleared their gear from Decker's Boarding House. Ma and Pa Decker shook hands with everyone and welcomed them to return. Ma Decker told Chivers that she, too, would ride in the helicopters to the front. Pat Moore, Eileen Chivers, and Bob Hunter flew to Montreal, then home. Walrus, Watson, Henrietta Nielson, Bonnie MacLeod, Dan Willens, Pablo Morse, Jet Johnson, and Carl Rising-Moore headed down the Great Northern Peninsula in vans, passing out Greenpeace pins along the way.

By March 23, the whitecoats who survived the sealing boats began to moult into ragged jackets. Two weeks later they had silvery new coats flecked with black spots. They were "beaters" now, and only slightly more valuable as pelts than the ragged jackets. From the ice pans, they plunged into the icy Atlantic and followed their mothers north to the Arctic Ocean for the summer.

1. Greenpeace logo, 1975, designed by Barry Lavender.

2. Paul Watson carries a harp seal across the ice, Bob Hunter blocks the *Arctic Endeavour* sealing ship, Labrador, 1976.

3. Swilers on the ice floes of Newfoundland.

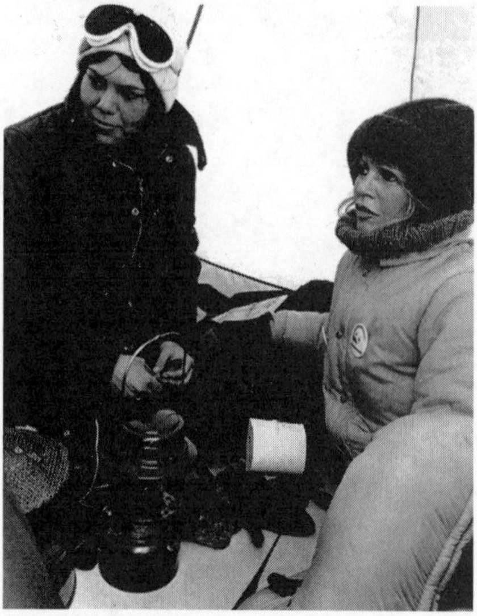

(Left): 4. Al "Jet" Johnson, led seal teams across the ice and dropped skydivers into nuclear power plants.
(Right): 5. Susi Newborn and Brigitte Bardot, Belle Isle,1977.

6. Patrick Moore arrested in Labrador by Canadian Fisheries officers for violation of the Seal Protection Act, March 1978.

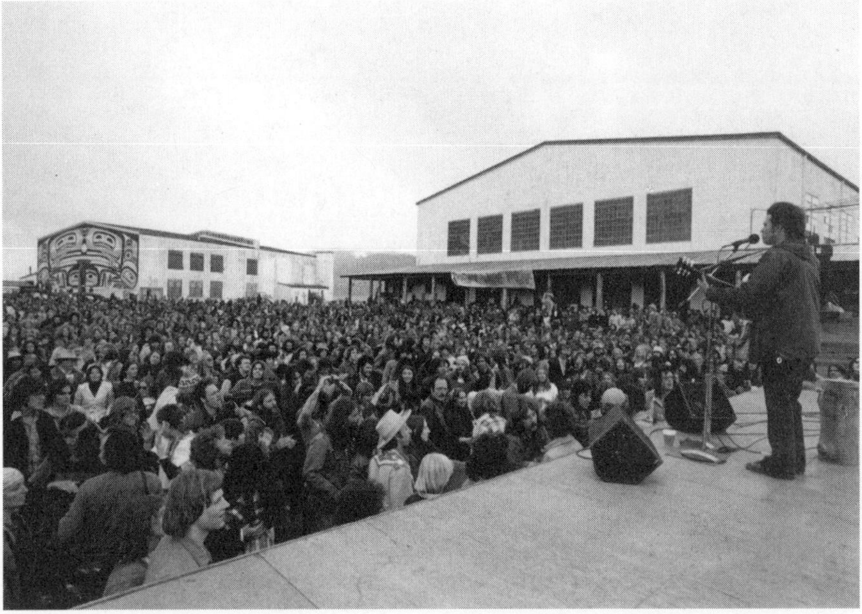

7. Country Joe McDonald at the send-off concert at Jericho Beach, in Vancouver, 1976.

8. Scraping and painting the *James Bay*, 1976.

9. The eco-navy, 1976: the *James Bay* and the *Phyllis Cormack*.

10. Gary Zimmerman in the engine room of the *James Bay*, 1976.

(Left): 11. Jerry Garcia plays a benefit concert in front of the James Bay, San Francisco embarcadero, 1977.
(Right): 12. Paul Watson and Marilyn Kaga in front of a Soviet harpoon boat, 1976.

13. Ron Precious and Rex Weyler, 1976.

14. *The Ohana Kai* is refitted in Honolulu, 1977.

15. The *Rainbow Warrior*, converted Aberdeen trawler, flagship of the eco-Navy.

16. Inside the Trident Nuclear Submarine Base, Bangor, Washington, 1978.

(Left): 17. Taking on Australian whaling, at the Cheynes Beach shore whaling station in Albany, Australia, 1977.
(Right): 18. Captain Nick Hill and Denise Bell on board the *Rainbow Warrior*, 1978.

(Left): 19. The Rocky Flats campaign achieved peaceful goodwill between protestors and police, Colorado, 1979.
(Right): 20. David McTaggart, Amsterdam, 1979.

21. Patching up the family feud. Greenpeace agreement committee: around the table are Rex Weyler, David McTaggart, Peter Ballem, Michael M'Gonigle, Walrus (David Garrick).

22. Greenpeace International meets in Amsterdam, November 1979.

BOOK THREE

POLITICAL ECOLOGY

CHAPTER NINE

HOTEL PAPA

"This is what you shall do: Love the earth and sun and animals. Stand up for the stupid and crazy."
— Aldo Leopold

We now had two months to launch our promised "bigger and faster" whale campaign for the summer of 1976. The element of surprise would no longer be working, so we needed a vessel that could keep pace with the whaling fleets.

On April 10, the Greenpeace Foundation board of directors met in our new office. Hunter presided and Eileen Chivers, Bobbi Innes, Michael Chechik, Paul Watson, Pat Moore, and other veterans participated. The photographs of baby seals, bloody seal pelts, Chivers attempting to save them, and Hunter and Watson standing in front of the *Arctic Endeavor* had pushed the seal hunt to front-page status around the world. Although the intention had been to promote the cause of seals, the pictures had also intensified the public spotlight on Greenpeace as an organization and the participants as media personalities. In the United States and Europe, Greenpeace appeared heroic for defending the seal pups, but in Canada, some former supporters returned crushed Greenpeace pins in the mail with angry letters.

Paul Spong had just returned from the inaugural Orca Symposium in Olympia, Washington. He reported that the gathering of whale enthusiasts had taken a bizarre twist when a Sea World team attempted to capture a pod of orcas in the inner harbour of Olympia, herding the whales by dropping explosives from airplanes. The imprudent incident lead to a popular uprising and a US federal court order to release the orcas, the last whales ever captured in Puget Sound. During the public uprising, Spong had forged new political alliances in Washington, D.C. One of these environmental lobbyists phoned our Vancouver office and told Hunter that he could obtain the location of whaling ships daily. "The information exists," a source told Hunter, "but someone in Washington has to see some political benefit from telling you." It seemed possible to us that the 200-mile fishing limit would be an incentive for the US, and if we could work our new contacts properly, we might be able to obtain coordinates of the whaling fleets while at sea.

George Korotva announced that he had located a 152-foot minesweeper in Seattle, the *James Bay*, which could be leased for $70,000. The ship, powered by two V-12 Lancaster engines, could reach a speed of 18 knots, but fuel for the summer would cost $30,000 or more. The entire whale campaign would cost roughly $120,000. We had spent $37,000 on the seal campaign in Newfoundland. We had exhausted our line of credit and remained in debt to local suppliers. Innes and Gannon had launched a new lottery and direct mail appeal, and money was coming in weekly. But we did not have $70,000 to lease a ship.

The *James Bay* was a Canadian minesweeper like the *Edgewater Fortune*, which had sailed as *Greenpeace II* in 1971, and like the French *La Paimpolaise* that rammed David McTaggart's *Vega*. The 390-ton, diesel-powered minesweeper had been designed for a crew of thirty-eight. It originally carried sophisticated surveillance equipment and 40-mm guns. The ship was now an empty shell, owned by retired businessman Charles Davis, who dreamed of fixing it up.

Following our meeting, Moore and Korotva made an arrangement with Davis that we would refurbish the ship, repair the engines, and replace the electronic gear in exchange for $50,000 of the charter fee. We knew we could do most of this with volunteer help and scrounged materials. We signed a deal, and Korotva brought the *James Bay* to Vancouver in late April. We immediately swarmed over the boat with paint scrapers and screwdrivers. Hewitt cobbled together radios and electronic equipment. Moore, Chivers, Easton, and a team of carpenters built berths and storage bins. We painted the hull white and added whales and rainbows at the bow. We rechristened the ship *Greenpeace VII*, but it was more affectionately known as the "Mind Sweeper."

Paul Watson proposed we purchase an S-55 Sikorski helicopter to carry on deck for spotting whalers. As a tactic, it was a sound idea, but $300,000 for a used helicopter was beyond our means. I noticed how military we had become for a peace group. One could argue, as we did, that we used the tools of industry to bring about an age of environmentalism. On the other hand, one might wonder if we were slipping into the very patterns of aggression that we opposed in our adversaries. Such discussions took place regularly. However, more than rainbows painted across the bow assuaged any fear that we had adopted too martial a style. Mel Gregory brought his pet iguana, Fido, to the Greenpeace boat, and since this was the Year of the Dragon, Fido became titular "Commander-in-Chief" of the campaign. Hunter posted written communiqués from our reptilian leader, headed "Secret Memo from Fido," in which he outlined strategies for the summer.

Greenpeace tactics had benefited from a host of influences, including Gandhi, Marshall McLuhan, Dorothy Day, the Quakers, and American populist Saul Alinsky. Alinksy had helped organize Chicago slum dwellers to improve their lot, and had compiled a keen set of "rules" for the disenfranchised to influence the rich and powerful. He had passed away in 1972, but his strategies, such as "Make the opposition live up to their own book of rules," "freeze the target," and "go outside their experience," became valuable reminders.

Our fundamental strategy for the whale campaign was to bring the whale issue before the Japanese public. We planned to do this by confronting the Japanese whaling fleet near Hawaii, then continuing on to Tokyo, where we would make alliances with peace groups in Hiroshima and Nagasaki. Meanwhile, the independent whale group from Mendocino would charter the *Phyllis Cormack* and patrol the California coast for the Soviet fleets. This plan, we thought, would turn the tide at the IWC. The Soviet and Japanese whalers had used Whaling Commission "scientific permits" and had stepped up pirate whaling to circumvent the quotas, but this also rendered them vulnerable. Catches during the previous summer had been the lowest in modern whaling history. Russia had announced it would dismantle its Antarctic whaling fleet. The Japanese announced in the *Japan Stock Journal* that six companies would consolidate into one. "Clearly," wrote Hunter in a public statement in the spring of 1976, "the end of whaling is near. Japan, Russia, and Norway could show tremendous goodwill to the world by stopping their whaling now, before they wipe out the last whales."

Peter Fruchtman, the political aide from California who had phoned Greenpeace earlier, now confirmed that he could deliver a government source in Washington, D.C. that would supply daily positions of the Soviet and Japanese whaling fleets. He asked us to send "glossy photographs from the previous year and $10,000." This request caused much hand-wringing in Vancouver. We did not have $10,000 for anonymous intelligence sources, and some, like Paul Watson, were suspicious. Watson claimed, correctly perhaps, that the information would come from the US military. Nevertheless, we decided to probe the source. Moore and I prepared documentation of the declining whale stocks and photographs of the undersized whales taken by the Soviets. We sent these to Fruchtman in Los Angeles with a photograph of our refurbished minesweeper. We told him we did not have $10,000. Fruchtman replied that, okay, he would pursue the contacts in Washington, D.C. even without the money, but he wanted a spot on the ship's crew. We agreed, provided that he could actually deliver the information. "The Mind Sweeper got to him," said Hunter.

HOPI FIRE

In April 1976, the rock music group Supertramp donated a share of their Vancouver ticket sales and let us sell T-shirts and lottery tickets at their concert. Meanwhile, event promoter Alan Clapp assembled 135 artists and builders, plus 9,850 volunteers, to convert the Jericho military base into a dazzling conference site for the non-governmental organizations attending the United Nations Conference on Human Habitat in Vancouver that summer. Builders salvaged enormous cedar logs from the coast and entire abandoned mining towns from the BC interior. Carpenters and artists converted the five WW II seaplane hangars into lecture halls and performance theatres. Volunteers split cedar shakes for roofs and siding. Haida artist Bill Reid carved sculptures. Fabric designers created 600-foot-long landscape murals. Thirty Cree from Manitoba set up camp and helped construct the site. A Greenpeace team built a traditional salmon barbeque pit designed by the Kwakiutl nation. Jim Bohlen returned from Denman Island and oversaw an alternative housing display. Clapp had planned that the "Habitat Forum" would culminate with a Greenpeace benefit concert on June 12, followed by the launch of *Greenpeace VII* on June 13, the final day of the UN conference.

During the conference, Mother Teresa delivered a blessing at the Habitat Forum site. Buckminster Fuller and Paulo Soleri extolled the use of recycled materials. Prime Minister Pierre Trudeau toured the grounds with guests from Europe and Asia. Conference Secretary-General Enrique Penalosa requested a ride "on the Greenpeace boat," and John Cormack took Penalosa's entourage for a tour of the bay aboard the *Phyllis Cormack*. The UN official wore a Greenpeace pin and proudly took the wheel with Captain Cormack at his side. Compared to the downtown hotels, where the official conference proceeded, Habitat Forum resembled the Land of Oz. For two weeks, the denizens of the Shire hosted the world, and the hand-hewn, recycled Habitat Forum became the crowning image of the UN summit.

A contingent of Hopi from Arizona set up a teepee camp in a meadow outside the forum grounds. The Hopi fire circle became a quiet congress of serious discussion, hosted by elder Thomas Banyacya, interpreter for the Hopi spiritual leaders. Tibetan Buddhists and Japanese Zen masters sat with politicians and intellectuals around the fire, where high-energy egos dissolved in the pool of Hopi dignity. The elders had come from Oraibi and Shungpavy, the oldest continually inhabited villages in North America. "We are not Third World," Banyacya responded to a visitor one day. "We are original people, indigenous. We don't seek the riches of the industrial nations. We never traded our spiritual teachings for material things."

Banyacya explained that after World War II, "People came to our land to take the uranium and coal. Our prophecies had warned us not to let those riches out from the ground as long as humans still practised warfare. The mining companies on our land were a sign that Earth was in such danger that we must warn the nations of the world. This is why we have come here. The destruction of the natural world is accelerating. The time has come for action."

The Hopi message seemed to validate the purpose of Greenpeace, but also reminded us of the warnings about humility, that although our message was important, we were no more than messengers. Media attention had brought us notoriety, but in the spiritual realm, compared to these Hopi elders, we were punks. On June 6, Banyacya spoke to the UN conference plenary session. "Mankind has a chance," he said, "... to move in a direction of peace, harmony, and respect for land and life. The time is right now; later will be too late. Humanity," he urged, "must return to the spiritual path as one to cure and heal our Mother Earth." The Hopi camp was closed to visitors on June 7, and the next day they were gone.

THE PLUTONIUM CAPER

A delegate at the UN conference told us of a movement to get nuclear waste on the agenda. He quoted a scientist who claimed the United States could not account for one percent of its plutonium inventory — enough plutonium to build an arsenal of bombs. The missing plutonium, the scientist said, was available on the black market. He claimed that he could get enough plutonium to build a bomb, and that if Greenpeace wanted to use this information, he could actually get the plutonium to demonstrate how easy it was. Hunter considered going along with this scheme and staging a news conference. Moore, however, convinced Hunter that even if it were true, we didn't want to have anything to do with obtaining plutonium.

As bizarre as this information appeared to be, it squared with other sources. I interviewed Ralph Nader, who told me that he was nervous about the possibility of nuclear terrorism. "Anyone can walk into a nuclear power plant," he said, "and there are 100,000 people who have enough knowledge to build a nuclear bomb." David McTaggart, in Vancouver on personal business, told *The Province* newspaper that he had twice been offered plutonium. "You can believe it or not," said McTaggart. "I don't care, but it's true." Physicist and science writer Walter Patterson confirmed that plutonium could be purchased on the black market. Hunter issued a media release in the middle of the UN conference, stating that Greenpeace had been offered plutonium. The report became a national story, and Canadian Justice Minister Ron Basford chimed in, stating that "if there is a black market in plutonium, that is a matter of great concern." Canada, meanwhile, flogged Candu nuclear reactors, contributing to the world supply of plutonium.

As the launch date for the *Greenpeace VII* approached, Bob Hunter and Bobbi Innes married in a small ceremony with friends and family. They had no time for a honeymoon as we prepared and provisioned the ship. Korotva, living on board, grew fatigued and short-tempered. We secretly referred to him as "Captain Cruel," but appreciated his determination to ready the ship by June 13.

Now that we were once again in the daily grind of ecological action, Hunter appeared exhausted with the pace. "We're all burning out," he told me, although he was speaking primarily about himself. Hunter had worked seven days a week on the whale campaign. For this he received $400 per month. He had trimmed his hair and beard and taken to wearing a sports coat over a black turtleneck sweater. Moore, too, had trimmed his wild Afro hairstyle and now wore a sports coat to press conferences, although most of the time he worked in his blue jeans, wielding a skill saw in the cabins of the *James Bay*.

In the midst of this activity, we published the second edition of the *Greenpeace Chronicles*, now our official voice. The issue included John Lilly on the rights of cetaceans, and stories on harp seals, orcas, jojoba oil, plutonium, nuclear power plants, mercury poisoning in Ontario, and oil drilling in the Beaufort Sea. Moore and Hunter wrote a Declaration of Interdependence. American politician Henry Wallace had coined the phrase in 1936 in reference to international political cooperation. Roderick Nash had borrowed it as a title of a television address after the 1969 Santa Barbara oil spill. Poet Gary Snyder had also referred to a "Declaration of Interdependence" in an ecology context. Moore began using the term during the 1975 whale campaign, and it now became the title of our Greenpeace ecology manifesto.

"It must be understood," wrote Hunter, "that the innocent word 'ecology' contains a concept as revolutionary as anything since the Copernican breakthrough ... As suddenly as Copernicus taught us that the earth was not the centre of the universe, ecology teaches us that mankind is not the centre of life on this planet."

Moore added Three laws of Ecology, borrowing ideas from Barry Commoner:

1. All forms of life are interdependent.
2. The stability of an ecosystem is dependent on its diversity.
3. Resources are finite, and there are limits to the growth of all living systems.

We were not yet fully aware — although Gregory Bateson had pointed this out in his 1972 *Steps to an Ecology of Mind* — that these laws applied to social organizations as well.

ARMOURED CAR

Greenpeace lawyers Marvin Storrow and David Gibbons advised that we register the Greenpeace trademark internationally. This led to philosophical conflicts with Watson, who argued that Greenpeace was "a movement, not a company," and we shouldn't trademark anything. Indeed, Watson, like McTaggart, had developed his own network of fundraisers under the Greenpeace banner. Storrow pointed out, however, that groups all over the world now raised money in the Greenpeace name without any accountability. "Some are sincere," he said, "but you've also got outright frauds." He cited a mystery man with a mailbox in Washington, D.C., who had raised thousands of dollars for "Greenpeace" and left no trace. Bobbi Innes, now Bobbi Hunter, freed up enough money to register the trademark in Canada, but it was deemed that there was no money for international trademark lawyers. This decision, or lack of a decision, would haunt Greenpeace for years to come.

Meanwhile, Storrow waged another, more immediate battle to secure insurance for the ship. Korotva said flatly we would never pass a Steamboat Inspection in the US by June 13, so we did what the pirate whalers did: we registered the *James Bay* in Panama. This caused a few raised eyebrows among the volunteers, and also required lawyers in Panama City. We made cash deposits, some of which were nothing more than payoffs to minor Panamanian bureaucrats. Storrow and Gibbons volunteered their time, but the foreign lawyers wanted retainers. The legal team swelled to nine lawyers and the legal budget inflated even without registering the international trademarks.

Bobbi Hunter distributed cash for the most urgent needs — a welder for the boat, a sycophant in Panama, or a courier to Washington, D.C. We had expected money from our US office in San Francisco, but their rent, salaries, and other expenses had reportedly consumed their revenue. Some of our local suppliers had reached their limit, but others extended our credit. Pentax replaced my ruined camera from the previous year, loaned me another one, and serviced my large format camera, all for free. Still, by June the Greenpeace Foundation was technically bankrupt. I didn't expect the bank to come after my guitars and yellow Volkswagen, but people with houses on the line were understandably nervous. We scrounged materials, borrowed cash from friends, and plunged forward.

Even as we dealt with our financial crisis, Greenpeace now enjoyed a high profile in global news reports. European magazines, inspired by the seal stories, demanded photographs of whales. Journalist Jack Richardson's story appeared not in the *New York Times* as we had expected, but in *Playboy* magazine, which caused more conflict. "The Great Whale Battle," spread among naked models and sexist jokes, lent credibility to the accusation that Greenpeace was "too macho." Nevertheless, through Richardson's story, the whale cause reached millions of new supporters.

Gannon redrafted our cash-flow projections, and went back to see the nervous bank manager. Hunter had already sent the banker the *New York Times Magazine* article by Charles Flowers, clippings from European magazines, and the Richardson article tastefully clipped out. He'd also included a press clipping quoting philosopher John Platt that international environmental groups were the next major social phenomenon. Gannon showed the banker the revenue figures, explained the bulging expenses, and pleaded our case for an overdraft. The manager agreed to a short-term overdraft of $10,000, to be paid down with receipts from the launch concert.

However, in the frenzied final week of preparations, Bobbi Hunter agreed to distribute blank cheques for supplies and equipment and we soon exceeded the $10,000 overdraft. The bank stopped honouring cheques, but agreed to hold them until Monday morning, after the concert.

A year earlier, 25,000 people had attended the launch of our first whale campaign. If we could sell that many $5 tickets, the $125,000 gate would finance the new campaign and pay off half the debt. Country Joe MacDonald, Ronee Blakley, Danny O'Keefe, and Paul Winter arrived the night before the concert. Popular local musicians — Susan Jacks, Valdy, Paul Horn, Bruce Miller, The Cement City Cowboys, and Pied Pumkin — were added to the show. The Habitat crew volunteered to run security. Time was short, so most of the tickets would be sold at the gate. Gannon took charge of collecting the money from ticket booths. He called the police and told them about the amount of cash that might be at the site, and he called Brinks Security to be on hand with an armoured car.

WARRIORS OF THE RAINBOW

On Saturday, June 12, the morning of the concert, I arrived at the Habitat site at dawn to meet with the security team. Black clouds hung over English Bay, and rain pelted down. Gannon set up ticket booths and assigned runners to deliver money from the booths. The rain forced us to move the concert into the converted hangers. Then, just as the gates opened at 11:00, the sun came out. We could not move the grand piano back outside, so some musicians played indoors. We ended up with three stages, and terrific confusion.

The police told Gannon that the concert crowd appeared to be 20,000 people, but this did not square with our 5,000 ticket receipts. Spong and I had turned security over to the Habitat crew, so I ran around to each gate. The head of security — a bearded, friendly giant known as "Bear" — had strung a rope around the perimeter, which he patrolled on horseback. He explained that the Habitat volunteers felt they should be let in for free, so the security team looked the other way as those volunteers, their families, and their friends and neighbours spilled over the rope. I asked Bear to send everyone through the ticket booths and put crew at the gates to usher in the legitimate freebies. "Okay," Bear said. He rode off on his horse, his magnificent black western hat bobbing and nodding at the revellers.

Danny O'keefe sang his haunting song about Hinmaton Yalatkit leading his starving Nez Perce families through the snow before the guns of General Howard. Ronee Blakely's voice and Paul Winter's saxophone echoed from the main hall. Country Joe McDonald sang his new song, "Save the Whales," incorporating the whaling shanty "Oo-Ray and Up She Rises" and closed the concert with his famous Fish Cheer: "Give me an F!" It was a glorious day, but we lost ticket sales because of the security breakdown. Gannon collected the money and counted it twice with the Brinks guards standing by. The total came to $27,200.

Sunday, June 13, the *James Bay* and the *Phyllis Cormack* stood at the pier, white hulls and rainbows blazing in the sun. Hunter delivered a zealous oration about extending human compassion to all beings. To our complete surprise, a Cree elder from Saskatchewan, Fred Mosquito, asked if he could address the crowd. Mosquito, wrapped in a ceremonial blanket, began to talk about the Cree legend of the Warriors of the Rainbow.

Hunter had read the Rainbow Warrior legend secondhand, from the Willoya and Brown book. Until this moment, we had not associated the legend with the Cree. Hunter feared that the Cree elder might rebuke us for being disrespectful, since we had never actually *asked* the Cree if we could use the legend in our campaign. As Fred Mosquito spoke, Marilyn Kaga and Walrus stepped forward. Jet Johnson and Peter Fruchtman from California stopped talking. Taeko Miwa stood with Japanese interpreter and photographer Kazumi Tanaka, who would sail with us on the *James Bay*. Byrd Baker from Mendocino, there to take command of the *Phyllis Cormack*, paid rapt attention. Two new crewmembers, long-haired Michael Manolson and smiling Mary-Lee Brassard from Montreal, stood with veterans Lyle Thurston and Myron MacDonald.

Greenpeace was already more varied than any of us could imagine. Seven thousand miles away in Paris, David McTaggart, Brice Lalonde, and Rémi Parmentier now attended environmental demonstrations together. In London, ecologists Denise Bell and Susi Newborn dreamed of their own boat and an Atlantic whale campaign. Greenpeace offices in Norway and Australia had their own concerns. Even in Newfoundland, where Greenpeace had been despised, Doug Pilgrim had formed a Greenpeace group.

"Our prophecies we take seriously," said Fred Mosquito. "To us it is not just a story. It is a foretelling." Fred Mosquito waved his hand over the crowd and held a stern look on his weathered face. "You *are* the Warriors of the Rainbow." Bob Hunter straightened. Mel, with Fido on his shoulder, bowed his head solemnly. Whispers and murmurs rippled through the crowd. Hunter stepped forward and gave the Cree elder a Greenpeace pin. After the speech, we filed down the pier and boarded the two boats, the seiner and the minesweeper. The *Phyllis Cormack* and the *James Bay* steamed out of the bay.

FIDO AND OTTO

On Monday morning, the bank manager called Gannon to announce that our account stood $27,000 overdrawn. "The Brinks truck is on its way," the accountant said, "with $27,200." The bank manager seemed satisfied, but Gannon knew we had launched the ship with only $200 in our coffers.

On board the *James Bay*, I claimed a bottom bunk, under Ron Precious. We had work yet to complete on the two ships, so we crossed the strait and tucked into the town of Sidney on Vancouver Island. On June 16, the *Phyllis Cormack* departed with the Mendocino Whale War team, who promised to patrol the coast of California. The next day, I found a spot on the deserted beach to meditate. *Breathe in, breathe out. Watch. Notice.* My meditations, however, were interrupted by an irritating noise, like a squeaky hinge. *Reeet*! *Reeet*! Annoyed, I stood up and looked around for the source of this sound. I squeezed through an opening in the salal and discovered a rusty, abandoned weather vane twisting in the sea breeze. The figure on the weather vane was not a typical rooster or a ship, but a sperm whale. *Reeet*! *Reeet*! Back and forth the whale turned on the metal rod. *Reeet*! *Reeet*! *Reeet*! The sound persisted as I walked back down the beach toward the ship.

On June 20, we rounded the southern tip of Vancouver Island, put into the port of Bamfield, and called our Washington, D.C. liaison, Peter Fruchtman. Through a sympathetic congressman, Fruchtman obtained daily coordinates for the Soviet whalers and transmitted them in code using pages from the San Francisco phone book. We felt like real international spies. We called the Soviet *Dalnyi Vostok* "Bear 1" and the *Vladivostok* "Bear 2." Fruchtman relayed numbers for north latitude and west longitude. A message of "10, 5" meant ten names down in the phone book and five numbers across, giving the first number of latitude. Each radio transmission consisted of eighteen such messages, revealing the position of the two Soviet fleets.

We could not, however, get positions for the Japanese fleet. The source in Washington D.C., whom we now called "Deep Throat" in honour of the Watergate scandal, would only divulge the Soviet positions. Clearly the Americans wanted us to confront the pesky Russians, not their Japanese allies, endangering our plan to confront the Japanese whalers. However, Saul Alinsky's rules applied: "Have an alternative. Avoid being co-opted."

We would confront the Soviets first, but unlike previous years, they had not ventured northeast of Hawaii. We planned to rendezvous with the *Phyllis Cormack* at Mendocino Ridge on the anniversary of our first encounter, then proceed southwest toward Hawaii. However, on June 23, as we prepared to depart Bamfield, a Canadian Coast Guard cutter steamed up beside us with two RCMP officers glowering from the deck. "I'm seizing this vessel," said the officer in charge.

"For what?" shouted an incensed Patrick Moore. The grim Mountie informed us that we had violated regulations by failing to complete a Customs form in Vancouver. The officers demanded to see our bonded goods — alcohol and other custom-exempt items — that could only be opened outside Canadian territory. The officers, or their bosses in Ottawa, had surmised we might have violated this regulation, providing them with another charge against us. But why? Was Romeo LeBlanc seeking revenge for the seal campaign? Why would the Canadian government want to stop the whale campaign? The bonded goods remained secure, but it took us all day to clear up the petty Customs infraction in Vancouver. In the meantime, Hunter sent out a media release attacking the "small-minded and niggling Canadian government" for siding with the whalers.

We paid our $400 fine and headed southwest that night for a shakedown cruise with Captain George Korotva at the helm, in a mild breeze over a tranquil sea. Ted Haggarty, chief engineer, had served on the ship in the Canadian Navy. On the first morning out of Bamfield, he informed us the minesweeper was farther from the coast of Canada than it had ever been in the navy.

Moore's carpentry crew had built double bunks for the couples: Moore and Chivers, Bob and Bobbi Hunter, Paul Watson and Marilyn Kaga, Rod Marining and Bree Drummond, Michael Manolson and Mary-Lee Brassard, and Walrus and Taeko. "Commander Fido" posted a schedule for "Captain Cruel's Honeymoon Cruise." Gary Zimmerman served as assistant engineer, Matt Herron as navigator and photographer, and Lance Cowan as helmsman. Ron Precious, Fred Easton, and Michael Chechik formed the film crew with new recruit Chris Aikenhead. Michael Bailey would pilot one of the Zodiacs. Dr. Don Webb from Vancouver was the medic. Bob Thomas and Alan Wade represented the Ottawa Greenpeace office, and Kazumi Tanaka, a photojournalist from Tokyo, helped Chivers run the galley crew. As a photographer, I was almost redundant, but I did have experience taking photographs from Zodiacs.

Melville Gregory, crew musician and keeper of the *I Ching*, put a "Dream Book" on the galley table, and instructed the crewmembers to write down their dreams. "Especially the important ones."

"How do we know if a dream is important?" asked Michael Bailey.

Mel pierced him with a wry look. "If you *think* it might be important, Michael, write it down."

Several crewmembers wore metal dragon pins we'd picked up in Vancouver's Chinatown for the Year of the Dragon, and Fido, as titular leader, had free run of the ship. Hunter built a nesting platform for the iguana under a skylight near his berth. The final crewmember, according to Hunter, was "Otto." The *James Bay* had been fitted with an electronic autopilot that would steer the ship on a set course. Hunter concluded that if we were in the hands of a machine, we should afford the device full crew status. His daily "Memo from Fido" quoted "sources close to Otto" revealing items such as "a rainbow was reported landing on Saint Melville … it might have been a dream … we don't know, it could *all* be a dream."

To engineer Ted Haggarty, the carnival atmosphere was disconcerting. He took to posting notices of his own. "A Friendly Reminder from the Chief Engineer," warned crew to conserve water and secure their gear. "The *James Bay* is a very lively vessel," he reminded us. "Things get flying around, sometimes lethally."

Fuel consumption at cruising speed would cost about $400 per day, at full bore $800 per day or more. The price of fuel would prove a key factor. When a whale group in Portland, Oregon, phoned the ship and offered to stage a benefit concert, featuring the notorious underground Holy Modal Rounders, we altered our schedule. The band, pioneers of social rock poetry, had influenced street-theatre activists like the Provos, who in turn influenced Greenpeace. So up the Columbia River we chugged, past the Trojan Nuclear Power Plant, into Portland.

City authorities waived our moorage fee and former governor Tom McCall presented us with an Oregon flag, which we hoisted up the mast to cheers from the crowd. The local whale group raised $1,500 in donations, and the concert at the Earth Tavern raised a modest $650, to bring our total to $2,100 in Portland. It seemed like a lot of money, but amounted to only a few days' fuel cost.

A local pilot flew Bob and Bobbi Hunter over the Pacific to look for the whaling fleets. They flew out fifty miles and south over Mendocino Ridge but saw no whalers. Reports came in from Deep Throat that the Soviet whalers remained west of Hawaii. The Soviets, it seemed, were avoiding us. This prompted Moore to announce to the media, "We can patrol the entire Western Pacific from a bar in Portland." His humour was lost on some of our supporters.

ECOTAGE

We arrived at the site of our previous confrontation with the Soviet whalers at sunrise on July 1. A pod of about fifty Risso's dolphins appeared, and crewmembers dove into the water. The dolphins swarmed around the swimmers. The Risso's dolphins are Delphinidea family, cousins of the orca and pilot whale. The adults were 10-12 feet long and weighed over 700 pounds. It was summer calving season and several of the dark grey adults swam with infants. One of the babies was pure white, a heavenly image breaking through the blue water. Mel played music from the deck as the dolphins poked their noses into our faces and darted around us for well over an hour.

Nothing could have pulled the crew together faster and more thoroughly than this encounter. All the talk of spirituality, ecological awareness, and being Warriors of the Rainbow paled in comparison to the physical experience of swimming with the playful cetaceans. A year earlier, we had been in this very spot, immersed in the stench of whale blood; now, no meditation could have been more therapeutic than the presence of the dolphins.

An hour after the dolphins left, the *Phyllis Cormack* approached from the southeast. We launched Zodiacs and buzzed around the fish boat. Byrd Baker hugged Hunter as cameras whirled. It was a euphoric day for both crews. For the first time in thirty years, the whalers had not arrived along the coast of California to intercept the summer migration of sperm whales. We called the media from the radio room of the *James Bay*. "Soviets didn't come to whale war," proclaimed the headline in the *San Francisco Examiner*.

We arrived in San Francisco that evening, during the run-up to the American Bicentennial celebration. Through Gary Zimmerman's efforts, Mayor George Moscone had proclaimed "Save the Whales Week." Greenpeace had opened a new office on Second Street, but was not in a position to provide funds for the campaign. The *James Bay* crew was left to hustle money to top up the fuel tanks for a run toward Hawaii.

Paul and Linda Spong, Will Jackson, designer Barry Lavender, and my wife, Glenn, met us in San Francisco with new T-shirts, whale pins, and other merchandise to sell to the Bicentennial crowds. Although it was probably illegal to sell lottery tickets in California, we did so. On July 4 we erected a Greenpeace booth in Union Square during the Independence Day celebrations. From the public stage, Paul Spong delivered an impassioned plea on behalf of the whales.

In San Francisco we learned that environmental politics in America had changed drastically in one year. The split between traditional conservationists and the innovative ecology activists had widened. The new eco-activists were inspired by Greenpeace, but equally by Edward Abbey's 1975 novel, *The Monkey Wrench Gang*, a humorous and presumably fictional story of four ecologists who used sabotage — "ecotage" — to defeat developers and save wilderness. Abbey, on a speaking tour, openly urged citizens to "wage war against industrialization." The veteran author and ecologist was one of our heroes, but his "war" against industrialization stirred a fierce backlash. A "Sagebrush Rebellion" among ranchers in Nevada had spread throughout the western US and into California. Many of the environmental groups in California distanced themselves from Abbey and Greenpeace. Over time, Greenpeace itself would also split along these very lines.

Now, Mel Gregory aggravated this schism. In Union Square he had too much wine, stripped off his clothes in an expression of personal freedom, and was summarily arrested. Rather than spend money bailing him out, we let Mel stew in jail overnight. The Warriors of the Rainbow navigated a delicate path. On the one hand, our willingness to take risks and challenge the status quo was a large part of our success. On the other hand, we believed ecology could appeal to a huge cross-section of the public. It was important that we not appear frivolous. Mel's indiscretion showed how easily we could sabotage our own cause. Korotva and a few others wanted to kick him off the boat, but Mel made humble apologies and we took him back on the crew. "Mel's a member of the Fellowship of the Piston Rings," pleaded Hunter. "We can't abandon him."

Cleveland Amory, founder of the Fund for Animals, came to our rescue with money for fuel. With income from T-shirt sales, we replenished our food stores. However, before we could depart, we had another problem to solve. As engineer Ted Haggarty had warned, the *James Bay* — too light without its original load of armaments — pitched and rolled wildly, throwing crew and equipment around. Korotva ordered 30 tons of sand as ballast. In borrowed trucks we hauled bags of sand from a local pit back to the dock. We handed the bags down through three decks into the hold, which made for a long, sweaty day for the crew and twenty volunteers.

During the loading, Alan Wade from Ottawa fell between the ship and pylons and was nearly crushed to death. He remained behind to recover. Taeko Miwa and Bree Drummond, both pregnant, left the crew because of morning sickness and concern for their babies. Michael Chechik and Dr. Don Webb also departed, and Eileen Chivers and Fred Easton took over paramedic duties. Dr. Norman Seaton, a physicist with the Fund for Animals, and Barry Lavender, who had designed the new Greenpeace logo, joined the crew.

As well, Dr. Paul Spong joined the ship for the first time. Spong may have inspired a mass movement, but he was a loner by nature. To gain some privacy, he built himself a tent on the raised sponson above the afterdeck of the *James Bay*.

The *Greenpeace VII* departed San Francisco on July 12, through the choppy waters of the Golden Gate and into a rolling sea. We headed northwest for two days, skirted the southern range of Mendocino Ridge, then turned southwest toward the last known location of the Soviet fleet, the seamounts south of Hawaii.

LATRINE OFFICER

On the minesweeper, the flying bridge sits over the wheelhouse, rather than forward, as on John Cormack's seine boat. On this upper bridge of the *James Bay*, we stood as high above the waterline as we had been on the mast of the fish boat. From this height, the horizon sat five miles distant. Depending upon the refraction of light through the droplets of mist over the water, we might see the mast of a ship ten miles away. At sea, the easiest objects to see at a distance are the lights of another ship at night. One of the more difficult things to see is the blow of a whale in any kind of choppy sea or mist. The observer learns, however, to pick out the tiniest discrepancy in the boiling grey patterns of water and atmosphere. On the second day out, I surveyed for whales and ships in a following sea and eight-foot swells. Even with the new ballast, the ship rolled incessantly. Norman Seaton, Kazumi Tanaka, and other new Rainbow Warrior recruits were in their bunks with seasickness.

On the forward deck, Hunter walked alone to the bow. He wore a white wool sweater and sandals. A brush dangled from his belt. He held onto the cable that served as a railing and stared out into the grey void of the sea. The pressure of leading this expanding movement had driven him to the edge of sanity. A year ago, the pressure had been to find the whalers. This year, we received daily reports of the Soviet fleet position, and we had a much faster ship. We knew exactly where to go, and when. Yet the publicity and success, as Ben Metcalfe had presaged, changed everything.

By 1976, administration had become the new Achilles heel of our movement. Our own organization had grown into a bigger mystery than finding the whalers. Twenty Greenpeace offices, big and small, grassroots or run by lawyers and political aspirants, now operated around the world. Most people who took up the Greenpeace flag were devoted ecologists of one stripe or another, some radical, others conservative. Yet even with supply lines and communication lines intact, which ours were not, the forward motion of a social movement can founder on the delicacies of administering these relationships. Hunter's natural style was to include and encourage everyone. "Let a thousand flowers blossom," he proclaimed, paraphrasing Mao Tse-tung, who had long since adopted iron-fisted tyranny. Hunter, at the hub of an expanding movement, and not prone to authoritarian rule, suffered exhaustion and private anguish.

We had been called "crazy" by more than one observer, but most of our antics — Commander Fido, the Dream Book, Deep Throat, the Whole Earth Church, the Greenhawks — were all in fun. Those of us serious about the value of the *I Ching* or the impact of miracles were not fanatical about any of this. The mystical wing of Greenpeace was not a cult or a collection of psychotics. We understood the importance of having a political strategy, a clear message, and a skilled team. But we also appreciated the value of a good myth and a good laugh. The debate between the mystics and mechanics in Greenpeace was a modern adaptation of classical mythos and logos, magic and science, the perennial play of novelty and tradition. Ecology was the mission, and in spite of a vast spectrum of styles, we remained resolute about delivering this message.

Part of the success of Greenpeace in the 1970s was an instinct to take the crusade lightly — an endearing quality of Canadian culture. American expatriates, like me, tended toward a more solemn or aggressive style. In contrast, the Canadians possessed a self-deprecating sense of humour. The unique blend that had become Greenpeace — ecology, media, spirituality, humour, and sea-going direct action — grew out of this blend of bold creativity and modest humour. Hunter embodied these qualities as much as anyone. However, our president was burning out like a meteor racing through the thick political atmosphere within the organization. His apparent madness on board the ship, however, concealed Hamletic method. As the burgeoning corps of volunteers proliferated, the competition for power intensified. Hunter had been influenced by Buddhist and Taoist notions of eschewing power. He had even queried his mentor Allen Ginsberg on the question. "What should we do," he had asked the beat poet, "with this power that is coming our way?"

"Let it go," Ginsberg had replied bluntly, "before it freezes in your hand." Hunter took this admonition seriously. As a theatrical retort to the crush for power on the ship, and within Greenpeace in general, Hunter had assigned himself the role of ship's "latrine officer" and took to wearing the latrine brush, which now dangled from his belt as he shuffled about the ship. He could be found each morning in the latrine, cheerfully scrubbing away at the sinks and toilet bowls. To some, this was pure delirium, and indeed, he had reached a fragile state, but his latrine officer act was a little internal mindbomb, not madness. "Don't take yourself too seriously," was the message.

HOTEL PAPA

We pushed on before the following northeast trade winds, which helped us make good time and conserve fuel. On July 15 we came upon an eight-foot giant squid, floating dead, or near dead, on the surface of the ocean, with seven albatross making a meal of it. Most of the crew favoured leaving the albatross to their banquet, but the oceanographers prevailed. Zimmerman and Watson hauled the squid on deck. Mary-Lee Brassard from Montreal and Bob Thomas from Ottawa leaned over their shoulders. The biologists marvelled over the translucent *Architeuthis dux*, eight feet long in the mantel, plus twenty feet of writhing tentacles and a long, drooping club. The squid likely weighed 300 pounds. With a large portion of the mantel torn away, Zimmerman hypothesized a sperm whale could have attacked it. Moore agreed and several observers nodded. Marilyn Kaga and Paul Watson cooked some of the squid, but no one other than Watson ate any.

Hunter could hardly believe his luck, getting a giant squid story just hauled up on the deck. He interviewed crewmembers about their impressions, and retired to his tiny sanctuary, below deck, where he typed a media release. Like the year before, Hunter cobbled together a story about giant squid and sperm whales, with quotes and impressions from the crew. He theorized that an unconsumed giant squid lying about in the ocean could be construed as evidence that the sperm whale populations were depleted. His premise, although not rigorous science, was not unreasonable. Moore, Zimmerman, and the other naturalists acknowledged that the sighting was at least consistent with a decline in whales. In any case, we possessed plenty of evidence from the whalers themselves that the sperm whale had been decimated. We had seen no sperm whales since leaving Vancouver, so reporting the decline in the whale populations seemed justified. Hunter filed the story by dictating it to a new volunteer in the Vancouver office.

A prompt media link in Vancouver had been an essential part of Greenpeace campaigns since Dorothy Metcalfe operated the radio during the Amchitka and Moruroa campaigns. Rod Marining and Bobbi Hunter had served that function during the whale and seal campaigns, but with them on the boat, media responsibilities had been left to a young, high-energy volunteer, Howard Arfin. He, however, had abandoned his post for Hawaii to meet the ship, leaving the media job to a volunteer, who considered Hunter's story about the squid too half-baked and refused to release it. The breakdown typified our new administrative problems. The Greenpeace media strategy, since the first campaign, had attached political and scientific arguments onto news stories that editors would run: action, personalities, and human interest. A year earlier, the squid and sperm whale dispatch had generated whale stories around the world. Having no professional journalist in our home office now proved a costly oversight.

On board the minesweeper, we had no idea that this critical link had failed. We busied ourselves about the ship, knowing that we now closed in on the Soviet boats. The *James Bay* provided an altogether different environment than the homey *Phyllis Cormack*. The military ship had a wooden hull laid up on aluminum frames, to foil magnetic mines during wartime. Its watertight bulkheads and metallic rooms felt hard and cold. Unlike the little fish boat, the crew berths had no portholes. The aluminum walls dripped with condensation. News clippings and "Memos From Fido" hung in the galley.

I took regular radio shifts along with Spong, Lance Cowen, Fred Easton, Marilyn Kaga, and Matt Herron. Old equipment, plastic knobs, and gauges lined the radio room. Posters of John Lennon and Apache leader Geronimo hung on the walls. The call letters of the *James Bay* were HP 2582, or in martial parlance, "Hotel Papa, 2582." In press releases we referred to the ship as *Greenpeace VII*, but among the crew, the "Mind Sweeper" had now become "Hotel Papa."

When we found out that the squid story had been censored by our office, Hunter raged briefly, then worked himself into a stoic acceptance. "The Truth Squad lives," he muttered. He began filing stories directly to his old colleagues at the *Vancouver Sun*. In the grand scheme, the media lapse was a minor setback. We knew that the coming confrontation would make the news. In the meantime, and fortunately, the whaling nations did our work for us. The Russians at the IWC meeting in London publicly called us "pirates," and the Japanese called us "religious fanatics." This greatly lifted our spirits. News also emerged from the IWC that the previous year's catches had failed to reach quotas, and that the quotas would be cut 14 percent to 28,050 whales.

"This is just a pretence of scientific calculation," said Spong. He talked to journalists via radio and pointed out that quotas for the larger whales — the sperm and fin whales — had been reduced the most, and that the whalers now turned to the smaller minke and sei whales.

From Deep Throat we learned that the Russian whalers had circled Hawaii and now moved east as if making for the coast of North America. On July 16 we turned slightly west, but otherwise kept our heading southwest toward Hawaii as if we had no idea of the whalers' location.

In the radio room we picked up Soviet coordinates from Deep Throat and scanned the frequencies used by the whalers. We regularly heard the two Soviet factory ships, the *Vladivostok* and the *Dalnyi Vostok*. The Japanese used at least twelve channels, but we picked up their transmissions, and Marilyn Kaga or Kazumi Tanaka translated. From the terse Japanese communiqués, however, we could not learn their location. We presumed they remained over the seamounts west of Hawaii.

At crew meetings, Spong insisted we had to find the Japanese whalers. "The Japanese whaling companies are running the Scientific Committee," he said. "We have to keep the pressure on them."

KRIEGSPIEL

As we headed southwest, physicist Norman Seaton rigged speakers outside the wheelhouse and piped Gustav Holtz's *The Planets* throughout the ship. The trade winds calmed to a moderate northwest breeze. A spontaneous ecstasy seemed to possess almost everyone. Even Moore and Watson got along, carefully poking fun at each other in a spirit of camaraderie. Hunter kept up his latrine duties, but ceased wearing the brush on his belt, the point having been made. His depression vanished, at least publicly, as we approached the whaling fleet. Bobbi Hunter, previously burdened by financial worries, relaxed. Eileen Chivers and Barry Lavender took control of crew routine in the galley. Tollhouse cookies appeared regularly on the galley table in the afternoon. George Korotva, the irascible Czechoslovakian skipper, had calmed down now that we functioned as a competent team at sea.

Moore assumed a leadership role and conferred with Matt Herron about navigational details. Moore's frizzy blond hair had grown back to an Afro style and he wore one of the airbrushed rainbow T-shirts given to the crew in Vancouver. Moore and Herron hauled the Pacific Ocean charts onto the galley table and pushed coloured cubes from the Risk game across the charts to represent ships. In military jargon, this is known as "Kriegspiel," or "war-games." Although we fully intended peace and ecology, not war, Eileen Chivers commented that the exercise of tracking down the whalers had taken on a militaristic style. Greenpeace played on a dangerous edge between Gandhian *satyagraha* and militant aggression. Furthermore, Chivers noted that gender justice within Greenpeace had not yet reached maturity.

A tradition of strong, smart women had existed in Greenpeace, dating back to Dorothy Stowe, Dorothy Metcalfe, Marie Bohlen, and others, but now, uncompromising women like Eileen Chivers, Bobbi Hunter, Marilyn Kaga, Susi Leger, and Mary-Lee Brassard comprised a quarter of the crew and served as a check on the tendency toward alpha-male bravado. Nevertheless, the militaristic Kriegspiel session was important. The Soviet fleet had approached within striking distance of the Greenpeace ship. The whalers would try to avoid us on their way to the coast of North America. Fuel remained our critical limitation, so we had to strike efficiently. Herron marked one day's running with the navigator's compass. Korotva traced the projected track of the whaling fleet. We could not afford to let them slip past us.

"Do you think the Russians know where we are?" Mike Bailey asked.

"We're not exactly the most low-profile boat on the ocean," interrupted Hunter. In fact, the Soviets carried an array of surveillance gear on the *Vostok* and could monitor our transmissions more easily than we could monitor theirs. On July 17, the *Dalnyi Vostok* factory ship and fleet of harpoon boats proceeded along the 30th parallel, due north of Hawaii, steaming toward the coast of California, 400 miles west of our position. We kept our heading southwest as if making for Hawaii. This evasive heading had been Korotva's idea. "Don't run at them," he said. "They'll just bugger off." The next day, the whalers closed to only 200 nautical miles northwest.

"Now we go to them," said Korotva. Lance Cowan swung the *James Bay* northward to intercept the projected path of the *Vostok* fleet. The Soviet ships, possibly because they had cheated north to steer clear of the *James Bay*, turned south, thinking they'd passed us. We were now on a collision course. By the evening of July 18, we could hear the Russians over the radio, less than four hours away.

That night, however, the whalers turned sharply north, as if responding to our new heading. *Hotel Papa* and its crew of Rainbow Warriors chased the Soviet fleet. "They know we're onto them now," said Korotva. He shuffled his feet on the bridge, in high spirits. Through the window glass, six pairs of eyes scanned the horizon. On the deck, at the bow, and on the flying bridge under the snapping flags, a dozen more pairs of eyes watched.

Korotva, Haggarty, Hewitt, Susi Leger, Bruce Kerr, Matt Herron, Gary Zimmerman, and Lance Cowan ran the ship. The film crew and Zodiac teams prepared their equipment. Pre-confrontation anxiety quickened everyone's pace.

WIND OVER WATER

As we approached the whalers, a new administrative problem surfaced. The makeup of the confrontation crews became a complex juggling of gender fairness, representation from the various offices, experience, and function. With the exception of Ted Haggarty, Al Hewitt, and skipper Korotva, who would remain with the ship, every member of the crew wanted to be in an inflatable, in front of a whaling boat, saving whales. We had three Zodiacs and an Avon inflatable. Two or three people would occupy each small boat. An experienced, durable operator was the first priority, and these roles fell to Watson, Zimmerman, Moore, Spong, and fervent new recruit Mike Bailey. One Zodiac, Bailey's, would be held back as an emergency rescue team. Bailey became so eager and competent with the inflatables that the crew referred to him as "Zodiac Mike." A photographer would ride in each of the confrontation boats, so that left three positions during each encounter to be filled by fifteen eager volunteers. Although everyone on the crew made an effort to remain magnanimous, tensions grew.

In the face of this dilemma, Hunter decided to consult the *I Ching* with the crew around the table in the "media room," where the film crew stored their gear. Mel played a meandering medley of sea shanties on his guitar throughout the proceedings. Most of the new ecologists appeared skeptical of the mystics. They were scientists, biology students, and political science majors. Between 1975 and 1976, the ranks of mechanics had swelled on the Greenpeace ship. As a slightly incognito mystic, I shared certain sympathies with the skeptics and saw this shift as a good sign. Nevertheless, I rooted for the *I Ching* to make a good showing.

Mike Bailey, Lance Cowan, and Susi Leger pushed forward to take a turn with the coins and Hunter turned to the fifty-ninth hexagram, "Wind over Water," implying the gentle over the abyss. We happened to be directly over the North Pacific Abyssal Plain, the seasonless ocean floor, 3,000 fathoms — three and a half miles — below.

The question at hand, however, was how to fairly apportion Zodiac crews. Hunter scanned the text: "Mmm … dispersing and dissolving divisive egotism. Okay. Religious forces are needed. Sacred music and rituals awaken a consciousness of the common origin of all creatures. Cooperation. Ah: When a boat is crossing a great stream, all hands must unite in a joint task … shaken by religious awe in the face of eternity. And the changing line says, take quick action to dissolve the misunderstandings." Hunter paused. "Mmm. Well, there you have it. As far as who goes on the confrontation Zodiacs, it sounds like we just need to lose our egos, sing, pray, and someone has to take quick action."

Magic or not, the *I Ching* reading engendered a celebratory and dignified spirit among us. No one wanted his or her ego to overshadow the mission. The Zodiac crews would be determined by practical considerations and as much fairness as we could collectively muster. Tensions drained away, the rum came out, and we sang together with Mel in the media room. Fido appeared as if to see what all the commotion was about. Hunter drew sets of Zodiacs into his notebook and assigned people into three confrontation teams and an emergency rescue team. Since the photographers and operators were all men, the next three spots went to Bobbi Hunter, Eileen Chivers, and Marilyn Kaga. Zodiac Mike's rescue team included Marining, Walrus, and a young cook, David Weiss.

We had learned the previous year that attempting to photograph from a distance, with a long lens, keeping pace at 15 to 20 knots in a bouncing inflatable is almost impossible. The photographers and film crew could achieve more with wide-angle lenses in the blockading Zodiac. We used fast film, even in sunlight, to keep shutter speeds fast. On a sunny day, we slightly overexposed the film to allow a shorter development time, which compresses the contrast. These were common photojournalist techniques, but in these conditions, every adjustment was difficult. Easton and I had refined our waist harnesses with padding to avoid rope burn, and we had used eyehooks and brass carabiners to snap them on and off.

Six years earlier, *Greenpeace* had been only the imagined name of an unknown boat. Four years earlier, the Great Whale Conspiracy had been a vision of Paul and Linda Spong and Farley Mowat. Two years earlier, finding the whalers had been considered a pipe dream. Now it seemed, for a brief moment, that we were veterans, that we knew what to do and how to do it. But this too was a chimera.

THE GREEN SHROUD

In the pre-dawn of Monday, July 19, we heard clear Russian voices on the radio. Korotva could make out the name "Vostok." Al Hewitt got an RDF fix on the signal to the northeast, no more than 30 miles away. We had been cruising at 11 knots to save fuel. Now we picked up the pace, but this meant we drained our fuel reserves. The Russians may have guessed or known precisely our fuel capacity, but in either case, we had no more than two days to chase them before we would have to make for the nearest fuel depot in Hawaii.

At dawn, Bob Thomas from Ottawa stood on the flying bridge with Matt Herron, Mary-Lee Brassard, and Susi Leger. The sky was overcast, the morning cold. At 06:15, Thomas pointed toward the northeast horizon. The cloud cover had opened, and golden light broke from the grey mist. There, in the glow, Thomas could make out tiny black dots. "Are those boats?" Herron looked through the binoculars and bolted below to the bridge to inform Korotva.

Fred Easton, Ron Precious, Kazumi Tanaka, and I packed gear in the media room when Hunter poked his head in. "We have a visual," he said and disappeared, and we followed. The sky cleared, the wind dropped to a gentle breeze, and the sea rolled in three-foot swells. On the horizon, the *Vostok* and nine harpoon boats circled and dispersed as if hunting. As we approached, a mile away from the factory ship, one of the harpoon boats turned toward us, and we saw the spray of whales running before it. We counted five whales, but assumed there would be more in the group. The crew dropped a Zodiac into the water, and Paul Spong tore away toward the harpoon boat with Bob and Bobbi Hunter. Pat Moore carried cameraman Fred Easton but no other rider.

The third Zodiac got hung up on a hook, suspended off the stern of the *James Bay*. I climbed out into the swaying Zodiac and pounded the hook with my fist until it came free, bruising my hand. Paul Watson, Marilyn Kaga, and I left in the third inflatable. As we came alongside the harpoon ship, we could read the number, ЛК-2007, the *Vlasny*, the ship we had confronted a year ago on Mendocino Ridge.

We prepared for a showdown, but when Spong and Hunter manoeuvred under the bow, the skipper of the *Vlasny* surprised us. The hulking, rusted harpoon ship stopped dead in the water. We circled to the stern, where a group of sailors watched. A young, blond sailor took photographs. They had a small, white Siberian husky with them. The little dog barked, and the sailors offered discreet waves. A few of the sailors spoke in halting English: "Where you from?"

"Canada."

"Japan," said Marilyn.

"Good ship," said one sailor, pointing to the *James Bay*.

The blond sailor with a camera, leaner and less soiled than the others, bent over the railing and spoke in English. "Got any acid?"

I patted my pockets and shrugged my shoulders as if he had perhaps asked for a smoke. "Uh, no. Sorry," I said and shook my head.

He nodded, as if to say, "Ah, too bad."

From my army fatigue jacket pocket I pulled two rolls of film and handed them to the Russian photographer. He tipped his hat and handed me a Soviet navy service pin, which I pinned to my jacket. I took off my Greenpeace badge and handed it to another sailor. The Russians smiled and chatted among themselves. Watson took off his Greenpeace T-shirt, which he wore over his sweater, passed it forward to me, and I handed it up to the sailors. Back came two packs of "Peace" cigarettes. The packages had been printed in English, with a golden dove carrying an olive branch. The rank and file Russians were buoyant and friendly. I wanted to invite them to the *James Bay* for a round of rum.

In the other Zodiac, Spong circled the *Vlasny* and approached the bow. Hunter reached out and placed the palm of his hand on the rusty metal hull. The gunner swung the harpoon sideways, locked it down with a pin, and covered it with a green tarpaulin. The wind had almost stopped and the sun shimmered on a bright blue, calm sea. Our situation felt surreal: "Peace" cigarettes, the hulking killer ship motionless in the water, tiny waves lapping against the hull, and the harpoon hidden under a green shroud.

The three Zodiacs converged, and we discussed our strategy. Perhaps, we hypothesized, someone in the Soviet political machine had read Marshall McLuhan or researched Greenpeace media tactics. Perhaps they assumed that if they denied us dramatic action photographs, we would go away. Before the shroud had covered it, I took photographs of Bob and Bobbi under the harpoon, but now, the visual drama had been drained from the scene. "We saved a pod of whales," Spong said. We circled the *Vlasny* several times and waved to the Soviet sailors. When the harpoon boat began to pull back toward the *Vostok*, we returned to the *James Bay*.

Back on board, I gave the Soviet service pin to Bob Thomas, as a prize for having been the first to spot the Russian ships. I gave one of the packets of Peace cigarettes to George Korotva. He, Hunter and Ted Haggarty each smoked one and gagged on the harsh tobacco. I displayed the other pack of cigarettes above the galley table. The image of the golden dove seemed like a bizarre historical twist. Ben Metcalfe had long ago pointed out that the dove, as a peace symbol, had been initiated by Picasso and adopted by the Bolsheviks in 1949. Now, it came back to Greenpeace by way of cigarettes from Russian whalers. Adding a touch of synchronicity to the surrealism was the fact that the cigarettes were made in Japan.

THE MECHANICS HUDDLE

Throughout the morning, Korotva kept pace with the *Vostok*, and a new group of volunteers prepared for a second encounter. Eileen gathered up whale pins, T-shirts, pamphlets, and other items for gifts to the Russian sailors. Moore took a bottle of rum from the stores and stashed it with his gear.

Paul Watson came up with an idea: We should disrupt the loading of whales from the harpoon boats to the *Vostok*. We approached in two Zodiacs. Photographers Kazumi Tanaka and Matt Herron rode with Watson. Moore, Eileen, and I followed in the Avon. While Watson was on a mission to stop the whalers from transferring dead whales to the flensing deck, Eileen intended to shower the sailors with gifts. The difference between the masculine and feminine styles could not have been more obvious. "Yin and yang," said Spong. "Perfect."

Two harpoon boats trailed behind the *Vostok*. Watson made straight for the stern slip of the giant factory ship. Workers watched from the decks and from openings in the metal stern plate that rose like a bastion wall before us. A dead sperm whale pitched in the blood-red wake of the factory ship. A line had been secured around its massive fluke to haul the whale toward the slip of the *Vostok*. Tanaka and Herron gagged from the smell of entrails. The two photographers clung to the lines of the pounding Zodiac as Watson gunned the outboard engine and vaulted forward onto the carcass in an attempt to foil the loading.

Heavy ropes snapped taut, the whale lurched forward, and the Zodiac was thrown back into the water. Tanaka saved himself from being cast adrift by clinging to the ropes, his cameras crashing about his neck. Herron fell to his knees to protect himself and his two Nikon cameras, but the small Zodiac took a wave that washed over him and Herron screamed at Watson to back off.

Meanwhile, Moore had approached the starboard beam of the other harpoon boat. Sailors gathered at the railing. Eileen reached forward and handed out whale pins, white oval badges with images of sperm whales, humpbacks, and fins. The sailors pinned them on their shirts. One bare-chested worker proudly wore his whale pin on his brief swimsuit, striking a theatrical pose for Eileen. The whalers crowded around for T-shirts. As Eileen passed up pamphlets with pictures from the previous year, the whalers passed back more service pins. Moore reached up with the bottle of rum, which earned cheers and thumbs-up salutes.

Back on board the *James Bay*, Herron fumed. The salt water had destroyed the motor drive on one of his cameras. He accused Watson of being reckless. "That's $2,000 worth of equipment, Paul!" Watson defended himself with a shrug. "We're here to save whales," he said. Herron let it go, but the tension between the two simmered. Tanaka, on the other hand, though soaked, seemed exhilarated and ready to go out again. Through the loudspeaker, Korotva pleaded with the whalers in Russian. When Tanaka spoke directly to the Japanese observers, they ducked behind the Russian crew and disappeared.

At sunset, with everyone back on the *James Bay*, Hunter got on the radio and phoned in a news report of the day's action. Patrick and Eileen danced on deck to the Rolling Stones as we followed the *Vostok*. The sea remained dead calm, not even a ripple on the water. The sky grew dark and the bow wave of the *James Bay* shimmered with phosphorescent light. I stood on the railing of the flying bridge with Marining, Susi Leger, Barry Lavender, Michael Manolson, and Mary-Lee Brassard.

As we rode through the peaceful, star-flecked blackness, Barry Lavender — now known as "Mr. Clean" because he rose early each morning and washed the dishes from the previous day — told us an ominous story about running into an old Greenpeace volunteer in Vancouver. The man was a financial advisor who had told Lavender he had tired of trying to bring corporate order to the band of anarchists. "The word is out," Lavender recalled the accountant telling him. "You guys are nothing but a bunch of renegades. No one respects you any more. That's why you were stopped by the RCMP in Bamfield. The Canadian government is ashamed of you idiots."

That night, the *Vostok* changed direction to the north and increased its speed to 18 knots. We kept pace, but this meant that our fuel efficiency plummeted. "They're running from us," Korotva proclaimed on the bridge at midnight. Ted Haggarty said, "Even if we turn back now, we'll arrive in Hawaii with dry tanks." Korotva convened a meeting with Herron, Moore, Hewitt, and Haggarty, the hard-core mechanics. Hewitt insisted that we had more fuel capacity than Haggarty claimed, and he hauled out the numbers to expound his point. He marked a line on the chart, his calculated point of no return. Haggarty, who was being conservative and prudent in the tradition of a Canadian naval officer, grumbled that Hewitt's calculation put us at risk of running dry at sea, "a dangerous gamble." The mechanics reached a compromise: We would steam north for no more than 24 hours, at which point, if the *Vostok* kept on, we would turn back and make straight for Hawaii.

JUST LIKE DANANG

On July 20, a bright, warm day, we followed 100 yards behind the *Vostok*. The harpoon ships had pushed ahead of us over the horizon but we knew, running at this pace, they could not be hunting whales. Hewitt calculated that we had cost the Russians at least 50,000 gallons of diesel fuel, worth some $30,000. Spong said the whales they failed to kill because of our presence were worth about $20,000 apiece. We had seen at least five whales escape. We could only guess at how much disruption we had caused by forcing the Russians to delay their run across the Pacific, or how many whales they would have killed if not fleeing northward. "We've cost them at least $200,000," said Spong, "maybe more, maybe $500,000. In any case, this makes it almost impossible for the Soviet fleet to operate profitably. We've done it." Moore poured rum and we drank a toast on the deck.

Watson and Herron shook hands. "I'm sorry about your camera," said Watson.

"It's just a motor drive," shrugged Herron. "Don't worry about it."

Shortly after 10:00 p.m., we received a radio call from Ed Daly, president of World Airways, who asked to speak to Hunter. Daly had seen the news reports about us and had called the San Francisco Greenpeace office to lend support. From Peter Fruchtman we had learned that the renegade businessman had made millions with his World Airways, mostly with US military contracts, flying soldiers and supplies. Reportedly, he had flown Hungarian refugees to Vienna in 1956 and airlifted mothers and babies from Danang, Vietnam, in 1975. According to the story, even when no military planes could land at Danang, Daly had flown in with a Boeing 727, dodged North Vietnamese anti-aircraft fire, and picked up refugees and soldiers. Daly's voice over the radio sounded slurred and gruff, but his tone all business. "Hunter?"

"Yes, sir," Hunter replied. The crew crowded around.

"Bob, I understand you need fuel in Hawaii."

"Yes, sir."

"Okay, here's the deal. I want you to know I'm not supporting any individuals in this deal. I'm supporting the cause. I want you to get back out there and stop those fools. How fast can you be in and out of Honolulu?"

"Twenty-four hours," snapped Hunter. The crew broke into snickers. Hunter hushed us with a wave of his hand.

"Okay, that's what I like to hear. What have you been paying for fuel?"

"We got a pretty good deal in San Francisco," said Hunter. "Sixty-five cents, I believe."

"You got ripped off," said Daly. "The navy gets it for less than that, and I get it for less than the navy." At this point, we could hear Daly talking to someone else in his office, presumably an aide. "Tell them we want the second price on 10,000 gallons of diesel in Honolulu." Then Daly spoke back into the phone. "Okay, it's set up, boy. When will you be there?"

"Friday," said Hunter.

"Okay Bob. Now listen, I don't want anyone to get hurt."

"No, sir."

"We want to make this a safe operation all around, just like Danang. You heard about Danang?"

"Yes, sir."

"Three-hundred and thirty-eight people, Bob. Last plane outta Danang before the NVA overran it. Took bullets. Got hit with a grenade. Not one person got hurt. Got 'em all back to Saigon. Had eight of 'em hanging in the landing gear wells. I like what you guys're doing. I been there."

"Yes, sir. I understand. Well, so far ..."

"Okay, Hunter. Our people in Honolulu will contact you. Good luck, son."

"Yeah, okay. Thanks. Roger, uh, out." Hunter cocked his head and looked at the radiophone, then around the room. "Okay, well, there you have it." He shrugged and handed the phone to Spong. "Money follows energy."

There was much talk about the mysterious Ed Daly and his links to the US military. Was he with the CIA? Had we become dupes of the Americans, used to embarrass the Russians? Watson went on about the CIA flying heroin out of Vietnam to fund covert operations. "It stinks, if you ask me," he said.

Near midnight, however, we agreed to turn back toward Hawaii. Lance Cowen, on the wheel, throttled down to 13 knots and we watched the *Vostok* disappear over the horizon. I had not slept in forty hours, so Fred Easton took my watch. I went to my bunk, lit a candle, and read from Lyall Watson's *Supernature*. After a few minutes, I pinched out the light, huddled in the rolling darkness, and slept.

CETACEAN ESCORT

On the afternoon of July 22, as we passed back through the area in which we had encountered the whalers, we came upon a pod of sperm whales heading southwest toward French Frigate Shoals, west of Hawaii. Korotva eased the *James Bay* westerly to stay with them. We counted five whales, including a baby. Spong felt certain this was the family of whales that had escaped the Russian harpoon ships three days earlier. The crew lined the starboard railing, hooted, cheered, and played flutes. The whales did not seem the least bit troubled by our presence.

The Greenpeace crew was in fine mettle now. We knew how to run the ship, we believed we had just chased the Soviet whaling fleet out of the mid-Pacific, we had given the media what they needed to help us tell our story, and on top of this, the whales had returned. Since the whales showed no fear, we could only assume they knew the difference between a harmless ship and the killer boats that could end their life in a single blow. Surely the sonar and roaring engines of the whalers would alarm the whales, but still we wondered: *How did the whales know that we would not harm them*?

Bob Hunter's spirits had revived. He insisted that we were witnessing a "turning point in human history. Human compassion is embracing nature."

In *The Storming of the Mind* he had written, "Ecological consciousness is the common denominator of the real revolution which is just now beginning inside the gates of the comfortable concentration camp fashioned by technique." Moore had condensed the idea in 1971 to "A flower is your brother." The family of sperm whales escorting us into Hawaii bolstered our belief that this era of ecology was dawning. After ninety minutes, cruising abeam of the minesweeper, the whales sounded with a flash of their flukes, and disappeared.

Seemingly, we had a simple job now: reach Honolulu for fuel, send out the pictures and film, tell our story, and go back out and do it again. But there was one complication: we desperately wanted to find the Japanese whalers. Spong, in particular, felt anxiety about this. Every two hours, we checked for radio traffic and gave interviews to media. Spong always asked the reporters if they knew where the Japanese whaling fleets operated. No one knew. The Japanese often used highly secure telex messages rather than voice transmission. We had no means of fixing them with Hewitt's RDF. We heard rumours of the vessel *Kyokuyo Maru #3* near Midway Island, another 2,000 miles west.

On the evening of July 22, we made landfall east of Oahu and watched the sun go down behind the island. I imagined what it might have been like for the first people ever to see these green cones rising from the misty mid-Pacific. I imagined the Polynesians on a chilly morning in a double-hulled canoe, navigating by stars and ocean currents from Marquesas or Tahiti, seeing these islands appear like a blessing from fisherman god Maui. In the quiet dusk, the world without humans, though an illusion, seemed tranquil and perfect, the world of humans so busy and strained. Could those two worlds make peace?

We sat off Diamond Head until dawn. A waning crescent moon hung over Honolulu as we entered the harbour. At 10:00 a.m. we tied up at Pier 9, dwarfed by towering grey warships in the throbbing inner harbour. Among throngs of reporters and television crews, Peter Fruchtman from Los Angeles stood on the dock with Howard Arfin and Taeko Miwa from Vancouver. Supporters arrived with fresh bananas, boxes of mangoes and papayas, and leis for the crew. Matt Herron, Kazumi Tanaka, and I rode with reporters to the *Honolulu Star-Bulletin*, where we processed our film and put photographs on the UPI and AP wires. The editors selected a photograph of Bobbi Hunter in front of the harpoon ship and a photograph of two sperm whale flukes lashed ingloriously to the gunwale of a Soviet whaler.

That afternoon, a World Airways car stopped on the pier. A well-dressed, finely groomed young man got out, made arrangements with Korotva and Haggarty to deliver the promised fuel, then left. The debate over Ed Daly continued. Watson was sure we had fallen into the clutches of the CIA, and who knew? Perhaps we had. On the other hand, Daly had rescued Hungarian refugees and found homes in the US for fifty-seven Vietnamese orphans. The US Department of Immigration had fined him $218,000 for violating regulations, and he had refused to pay. We admired his stubborn heroics. "Besides," said Hunter, "there are no strings attached. They're filling our tanks with fuel. Period. If anyone has a problem with that, they need to come up with $7,000."

MIDWAY

The next morning Marining and I took a cab to the *Star Bulletin* office and met with UPI bureau chief Kay Lynch and stringer Hal Ward. Lynch, a hard-nosed journalist, told us that the Japanese whalers had been seen 600 miles to the northwest at French Frigate Shoals. Ward, a young, blond man in sunglasses, told us that media representatives could get on routine Coast Guard flights to Midway Island, flying right over the archipelago. Lynch conspiratorially pressed us for our plans. Caught up in the intrigue of the moment, I let slip that, yes, we intended to go out after the Japanese if we could find them, but that we wanted them to think we intended to go after the Russians. This blunder would backfire on us later.

The next night we held a crew meeting on the forward deck of the *James Bay*. Paul Spong presented a plan to confront the Japanese vessel *Kyokuyo Maru #3*, last seen two days away at the Shoals. We agreed that to simply run out 600 miles on a rumour would be foolhardy. Instead, we would announce in the media that we were going back out after the Russians. Taeko Miwa and Kazumi Tanaka would tour Japanese ships in Honolulu, pose as journalists, and attempt to uncover information about the whaling fleet. We would then head northwest to Kauai, 100 miles closer to French Frigate Shoals. Fred Easton and I would stay in Honolulu and use our media credentials to get on the Coast Guard flight to Midway.

The *James Bay* departed Honolulu harbour on the night of July 29. Hal Ward had joined the crew as a reporter, saying that he would file news stories back to UPI. I stayed behind in port with Easton and Peter Fruchtman. The next morning, the *Star Bulletin* story revealed that we intended "to confront a sophisticated Japanese whaling fleet known to be operating near the Hawaiian Islands." Although this was no real secret, the news story undermined our ruse that we were searching for the Soviet fleet. The leak had been my fault. As a journalist, I should have known that Lynch would not keep our secret.

Easton, Fruchtman, and I drove to the Barber's Point Naval Air Station to catch the Coast Guard flight to Midway. Although we presented ourselves as journalists, the flight crews knew exactly who we were and grilled us about the Greenpeace ship. We boarded a Lockheed C-130 patrol plane and dove down over French Frigate Shoals. Pilot Lieutenant Richard Mattingly talked to other pilots in the area, but none reported seeing the Japanese fleet.

Over Midway, we could see shimmering turquoise lagoons and two islands, remnants of an eroded volcano, surrounded by a reef about six miles in diameter. On the approach, we flew into a flock of albatross, some of which splattered onto the C-130 wings and window. "Oh yeah," the navigator said, "we wipe out a few of those guys every time." We landed on Sand Island, where we watched albatross, brown boobies, and frigate birds loping laconically over the white coral sand. The US Navy had blasted a 200-yard channel through the reef in 1870 and built the naval station in 1941. "They used to push the goony birds off the beaches with a steam shovel," the navigator told us. Poachers had decimated the birds, collecting feathers for the high-fashion hat industry. A population of some 500,000 Bonin petrels that burrow in the atolls at night had been reduced to a few thousand by rats from the poachers' ships. The Midway Islands, as isolated as any place on the planet, were themselves an ecological disaster.

In a Quonset hut, enlisted men sat around a table playing Risk and listening to "Marrakesh Express" from the 1969 Crosby, Stills and Nash album. I handed out whale buttons and several sailors asked how they could get onto a Greenpeace ship. The seamen told us the Japanese whaling fleet had sailed off to the south, possibly toward the seamounts around the Wake Islands. Still, no one had — or at least, no one revealed — any precise information. We ate dinner with the Navy crew, slept the night at Midway, and returned to Honolulu the next morning.

NAWILIWILI UPRISING

Fruchtman stayed in Honolulu to continue intelligence gathering, and a local volunteer flew Fred and me to Kauai. When we rejoined the *James Bay* in Nawiliwili Bay, we found the crew in turmoil. Spong chastised me for leaking the *Kyokuyo Maru* information and Mike Bailey was in open revolt.

"No Japanese?" asked Hunter.

"Nothing we saw," I told him. "The guys on Midway told us the fleet moved south, but where? We didn't see them south of the archipelago. The next closest seamounts south are a thousand miles away." I told Hunter that the navy seamen had confirmed that the military knew the location of every ship on the ocean, but that the Americans would not likely reveal the location of the Japanese whalers. "The bosses don't want us to find the Japanese," I said, "but the rank and file navy guys think we're heroes."

"More than I can say for our own crew," said Hunter. Many on board, especially Michael Bailey, had grown frustrated with sitting in port and suspicious of all the clandestine intrigue. Watson vowed to leave, still complaining about CIA money. Bailey and Watson wanted to move northwest, along the seamounts and atolls, to look for the Japanese whalers. Bailey took it upon himself to call a full crew meeting and openly questioned Hunter's leadership. A humbled Hunter faced the crew.

"Look," he said, gesturing to the charts out on the hatch cover. "We're almost 1,500 miles from Midway. Matt estimates they could be anywhere within a thousand miles of Midway, from the French Frigate Shoals to the Suiko seamounts, halfway to the Aleutians. Hewitt says that's about three million square miles of ocean."

"It's a lot of ocean," said Matt Herron.

"Private pilots all over the Hawaiian Islands have offered to fly missions for us," Hunter continued. "We have a volunteer air force, but we don't know if the Japanese are north or south of Midway. Rex and Fred heard they had gone off to the south, but that could be a con job by the Americans. Charging off after the Japanese solves nothing. We burn up $500 a day in fuel. If we run all the way to Midway, we still might not find them. However, we could find the *Vostok* again. And we still might be able to continue on to Tokyo and carry the issue to Japan that way. Sorry, but I still say the best thing we can do right now is sit tight and try to gain some information. A voyage with no destination would be crazy."

"It's not like we can just spend more money," Bobbi Hunter warned. "We're broke. Bill can't get any more money for us. We're on our own."

"Peter said Daly will refuel us at Midway if we go there," said Bailey.

"Right, but what does that accomplish?" said Moore. "We're five days to Midway at cruising speed. If we spend a few days looking around, and come back, that's two weeks flat out running round trip, only to get back here with empty fuel tanks." Navy veterans Haggarty and Lance Cowan agreed. The older Greenpeace crew, with the exception of Watson, agreed. Most of the new crew, even those frustrated with sitting in port, appreciated the logic. Susi Leger, who had worked tirelessly in the engine room, spoke up. "Maybe we don't see how much we've already done," she said. "Look at how many people we've inspired. Everyone wants to help. It's incredible."

Walrus announced that he and Taeko Miwa were organizing a "Japan Committee," to fly to Tokyo. "If the *James Bay* does not get to Japan this summer," he said, "we'll fly to Japan anyway in September. This battle will be won over the next few years. Ya' gotta see the big picture."

Moore claimed the summer's campaign was already a success. "It's almost August," he said, "and neither the Russian nor the Japanese whalers have come within 800 miles of the coast of North America. The Japanese fleet, which generally operates along the Hawaiian archipelago, is nowhere near Hawaii. We've covered 200,000 square miles of ocean by air. We've completely disrupted both whaling fleets. The IWC is in disarray over all of the public scrutiny. We're winning."

Bailey shrugged. His revolt claimed few committed backers. If Hunter took the insurrection personally, he didn't show it. Bailey gained prestige with most of the crew because he had, at least, called on the veteran leadership to account for itself. Hunter began calling the former "Zodiac Mike," "Generalissimo Bailey."

Spong fell noticeably silent. Finding the Japanese whalers had been his single vision for the last twelve months. He was not prepared to abandon it.

THE ART OF BATTLE

We left Nawiliwili and steamed for 24 hours southwest, past Oahu and Molokai and into Lahaina harbour on the Island of Maui. Hunter posted a Bulletin: "Schedule for next 24-hour period: Hang loose. Do what George says. Possibilities inherent in field situation: Limitless ... Recommended mental attitude: Positive."

In Maui, Watson departed for Vancouver to work on the spring harp seal campaign. Rod Marining returned to Vancouver to be with Bree, now three months pregnant. Norman Seaton flew back to California with his Gustav Holtz cassette tapes. Two Americans joined the crew, activist Ross Thornwood and political insider Peter Fruchtman.

Despite his recent upbeat messages to the crew, Hunter felt frustrated. "We need to get back out to sea before the crew kills each other," he told me under the banyen tree in the centre of Lahaina. Korotva and Walrus had come to blows over some dispute that neither would discuss. Tanaka was upset that we had not found the Japanese, and Spong nearly inconsolable. "He refuses to come out of his Hobbit hole," said Hunter. "I have a feeling that if we stay here much longer, something bad is going to happen." We both knew there was little chance of tracking down the Japanese whalers. They could be halfway to Kamchatka, and probably received daily coordinates on *us*.

"But it's worse than that," said Hunter. "We're more broke than ever. Bobbi can't get any money out of either San Francisco or Vancouver. There are vicious political battles in California. Will Jackson has been booted off the board and Jet Johnson has quit in protest. Bobbi's nervous about the situation in the Vancouver office as well. Gannon's trying to squeeze out some money to send us, but right now, all we have is a tank of fuel and enough friends that we can load up on food. We should get out of here and find the Russians again." Hunter turned solemn. "Every army that goes into battle has strengths and weaknesses," he said. "The art of battle is to steer the thing in such a way that it favours our strength and covers our weakness. Our strength is the media, not international espionage. Our weakness is that we have no money — and our organization seems to be falling prey to the lowest level of Machiavellian bullshit. But the whalers don't know that. We should just get back out there and do our mindbombing thing. It's what we do best."

"What about Tokyo?"

"Even if Daly bought the fuel, we have no reserves. The Russians are still up north, according to Deep Throat. They haven't dared go near the coast of California. We can strike at the Russian whalers, but our press releases can expose the Japanese. We've disrupted the Japanese hunt just by being here. Spong feels defeated right now, but even Paul believes we are winning this at the IWC. Taeko, Kazumi, and Walrus are prepared to set up in Japan. Taeko has friends there in the environmental movement. I believe the best thing we can do right now is get home and prepare for next year. We'll hit the Russians one more time on the way."

The next afternoon, August 7, we departed Lahaina and rounded Cape Halawa on the island of Molokai. That evening, a nearly full moon sat over the horizon to the east and a pale pink sunset to the west. David Weiss made dinner with Chivers, Barry Lavender, and Matt Herron. Around his waist, he wore the small, white, linen apron that he had worn for most of the voyage. Weiss — strikingly handsome, fit, youthful, with dark hair and eyes — had joined the crew from Woodstock, New York, and served tirelessly with the galley team. He picked up a bucket with a rope on the handle that had been used to fetch sea water while in port and slipped out onto the deck after water for the clean-up. Weiss wrapped the rope around his hand and tossed the bucket into the sea. As soon as it hit the water, the bucket stopped like a sea anchor, and the rope snapped the ring finger from his right hand in an instant. He shrieked, held the mangled hand to his stomach, and slumped to the deck. Blood poured down his shirt and soaked into the white apron.

Barry Lavender, Eileen Chivers, and Lance Cowan pulled him inside. Fred Easton, acting as paramedic, administered first aid. The strong painkillers had been padlocked in a metal cabinet, but no one could remember where Dr. Webb had secured the key. Moore and Bailey broke into the cabinet with a hacksaw blade. Korotva ordered the ship around, called the Coast Guard, requested an ambulance, and steamed back toward Lahaina at full bore. Weiss refused painkillers due to his belief in the body's natural healing powers. "We'll do it on love," he muttered weakly. Hunter cradled Weiss' head in his lap at the galley table. Chivers stroked his forehead. He seemed to go into a shock that dulled the pain. "It's like you're all angels," he murmured. In Lahaina, the ambulance transported Weiss to the hospital. Other than the beatings of Rod Marining, David

McTaggart, and Nigel Ingram by French thugs, this was the worst physical calamity yet to befall a member of a Greenpeace expedition. We stayed in port the next day, until Weiss was out of the hospital and safely in the private home of two young women from the Lahaina B'nai B'rith camp.

On August 9, we moved to Kahului on the north side of the island. We intended to leave at first light, but at 23:00, a fan in the crew berths overheated and caught a towel on fire. Bobbi Hunter smelled the smoke and sounded the alarm. Lance Cowan stormed in with a fire extinguisher and Hunter followed with the salt water hose.

The fire caused no serious damage, but black soot covered the berths and bedding. Worse, it felt to us like the voyage was disintegrating. We spent most of the night cleaning the bunkroom, scoured the entire ship the next day, and departed Kahului at sunset. Then, things got really crazy.

CIA GETS HIGH

We learned that the *Vostok* had turned toward Mendocino at the 40th parallel, so we increased our pace. A dense fog settled over the North Pacific. For days, we moved closer to the Soviet ships, through the mist. A strange black object appeared from time to time whenever the fog lifted, far at sea near the horizon. Korotva, Haggarty, Herron, and Lance Cowan studied this object through the binoculars and came to the conclusion that it was the "sail" — the upper observation deck — of a submarine. Whatever the object was, it spooked us, appearing and disappearing back into the fog. It would appear on the radar screen, then vanish. There was a great deal of cogitation over this mystery. Was it an American submarine? Moore speculated that the Soviet Union had dispatched a submarine to keep track of our location. "The eye of Mordor," we called it.

In any case, *Hotel Papa* was back at sea. Engine room watches continued. Kazumi Tanaka began a regular Japanese language class. Easton, Spong, Leger, and I monitored the radio. Fido came out of hiding, but shat all over the Hunters' bed. Bob Hunter returned to latrine officer duty, with the brush back on his belt.

Hunter's communiqués became *The James Bay Daly Bulletin*, named after our mysterious benefactor. He secretly posted his supposedly anonymous chronicle in the Ward Room at odd hours, filled with gossip, news, comics, and analysis. Hunter poked fun at everyone, including himself, "El Presidente," and "Generalissimo ('Zodiac') Mike Bailey," leader of the "abortive Nawiliwili Uprising." Hal Ward had become known as "KGB." We sensed something strange about Ward, and many on the crew thought he was an American intelligence agent, perhaps CIA. I became suspicious because he seemed to have no journalism experience. He had a dream job for any journalist, that of UPI stringer in Hawaii, yet he rarely interviewed anyone, never took notes, and never filed any stories. Nevertheless, everyone liked him, so KGB became a regular member of the crew.

By the time we reached 40 degrees north, the Soviets had changed direction, now returning west toward Kamchatka. But something had gone terribly wrong with our fuel calculations. We had burned diesel fuel twice as fast as expected. Hewitt researched the problem and determined that the engines had carboned up, cutting our fuel efficiency. Rather than chase the whalers, we stopped and waited, on the advice of Hewitt and Matt Herron. "If they run all the way back to the Sea of Okhotsk," said Herron, "fine. We keep them away from North America. If they turn back, we're waiting for them and we won't waste any fuel chasing them." This made sense to everyone. We drifted in the fog on the easterly current. On the aft deck, we lounged in Zodiacs and listened to rock and roll music — Bob Dylan, Pattie Smith, Supertramp — that had replaced *The Planets*.

The fog, the submarine, and CIA paranoia put Melville Gregory on edge. He suspected Hal Ward of being a snoop, and I confided in Mel that KGB didn't seem to be a real journalist. During the 1960s, when the FBI had infiltrated the civil rights and anti-war movements, some activists had used drug sessions to vet out infiltrators. Most undercover agents would smoke marijuana to protect their cover, but few would take LSD. It became part of the underground mythology that offering an infiltrator acid was a sure way to expose him or her. Mel Gregory offered Hal Ward a blotter tab of LSD, and to his surprise, the new crewmember accepted. Mel and KGB spent a seemingly pleasant evening wandering about the ship, watching the sunset, and marvelling at stars. Late that night, in the media room, Ward confessed to Mel that he was indeed with the US Central Intelligence Agency. According to Mel's account, Ward said, with tears in his eyes, "You all are good guys. You're not doing anything wrong. I don't know why they wanted me to report on you. There are enough people screwing up the world. I don't know why anyone would be worried about you."

We still did not know if Ward's story held true. Was he really CIA or was he just playing into our paranoia and naiveté? Oddly enough, the confession clarified nothing. "Who gives a shit," said Moore. "We don't really have any secrets." In any case, KGB now had glowing red cheeks and a bright look in his eyes. He seemed to settle in and thoroughly enjoy his cruise. He worked hard in the engine room and never complained. The *Daly Bulletin* reported:

"The astonishingly handsome and versatile young Hal Ward, Ace News Dick, seems to have recovered nicely from his, ah, trip …"

IN A FOG

On August 18 the Soviet factory ship *Dalnyi Vostok* and its armada of twelve harpoon boats abruptly turned back toward the coast of California. We sat in their path. Overnight, they dodged south and we followed through a thick fog. "We're being way too nice," said Spong. "Let's don't forget, these people are murdering whales. We need to be more aggressive." Herron and new crewmember Julliette Williamson spoke up for non-violence. "I'm not talking about violence," said Spong. "I'm talking about being aggressive." No one questioned that Greenpeace was committed to non-violence, and there ensued a long discussion about Gandhi, the Quakers, and bearing witness.

"Harass dem, harass dem, harass dem," said Korotva. "Dat's the only thing will work." Bailey came up with a plan to "launch all the Zodiacs at the *Vostok* at night. It'll freak out whoever is on radar. They'll think they're being torpedoed." Bailey, previously skeptical of the mystics, asked to throw the *I Ching*. He drew hexagram number four, *youthful folly*. "In the first oracle I inform him," reads the text. Bailey scanned the commentary. "In the time of youth, folly is not an evil. One may succeed in spite of it, provided one finds an experienced teacher and has the right attitude." The changing line in the second place advised, "Tolerate with kindliness the shortcomings of human folly."

"Okay, wow," said Bailey, slightly stunned by his first *I Ching* reading, which seemed to speak directly to him.

On August 19, the mystery submarine, if that's what it was, appeared behind us for three hours as we moved south toward the approaching Soviet whaling fleet. Then the fog closed back in, cutting visibility to no more than a few hundred yards. At 17:00 we picked up Russian broadcasts, and an hour later, we saw a 12-foot blue shark, a possible sign that we were near the blood trail of the factory ship. At 23:00, we picked up what looked like a Soviet harpoon ship on the radarscope, three miles away, but invisible in the fog. Our ship sat dead in the water at 41°21' north, 162°38' west, the middle of the North Pacific. Just before midnight, the harpoon boat moved off to the north and we followed. Lance Cowan stayed at the wheel, with Hewitt monitoring the radar, Easton on the radio, and Leger and Zimmerman in the engine room. More ships appeared on our radar, as if we cruised in the midst of the fleet, although we could not see a single ship. Their radar would be good, but that didn't mean they knew who we were. We would look just like them. We imagined a Russian sailor huddled over his radar screen, counting, "twelve, thirteen ... hey there's an extra ship!" We broke radio silence a half hour after midnight, phoned Vancouver, and told Marining we were with the whaling fleet.

Most of the crew stayed up all night. In the pre-dawn, the mystery submarine appeared, and then vanished from the radar screen. At daybreak, Mel, Bobbi, and I watched an albatross arrive through the mist, gliding slowly from the east. It stayed at our boat for only a few minutes, and then returned toward the direction from which it had come. We surmised the albatross headed back to the Soviet ships and I relayed this news to Herron on the bridge. We followed the seabird and soon saw an oil slick, garbage, and another shark. Then, the *Vostok* appeared on radar, moving east at 15 knots, at a heading of 80 degrees. The harpoon ships fanned out north and south, hidden in the fog.

This would be our last charge, and we knew it. Chasing the *Vostok* at this pace would deplete our fuel. The closest fuel depots were Midway Island to the south and Dutch Harbor in the Aleutians. The harpoon ships worked in a circle pattern as if herding their prey. The fog would not impede the whalers since they could still hunt whales with sonar and get close enough to visually track them. In the afternoon, the fog suddenly dissolved, as if curtains had opened on a stage. Under a clear sky, we stared directly at the *Vostok* and five harpoon ships.

Moore, Fred Easton, and Peter Fruchtman climbed into the Avon and proceeded toward the closest harpooner. Paul Spong, Susi Leger, and I followed in a Zodiac. The Russian ship moved away and we pursued.

However, the break in the fog had been an illusion. The conditions were such that, as the afternoon air cooled, the fog almost instantly condensed around us. When Korotva saw this happening from the bridge of the *James Bay*, he radioed the Zodiac. Leger received the call. "Immediately get back to the *James Bay*!" shouted Korotva. Spong got on the radio, agreed to return, but said we should chase down Moore and the others first. "Yeah, okay," said Korotva, "but hurry. This is dangerous. We can't see you. We don't know where you are."

I could barely make out the vaporous image of the minesweeper behind us as we chased after the Avon. Then, when I turned again to look, our ship was gone. Now the only indication of our heading was the direction of the ocean swell itself. It would have been a wise move to carry a compass in my gear, but I had not done so. I looked down at the water. We ran before a slight swell that came in off our port stern at roughly a 30-degree angle to the line of our heading. Instinctively, I fixed the image of this angle in my memory. I knew that if we reversed this heading later we could get back to where the *James Bay* had been when I lost sight of it.

By the time we caught Moore's inflatable, Easton was filming Russian sailors hauling a dying sperm whale from the water and lashing its flukes to their steel ship. The agonized giant thrashed helplessly. We pulled alongside Moore and relayed the order to get back to the *James Bay*. However, our ship had disappeared into the fog. Moore, Fruchtman, and Spong debated what to do, all three talking at once. "I know the way back," I shouted. "The swell ..." Moore looked at me, but Spong was now back on the radio to the bridge of the *James Bay*.

Hunter, over the radio, recommended we stay with the harpoon boat. "At least we can track them on the radar." There were two problems with this plan. One, the *James Bay* didn't know which harpoon boat we sat with, and furthermore, nightfall approached. If the harpoon ship decided to take off, we could be left in the middle of the Pacific, lost. Korotva spoke of Hewitt trying to get an RDF fix on our radio, but our signal was too weak. Spong had figured out how to turn our radio in an arc and get a crude fix on the *James Bay* signal, but the results were ambiguous. Easton suggested asking the harpoon boat to take us aboard, a safer plan than to risk getting left behind. I butted in again and insisted that I knew the direction back to the *James Bay*. With everyone talking at once, however, my voice was lost, or so I thought.

Susi Leger looked up at me from her seat in the Zodiac and whispered, "Do you really know?" I explained briefly.

She turned toward Spong and screamed, "Stop!" Spong, Moore, and Fruchtman quieted. "Just listen to Rex for a minute," she said. I explained the direction of the swell and pointed to the heading that would take us to the *James Bay*. Spong and Moore nodded. "Are you sure?" asked Spong.

"Yes," I said.

"The problem is," Moore said, "the *James Bay* is moving."

I shrugged. "Yeah. Hopefully, toward us," I said, and I felt confident that we could get back to within sight of the *James Bay*. "If we're going, we should go now," I said. "Otherwise, get prepared to spend the night with our Russian friends." We decided to make a run for our ship. Back we headed, roughly 30° across the steady sea swell. Spong raised Hunter on the radio and told him what we were doing. "Okay," said Hunter. "George is sounding the horn, do you hear?"

"No," said Paul. "Keep sounding the horn. We think we're approaching you."

"Keep your radio on," said Hunter. "Keep transmitting. Al's trying to fix you."

On the bridge of the *James Bay*, Hunter paced and Korotva snarled at the film crew that cowered in the corner where they could catch the action on film without interfering. The rest of the crew lined the flying bridge and bow railings to look for us.

In the Zodiac, I quietly panicked as I guided Spong across the swell. I stood in the bow, clung to the rope, and pointed left or right to keep the angle as I remembered it. My heart pounded. Had I done the right thing? If this failed, I would be to blame. We'd be lost at sea, at night. The sky had already turned dark. Susi Leger gazed at me expectantly. I gave her the most confident look I could conjure. Then, we heard the faint horn through the mist. "That's it!"

"Did you hear it?" Leger shouted. Spong and Moore slowed the engines. "We hear you," Spong called over the radio. The sound of the horn became louder. Then, we saw the bow of the *James Bay* emerge from the fog.

In my berth that night I imagined the other scenarios: sleeping on our coats on the deck of a harpoon boat or drifting in the vast blackness of the mid-Pacific.

THE INDUS RIVER

We dogged the *Vostok* and its fleet the next day. They killed one sperm whale in sight of Bailey, Hunter, and Herron, but otherwise the Zodiac teams frustrated the harpooners. Michael Manolson, Bob Thomas, Tanaka, Julliette Williamson, and the other new crewmembers rode in Zodiacs and blockaded the whalers. Whereas the day before we had been shamefully unprepared for the fog, on this day, we struck decisively. The harpoon ships abandoned the whale hunt in our presence. However, we knew the Soviets had two fleets of some dozen harpoon boats each. Even on a successful day we could slow down only one or two harpoon ships.

That afternoon, Hewitt informed us that we had just enough fuel to reach either Midway or Dutch Harbor. Ed Daly had agreed to pay for a refueling, and the Midway base commander, a Captain Fischer, spoke to us by VHF radio and cleared us to enter the naval port. I pressed Hal Ward on Daly's relationship to the CIA. "Everybody knows everybody," he said. "The CIA and the military are partners and are merged through personnel. They all know what you're doing, and they all know what Ed Daly's doing. Daly knows lots of military and intelligence people. He flew charters for 'em. But that doesn't mean he can't do things on his own. He can certainly give away $10,000 on his own. It's pocket change. He probably likes what you're doing."

The *Vostok* steamed northeast at 16 knots. Before we turned away to run for fuel, we made one final gesture. Barry Lavender designed a banner with a dying whale and the Russian word "HET" in Cyrillic script, pronounced "Nyet," meaning "No." Eileen, Pat Moore, and Fred Easton took the sign in the Avon and approached the stern of the *Vostok*. The Russian crew lined up to see the floating protest sign. A few Russian crewmen returned insults, but most just watched. Some waved and gave us the thumbs up.

Later, with everyone back on board, we cut our engines and bobbed in the swells as the *Vostok* disappeared over the northern horizon. That night, news of our encounter aired on "Voice of America," following news that US troops had been placed on combat-ready DEFCON-3 status after axe-wielding North Korean soldiers killed two US Army officers.

The next day we headed southwest for Midway, enjoying the feeling that we had hounded the Russians from the whaling grounds. Bobbi

Hunter talked to the office in Vancouver and discovered we were $140,000 in debt, dousing our sanguine spirits. The bank had financed us for $15,000 beyond the amount covered by the guarantors, but we had reached the limit. Watson had launched the seal campaign and had already amassed new expenses. The office faced a $3,000 phone bill, and the phone company had threatened to cut us off.

Our San Francisco group had $7,780 in the bank. Gannon knew this, phoned, and asked for $5,000 to be sent to Seattle, destined to refuel the ship. However, political battles raged in San Francisco, where our old friend Will Jackson had been axed and Jet Johnson had resigned. We learned that Paul Krassner, the most experienced social crusader in the group, had also quit. Gannon spoke to Cindy Baker in the San Francisco office, a devoted whale advocate, who told him she was under strict orders from lawyer David Tussman not to release any money, not even to the Greenpeace Foundation in Canada.

Our organization had reached the precise limit of its ability to manage itself from a ship in the middle of the Pacific Ocean. Like Alexander of Macedonia at the Indus River, we had marched across more territory than we could administer. We had no money and our main foreign office operated in turmoil, if not open rebellion. To compound these problems, virtually the entire administration of the Greenpeace Foundation served on the ship crew, leaving no one to sort out disputes at home. Gannon, Michael Chechik, and John Cormack, the only board members not on the *James Bay*, could not even form a quorum. By now, Cormack had returned to Vancouver, but had not been paid his charter fee by the Mendocino Whale War group. In the media room of the *James Bay*, we held the first official board of directors meeting of the summer, attended by Bobbi Hunter, Bob Hunter, Paul Spong, Pat Moore, Eileen Chivers, George Korotva, Ron Precious in proxy for Chechik, Michael Manolson and Bob Thomas representing the Canadian offices, Gary Zimmerman representing the United States offices, and me.

Before the meeting, Zimmerman had phoned San Francisco. Aside from the money that we could not access, some volunteers in San Francisco had been miffed that a story appeared on the front page of the *San Francisco Chronicle* without the media release having been approved by the local office. "I don't think anything in the story offended anyone," said Zimmerman. "I think it was the principle of the thing."

"It starts," lamented Hunter. "Our own organization is now the filter through which our communiqués must pass." Our Vancouver office had censored Hunter's squid story, and now the San Francisco group demanded similar media veto powers. Hunter questioned his own leadership, graciously perhaps, so no one else would have to. "Look," he said, "there are things I can't do. I never claimed to be an administrator."

"The problem is," said Bobbi Hunter, "we're broke without support from all the other offices. We can't go on. Forget Midway and Tokyo. I don't even know how we're going to get Taeko and Walrus over there. Money's coming into Vancouver, but it's just paying the rent and the wages — a few hundred dollars a month for Starlet to do the books and Betty to run the office. Bill Gannon's working for free. The line of credit is used up, and there's no money coming out of San Francisco. So that's it. We have to go back."

Spong fumed for a while but turned philosophical. "Next year, we'll start from Hawaii. We'll track the ships all the way from Japan if we have to."

We turned back toward North America. We now had no fuel margin at all. Ironically, or perhaps auspiciously, the closest points of land were Mendocino and Moore's home of Winter Harbour. We made for Winter Harbour, a heading of 40 degrees, north-northeast.

GOODWILL MISSION

In spite of our financial and political turmoil, we believed we were winning the battle for the whales. The US Congress had enacted the 200-mile fishing limit, which gave them the authority to prohibit whaling on the continental shelf, and would inspire similar controls by other nations. The conservationist Netherlands had joined the International Whaling Commission, putting more pressure on Japan and Russia.

We learned from our office in Vancouver that three Soviet warships arrived in the Shire for what was supposed to be a "goodwill mission." The director of the Vancouver Maritime Museum had spent three years arranging a visit by Soviet ships. On August 25, two Soviet destroyers, the *Gnevny* and the *Sposobny*, and a tanker, the *Ilim*, entered the harbour. Paul Watson and a friend slipped past Harbours Board police, brandishing a protest sign. The police ordered Watson to leave, and when he refused, they arrested him. At a press conference on board the *Sposobny*, following statements from the hosts and guests, the first question from the media was, "Do you know about Greenpeace?" Vancouver organizers bowed their heads in despair, but Rear Admiral Vladimir Varganov responded. "Yes," said Varganov, "Greenpeace is respected in the Soviet Union."

Then Nikolai Makarov, chargé d'affaires from the Soviet Embassy in Ottawa, grabbed the microphone and said they couldn't talk about whaling because it was a political issue. Attempting to explain, he unwittingly dropped a bombshell: "The Soviet Union," he revealed, "is already getting ready for the eventuality that we will have to stop whaling and we're doing our best to find other sources — synthetic ones — to replace the products that we get from the whales. But our industry will need time to make these changes."

"How much time?" a reporter asked.

Makarov revealed that the Soviets would likely quit whaling "within two years." The goodwill visit to Vancouver went quickly downhill. Reporters rushed off to announce that the Soviets would stop whaling within two years. Rod Marining called the *James Bay* and reported the news. Hunter issued a media release announcing that Greenpeace welcomed the Soviet announcement. Then, a fisheries minister in Moscow denied the report that the Soviet Union would end whaling within two years. When reporters pressed *him* for more information, he acknowledged that they might quit whaling within *four* years, by 1980.

In Vancouver, Makarov, covering his tracks, said, "I don't see any contradiction between my statement and what was stated in Moscow by the fisheries minister who said the date would be 1980." Making things worse for himself, he added, "The Soviet Union observes the quotas set by the [International Whaling] Commission, which have been reduced recently. These quotas are based on exact scientific information obtained by the Commission. In the case of diminishing numbers of whales, these quotas will be reduced even further." Poor Makarov sank deeper into this mire as he explained that if and when whale populations got to a dangerously low level, the IWC would curtail whaling altogether.

Marining immediately sent a news release around the world quoting the unfortunate diplomat that whale numbers were "diminishing," which we knew was true, and that, according to the Soviets, the IWC would soon curtail whaling altogether.

The flap embarrassed the Soviet whaling industry and also exposed the Soviet military to unwanted media scrutiny. News reports revealed that the visit by the Soviet ships was not a goodwill mission at all. There had been a cold-war rumour that the Soviet Union had planted nuclear warheads in the coastal waters of twenty-five countries around the world, including the United States and Canada. This rumour turned out to be true. On August 17, 1976, the Canadian Navy found one such warhead near Crescent Beach, south of Vancouver. Prime Minister Trudeau had called Makarov in Ottawa and demanded that the Soviet Union remove the missile. The "goodwill" mission had been a cover for a team of Soviet divers who removed the warhead. The Soviet Union summarily recalled Nikolai Makarov to Moscow. "I feel sorry for the guy," said Marining. "He'll probably end up in Siberia."

STILL A TRIBE

On August 30, we caught sight of North America at Kwakiutl Point, south of Winter Harbour. On September 6, eighty-four days after leaving the beach at Jericho, we arrived in Vancouver. I found it difficult to depart, and sat up late with Glenn and others in the ship's galley. *Hotel Papa* had become our home and leaving felt like a loss. When I mentioned this, Hunter said, "Of course. It's like the guys who came back from the war. As horrible as it was, some of them didn't want to come back." He told about a story he had investigated as a journalist in Winnipeg a decade earlier. "The amputees from the war shared a bizarre camaraderie," he said. "They all lost something in the war, and this became their bond. They had a club, but the only way to get into the club was to get your leg blown off, or something, so it was a tightly knit group."

We had not suffered such losses, but we had lost our innocence and exposed our foibles. We had seized the power of our convictions but had been duped by that same power. The clout to make headlines and sway governments had made us feel invincible. The financial and political mess that awaited us would soon make us wish we were back at sea. We now returned home drained of energy and financially insolvent. The bank demanded regular payments to reduce the loan. Our foreign offices wanted their freedom. Our local suppliers had lost patience and wanted to be paid. Our spouses wanted us back. We all had rent to pay, but most of us had no jobs to return to.

"We're still a tribe," said Hunter. "We know each other's dark secrets now. Like a family, we've all been pissed at each other, one time or another. But we're all we've got. Like the amputees. We're all slightly crippled, so all we can do is just remain a tribe and go on from here."

CHAPTER TEN

A NAME FOR WHAT IS NATURAL

"If i dreamed natural dreams of being a natural
woman doing what a woman does when she's natural
i would have a revolution."

— Nikki Giovanni

By the time the *James Bay* docked in Vancouver, our compatriot Paul Watson had flown to Bergen, Norway, for the UN Marine Mammals Conference. Before he left, however, Watson had opened his own Greenpeace bank account and initiated his own fundraising. He had convinced the Greenpeace bookkeeper to part with several blank cheques, against the instructions of accountant Bill Gannon. The Greenpeace Foundation board supported the seal campaign, but not a private bank account. Had our bankers found out about this second account, they would likely have taken their own legal action to close it. The Greenpeace lawyers advised Hunter to write a letter to Watson on September 13, insisting that the illicit account be closed. Meanwhile, Bobbi Hunter fired the bookkeeper and hired a new one. These moves were painful, as Watson remained an admired comrade and the bookkeeper, Starlet Lum, had meant no harm. Nevertheless, the Warriors of the Rainbow had to grapple with financial accountability.

In Bergen, Watson and Jet Johnson, who spoke fluent Norwegian, posed as journalists and met with sealing company owner G. C. Rieber, from whom they coaxed valuable information about the sealers' departure plans in the spring. They also conspired with animal rights activists from around the world about tactics to keep pressure on Canada and Norway. When Watson returned to Vancouver, however, he discovered the legal letter from Hunter. He agreed to close down the bank account, and the board of directors welcomed him back, but loyalties had been strained, particularly between Watson and Gannon and Bobbi Hunter. Watson's fear of losing control of the seal campaign would later lead to a peculiar, and brief, alliance with his rival, Patrick Moore.

Meanwhile, Walrus, Taeko Miwa, and Kazumi Tanaka had arrived in Tokyo to carry out our whale campaign strategy. There, they faced a skeptical public. Whaling companies in Japan had portrayed Greenpeace as anti-Japanese, and some journalists — maliciously or not — linked us to the infamous Red Army radicals who had hijacked a Japan Airlines plane. Miwa and Tanaka felt that before they could successfully deliver the whale message in Japan, they needed to clarify that Greenpeace promoted ecology and disarmament, not political revolution. From Tokyo, they made arrangements to meet pacifists in Hiroshima, the families decimated by mercury poisoning in Minamata, and members of the small but robust Japanese ecology movement.

However, the biggest problem facing the Japan Committee was — typically now — internal. Howard Arfin, who had been left in charge of communications in Vancouver during the *James Bay* voyage, had joined a group of disenchanted volunteers in San Francisco and formed his own Greenpeace delegation to Japan. Their presence in Tokyo created confusion among journalists and environmentalists, and from a financial point of view, having two competing delegations in Tokyo was absurd. Lawyer Marvin Storrow convinced Hunter that if we did not protect our name we would lose it. With Zimmerman back in San Francisco, the US board approved a letter from Hunter to Arfin designating Miwa's group as the official representatives of Greenpeace in Japan. The letter emphasized that the name "Greenpeace" had been copyrighted in Canada and in the US, and that we would defend it legally, the opening salvo in a legal squabble that would persist for three troubling years.

FIRE DRAGON BITES

In October of 1976, Hunter, exhausted and frustrated by the political disputes, accepted an offer from David McTaggart to spend two months in the Welsh countryside, near Corwen, to work on a book about McTaggart's battle with France. McTaggart brought photographs, ship logs, and court documents. In Wales, Bob Hunter wrote *Greenpeace III: Journey into the Bomb*, based on McTaggart's voyages to Moruroa and his subsequent victory in a Paris court.

McTaggart and Hunter had quite different views on the history of the Moruroa campaign, as was revealed in the book. The prose is pure Hunter, but the selection, and in some cases revision, of history is McTaggart's. There is no record in the book of the Greenpeace delegations to Paris, Stockholm, and London, or the protests in Vancouver. Ben Metcalfe, whom McTaggart despised, is dismissed as a fraud. Dorothy Metcalfe, who fashioned the "Mururoa Mon Amour" campaign and ran media communications for two years, is not mentioned. Rod Marining, who spent half a year in Paris and London rallying support, and was severely beaten for his troubles, is expunged. The Greenpeace Foundation, which was sending money to McTaggart regularly, virtually disappears in his book. To the extent that Hunter included these historical points, McTaggart later deleted them from his manuscript.

Hunter and McTaggart also held different views on the future of Greenpeace. McTaggart told Hunter the organization would "fall apart sooner or later," but asked the Greenpeace Foundation in Vancouver to send him $6,000 to organize Greenpeace in Europe. He spurned what he called "the ecology fad" and he did not like the "hippie element" in Canada. In 1974 McTaggart had been against the whale campaign because he thought it would drain money away from his battle with France. Now, the whale and seal campaigns had raised the Greenpeace profile in Europe enormously, and McTaggart realized he could leverage this popularity into a Greenpeace presence in Paris. Over beer at the local Welsh public house, Hunter the journalist and McTaggart the entrepreneur debated these strategies. Hunter argued that public recognition of Greenpeace had reached a new level with stories in *National Geographic Magazine*, *Smithsonian*, and *The Wall Street Journal*. Charts, graphs, and scientific evidence about the demise of the whales had been printed with the dramatic confrontation pictures. The public mindbombing strategy was working just fine.

Hunter left the manuscript in McTaggart's hands and joined Bobbi Hunter, in London with their friends Walt and Cleone Patterson. From nuclear scientist Walt Patterson, Hunter learned that the US General Accounting Office had revealed that plutonium was indeed missing from the US inventory, just as Greenpeace had claimed six months earlier. The GAO reported two tons of plutonium "unaccounted for." The US Atomic Energy Commission surmised that the missing plutonium was "embedded in machinery or lost in crude statistical controls."

"Right," laughed Hunter. "Missing in the pipes? Two tons of plutonium?" This represented enough fissionable material for several hundred nuclear bombs. Hunter had taken a lot of criticism inside and outside the organization for repeating the plutonium rumour, but now felt vindicated.

The Hunters returned to Vancouver, and in December 1976, we published the third issue of the *Greenpeace Chronicles* newspaper, with articles about wolves shot from helicopters in Alaska, the vanishing Mediterranean monk seal, porpoises caught in tuna nets, the extinction of the Bali tiger, mercury poisoning in Japan and Canada, the Mackenzie Valley gas pipeline, and the Greenpeace whale and seal campaigns. Hunter wrote about David McTaggart's court case in Paris, and Ben Metcalfe wrote about the "first-strike" capabilities of the Trident nuclear attack base at Bangor, Washington. Privately, Metcalfe warned us about the Trilateral Commission, a new global trade cabal, which he believed would ultimately undermine the environmental movement. It was fine, Metcalfe alleged, for the ecology message to be apolitical, neither rightist nor leftist, "but don't be naïve," he said. "It's no accident you didn't find the Japanese whalers."

Meanwhile, the Mendocino Whale War group still failed to pay the charter fee from the previous summer to our mentor and father figure, John Cormack. Hunter made repeated pleas on Cormack's behalf, but to no avail. The skipper, facing bankruptcy, sold the *Phyllis Cormack*. He said he felt ready to retire, but seeing the *Phyllis Cormack* disappear from the "tribe" was painful. This, however, paled against the final dark stroke of the year of the Fire Dragon.

Mel Gregory, his partner Sybil Maier, and their two boys had moved north to Powell River on the coast of British Columbia. On December 27, with Maier out doing laundry and Mel across the street at a friend's home, a floor heater caught fire and the cedar A-frame burst into flame. Four-year-old Nathaniel and three-year-old David perished. Mel Gregory attempted suicide but was taken in and looked after by friends. No one dared question what cruel karma had led to the disaster. We just lived quietly with the absolute horror and anguish.

The Chinese year of the Fire Dragon ended on Feb. 17, 1977. In seven years, Greenpeace had passed through two incarnations, as a post-WW II disarmament group, then as a counterculture ecology group. The little band from the Shire had made global waves and helped usher in a new era of ecological awareness. Greenpeace had orchestrated seven campaigns in the previous seven years. In 1977, we would launch eight more, and the pace of our activities accelerated dramatically. Nine Greenpeace offices operated in Canada, five in the US, one each in Paris, London, New Zealand, and Australia, and an extended mission in Tokyo. However, the tough political work — the stuff most of us loathed — lay ahead.

MONEY DOESN'T TALK, IT SWEARS

In January 1977, the Greenpeace Foundation held an Annual General Meeting in a room donated by the Plaza Hotel in North Vancouver. Patrick Moore ran for president against Hunter. Each gave a short speech regarding his vision. Hunter knew his administrative shortcomings, but was slightly miffed that Moore would challenge his leadership. The vote presented a dilemma. Hunter remained our emotional and intellectual leader. Moore, however, possessed a methodical, rational style that perhaps the organization needed. Watson shocked everyone when he supported his nemesis, Moore. Following the bank account conflict, Watson was concerned that Bob and Bobbi Hunter might restrict his control of the seal campaign. His expedient alliance with Moore ruffled Hunter even more. I supported Hunter, feeling that he embodied the fundamental philosophy of Greenpeace, and that administration remained safely in the capable hands of Bobbi Hunter, Gannon, Storrow, and others. Hunter won by one vote, Moore was gracious in defeat, and we moved on to other business. Gannon produced financial statements that showed Greenpeace revenues for the year 1976 had surpassed the budget of $300,000, to $302,129. Money now came into the office at the pace of $50,000 per month, which meant that the next year's revenues might reach $600,000. That was the good news. Fundraising costs had consumed one-third of the income and office overhead had cost us $51,883. We paid $7,139 in interest for our loans, $8,157 to set up the branch offices, sent $6,280 to David McTaggart in Paris, and spent another $22,164 for promotion, film, photography, and the *Greenpeace Chronicles* newspaper. We spent $37,712 on the harp seal campaign and $147,494 on the whale campaign. Our total expenses for the year — also budgeted for roughly $300,000 — had swelled to $384,925. Our deficit had grown by $82,796. We now owed roughly $136,000 to the bank and commercial suppliers.

In spite of our troubles, Gannon and Bobbi Hunter remained upbeat. The bank was satisfied with our progress. We had proven that we could raise money for our campaigns, and the cost overruns were "not unusual," said Gannon, for such an untested expansion. We were solvent and had $14,762.67 in our operating bank account. The pressing concern at the bank, and with us, was the status of the new Greenpeace offices. We had borrowed money a year earlier on the promise of creating an international organization, yet we had no record of the revenues or expenses in the offices outside Vancouver. The bank did not yet know that we had no control over the assets acquired in the Greenpeace name. From their point of view, raising and spending money that was sheltered from them could be considered a breach of our obligation. We kept the bank at bay by making our monthly interest payments.

Spong reported that a new Greenpeace group in Hawaii had just raised $50,000 in a single fundraising drive, but the people who raised this money naturally wanted to spend it themselves. Herein lay the crux of the internal political dispute that would haunt the expansion of Greenpeace: From the point of view of the Greenpeace Foundation in Canada, five years of expensive campaigns had established the organization and made it possible for a group of people in Honolulu or London to raise large sums of money without having to actually launch a campaign themselves. The Greenpeace Foundation board naturally expected some share of that income. Money, however, is a sticky obsession. In a typical case, a young man from California had visited the *James Bay* in Maui and dreamed of joining Greenpeace. When he later died tragically at sea, his family directed donations in his honour to the Greenpeace Foundation. The money, however, went to the San Francisco office. If it could not be used to relieve our debts, we insisted it be held in trust for the 1977 whale campaign, as it had been intended, but this led to disputes with the California office. To resolve these problems, Storrow, Gannon, and Bobbi Hunter insisted that our organizational priority must be to consolidate all Greenpeace operations.

In the end, though, it proved easier to take the campaigns to the money than to coax the money to Canada. Since we wanted to launch the next whale campaign ship from Hawaii anyway, George Korotva flew to Honolulu in January 1977 to find a ship and crew. Ross Thornwood, who had sailed on the *James Bay*, provided a free office in a mental hospital in Waikiki. Here, Korotva met Don and Sue White, who administered Greenpeace Hawaii and their own group called Save the Whales Hawaii. There seemed to be a great deal of money, but Korotva found the politics bewildering, so he summoned Spong, who joined him and negotiated with the US offices — Hawaii, San Francisco, Portland, and Seattle — to help fund the campaign. While Spong met with media, staff, and volunteers, Korotva searched for a suitable ship.

YOU ARE CRAZY

The Greenpeace Foundation in Vancouver turned its focus on the Canadian seal hunt. Watson remained in charge of the campaign, but agreed to answer to the board. Watson, Hunter, and Moore wrote a formal Greenpeace seal policy so there would be no conflict once teams were on the ice floes. We demanded a six-year moratorium on sealing and maintained that killing infant seals in their nursery was fundamentally wrong. In alliance with World Wildlife Fund, we initiated a campaign to educate the public about the ecological cost of buying sealskin coats. Because the seal populations had been so thoroughly decimated — to less than five percent of their original numbers — Watson wanted to oppose the landsman hunt as well as the Norwegian ships. Hunter and Watson differed on this point. A year earlier, Hunter had crafted a delicate alliance with the fishermen's union in Newfoundland. He was an idealist, but a pragmatic one. He believed stopping the massive pelagic hunt, while keeping the peace with Newfoundlanders, would be a victory. Watson, on the other hand, wanted no half measures. He and most Greenpeace members, including Hunter, opposed the killing of infant seals by anyone. But Watson saw nothing to be gained by making deals with the Newfoundlanders. He won this battle, but as a compromise, we proposed a subsidy or business investment from the Canadian government to make up the financial loss to Newfoundlanders. Hunter advised Watson to keep the landsman issue low profile. "Why stir a hornet's nest?" he counselled his comrade. He remained uneasy, however, as he knew from the Taoist philosophers: What doesn't bend, breaks.

Watson did not want Hunter or Moore along on the campaign, but Moore insisted on going to Newfoundland as the Greenpeace scientist. Hunter agreed to stay behind, run the media link that had failed during the summer, and preside over the organization. Watson was free to select the rest of his crew. To secure funds from the foreign offices, he promised positions on the campaign. Although he only needed a dozen crew for Newfoundland, he enlisted thirty-five people from the US, London, Norway, and eastern Canada. With Hunter in Vancouver, Bob Cummings, who had sailed on the Amchitka voyage, acted as media coordinator in Newfoundland. Patrick Ranahan from San Francisco and Erol Baykal from Vancouver were the photographers. I stayed in Vancouver to receive the film and supply the media.

The affair got off to a smashing start when Margaret Trudeau, wife of the Canadian prime minister, announced that *she* would "never wear a baby seal." The International Fund for Animal Welfare posted a billboard across the street from Canada House on Trafalgar Square in London, showing a swiler clubbing a seal pup and announcing: CANADA'S SHAME. But even as Greenpeace memberships swelled in London, Hunter's fragile Newfoundland détente crumbled in Canada. In the first week of March 1977, Watson and Walrus led their crews to the small Québécois town of Sept-Îles on the icy St. Lawrence Seaway. Five volunteers flew in from Europe: Canadian expatriate Allan Thornton, Susi Newborn from Friends of the Earth in London, and three women from Norway — Vibeke Arviddsson, Elizabeth Rasmussen, and Kirstin Aarflot.

Rather than face angry Newfoundlanders, Watson calculated he would be better off across the Strait of Belle Isle in the tiny outpost of Blanc Sablon, Quebec. He proceeded to set up camp there. However, the denizens of Blanc Sablon were no more indulgent of outsiders than the Newfoundlanders. Quebec native and Greenpeace advance agent Laurent Trudel received a punch in the face on his first day there. Fifty journalists from Europe filled the tiny hotels and beer parlours. Few of these Europeans had a clue about how to get onto the ice floes. They lined up all day in front of every pay phone in Blanc Sablon and mercilessly hounded Bob Cummings, the media coordinator, to fly them into the action. A frustrated German photographer paid a local swiler to pose with a hakapik over a stuffed toy seal. The seal campaign had turned into a media circus long before the hunt and the formal protest had even started.

Meanwhile, Walrus, Jet Johnson, and a team of volunteers, including Susi Newborn, set up camp on Belle Isle. Newborn's Argentinean father, a trade diplomat to England and Italy, had been killed three years earlier in what Newborn felt were suspicious circumstances. The apparent assassination had radicalized her. She told Walrus that she had dedicated her life "to the struggle for a healthier planet." She had been a campaign assistant for Friends of the Earth, but the action politics and spiritual foundation of Greenpeace appealed to her. She had met Paul and Linda Spong at the IWC meetings in 1975 and Bob Hunter in London on his way to Wales only a few months earlier. Newborn was a hard-core, grassroots ecologist who would help lead the next generation of Greenpeace actions from Europe. She and Walrus explored the frozen caves of Belle Isle, and wrote the "Declaration of Freelandsea," a free-spirited manifesto of ecology.

On March 15, the hunt opened. Watson led a crew of eleven to the ice floes in the helicopters, including renowned photojournalist Arthur Grace, who had covered the Vietnam War for UPI and now worked for *Time* magazine. Since the Orwellian Seal Protection Act had made it illegal to land a helicopter anywhere near a seal, the pilots put down on a large ice pan far from the hunt. The biting winds stung the faces of the crew and the Labrador Sea heaped up in 12-foot swells under the ice, sending enormous blue-white shards into the air. When Watson waved everyone out of the helicopter, the two journalists declined. Grace, the veteran of Vietnam, thought that trekking across the heaving ice floes was a suicide mission. "*You*," he told Watson, "are crazy."

Watson, in his typical manner, bolted across the ice, leaving his crew strung out behind him. One by one, they ran into trouble. Michael Bailey crossed several small leads but soon found himself alone at the edge of a wide expanse of frigid black water, and he turned back. Jet Johnson, who had twisted his ankle on Belle Isle, could not keep up. He too turned back to find the helicopters. Canadian lawyer Peter Ballem, a stocky ex-rugby player, dragged a small inflatable with him, which proved useful for crossing the leads, but slowed him down over the ice. He shepherded the film crew — Chechik and Easton — and Londoner Allan Thornton over the ice floes. In the final sprint to the sealing ships, only Ballem kept pace with the fanatical Watson.

Watson approached the first sealer he saw, scooped the man's club from the ice, and threw it into the water. Ballem warned his client about destroying property, but Watson, in no mood for a legal briefing, waved him off. He made for the sealing ship *Martin Karlsen*, hurled himself onto a pile of bloody pelts, and handcuffed himself to the cable that lifted them from the ice. Sealers on deck laughed and jeered as Watson was dragged across the ice, hauled ten feet in the air, then plunged into the icy water. Four times they hoisted him up and dropped him, sealers squealing with delight.

The film crew lagged behind, hauling gear across the ice, sweating in their survival suits, so the world would be denied the spectacle of Watson hanging in mid-air on the pelts. Ballem screamed at the sealers to haul Watson aboard and he took still photographs with a small snapshot camera. The sealers were having fun dunking their hooked protester and seemed to have no intention of saving him from freezing to death. By the time Easton and Chechik arrived, they had to help in the rescue. Ballem launched the inflatable and ordered the sealers to cease under threat of being charged with attempted — or actual — murder. An officer of the ship intervened, and Ballem pulled Watson from the water onto the ice. He found a fisheries officer and browbeat him for thirty minutes before the functionary agreed to order the captain of the *Martin Karlsen* to take Watson aboard.

Ballem insisted that the fisheries officer allow the helicopter to pick up Thornton and the freezing film crew and that he be allowed to join his cataleptic client on board the sealing ship. They spent the night in a small, frigid cabin on the *Martin Karlsen*, Ballem nursing Watson's frozen hands and feet. The film crew slumped back to Belle Isle without a single frame worthy of network news. Meanwhile, Thornton radioed Blanc Sablon and announced that Watson had suffered back injuries and a broken arm, neither of which was true. When Watson showed up in Blanc Sablon the next day with nothing more visible than bruised wrists — although he went into the hospital with pneumonia — the media turned skeptical of the whole affair. The next day, when a second crew led by Walrus forced the sealing ship *Theron* to stop hunting and abandon some hundred white-coat pelts on the ice, most of the media ignored them. Hunter released the story in Vancouver to some success, but by now the journalists in Quebec and Newfoundland pursued a new angle: Brigitte Bardot had landed in Blanc Sablon.

VIVE ÉCOLOGIE

Brigitte Bardot's appearance in the normally quiet harbour town spun the Greenpeace media plan wildly out of control. Bob Cummings staged a press conference at the Alexander Dumas Hotel, but journalists no longer wanted to talk to him or Watson; they wanted to talk to Ms. Bardot. Canadian journalists vilified the actress in beer parlours. "The idle rich," they laughed. "Second-rate movie actress trying to revive a dead career." Her opening news conference was as much a bloodbath as the scene on the ice floes.

Bardot had arrived with her boyfriend, *Sygma* photographer Miroslav Brozek, and Swiss conservationist Franz Weber. Weber had raised $240,000 by selling toy seals and used the money to fly journalists and Bardot to Canada. He met with Fisheries Minister Romeo LeBlanc and offered to build a $2.5 million fake fur plant in Newfoundland to offset the loss of income if Canada ended the seal hunt. The factory, he said, would employ 600 Newfoundlanders, year-round. "Blackmail," scoffed LeBlanc. "Canada refuses to be intimidated by pressure from abroad." In Newfoundland, Richard Cashin, the union leader who had cut a deal with Hunter the year before, also dismissed Weber's offer.

At the news conference in Blanc Sablon, journalists mocked the actress for interfering with the sealers' income. "Do you eat meat, Miss Bardot?" they asked. "Will you attend the massacre?" In this bastion of hard-working rural families, Bardot was an easy target. From the back of the room, local swilers stepped forward. "Miss Brigitte," one asked, "would you like to show the journalists a baby seal who has been freshly killed this afternoon?" From a plastic bag, the swilers produced the carcass of a skinned seal, dripping in blood, black eyes rolling in the dark red skull. Bardot gagged. The assembly snickered. Fighting tears, the actress rose, thanked the audience, and disappeared.

Because of the Seal Protection Act, Franz Weber could not find a helicopter company willing to fly Bardot and his journalists to the ice floes. When Patrick Moore heard this, he phoned Hunter. Greenpeace did not care who delivered the seal issue in the media. Bardot, we felt, was as sincere as any of us. She had leveraged her notoriety into public exposure for the seals, at no small cost to herself. Our mission was not to get Greenpeace into the news; it was to get the seals into the news. One of Saul Alinsky's rules for successful protest again applied: "Utilize all events of the period. Move with the action." To move with the action in this case meant helping Bardot do what she came to do. In Blanc Sablon, Moore and Ballem walked through the swirling snow to the small house outside of town where Bardot and Weber fretted impatiently. Moore offered the Greenpeace helicopters to fly Bardot to the ice floes to see seals and witness the hunt.

Watson left the hospital and confronted Moore. Their later versions of this argument diverged: Moore felt Watson resisted helping Bardot, but Watson claimed he only resisted Moore's presumed leadership. In any case, Cummings sided with Watson and questioned Moore's plan to help the French actress. "We'll look bad," Cummings worried.

"Gee, Bob," Moore argued, "we already look bad. Besides, the point isn't to *look* good; the point is to raise the issue in the media and the way to do that is not Greenpeace right now, it's Brigitte." Still, the idea did not go over well with some of the crew on Belle Isle. Jet Johnson argued profusely with Moore, claiming that we were selling out to a movie star. In the end, Moore simply pulled rank as vice-president of the organization. "Hunter and I have discussed it," he said. "We're helping her."

When Bardot finally arrived on Belle Isle, however, everyone wanted to be photographed with her. Watson nudged in beside the actress for photographs. In fact, Bardot wrote later in her account, she had been terrified in the helicopters throughout the storm and arrived at the camp stifling tears and with frozen fingers. Walrus gave her a cup of hot chocolate, and she huddled in a tent with Susi Newborn, who explained practical tips such as how the women managed to pee at night on frozen Belle Isle. Bardot and the Greenpeace activists, once out of the glare of cameras, hit it off splendidly. Laurent Trudel, still suffering from the punch in the eye in Blanc Sablon, played his flute for the appreciative actress. "They give me courage," Bardot wrote that night in her journal, back in her rented house in Blanc Sablon. "We will fight together."

Brian Davies, president of the International Fund for Animal Welfare, later flew her to the front with a camera team and photographer Brozek. They avoided the swilers, but found a colony of baby seals. Bardot slipped through the ice, and her boots filled with water. She shivered and wept as she held a docile infant seal to her cheek. Later, Miroslav Brozek's photographs of Bardot and the seals circled the globe. Not all news reports flattered the actress, and *Le Figaro* ridiculed her mercilessly, but in Paris, Giscard d'Estaing's government announced that France would ban the importation of harp seal pelts. The ensuing European ban on harp seal pelts would eventually lead to a moratorium on the killing of the infant whitecoats. A tidal wave of dramatic images and ecological awareness broke across Europe following the seal campaign. "*J'ai atteint le paradis*," Brigitte Bardot wrote in a Paris magazine. I have reached paradise. "*Vive* Greenpeace!"

"Almost," remarked Hunter wryly over a beer on a Fourth Avenue in the Shire of Kitsilano, "*Vive Écologie*."

STARK JUSTICE

After Greenpeace and Bardot left Newfoundland, fisheries officers arrested Brian Davies for breaking the Seal Protection Act. In Vancouver, Hunter took the opportunity to lambaste the supercilious fisheries minister, Romeo LeBlanc: "LeBlanc," snarled Hunter, "is boss swiler, the brains behind the most diabolical legislation ever cooked up in Canada. The Seal Protection Act is designed to protect the hunters from *us*. The minister has suspended liberties, stomped all over civil rights, and cordoned off the Western Atlantic from the world media. This Orwellian bundle of regulations is enforced, they tell us, 'at the discretion of the minister,' which means the government can break its own laws any time it wants, and arrest protestors any time it wants. If we devise a new tactic, they belch out another Order-in-Council making it illegal. They know these arrests won't hold up in a court of law. This is just a convenient way of sidelining protest until the media goes away. It's the sort of trick authoritarian regimes use all the time to crush dissent and tramp all over the rights of people who don't happen to agree with them."

For our actions in Newfoundland, we received hate letters and more crushed Greenpeace buttons from across Canada. Most Canadian journalists attacked us for depriving the Newfoundlanders of their honest income. Canadians who had once applauded Greenpeace now vilified us, and this provided an important lesson. By 1977, we had realized that nationalism, regional self-esteem, and local jobs would be forces in opposition to ecological transformation. I discovered a stark example on a trip to visit my family in Colorado. Near Denver, local peace activists were attempting to shut down the Rocky Flats nuclear weapons plant that leaked tritium and other contaminants into the air and water. Local workers claimed the protests endangered their livelihoods. In Canada, almost everyone was in favour of stopping nuclear bomb tests and slowing the American war machine, but in Broomfield, Colorado, there were *jobs* at stake. Likewise, in Colorado, virtually everyone wanted to see the seal hunt stopped, but in Canada the hunt had become sacrosanct. Canada spent more money policing the seal hunt, some $6 million annually, than Newfoundland swilers earned from it. The mulish resistance to ecological change wasn't just about money and jobs, but turned on local pride and resisting outsiders.

Every uranium mine or bomb factory in the world put food on the table for innocent families attempting to survive and raise their children. Every leaking supertanker and belching smokestack paid wages to someone. Even the Russian whalers were just working-class men and women supporting poor families. What seemed obvious from the point of view of ecology, turned complex in the realm of politics. And pointing out the ecological crimes of another country proved far easier than turning the critique upon one's own nation, community, or even on oneself.

Where would the industrial steamroller stop? Walrus and I discussed this on a sunny spring day in Kitsilano. Where would people actually make a personal sacrifice to create a sustainable society? "Here," said Walrus. "We're not going to let them tack down the industrial carpet in this corner of North America, and we'll roll it back from here." His was a bold vision, perhaps grandiose, but he believed it.

After the spring seal hunt in 1977, Bob and Bobbi Hunter decided to step down from their respective positions within Greenpeace. Bobbi had been the organization's treasurer since the summer of 1974. She handed the job over to Bill Gannon. Bob Hunter had led Greenpeace for four years, after taking over from Ben Metcalfe. He remained on the board and agreed to manage media affairs for the organization, but he handed the presidency of the Greenpeace Foundation to his comrade of six years, Patrick Moore. There was no vote or visible competition for the job. Paul Watson groused about Moore but did not pursue his argument. Hunter told a reporter for *The Province*, "I'm afraid that as a business manager I'm no good, which has been recognized by the fact that ... I've been stripped of all my financial decision-making abilities because I've demonstrated repeatedly that I don't have any."

Despite his self-criticism, the truth was that since 1973, Hunter had led the transformation of Greenpeace from a single-issue disarmament group into a global ecology action organization with offices all over the world. Like Irving Stowe, he had an inclusive and tolerant attitude toward his compatriots, and like Metcalfe he possessed a keen instinct for translating radical ideas into the everyday language of newspapers and television. He had discovered and inculcated the Rainbow Warrior ideal. He was unconventional and prone to excesses, but he provided Greenpeace with a mythology to believe in, a vision that helped define the ecology movement of the era. He told the *Province* reporter, "Greenpeace's success can be traced to a few people who know how to play by the rules and who understand the limitations that people in the media have to deal with. Most environmental groups are so busy beating their chests in righteous indignation that they don't take the time to find out what makes the media tick. The media are a courtroom. You've got to prove your case. There is stark justice at work."

I took to meeting Hunter at the Port Moody Pub in late afternoons, ostensibly to chat and drink beer, but perhaps emotionally to keep our little tribe from dispersing. "Henry Kissinger brags that power is an aphrodisiac," smirked Hunter one day. "Well, *giving up* power is an anti-depressant."

AMBUSH AT DOUGLAS CHANNEL

Immediately after assuming the presidency, Patrick Moore announced that the Canadian group should focus on urgent local issues. As the

Greenpeace empire swelled around the world, we returned to our roots. Moore announced we would challenge a proposed supertanker route along the coast of British Columbia. We had forged a strong alliance with fishermen, Native groups, the United Church, and rural environmentalists dedicated to stopping the supertanker route up the twisting, 100-mile inlet of Douglas Channel into the coastal town of Kitimat.

Our old nemesis Jack Davis had promoted the treacherous route. As Fisheries Minister in 1971, Davis had tried to cancel the insurance on the *Phyllis Cormack*. In Stockholm in 1972, he had refused to help Greenpeace put nuclear weapons testing on the UN agenda and had mocked Greenpeace for being "sensationalists." Now, in the spring of 1977 he told a meeting with the State of Washington, "If I was an oil company I would much prefer Kitimat because the damages in the Puget Sound area have some dollar signs on them. People with property, waterfronts, and so on. In Kitimat there's practically nobody."

Davis' comment did not play well in Kitimat, and it infuriated the Gitga'at people in Hartley Bay. Chief Clifton and his son Oliver offered to host the blockade. The Gitga'at fishermen knew John Cormack, and in 1975, during the first whale campaign, we had stopped there on the *Phyllis Cormack*. The pristine channel provided their food and livelihood: salmon, cod, herring, clams, and abalone. Northerly winter storms raged down narrow Douglas Channel — where tides ran swiftly around the rocky points — and the idea of bringing oil tanker traffic through here was dubious, if not completely insane.

We knew from our research that over the previous five-year period, some three billion gallons of oil were *known* to have been spilled into the world's waterways. Estimates of chronic leaks and undocumented spills doubled that horrific figure. In December 1976, the Liberian tanker *Argo Merchant* broke up and dumped nine million gallons off Nantucket Island, and a Standard Oil of Ohio tanker spilled 134,000 gallons into the Delaware River. Samuel Baker, a spokesman for Standard Oil had commented, "It's just one of those things that happens."

"Not here," declared Walrus in the Greenpeace office. In May we found out that the Kitimat Pipeline Company, a consortium of fifteen oil companies, would host the annual conference of the North Central Municipal Association of Mayors, including their partners, friends, and aides — 250 people — on a Canadian Pacific cruise ship, the MV *Princess Patricia*.

The civil servants gleefully extended their junket for two days so the pipeline consortium could show them how safe it would be to take a boat up Douglas Channel to the proposed pipeline head at Kitimat. Drinks flowed and a band played. The oil consortium's public relations firm brought the media along to ply them with single malt scotch and show *them* what a good idea it was to bring supertankers into the channel.

Hunter and Moore flew to Prince Rupert and joined a United Church vessel, the 90-foot *Thomas Crosby*. The United Fishermen and Allied Workers sent their own boat. Fishermen along the coast, communicating over marine radios, headed for Douglas Channel. Oliver Clifton organized the Gitga'at band members in Hartley Bay, who brought trollers, seiners, and herring skiffs. Rural homesteading families arrived in sailboats, prams, and dinghies. From Vancouver, a Greenpeace crew steamed north in the 67-foot *Meander*, a cruise ship with teak finishing, stained glass windows, and a comfortable lounge. Skipper Dennis Feroce, the man who had rescued us from the beach at the launch of the first whale voyage, donated the use of the *Meander*. Marining, Walrus, Mel Gregory, Bill Gannon, and Linda Spong formed the crew. Hunter believed that Greenpeace could only maintain its focus if office workers and administrators integrated with activists on the campaigns, and he had urged Gannon and Linda Spong to accompany the campaign. "It's a visceral thing, standing up on the front line for Mother Nature," he said. "Hard to translate."

On May 10, 1977, the flotilla converged near Promise Island at the mouth of Douglas Channel. Fishing boats along the coast relayed reports of the *Princess Patricia's* position. Marining and Mel Gregory climbed into a Zodiac and prepared to move quickly to blockade the ship's passage. When the oil consortium's cruise ship rounded Promise Island, thirty boats awaited them across the mouth of the inlet. The United Church skipper radioed the *Princess Patricia* with a request from Chief Clifton for the vessel to stop so the Gitga'at leaders could speak to the visitors about the proposed supertanker route. The captain on the bridge of the 6,000-ton cruise ship refused to stop or even slow down. He throttled forward at 15 knots.

Feroce moved the *Meander* into the path of the oncoming ship and the smaller, faster boats darted to fill the gap in the line. Feroce then radioed the *Princess Patricia* that he was "dead in the water," which legally placed responsibility on the harried cruise ship captain to avoid a collision. Marining and Mel gave chase and positioned themselves directly under the bow of the cruise ship. Twenty feet above, startled cocktail party guests leaned over the railing to watch. The television teams on board, jaded by the consortium's promotional show, now rushed into position to film the protest. A CBC helicopter swept in through the fog, cameras rolling. Somewhere on the *Princess Patricia*, the public relations team realized that their carefully crafted cabaret had been ambushed and that they had unwittingly supplied the media that would document their downfall.

At the last minute, Feroce thought better of sacrificing his vessel to the towering cruise ship and backed out of the mad captain's way. Mel, however, maintained his Zodiac's position at the bow, while Marining screamed up to the mayors and media. Oliver Clifton and his friends zipped back and forth in front of the bow of the steaming cruise ship. Waves pounded the Greenpeace Zodiac until the wooden floorboards cavitated, the bow of the cruise ship slashed down over the top of Marining and Gregory, and the two protestors disappeared under the steaming ship.

Marining told me later that his first thought, once under water, was how to avoid the propellers, but as he looked around, he could see only the massive hull above and a galaxy of bubbles and foam. He dove straight down as hard as he could until he felt clear of the boat, then stroked for the surface to breathe. He saw horrified onlookers at the stern of the cruise ship, and off to the side he saw the empty Zodiac, engine still running, turning circles in the water. He could not see Mel Gregory. Oliver Clifton, however, had located the panicked, choking musician and dragged him from the water into his skiff. He now found Marining and pulled him in. Mel vomitted profusely over the side. Clifton delivered the two sodden Rainbow Warriors to the *Meander*, where Walrus and Linda Spong tended to them. Mel choked up salt water and Marining had a bruised hand. Otherwise, they survived unscathed.

Journalists lined up at the cruise ship's radio to file their stories, but an irate captain refused them. Film from the CBC helicopter, however, appeared on the news within three hours. By the time the *Princess Patricia* arrived in Kitimat, the entire town had seen or heard the news. An angry multitude met the oil consortium and mayors, waving picket signs and shouting, "No supertankers!" Journalists bolted from the boat to pay phones. As the mayors trundled from the boat to a waiting bus, the crowd closed in. "No supertankers! No supertankers!" The politicians and their entourage slouched in their seats as the bus pulled away with demonstrators pounding the windows with placards. The oil consortium cruise may have been the least successful public relations event in the history of Canada.

The pipeline at Kitimat was doomed. No supertanker ever plied the waters of Douglas Channel. A year later, the plan was permanently scrapped. "Greenpeace three, Jack Davis zero," crowed Moore.

EARTHFORCE

The *Meander* had supplied its own funding by staging dockside musical shows along its route. Within days of its return, Greenpeace volunteers hitchhiked and drove up the Fraser River, where provincial forestry managers intended to spray 50 square miles of forest with chemical insecticides to halt the spread of spruce budworms. Moore, who had grown up in a forestry family, knew that the budworms advance and decline in a routine cycle. "The budworms are part of the native biological community," said Moore. "Weather, diseases, predators, and parasites will control them."

In towns like Spuzzum and Lillooet, where prospectors, loggers, homesteaders, and hippies mingled, Greenpeace formed alliances with the St'at'imx and Nlaka'pamux Native nations. From reservation land, young Natives lead twenty mobile camps to undisclosed locations in the forests. Crews floated helium balloons above the treetops to signal their presence. The provincial government hired Pinkerton security guards to comb the region, but one guard, a Greenpeace member, called our office with their locations, allowing our campers to avoid them. Finally, rather than expose their half-baked plan by dumping poison on environmentalists and Native people, the government called off the spray program. As predicted by Moore, the budworm infestation ran its natural course. "They can't say we only care about animals that are smart or cute," said Moore.

In three months, we had pulled off three successful campaigns. "We're getting this protesting thing down," chirped Hunter, much happier now in his media role, not having to deal with internal politics.

Moore, however, faced the ongoing political pressures over claims on the Greenpeace name. The most painful clash, between Moore and Paul Watson, escalated to a showdown. Watson tended to push the edge of non-violence. Throwing the sealer's club and pelts into the water in Labrador had exposed him and Greenpeace to federal charges for destruction of property. Although the charges were petty, the impact could be huge. The group in California claimed that the FBI had inquired about Greenpeace's use of violence, which threatened their tax-exempt status, and millions of dollars in fundraising potential. But more to the point, Greenpeace's policy remained strictly non-violent. Most of us sympathized with Watson's outrage, but if Greenpeace lost its claim to non-violence, we would crumble. The strength of Gandhi or Dorothy Day had been their absolute commitment to peaceful protest. Greenpeace simply could not afford to lose the moral stature of *satyagraha*, absolute non-violence.

The Greenpeace Foundation board censured and removed Watson by a vote of 11–1, his being the dissenting vote. Ostensibly, the group took this action because of the destruction of property in Labrador, but more personal motives, the Watson/Moore clash, clouded the affair. Watson had been on a mission to preserve what he considered the grassroots nature of the ecology movement. In his travels to other offices, as the radical among radicals, he had advocated rebellion against Moore and the Greenpeace Foundation. Naturally, he found support almost everywhere, as most of the new Greenpeace activists wanted to govern their own affairs. A San Francisco faction, in particular, threatened secession, but they also faced internal disputes of their own. Don and Sue White, who controlled Greenpeace Hawaii, had openly defied the US hegemony of San Francisco. The Greenpeace Foundation board could see that its organization flirted with chaos and had taken offence at Watson's internal insurgency. This was no "Uprising of Nawiliwili." He wanted to bring down his rival, Moore.

Watson, understandably bitter, formed "Earthforce," with Walrus and Jet Johnson on his board of directors. Former Greenpeace bookkeeper Starlet Lum, with whom Watson now lived, ran the Earthforce office. Watson had secured backing from the International Fund for Animal Welfare and claimed scores of grassroots supporters. He vowed that his first action would be to halt the slaughter of elephants in Kenya, and he talked about going after the pirate whalers.

DOUBLETHINK

Charles Dickens characterized 1775, the eve of the French Revolution, as "the age of wisdom and an age of foolishness." This description applied to the mid-1970s as well. Greenpeace had the right idea at the right historical time. Runaway industrialism had to concede some authority to ecology in 1977, just as European royalty had to concede power in 1777. Like the French revolutionaries, however, the new ecologists faced the constraints of their own cultural habits, desires and fears, and measured abilities to handle success. With international notoriety, we became like a suddenly famous rock band, but with scores of hopeful lead singers crowding the stage. Those with a measure of political foresight and distance from the battles knew that Greenpeace was poorly managed. A nationally prominent financial analyst in Vancouver told Gannon, "You've exposed a huge public interest. You people are onto something like plastics in the 1950s. We're just wondering when you're gonna go for it."

Of course, we *were* going for it, but we had each reached limits of our knowledge and experience. Author Laurence Peter had described the phenomenon in his popular 1969 book, *The Peter Principle: Why Things Always Go Wrong*. By being competent, people advance in organizations until they reach a level at which they are incompetent, and there they stay. Thus, persons operating just beyond their prime effectiveness populate bureaucracies. Hunter's retreat to a more modest role was rare. Most people want to *advance* in an organization, to have more power, more prestige, and more influence, until they are spread so thin they lose effectiveness.

Our particular dilemma proved even more complex. What would happen if we all backed off, gave it away, as Allen Ginsberg had advised? Someone had to step up and take on more organizational roles. One theory of creative organizations recommends that the creative personalities back away from administration and allow professionals to manage business affairs. However, in a social movement there is something inherently risky about this. The business managers and lawyers may not be equipped to carry forward key principles or the innovative style that launched the organization in the first place. Business consultants know that successful corporations keep a cultural link to their core values.

For example, our tough new office manager, Betty Rippey, had installed a tight regime, but she had become so pushy and dictatorial that most people avoided the office. This might be fine in a corporation, but we were a public movement. We *wanted* to interact with the public in our office. When Rippey refused to hand out office keys to certain board members, the old-timers revolted. The board passed a resolution instructing her to release keys so people could work at night. Rippey, with the best of intentions, could be rude to allies who did not possess certain social graces but who, nevertheless, were important to the movement. There are key differences between a dynamic corporate structure and a dynamic political structure. Had we been a fast-food franchise, we would have issued shares and dictated policy to our branches. Had we been a rock band, we would have hired a manager to negotiate our deals and contracts. But we were neither. We were an international ecology movement that had evolved far beyond anyone's blueprint. No hierarchical management chart could answer our dilemma. We had to create a solution.

It occurred to some of us that the solution should be "organic," and speak directly to the issues we espoused. We talked about "biocracy" and "ecological society." Murray Bookchin's *Ecology of Freedom* was still a few years off, although he was obviously thinking similar thoughts. How do we organize ourselves in ways that reflect the lessons and demands of ecology? It was, to us, the "Big question."

Although Greenpeace had not created the ecological wave that had grown over centuries, it now added considerable volume to the swell. It was clear that some of our fellow ecologists resented Greenpeace, which garnered so much attention, but most identified with Greenpeace and many found advantages in adopting the name. In many cases, Greenpeace simply lent its easily recognizable name, and attendant fundraising muscle, to people doing the ecology work anyway.

In Vancouver, Gannon negotiated to increase our bank line of credit to $150,000 and to release the personal guarantors in exchange for a claim on Greenpeace assets, including future revenues. We believed in a form of benign doublethink: the ability to hold contradictory thoughts in one's mind simultaneously. Some of us — Bob and Bobbi Hunter, Pat Moore and Eileen Chivers, Paul and Linda Spong, Marining, Gannon — believed we could be grassroots ecologists and still manage hundreds of thousands, soon to be millions, of dollars. We could not tell, in 1977, if this doublethink was naïve or innovative.

AMERICAN SPORTSMAN

Had we been able to take a year off from our ecology campaigns, we might have fared better with our internal political morass, but this was not to be. We stood on the verge of winning liberty for the whales, and letting up the pressure was out of the question. Meanwhile, Elton John performed a benefit in Lahaina and Greenpeace Hawaii prospered. The local leaders in Hawaii included Ross Thornwood, from the James Bay crew; two gritty activists, Dexter Cate and Nancy Jack; and Don and Sue White. Don White, a former petroleum geophysicist from Texas, was the president of "Save the Whales – Hawaii," a group founded by Cate. The two whale advocates had visited the *James Bay* in Honolulu the previous July, and Spong had urged them to look for a ship. By November, they had located a World War II subchaser, the *Island Transport*, available for $70,000.

In the meantime, George Korotva located an ex-whaling ship in good shape. Back in Vancouver, we liked the idea of using the whalers' castaway to confront them. However, Zimmerman in San Francisco balked and controlled the money needed to make the purchase with Greenpeace Hawaii. In April 1977, Korotva, Spong, Zimmerman, and the Hawaiians purchased the *Island Transport*, the first ship owned by Greenpeace. The sleek, 176-foot vessel, with twin diesel engines, could reportedly achieve 26 knots, faster than the *James Bay* and the whaling ships. However, the thirty-five-year-old ship languished in decrepit condition. The engines and their moorings sagged; the rusting hull and bulwarks required re-welding.

At Pier 40 in the heart of Honolulu, the *Island Transport* was re-christened as the *Ohana Kai*, translated as "Family of the Sea." Hundreds of volunteers came forward to sandblast, scrape, weld, and paint the superstructure of the ship. They repaired engines, reinforced the hull, removed armament mounts, and installed extra fuel tanks to extend the ship's range. They painted the now customary rainbows at the bow. On the side of the wheelhouse, workers applied the Greenpeace logo designed by Barry Lavender, but left off the outer ecology oval. Artists painted whales on the side, and the words SAVE THE WHALES and SAVE THE EARTH in English and Japanese.

Months earlier, in March 1977, a letter addressed to Bob Hunter had arrived at the San Francisco Greenpeace office from the American Broadcast Corporation. The letter, from ABC's "American Sportsman" television show, offered to pay $60,000 for the exclusive rights to film this year's confrontation with the whalers. Had this letter reached Hunter, Greenpeace history would likely have taken a different path, but Zimmerman in San Francisco had sent the letter to the new Greenpeace office in Hawaii. They accepted the deal on behalf of Greenpeace, and received the $60,000.

When we heard about this from Spong, we could not help feeling duped. Bobbi Hunter, Bill Gannon, and other board members wanted to know why the money from ABC should not come to us. The Hawaii whale campaign had burned through, as far as we could account, $150,000 — equal to our bank debt and more money than we had spent on the entire 1976 whale campaign — but the ship was not yet off the dock. Far from it. Gannon pointed out we could have launched the *James Bay* for half that amount and used the rest to pay down our debts. Bob Hunter, typically magnanimous, argued to placate the Hawaiian ecologists who wanted to run their own campaign. We intended that the swift *Ohana Kai* would track down the Japanese whalers, Spong's obsession. ABC would bring an eight-person film crew and their own helicopter. A landing pad would be built on the stern of the subchaser. Gannon acquiesced and assured us that as long as we made our interest payments at the bank, we were okay. Bobbi Hunter, however, felt that even a small share of the $60,000 would go a long way toward appeasing our creditors. In the end, we made no claim on the money from ABC. "Let them have it," Hunter argued. "If they can launch a fast ship and find the Japanese and get all this on ABC, then it's worth it."

"And if they can't?" sniffed Moore.

"Then, we've blown it," said Hunter.

BROWN BAG

Spong called and reported that the launch date, originally set for May, had been pushed to June. Moore fretted that the group in Hawaii might "go through $200,000 and never leave Honolulu." Hunter shrugged. Have faith. "Fine," said Moore, "but we need a backup." He negotiated with Charles Davis, owner of the *James Bay*, and Davis agreed that the *James Bay* would stand by in case it was needed.

Progressively more cryptic communiqués from Hawaii made it difficult to know how well the transformation of the ship progressed. Korotva sounded confident that the team would solve the mechanical problems and that the ship would pass Coast Guard inspection, but was not certain about when this would happen. Don White and others in Hawaii objected to a media release from Hunter and a brief spat ensued over who could speak publicly on behalf of the campaign, further souring our faith.

The launch date had been pushed into July, and the whaling season had long since begun, when Moore proposed to the Greenpeace Foundation board that we launch the *James Bay*. The board supported the idea, although concerned about the financial implications. Moore, however, cut a deal with owners Charles and Patsy Davis from Seattle. The two retirees had become whale advocates and wanted to join the crew. They made the *James Bay* available on the condition that Greenpeace cover the operating costs. Following the experience of the *Meander* campaign, we intended to pay our way as we travelled the coast. "We should have launched the *James Bay* from the beginning," Moore grumbled. The $200,000 spent in Hawaii would have retired the debt. "No," argued Hunter — "having *two* ships makes it an escalation of tactics."

"But we don't even know if we have two ships," said Moore.

"Momentum," responded Hunter, "is a perceptual thing."

John Cormack agreed to skipper the *James Bay*. We issued media releases about two ships, faster speeds, and a "pincer movement" on the whalers in the North Pacific. In coordination with Spong, we declared that we would stalk *both* the Soviets and the Japanese. Within two weeks, a crew for the *James Bay* assembled, and on the moonless night of Sunday, July 17, we slipped out of Vancouver, escorted by a modest flotilla of supporters.

Bob and Bobbi Hunter stayed in Vancouver to communicate with the media and mind the office. This proved no small task. Amy Ephron continued to pitch the Paramount film deal and said she could guarantee $70,000 in July, but we failed to produce the character releases. Hunter complained that petty bickering had allowed the film to slip away.

Furthermore, to purchase provisions and fuel for the *James Bay*, we had spent the money Bobbi Hunter had planned to use to launch a direct mail funding drive. Gannon asked the bank manager for a $15,000 extension on our line of credit but the sympathetic banker had reached his limit.

A few days after the *James Bay* departed, however, our new volunteer office manager, Julie McMaster, discovered a brown paper bag in the morning mail, tied up and addressed to: "Greenpeace, Vancouver, Canada." Inside the bag, she discovered a bundle of worn Canadian and US dollar bills in small denominations. A handwritten note from a hermit in a mountain cabin in Washington State read: "I'm dying from cancer. This is all the money I have. I know you can use it. Thanks for what you are doing." There was no name. McMaster showed the bag to Bobbi Hunter, who called Gannon. When Gannon later carried the brown bag into the office of the Royal Bank manager, the banker expected him to beg for an extension on the line of credit. He shook his head before Gannon spoke, held up his hand, and said, "No way."

"Not a problem," said Gannon. "We have other sources." He showed the banker the hermit's notes and, for dramatic effect, emptied the cash from the bag onto his desk. The manager asked a teller to come in and count it. The total, in Canadian dollars, came to $15,500. And change.

PINCER MOVEMENT

In Honolulu, restless ABC film director John Wilcox joined the engineering team battling to get the subchaser off Pier 40. Finally, on July 26, with a helicopter and eight speedy Zodiacs aboard, the *Ohana Kai* stood ready to sail. Ross Thornwood broke his foot and could not go, but the other volunteers remained aboard, so the Family of the Sea swelled to fifty, including the ABC crew, Korotva, Spong, Zimmerman, Kazumi Tanaka, Nancy Jack, Dexter Cate, and scores of volunteers from Hawaii.

We knew that two Japanese factory ships, the *Kyokusei Maru* and the *Kyokuyo Maru #3*, operated northwest of Hawaii, but we had no precise coordinates for them. We also knew that the Soviet *Vladivostok* was steaming toward the coast of Baja. Our friend Deep Throat from Washington, D.C. provided the usual daily positions for the Russians. Our plan was to rendezvous the two Greenpeace ships in the so-called "pincer movement." However, on the first day out, the *Ohana Kai* suffered a fuel leak and returned to port for repairs.

Meanwhile, after leaving Vancouver, the *James Bay* had headed directly toward Baja, where we expected to intercept the *Vladivostok*. On July 26, we discovered that the Soviets had slipped past us and were hunting sperm whales over the seamounts about 800 miles off the coast. We pushed toward them, and at midday on Friday July 29, we sighted harpoon ships. We stayed with them, in rough seas, through the day and through the night of the full moon. We located the *Vladivostok* on radar at 04:00 on July 30. By 11:00 we had caught up with the factory ship and could see two harpoon ships chasing a pod of eight to ten sperm whales. We launched two Zodiacs, Moore and cameraman Bill Roxborough in one, Michael Bailey and I in the other. After fifteen minutes, the whales sounded. A third harpoon ship joined the hunt, and the three ships waited, tracking them, we knew, on their sonar screens.

Then, black smoke bellowed simultaneously from the stacks of the three harpoon ships, the whales surfaced, and we raced in front of the Russian ships. Fresh harpoon ships steamed over the horizon toward us. Apparently, the Russians had changed their strategy. Rather than shut down the hunt in our presence, they attempted to out-number and over-power us. Ten ships chased the pod of whales in a V-formation, like geese, with us in front of the lead goose, the sperm whales frantic before us in the choppy four-foot swells.

After we had been in front of the ships for over an hour, my legs had become knots of lactic acid. Bailey pushed the Zodiac among the whales, so close I wondered if a whale might surface directly under us. I had my back to the harpoon and trembled when I heard the whaling captain's horn. I prepared for the harpooner to fire, arching my back as if to pull away from the threat. I imagined what a harpoon or even a slashing cable would do to me. How accurate was the harpooner? I didn't trust his judgement or skill. Gripped in this terror, I began to see the faces of my friends and family: my wife, Glenn, Bob and Bobbi, Rod and Bree, my siblings and parents, my grandmother. I thought of old high school friends. Behind the parade of these imagined faces, I heard Bailey singing, "Michael row the boat ashore, hallelujah ..."

By the time I realized they had shot, I knew they had missed us.

My right ear rang with the explosion. The whales panicked and plunged below. The sea became a froth of grey water and grey bodies, flukes thrashing. The harpoon cable cut through the water beside us. I felt certain a whale had been hit and screamed for Bailey to get out of the way. But once the whales had sounded, we could see that the Russian harpooner had missed.

While ten steel-hulled whaling ships circled and waited, Bailey and I, and Moore and Roxborough, returned to the *James Bay* to change crews. For two hours we had been in the Zodiacs. I could not stand, even on the deck of the *James Bay*, without clinging to a halyard.

Two more crews leapt after the whalers, but before they arrived an explosion rang out, a whale was hit directly, and the sea under the killer boat bow turned red with blood. I leaned against the gunwales of the *James Bay* and took photographs. The Zodiacs hovered near the wounded whale as it thrashed and shrieked. Blood sprayed over the Greenpeace Zodiac crew. The gunner loaded another harpoon, aimed directly down from the bow at the ship, and fired another exploding missile into the whale. On the *James Bay*, the crew watched, silent. I felt Eileen Chivers grab my arm. A final, desperate geyser of red foam issued from the blowhole of the dying whale, then the animal fell silent.

For another four hours we fought the harpoon boats over every shot, but they hunted down and killed the entire pod of whales. It seemed the most miserable day of my life, of all our lives. Many among the crew wept or screamed. That night, the *Vladivostok* and its fleet moved southwest at full speed. We followed until we had just enough fuel to make San Francisco, then turned for the coast.

The *Ohana Kai* had returned to Hilo, picking up a new RDF and waiting for parts to repair a burned-out clutch on their Zodiac launching crane. On August 1, they departed and made straight for the *Vladivostok* fleet. Our pincer strategy changed to a "tag-team" strategy. Alinsky again came to mind: "Observe and stay open … because the ultimate action is going to be the *reaction* of the opposition."

FAMILY OF THE SEA

In Hilo, with the crew of the *Ohana Kai* trimmed to thirty-five due to seasickness, Korotva stormed across the bridge and decks, frustrated with the breakdowns. The subchaser had been in horrific condition, and virtually every piece of equipment on the vessel had been repaired, replaced, or rigged to work. Nevertheless, the Family of the Sea pulled together and departed again, heading north after the *Dalnyi Vostok*. However, the *Ohana Kai* did not achieve 26 knots, as some had hoped. At full throttle, the ship reached 18 knots, but at a tremendous cost in fuel. Nevertheless, they closed the gap on the *Vostok*.

Century-old logbooks document sperm whales, blue, humpback, fin, sei, and minke in the North Pacific, but the Family of the Sea saw almost nothing, other than some flying fish and jellyfish. The ABC documentary team flew sorties in the helicopter and saw no whales. John Wilcox, running the ABC crew, could see that the great grey emptiness of the Pacific shaped its own bleak statistic, but not the stuff of ABC specials. He fretted over what he would get for his $60,000.

Two thousand miles to the east, the *James Bay* arrived in San Francisco. Bob and Bobbi Hunter had flown from Vancouver and ran the media hub at Fort Mason with radio technician Dick Dillman. Michael Chechik had flown in to process and distribute the film that had been shot on the *James Bay*. On October 3, ABC executives in New York phoned and insisted they had paid for the rights of the "campaign," not just the *Ohana Kai* voyage. We had sprung a second boat on *them* as well as on the whalers. ABC wanted the film. Chechik argued that he had invested his own time and money, and the team in the San Francisco office did not want to "give the film away."

"The original letter from ABC was sent to *me*," Hunter said, taking charge. The television deal with Greenpeace Hawaii, argued Hunter, bound all Greenpeace entities. "We accepted their money," he said, "and I don't think a media-based ecology group wants to piss off ABC. Besides, this is about the whales." In the end, Chechik released the dramatic *James Bay* film to ABC, who in turn released clips to the agencies.

Meanwhile, half the *Ohana Kai* crew was seasick as the North Pacific heaved under a northwesterly storm. The svelte ABC men were among the more reliable deckhands, and Korotva relied heavily on them. On Monday, August 8, 1,000 nautical miles north of Hawaii, with foam blowing across the wheelhouse windows, the steering linkage snapped. The *Ohana Kai* was adrift. In high seas, the safest orientation is either directly into the storm or running with it. The worst orientation is to be blown abeam of the wind, which is exactly what happened to the long, narrow *Ohana Kai*. When the winds increased to 40 knots, and the wheelhouse door dipped to within a few feet of the dark water, Korotva secretly feared the ship could capsize. He advised Spong to have all the Zodiacs ready, but took no one else into his confidence.

Gary Zimmerman and Dino Pignataro from San Francisco climbed into the aft compartment where two mechanical tillers drove twin rudders at the stern. Unable to repair the steerage system with the ship pitching over, they rigged a chain hoist to each rudder. Two crewmembers sat in the tiny compartment, took instructions by walkie-talkie from Korotva on the bridge, and hauled on the chains to steer the ship. For four hours through the night, Nancy Jack and Bobby Baker, both from Maui, huddled in the damp bilge and hoisted the chains. Korotva stayed up all night. They turned the subchaser back into the gale and managed to push north after the whalers. Though they may have lacked maritime poise, there had never been a more heroic charge in the history of sea-going ecology campaigns dating back to the *Golden Rule* in 1958.

Five days later, on Saturday, August 13, 1,800 miles north of Hawaii, the crippled *Ohana Kai* intercepted the factory ship *Dalnyi Vostok*. For an hour in moderate seas, the Greenpeace crews blockaded the harpoon ships from transferring two dead whales to the factory ship. Photographs of the earlier confrontation now circulated on the wire services. For all our foibles, the pincer, tag-team, two-pronged protest had worked, and the Soviets stopped whaling and headed east at full speed. For six days, the helicopter and zodiacs from the *Ohana Kai* buzzed the harpoon ships. They saw no whales. On August 20, low on fuel, they made a farewell statement.

Paul Spong, Nancy Jack, Kazumi Tanaka, Dexter Cate, and an ABC cameraman gunned two Zodiacs up the stern slip of the factory ship. They tied their little inflatables to a rail in the dark cavern and climbed to the flensing deck. Curious Russian crew gathered around. Spong and Nancy Jack handed out Russian language literature and whale pins. The whalers stepped forward to shake hands and accept the gifts. Some spoke in halting English. "The whales are your comrades," Spong told them.

A short, well-groomed political commissar in a civilian sports coat arrived on the deck and escorted the boarding party to a lounge. Spong asked to speak to the captain, who arrived in dress whites and braided collar.

They exchanged polite greetings in English. Spong apologized for the intrusion, but said they had urgent concerns about the whales. "Even you," Spong said, "can see there are few whales left ... People from all over the world are asking you to stop killing the whales ... You know that we are determined, that we'll keep coming back. Please stop." Kazumi Tanaka asked the captain why, for days, they had found no whales. The Russian captain shrugged. He was just a sea captain. Resource management policies were made elsewhere, he explained. Kazumi saw the Japanese observer peeking through a group of Soviet officers, and he asked him about the evidence Greenpeace had of illegal, undersized whales taken by the *Vostok*. The man ducked away and did not reappear. The political commissar stepped in, announced the meeting was over, and escorted the visitors back to their Zodiac. As they shook hands and said goodbye, Spong pinned a whale button on the jacket of the commissar. He did not object.

The next day, with only enough fuel to make Hawaii, the *Ohana Kai* turned south for Honolulu.

ROCK AND ROLL HEAVEN

Meanwhile, the *James Bay* crew in San Francisco raised money for fuel to maintain the tag-team strategy. We needed to raise $10,000 in a week. Bob Hunter, Cindy Baker, and radio operator Dick Dillman churned out media releases from Fort Mason, while ABC News aired its special on the whale campaign. Meanwhile, two women from Marin County painted stars and rainbows on the bulwarks of the minesweeper at Pier 31. One of them, Caroline Keddy — smart, funny, beautiful, and in thick with the rock and roll elite of the Bay Area — urged us to go see the Jerry Garcia Band, playing at the Keystone Club in Berkeley. "Ask Jerry if he'll do a benefit. You're not going to get out of here selling T-shirts."

On the evening of August 6, Mel Gregory, Caroline Keddy, and I drove to Berkeley, pulled up Shattuck Avenue, and spotted the marquee that announced, JERRY GARCIA BAND. A crowd milled about outside. Keddy did all the talking at the entrance, and we followed her through the cavernous rock and roll club to the backstage door. A towering, burly biker in a Hell's Angels leather jacket gave us a curious sneer and said, "Yeah?"

Mel stepped forward and looked up at the biker. "We're from Greenpeace, and we ..."

"Yer from Greenpeace?"

"Yeah."

"Really?"

"Yeah."

"Were you out there on those boats?"

"Yeah," said Mel. "We want to talk to Jerry."

"Just a minute." The Hell's Angel biker disappeared, returned, and waved us in. "Shit, man, this is cool."

Back stage, Jerry Garcia sat with his band, renowned rock bassist John Kahn, vocalists Keith and Donna Godchaux, and drummer Ron Tutt. They gathered around to meet the Greenpeacers. "Look, man," said Mel after a few whale stories. "We're broke. We need about $10,000 to fill the fuel tanks, buy some food, and go back out. We want you to do a benefit."

Garcia and his manager conferred and came up with the idea to do the concert right on the pier, in front of the boat. "Yeah," said Garcia, "we could do it next Friday if Tom Campbell will produce it. Do you know Tom?" We didn't, but I sat with the manager and discussed details while Mel entertained Garcia and the bikers with Greenpeace stories. Hells Angels and hippies didn't always get along, but in this case, Mel delighted the bikers, and they proudly wore their new whale pins.

The next morning, Sunday, I called Tom Campbell, imagining a flashy rock and roll impresario on the other end of the phone. That afternoon, Keddy and I met him at his home near Sebastopol, 50 miles north of San Francisco. We drove up a dirt road toward his rural home and met a ramshackle red pick-up truck. Out stepped lanky, dusty Tom Campbell, a red bandana wrapped around long red hair. Inside his home, concert posters hung on the walls. He introduced his partner Janis and offered us a beer. We told him our dilemma and explained that Jerry Garcia would help us if he would produce the show. "Yeah, okay," he said. "When?"

"Friday," I said.

"Which Friday?"

"This Friday."

Campbell grimaced. "Impossible. You want to produce a Jerry Garcia concert on the dock in San Francisco, build a stage, promote, secure the site, sell tickets, the whole deal in, uh, five days?" He rolled his eyes.

"Yeah," I said, completely naïve about what I was asking him to do.

Campbell, thirty-seven, had grown up in a progressive, political family of community organizers and musicians. At twenty-two, he became the entertainment production coordinator at Disneyland, and later, in the late 1960s, he played the folk music circuit. Linda Ronstadt and Taj Mahal had recorded his songs. In 1974, he produced his first benefit concert — with Ronstadt, Pete Seeger, the Nitty Gritty Dirt Band, and Steve Martin — to support a group attempting to stop the strip mining of Black Mesa in New Mexico. Later, in California, he produced shows for the Sierra Club and the California Nuclear Safeguards Initiative, with Jackson Browne, Jesse Colin Young, Maria Muldaur, Danny O'Keefe, Bonnie Raitt, and The Eagles. He had put hundreds of thousands of dollars into the hands of grassroots activists, but most of these shows took months to organize. The last thing a popular musician wanted was to donate time to something poorly organized, like our send-off party a year ago with mix-ups in the program and a porous perimeter. Musicians who donated time wanted results. The professionals like Garcia trusted Campbell's ability to create a successful event. I didn't know any of this at the time, and Campbell did not boast of his accomplishments. He sat in a large overstuffed chair and thought about what we had asked of him. He stood up, grabbed a large notebook, and scribbled a long list of items. He ripped the page out of the notebook and handed it to Caroline Keddy. "Okay," he said, "if you guys can do everything on this list by Wednesday, I'll be down on Thursday, we'll build the stage, and do it."

Keddy managed work crews, had tickets printed and distributed to sellers the next day. Campbell planned to use the *James Bay* itself as the backstage area. Volunteers constructed a security perimeter. KSAN and the other FM radio stations spread the word, and the show sold out by the time Campbell arrived on Thursday morning. Even in our most harried moments, we had never experienced such a hurricane of proficient energy. Carpenter crews erected a stage, speaker platforms, a table for the mixing board, and a small technician's hut. Security teams walked the fences and gates, roadies dropped off gear, crowds milled about to watch and the Greenpeace crew decorated the dressing rooms on the *James Bay*. Towering Scottish redhead Tom Campbell directed the concert team with shouts and waving arms.

By Friday morning, August 12, Pier 31 had been transformed into rock and roll heaven. The public crowded through the gate and those without tickets climbed onto nearby buildings for the show. The sun burst out with the first electric notes of the sound check. Legendary musicians — Maria Muldaur, Billy Kreutzmann from the Grateful Dead, and Jack Casady from the Jefferson Airplane — toured the *James Bay*. I stood on the flying bridge with my wife Glenn and Pete and Jeanette Sears, songwriters for the newly formed Jefferson Starship. Jeanette held their new baby, Dylan. Below on the stage, Jerry Garcia and his band played the reggae classic "Sitting in Limbo," and the crowd spontaneously danced.

Pete and Jeanette Sears talked about ecology and asked how they could help. Pete Sears told me they abstained from drugs and seldom drank, which was not easy in the San Francisco rock music world, and that they tried to live a spiritual life. Jeanette Sears cuddled her new baby. "Don't gain the world and lose your soul," she said casually, not to anyone in particular. "Don't *save* the world and lose your soul, either."

"This," said Pete Sears, casting a glance over the ship, "is more important than being a rock star."

The concert raised $20,000. We provisioned the ship and filled the fuel tanks. At 11:30 a.m. on Friday August 19, we pulled away from Pier 31. California Governor Jerry Brown and US Congressman Leo Ryan stood among the well-wishers and media. Ryan carried a report we had produced for him, destined for President Jimmy Carter, documenting the taking of undersized whales in violation of IWC regulations.

By mid-afternoon, we were off Point Reyes heading due west toward the *Vladivostok*.

KANGAROOS & POINTER SHARKS

A few days before the *James Bay* left San Francisco, Bob and Bobbi Hunter had received an urgent phone call from French entrepreneur and environmentalist Jean-Paul Fortom-Gouin in Australia. Fortom-Gouin wanted the Hunters to lead a group of Australian whale-savers in a campaign to shut down Australian shore whaling. He said he had studied Greenpeace tactics and he had a boat, Zodiacs, and crew ready to go. This appeared as a golden opportunity: We knew that another encounter with the Soviet *Vladivostok* would not significantly amplify the international pressure already on the whalers. However, it so happened that whaling politics might hinge on sentiment in Australia. The IWC meetings had just been held in Canberra, Australia. Jean-Paul Fortom-Gouin had insinuated himself into the IWC by funding a Panama delegation and having himself appointed commissioner. He had financed activists in Canberra, and thousands of protestors had stormed the meetings with a life-sized whale balloon, "Flo," that floated above the assembly hall. The Canberra sessions had resulted in a 36-percent reduction in quotas — a major victory for the anti-whaling movement. The events also galvanized Australian environmentalists. The wealthy Frenchman had spent $100,000 on whale campaigns, including a $20,000 gift to the *Ohana Kai*. He now believed that if Australia could be persuaded to stop whaling, the resistance of other whaling nations would crumble. Fortom-Gouin wanted Greenpeace to help him eliminate Australian whaling.

When the Hunters arrived in Sydney, they felt as if they had stepped into a remake of their own lives, ten years earlier. Like disarmament and ecology committees of the 1960s, the Australian Greenpeace crowd remained fanatically grassroots, led by a lanky radical named Jonny Lewis and a seasoned activist from California, Pat Ferrington, who had marched in civil rights rallies and led feminist uprisings. The office was a chaotic clubhouse of whale lovers and dispossessed proletarians preparing to drive to the Cheynes Beach whaling station in Albany, at the southern tip of Western Australia on the Indian Ocean.

Jean-Paul Fortom-Gouin, whom Hunter called "the Godfather," paid the bills and commanded the legion of ecologists. He informed the Hunters that *he*, along with Lewis and Ferrington, would fly to Albany as an "advance team," and that *they*, the Hunters, would lead the action team across the desolate interior deserts with the gear loaded on a flatbed truck. The Hunters had not been informed that their destination lay almost 3,000 miles by highway through Adelaide, past desert tank towns like Nundroo and Cocklebiddy, to the dusty coast at Albany. They were not impressed that the so-called leaders would be lounging in a hotel while they crossed the continent. Bob Hunter thought that perhaps he and Bobbi should go ahead to Albany to reconnoiter the media environment, but he did not mention this to the single-minded Godfather. Besides, the Australian volunteers had grown so animated with purpose, the Hunters found themselves inspired to push through. The Canberra IWC meeting represented a milestone. Perhaps they could deliver the *coup de grâce* to the whaling industry with this action in Australia.

Across the Great Victoria Desert they sputtered, Zodiacs and survival gear stacked high on the 1961 Ford flatbed, food and water in a station wagon. Bobbi drove the car. Truck breakdowns started at one per day then increased to two or three per day in the searing heat of the Nullarbor Plain. Nullarbor means, simply, "null arbor," no trees. "Good name," observed Bobbi Hunter. On the outskirts of Ceduna stood a sign warning the "last reliable water," with Albany still 1,200 miles away. The two team mechanics, Tom Barber and Allan Simmons, repaired the truck near the ghost towns at Fowlers Bay and Eucla, where the original city had been swallowed by sand dunes. Now, in the summer of 1977, drought in the desert interior was driving hoards of kangaroos south across the highway at all times of day and night. Bobbi Hunter insisted on following behind the flatbed, which occasionally took out a kangaroo with a sickening *thud*.

Finally, east of Esperance, 300 miles from Albany, the 1961 Ford sputtered to a stop and defied the mechanics. The Hunters drove to the nearest settlement and hired an elderly repairman to drive them to Albany for $100. The station wagon followed, crammed with people and gear. Barber and Simmons stayed behind with the truck and the rest of the gear.

Fortom-Gouin greeted the grimy road team in Albany. The Cheynes Beach shore whaling station stood directly across King George Sound, and Fortom-Gouin wanted to launch the Zodiacs immediately and charge across the bay. Bob Hunter's celebrated sense of humour had evaporated along with his bodily fluids. He and Bobbi wanted nothing more than a shower and a cold beer. Fortom-Gouin, however, instructed volunteers to drag the Zodiacs onto the beach. With television crews watching anxiously, the Frenchman directed the tired Canadians to assemble the inflatables. The Godfather was aghast to learn that the Hunters — the famous Greenpeace whale savers — had never assembled a Zodiac in their lives. Hunter was equally aghast that their patron had failed to plan out any of this or assemble a team with the necessary skills. Into this stalemate, Barber and Simmons rolled up in the smoking flatbed and went to work on the inflatables. On their first run across the bay, Hunter and

Fortom-Gouin hit a submerged pipe, damaged the propeller, sputtered back across the bay in the dark, capsized in the surf, and staggered wet and miserable into the motel to be met by chortling journalists.

That night, Hunter discovered that the steady flow of blood from the whaling station attracted 3,000-pound Great White Pointer sharks. No locals swam in the area nor did they travel on the water in anything without a steel hull. The journalists could scarcely believe that the ecologists would risk their lives in the shark-infested waters. Great White sharks grow to well over 20 feet long, possess six rows of razor-sharp teeth, and are considered the most dangerous shark in the world, nature's ultimate predator. They feed on seals and sea lions, have been known to ram small boats, and have killed humans in a single bite.

Nevertheless, the next day the Hunters, Jonny Lewis, and Rosie Dekanic piloted a Zodiac across the bay, in the drizzling rain, to meet up with 200 protestors who assembled at the entrance of the Cheynes Beach whaling station. Three dead sperm whales floated in the bay. Bobbi Hunter became so frightened of the sharks that she trembled and wept. Still, remarkably, she drifted in the bloody effluent from the flensing plant, and held up placards. At the whaling station, angry bikers from the God's Garbage motorcycle gang, many of whom worked at the plant, confronted the protestors. Hunter attempted to reason with the gang, even explaining that in California some bikers supported us, but the gang members scowled and told him to go back to California.

Just as Hunter felt the campaign was hopeless, the clouds parted and a tremendous rainbow arched across King George Sound. *Okay*, he thought. To add to the magic, four dolphins arrived in the bay, which explained to the locals why the sharks had not shown up on this day. Pods of dolphins have little fear of sharks and can easily drive them away. Fortunes turned even more favourable when Hunter discovered that the public relations firm hired by Cheynes Beach Whaling Company Ltd. had invited journalists from across Australia to come to Albany and see the whaling operation. The evening news carried the entire protest across Australia, including the rainbow and the "dolphin patrol." *Maybe*, thought Hunter, *we can turn this around*.

Throughout the next week, the protestors grew more confident with the Zodiacs. They followed whaling ships 50 miles into the heaving Indian Ocean. The Zodiacs climbed 10-foot swells that dropped off into dark, windless troughs. When they shielded a pod of fleeing sperm whales, the Aussie whalers fired a harpoon past Fortom-Gouin and Tom Barber. The camera teams on board the whaling ships, courtesy of the whaling company, captured each encounter and delivered images of protestors and slaughtered whales into virtually every household in Australia.

The entire country rose up against whaling. Few national politicians dared defend the industry. Even forty-six-year-old Kase van der Gaag, the Dutch captain of the *Cheynes 2* whaling ship, cornered Hunter in a bar and told him "I love being at sea, but I do not enjoy killing whales. It's just my job. You don't have to remind me," the remorseful skipper told the ecologist, "that that's what the Nazis said, too."

A year later, the national government ended whaling in Australia, and the Cheynes Beach station closed, at a cost, mind you, of half a dozen kangaroos, sacrificed on the Nullarbor Plain.

TALE OF TWO CITIES

In fact, Fortom-Gouin's strategy had been sound. As Australian whaling crumbled, the Russian and Japanese whalers grew more isolated. Iceland became the next target. Meanwhile, Greenpeace groups sprang up around the world, with their own distinctive styles and tactics. In Vancouver we became progressively aware that a new era of Greenpeace was taking shape in Europe. In London, Susi Newborn and Allan Thornton, who had joined the seal campaign, met with Denise Bell from Friends of the Earth in Harrow, northwest of London. Bell wanted to find a boat to confront the Icelandic whalers in the North Pacific. Newborn tracked down the activists from *Peace News*, who had supported the Amchitka and Moruroa campaigns and had adopted the name Greenpeace.

She met with the charismatic leader of *Peace News*, Albert Beale, a hard-core revolutionary loyal to his trade unionist friends. The *Peace News* journal avowed non-violence, but one of its activists, Ronnie Lee, had been arrested for causing £52,000 in damage to vivisection laboratories. Lee spent fifteen months in jail and later founded the more militant Animal Liberation Front. Nevertheless, the *Peace News* group displayed a proclivity for creative protesting. They held a "Mutants March" mocking the notorious Windscale nuclear power accident and taunting the government about the link between "nukiller power" and "nukiller weapons." Beale had met David McTaggart during the Moruroa campaign, but did not like his imposing personality or the "box office" image of ecology depicted in glossy magazines during the seal hunt. "Greenpeace," Beale told Newborn, "is an imperialist impostor." Newborn didn't argue the point since she considered the *Peace News* activists to be her allies.

Beale's disdain, however, implied to Newborn that no active Greenpeace group existed in London. She, Thornton, and Denise Bell decided they were it. Her experience on Belle Isle had convinced her that Greenpeace was staunchly non-violent, creative, media savvy, and successful, and this appealed to her. In May 1977 they opened an office at 47 Whitehall Street in London and put out a shingle that said, simply, Greenpeace.

That spring, filmmaker Michael Chechik arrived in the UK with a copy of the new Greenpeace documentary film about the whale voyages. The BBC aired the film, with an introduction by British naturalist David Attenborough. Chechik gave a copy of the film to Bell, Newborn, and Thornton, and they used it to raise money. At a Country Joe and the Fish concert, they met Charles Hutchinson, a soft-spoken, young environmentalist in wire-rim glasses, who joined them.

David McTaggart, who now visited London regularly, proposed that they establish Greenpeace UK Ltd., and that they each hold shares in the "company." McTaggart directed the lawyers and issued one pound shares to Bell, Newborn, Allan Thornton, Charles Hutchinson, and himself. Newborn grew suspicious of McTaggart and resisted his control. She had met Walrus, Bob Hunter, and the Spongs, and was aware of the Quaker and Native American influence on the Greenpeace Foundation in Canada. She objected, on ethical grounds, to owning a share in Greenpeace, and gave hers to Denise Bell.

For his part, McTaggart organized things the way he knew how, as an entrepreneur. His tenacity had carried him to Moruroa twice against tremendous odds and helped him prevail over the French government in its own courts. Europe was fertile ground for an ecology movement and, as far as McTaggart was concerned, it was *his* ground. He admired Hunter, but otherwise had no interest in aligning with the Greenpeace Foundation in Canada. Although he drank beer and smoked marijuana with the rest of the activists in Europe, he did not like hippies or grassroots militants. He considered the mystical and Native American motifs within Greenpeace to be flaky pretensions. He clashed with Newborn over relations with the *Peace News* activists and other potential allies in London. At the same time, he could be exceedingly charming, confident, charismatic, bright, and full of energy. But his charms led to other conflicts. Newborn resented what she called his "playboy attitude," with women. She didn't like it that he hit on the female volunteers, and when she refused his advances, he asked her, "Are you gay?" On the other hand, Newborn recognized that his charisma could move people to action and that he seemed to genuinely care about the issues. He had certainly proven his courage. David McTaggart was perhaps the most self-contradictory personality in the ecology movement.

A year earlier, and 500 miles away, in Paris, activist Brice Lalonde from Les Amis de la Terre and his friend, student Rémi Parmentier, had attended a demonstration by workers of the Commissariat à l'Energie Atomique, who claimed the loss of jobs at French nuclear facilities affected worker safety. Lalonde and Parmentier began to forge an alliance with the trade unionists, who had published a critique of the nuclear industry, and unionists joined Les Amis de la Terre's "Energy Commission." Lalonde introduced Parmentier to David McTaggart, who rented a room at Lalonde's flat on rue de l'Université. McTaggart showed Parmentier a truncheon like the one the French used to beat him up and told Parmentier that he had started Greenpeace. He claimed the first office was in Paris and revealed nothing about the Greenpeace Foundation in Canada. The two became friends, and Parmentier abandoned his law and English studies at the Sorbonne to join McTaggart in building Greenpeace. Parmentier told his friends, "I want to be a doer. There are enough thinkers in the environmental movement." Over the next year, Lalonde and Parmentier backed renowned agronomist René Dumont to run for the French presidency under the "*Écologie*" banner, and they garnered almost 14 percent of the vote, a signal to French politicians that the ecology constituency could spell the difference in a French election.

By the summer of 1977, after two whale and seal campaigns and Brigitte Bardot's return from the Labrador ice floes, Greenpeace enjoyed fame in Paris. McTaggart brought Parmentier to London, where they met at the Whitehall office to establish ground rules for Greenpeace in Europe. McTaggart presided at these meetings as the Greenpeace activist with seniority, although he abandoned his story about being the founder. From

Newborn, Parmentier learned about the Greenpeace Foundation, but McTaggart told him, "Don't worry about those wankers in Canada. They don't know what's going on in the world beyond Alberta." This lack of cohesion within Greenpeace would wound the organization over the next two years, but in the meantime, the group in Europe prospered. They worked tirelessly like a small tribe, travelled on cheap night trains, and slept on each other's sofas. They listened to music, drank beer, smoked joints, and plotted ecological insurgencies. Like our gang in Kitsilano, like any extended family, they had sharp disagreements that often boiled over into fights, but they held together and achieved results. "We're faster and freer than others in the environmental movement," Parmentier told his friends. They were doers.

THE ABERDEEN TRAWLER

Meanwhile, in London, Denise Bell scoured maritime journals for ships for sale. On the Isle of Dogs, in the Thames Docklands, she found a rusting, 134-foot trawler that had been converted to a research ship by the Ministry of Agriculture, Fisheries, and Food. The diesel-electric, 400-metric ton *Sir William Hardy* was available to the highest bidder. From a nearby phone box Bell called Newborn. "It's perfect," she told her friend. Newborn leapt onto her bicycle and headed for the East London Docklands.

On board the Aberdeen trawler, they spun the wooden wheel on the bridge. The ship listed slightly to port. Neither of them knew anything about boats, but they had an intuition. This was the one. Newborn phoned childhood friend Athel von Koettlitz, a qualified mechanic who might know how to get the generator started. He arrived and clambered down into the pitch-black engine room with a flashlight. The hovel was a rust bucket and the 800 horsepower electric-diesel engine had not been fired in years. He wiped moisture off gauge glass and kicked at loose equipment. The mechanic got the two-stroke diesel engine running and the generator working so they had light on the ship. In the galley sink Newborn found egg-encrusted plates and mouldy teacups. Bell tenderly wiped dust from the chart table and brass fittings.

The Department of Trade accepted their bid of £42,725, and Charles Hutchinson introduced them to the manager at Lloyds of Pall Mall bank.

They received a bank loan, secured by the life insurance policies of Hutchinson and Bell, and put down a 10 percent deposit on the ship, £4,272, setting in motion a new era of Greenpeace actions in Europe.

Hutchinson later negotiated to reduce the price of the *Sir William Hardy*, including all spare parts and remaining fuel on board, to £32,500, about $56,000 US at the time. To raise funds, Thornton and Hutchinson toured European cities with a copy of the Chechik documentary, *The Voyage to Save the Whales*. In the Netherlands, the World Wildlife Fund established a trust account for Greenpeace donations and financed a fundraising campaign. Greenpeace UK would get the first £45,000, enough to purchase the *Sir William Hardy*, pay off the bank loan, and launch the ship. Bell, Newborn, von Koettlitz, and Hutchinson brought the Aberdeen trawler back to life, removed the trawling gear, scraped off rust, repaired loose fittings, and shopped around for second-hand parts. They passed long, happy days on the boat through the summer and fall of 1977. Bell sometimes stood at the bow, looking out across the grey Thames and imagining they were already at sea, chasing down Icelandic whalers.

As the WWF fund approached the critical £45,000, a Dutch television station agreed to host Bob Hunter on a broadcast appeal to reach their funding goal. The WWF also wanted someone from the Greenpeace Foundation to receive the cheque. Newborn caught up with the Hunters in Australia and flew them to London. Newborn and Bell took the Hunters to see the ship. When they stepped onto the old trawler, it rocked against its ropes. The metal felt cold and damp in the river fog. Newborn had received Greenpeace banners and the Kwakiutl designs from Walrus in Newfoundland and from the San Francisco office. Hunter had told her about the *Warriors of the Rainbow* book, which Newborn found in the library.

In Amsterdam, they appeared on Dutch television and Hunter accepted the cheque from the World Wildlife Fund. Bob and Bobbi Hunter conferred, agonizing over the fact that a portion of this money would ease our debts in Vancouver. But the money had been raised to purchase the boat, and asking would have felt crass. As Hunter would recall later, it is the tension that makes history interesting. When Newborn told him they would call the vessel the *Rainbow Warrior*, he did not mention anything about debts. "Great," he said. "Go for it."

After the Hunters departed, David McTaggart arrived in London and found Newborn, Bell, and the others at the dock, painting rainbows on the ship's deep green hull. Newborn had added a white dove copied from the library book and the name Rainbow Warrior at the bow. McTaggart scoffed at the name and told Newborn they should come up with something else, but Newborn wouldn't hear of changing it. McTaggart shifted from one foot to another with his hands in his padded vest, a characteristic jig he danced when roused. He argued with Newborn, cursing the "goddamn rainbows." Newborn went back to painting. "It's those flaky hippies in Canada," he told Newborn. She ignored him and this only stirred him more. "Waste of time," he said. "You should be getting this ship ready for service." Newborn huffed at this and waved him off.

Later, in a manner also typical of McTaggart, he apologized and reasoned with her. As much as Newborn harboured misgivings, she resigned herself to working with McTaggart. He asked her who she thought should run their European nuclear campaigns. "Who's that tough guy at Friends of the Earth? The one who's really good at campaigning?"

"Pete Wilkinson," said Newborn. Wilkinson had grown up near the docks in South London, the son of a skilled engraver fired by a firm after thirty years faithful service. Young Pete had become the radical among his South London friends. He found a constructive outlet for his rage when he read the Friends of the Earth *Environmental Handbook*. "Perhaps," he thought at the time, "the source of my frustration is that I live in an artificial world." He set out to understand the natural world, but among environmentalists, he told Newborn, "I feel like the token working-class guy."

In the fall of 1977, Wilkinson came to work for Greenpeace and began to research European nuclear issues. He came upon evidence that the UK nuclear industry was dumping dangerous radioactive waste at sea. "We gotta stop this shit," he told McTaggart.

When Charles Hutchinson ran into trouble with the dockworker unions in London, who told him that work on the ship had to be carried out by unionized labour, Wilkinson sorted it out. "You have to speak to them in an accent they understand," he told Hutchinson. The workers agreed with Wilkinson to "turn a blind eye" to the non-union Greenpeace labour. There had been plenty of proletarians in Greenpeace before, but Wilkinson made a point of inculcating his values into the organization. In class-ridden London, armies of young people and unemployed labourers stood poised to support social change.

A NAME

In each new place that a Greenpeace office emerged, it assumed a local personality. Newborn and Wilkinson recruited from London youth clubs and dockworkers. French ecologists like Lalonde and Parmentier formed complex political and intellectual alliances. Ecology parties, the Greens, had emerged in Tasmania, Belgium, Netherlands, Switzerland, Austria, France, and New Zealand. The deterioration of the environment had become as much a sensate trauma as a tooth infection. Common armies of citizen ecologists around the world sensed something fundamentally wrong with the status quo — a runaway human population, deteriorating air and water, disappearing seas, vanishing species, and an apparent industrial disregard for the general health of the planet.

Greenpeace had long since noticed that ecology broke down established political alliances and created new ones. We had bikers, presidents, hippies, ranchers, liberals, capitalists, and socialists all supporting us. Although ecology was a global phenomenon, the social environments for ecology remained local. To Susi Newborn, London in the mid-1970s was a filthy, squalid place. The rubbish everywhere sickened her. Clocks in the tube stations didn't tell the right time, trains ran on no discernible schedule, and young people grew angry and restless. The chaotic street life in London had already spawned a new wave of fury expressing what Newborn called "an in-your-face, loud, discordant, rude, shocking message." Newborn noticed a contrast, in her words, between "the bare-footed, incense-burning hippies protesting the war in Vietnam or the slaughter of whales, and the heroin-fueled, anti-Christ, anti-Monarch, anti-everything youth with safety pins through their flesh."

Newborn understood Greenpeace as a mix of Native American spiritual mythology, Gandhi's *satyagraha*, ecology, and the Quaker philosophy of "bearing witness." Greenpeace had developed a formula that appealed to people, but Newborn felt that simply following the formula would dull the cutting edge. "Tactics get old," she warned. She didn't want to see Greenpeace in Europe live off a formula. The street punks of London, it turned out, appreciated the environmental movement as much as anybody; they just had their own way of saying things. When the Sex Pistols produced a badge that said, "Fuck the Queen," Newborn produced one that said, "Fuck the Whalers." It wouldn't necessarily work at cocktail parties in

Carmel or Connecticut, but it played well among the housing estates in London, the docks of Hamburg, and among the Sharpies in Perth and Sydney. "Our gut reactions to injustice are the same," Newborn told her allies.

Ecology challenged *all* the political blocs — Aboriginal, peasant, proletarian, bourgeois, the famous, the powerful, the strong, the weak, the merchants and capitalists — to find a new relationship with the earth. Even the sons and daughters of European royalty embraced ecology. Ecology found champions everywhere because it touched everyone. Greenpeace simply became a name for what took form naturally in the human spirit and human psyche of the age.

CAPTAIN NO FACE

Off the coast of North America, the *James Bay* steamed back to Vancouver from San Francisco after a brief, final encounter with the Soviet *Vladivostok*. It had become painfully clear to us while at sea that the whalers were finding few whales. For three full days we had watched eleven Soviet harpoon ships, lined up abeam at 10-mile intervals, sweep a 100-mile swath across the ocean at 15 knots, without sighting a single whale.

During a brief stop in San Francisco, poet Lawrence Ferlinghetti joined the ship. The fifty-eight-year-old Ferlinghetti had been one of my cultural heroes since my days as an apprentice engineer at Lockheed in 1967, when I had ventured into San Francisco's North Beach, purchased his *Coney Island of the Mind* at City Lights Bookstore, and discovered the beat generation writers. He had been arrested for publishing Allen Ginsberg's *Howl*, resulting in a landmark case that established a legal precedent for freedom of speech in America. Now, sharing a coffee and casual conversation on the *James Bay* with such a literary mentor felt like a great gift. Ferlinghetti told me he had arrived in Nagasaki with the US Navy just weeks after the bomb had been dropped and the experience had turned him into a lifelong pacifist.

On the morning of October 14, off Cape Flattery at the entrance to Juan de Fuca Strait near Vancouver, Ferlinghetti sat at the galley table and opened the second volume of Mel's "Dreambook" that had toured with us for three years. The elder beat poet wrote down his misty recollections from the night before. His dream became one of the more poignant expressions of the ecological turmoil of the era:

Dreamt of
Moby Dick the Great White Whale
Cruising about
with a flag flying
with an inscription on it
"I am what is left of Wild Nature"
and Ahab pursuing in a jet boat with a ray gun
and jet harpoons and super depth charges
and napalm flamethrowers and electric
underwater vibrators and the whole gory
glorious efficient military-political
industrial-scientific technology
of the greatest
civilization the
earth has ever
known
devoted to
the absolute extinction and
death of the natural world as we know it
And Captain Ahab Captain Death Captain Anti-Poetry
Captain Dingbat No Face Captain Apocalypse
at the helm
of the Killer Ship of Death
And the blue-eyed whales
exhausted and running
but still
singing
to each other …

We had just arrived in Vancouver when we became embroiled in one final permutation of the Australian campaign. On September 8, 1977, 1,200 tons of sperm-whale oil, valued at $1.2 million Australian and representing one-third of the annual production of Cheynes Beach Holdings Co.

Ltd., left Australia on a Norwegian chemical tanker, the *Stolt Llangdaff*, owned by Stolt Nielson in New York City. The tanker arrived in Portland to offload palm oil on September 24. The US Marine Mammal Protection Act prohibited whale products entering the country, even in transit. The Customs office in Portland found sperm-whale oil on the ship's manifest but inexplicably let the ship enter the port. Someone tipped off Portland Greenpeace, but a Customs officer claimed the shipment was "fish oil."

The ruse unravelled with mercurial speed, and US Customs heavies in Washington, D.C. ordered the *Stolt Llangdaff* to get outside the new US 200-mile limit and not return with whale oil. Someone working for Stolt Nielson's company decided to send the ship into Vancouver to solve their problem. The wayward tanker entered Burrard Inlet under the pretence of having a leaky tank of fish oil, and convinced West Coast Reduction, owned by Vancouver horse breeder Jack Diamond, to store it. A dock-worker phoned Greenpeace on Fourth Avenue. When Moore exposed the sperm-whale oil, Diamond, a life member of the Horsemen's Benevolent and Protective Association, told the Customs office, "We wouldn't have touched it with a 10-foot pole if we had known it was whale oil." As well, the BC longshoremen and BC Federation of Labour refused to touch it.

Moore sent Stolt Nielson's New York phone number to all the Greenpeace offices, flooding the Norwegian shipper with calls. Nielson abandoned his cargo, and the fiasco sent Cheynes Beach spinning toward bankruptcy. "The oil represents 200 sperm whales," Moore said. "We hope and pray they are the last of their kind to fall under the Australian harpoons." They were.

This final victory capped a successful year that had started with the Japan whale mission and supertanker campaign. Most of us in Vancouver were giddy with how well our work progressed, though slightly troubled by the mounting political nightmare ahead of us. Over the past year, the Greenpeace Foundation had sent $7,000 to the *Ohana Kai*, spent $1,000 on the Budworm Campaign, $7,000 on the Harp Seal Campaign, $20,000 on the Japan whale missions, $67,854 on the *James Bay*, zero on the whale oil embargo, and had made a $3,000 profit on the ambush at Douglas Channel. We shrugged off the $150,000 in debts. Worldwide, Greenpeace revenues approached a million dollars per year, and we had a new ship in London, prepared to work in the North Atlantic. We concluded that the time had come to host a meeting of international Greenpeace representatives in an effort to unravel our internal political knots.

THE FIRST GLOBAL

Twenty-eight volunteers from Canada, San Francisco, Hawaii, Portland, Seattle, Toronto, Australia, France and England arrived in Vancouver to plot the future of Greenpeace. Participants included David McTaggart, Gary Zimmerman, Don White, Nancy Jack, Dexter Cate, Elaine and Margaret Tilbury from Portland, lawyer David Tussman and whale-advocate Cindy Baker from San Francisco, Campbell Plowden from Seattle, Dan and Patty McDermott from Toronto, and others. From October 14 to 16, 1977, in Kitsilano, at the home of Bill Gannon, we held the first global Greenpeace meeting. A governance committee formed with Gannon, Robert O. Taunt III from California, Margaret Tilbury, and our former Zodiac expert Carlie Trueman, now a law student. Twenty-one delegates held a vote.

Moore circulated a paper on "Organization," making reference to patterns of "ecological organization," diversity, interdependence, and specialization. Don White proposed that "Greenpeace International should be *communicative*, not directive," meaning there should be no central Greenpeace authority, and every local organization should be independent. Margaret Tilbury from Portland objected, saying the Greenpeace Foundation in Canada remained the rightful centre of policy and decision-making. "If that changes," she said, "we need a strong international office and each office must surrender some autonomy." Seattle and Toronto agreed with Tilbury. The San Francisco group felt torn: they wanted independence from Canada, but they wanted control in the US.

Gannon pointed out what we all knew but had not said: the name Greenpeace had tremendous social, political, and financial value. Anyone could start his or her own environmental group. Such groups sprang up everywhere. "But if you call yourself *Greenpeace*," said Gannon, "you're attaching yourself onto something with a history. That history includes an investment of time, energy, vision, and money." Thus, the fundamental political dialectic of this gathering — local autonomy versus coordinating authority — consumed everyone's attention, with the exception of nine-month-old Marissa, Rod and Bree's baby, who slept at our feet under Gannon's antique dining room table.

"International isn't the right word," I argued. "Global is a better word. I don't think an ecology organization wants to organize itself along geopolitical boundaries. This would be a mistake, or at least a missed opportunity. We can send another message by the way we organize ourselves. We should observe ecological regions and get creative about how to make that work." My idea may have been politically naïve, but I believed it. "BC environmentalists have more in common with Pacific Coast communities than with Toronto or Ottawa," I suggested. "The way we organize ourselves is going to shape people's thinking for years to come. We should organize around ecology, not established national politics."

"Successful anarchy," said Hunter, leaning against a wall and summing things up with his usual economy.

For the time being, we agreed that we would simply call ourselves Greenpeace. Don White and David McTaggart insisted that all decisions had to be ratified by the local groups. We agreed to this, knowing full well it undermined our authority and presaged trouble down the road. McTaggart moved that we meet in January 1978 to ratify a plan, with two votes from each country. The jockeying for control had begun. McTaggart preferred a votes-per-country format because he felt he could control Europe and arrive with ten or twelve votes. Everyone knew this, and McTaggart's motion was defeated 4-to-ll with 6 abstentions. McTaggart's face never once betrayed concern at the defeat.

We formed an Executive to oversee the structure of Greenpeace, the global organization: Bill Gannon, finance; Cindy Baker, administration; Bob Hunter, media and communications; Patrick Moore, policy; Paul Spong, research; and Robert O. Taunt III, political affiliations.

An advisory board consisted of John Cormack, ships; Carlie Truman, legal; Gary Young, finance; Bobbi Hunter, fundraising; Michael Chechik, film and broadcast productions; and me to coordinate the photography archives and musical events. Margaret Tilbury and Don White headed a committee to draft rules for affiliate offices. Dexter Cate accepted responsibility to oversee the *Ohana Kai*, now an expensive and fast-depreciating asset in San Francisco Bay.

We approved Bill Gannon's accounting system unanimously, which called for 50 percent of all net revenues from each office to go into a "Global Fund," to be administered by the global entity when it emerged. The $1-million consolidated annual Greenpeace revenue was on everyone's mind. Most people knew that this revenue stream would swell dramatically over the next few years. Hawaii reported an $88,000 debt, but projected $250,000 per year in income. The IRS had notified Greenpeace Hawaii that they would be audited. I queried White about Save the Whales Hawaii, and he explained it was a private organization with separate accounting. Gannon agreed to go to Honolulu and account for the estimated $200,000 that had been spent on the *Ohana Kai* voyage.

We had come up with a decent plan to solve our internal conundrum. We had committees to dig into the tough questions. We had a financial system and plan to retire our debts and move forward. The *Rainbow Warrior* was paid for and refurbished. Had we followed through on what we had just agreed to do, the Greenpeace saga might have been spared two years of turmoil. However, once everyone got back home and faced their local factions, the agreement deteriorated as methodically as the hull of the *Ohana Kai*. Self-interest, like rust, never sleeps.

Gannon asked our lawyers to draft affiliation contracts, which the Greenpeace Foundation signed with offices in Los Angeles, Denver, Pennsylvania, and Toronto. However, the larger offices, with more to lose — San Francisco, London, and Paris — stalled. Greenpeace in San Francisco copyrighted the name "Greenpeace USA" and moved toward quasi-independence. McTaggart handed out "Greenpeace Europe" business cards. The carving of the pie had begun.

This failure was our own. We could not blame this on the military-industrial complex or the Trilateral Commission. Our political shortcomings were personal: fear of each other's motives, desire for control, and the sheer ignorance that haunts human enterprise. Virtually everyone involved attempted to rise above his or her own superficial self-interests. Every one of us, to some extent, failed.

Later, in Honolulu, Gannon sifted through stacks of account transfers, odd receipts, and intermittent bank statements to account for the *Ohana Kai* campaign. After a week, he completed a financial statement and balance sheet for the organization. The back-up documents were replete with estimates that he had gleaned from the office workers in Honolulu. Nevertheless, Gannon guided Greenpeace Hawaii through the federal government audit, and they survived the scrutiny unscathed.

The San Francisco office sold the *Ohana Kai* to a crab fisherman, who lived aboard the subchaser in Berkeley. In a storm, the vessel ripped free from its moorings, drifted like a ghost ship, and came to rest in the Emeryville mudflats near the Bay Bridge. There it sat, with whales and rainbows rising out of the mud, until radioman Dick Dillman had the sense to paint out the desecrated icons of the Family of the Sea.

Nevertheless, 1978 would prove to be the most successful year of campaigning yet. The words of Charles Dickens still rang true: The epoch of belief, the epoch of incredulity. We had everything before us, we had nothing before us. The strength of Greenpeace over six years had been in its victories. The American military had abandoned nuclear bomb tests in the granite belly of Amchitka Island. The French had backed down from contaminating the South Pacific with fallout from atmospheric nuclear blasts. The sealing and whaling industries stared now into the face of global public opinion. We felt confident we would achieve a moratorium on pelagic whaling. Paul Watson announced he would go after the renegade pirate whalers. Half-baked plans for supertanker routes along the BC coast had been scrapped and toxic aerial bombardments halted. Now, the *Rainbow Warrior* sat poised to break all Greenpeace records for swift, successful campaigns.

Susi Newborn was right: Greenpeace had a formula that worked. She was also right that the formula could be a liability if we blindly repeated it. The politics of ecology had changed significantly in the last six years. *Staying* effective, and *staying* on the cutting edge of the issues would prove to be the genuine challenge. As our old captain John Cormack said whenever we appeared moderately successful: "Waaall, we'll see how much *stayin' power* ya have."

CHAPTER ELEVEN

LAWYERS OF THE RAINBOW

"Nature is the first ethical teacher of humanity."
— Peter Kropotkin

The days of Greenpeace being run from Vancouver were coming to an end. Politically savvy ecologists in Toronto, Seattle, San Francisco, London, Paris and Hamburg represented the new Greenpeace. Our little tribe in the Shire knew this. We were now the country cousins and already a bit old-fashioned. We each dealt with these developments in our own way. Nevertheless, we agreed that there should be a single Greenpeace entity and that it must adhere to the fundamental values — peace, tolerance, bearing witness, ecology, innovative direct action, non-violence — upon which the movement had been founded and for which we felt responsible.

On Sunday, December 18, 1977, Pat Moore and Eileen Chivers were married in a Whole Earth Church ceremony at Bob and Bobbi Hunter's new rural home east of Vancouver. Snow fell as Bob Hunter delivered ecological nuptials: "We are not separate from the Earth or from each other … There is no greater temple than the Earth itself … we are not just living on or in the world, we *are* the world … a flower is your brother *and* your sister … For *you* I live," and finally, the erstwhile "Zap!" Mel Gregory and the Migrating Whale Medicine Band played, the music tighter than ever. Huge snowflakes drifted through the waning light as we sat before an open fire, told stories, and drank champagne.

The ecology movement had emerged from the underground, academic halls, and beer parlours into the public arena. Factions now debated the presumed correctness of strategies and tactics: animal rights, deep ecology, scientific ecology, social ecology, eco-feminism, and so forth. Ecologists debated the virtues of lobbying, direct action, non-violence, and Edward Abbey's more radical "war" on industrialism. In 1978, all these factions, and more, existed within Greenpeace.

By the year's end, one of our key allies would be murdered. Greenpeace would no longer represent the radicals of the environmental movement as anti-nuclear alliances, Abbey's army of ecotage activists, and ex-Greenpeace militant Paul Watson stretched the boundaries of citizen dissent. Nevertheless, as we fumbled internally with raging egos and lumbering politics, the organization secured its niche in the ecology of ecologists: non-violent, creative, and media savvy direct action. And now, at the West India Dock in London, a crew of inspired environmentalists prepared the *Rainbow Warrior* for a voyage that would change everything.

BEFORE COMPLETION

In January 1978, Greenpeace delegates worldwide returned to Vancouver to resume the talks we had begun in the fall of 1977. Although everyone maintained civility, the competition for slices of the Greenpeace pie seethed behind the hugs and smiles. Vancouver volunteer John Frizell had taken over radio communications during the 1976 whale campaign, served on the Greenpeace Foundation board in 1977, and had become a "coordinator" of the offices in North America. Frizell lived across the street from my flat on First Avenue, where he grew psilosybin mushrooms. He told me, "No one on the board appreciates how much work I've done." This was probably true. Most of the Greenpeace Foundation board members felt that Frizell had undermined the organization by fomenting revolt among the offices, although Frizell claimed he had simply provided access to the many new voices. When he ran for the board in 1978, he was not elected, but this action may have backfired when he became more aggressive about aligning with dissidents. To appease the rebellious factions, and to show good faith, the board named Frizell as a Canadian delegate, along with Moore, at the January meeting. We convened at International House at the University of British Columbia, under towering cottonwood trees.

The formal sessions simply ratified or unravelled deals made in private trysts, often over beer at the pubs or on walks along the blustery winter shoreline of Kitsilano Beach. Hunter met with Tussman and Baker from San Francisco. Moore talked with the Canadian delegates. Other groups worked out political deals that would satisfy all the factions. The Greenpeace Foundation now faced the reality of conveying authority to some new entity, but complex questions remained: How much authority? To whom? When? Under what conditions? Who gets the money? Who assumes the debts? And the big one: Who controls the use of the name?

The returning international delegates had new aspirations and alliances, but the political goals were simple: Tussman, Zimmerman, Baker, White, and others from Greenpeace USA did not want the Greenpeace Foundation in Vancouver to control the name Greenpeace. Conversely, some of us believed that if a single Greenpeace body did not control the name, the enterprise would spin off into fiefdoms: McTaggart's UK Inc., the semi-autonomous Greenpeace Hawaii, and myriad splinter groups including the mysterious huckster still operating in Washington, D.C. Some, who felt disenfranchised, found it expedient to encourage the breakaway factions. Others waited to see which way the wind would blow.

Ultimately, the second global Greenpeace gathering broke into two meetings. The plenary gatherings at UBC addressed politics. Those not captured in the gravity of power-sharing met in cafés and pubs to talk about ecology and future tactics. I found the political meetings almost unbearable but attended, took notes, and ducked out to the far more appealing strategy sessions. Since our agreement from the previous fall had broken down, the Greenpeace Foundation board proposed an interim "International Board" to preside over a process of creating a solution. This amounted to a considerable act of good faith. Pat Moore was the only long-standing campaign veteran appointed. The other delegates were Tussman, Frizell, Bob Taunt, Deborah Jayne, and Greenpeace merchandise coordinator Karol Sinats. The seventh, and final, position on this board remained contentious because the vote could swing the entire organization one way — in favour of a single Greenpeace — or another — in favour of the ostensibly independent offices.

Bob Hunter declared no interest in the seventh position on the interim board, but after long debates without resolution, he offered to resign from the Greenpeace Foundation board and serve as a delegate-at-large for the seventh position. Perhaps naively, Hunter assumed the delegates respected him as a committed, non-partisan, global-thinking environmentalist who would not be swayed by political affiliations. Some of the delegates clearly did; others did not. Tussman and Jaynes opposed Hunter, perhaps because they feared that a bloc comprised of Hunter, Moore, Sinats, and Taunt would control the organization.

Some visiting delegates, understandably, viewed the Greenpeace Foundation as the old guard, out of touch with the "new Greenpeace." This had the effect of frustrating people like Hunter and Moore, who had a decade of environmental research and action behind them. Particularly galling for the Greenpeace Foundation board were attacks for "being in debt," which allegedly proved the Canadians were "disorganized" and "irresponsible." This point annoyed Gannon and Bobbi Hunter, who had spent the last three years managing the financial growth of the organization under enormous pressures.

The Greenpeace Foundation lawyers — Gibbons, Storrow, and Peter Ballem — assured us the Foundation legally owned the rights to the name and history. The new Greenpeace factions, however, did not see it this way. Hunter became so frustrated by what he considered "low-level politics," he convened the Greenpeace Foundation at Bill Gannon's home. "It's kind of hard to give it away when it's being ripped out of our hands," he fumed. Angry with Frizell, whom the board felt had used his delegate position to once again undermine the Greenpeace Foundation, we removed Frizell as a Canadian delegate at the meeting. More significantly, we decided at Gannon's home that if the international delegates rejected Bob Hunter — in our view the person more responsible than anyone for creating the phenomenon they now divvied up, a committed ecologist who had risked his life many times for the cause — then we would not proceed.

From Gannon's kitchen I heard the *clink, clink* of Mel's *I Ching* coins. He ambled into the meeting room, and said, "Before completion. The situation is in transition. Things are being differentiated so each finds its place. It's okay." This was scant comfort but perhaps a fair reading of events.

We returned to the meeting at UBC and proffered once again that Bob Hunter represented the only reasonable choice for the final spot. "Anyone who doubts Bob's impartiality is crazy," said Patrick Moore. When the delegates rejected the proposal, Hunter delivered a short speech in which he chastised all of us, and himself, for allowing our ecology work to "fall victim to petty, Machiavellian politics." No one appeared particularly proud of what we had achieved. "We've got campaigns to run," said Hunter. "Maybe we should all just go home and do the work and see if we come to our senses." The second global Greenpeace meeting was over.

We had no political strategy to pull the organization or the vision together, so the bickering only grew worse. McTaggart had not attended, but we knew that he too had political aspirations within the new Greenpeace. Hunter became so disgusted that he wanted nothing more to do with internal Greenpeace politics. Bobbi Hunter, we soon learned, was pregnant, and the Hunters wanted to focus on their family. However, as the undisputed moral leader, Bob Hunter would soon get drawn back in.

FUN AGAIN

Though clumsy in politics, we remained seasoned campaigners and felt much better when we headed off to Newfoundland to challenge the notorious Seal Protection Act. On February 26, 1978, Fisheries Minister Romeo LeBlanc pushed through a new Order-in-Council, Canada's well-worn tool for declaring laws on short notice, making it a crime to be on the ice floes in the seal nursery without a permit from LeBlanc's department. The regulations stated that "applications" for permits had to be submitted by February 20, a week before the law passed. The Greenpeace lawyers won the opening salvo when they forced the government to waive this unachievable requirement. With Romeo LeBlanc cursing and threatening us from Ottawa, we were back in our comfort zone.

"Seals are vermin," proclaimed Newfoundland Chief Fisheries Officer Alfred Cross. Newfoundland Premier Frank Moore announced in Germany that the killing of pups was "repulsive but necessary for ecological reasons." Patrick Moore slammed the bureaucrats in the media for not having a clue what they were talking about. The quota for 180,000 whitecoat pelts, he insisted, was not based on science.

Greenpeace ran ads in Newfoundland newspapers accounting for the revenue from the harp seal hunt. The government's own Marine Service statistics showed that most of the Newfoundland sealing income, 88 percent, went to the ships, agents, and pelt processors. For two weeks' work, landsmen made about $200 each, welcome winter income for the fishermen, but negligible economic return for the government's expense. The Federal budget to monitor the hunt and enforce the idle diktats from Ottawa came to, we heard through lawyers in Ottawa, $6 million each spring. "Too bad the politicians didn't go for the fake fur factory last year," said Hunter. The plant would have provided some $8 million annual wages for the region, requiring no public investment or enforcement cost.

Craig Van Note, from the Monitor consortium in Washington, D.C., told us, "Keep up the pressure. The boycott in Europe is going to work." In Paris, Brigitte Bardot joined the popular revolt demanding a ban on seal pelts. In Ålesund, Norway, on February 27, when sealing ships attempted to depart, Greenpeace members Elisabeth Rasmussen, Vibeke Arviddson, Rémi Parmentier, and Allan Thornton chained themselves to the propellers for 11 hours before the manacles were cut with a welding torch. In Halifax, Nova Scotia, angry sealers drenched Canadians Dan McDermott and Michael Manolson with a firehose and backed the sealing ship *Martin Karlsen* over a Greenpeace Zodiac. The war of images was on.

One of our lawyers, Peter Ballem, travelled with us to Newfoundland to do battle with the Fisheries mandarins. I went as photographer. Taking a circuitous route, our first stop was in San Francisco, where popular actress Pamela Sue Martin, her colleague Monique van der Ven, political liaison Robert O. Taunt III, and a contingent of American Greenpeacers joined us. We flew to Washington, D.C. and picked up California Democratic Congressman Leo Ryan, Vermont Republican Senator James Jeffords, and Ryan's aide, Jacqueline Speier. Through diplomatic channels, the US legislators had wrested permits from a bitter Romeo LeBlanc who sneered at "American interference" in Canadian affairs.

We stopped for press briefings in Ottawa and Halifax, and pushed on to St. Anthony, Newfoundland, where we settled in at Decker's Boarding House. Twenty-one rugged Royal Canadian Mounted Police bolstered the St. Anthony police force of three. Hunter arrived and joined the journalists at the Vinland Hotel. We learned that our St. Anthony supporter and former guide, Doug Pilgrim, had been ostracized and so badly beaten that he could not walk on his damaged legs for months. The mild-mannered Newfoundlander moved away to avoid further reprisals, perhaps the most tragic unsung Greenpeace hero to date. "To Doug Pilgrim," said Moore, raising his glass in the Vinland lounge.

Understandably, no Newfoundland supporters came forward to join us on the ice floes, but Ma and Pa Decker remained as gracious as ever. They charmed the visiting congressional representatives and actors, who magically transformed before our eyes from Hollywood and Washington celebrities into modest, hard-working, and astoundingly smart campaigners. The actors gave inspired, mind-bombing interviews, then turned into scullery maids and supply officers. The American politicians hauled gear to the helicopters and peeled polite strips off petty fisheries officers who stood in their way. Speier waved the federal permits and charmed the local cops. Pamela Sue Martin and Monique van der Ven entertained us like players from a travelling chautauqua. Martin had a biting sense of humour. "Get your finger off my fortune," she snapped at Ballem when the rugged lawyer attempted to examine her *I Ching* reading. Ecology was fun again.

THE SYCOPHANT

The big fight this year pitted Ballem against Ottawa over permits for the Greenpeace crews. The parley became a slugfest of telexes, phone calls, and meetings in a makeshift office with LeBlanc's commissar, Charles Friend, a bearded, well-fed bureaucrat, who could turn from charming to vicious in an instant. Friend served as "Information and Media Officer," the public relations guy, but his role seemed to encompass permit policy. Ballem and Friend contested every infinitesimal nuance of the laws. Friend insisted that the Americans' permits were good for only one day, although the documents said nothing of the kind. "It's policy," snapped Friend. Ballem, however, possessed a copy of the regulations.

"Why? What policy?" said Ballem, unmoved. "When was this policy established? By whom?"

Strangely, after these red-faced battles, Friend would join us in the pub and laugh about the entire charade. I had never before witnessed such polite delivery of insults. Friend slouched in his chair and chided Moore. "Your family's in logging, isn't it?"

"Yeah," said Moore, "but we wait more than two weeks before we cut our trees down."

Friend raised his glass. "Maybe you should get that Swiss guy to build you a fake wood factory in BC."

The Americans had four permits, so Friend could not stop them from going to the ice floes. On Sunday, March 12, Ryan, Jeffords, Pamela Sue Martin, and Pat Moore flew to the Labrador front with Canadian Press and AP photographers. However, Newfoundland Minister of Rural Development John Lundrigan, wearing a swiler's toque and licence badge, waited on the ice to spring a trap. When the Greenpeace party approached, Lundrigan stepped before the cameras, blood on his cheeks and knife in hand, and claimed to have already killed 100 seals that morning. He scorched Leo Ryan with Newfie indignation. When Ryan said he had come to Newfoundland "to learn the facts," Lundrigan jabbed a blood-caked finger in the towering US Congressman's face. "You should go to the Pribiloff Islands in Alaska and learn the facts. Take a look at your own fishery. You're not *there* because those seals are ugly bastards and nobody gives a damn. If the whitecoats weren't so cute, these outfits," Lundrigan shot a thumb at Moore, "wouldn't get any support. If you represent a typical American attitude, it's no wonder you're in such a bloody mess back home."

He accused Ryan and Jeffords of "cheap political tricks," while he won headlines across Canada and earned voter sympathy in Newfoundland. "He out-mindbombed us," Moore admitted to Hunter back at Decker's.

"In Canada, yeah," said Hunter. "Internationally, it's irrelevant." That night, I talked with my sister, Kaye, at the Rocky Mountain Greenpeace office in Denver. She had gone on a one-hour talk show fielding calls from Texas to Canada. The response had been so overwhelming that the station extended the show for a full five hours. Throughout the week, protestors marched in Denver, San Francisco, New York, Paris, London, and other cities.

"We need to get back on the ice," said Hunter, "and challenge the Seal Protection Act." We would have tested the permit rule, but the pilots could not afford to have their helicopters seized, even if they could later prove the government acted improperly. Charles Friend's tactic in denying us permits was simply to stall, but he squirmed before the incessant questioning of Senator Jeffords, Ryan and our lawyer Ballem. He knew that *they* knew he was on thin ice. Ballem finally wore the system down and scheduled a meeting with Friend to receive our promised permits.

On May 13, Moore, Ballem, and I arrived at Friend's makeshift St. Anthony office. Friend, typically, kept us waiting, then attempted to equivocate and dither, but Ballem demanded the permits. When Friend refused, Ballem asked him "on what authority."

"I'm the spokesman for the ministry."

"And spokesmen decree policy?"

"The meeting's over," sniffed Friend, and ordered us out of the office. None of us moved.

"We're here to receive our permits," Ballem insisted. "We're not leaving." Friend told us to leave or face arrest. Fifteen minutes later, two slightly apologetic RCMP officers arrived and asked us to leave. Ballem told them that he was an officer of the court and that he had a scheduled meeting with the minister's agent, Friend. We refused to leave. Friend stormed into his private office, where we could hear him thunder at one of his underlings. I took photographs. Ballem stepped aside to avoid arrest, the RCMP took Moore and me into custody, and we walked back to the RCMP detachment with our enraged lawyer. There, we met a smiling Hunter with CP photographer Doug Bell. The news and pictures of the bizarre arrest made the wire services within an hour. The ministry charged us with "breech of section 171(1)(c) of the Canadian Criminal Code, causing a disturbance by loitering in a public place, the Fisheries office."

In the Vinland lounge, Ballem, a traditional lawyer who had believed in the sanctity of law, shook his head in dismay. "I've never witnessed anything like this," he said. "The government has mocked the rule of law, to which I've sworn allegiance. I feel like I just woke up."

"Cheer up," Hunter teased him. "We just won." We toasted our good fortune. "When the police state draws a line," said Hunter dryly, "you either cower, or you step over it."

"Well," Ballem mused, "I suppose it isn't against the law to get arrested."

We held a press conference in the Vinland. "Civil rights have been suspended in Newfoundland," Moore ranted to the journalists. "Freedom of the press has been suspended and minor public officials are passing laws in beer parlours."

Ballem, Davie Gibbons in Vancouver, and their colleagues in Toronto and Ottawa besieged Prime Minister Pierre Trudeau with urgent telegrams. Stories appeared in the newspapers, referring to "Gestapo tactics," and "suspension of civil rights." After four days of intense negotiations, media battles, and telegrams arriving from around the world, the federal Liberal government capitulated and issued four Greenpeace permits to visit the ice floes.

We met Charles Friend in the pub to fill out applications and receive the permits. He hated to lose, but shrugged it off. During the conversation Friend groused about how much money we must be making off the publicity. Moore explained that we were all unpaid volunteers. "I won't even have a job when I get back home," Moore said.

"Who will?" said Friend.

THE LIGHT OF DAY

The final arrow in the government's quiver of obfuscation was to issue the Greenpeace permits for a 24-hour period during which a violent storm had been forecast over Labrador. It was a cunning move: if we refused the permits because of weather, we would look foolish. "Screw 'em," said our pilot, "I've got survival gear." Hunter and I ducked into his room at Decker's and tossed the *I Ching* coins. *Dispersion*: Quick and vigorous action dissolves misunderstandings. "I guess it's a go," shrugged Hunter.

At 2:30 p.m. on March 17, we lifted off in the Bell Jetranger helicopter. The intrepid Paul Watson, having launched his elephant campaign, was not with us this spring. No independent media permits had been issued for the day — another clever government tactic — so I went, along with cameraman Steve Bowerman, Taunt, Moore, and Ballem, who continued to negotiate for his own permit. We arrived at Cartwright, on the Labrador coast, at 5:10 p.m. The outpost crawled with RCMP officers, ministry of transport officers, fisheries officers, and chopper pilots with their sleek rigs ringing the compound. A visibly sick RCMP officer showed us to our rooms in the Hudson Bay House. As predicted, the storm raged all night.

At dawn, Ballem woke me singing, "Everything is beautiful, in its own way…" He waved a fistful of telegrams. "Lead editorial in the *Vancouver Sun*," he chirped, "accusing Ottawa of, and I quote, 'bloodying this country's image … for a hunt that brings so little to Canada,' end quote, and gentlemen it's a fine day …"

Indeed, the storm had blown out over the Labrador Sea and sunlight shimmered through the curtains, but the source of Ballem's cheer was that his own permit had been issued in Ottawa. He would go to the ice with us. We had coffee, bread, and cheese in the kitchen. Ballem, the tough rugby-playing lawyer, insisted on an *I Ching* reading of his own and tossed the coins on the table. *Grace*. By contemplating the forms in human society it becomes possible to shape the world. However, there is always a reason for caution. Not all important questions can be decided by simple grace. They may require greater earnestness."

I watched the strapping lawyer choke back tears.

At 8:20 a.m. we departed Cartwright, followed by three RCMP and fisheries helicopters. Within ten minutes, we saw sealing ships nosed into the ice, rivulets of blood streaking the great whiteness, and piles of bloody pelts. At 8:40 a.m. we set down and trekked past carcasses toward the sealers. Even touching a seal could lead to our arrests, so we waited. Moore stopped to debate with swilers and fisheries officers about harp seal data. Swilers hauled seals across the ice followed by wailing mothers. "Grace," nodded Ballem. I wandered off alone, got down on my hands and knees, and stared into the eyes of an infant whitecoat. The seal sniffed me, curious. I took a photograph, sat by the seal, meditated, and could hear the *thwacks* of hakapiks and the cries of seals. Bowerman found me and said, "We're ready."

At 12:15 p.m. Moore moved toward a seal, and announced to a fisheries officer, "I want this *one* pup to live. For three years we've watched the sealers come through here. They leave nothing but carcasses behind. This is a nursery, for God's sake. Just this *one*. For all the people of the world who have demonstrated their opposition to this hunt." Moore climbed on the back of the stunned whitecoat and held on.

The fisheries mandarin flipped through his notebook and demanded that Moore release the seal. The ecologist held fast. The officer asked him a second time, then said, "I ask you one more time to let the seal go." Moore shook his head firmly. "I will not," he said and stared at the sad public servant in his sunglasses, earflaps, and wool pants. Two swilers stood nearby, an older man with a coiled rope and young man, maybe seventeen or eighteen years old, with a hakapik. With little enthusiasm the fisheries officer asked the young swiler, "Do you want to kill this seal?" The young man nodded, but turned his eyes away. I took photographs, Bowerman ran film, and Taunt jotted seriously in his notebook. The fisheries officer read out the violations of the Seal Protection Act and senior RCMP officer Alfred Ollerhead, with a tape recorder dangling from his neck, stepped forward and arrested Moore.

"Kill 'er, b'y," said the elder swiler. *Thwack*. The seal went limp on the ice. The older landsman pulled out a long knife, flipped the whitecoat on its back, slit up the middle of its belly, emptied entrails onto the ice, skinned it, and left the bloody carcass on the white snow.

An hour later, Moore sat in a makeshift jail in Cartwright. Ballem bent over the commanding officer's desk, gracefully but earnestly demanding a phone. By 3:00 p.m., Moore was out of jail and at 4:55 p.m. the helicopters set down at Decker's. A half-dozen grim RCMP officers stood in the welcoming crowd at the icy cove in front of the boarding house. As I stepped out of the helicopter, Hunter's eyes riveted on mine. I nodded. Hunter patted CP photographer Doug Ball on the shoulder. Ball steered me away from the crowd and explained that the RCMP were talking about "collecting evidence." I handed him the film in a canister and met him later at the Vinland, where he had assembled a makeshift darkroom, complete with a vintage 1950s-era AP wire photo transmitter. By 6:30 p.m., pictures of Moore being dragged off the seal pup reached Toronto, on their way to every major news centre in the world.

Hunter phoned the Vinland, concerned that the RCMP would come for the photographs. "Get back here with all the film," he said. "We'll put Peter at the door." At the boarding house, Ma Decker served dinner and Pa Decker watched a hockey game. I asked him which team he was rooting for. "I don't wanna see anybody win," he said. "I wanna see 'em tie."

Two days later, I caught a plane to Halifax, and from there to Montreal. On the Air Canada flight to Montreal, a man across the aisle read the *Globe and Mail* with the picture of Moore and the seal on the front page. I remained in shock, but the picture of the arrest in the newspaper gave me a sense of surreal equanimity. I was too rattled by what I had witnessed to feel satisfied. Influence, I understood, is not about forcing one's will on the world. We could not stop the sealers from slaughtering infant seals or the bureaucrats from dictating duplicitous edicts, but we had forced them to do these things in the light of day.

I asked the man for his newspaper when he finished. I read that seventeen high school students had left Toronto for St. Anthony to protest the hunt. Forty-one members of the US Congress had co-sponsored a resolution urging Canada to end the annual carnage. Labour MP Arthur Latham had introduced a motion in the UK House of Commons to ban all imports of seal products.

Hunter's theory, spoken often in casual meetings as well as in the heat of conflict, maintained that our job was not to resolve the nuances of ecology. Our job was to expose ecology by delivering images to people's minds. "Let the scientists and politicians sort out what to do," Hunter often said. I offered the man across the aisle his newspaper, but he said I could keep it. On the midnight run from Montreal to Vancouver I cut the photograph and stories from the paper, pasted them into my notebook with a glue stick, sipped a Jameson's Irish whiskey, and fell asleep somewhere over Lake Winnipeg.

THE NEW GREENPEACE

In Europe, along the Seine, the Elbe, and the Thames rivers, ecology activism was about to take one of John Platt's self-structuring hierarchical leaps. In Germany, the ecologists of the 1970s tended to be well-informed, politically smart, and highly organized. Northern Germany, one of the most heavily polluted regions on the planet, faced deforestation, pesticide runoff, and acid rain that had reached Scandinavia and sparked the 1972 Stockholm conference. By 1978, in the village of Bielefeld, near the German-Dutch border, young ecology activists gathered regularly in a popular intellectual beer hall. Among them were Monika Griefahn, Petra Kelly, and a group called Grüne Tätigkeitszukunft, "Green Action Future." Kelly and her friends made alliances with populist, right-wing ecologists and formed Die Grünen, which became the highly successful German Green Party, while Monika Griefahn joined forces with a young fisherman and dockworker from Hamburg, Harald Zindler, to protest nuclear power risks. They would later meet educator Gerhard Wallmeyer and communications professional Christian Krüger in Hamburg and form the core of Greenpeace Germany.

In Paris, Brice Lalonde forged alliances with the French labour-ecology coalition l'Alternative Rouge et Vert, the electoral Mouvement d'écologie Politique, and other pacifists, anti-nuclear groups, and the radical ecologists at Les Amis de la Terre and Greenpeace. Lalonde entered the French general election with a coalition called Collectif écologie 78. Rémi Parmentier and David McTaggart supported Lalonde but remained aloof from the partisan political groups. Parmentier's philosophy was: "Don't argue with the other ecology groups, in public or in private. Preach with example." Parmentier had a mission and he infected his friends with enthusiasm: "Go out there and bear witness."

Four hundred miles to the west, on the Thames, the trawler *Sir William Hardy* had been transformed into the *Rainbow Warrior*, fitted for its first ecological campaign, and moved into the centre of London. The Kwakiutl orca totem from the *Phyllis Cormack* sail had been painted on the smokestack. In January 1978, Susi Newborn, Denise Bell, Charles Hutchinson, and Allan Thornton had delivered a bank draft for £32,500 to the UK Department of Trade on Parliament Street in London, which, along with the £4,372 deposit, completed the purchase of the ship, now owned by Greenpeace UK Ltd. of 47 Whitehall Street.

On May 2, 1978, Bob Hunter flew to Heathrow Airport and raced into London for the launch. Meanwhile, due to the tides, the ship departed without him. From the empty dockside, he urged a taxi east along the river until he passed the ship. He raced for a small bridge, stood out over the river, and as the *Rainbow Warrior* passed under, he leapt onto the foredeck to be greeted by Susi Newborn and his old colleague, cameraman Fred Easton. They slid down the Thames, into the North Sea.

"Make a note of everything that happens," Hunter advised Newborn. "This is history in the making." Hunter urged her to accept the role of "chronicler" on the *Rainbow Warrior*. Newborn took the job seriously. Bell and Hutchinson called her the "spiritual advisor."

However, the organizers in Europe wanted to shed what they called the "amateur image" of the early Greenpeace actions. Hunter shrugged and rooted them on. The balance of mystics and mechanics had shifted toward seasoned sailors who could run an ecology ship like a precision naval vessel. The London office had drafted Nick Hill, former skipper on a North Sea seismic ship; Peter Bouquet, a mate off a tanker; Alastair Hamilton, with a master's ticket; experienced chief mate Jon Castle; and cameraman and mechanic Tony Marriner. Nurse Sally Austin left her Devon country home to join the crew as medic. Vegetarian Hilari Anderson from New Zealand served as cook. Experienced engineers came aboard to assist Athel von Koettlitz. Newborn, Bell, Hutchinson, and Thornton formed the UK core of the crew, and Parmentier joined them from Paris. Fred Easton had arrived from Vancouver with his camera and three years of experience as a Zodiac cinematographer. David McTaggart joined the ship the day it departed London. The crew of twenty-four represented Holland, France, England, Scotland, South Africa, Switzerland, New Zealand, Australia, the USA, and Canada.

Crowds welcomed the ecologists in Amsterdam, Copenhagen, and Hamburg, as the crew showed films from earlier Greenpeace missions. In Hamburg, local environmentalists organized a welcoming party, lowered a piano onto the deck, rigged spotlights on the mast, and staged a concert by a popular German jazz band. Harald Zindler and the Elbe fishermen fighting river pollution mingled among the visitors on the ship. Hunter toasted their success and flew back to Vancouver.

The *Rainbow Warrior* then crossed the North Sea to the site of a proposed 1400-megawatt nuclear reactor at Torness, Scotland. The crew joined an anti-nuclear rally of 3,000 citizens in Dunbar, where McTaggart took the microphone and introduced himself as the "Director of Greenpeace Europe" — a declaration that took Newborn and the others by surprise. It was the first public political speech McTaggart had ever given. He had observed Lalonde, René Dumont, Hunter, Newborn, and others move crowds. McTaggart had always been a private person, but he was smart and charismatic. He could convince a room of investors to part with their money, he could run a company and skipper a boat crew, and he had not once flinched under the treacheries and truncheons of the French Navy, but addressing the masses was new to him. He spoke to the crowd about their right to protect their environment from radiation. The denizens of Dunbar roared approval. "You have the power," he cried. They roared again. McTaggart quickly got the hang of public speaking.

Like the old Greenpeace, the new version faced conflicts of style. "I wish he'd shut his gob," Newborn complained of McTaggart's speech. The hard core smoked hash in their cabins and consulted the *I Ching*, the maritime professionals ran the ship, and more than a few crossed this cultural boundary travelling both directions.

ICELAND: ABSOLUTE NONSENSE

The *Rainbow Warrior* pushed north to its birthplace at Aberdeen, then rounded Kinnaird's Head, and put into Lerwick, Shetland Islands. The crew spent a day manoeuvring the Zodiacs and new Avon inflatables that featured steering wheels and windscreens. On June 1, they headed northwest to confront the Icelandic whalers. In 1972, Iceland had supported the UN whaling moratorium in Stockholm but opposed the same moratorium two weeks later at the IWC meeting. They still hunted the decimated fin whales, protected in every other ocean in the world. Icelandic communities, like the swilers of Newfoundland, defended their cultural autonomy and maritime resources. Icelandic gunboats had recently cut British trawl lines and faced down the British Navy over cod and herring stocks. The *Rainbow Warrior* crew did not expect a warm welcome, even though Greenpeace enjoyed support in Reykjavik, including a Greenpeace group that had endured since Paul and Linda Spong had visited three years earlier.

In Reykjavik, Greenpeace diplomats from London and Paris met with Iceland's IWC delegate Kristján Loftsson. Loftsson offered no hope that Iceland would reconsider its position on whaling, not surprising, given that Loftsson owned Iceland's only whaling company, Hvalur Ltd. In 1915, the Icelandic parliament had banned whaling until Loftsson's company began operations in 1948. Four 600-ton harpoon ships supplied a shore station in Hvalfjördur (Whale fjord), north of Reykjavik. Loftsson attributed the "great over-harvesting" of whales to "the mistakes others made 70 years ago." He denied that Iceland had participated in the decimation of North Atlantic whale species, along with Norway, the US, and Canada. In 1978, the Icelandic and Norwegian fleets expected to kill 2,500 whales in the North Sea. Spanish and pirate whalers, operating outside IWC scrutiny, also plied these seas.

The *Rainbow Warrior* waited outside Hvalfjördur and followed the whaling ships that bolted south to the Reykjanes Ridge and west along the Greenland-Iceland Rise, where migrating fin whales became easy targets. Each of the four whaling ships harpooned three whales per trip, lashed them down, and steamed back into the Hvalfjördur plant, where the meat was frozen for export to Japan. The *Rainbow Warrior*, at 10 knots, could not keep pace with the speedy whaling ships, but by monitoring radio transmissions, the crew intercepted the *Hvalur 9* over a pod of fin whales.

Charles Hutchinson crashed over 10-foot swells in an Avon with cameraman Fred Easton, followed by a second Avon piloted by Chris Robinson, with Allan Thornton and photographer Jean-Paul Ferrero. For six hours, in nearly impossible conditions, the ecologists frustrated the whalers until the *Hvalur 9* returned ashore unburdened by fin whales. The *Rainbow Warrior* put into Reykjavik with film and photographs, then raced back out to the seamounts.

For a month under the Arctic summer sun, the *Rainbow Warrior* disrupted and exposed the Icelandic whaling industry. The story of declining fin whale stocks appeared in Reykjavik newspapers. Greenpeace promoted the IWC moratorium and talked about the intelligence and culture of whales, which Loftsson called "absolute nonsense." Hvalur Ltd. sought a court injunction against the *Rainbow Warrior*, but the Icelandic gunships that had defended the cod fishery from the British stayed in port. The *Rainbow Warrior's* first campaign proved a triumph.

At the end of June, as the whale campaign wound down, Greenpeace nuclear researcher Peter Wilkinson joined the crew in Reykjavik. He told Newborn, new skipper Peter Bouquet, and Chief Mate Jon Castle about the British dumping of radioactive waste into an ocean trench 1,500 miles to the south. The clandestine dumping had been underway for a decade and would resume in July. The *Rainbow Warrior* took its next assignment. The crew put into Dublin for fuel, and then pushed south. The ecology ship would soon blow the lid off one of Britain's nastiest little secrets.

THE GEM

Months earlier, Peter Wilkinson had been poking through shipping records and discovered that the United Kingdom, Belgium, Switzerland, and the Netherlands pooled nuclear waste and dumped it over the edge of the continental shelf, 400 miles west of Cabo de Finisterra, the "end of the earth," in northern Spain. In 1972, the London Dumping Convention had banned the discarding of so-called "high-level" radioactive wastes at sea. The UK Atomic Energy Authority (UKAEA) claimed the "low-level" waste was "general trash and residues from the nuclear industry, medical therapy, research, etcetera." The "etcetera" would prove the interesting part. No one outside the industry had monitored the deep-sea dumping program. Wilkinson suspected that while the European nuclear powers claimed to be safe and responsible, they systematically contaminated the North Atlantic seabed with the world's most toxic isotopes, plutonium, and other elements.

For years, a ship called the MV *Topaz* had been the nuclear garbage scow, but several 600-pound drums of radioactive waste had broken apart and contaminated the ship. The replacement, a 300-foot freighter, *Gem,* arrived at the port of Sharpness in the Bristol Channel on July 10, 1978, bound for the coast of Spain on a covert assignment.

On July 11 the *Rainbow Warrior* slipped south past Wicklow Head with Peter Bouquet at the helm. Jon Castle studied charts. Wilkinson and Newborn discussed strategies. Tony Marriner prepared the Avons and Zodiacs, Sally Austin restored her medical supplies, and Fred Easton cleaned his camera gear. They passed south of Sharpness and tucked into Falmouth Bay. They had learned that the *Gem* could cruise at 12 knots, so they knew they would lose 50 miles per day to the faster *Gem* at sea on their way to the dumpsite. They now had a 200-mile lead and planned to depart the same day the *Gem* departed Sharpness.

Newborn and Denise Bell returned to London to shore up the busy office. Easton, Thornton, and Marriner drove north to Sharpness, where the *Gem* sat in port. Anti-nuclear groups had demonstrated a week earlier, and the news media had been around the dock, so the Greenpeace trio posed as a news team and filmed workers loading drums of nuclear waste. A friendly Customs inspector alerted them that "two special drums" were on their way. On July 13 a flatbed lorry arrived with two six-foot diameter, seven-metric ton yellow drums labelled: RADIOACTIVE WASTE and UKAEA HARWELL, indicating that the drums had passed through the central UK nuclear waste disposal facility. It would later be revealed that this was not true.

Near the dock, Easton met an artist who made a living selling his sketches of ships to sailors. The artist introduced Easton and Marriner to the Scottish skipper of the *Gem*, Captain McKay. The captain, a veteran of thirty-nine nuclear dumping missions, invited them on board. Easton asked him what was in the large, yellow drums. Without hesitation, McKay told them, "The big ones contain spent nuclear fuel rods from nuclear submarines." The three Greenpeacers choked back gasps.

When the *Gem* departed Sharpness, the Greenpeacers raced back to Falmouth, and the *Rainbow Warrior* set out for the dump site. The *Gem* passed them during the night of July 14. The next day, they came upon the *Gem* at the dump site, creeping along at two knots. The big yellow drums were gone. Deck crews hoisted pairs of smaller black drums onto a platform, rolled them out over the water, and dropped them into the ocean. Easton could see lids bursting off when barrels hit the water. Every few minutes, more drums dropped into the sea and disappeared below. Pete Bouquet radioed the *Gem*, requesting they suspend the dumping, and requesting that Greenpeace members be allowed aboard to explain their concerns. Captain McKay refused. Marriner's team launched four Greenpeace Zodiacs and positioned them under the dumping platform, where protestors spoke with deckhands on the *Gem*. Fred Easton filmed from the bridge of the *Rainbow Warrior*. A 600-pound, concrete-lined drum rolled off the platform onto the Zodiac piloted by Athel von Koettlitz. The nuclear waste drum destroyed the outboard engine and wooden transom, burst open one side of the inflated Zodiac, and sent von Koettlitz sprawling, clinging to the dinghy.

Easton, Tony Marriner and Jean-Paul Ferrero captured the sequence on film and in photographs. In London, the pictures stunned journalists, and the subsequent stories aroused the public. The UKAEA sent the head of the Harwell waste facility, Dr. John Lewis, to London for a press conference. Confronted with the evidence, Dr. Lewis admitted that the mysterious large yellow containers had not passed through inspection at Harwell but had been shipped to Sharpness directly from the navy. Easton debated the UKAEA scientist on the BBC, and Dr. Lewis admitted, plutonium was present in the so-called "low level" waste. Each year, approximately 80 kilograms of plutonium-239 had been dropped into the Atlantic trench. Lewis claimed that the sea would disperse the plutonium and talked of minute "nanocuries" of radiation, but the lid was off the secret. In a single day, with a few cameras, the *Rainbow Warrior* had opened a new era of scrutiny for the European nuclear industry.

As the media in London focused on nuclear dumping, the *Rainbow Warrior* launched its next mission in the Bay of Biscay, where five harpoon ships out of La Coruña hunted whales in open defiance of IWC regulations. Spain did not belong to the IWC, and the Spanish Marine Institute had revealed to Greenpeace that the brigand whalers took endangered species like humpbacks and sold the meat to Japan in violation of Commission rules. Whaling company owner Júan Masso filed for an injunction to prohibit the *Rainbow Warrior* from interfering with his ships. For several days in August, however, Greenpeace inflatables blockaded the harpooners.

Then, Spanish Navy frigates arrived, slashed ominously across the bow of the *Rainbow Warrior*, and ordered the Greenpeace crews to desist. Greenpeace ignored them, and the majority of La Coruña citizens supported the whale-savers. Newspapers and television stories in Spain created a public outcry that Spain would tarnish its name by disregarding international protocol. Nevertheless, Masso received his injunction and the Spanish Navy ordered the Greenpeace ship into the military harbour. Naval officers insisted that Bouquet tie up at the navy dock, but the Greenpeace skipper stalled and remained anchored in the harbour. When the military police went ashore that night to receive instructions, Bouquet and the crew turned off the lights, lifted anchor, slipped quietly out of La Coruña harbour, and entered French territorial water before the Spanish Navy caught them.

In September, the *Rainbow Warrior* returned to London after four months at sea. The crew had completed the most comprehensive Greenpeace mission ever, touring northern Europe and exposing nuclear power risks in Scotland, Icelandic and Spanish whaling, and Britain's nuclear misdeeds. They had literally saved scores of whales, and their speed and efficiency set a new standard. Despite these achievements, the *Rainbow Warrior* crew hardly had time to recover and visit their families before they pushed north to confront the proposed British cull of 30,000 gray seals on the Orkney Islands. The seal hunt represented a desperate attempt by the British Ministry of Fisheries to salvage depleted fish stocks and blame seals for decades of poor resource management.

Meanwhile, in the Pacific, the 145-foot *Peacock* sailed out of Los Angeles under the Greenpeace banner and chased the Soviet whalers from Baja to Midway. In Vancouver, we cheered as the dream of an Eco Navy came true.

NO NUKES

When Easton returned and revealed the full scope of the *Rainbow Warrior's* campaign, my first impulse was to fly to Europe and get on the new Greenpeace ship. But we had work to do at home and very little of it involved ships. Ecology had come full circle in the last decade, back to nuclear waste, uranium mining, and nuclear weapons. But our circumstances had changed: Greenpeace now had clout.

On April 17, 1978, *US News & World Report*, a conservative US business weekly, ran a four-page spread, "Preserving Wildlife, A Worldwide Struggle," with photographs of polar bears, elephants, tigers, orangutans, whales, and bald eagles. The article served notice that economic conservatives could be ecologists too. The lead photograph was the now-familiar picture of Moore being arrested with a seal pup on the Labrador ice.

Ironically, our promotion of ecology had not been an exercise to gain political power or economic muscle. It had been an exercise to engage the collective human mythology about who we are. Greenpeace had helped link disarmament to ecology, link ecology to the spiritual, and link the spiritual to action. Its purpose, at least up to this point, had been to assist in a great awakening about the world's story. For how long Greenpeace would play this role, or how that role might change, we didn't know.

In any case, the world had embraced ecology. Schoolchildren wanted to grow up and be marine biologists. Ecology was cool. Local battles were virtually infinite in number and sometimes infinitesimal in size. In 1978, a tiny endangered fish, the snail darter, halted the opening of the Tellico dam on the Little Tennessee River when the US Supreme Court upheld the Endangered Species Act. Tennessee business leaders fought back to exempt the dam on economic grounds, casting a new social dialectic. Clearly, ecology had to negotiate with economy, and a delicate line had to be drawn between nature and human enterprise, from Love Canal to the Aral Sea.

In North America, ecology and economy clashed most fiercely in the nuclear industry. In 1978, our new friend Leo Ryan had completed an exhaustive study of nuclear power costs for the US House of Representatives. His report documented safety failures, cost overruns, and veiled government subsidies. Residential customers of US private utilities now paid up to 71 percent of their energy costs for delivery from centralized generators. Only three states — New Mexico, Nevada, and Washington — had agreed to accept nuclear waste, while costs for waste disposal soared. Nuclear power promoters had once promised power "too-cheap-to-meter," but the experts continually revised the cost of nuclear power upward, even before considering accidents and decommission costs. Insuring the plants became too risky for private companies, so US taxpayers provided $560 million to insure *each* US plant. However, industry data showed a meltdown could result in thousands of deaths and billions of dollars in damages. By 1978, practically every schoolchild knew that plutonium was an extreme carcinogen and had a half-life of 24,000 years. The nuclear industry played a risky game with public health.

By 1974, the United States had 236 reactors operating or planned, but as risks and costs soared, utility companies cancelled scores of orders. After several nuclear boondoggles were exposed, some citizens had revolted. In 1974, at a proposed reactor site near his farm in Montague, Massachusetts, farmer Sam Lovejoy toppled a utility tower. He then walked into the local police station and turned himself in, and the American anti-nuclear movement swelled.

On August 1, 1976, New Hampshire citizens occupied a proposed reactor site on a delicate tidal estuary. The citizens called themselves the Clamshell Alliance. Eighteen were arrested. The next spring, 2,000 people occupied the site and a thousand were arrested and held in five National Guard armouries. This prototype No Nukes group was replicated by the Palmetto Alliance in Barnwell, South Carolina; the Crabshell Alliance in Seattle; the Abalone Alliance in California; the Trojan Decommissioning Alliance in Oregon, and countless others. These groups were intentionally "leaderless." Whereas Greenpeace evolved into an organization throughout the 1970s, the No Nukes movement remained unambiguously decentralized. The alliances included small neighbourhood squads, called "affinity groups," trained in non-violent direct action. Every affinity group had its own spokesperson. Activist concert promoter Tom Campbell's Pacific Alliance production team — which had produced our Jerry Garcia concert — fueled a great deal of this public activity through benefits with The Eagles, Linda Ronstadt, Jackson Browne, Jessie Colin Young, Bonnie Raitt, Danny O'Keefe, Graham Nash, and other musicians.

The Greenpeace Foundation, with its own disarmament pedigree, was cautious about horning in on the No Nukes movement, but we supported the anti-nuclear alliances with resources, volunteers, and sometimes media presence. In the *Greenpeace Chronicles*, now a monthly newspaper going to 50,000 North American environmentalists, we published global No Nukes reports and local contacts. And a year earlier, in 1977, John

Bennett, Doug Saunders and Rick Curry from Greenpeace Toronto had paddled ashore from Lake Huron, wandered through the Douglas Point nuclear plant in Ontario, and placed Greenpeace stickers in supposedly secure areas of the plant to expose the lax security. Four months later, they struck again at a proposed Ontario Hydro reactor site, where a dozen Greenpeacers were arrested.

In my hometown of Denver, my sister, Kaye, and brother, Bruce, had opened the Rocky Mountain Greenpeace office in 1978 and joined a group called the Rocky Flats Truth Force and the Native American Black Hills Alliance in an attempt to shut down the Rocky Flats nuclear bomb trigger plant west of Denver. Radioactive waste from the plant had polluted local water and citizens had blockaded the rail tracks into the weapons facility. At a rally, nineteen-year-old Anishinabe leader Winona LaDuke, from the White Earth Reservation in Minnesota, delivered a moving speech. On May 5, 1978, police arrested thirty-five protestors including Daniel Ellsberg and three Michigan Greenpeacers.

On the West Coast, I accompanied Walrus, Linda Spong, Bill Gannon, and Eileen Moore to the Trident Nuclear Submarine Base in Bangor, Washington. In another typical shift of partners, Bill and Mary Gannon had separated and Mary had moved in with publisher Peter Speck. Paul and Linda Spong had separated, Paul had taken up with Nancy Jack in Honolulu, and Linda with Bill Gannon. Also typically, the ex-couples remained friends and working colleagues. Eight-year-old Yasha Spong and Gannon's daughters Maureen and Patrice joined us on our excursion to Bangor.

The arrival of first-strike nuclear submarines rendered Puget Sound a nuclear target. Five thousand people assembled at Ground Zero to protest. At 6:00 a.m. on Monday, May 22, 290 people went over the US Navy perimeter fence and occupied the grounds. Walrus led a group up a small hill where they unfurled the UN flag. I carried my press pass over the fence, flashed it to the military police, and avoided arrest. Schoolbuses carried away cheering detainees and the photographs went out on the wire services.

Then, a disturbing story in The *Washington Post* seemed to validate the anti-nuclear movement. Twenty-four years after the thermonuclear blast on Bikini Island, eighty-two inhabitants of Rongelap — 40 percent of the population — had developed thyroid cancer. Among twenty-one children who were under twelve at the time of the blast, nineteen had cancer. Two decades after the Bravo blast, strontium-90 and plutonium persisted in the Islanders' bodies and still devoured living flesh.

CHRONICLES

By May of 1978, I devoted most of my time to our newspaper, the *Greenpeace Chronicles*. We published stories about Antarctic ecology, Australian uranium mining, and the American Indian "Longest Walk" to Washington, D.C. Hunter began a series of essays on environmental policy for the coming decade. Moore wrote a humorous column under the *nom de plume* "Earnest Greenlaw," Ferlinghetti and Ginsberg submitted relevant poetry, and distinguished ecologists and writers Barry Commoner and Helen Caldicott contributed essays. Ron Cobb donated political cartoons. Dispatches and letters arrived from all over the world.

New Zealand claimed the first nationally elected Green candidates that summer. The European Green Parties commanded between 5 percent and 10 percent of the popular vote, and gained strength in the wake of ecological disasters — an explosion at a propane plant in Tarragona, Spain, and the 68-million gallon *Amoco Cadiz* oil spill off the coast of France. It seemed that ecology disasters did more to fuel the public ire than the environmental groups. In New York, the Department of Health declared the Love Canal area a threat to human health, and in August they closed the local school.

Meanwhile, Nick Carter, a quiet, inconspicuous observer at the International Whaling Commission, had documented renegade whaling conducted by Japan from non-IWC countries like Spain, Portugal, Chile, Peru, Taiwan, South Africa, and Korea. At the IWC meeting in 1978, the French delegation revealed Carter's findings. The walls of public scrutiny closed in around the whaling countries. Within the Greenpeace extended family, creative new tactics sprung up unannounced. When Japanese Prime Minister Fukata visited Chicago in May, ex-Navy sailor Joe Healy scaled the Sears Tower at 2:00 a.m. and hung a "Green Peace" banner — written in English, Japanese, and Russian — urging an end to whaling. He had conceived and financed the protest on his own. His action was the sort of spontaneous social theatre that had made Greenpeace work all along. We printed Healy's story in our June 1978 *Greenpeace Chronicles*.

In a later issue, Hunter wrote: "With the *appearance* of so much going on in the name of 'saving the environment,' how is the danger of lulling the public at large back to sleep to be overcome? ... There are good people among all the environmental groups — Sierra Club, Friends of the Earth, Fund for Animals, World Wildlife Fund, and the ubiquitous Greenpeace Foundation — doing their very best to counter the tremendously destructive tide of industrialism and its impact on nature. And they — we — are getting better all the time at getting our message across." But Hunter longed for this era to be "a time of fundamental re-thinking ... [not] merely a time of desperate crying out." He voiced concern about the day when "suddenly, instead of being able to afford the luxury of worrying about other endangered species, the folks in the big cities will be scrambling to stay alive themselves. This is going to make one hell of a difference for the environmental movement."

At the Port Moody Pub near his home in Anmore, Hunter told me: "The biggest threat to the environment now might be that the environmental movement becomes another NGO, hawking statistics and special interests." Fundamental to our understanding of ecology — which Hunter and I shared with most of our compatriots — was the belief that there existed laws more fundamental than human law. The Declaration of Interdependence was nature's declaration, not ours. We carried the UN flag, but more importantly the Earth's own flag. We believed that Greenpeace spoke for the Earth. The whale campaign was more of an *alliance* with the whales than a human political movement, although we were cautious about saying such things in public. History showed that the powerful did not relinquish power willingly, and rarely peacefully. Ecology became popular, but it seemed that "biocracy" was a dream as idealistic as democracy had once been.

WORLD RECORD

The clash of the status quo paradigm with the new era of ecology went on full display that summer of 1978 in the quiet town of Corner Brook,

Newfoundland, where Moore, Ballem, and I faced criminal charges for our alleged misdeeds during the spring seal campaign. Moore and I had been indicted for loitering in the Department of Fisheries office. Moore had been charged with violating the Seal Protection Act, and our lawyer Peter Ballem had been charged with "aiding and abetting" Moore in his alleged crime on the ice. This apparent attempt to intimidate our lawyer infuriated the BC Law Society. Greenpeace stalwart Davie Gibbons led the defence team that included his fiancé, Janice Dillon, from Ottawa, colleague Tom Heintzman from Toronto, and Randy Earl from Newfoundland. The fun started right away when Newfoundland Law Society boss Bob Wells denied our lawyers the right to practise in Newfoundland. Terse telegrams from the BC and Ontario Law Societies, copied to Pierre Trudeau, removed the impasse and we proceeded to argue the case.

Each morning in Corner Brook, Moore, Gibbons, Dillon, Heintzman, and I had a pleasant breakfast in the Glynmill Inn, an English Tudor hotel, with swans outside in the lake. The waitress, Irene, would arrive with the coffee pot and ask, "Cap a'caphy?" She gleefully accepted a seal pin, and we picked up the Newfie dialect.

At breakfast the first morning, Gibbons explained the loitering case: "You see, Section 171(1)(c) of the Criminal Code of Canada states that anyone who loiters in a public place and in any way obstructs persons who are there is guilty of an offence."

"So are we going to do jail time, Davie?" asked Moore.

"Well, the thing is," said Gibbons, "if Charles Friend had the right to order you out, it's not a public place, is it? It's a private place. You can't technically loiter in a private place. You can trespass, but you can't loiter."

"Well, we had an appointment," said Moore.

"Exactly," said Gibbons. "So you weren't trespassing either. These guys are sweatin' bullets having to argue this case."

"Don't win it too fast," Moore said.

"Oh, no, we have to go through their whole case," said Janice Dillon, who did the tough legal work of digging into the laws and precedents for the trial. Winning the case was not the point of our mission. The trivial charges reflected vital principles. We were spending our supporters' money on these pleasant breakfasts and felt duty bound to make it count. The trial provided an opportunity to express our ideas and expose the Seal Protection Act as an abuse of power. The trial was a campaign.

Before magnanimous Judge Gordon Seabright, the Crown called Charles Friend as its first witness. He identified himself as a "public relations officer," and said he was "just following orders," and "trying to help Greenpeace." Under cross-examination by Gibbons, he revealed that his responsibilities in Newfoundland were to "handle the news media."

"Do you have the authority to issue permits, or to set or interpret fisheries policy?" asked Gibbons.

"No."

"From where do you derive your authority to demand that citizens of Canada remove themselves from a fisheries office?"

"I was busy," said the rattled p.r. man.

Judge Seabright broke in softly: "You are skirting the issue, Mr. Friend."

"I'm a servant of the department. I assume I have some authority."

"You can't assume that, sir," said the judge.

When Moore, Ballem, and I took the stand, we told our stories and were cross-examined by prosecutor Gerard Martin. Ballem and I had kept extensive notes in our journals of every encounter with the government officials. Ballem had written out an agenda for the meeting with Friend. These notes helped our case, as we supplied details of events, which the bureaucrats could not match. When prosecutor Martin repeatedly interrupted Moore, Judge Seabright admonished him, allowing Moore to describe the pattern of obfuscation and avoidance that we faced in St. Anthony.

Perhaps the climax of the first trial was on day two, when Gibbons told the court: "Your Honour, ten minutes elapsed from the time Mr. Friend left the room, and before the RCMP arrived. The accused hardly had time to work up a good loiter. We've done some research and, if I may, I'd like to point out that if my clients are convicted, this will be a world's record, the shortest loiter ever recorded in the history of British or Canadian jurisprudence."

The defence table cracked up, the prosecutors bristled, journalists scribbled in their notebooks, and even Judge Seabright could not hide his mirth. In a more solemn moment, Gibbons pointed out that Charles Friend had "set up the accused. He invited them into his office, refused to meet with them, left, and then had them arrested." The next morning, July 14, Judge Seabright delivered his ruling: "I find the evidence before me no proof of either loitering or obstruction, and therefore I dismiss this case."

"There goes our world record," said Moore.

NEVER ON SUNDAY

In the break between trials we packed a lunch and drove north to the Gros Morne cliffs. What had been a frozen, hostile coastline in March was now a wonderland of wildflowers and green hillsides overlooking blue Bonne Bay. The granite cliffs, previously covered in ice, now glistened with feldspar crystals and bright orange lichen. We ate lunch among the buttercups and bellflowers, listened to invisible warblers, and watched thick-billed puffins on the cliffs over the bay. Dillon and Gibbons entertained us with bizarre courtroom tales. While researching our case, Dillon had discovered a section in the Revised Statutes of Newfoundland, Section 15, Chapter 347 of the Seal Fisheries Act: it was against the law to kill seals on Sunday. "Did any of those guys ever kill seals on Sunday?" she asked Moore.

"Sure. They killed seals every day." Moore thought about it. "They killed seals on Sunday, March 12, the first day we were on the ice with Leo Ryan and Pamela. In fact, John Lundrigan, the Newfie cabinet minister, killed seals that day. He was out there getting his mug in front of the cameras and telling how he had just killed 100 seals. He had blood all over him. There are photographs. Doug Ball at CP has 'em."

The lawyers looked at each other. Dillon buried her eyes in the palms of her hands, shaking her head in disbelief. Moore had a wide grin on his face. "Lawyers of the Rainbow," he said. We walked along the bluff and saw the white mist from the breaths of a pod of whales about a mile out in the Gulf of St. Lawrence. They could have been humpbacks or even rare blue whales on their summer Arctic feeding tour. We watched in silence as the whales moved south toward Cabot Strait and the open Atlantic.

That evening, Moore and I went out to a pub in Corner Brook, where we met members of Codpeace, a group that had formed three years earlier to poke fun at Greenpeace. We bought them beer, listened to their Greenpeace satire, and told them about our trial. They invited us back to a private home, where we drank Newfoundland screech rum while they performed bits of their Brigitte Bardot routine and gave us a Codpeace poster. I gave one of the young men my Greenpeace pin and for one evening there was a heartfelt détente.

On Monday morning, Moore skipped breakfast, walked to the magistrate's office with our Newfoundland lawyer Randy Earl, and swore out charges against Progressive Conservative member of the Newfoundland legislature for Grand Falls, John Lundrigan, and Captain Morrissey Johnson, skipper of the vessel *Lady Johnson*, for sealing on Sunday. "Wait'll Leo Ryan hears about this," Moore said when we met him in the courtroom.

The new prosecutor, Clyde Wells, was the son of Bob Wells, who had attempted to deny Gibbons and our BC lawyers the right to practise in Newfoundland. For the second trial, on charges that Moore and Ballem had violated the Seal Protection Act, the Newfoundland Law Society had insisted that Gibbons could not act. Wells sat resolutely at the Crown table as we waited for the judge. "Going to send me back to BC, eh Clyde?" said Gibbons.

The stiff prosecutor, caught off guard, did his best to make a joke of it. "On your way, boy," he said, waving with the back of his hand.

Judge Seabright entered, not in a good mood. He was bound by the law and explained that Gibbons could not act without an invitation from the Newfoundland Law Society. "I regret the action," the judge said to Gibbons. He glared at Clyde Wells, who sank in his seat. Everyone knew that the Newfoundland Law Society had just embarrassed itself. To snub a lawyer from another Canadian province was no small matter. We counted it as a victory, another exposure of iniquitous scheming by a government shoring up its patchwork Seal Protection Act. Randy Earl, the Newfoundlander, took over our case in the courtroom. The Lawyers of the Rainbow never faltered. Dillon, Gibbons, and Heintzman supplied research. Even Ballem, the defendant, pitched in, poring over discovery documents and regulations. The lawyers seemed to be having more fun than we were. The journalists arrived from Corner Brook, Toronto, and Ottawa. Children sat in the courtroom, wearing Greenpeace buttons.

Peter Ballem had never before been charged with a criminal offence. On the stand, he detailed the litany of changing regulations that he had been forced to learn on behalf of his clients. "I've never seen anything like it before in my life," he told the court. "I had an obligation and a right to be on the ice floes with my clients, who were being constantly harassed by fisheries agents and RCMP officers, and threatened by sealers. I was there to clarify legal points for my clients. I had been abused and slandered by Charles Friend. I was in a very difficult situation, attempting to remain professional."

Under cross-examination, Wells characterized Ballem as a radical troublemaker using his lawyer status as cover. He pointed out that Ballem was not getting paid. "How could you put in so much time and effort? You must be dedicated to the cause."

"The cause I'm dedicated to, Mr. Wells, is that every citizen of Canada gets a fair shake and does not get silenced by their government and does not have laws passed just to stop them from speaking out."

"Regulations allow discretion –" Wells began to argue, inappropriately.

Ballem cut him off: "The law cannot be applied arbitrarily, Mr. Wells."

Seabright clarified Ballem's point. "Discretion must be applied to a specific *type* of conduct," said the judge.

Wells and Ballem argued over whether or not Friend had used appropriate discretion in stonewalling our requests, and Seabright let it go on. The reporters scribbled notes. This was exactly the sort of debate we wanted and Wells, now emotionally invested in making his points, seemed to have forgotten about asking questions. He did, however, have one bomb left. Charles Friend had revealed to Wells that Ballem had once threatened him in rage. Wells paused as if he were done, then turned and offhandedly gestured to Ballem.

"Here it comes," whispered Gibbons.

"Mr. Ballem," drawled Wells, "did you ever *threaten* Mr. Friend?"

Ballem knew what was up, but he savoured the moment. "Well," the Greenpeace lawyer said slowly, "there *were* rumours circulating that the fisheries officers might confiscate our film, which we assumed would be consistent with their attempts to silence and obstruct us, and to keep these images from the public. Now, I believe I might have told Friend that if he tried this," Ballem paused, "I'd have his nuts." The courtroom remained silent except for the scratching of pencil lead. Ballem grinned. "Now, of course, I didn't mean that *literally*."

The courtroom broke into laughter, and the ambush fizzled. The examination of witnesses went on for another three days. Seabright postponed his decision. Before we left Corner Brook, Moore swore out charges against the captains of two more sealing ships, the *Endeavor* and the *Arctic Explorer*, for sealing on Sunday, although we had no eyewitnesses that they had done so. "Well, if we find out one of 'em was observing the law, wouldn't that make it worse for the others?" Moore asked Dillon at breakfast.

"You'd make a good lawyer, Pat," she said.

Our familiar waitress, Irene, came around. "Caphy? Caphy?" She had the seal badge pinned discreetly on the pocket of her apron.

A month later, Judge Seabright dismissed the case against Ballem, but ruled that Moore "did minimally interfere with the seal hunt" in violation of the Seal Protection Act. He sentenced Moore to a $200 fine, like an overblown traffic ticket. Randy Earl filed an appeal, which the Minister of Justice in Ottawa ignored, and the fine was never paid. The sealing on Sunday charges remained pending.

THE MONKEY WRENCH GANG

Ecological action around the world now moved so quickly that by the time we got home from Newfoundland several new milestones had been reached. Craig van Note called from Washington, D.C. and told us the European Economic Council would declare a two-year moratorium on harp sealing. The Australian whaling inquiry had ended whaling at Cheynes Beach. Japan was caught in an embarrassing public denial over their complicity with pirate whalers. The Soviets had announced that one of their North Pacific whaling fleets would be scrapped. *Time* magazine featured Clamshell Alliance nuclear power protestors. On Sunday, August 6, pacifists all over the world observed the anniversary of the Hiroshima bomb. Japanese geneticist Dr. Sadao Ichikawa used the opportunity to announce his method to accurately monitor radiation levels around nuclear power plants, by counting mutations in the cells of spiderwort plants. Robert Bullard wrote a report called "Cancer Alley," about DDT contamination in Triana, Alabama. His campaign helped launch the "environmental justice" movement, pointing out how low-income communities suffer the bulk of environmental injury. The US Congress passed the National Energy Act, the Endangered American Wilderness Act, and the Antarctic Conservation Act. The era of ecology, or so it seemed, had arrived.

In September 1978, *Newsweek* magazine featured "the Vancouver-based environmentalist group known as the Greenpeace Foundation," with a 1977 picture of Moore in front of a whaling ship and a reproduction of the original Greenpeace button with the peace and ecology symbols. Ecology stories appeared regularly now in European magazines and newspapers. The *Rainbow Warrior* had made headlines during its confrontation with the Spanish whalers and navy gunboats. Following this, the citizens of the Orkney Islands, with the support of the *Rainbow Warrior*, had stopped UK fisheries managers from culling 30,000 gray seals. Not a single seal had been killed.

That summer I spent four days in Louisville, Kentucky, with 300 ecology and anti-nuclear activists to coordinate a nuclear power strategy. We discussed plans to expose the dangers of the entire nuclear cycle: from uranium mining and nuclear power plants to weapons and waste. We planned a march on Washington, D.C. for the spring of 1980, in the tradition of the 1969 "mobilization" against the war in Vietnam. In Louisville, I met Barry Commoner, a hero and mentor to us younger ecologists. Commoner gave me a copy of Leo Ryan's nuclear report. "The scientists know this stuff," he said. "So do the politicians. It's like leaded gasoline. Everyone knows, but the whole system is in denial, like a bunch of drug addicts promising to get better." Commoner offered to write an article for the *Greenpeace Chronicles*, which we published in November.

Tom Campbell introduced me to investigative writers Ada Sanchez, Anna Gyorgy and Harvey Wasserman; activist Sam Lovejoy, who toppled the tower at the nuclear site in New Hampshire; Becky Hardee, who staged her own brand of political street theatre as "Ready Kilowatt;" and lawyer-activist Kitty Tucker, who helped organize the National Organization for Women. From Tucker I learned about the assassination of Karen Silkwood, a whistle-blower at the Kerr-McGee plutonium processing plant near Crescent, Oklahoma, where safety monitoring was rudimentary and workers used uranium for paperweights.

Anna Gyorgy gave me a thumbnail history of accidents at nuclear power plants, going back to a uranium fuel rod meltdown at Chalk River, Ontario, in 1952 and a fire at the Windscale plutonium production reactor in the UK, now blamed for thirty-nine cancer deaths. Using the Freedom of Information Act, Gyorgy had learned from CIA files about an explosion at a Soviet plant in the Ural Mountains that killed hundreds of people. Rather than expose the Soviets, the CIA had kept the secret, presumably to protect Western nuclear interests. From Gyorgy I also learned about the death of a worker in an accident at Los Alamos, three dead at a government reactor in Idaho Falls, and a fire in 1975 at the Brown's Ferry reactor in Alabama, which nearly exposed the reactor core. A fuel-core meltdown at any of these reactors could cause a 5,000 degree inferno dubbed "The China Syndrome," imagining a hole right through the centre of the Earth. "A meltdown is going to happen," said Gyorgy matter-of-factly. "The safety record points to it." Most anti-nuclear activists understood the general problem; Gyorgy had the particulars.

Delegates formed networks around special interests: writers, lawyers, philosophers, strategists, women, Southerners, and other natural blocs. Writer Howard Kohn's series of stories in *Rolling Stone* magazine had alerted a broad base of the music community to the seriousness of the nuclear threat. Bonnie Raitt, Jesse Colin Young, Jackson Browne, Danny O'Keefe, John Hall, and *Rolling Stone* publicist David Fenton organized the musicians and planned a two-night extravaganza in Madison Square Garden the following year. Campbell, Tucker, Sanchez, Gyorgy, Wasserman, Brett Bursey from South Carolina, and I formed a small North American news network with half a dozen other people, to relay information, stories, data, and plans. We named our ad hoc group "The Natural Guard." Once back in Vancouver, I received in-depth environmental stories from these contacts and published them in the *Greenpeace Chronicles*.

In the meantime, tactics had escalated within the ecology movement. Greenpeace and the No Nukes movement continued to adhere strictly to Gandhian non-violence, which precluded the destruction of property, but others, like Paul Watson, did not. In Wyoming, Mike Roselle, Howie Wolke, and Dave Foreman discussed a new type of ecology group in response to what they called the "namby-pamby environmental groups." Like the punks in London, they resented what they saw as "a lethargic, compromised, and corporate environmental community." They would call their new group "Earth First!" (with the exclamation point permanently fixed). They were prepared to crank up civil disobedience to actual "eco-tage" as described in Edward Abbey's *The Monkey Wrench Gang*. Abbey's fictional "war" against industrialization was about to turn startlingly real.

In the meantime, Paul Watson had raised enough money to buy his own boat, the British deep-sea trawler *Westella*, which he renamed *Sea Shepherd*. Among his benefactors, Bob and Bobbi Hunter let him use their home as collateral to borrow money. That fall, Watson filled the bow of the *Sea Shepherd* with three tons of concrete so he could hunt down and ram the pirate whalers. Was it illegal to stop an illegal act with force? Was it morally wrong? Watson would probe this realm of righteous aggression for the next several decades, but for now, he had the pirate whaler *Sierra* in his sights.

In September 1978, I read that the FBI, acting on a tip from an informant, had caught thirty-one-year-old ex-Navy diver James Rose with a submarine, pictures of Japanese and Russian whaling vessels in Chile, and enough C-4 plastic explosives to blow up the fleet. "Here we go," said Hunter, on the back porch of his rural home, when I returned from Louisville and showed him the magazine article about the submarine.

PEOPLE'S TEMPLE OF DOOM

In November, the Hunters had a new baby, William, affectionately called "Little Will." Bob Hunter was writing his personal account of the last decade, *Warriors of the Rainbow*, which would be published by Holt Rinehart and Winston the following year. It was the one deal he had salvaged from the Amy Ephron movie fiasco. He handed me the second installment of his "Environmentalism for the 1980s" column for the January 1979 *Greenpeace Chronicles* — something about a "Triage Strategy." Hunter had discovered the work of biologist Norman Myers, who had estimated the rate of species extinction worldwide caused by human activity.

Myers had pointed out that here have been five major extinction events on Earth since life got rolling 550 million years ago. The first species crash occurred 440 million years ago, during the age of nautiloids and trilobites, when a quarter of the family types perished, comprising some 85 percent of the species. The last great species extinction took out the dinosaurs 65 million years ago, leaving the tiny mammals that evolved into primates and whales.

Now, according to Norman Myers, a sixth massive extinction was underway; caused by human activity. Myers estimated that one species per day was lost as wild habitats vanished, a rate one hundred times greater than had been generally accepted. He suggested a strategy of identifying and preserving biodiversity "hotspots," such as tropical rainforests. His ideas seemed radical at the time, but he would later receive the UN Environment Prize and the Order of St. Michael and St. George from Queen Elizabeth II for "services to the global environment."

Hunter had been shocked reading all this. "Jeez," he said, "while we've been trying to save the whales and seals, 1,500 species have probably vanished forever." There were about 1.5 million identified species on Earth, perhaps twenty times that many unknown. Half of them were insects and half of those were beetles. Naysayers might claim, and some did, that losing a few hundred of the 400,000 beetle species was irrelevant to evolution. Ecology, however, is not simple addition and subtraction. Ecosystems are held together not by individual species, but by relationships, millions of fragile relationships, and disruption to a part is disruption to the whole. History tells us that diversity can bounce back from devastation, but these "bounce-backs" took millions of years. Our hunter-gatherer ancestors caused local extinctions in Africa and Europe with wooden spears and fire. Ancient forests were levelled by hand axes and goats. But the modern demise of diversity is directly linked to pollution, industrialized resource harvesting, human farming, and urban sprawl.

"We've come all this way," said Hunter, "and now it looks worse than I ever imagined. We need a thousand Greenpeaces just to keep up with everything." Worldwatch Institute researcher Erik Eckholm had written that "consciously writing off some life forms in order to save many more may be the best among unpleasant alternatives." In his column, Hunter proposed a "triage" strategy like the system used on battlefields to focus medical resources on the worst victims who have a good chance of surviving. The others either perish or get well on their own — a sobering thought.

On the cover of the December *Chronicles*, we printed a leaping *Orcinus orca* and the greeting:

PEACE ON EARTH

GOODWILL TO ALL CREATURES

However, as the issue went to the printer, on November 18, 1978, we got the worst news of the year. Senator Leo Ryan — the man who had saved redwood forests in California, supported the whale campaign as a Washington, D.C. insider, joined us on the ice in Newfoundland, and exposed the dark secrets of the nuclear power industry — had been murdered in Port Kaituma, Guyana. His colleague Jacqueline Speier had been seriously wounded and had crawled into the forest to hide and survive. Many of us doubted the official story that the murders were an attempt to stop him from exposing the mad prophet Jim Jones, alleged mastermind of the creepy People's Temple at Jonestown. Television clips of the Ryan assassination showed highly trained marksmen in clean khaki uniforms standing tall in a moving trailer pulled by a truck, picking off Ryan's party from a hundred yards at the Port Kaituma airport in Guyana. We shuddered at oblique news reports that the killings had been masterminded by the now-dead Jim Jones. And why had Jones been shot? Who gave *that* order?

One thing we did know: Leo Ryan was in Guyana to help people in desperate need. He was a man of immense compassion, who died serving society's outcasts, a truth-teller, a hero of ecology and common sense. We had lost one of our Warriors of the Rainbow. We stopped the presses and inserted a eulogy.

"He was a reasoned man who was not ruled by reason, a sensitive man who was not ruled by emotion, but, most important of all, he was a powerful man who was not ruled by power."

SATORI IN BAJA

Our colleague from Seattle, Campbell Plowden, ventured to San Vicente to investigate the pirate whalers in Chile. There, Augusto Pinochet's notorious DINA secret police invaded his hotel room in the middle of the night, ransacked his belongings, and interrogated him for four hours. Was ecology such a threat? Were vigilantes now protecting the marketplace for whale meat and nuclear power? Perhaps Paul Sears had been prophetic in 1964 when he called ecology a "subversive subject."

The dangers, however, were not all external. The growth rate of Greenpeace had far outstripped our ability to organize ourselves politically. The pace of our work and the internal tensions of Greenpeace had exhausted me. When Paul Winter invited me to Baja for two weeks, to play music and watch the gray whales, I accepted without hesitation. My wife Glenn and I had been on the verge of separation for months. We needed a break and an opportunity to revive our faltering marriage. We packed clothes, a guitar, flutes, and cameras, and flew to La Paz, where we met Winter and twenty-two others. We crossed the arid peninsula by bus to Puerto Lopez Mateos, chartered a boat across to Isla Santa Magdalena, and pitched tents on the beach.

Paul Winter and his band were working on a new recording, *Callings,* with musical structures built from the voices of whales, wolves, eagles, and other wild creatures. On Santa Magdalena, Winter, oboist Nancy Rumble, and guitarist Jim Scott coaxed melody, rhythm, and natural harmonics from the rest of us. When a seal barked, Winter answered with the alto saxophone and wove the new line back into the fabric of voices. After a morning of this, I felt transported far away from the politics of ecology, back to wilderness itself. Quietly, I experienced a breakdown, as the emotions that had built up over the last few years found a new equilibrium.

Glenn and I walked on the beach and saw two gray whales making leviathan love as they drifted out to sea on a tidal current. We saw horned lizards and geckos among the rocks and sparse island plants. Along the shore we saw an egret. A turkey vulture passed overhead and a gopher snake slid over the sand into the shadows. Glenn carried large dried seedpods from La Paz that made fine rattles. I cajoled notes from a shakuhachi that Fred Easton had given to me.

Over the next few days, Winter's fundamental message — to pay attention — began to sink in. The weight of the world slid from my shoulders. The Taoists say that all action breeds opposition. It suddenly seemed clear to me that we should not have been surprised by the external violence and the internal squabbling. I thought of the Quakers and their severed ears, of the suffragettes, and Rosa Parks refusing to give up her bus seat in Montgomery, Alabama. Gandhi and Martin Luther King assassinated. My own troubles seemed petty in comparison. Opposition would never cease, and as ecology became embraced by more people, it would only become more fierce. The bickering within and among ecology groups might endure for decades.

As American black leader Eldridge Clever had once declared, there are "no innocent bystanders." A witness is involved. No one could predict what resistance — violence, jail, or ridicule — a witness might suffer. Standing on a principle, which only days before had seemed unspeakably complex, now seemed simple, as long as one was not intimidated by the consequences.

On Isla Santa Magdalena I stumbled onto the shards of a forgotten epiphany in my own heart. I recognized some ineffable calm in seeing the world again without wanting to plan its course or fix it. The Green Robes, if that's what we were, had only to bring the light of day to what we witnessed, nothing more. The vision was important, but we were expendable. The Earth could tell its own story, and would, even without us. Greenpeace was about to be recast as a global organization. I wanted it to be something we would all be proud of, but wanting things to turn out a certain way was perhaps the biggest problem of all. The dilemma — how to structure innovation — was a contradiction, a koan, a trick of nature.

One night, around the fire, a businessman from Scarsdale, New York, said, "I'm looking for the Whole Earth Church." I thought this was odd, since no one had mentioned that such a thing existed. Then Peg Post from Tallahassee, Florida, responded, "We're it."

CHAPTER TWELVE

THE SCEPTRE

"You are empowered to remind people that they are utterly free."

— Jack Kerouac

By 1979, the *Rainbow Warrior*'s presence on the high seas provided the most visible evidence of Greenpeace's new global influence. In February of 1979, the flagship of the Eco Navy arrived in Ålesund, Norway, to delay the departure of the sealing ships bound for the harp seal nursery off the Labrador coast. On February 27, fifteen Norwegian, British, French, and Dutch volunteers chained themselves to the sealing ships. Eleven were arrested, but four protestors chained themselves high on the mast, out of reach of the police. These four were carried to sea, where frigid Arctic winds forced them down. The Norwegians dropped the activists off on the Faeroe Islands, where the *Rainbow Warrior* crew retrieved them.

In Canada, we had shifted our tactics. Rather than confront landsmen swilers on the ice floes, we slipped into St. John's, Newfoundland, to blockade the sealing ships that would depart on March 4. To counter the environmentalists, Newfoundland Premier Frank Moores had hired a delegation of public relations consultants to tour America. Head consultant Larry Dworkin claimed that he did not know "the difference between a seal and a cow," but he assembled a team of credible marine experts.

A skirmish of mindbombs ensued. Newfoundland's initial sound bite claimed the seal hunt was "a harvest, not a slaughter," but the consultants came under attack when one of them said, "There is little difference between someone in Florida harvesting oranges and someone in Newfoundland engaging in the seal hunt." *Oranges*? CBS ran the comment over footage of harp seal pups bludgeoned to death before their wailing mothers. Round one went to Greenpeace. Dworkin wore a sealskin parka, but the ploy backfired when authorities in New York arrested him for violating the US Marine Mammal Protection Act. Two-nil Greenpeace. Nevertheless, Dworkin's group inspired positive editorials in the *New York Times*, the *International Herald Tribune*, and the *Christian Science Monitor*, and the clash of paradigms proved an even match.

In February, the Fund for Animals called for an international boycott of Canadian goods. Paul Watson rekindled the spray-paint idea to render the seal pelts worthless and steamed for the ice floes aboard the *Sea Shepherd*, armed with organic red dye and a helicopter. In Bonn, businessman Franz Weber convened a citizen's tribunal comprised of Swiss, Danish, German, Japanese, and French clergy and lawyers. The panel censured Norwegian and Canadian Fisheries Ministers, Eivind Bolle and Romeo LeBlanc, for presiding over the last mass slaughter of infant marine mammals on the planet. In Paris, twenty-three-year-old American Douglas Allen climbed the Eiffel Tower, suspended a "*Sauver les phoques*" banner, and was arrested. With every action and arrest, stories and photographs appeared in newspapers and magazines around the world.

In Europe and America, the Canadian government was cast as the scoundrel, but to many Canadians, the environmentalists represented the villains. In the House of Commons, Tory MP John Crosbie from Newfoundland demanded that the Canadian government arrest the Greenpeace protestors and seize Watson's ship. "They have to commit a crime first," LeBlanc conceded. Fisheries officers and RCMP stormed into St. Anthony expecting Greenpeace to arrive. Meanwhile, volunteers from all over North America made their way into the Newfoundland capital of St. John's.

On March 1, Moore and I arrived with our old friend Don Franks, our lawyer Davie Gibbons, lawyer Joanna McFadyen from Ottawa, and veteran underground journalist Bob Cummings. My brother, Bruce Weyler, arrived from Denver with rock climbers from Montreal. Annie Linton and

Steve Sawyer arrived from Boston, Vivia Boe from Seattle, Dan and Pati McDermott from Toronto, and more. Forty Greenpeace members were camped and billeted around St. John's.

"The whole world is asking Canada to be reasonable," Don Franks, a.k.a. Iron Buffalo, said on St. John's radio the next morning. "If you're at a party and one person says you're drunk, you might say, 'Oh, I'm fine.' But if *three* people tell you you're drunk, you should listen." Moore, Gibbons, and Don Franks held a press conference at the Newfoundland Hotel. As far as anyone knew, or so we thought, they were the only Greenpeace delegation in St. John's. I blended in with the photographers in the press corp. Codpeace members showed up with "Cuddles the Cod" and sealers heckled Greenpeace. Newfoundland Cabinet Minister John Lundrigan told Moore, "You and the rest of your outsiders can go home."

"Been sealing on Sunday lately, John?" taunted Moore.

"You call us 'outsiders'?" Don Franks smiled. "Outside what? Are you outsiders when you're in the harp seal nursery? Do you think you are the original people of this land?" The crowd rumbled, but Franks had their attention. "Are there any Beothuk here? They were here when your ancestors came." Franks knew, as did many in the room, that the European settlers of the Atlantic provinces had exterminated the indigenous Beothuk. It was not a polite subject in Newfoundland. Some in the crowd grumbled, but the room fell silent. "It's time we learned to take care of the Earth," said Franks, "not diddle around with so-called old traditions."

On Friday, March 2, in the dead of night, the rock climbers scaled the granite face at the harbour entrance and set pitons where they intended to drop a large banner. In the morning, the crews that planned to chain themselves to the ships, the "chain gangs," cased the *Lady Johnson*, *Gulf Star*, and the *Arctic Endeavour* at the wharf. On Saturday afternoon, thirty-five Greenpeace volunteers met at a supporter's private home overlooking St. John's to coordinate the advancing spectacle. Bob Cummings and Jeff Kunz from Indiana would create a diversion by leaping into the water from the wharf. Zodiacs would arrive from the harbour as additional diversion. The chain gangs would slip casually aboard the ships with the local crowd.

That evening, the Chief of St. John's Newfoundland Constabulary visited Moore and Gibbons in the hotel. "Look," the officer said, "do you think you can sneak thirty Greenpeacers into our town and I don't know about it?"

"Obviously not," conceded Moore.

"Tell me what you're going to do," the police chief told Moore, "and I'll make sure no one gets hurt." Moore revealed the Zodiacs and the plan to chain protestors to the ships. He did not mention the banner on the rocks or precisely how chain gangs would gain access to the ships. "Okay," said the chief. "If we have to arrest anyone, it will be done properly. Keep it peaceful." Moore and the police chief shook hands.

By noon on Sunday, March 4, 5,000 people had gathered at the wharf for a 1:30 p.m. ecumenical blessing of the sealing ships. The sun shone bright, the sky and water were blue, but the frigid spring air chilled our faces. Policemen in thick coats blew through their hands and slapped their arms. A rope cordoned off the dock in front of five sealing ships. Moore and Franks stood at the rope, surrounded by an agitated crowd of jeering spectators. Bruce Weyler and Jeff Kunz stood on either side of them. Cummings scribbled in his notepad as he stood against the rope at the edge of the wharf.

Outside the cordon, a gangway led to the *Arctic Endeavour*. Vivia Boe and her chain gang filed onboard with the public tours. Inside the cordon with the other reporters, I worked my way aboard the *Lady Johnson II* in the middle of the wharf. Skipper Morrissey Johnson stood at the gangplank with Newfoundland Premier Frank Moores in his sealskin coat. Canadian Press correspondent Ed Walters asked me what was going to happen. I told him. A sealer poked me and said he'd heard I was with Greenpeace. Walters came to my aid and sent the man away.

After the Catholic priest's blessing, the band struck up "Ode to Newfoundland." The crowd cheered. A second chain gang pressed in near the gangway of the *Gulf Star* on the far side of the dock, watched over by lawyers Gibbons and Joanna McFadyen. Moore and Franks unfurled a Greenpeace flag at the rope, and the crowd nearby roared insults and grabbed for the flag. Constables moved in to protect the Greenpeacers. Cummings slid under the rope and broke for the water, but was tackled by a dozen constables. Jeff Kunz slipped quietly to the edge of the wharf, stepped past the rope and leapt into the icy water. Zodiacs appeared. The distraction in the water left the *Gulf Star* chain gang free to board, and both groups chained themselves to the ships. On the *Lady Johnson II*, Captain Johnson bear-hugged Annie Linton, kneed her in the stomach, and shoved her tumbling down the gangway. Police officers yelled at the skipper to back off and arrested Linton. Premier Frank Moores beat a hasty retreat, his sealskin coat flapping behind him.

Police arrested a dozen protestors, six men and six women. Angry citizens attacked Moore, Franks, Bruce Weyler, and Joanna McFadyen, and police took them into protective custody. Horns blared as the ships moved away from the dock undaunted by the Zodiacs still attempting to block their way. Photographers and film teams raced back to their offices. Trial dates were set for the summer, Gibbons got everyone released that evening, and we left St. John's the next morning.

Meanwhile, Paul Watson and Cleveland Amory had manoeuvred the *Sea Shepherd* into the ice floes and dyed about 1,000 seals before Watson, photographer Matt Herron, and seven others were arrested. In the airport at Cap-aux-Meules, Quebec, irate sealers doused red paint over four unsuspecting journalists. American Eddie Chavies persisted in obtaining a fisheries permit, visited the Labrador seal nursery, and marked one single seal pup with an indelible green marker before an RCMP officer arrested him.

Over three weeks, thirty-four seal protestors had been arrested in France, Norway, and Canada. Four more had been taken to sea, chained to ships, and four had been taken into protective custody. New protests erupted across North America and in Europe. The Canadian parliament announced "unanimous" support for the seal hunt, until MP Marke Raines from North Vancouver protested that this could not be so because *he* did not support the seal hunt. The Speaker of the House refused to acknowledge his protest and his colleagues shouted him down.

OVERDOSE

As Greenpeace championed animal rights and "deep ecology" issues like the seal hunt, we had simultaneously returned to the concerns that founded our movement: nuclear contamination and nuclear weapons. The United States pressured the Europeans to accept new Pershing missiles with nuclear warheads. The US, France, and the Soviet Union were conducting research into a nefarious "neutron" bomb, a new class of nuclear weapon that would kill people without destroying buildings. As Greenpeace came full circle, back to the nuclear weapons issue, the public imagination in North America and Europe seized upon the inherent fears of radiation poisoning from a major accident at a nuclear power plant. The nuclear industry, meanwhile, continued to insist those fears were groundless.

On March 17, 1979, the movie *The China Syndrome* was released, starring Jane Fonda, Jack Lemmon, and Michael Douglas. The film depicted a near meltdown at the fictional "Ventana" nuclear power plant. It was a huge success with the public but scorned by the nuclear power industry as alarmist propaganda. Eleven days later, however, a valve failed to close at the brand new Pennsylvania Met-Ed 900-megawatt pressurized water-cooled nuclear reactor, Unit-II on Three Mile Island in the Susquehanna River.

At 4:00 a.m. on Wednesday, March 28, a malfunction in the cooling water circuit caused the fuel core temperature to rise, creating steam. Computers automatically vented the pressure and shut down the reactor, but the pressure relief valve that failed to close allowed cooling water to drain from the uranium core, heating it even more. Superheated steam reacted with the zirconium cladding around the exposed fuel rods, creating an abundance of hydrogen gas. Injection pumps automatically pushed replacement water into the reactor, but because the valve remained open, the water flowed back out. The uranium core began to melt.

Control room operators believed the relief valve had closed, as their instruments indicated, so they manually reduced the flow of water. The exposed core cooked, and gas pressure caused vibrations in the cooling pumps. The operators shut down the pumps to save them, but thereby ended the cooling of the reactor core. Astonished technicians watched helplessly as their computer printed out lines of questions marks: "??????? ..." They called system designers Babcock & Wilcox to find out what the question marks meant. No one knew. They now presided over a controlled nuclear bomb that had just gone *out* of control. They were within 150 miles of 25 million people.

By sunrise, the technicians realized the valve had stuck open, but it was too late. Pressurized gas blocked the flow of water throughout the system. By noon, the reactor went to full emergency shutdown.

That morning, as we packed our entire Vancouver office for a move down Fourth Avenue to a new office, Ada Sanchez from the Natural

Guard called with the news from Three Mile Island. I sat on the empty floor most of the day, talking on the telephone and attempting to find out what had happened in Pennsylvania. I heard talk of Iodine-131 in the atmosphere, 125-millirems per hour of radiation, and a public evacuation. Scientists supporting both sides of the issue flew into Harrisburg to sort out the crisis. That night, Walter Cronkite said on CBS *Evening News*, "It was the first step in a nuclear nightmare; as far as we know at this hour, no worse than that. But a government official said that a breakdown in an atomic-power plant in Pennsylvania today is probably the worst nuclear accident to date. There was no apparent serious contamination of workers."

At the plant, however, the employees worked in a near panic. The emergency crew restarted one pump and restored cooling to the reactor core, but the chemical reaction with the zirconium cladding continued to create hydrogen gas. Workers pumped the hydrogen to holding tanks, but their compressors leaked radioactive gas. Over the next two days, March 29 and 30, Nuclear Regulatory Commission officials believed the hydrogen bubble could explode, so they periodically vented the hydrogen, along with iodine, krypton, xenon, and other radionuclides. The winds blew north along the Susquehanna River toward Middletown and Harrisburg. Monitors reported strontium-90 and cesium in the river, indicating that the core stood close to a meltdown. The populations of New York City, Philadelphia, Baltimore, and Washington, D.C. went on full alert.

Medical biochemist and Nobel laureate George Wald flew to Harrisburg to warn people to leave. President Jimmy Carter visited Harrisburg and urged Governor Thornburg of Pennsylvania to "err on the side of public safety." Thornburg recommended all pregnant women and preschoolers within five miles of the plant evacuate. People began to pour out of nearby Goldsboro, Pleasant Grove, and Woodside. Few people knew if they were safe or not. No one knew how far away they should go. A reading directly above the reactor stack indicated 1,200 millirems of radiation, but few citizens knew what that meant.

The citizens could be excused their bafflement. The health effects of nuclear radiation are complex and were not entirely understood even by the scientists. Communications among agencies were confused. The public picked up snatches of facts from the media. What's a millirem? What's an off-site reading? Was a hydrogen explosion possible? Was a meltdown possible? Did the Nuclear Regulatory Commission order an evacuation? When the Department of Energy announced that they had detected "virtually no iodine," was that good news?

Calculating the health effects of radiation must account for the varieties of energy — alpha, beta, X-rays, and so forth — measured in Roentgen. A human dose is measured in "rems" or "roentgen equivalent-in-man," meaning the amount of energy actually absorbed by the body. A thousand rems of radiation, a few miles from a large nuclear explosion, would cause death within hours. A hundred rems absorbed in a short period will cause severe radiation sickness and some fatalities. This is approximately the dose received by the Rongelap Islanders and Japanese fishermen on the *Lucky Dragon* in 1954, causing death and cancers that manifested over many years.

The NRC had set a maximum limit for industry workers at 5 rems per year. For the general public, on average, the limit was 0.17 rem (170 millirems). These doses were not defined as "safe," but only "permitted." By 1979, any serious science student knew there was no absolutely safe level of radiation. "Every dose is an overdose," Dr. Wald told the journalists in Harrisburg. Dr. John Gofman — Medical Director at the Lawrence Livermore laboratory in the 1950s — had been hired by the Atomic Energy Commission to determine just how much cancer and genetic injury would result from a robust nuclear power industry. He determined that if everyone in the United States received the allowable dose, there would be an additional 16,000 to 32,000 fatal cancers. Roughly one out of ten thousand people who received that dose would die of cancer.

The NRC "permitted public dose" was approximately equal to the background radiation everyone receives from the earth and cosmic sources. This background radiation undoubtedly causes some cancers, and doubling it with human-generated radiation will roughly double that cancer rate. A nuclear worker's allowable dose of 5 rems posed a proportionately greater cancer risk. Radiation is like millions of infinitesimal bullets. Most of them might not penetrate, might go right through, or might not cause damage. The reason there is "no safe dose" is that a single ingested alpha particle, for example, can cause damage to the DNA of a cell. The tiny bits of atomic energy can knock an electron off an atom or break apart a molecule. The damage is immediate and permanent but may not manifest for years. A cell with damaged DNA may not get the message to stop multiplying, and thus become malignant.

The promoters of nuclear power, however, could claim that no one had ever proven that radiation had caused a case of cancer, because the damaged cells did not reveal the source of the damage, and the symptoms sometimes did not appear for decades. The statistical data, however, remained unequivocal on one point: radiation caused cancer. According to the US Environmental Protection Agency, even a single millirem of radiation, what a person might receive from a television set in a year, will increase fatal cancer by four people per ten million. The odds are long, but the game is deadly. The citizens of Pennsylvania were understandably confused and afraid.

A fisherman on the river near the plant received 100 millirems of radiation. A few miles away from the plant, where the NRC, Met-Ed, and other agencies parked their emergency trailers, the radiation exposure reached 100 millirems per day, primarily from xenon gas. At the core of the plant, the radioactivity of the coolant water surpassed 1,000 rems, comparable to a nuclear explosion. The filter systems became saturated with iodine and no longer worked, but were too hot to change. There was virtually no filtration inside the plant for a month.

By April 27, operators had bypassed the mechanical pumps and returned coolant circulation to the reactor core, a so-called "cold shutdown." In July, four months after the accident, the first human re-entered the reactor building in a radiation suit. The Department of Energy and other agencies would spend about $1 billion to clean up and entomb the ravaged reactor. They removed a hundred tons of damaged uranium fuel from the core. Millions of gallons of contaminated water flowed into the Susquehanna River. And there, in the forest of William Penn, in the countryside of the Quakers and the birthplace of democratic visions, the promise of nuclear power was fatally wounded. The vagaries of radiation exposure aside, the sheer cost of dealing with the mess was more than most communities or utility companies wanted to contemplate. Who would insure these monsters? Who wanted to live near one?

The only winner was Columbia Pictures, whose stock gained five points over the weekend of the accident as an alarmed public lined up to see *The China Syndrome*.

Throughout North America, the Three Mile Island incident pulled Greenpeace back into the nuclear issue. Ironically, to some of our new supporters in the US, who associated Greenpeace with saving whales, the nuclear power and disarmament campaigns seemed almost too radical. In San Francisco, I met with Gary Zimmerman, Cindy Baker and some of the Natural Guard group to discuss the issues. Anna Gyorgy had just published *No Nukes: Everyone's Guide to Nuclear Power.* We learned from her that a uranium mill in Church Rock, New Mexico was leaking 60,000 gallons of radioactive waste per month into streams and underground aquifers. The nuclear industry appeared out of control.

Tom Campbell staged "safe-energy" rallies across the United States featuring stalwarts Bonnie Raitt, Jackson Browne, and others. On May 6, at a Washington, D.C. rally, Joni Mitchell — whose inaugural Greenpeace concert had funded a good portion of the first Greenpeace voyage — joined the troupe. In the midst of this, I arrived in Washington, D.C. to find and close down the spurious "Greenpeace" huckster selling bogus memberships. Tom Campbell, Sam Lovejoy, and I arranged a meeting with a reluctant President Carter at the White House. Popular support had made ecology not only acceptable but also important to politicians in democratic nations.

Back in Vancouver, Walrus Oakenbough launched a full-fledged campaign to stop uranium mining in British Columbia, declaring, "We have to put the peace back in Greenpeace."

TRIBAL WARS

Citizens of Europe confronted the same environmental horror stories that haunted North Americans. A string of nuclear mishaps and the confrontation between the *Rainbow Warrior* and the *Gem* had aroused the European public. In January 1979, the *New Ecologist* revealed that Lake District residents in the UK had been exposed to radiation levels fifteen times higher than originally reported from the Windscale accident. *New Scientist* published a study showing that British nuclear submarine workers suffered chromosome damage even with radiation doses below safety standards. Nuclear accidents caused shutdowns in Sweden, Holland, and France. The most chilling news came from Russia, where ex-inmates of the Gulag, forced to work in uranium mines and nuclear submarines, were now dying from the radiation exposure.

New Greenpeace recruits from Amsterdam and other European centres joined the veteran crew of the *Rainbow Warrior* — Susi Newborn, Jon Castle, David McTaggart, Tony Mariner, Denise Bell, Alan Thornton, and Athel von Koettlitz — for the second summer of confrontations with the nuclear garbage scow, *Gem*, and the Icelandic whalers.

In the London and Paris Greenpeace offices, however, internal political tensions simmered. Susi Newborn remained frustrated with what she felt was an elitist style within Greenpeace. Newborn and Denise Bell had wanted to make the *Rainbow Warrior* available to Amnesty International, CND, Greenpeace New Zealand, and to the original "Greenpeace London" activists for campaigns. Newborn had organized another meeting with *Peace News* leader Albert Beale, but she felt McTaggart showed no interest in cultivating the coalition. Beale and McTaggart clashed and the alliance broke down.

In Paris, Rémi Parmentier told McTaggart, "I should return to my studies," but McTaggart convinced him he should stay with Greenpeace. "You won't learn half as much at university," the Canadian said. McTaggart revealed to Parmentier a larger plan to take control of Greenpeace worldwide. The potential was huge: "We'll show those hippies in Vancouver how to do things right," he said. McTaggart believed the public would be alienated by mystical talk and Native traditions. Indeed, McTaggart had made it clear to us earlier in Vancouver that he wanted a "tough, politically mature Greenpeace. Not that airy-fairy crap." When Greenpeace Netherlands formed in late 1978, McTaggart gave each director business cards that said "Greenpeace Europe." He had long since established himself as the "Director." Parmentier remained loyal to both Greenpeace and to McTaggart. He did not always agree with the aggressive Canadian entrepreneur, but he respected McTaggart's tenacity. "We're like a small tribe," he told his friends. "But tribal life includes tribal wars, and they can be bloody."

Susi Newborn was not so conciliatory. She knew McTaggart had designs to control Greenpeace, and she feared the direction he might take it. She felt that any decision about a "Director" of "Greenpeace Europe" should come from a formal vote. Greenpeace cohesion cracked along a philosophical faultline between the political "realists" and the more spiritually inclined "deep ecologists." The political wing, Newborn feared, would soon oust the spiritual elements, and a superficial form of ecology might replace the Gandhian and Quaker roots. She fought back and found allies in Denise Bell and others. Newborn had hit upon a fundamental paradox faced by any social innovator, and known well to some of the ecologists in Vancouver: How do you sustain innovation? Religions and republics throughout history had stumbled over this contradiction. A bargain would have to be struck between the visionaries and realists. Newborn did not want competition for control of the organization to cripple the spontaneity that had created it. In the spring of 1979, she left London, weary of the power struggles, and retreated to the Greek island of Samos for a rest.

By chance, on a beach near Ayios Konstantinos, Newborn met enthusiastic young environmentalist William Johnson. When Johnson discovered Newborn was a director of Greenpeace UK, he wanted to talk about ecology actions. At first, she discouraged him. "It's all politics," she said. Johnson, however, persisted and said he wanted to do something "like Greenpeace" for the environment. "Have you ever seen an Aegean monk seal?" Newborn asked him.

Newborn had heard from fishermen about an incessant massacre in the Mediterranean. Fishermen from Naxos reportedly set nets at night, enticed seals with trapped fish, and then tossed dynamite into the water to kill them. Like the harp seals in Labrador and the grays in the North Sea, the monk seals had become scapegoats for the decimated Mediterranean fishing stocks. Newborn and Johnson made a pact to stop the slaughter.

Johnson visited Allan Thornton in London and accepted the job of coordinating a monk seal crusade for Greenpeace. Dr. Keith Ronald at Guelph University in Ontario had coordinated an international alliance on behalf of the monk seal, including the World Wildlife Fund, the UN, the Greek government, and twenty-one other countries. "But," warned Thornton, "among the politicians, there's no motivation. Without a public action, not much will happen."

By the summer of 1979 Johnson and Newborn had established "Greenpeace Aegean Sea" on Samos. The campaign was an act of internal defiance as well as a rescue for the monk seals. McTaggart opposed the opening of new offices in Europe until the political structure of Greenpeace had been settled. But Newborn and Johnson pushed ahead, exposed the Turkish dolphin hunt as well as the monk seal slaughter, and ultimately halted both marine mammal massacres.

AN ECOLOGY OF ECOLOGISTS

Meanwhile, in Hamburg, thirty-four-year-old shipyard organizer Harald Zindler and his friends who fished the Elbe collected scores of deformed fish, and dumped them outside the German Hydrographic Institute in Hamburg, the agency responsible for monitoring the river's water quality. The action created an immediate public outcry in the fishing communities along the Elbe and Wesser rivers.

Harald Zindler was born near the docks in 1944, where his family hid in a concrete bunker from the phosphorous bombs and firestorms in Hamburg. He became a pacifist, studied for the Catholic priesthood, and refused to register in the German army on moral grounds. "I had to go before a committee," he told his friends, "to prove I have a conscience." When the German post office forbade the use of peace signs on envelopes because they were "political," Zindler challenged them. "The veterans' groups get to put *guns* on *their* envelopes," he argued. Zindler discovered the greatest inspiration for a social activist: he could win. He had seen pictures of the Greenpeace confrontations with the Russian whalers and had visited the *Rainbow Warrior* in Hamburg the previous summer. The fishermen gave Zindler a boat to use for ecology actions. He named the vessel the *Moby Dick*, fitted it with monitoring equipment and navigated the Elbe with the intention of busting every polluter from Lauenburg at the East German border to Cuxhaven at the mouth of the North Sea.

Zindler and his partner Monika Griefahn planned a boat action against a polluter in Bremerhaven. At a demonstration, Griefahn met a schoolteacher with a Greenpeace button. She took the young man's phone number, and Zindler called him. David McTaggart had given the teacher responsibility to start Greenpeace Germany. However, during their protest at Bremerhaven, the teacher got nervous about the potential 200 deutsche mark fine, and wanted to halt the protest. Zindler and Griefahan thereafter became Greenpeace Germany and later formalized the organization with Gerhard Wallmeyer and Christian Krüger in Hamburg.

In Germany, the national Die Grünen grew into a broad-based political party. In France, Europe-écologie led by Solange Fernex, won enough popular support to become a balance of power between the Gaullists and socialists. However, with political success came pressure to conform to various blocs. Philosophical differences broke down into endlessly tedious nuances. Since almost everyone in the culture now saw himself or herself as an environmentalist, the platform for "political ecologists" became complex. The German Greens incorporated the far right-wing Aktion Unabhaengiger Deutscher, Petra Kelly's committed environmentalists, and the leftist Communist Alliance. By 1979, progressive capitalists talked about "sustainable development" as a strategy for achieving a stable world economy. Ecologists throughout the world faced the fact that history does not wait for the nuances to be sorted out, elections come and go, moments of change are seized or lost.

All the Greenpeace offices wanted autonomy, but how, we wondered, could all that autonomy exist under a single name? Could Greenpeace be simultaneously business-like and radical? The solution might have been right under our noses, in the lessons of ecology itself. Famed anthropologist Gregory Bateson, who had just written the groundbreaking *Mind and Nature*, addressed these very questions in his connection between the patterns of nature, mind, and human society. Bateson pointed out that nature is both creative and conservative. "Embryology," he said in a lecture at the University of California "demands that every new thing shall conform or be compatible with the regularities of the *status quo* ante." Meanwhile, said Bateson, the outside world is changing and "ready to receive creatures which have undergone change." Our human systems, he encouraged, must honour *coherence* in their structure and *imagination* in their function. This might have been the magic formula we sought, the means to keep creativity alive. However, Bateson's analysis had not been widely read and certainly had not yet taken root in Greenpeace.

For the most part, in fact, during the summer of 1979 our attention remained not on politics at all, but on the environmental issues. We felt tantalizingly close to winning an end to whaling. At the IWC meeting in London, in June, Patrick Moore, Paul Spong, and fiery French entrepreneur Jean-Paul Forton-Gouin marched with Greenpeace UK and 15,000 demonstrators to Trafalgar Square. Veteran whale advocates — Joanna Gordon Clark from the Marine Action Centre in Cambridge, Christine Stevens from the US Animal Welfare Institute, Sir Peter Scott from the World Wildlife Fund — lobbied the twenty-three IWC member nations. Since Panama had abandoned the whale's cause for a sugar deal with Japan, environmentalists had recruited the Seychelles into the IWC, with financial help from Prince Sadruddin Aga Khan. The Seychelles chose avant-garde naturalist Lyall Watson as their plenary delegate and marine biologist Dr. Sidney Holt as their scientific delegate. On July 11, the Commission passed a motion by the Seychelles to declare the Indian Ocean a whale sanctuary. Then, in a vote of 18-2 — with Japan and the Soviet Union opposed and three abstentions — the IWC passed a US motion for a ban on the deep-sea sperm whale hunt. Panama, in the service of Japan, amended the motion to exempt shore whaling and minke whales.

Nevertheless, the vote represented a day of liberty for whales. Seven thousand sperm whales would be spared the following summer. A celebration among the environmentalists lasted all night, into the next day, and reverberated around the world. The environmentalists, in spite of their differences — perhaps because of their diversity — proved they could rally their forces and win a victory for those beings with no other political voice in human affairs.

OH, PARDON ME

Even so, we had good reason to be skeptical about the victory. In our celebration, we knew that renegade whalers operated outside the scrutiny of the IWC, and Greenpeace had no complete answer to their destructive impact on the whales. Our tactics could shine the light of day on the Japanese, Soviet, and Icelandic whalers; Nick Carter's research at the IWC could link the Japanese whaling companies to the pirate ships; but neither Greenpeace exposure nor Carter's evidence yet threatened the pirate whalers themselves. Their company owners could move around the planet almost as fast as our electronic images. Many ports of call opened to them, where a deal could be made for cargo. The pirate whalers had no national honour to defend and answered to no one.

Since 1948, the International Whaling Commission had been little more than a whalers' club, but in 1964 the Japanese agreed to cease hunting the nearly extinct blue whale. Immediately, pirate whaling began. Seven years had passed between the first UN whale moratorium at the Stockholm Conference in 1972 and the IWC ban on sperm whale hunting in the North Pacific. However, the exemptions for shore whaling stations and the minke whale hunt were only the most obvious loopholes. Japan and the Soviet Union held "scientific" permits for protected Byrde's and fin whales. Their combined contribution to science in 1976 consisted of 114 Byrde's whales measured, thirteen weighed, and bones collected from six. The scientists, however, failed to notice, or failed to reveal, that the rare Byrde's whales represented three separate species that did not likely interbreed. This fraudulent "scientific harvest" of Byrde's whales netted 1,128 tons of prime whale meat for the Japanese markets. Meanwhile, along the coast of Chile, the Japanese discovered a remnant population of blue whales. In 1978 the carcass of a 75-foot blue whale washed ashore on the beach of a Peruvian resort, mortally wounded by an exploding harpoon. Craig van Note and Nick Carter suspected the Nippon Hogei Co. under Panamanian registry had killed the protected whale.

The outright pirates operated in Spain, Portugal, Chile, Peru, Taiwan, South Africa, Korea, Somalia, and Cyprus. Norway and Japan financed and supplied them. While the IWC quotas had been trimmed over the previous five years from 43,000 whales to 20,000, the covert industry had grown to over 5,000 whales per year, plus the whales wounded and left for dead. Although IWC regulations prohibited member countries from importing their products, Japan refused to comply and claimed the restrictions violated "free trade."

The most notorious and productive pirate whaling ship of them all was the *Sierra*. In 1964, the bankrupt Dutch harpoon ship *A.M. #4* had been converted to a harpoon/factory ship in Norway, ostensibly sold to a Liechtenstein shell company, and registered as a "fishing boat" in the Bahamas. The ship worked the coast of Angola, taking 500 whales per year, until an embarrassed Bahamian government pulled the registration. The ship took up the Somalian flag and the new name, *Sierra*. In 1977, the *Sierra* shipped 586 tons of prime whale meat to Japan in 50-kilogram bags illicitly labelled "Produce of Spain."

A Norwegian skipper commanded the *Sierra*, with Japanese officers, harpooners, and buyers. At the Ivory Coast port of Abidjan, Japanese freighters picked up the meat, without processing the transactions through any country. Taiyo Fishery and Nippon Hogei controlled the pirate operations in Chile and Peru. The United States, France and the Netherlands had complained, but Japanese IWC delegate Kunio Yonezawa claimed he knew nothing about the operations. Nick Carter later confirmed that Taiyo Fishery in Japan owned 75 percent of the *Sierra*, and the Foreningsbanken in Norway 25 percent.

Although Greenpeace adhered to a strict philosophy of non-violence against person or property, by 1979 environmentalists had grown frustrated at the dithering while whales perished. A popular leaflet at the time quoted a despondent Mark Anthony from the third act of Shakespeare's *Julius Caesar*:

> O, pardon me, thou bleeding piece of earth,
> That I am meek and gentle with these butchers!

Paul Watson, whose aggressive tactics had strained his relationship with Greenpeace, now pursued his own methods. In July 1979, Watson's 206-foot *Sea Shepherd*, a converted trawler with reinforced concrete bow, plied through the eastern Atlantic looking for the *Sierra*. The *Sea Shepherd* carried a crew of eighteen. On July 15, they came upon the whaler over the Azores-Gibraltar Ridge, 300 miles off the coast of Portugal. As they approached, the ship fled east for Porto De Leixoes. There, a local pilot escorted the *Sea Shepherd* into port with the *Sierra*, but the pirate whaler suddenly turned and headed back out to sea. The Portuguese authorities, however, refused to clear the *Sea Shepherd* for two hours and ordered them into the dock. Watson had been duped. He, Peter Woof from Australia, and Jerry Doran from Hawaii departed, in defiance of the authorities. The other fifteen crewmembers stayed in port to avoid arrest.

The three renegades caught the *Sierra* only a quarter mile outside De Leixoes, the whalers lounging on deck in the sun. To warn the crew that they were about to be rammed, Peter Woof guided the *Sea Shepherd* across the whalers' bow, glancing off the rusted metal hull and jarring the harpoon. They circled the stern of the whaling vessel as startled workers lined the decks. They took dead aim at the forward bow, hit the ship at 12 knots, tore a six-foot gash in the infamous *Sierra,* and stove in 45 feet of the hull. The *Sierra* was out of business. As Watson, Woof, and Doran raced for Spanish territory, a Portuguese destroyer caught them and forced them back to Porto De Leixoes. A Liberian shell company, Ultra-marine Shipping, filed a suit and Portuguese police seized the *Sea Shepherd* along with the crew's passports. Watson and his accomplices slipped out of the country. The *Sea Shepherd* was looted in the Portuguese harbour until Watson and Woof returned weeks later and scuttled the ship to keep it out of the hands of the Japanese fishing companies that had sued them.

The publicity proved decisive. Even conservative *Time* magazine cheered the demise of the "loathed" whalers and called the ramming a "Victory at Sea." The Japanese and Norwegians came under such scrutiny that the IWC responded. The detective work of Nick Carter left the banks and financiers no room to wiggle out. In the September 1979 *Greenpeace Chronicles*, we ran Watson's story and photographs. In spite of the Greenpeace policy of non-violence, none of us had been sorry to see the *Sierra* meet its ignoble end. Some who had opposed Watson inside Greenpeace cheered his audacity. Perhaps the *Sea Shepherd*'s brief life and the *Sierra*'s scars were fair measure for the life and freedom of whales. In any case, it was done, and whale lovers worldwide rejoiced.

A RIP IN THE FABRIC

In Vancouver, we considered a campaign to stop the Pribilof Islands fur seal hunt in the Bering Sea. American schooners once took 250,000 seals from the Pribilofs each year, but the annual harvest now stood at 30,000, and dropping. Craig van Note told us that the US government secretly longed to end the hunt and that a Greenpeace protest there would help force their hand in negotiations with Alaska, Japan, Canada, and the Soviet Union. We intended to go, but had to raise at least $20,000 even if we could get the *James Bay* for free.

I had been away from home half of the last two years. At a critical time in my marriage, when Glenn and I needed to make the transition out of romanticism, I had been gone. We loved each other, but had not understood what love required to endure, and our pilgrimage to Baja had not saved our marriage. She left that summer for Amsterdam, and I lived alone on First Avenue.

I had been without income for a year, but now received $500 per month from the *Greenpeace Chronicles*. I worked with Bill Gannon's sister, Shivon, and her husband Lee Robinsong to produce the newspaper each month, gleaning stories from our Greenpeace and Natural Guard networks.

In July, the United States experienced the worst radioactive waste spill in its history when 100 million gallons of contaminated water breached a uranium mine tailings pond and spilled into the Rio Puerco. The *Greenpeace Chronicles* would later earn a Columbia University School of Journalism award for breaking the story about the disaster. We continued to cover Karen Silkwood's unsolved murder case, in which Kitty Tucker's legal team eventually won an $11 million settlement from Kerr-McGee for Silkwood's three children. The case was made into a feature film starring Meryl Streep.

Environmental horror stories bubbled to the surface like the dioxins in Love Canal. In Philadelphia, an enterprising disposal agent accepted $213,000 to dump 730,000 gallons of toxic sludge into the Delaware River. He was caught and jailed for six months, the first conviction under the EPA's Clean Water Act. At the Aldermaston Atomic Weapons Research Station in the UK, where the European disarmament movement had begun twenty-five years earlier, an explosion killed government scientist Peter Allen.

When the Canadian Ministry of Agriculture announced a plan to eradicate Gypsy moths by spraying 150 blocks of Kitsilano — directly over the top of our Vancouver office — with the insecticide diflubenzuron, or Dimilin, we rose up overnight. In the Shire? "No way," Shivon said, four months pregnant. We dressed up in animal costumes for city council meetings, and citizens rose up in spontaneous displays of disapproval. One family wrapped their entire home in plastic. Signs posted block votes: "Yes-0, No-63." In the end, the ministry did not spray the neighbourhood and the alleged Gypsy moth disaster never materialized.

In June 1979, pilot Al "Jet" Johnson dropped ten Greenpeace skydivers over the construction site of the Darlington Nuclear Generating Station in Ontario. Five of the ten parachutists landed inside the perimeter fence and were arrested by Ontario Hydro private security as Don Franks led a rally of 2,000 people at the front gate.

Following the Greenpeace success in the North Sea and Mediterranean, and since the Americans had censured the Canadian seal hunt, it only made sense that the US should end the Pribilof hunt. We sent a letter to President Jimmy Carter and prepared to launch the *James Bay*. But in Vancouver, in the summer of 1979, we reached the decisive point at which our internal crisis precluded our ecology activities. Without cash support from our American groups, we could not launch the ship to the Pribilofs.

The backlash from our harp seal campaign had cut our Canadian revenues by half. We never once considered backing off the seal campaign for the sake of local fundraising, but since we had lost control of our global revenues, which boomed during that same period, we were broke. The Seattle and Denver offices agreed to help, but they did not have the resources. We needed San Francisco, which had just received a $150,000 bequest to Greenpeace, and had launched a national direct mail fundraising campaign. Consolidated annual Greenpeace revenues had reached $5 million.

To us on Fourth Avenue, of course, the situation seemed unfair, but we knew few others saw it that way. The *Rainbow Warrior* remained busy in Europe, where McTaggart now had enough revenue to be independent. The Hawaii group considered themselves a sovereign entity. The San Francisco group had money but was in no mood to finance a campaign from Canada directed at the US, which might endanger their own funding drive. This inclination to protect local funding had represented our primary fear about organizing around national identities. "It's convenient to believe that the environment should be cleaned up somewhere else," Hunter observed. Over the phone, I pleaded with Gary Zimmerman, who was sympathetic but not encouraging. He had his own board to appease.

The Canadian Greenpeace Foundation finally reached the impasse where we could go no farther without settling our political mess. No one in Vancouver wanted to face it, but the time had come. On June 15, 1979, the board of directors — Bob and Bobbi Hunter, Pat and Eileen Moore, Bob Cummings, Michael Chechik, Bill Gannon, Rod Marining, Mel Gregory, Paul and Linda Spong, Lyle Thurston, John Cormack, and I — cancelled the Pribilof campaign and set to work to solve the internal political chaos.

THE PATH NOT TAKEN

Greenpeace in San Francisco had incorporated three new entities: "Greenpeace Foundation of America," "Greenpeace USA," and the "Fund For Greenpeace." We were not privy to the directors or financial records of these organizations, and though we trusted our friends' intentions, we wanted to see the accounting trail. Furthermore, just as the Greenpeace Foundation faced rebellion everywhere, the San Francisco group faced rebellion from the other American offices. In Europe, McTaggart's claim to "Greenpeace Europe" faced rebellion from two UK groups, "London Greenpeace," and "Greenpeace UK Ltd," as well as "Greenpeace Aegean Sea." It became Pat Moore's unhappy job to sort this out on behalf of what we longingly called "one Greenpeace."

With the help of our lawyer Peter Ballem, we negotiated an agreement with the three San Francisco entities, which agreed to reveal their boards of directors and provide monthly financial statements. We confirmed regional editions of the *Greenpeace Chronicles*, with each region retaining editorial and advertising rights in their inserted sections. According to the deal, all local groups would match local overhead and campaign costs with equal deposits to an international fund overseen by an executive committee comprised of representatives from the US and Canada. We would then integrate other Greenpeace groups. Toronto, Rocky Mountains, and Seattle agreed. The international fund would solve, we hoped, the problem of local offices being hurt financially by particular campaigns. Ballem drafted the agreement in a seventeen-page document, a well-conceived blueprint for Greenpeace to move forward as a single entity. Had we signed the accord, we would have saved ourselves tremendous heartache, but once again, on the verge of solving our problems, we balked.

After long negotiations, the San Francisco group claimed they could not sign the document until all the other US groups agreed. We all knew Hawaii would refuse. In Vancouver we suspected the delay was a ruse. Millions of dollars now hung in the balance. Moore lashed out at Zimmerman and lawyer David Tussman. Diplomacy was not Moore's strength. He was the brightest ecologist we had, able to face down industry scientists and witty with the media, but the very characteristics that made him a tough negotiator, worked against him in the delicate arts of diplomacy. Moore ruffled feathers with his insistence that the Greenpeace Foundation rightfully coined the name, established the reputation, financed the growth, and therefore owned the rights worldwide. Legally, all of this was true, but diplomatically, better left unsaid.

David McTaggart, on the other hand, was the consummate diplomat, tough with his enemies, soothing and encouraging to his allies. He had support in Europe and he now courted the dissenters in North America. I went to San Francisco to coax Tussman, Baker, and Zimmerman toward a resolution. I had common cause with them because of our deal for regional editions of the *Chronicles*. Zimmerman understood the Greenpeace Foundation position, since he had known us since 1974, and he supported a resolution that would share the financial bounty from the United States. Tussman remained cautious. Cindy Baker, I discovered, had cancer. She had dedicated the last months of her life to the whale campaign and I could not bear to drag her into the internal conflicts. In contrast to our tensions, Cindy Baker seemed bathed in some ethereal light, soft-spoken, and on a sacred mission to save the whales.

Zimmerman and Tussman advised me on their direct mail campaign worth millions of dollars. We discussed tying this into a *Chronicles* subscription drive. With Erol Baykal — the 1977 seal photographer, now living in San Francisco and running the *Chronicles* office there — I met with Bill Dodd and Sherry Morely at the Parker-Dodd direct mail office. Indeed, they had big plans. The initial test mailings had been successful. "Direct mail is a simple science," Dodd told me. "You send the appeals with the best proven results to the best markets." What appeals got the best results? I wondered.

"Seals and whales," he said. Dodd talked about sending millions of pieces of mail, getting a two percent response, and maybe $20 or $30 per response. Yes, in round figures, that came to millions of dollars, but I had concerns. Where would the lists come from? What were the costs, fee structure, and net income? Parker-Dodd seemed like a legitimate organization, but here the answers became vague. When I questioned his right to proceed before we had a confirmed deal with the Greenpeace Foundation, Dodd seemed perturbed. "Greenpeace doesn't really belong to anyone, as far as I can see," he said. "It's in the public domain." Baykal and I looked at each other and I felt a shudder. The man obviously believed what he had just said.

"Yeah, okay," I said. When I told Tussman about my conversation with Dodd, he said, "Don't worry about it. He doesn't know what he's talking about." I felt confused. Why wouldn't San Francisco sign the deal with the Greenpeace Foundation? What was going on?

Moore lost patience. He travelled to San Francisco, but I later heard from Dick Dillman that he had alienated people in the office by demanding that they send money to Vancouver. Moore, on the other hand, said he had made no such demand, but had merely explained to the Americans the financial situation we were in. Over the phone, Tussman claimed we must have mismanaged our money since we were in debt. It was a gratuitous argument, but Moore slammed down the telephone. He told the Greenpeace Foundation board he was going to "give San Francisco one more chance." Tussman was coming north for talks. If he failed to sign the deal as negotiated, Moore wanted to launch a lawsuit. "We'll put it to the courts," he said. "Our lawyers say we have the right to insist they make a deal with us." Legally, yes, we knew, but politically and publicly, a lawsuit could be a disaster. Moore and Ballem assured us they had to use the threat of a suit to force San Francisco to the table. The board agreed to let Moore and Ballem negotiate a final deal. Mel Gregory dissented. We sympathized with his opinion that a lawsuit could be damaging, but we expected Tussman, in the end, to agree.

Tussman arrived in Vancouver in August 1979. Gannon and I met with him to confirm the *Chronicles* agreement. Then he disappeared into Moore's office. When he emerged, he left the office without saying a word. It was the last time I ever saw him. "We're going to file the papers," Moore said, storming through the office. "Let the courts settle this."

RUBIK'S CUBE

With the lawsuit filed, there was no more need for pretence. Tussman, McTaggart, and Don White in Hawaii felt their interests would best be served if each region operated its own Greenpeace organization. "No," insisted Moore, "there has to be *one* Greenpeace." On that point, the Greenpeace Foundation board agreed. There were legitimate dissenters in Canada, like Walrus, who felt that Greenpeace was "a movement, not an organization." Walrus Oakenbough, formerly and later known by his given name David Garrick, had been involved since the beginning, even before the first Greenpeace ship had sailed to Amchitka. He represented the heart and soul of the first decade of Greenpeace as much as anyone. I sympathized with his position that Greenpeace was a movement, more like the No Nukes movement than the Sierra Club, but I did not entirely agree. Walrus and I discussed these matters on the front lawn of his communal "Kitsilano Harmony House." Taeko Miwa was pregnant with their first child. "I don't think we can change the fact that Greenpeace is an organization," I said. "There are bank accounts, fundraising machines, and boards of directors. None of that is going to go away, no matter what we do."

"Stop the lawsuit," he insisted.

I met Bob Hunter in Port Moody. He did not blame Moore for the impasse with San Francisco, but he seethed over his last meeting with his old buddy. "Pat told me to butt out," Hunter complained. "Butt out?! Jesus! The environmental navy is about to go to war with itself! You'd think Uncle Pat would be taking some advice from his oldest comrade." Hunter believed that Moore had done everything he could but did not possess the political personality to rally the rebellious new environmentalists. "He's right about forming one Greenpeace," said Hunter, "but the lawsuit is a nightmare." We had agreed that Moore and Ballem should prepare to defend the Greenpeace name. The Royal Bank of Canada had assured us they would increase our credit line to cover attorneys' fees. The entire plan for paying back the loans in 1975 had been to develop a global ecology organization. But now, like the baby before Solomon, Greenpeace hung in the air, the sword raised. Like a parent, Hunter said "No. Wait." He wanted a political solution. "We're now seen as the oppressor," he said. "They're using liberation language like 'autonomy' but the naked truth is that most of them are little eco-fiefdoms looking after their cash flows. It's disgusting."

Hunter buried his face in his hands. "McTaggart's coming to Vancouver," he said, looking up. "I'm going to talk to him." He must have read the look in my eyes. "I know. He doesn't get it. He treated us poorly in his book, which I helped him write, by the way. But it doesn't matter. We have to make peace with David and with the Americans. David has nothing to gain by compromising with Moore. He's set up as the king of Europe. They've got a boat, they're on the news, and they can raise money. They don't need us. Neither do the Americans. The only thing we really have now is the moral right to the name. The legal route is the last, last, *last* resort. I'm going to see if I can convince David to make a deal."

I had come across an essay, "A Good Solution," by farmer-philosopher Wendell Berry, who pointed out that a complete solution to a social problem followed certain ecological principles: a "good solution," said Berry, maintained patterns and harmony, solved several problems at once, did not create new problems, allowed for changing circumstances, was frugal with time and money, and interdependent in many realms. I mentioned Berry's ecological approach to problem-solving to Hunter.

"Yeah, sounds nice," the disenchanted ecologist said. "Be prepared: the subtleties of ecology may not survive the politics." Hunter raised his beer and we clinked the bottles on his back porch overlooking the head of Burrard Inlet. "I'll call you when David's around."

Moore's recollection of the meeting with Hunter was, understandably, different. "Bob's right that they don't need us," Moore said, "but that doesn't make it right that Greenpeace gets chopped up into little camps with their own purposes. If people want to go off on their own, they should do what Watson did, form their own group with their own name. Greenpeace has fundamental values and policies. Those aren't negotiable as long as I'm involved." Moore thought Hunter's political interference confused things. "I didn't tell him to butt out. Well, maybe I did, but I didn't mean any disrespect. Hunter's too soft. If he undermines me, that just makes our case weaker."

Eileen, pregnant with their first child, had grown weary of the politics, but knew her young family would not soon be extricated. Aside, she told me, "Pat's as sick of this as anyone. He doesn't want to sue anyone. He wants to get this bloody thing settled." Eileen and Pat had worked odd jobs for five years as they helped build Greenpeace into an international force for ecology. Now, as full-time president, Moore received a modest salary of $1,000 per month. They were settled in a home in Kitsilano, prepared to raise a family.

No single person could be blamed for the impasse. Our successes and failures were collective. In San Francisco, Tussman was bright and well-spoken, yet Moore felt that the lawyer had betrayed our trust. We didn't really know the political pressures to which he might have been responding. Susi Newborn and David McTaggart represented the spiritual and political extremes in Europe, but there were myriad positions between those two. The interpersonal dynamics of organizing a global ecology force seemed as complex as the Rubik's cube that had become popular at the time.

DAVID

Rémi Parmentier and David McTaggart knew a public scrap over control of Greenpeace would hurt everyone and the cause. They envisioned a "political" Greenpeace, along the lines of le Mouvement d'écologie politique in France. McTaggart and Parmentier forged a plan to formalize a single European Greenpeace that would speak with one voice and "pick up the pieces," as McTaggart told Parmentier, from the two competing entities in North America. They met with Allan Thornton and proposed the plan. Thornton had somehow obtained Susi Newborn's original Greenpeace UK Ltd. share certificate, from Denise Bell. They ratified the Greenpeace Europe proposal with McTaggart as director. Newborn resigned from the UK board but kept her place on the *Rainbow Warrior* crew. "What's on this boat," she told her friends, "is the true spirit of Greenpeace. I don't care what anyone says. This is the thing we can't lose."

Parmentier, McTaggart, Thornton, and new Greenpeace Netherlands executive director Art van Remundt arrived in Vancouver in July. They met with Fred Easton and post-graduate student Michael M'Gonigle to get a debriefing of the local political climate. M'Gonigle had accompanied Spong to the IWC for three years. He had worked closely with the European environmentalists and understood the European perspective. McTaggart learned quickly that there was scant enthusiasm in Vancouver for a long, embarrassing legal stand, and he knew that Hunter likely held the balance of power.

The four Europeans made a quick trip to San Francisco and met with Tussman, Zimmerman, Baker, and Dillman. McTaggart secured approval to speak on their behalf in negotiations with the Greenpeace Foundation in Canada. Parmentier and the others returned to Europe, but McTaggart came back to Vancouver and met with Hunter at the Cecil Pub. The old pub had been transformed into a cheap strip bar, the tiny avant-garde corner desecrated with strobe lights. Hunter and McTaggart sat near the door and negotiated. "Moore is marked for a battle," McTaggart warned Hunter, explaining that the Greenpeace groups in the United States and Europe "are aligned." Hunter told McTaggart that the Canadian group had a legitimate claim and that the Royal Bank would finance the Greenpeace Foundation to protect its financial interest. Greenpeace, as far as the bank and *their* lawyers were concerned, was a single entity.

"Fine," McTaggart said, but there had to be a political structure that everyone would agree to. He proposed "one country, one vote," the same proposal that had been defeated by a 4–11 vote at the first global Greenpeace meeting two years earlier. However, the political landscape had changed. The lawsuit had forced McTaggart to the table, but it also had isolated Moore. San Francisco and Hawaii, the richest American groups, would rally around McTaggart, their best hope of retaining autonomy.

It was our own fault that Greenpeace had developed in such a muddled fashion. We were ecologists, journalists, and activists. Few among us — perhaps only Gannon, McTaggart, and our lawyers — were experienced business managers. Gannon had drafted a Greenpeace accounting system and the lawyers had drafted a reasonable organizational model, but that deal remained unsigned. The vagaries of personality and self-interest had carried more influence than business logic.

I arrived at the pub at 4:00 p.m. Hunter shrugged and looked satisfied. McTaggart was in good spirits. We toasted the demise of the *Sierra* and talked about an underground bomb test at Moruroa that registered 6.3 on the Richter scale in Wellington, New Zealand. "We have to go back there," McTaggart said, "and finish that crap."

Marining arrived and McTaggart left at 5:00 p.m. "David wants one-country, one-vote," Hunter told us. The proposal would put McTaggart in charge of Greenpeace. Marining wondered out loud what others felt: Which countries will be included? Why should some country that has never launched a single campaign be given a vote equal to the Greenpeace Foundation? "Yeah, I know," said Hunter. "If we do this, we're giving it away. The centre will shift to Europe, with David in charge. We have to talk to Moore and Ballem, and everyone else."

Ballem advised we make a deal. At first hearing this, Moore said he felt betrayed by his lawyer. Hunter argued that the goal was to have a single, cohesive organization, not to control it. "Maybe the only way to have one Greenpeace," Hunter said to Moore, "is to give it to David." Eileen Moore, six months pregnant, devoted what energy she did have for Greenpeace business to console her husband, who now felt unappreciated and undermined by Hunter's interference.

Bobbi Hunter and Gannon were against the deal without a guarantee that the debts would be retired by the money sitting in bank accounts in the US and Europe. Gannon wanted a promise of monthly financial statements from every national group that had a vote. He recommended the organization adopt the financial planning and revenue sharing guidelines already drafted. The rest of the board members were willing to go along. No one wanted a lawsuit, but everyone on the Greenpeace Foundation board aspired to preserve what he or she regarded as the core values of Greenpeace.

Paul Spong wanted to make sure the whale campaign was not compromised. A complete whaling moratorium seemed imminent, but political momentum is fickle: if Greenpeace let up, the whaling nations would gain strength. Although Greenpeace was not alone in bringing the whaling industry to an end, Greenpeace bravado had become the symbol of the movement. Without the public pressure, the whalers could simply ignore IWC rules.

I wanted to preserve the *Greenpeace Chronicles*, and I held out hope that we could devise an organization based on ecological regions, not national offices. Gannon said the accounting could easily flow across borders and currencies. "No big deal," he assured me. Perhaps romantically, I invoked the Wendell Berry checklist and Bateson's natural order. One thing Bateson had said was certainly true: "Any answer which we promote, as it becomes partly true through our promoting of it, becomes partly irreversible."

History would not abide our dithering. History, like Hunter's description of journalism, exacted "stark justice." Humanity is pushed by complex drives and impulses, and events turn on the sum of myriad accidents and decisions, on personal stamina and popular versions of partially formed ideas. Change, as Spong had said, may happen at the speed of thought, but social change involves a tangle of competing and contradictory thoughts.

"David may get his way," shrugged Hunter, "simply because he's the smartest politician." With Hunter and Ballem prepared to make a deal, momentum would swing away from the Greenpeace Foundation in Canada. Europe would become the organizing force for the new Greenpeace. It was a bitter pill for Moore, even though he would achieve his vision of one Greenpeace. McTaggart promised to return in October, at which time we would meet with our lawyers to draw up the deal and create the new Greenpeace structure.

TO THE MARROW

Between July and October, when McTaggart would return, most of us in Vancouver simply turned our attention back to the reports of environmental disasters that arrived daily in our office. Among these communiqués from around the world, I received a telegram from Carolyn Tawangyawma, an elder of the Hopi Nation in Arizona: "I HOPE AND PRAY THAT THE GREEN PEACE FOUNDATION WILL HELP TO BRING ABOUT PEACE IN HOPI LAND." The message seemed cryptic. What were we to do? I stuffed the telegram in my notebook in August when I returned to Colorado. The Greenpeace group in Denver had discovered their own Love Canal disaster in Sand Creek, which runs between two oil refineries northeast of the city centre. Typical of the era, the creek was the sewer for the refineries, a pesticide dumping site, a city landfill, and contained an abandoned acid storage pit. Two years earlier, gas from the dump had exploded in a city water conduit and killed two workers. Rocky Mountain Greenpeace staged public demonstrations in the creek to force a cleanup.

I felt at ease working in Colorado, where the focus remained clearly on ecology. A study in the Denver suburbs, downwind from the Rocky Flats plutonium trigger plant, had shown a 45 percent increase in congenital birth defects compared to the rest of the state. I visited Dr. Carl Johnson, director of the county health department. Johnson had found increased cancer rates close to the plant — 24 percent higher for men, 10 percent higher for women — including leukemia, lymphoma, and lung cancer. Johnson estimated 491 excess cancer cases where the DOE had estimated one. Real estate interests, however, pressed the county to fire Johnson, claiming his public statements hurt their industry.

Meanwhile, farmer Lloyd Mixon in Broomfield, directly downwind from the plant, had his thyroid removed and tumours removed from his chest. He complained of a bizarre string of malformed animals: piglets with twisted snouts or with five toes, a hairless calf with an enlarged liver, eyeless chickens, and crippled lambs. State health inspectors blamed bad feed and inbreeding, but Mixon scoffed at this. He had talked to other "downwind farmers" in Pennsylvania, Vermont, and New Hampshire, who had reported similar deformities. "It's that factory," Mixon said.

Eleven-year-old Kristen Haag, whose family lived six miles downwind from Rocky Flats, had her leg amputated to stop the spread of bone marrow cancer. It was impossible to conclusively link her cancer to Rocky Flats, but her father blamed the plant. In 1969, a fire at the plant killed two workers and released plutonium into the winds that blew past their home. Kristen had been two years old. In the summer of 1979, Denver citizens had no proof that plutonium had caused the strange ailments. All they had were the sad, peculiar stories.

From Broomfield, I attended the Rocky Mountain Healing Arts Festival, northwest of Boulder, a gathering of humanistic psychologists and holistic doctors. There, I ran into Paul Winter and through him met a woman from

California, who asked me, seemingly out of the blue, "Are you working with the Hopi?" From my notebook I pulled the cryptic telegram from Hopi elder Carolyn Tawangyawma. The woman gave me the name of Joan Price in Denver and told me, "She'll know what to do."

A week later, I met Price in Denver, and through her met Hopi, Navajo, and Lakota activists battling to save their traditional lands from the ravages of uranium mining, including the disaster on the Rio Puerco. Price introduced me to Winona LaDuke, the woman who had given a rousing speech at the Rocky Flats gathering a year earlier. She introduced me to Lakota elders in Pine Ridge South Dakota and spiritual leader Richard Kastl, who worked with the Hopi. The ecology struggle on Native American land had taken a much darker turn than even the worst of what I had witnessed in the much more tame peace and ecology movements. Treaty land had been leased away to resource companies. Traditional Native leaders had been shot, jailed, and driven underground. "It's outright land theft," LaDuke told me. "Hopi and Navajo families are being forcibly removed from their homes. The Department of Interior calls their reservation land a 'National Sacrifice Area.' It's genocide."

Although I did not suspect this at the time, over the next three years, my own life and work would be linked with these people I had just met: Joan Price, the Hopi, and the Lakota. Throughout North America, the middle-class ecology movement found a natural link to the indigenous peoples' struggle for their heritage land. For those of us who considered ourselves Warriors of the Rainbow, we had little choice but to help.

LaDuke and activist Mark Tilsen worked with the Lakota leaders and musicians — Browne, Raitt, O'Keefe, Campbell — to stage a Survival Gathering in the Black Hills. Later, in September, the Musicians United for Safe Energy, MUSE, performed over five nights at Madison Square Garden, with a rally at New York's Battery Park, featuring Ralph Nader, Bella Abzug, Dr. Dr. John Gofman, Native leader John Trudell, and Grey Panthers founder Maggie Kuhn. "Old age is an excellent time for outrage," Kuhn told the crowd. The evening concerts featured — in addition to the regulars like Raitt and Browne — James Taylor, Carly Simon, Stephen Stills, Graham Nash, David Crosby, Pete Seeger, Ry Cooder, The Doobie Brothers, Chaka Khan, Tom Petty, Poco, Raydio, Nicolette Larson, Peter Tosh, Paul Simon, Sweet Honey in the Rock, and Bruce Springsteen. The musicians assembled on stage for John and Johanna Hall's safe-energy anthem "Power." The concerts raised over $600,000 for ecology and Native groups. A recording was released in December, followed by a feature film, with royalties and profits donated to the activists.

Before the end of the year, Kristen Haag, the eleven-year-old girl downwind from Rocky Flats, died from her bone marrow cancer. Her body was cremated and, at the request of her father, tested. Plutonium-238 was found in the ashes. An EPA autopsy study by Dr. John Cobb at the University of Colorado found plutonium in other downwind citizens, traceable by isotope-ratios to Rocky Flats.

THE SCEPTRE

Fall came to the Shire with steady rain and silver-grey overcast days. Taeko Miwa gave birth to Cedar Akifumi Miwa Garrick. Our little tribe had grown older, and responsibilities for children would change individual roles. Serendipitously, the United Nations had declared 1979 the Year of the Child. Nothing connected one to the future — or to nature — more clearly than the eyes of a newborn. In keeping with this, we planned a special edition of the *Greenpeace Chronicles* for December, dedicated to children and to optimism for the future of human life on Earth.

Meanwhile, we had time for one quick campaign before our scheduled meeting that would end the era of the Greenpeace Foundation. On the first day of October, 1979, I flew 450 miles north to Smithers, British Columbia, with naturalist Jim Allen, filmmaker Michael Chechik, cameraman Colin Wedgewood, veteran eco-warrior Al Johnson, nature photographer Jim Wright, and Greenpeace stalwarts Jim Taylor and Judy Drake. We joined the Hagwilget First Nation in New Hazelton and launched a campaign to stop trophy hunting in Spatsizi Plateau Wilderness Provincial Park. The park had ostensibly been established as a "wilderness landscape in which natural communities are preserved intact." A hunting lobby had negotiated an amendment that allowed trophy hunting, but the parks branch chief biologist was "concerned" about the decline of caribou and sheep. A study by the University of Victoria and UBC had concluded, "hunting should cease." The local guide outfitters had seen the writing on the wall and began offering photography excursions, but the big money was still in killing big mammals — the stone sheep, timber wolves, grizzly bears, caribou, and moose. On October 3, we confronted American and Swedish hunters in the park. The Swedes called us *Gröntmän*, "the Greenmen." By October 5, we were back in Vancouver with the film footage that would eventually force the provincial parks branch to declare Spatsizi a true wilderness.

After this effective jaunt, we took a deep breath and plunged into meetings with lawyers to prepare for our showdown with McTaggart, scheduled for October 14. Walrus was committed to the McTaggart plan, as were Fred Easton and our IWC delegate, Michael M'Gonigle. Paul Watson arrived in Vancouver, a hero for putting the *Sierra* out of business. Although he had declared Greenpeace "a movement, not an organization" and now claimed to be "out of Greenpeace," he backed McTaggart. Bob and Bobbi Hunter wanted the issue settled without a lawsuit, and saw McTaggart's "Council" of national groups the only viable solution.

Gannon, Chechik, Linda Spong, Paul Spong, Rod and Bree Marining, and the Moores either opposed the plan or had strict conditions. On October 11, three days before our scheduled talks with McTaggart, we assembled as a board at Gannon's home. Lyle Thurston held the gavel that had been used at Greenpeace Foundation meetings for seven years. Thurston invoked Dorothy and Irving Stowe, Dorothy and Ben Metcalfe, and others who had held the responsibility in the early years. "The heart of the matter is trust," he said. "We either trust a Council to carry the name and principles forward, or not." With this, Thurston let drop the gavel in a gesture of relinquishing hold on the sceptre. Moore held open his palms as if agreeing to let go. One by one, silently, we nodded. There was no vote. Everyone knew there were issues to resolve, but the intention was clearly to let it go. Hunter reached his thin fingers into the air, and with a pinching movement, pulled some invisible thing back out of the air. "We'll keep the *Foundation*." The new organization would be called, simply, Greenpeace. "The Greenpeace Foundation has done its part," said Hunter. "It's over."

The McTaggart plan now stood as a *fait accompli*. "The final test," Hunter said later, in the pub, "is to give it away without any expectation."

On Friday, October 12, McTaggart came to my flat on First Avenue at about 8:00 p.m., dripping wet from the rain. This, I suspected, would be my last chance to negotiate with the future leader of Greenpeace. There was still a chance that the deal could falter if the Greenpeace Foundation did not reach consensus. Ballem advised we accept the Council, but still took instructions from the Board. McTaggart knew this and was prepared to compromise if he had to. He also knew that he had the whole thing within his grasp if he remained reasonable.

McTaggart told me about the adventures of the *Rainbow Warrior*. "The Europeans are bloody serious," he said. I tested my idea about eschewing the national format. We discussed the potential conflict between nationalist priorities and ecological priorities. "Too complicated," he said flatly.

"What are we going to do," I questioned him, "when the Canadians want to compromise the seal policy to solve their fundraising problems, or the Japanese want to compromise the whale policy, or the Americans want to go easy on their own fishing industry?" McTaggart said he believed the Council could sort through these conflicts as they came up. On the one hand, I doubted him, but I let it go.

I told McTaggart about the finances and organization of the *Greenpeace Chronicles*. There had been talk of abandoning the news format for local fundraising newsletters. Some people didn't like the idea that we sold advertising, even to our supporters like Zodiac and health food companies. "I've heard some complaints about some of the opinions expressed," McTaggart told me.

"I would hope so!" I responded. "We can't publish a decent magazine without controversy. The idea is a contradiction." He did not appear convinced.

"You just keep doing what you're doing," he said. "I can't guarantee that the European groups won't want to do their own thing." I had envisioned an international ecology magazine that would break important stories every month. I explained the concept. It would not be simply about Greenpeace. It would be about ecology. McTaggart was not a journalist, but he possessed a sharp business mind, and he understood the point. "Yeah, I'll support that," McTaggart told me. I clinked his coffee cup.

We talked wistfully about the future. "There's one other thing," I said. In the discussions about trademarks, it had been suggested that "Rainbow Warrior" should be registered. "This would be a mistake," I told McTaggart. "Greenpeace" was a legitimate trademark. The organization originated the name, gave it meaning, and created the public goodwill for it since 1971. "But 'Rainbow Warrior' is different," I said. "That's a legend we borrowed."

"Well, yeah, but protecting its use is necessary."

"No," I insisted. "It would be wrong. Don't do it. We don't own it and we shouldn't pretend to."

"I'll have to talk to the lawyers."

"It's not a decision for the lawyers." I was adamant, if somewhat polemic. "It's a sacred tradition. You can *be* a Rainbow Warrior, but you can't *own* Rainbow Warrior."

McTaggart shrugged. I had lost him, but I knew I could count on Hunter, Walrus, and others to back me up. "Talk to Bob," I said. "Be careful with this one."

"Yeah, okay."

I doubted that I had convinced him of anything, although I had solicited his support for the *Chronicles*. I drove him to his relatives' home near Kitsilano Beach and we talked in the front seat of my yellow Volkswagen beetle, rain blowing in from English Bay. We did agree that nuclear weapons needed to be addressed with a fresh campaign. High-technology saber rattling threatened global security. I told him about the neutron bomb. "Well," said McTaggart, "let's sort out our organization so we can deal with these things." McTaggart, I believed, was sincere about this point. He saw how powerful and effective Greenpeace could be internationally, but only if we quelled the internal bickering. We shook hands, and McTaggart disappeared into the darkness and rain.

The next morning I met with Pat and Eileen Moore, and lawyer Peter Ballem. Eileen served tea at the kitchen table. I recounted my meeting with McTaggart. "Sooner or later," said Ballem, "in these kinds of things, someone has to trust someone." McTaggart, Moore, Ballem, Gannon, and I met that afternoon to discuss the debts, revenue sharing, and financial reporting. Our final meeting, to draw up a document with Davie Gibbons, was scheduled for the next morning. That night, at Gannon's home, we took out the Greenpeace Foundation seal and passed one final resolution, sentimental perhaps, and ceremonial, but with solemn intent: "Planet Earth be hereby declared a preserve for all sentient beings." We sealed the resolution and signed it: Gannon, Moore, Linda Spong, and I.

THE MEETING

On Sunday, October 14, I arrived at Davie Gibbons' Vancouver office just before noon. Hunter, Thurston, and Marining conversed by a large window.

Moore arrived with Ballem. McTaggart arrived with Walrus and Michael M'Gonigle. Gibbons presided. He had been the senior Greenpeace lawyer since 1972, the counsel of choice in a crisis. "Okay," said Gibbons, "I think the best thing would be to go around the table and let each person speak, and let's see what we can all agree on."

"Well, I still believe in miracles," Hunter said cheerfully, "although my spiritual beliefs have come under fire lately." Hunter could be counted on to set the ethereal context. He told us about his life as a new father, and an epiphany he'd had in a sweat lodge erected by three Cree men on his land. "Basically," he said, "I realized the Earth really *is* God. Miracles are about timing. You just have to be there to see them."

Lyle Thurston, a devoted advocate since the first Greenpeace voyage, was brief and jovial, but then turned serious: "We're putting our trust in people who say they want to be Greenpeace. Fine, but a responsibility goes with it."

Rod Marining pointed out, "There are no women at this meeting, you notice." He and Bree had cast the *I Ching* coins over this and obtained the hexagram of the Marrying Maiden. "Understand the transitory in the light of eternity," Marining quoted the oracle. "Every relationship between individuals is fraught with danger that wrong turns may be taken. It's necessary to remain mindful of the end that endures." This was just the sort of mystical distraction that McTaggart detested, but his raised eyebrow was discreet.

Walrus called the current era "the decade of survival." He no longer insisted that Greenpeace remain a movement, and supported the idea of a Council. He did not entirely support the idea of national offices, but did not mention it.

Michael M'Gonigle called for "the independence of the national groups." The questions that followed this premise comprised the heart of the matter. What is "independence?" What collective responsibilities apply? What policies are non-negotiable? There were hundreds.

I spoke next and said, "*Inter*dependence." M'Gonigle interrupted and said, "Yes, of course, but." I recounted my concerns about the conflict between nationalism and ecology. "No system is perfect," M'Gonigle said. I championed the *Chronicles* as a voice for ecology and repeated my view about the proposed "Rainbow Warrior" trademark. As I expected, Hunter and Walrus nodded support for both those ideas.

McTaggart had thought about the eco-region idea. "Trying to decide the form of the international is premature," he said. "We should just put the hat on the table and put everything into the hat. We'll sort out all the details as we go." This was a convenient position for him. In fact, we *were* deciding the form of the international. Agreeing to the Council of national offices sealed the issue, or as Bateson had said: "Any answer which we promote ... becomes partly irreversible." The national structure had been McTaggart's position for two years and it would put him in control of Greenpeace. Everyone knew this, but there was no other proposal that would achieve a consensus, and few of us had the patience to endure another year of negotiations.

Paul Watson arrived just after 1:00 p.m. He did not, formally, have any status within Greenpeace. However, he'd been involved since the beginning. Watson, perhaps sensing the mood and understanding that McTaggart was in control, had little to say. He did repeat his belief that "the environmental movement is too conciliatory" with the perpetrators. No one argued with him on this point.

Ballem had little to say, except that "things appear to be heading in a positive direction."

Moore spoke last. He had already let go the reins of power and had accepted that he would step down from the presidency of the Greenpeace Foundation to become president of Greenpeace Canada. Perhaps to get it on the record, he said, "The root cause of the court case was the refusal of the American group to come to an agreement. It was not fair that we be left shouldering debt while others rode off with the name and the money. The lawsuit was necessary to force this meeting." No one objected. "We'll go along with the Council."

That was it. Davie Gibbons summed up the discussion and made notes: The lawsuit was stayed. A single Greenpeace USA would be created including all existing offices and entities. The Greenpeace Council would be formed, and Greenpeace Foundation would assign all rights to the Council. The charter members, it was agreed, would be Canada, France, the United States, the United Kingdom, New Zealand, and the Netherlands. The Greenpeace groups in Australia, Denmark, Germany, Belgium, Japan, and Switzerland would be eligible for later admission to the Council. The debts of the Greenpeace Foundation would be paid out in full from cash available in the US and Europe. The Council would settle the *Greenpeace*

Chronicles and Rainbow Warrior trademark issues. We pledged to meet in November in Amsterdam to form the Council with the national groups. We milled about and talked as Gibbons typed out the terms, and then we signed the document.

The *Globe and Mail* ran a story under the headline: "Greenpeace factions patch up family feud." On October 17, the Greenpeace Foundation ratified the deal and three days later, the Greenpeace USA groups met in San Francisco and ratified the deal. Kaye Moss, my sister in Denver, was proclaimed executive director in the US, but immediately declined the job. Kay Treakle from Seattle became interim director. Don White signed for Hawaii, but later pulled out and reclaimed his independence. Turf battles in the US persisted for several years, and the headquarters eventually moved to Washington, D.C.

On October 20, Eileen Moore gave birth to a boy, Jonathan. I took pictures in the hospital and later that day stopped into a bookstore and found James Lovelock's *Gaia*, which lent considerable scientific credibility to the notion that the biosphere of the earth was itself a living organism.

The new Greenpeace, I understood, would not fulfill our every vision, but it would exist and it would continue to be influential. We had little else to do but plunge forward with our work. On Sunday, October 21, Walrus, Marining, and I met with John Moelaert at Dorothy Stowe's home on Courtney Street in Point Grey to discuss Canadian uranium mining. The first Greenpeace meetings had been held in this house nine years earlier. Moelaert had been a writer and ecologist in Vancouver since the 1960s. Dorothy Stowe was as gracious as ever, putting tea and cookies on the table. Moelaert insisted the time had come to force the Canadian government to reveal its uranium policy. The cancer death rate among uranium miners was over five times that of the general population. "They're using the remote Native communities like guinea pigs," said Moelaert. We drafted a plan to expose the issue in Canada, which we now knew was part of the notorious uranium cartel in Paris.

We felt back in stride. Hunter came by my Kitsilano flat, and we walked around the corner for a traditional and celebratory beer. We made plans to leave for Amsterdam, where we would ratify our new agreement with the European ecologists. The former Greenpeace president and *James Bay* latrine officer bounced as we walked. In the pub, he laughed at his own lively stories. His theory that "giving up power is an anti-depressant" had proved convincing. "Personally," he said, "I'm going back to freelance mindbombing. I'm redundant. We've been cloned. It's perfect."

I told Hunter about the meeting at Dorothy Stowe's home, and he turned sentimental. "I don't think I fully appreciated Irving and Dorothy and Ben at the time," he said. "I hope Irving's disembodied consciousness is floating around the universe somewhere witnessing what has become of this thing." He raised his glass to his mentors.

"The mystical experience itself," he said, thinking out loud, "can't be institutionalized. You just more or less have to be there for it."

CHAPTER ETERNITY

WERELDRAAD

"When one tugs at a single thing in nature, he finds it attached to the rest of the world."

— John Muir

I departed Vancouver on November 9, 1979, on my way to Amsterdam, but stopped in Boston to see Peggy Taylor, whom I had met in Colorado. Taylor published *New Age Journal*, a progressive magazine of social and personal change, with a spiritual theme. Taylor and her partner Rick Ingrasci had invited me to attend a meeting at the home of Helen and Bill Caldicott to talk with California Governor Jerry Brown about nuclear weapons and nuclear power. The Caldicotts had founded Physicians for Social Responsibility, and the fiery Helen Caldicott was a popular speaker on the health effects of radiation. At the meeting we met writer Harvey Wasserman from the Natural Guard group and Bill Whitson, an ex-Pentagon analyst, who had taken up Buddhism and become a pacifist.

Jerry Brown was running for the Democratic presidential nomination against incumbent President Jimmy Carter. The Carter administration had badly botched the neutron bomb issue, and Brown included global disarmament as a plank in his platform. The guest of honour, nuclear physicist George Kistiakowsky, who had attended the first "Trinity" nuclear explosion in 1945, explained that the US military wanted to deploy 572 new

Pershing missiles in Europe, to "modernize" their arsenal. "The loophole in the arms agreements," he said, "is that each country retained the right to *modernize*." This provision had been used to develop the neutron bomb, the MX missiles, and now the Pershing missiles. "The Russian and American military hawks use each other to stir up fear and justify their own existence," said Kistiakowsky. "But new technology doesn't make things more secure. It makes things *less* secure." In fact, the day before this meeting, an early-warning computer mistake had fooled American generals into believing the Soviet Union had attacked. Planes had been launched and missile bases put on alert. "The new missiles reduce react time from 30 minutes to 8 minutes," said Kistiakowsky. "System errors increase with technology."

Governor Brown scribbled notes. "What's the world military budget?" he asked.

"Something like $360 billion a year," said Kistiakowsky. Whitson pointed out that this represented "half the entire Third World gross national product for 70 percent of humanity." According to Whitson, escalating the cold war in Europe was part of the US strategy to bankrupt Russia. However, 100,000 peace activists had marched through Bonn on October 14, French nuclear workers had gone on strike in two plants, and an awakened disarmament movement now influenced European politics.

"The same thing has to happen here," said Brown. "The anti-nuclear movement has to address weapons, to put pressure on the politicians. How many nuclear warheads in the US arsenal?" he asked.

"Thirty-five thousand," said Bill Whitson, "twenty-five thousand in Russia."

Brown looked around the room at us ecology activists. "Disarmament can't be partisan," he said, shaking his finger. "The Soviets and China have to be a target of protest as well as the US." No one argued with this. We each took our opportunity to explain to Brown what we believed to be the urgent environmental issues. I urged Brown to remain firm on the marine mammal issues, but to look into the uranium mine tailings, Native land rights, and a new story that I was preparing for the next *Chronicles*: carbon dioxide in the atmosphere. He asked pointed questions and took notes throughout.

At 5:00 p.m., Brown left abruptly and Taylor, Ingrasci, and I stayed to talk with Wasserman and the Caldicotts. Wasserman had been a key organizer in the Clamshell Alliance opposing the Seabrook nuclear power plant. The nuclear industry was now on the verge of bankruptcy. The fight for oil reserves in the Middle East, however, had heated up. It made sense to refocus on nuclear weapons and militarism. Wasserman revealed that the No Nukes alliances planned a mass demonstration at the Pentagon early in the New Year. Helen Caldicott told us about her detractors calling her "crazy."

"We have to be crazy," she said. "There's not enough time *not* to be crazy!"

AMSTERDAM

On Monday, November 12, I flew through London Heathrow to Amsterdam, reading The *Daily Telegraph*: 100,000 people fleeing a chemical explosion train wreck in Mississauga, Ontario; the US Department of Defense explaining how they had fed a computer test tape back through the Early Warning System that had triggered the nuclear alert and scrambled missile silos two days earlier; the Palestinians and the Pope vying to serve as mediator in the Iran hostage crisis.

I met my now-ex-wife, Glenn, in Rembrandtsplein and stayed at her flat on Jacob van Campenstraat in the working-class and student neighbourhood of De Pijp. We had tea in the morning, cheese and chocolate on toast, talked and looked out at a tour boat captain bent in the rain on Amsteldijk. Her goodwill toward me, in spite of my previous failures, seemed to have no bounds. I saw her as the embodiment of a deep compassion and grace that I aspired to achieve.

On Tuesday, November 13, I met Bill Gannon at the train station and walked past "*Stop de kernraket*" posters denouncing the Pershing missiles, to the Greenpeace office at 98 Damrak. There we met cheerful Geert Drieman, Greenpeace Netherlands's executive director Art Van Remundt, *Fri* skipper David Moodie, and others arriving from around the world. Later, we walked along the Amstel River, I showed Gannon where I had lived on a boat in 1970, and we had an Indonesian dinner with Glenn.

On November 14, the *Rainbow Warrior* arrived with Bob Hunter and Susi Newborn at the bow, Jon Castle on the bridge, and Tony Marriner, Athel von Koettlitz, Pete Wilkinson, and others from Europe on deck, anticipating the meeting two days hence. McTaggart and Rémi Parmentier arrived from Paris. Their associate Brice Lalonde had just declared himself a candidate for the presidential election of 1981 with Philippe Lebreton from le Mouvement d'écologie politique, creating a new electoral bloc called Aujourd'hui l'écologie, "Ecology Today." This alliance would soon change French politics. Parmentier claimed that under Valéry Giscard d'Estaing, a technocratic elite ruled France, characterized by lax environmental laws and an aggressive nuclear weapons program. Former right-winger, turned leftist, François Mitterrand courted the ecologists. A year later he would prove successful, but the French love affair with nuclear weapons would eventually sink even Mitterand, as well as the *Rainbow Warrior*, which now sat in the port of Amsterdam a short walk from the office on Damrak.

Campbell Plowden and Kay Treakle arrived from Seattle. Now that the Greenpeace Foundation no longer posed a threat to anyone's autonomy, most of the tension had dissolved. But not all. Newborn, Wilkinson, and Castle did not want the new Greenpeace International to separate the ecology struggle from social justice. Jon Castle felt there was a danger the bureaucracy would supplant the activists. He wrote a poetic essay, "Why Greenpeace is bad for the environment" to express his concerns. Castle would spend the next two decades leading Greenpeace campaigns. David Moodie groused about why Australia and Germany had been left out of the new Council.

By now, Harald Zindler, Monika Griefahn, Gerhard Wallmeyer, and Christian Krüger had formed a Greenpeace Germany group. They possessed an effective mix of skills: Zindler a clever and fearless activist, Monika Griefahn an articulate public voice, Krüger a deft media strategist, and Wallmeyer, an able administrator and accountant. Physicist Gerd Leipold from the Max Planck Institute, had joined them to guide scientific policies. Over the next decade, this group would provide a partial answer to the paradox of sustaining innovation, and would largely redefine Greenpeace in its international form, but in 1979 they were not represented at the Amsterdam meeting.

The Greenpeace Foundation delegates — Hunter, Moore, Gannon, and I — had ostensibly let go. We no longer controlled, or imagined we controlled, the fate of the Greenpeace name. However, we clung to certain hopes. Aside from saving the *Chronicles* and forestalling the attempt to register a copyright claim on "Rainbow Warrior," I hoped the Council would address the nuclear weapons issues that Kistiakowsky had outlined.

Gannon wanted sound financial management, Moore wanted Greenpeace to maintain a tradition of strong science, dating from Jim Bohlen, Terry Simmons, and Lille D'Easum during the Amchitka campaign. Hunter, who seemed most genuinely to have relinquished his attachments, still harboured hopes that Greenpeace would preserve its place on the cutting edge of cultural change. "I also hope it retains its sense of humour and willingness to take risks," he said.

Yet, we were not in Amsterdam to quibble over any of this, but to pass on the peace and ecology symbols, as they had been passed to us. Perhaps we overestimated the importance, but in the moment we believed the ceremony conveyed historic responsibilities to traditions that predated any of us: the Quakers, CND, Ecology Action, Rachel Carson, Ron Cobb, the *Golden Rule*, Provos, White Rose, the grandmother Eyes of Fire, and so forth.

WERELDRAAD

Greenpeace delegates and onlookers arrived for the formal meeting on Friday morning, November 16. Peter Woof, representing the *Sea Shepherd*, sat with David Moodie from the *Fri* and Jon Castle from the *Rainbow Warrior*, the skippers of the Eco Navy, heirs of Captain John Cormack, and like the old skipper in 1971, they had no vote. The delegates hugged and talked and took their seats. McTaggart arrived, dressed in white shirt and trousers, neatly pressed. He greeted everyone, and sat down.

The delegates from France, the Netherlands, and the UK formed the Council of Europe. Into this, the Council accepted the US and finally Canada. The new "Greenpeace Council" awarded New Zealand and Denmark non-voting status. We had previously agreed that New Zealand would join, but McTaggart had convinced the European delegates to wait. The Council as constituted provided an unambiguous majority. Parmentier nominated McTaggart as executive director of the Council, and we unanimously proclaimed it so.

Most of the administrative issues had been settled: $75,000 would be sent to Canada to retire a portion of the bank debt. The international campaign budget for the following year was set at $340,000 with a $500,000 contingency. Gannon estimated the consolidated Greenpeace income for the year at just over $5 million. This seemed like an enormous amount of money. The Council set an overhead budget of $2 million, which Hunter questioned, and the group referred the matter to an executive committee. My nuclear weapons motion went to a nuclear committee, and the fate of the publication went to the publishing committee. My motion that we refrain from registering a trademark for "Rainbow Warrior" lost 4-1, with Canada opposed. I rose to protest but Hunter elbowed me. *Be nobody. Let it go*. Later, delegates cornered me privately and told me they agreed that "Rainbow Warrior" was a cultural myth, and variously shrugged. Even McTaggart said, "Look, I understand, but it's better to control it legally."

The meeting ended quickly, most matters referred to committees. In the hallway, during a break, Allan Thornton from London floated the idea that Toronto should be the new centre in Canada, a move that would make the Shire of Kitsilano a distant province in the new Greenpeace galaxy and could possibly oust Moore as future Council delegate for Canada. It was no secret that McTaggart and Thornton would be happy to see him replaced. However, at the suggestion of his demise, Moore bristled. "Stay out of Canada's business," he told Thornton.

"Greenpeace *sticht wereldraad*," announced the Amsterdam newspapers, "Greenpeace forms world council."

The next day, Peter Wilkinson chaired the nuclear committee, which undertook an international spent-fuel campaign, a high-priority global mess, comprising a hodgepodge of international dumping regulations, and virtually no enforcement. The *Rainbow Warrior* had already exposed Western Europe's complicity, the issue linked back through the entire fuel cycle to North American uranium mines and the "Sacrifice Area" on Hopi and Navajo land in Arizona and New Mexico. Wilkinson intended that the *Rainbow Warrior* would blockade the Dutch nuclear dumping ship *Bayer* and sail into the French port of Cherbourg to stop shipments of nuclear waste from Japan. The action the following summer would provoke the French navy to ram the Aberdeen trawler as they had rammed the *Vega* eight years earlier.

Hunter proposed hot-air balloons and a dirigible to enter nuclear weapons sites. "The Zodiac thing is already old," he said. The committee rejected the idea for the time being, but respectfully. I proposed a campaign to halt the Pershing missiles in Europe and to include the Soviets and China as disarmament targets, but the committee had its budget limits, and the nuclear dumping campaign seemed enough. Later we laboured over a policy statement, down to the fine points of whether we should use the phrase "alternative energy," or "appropriate," "renewable," or "sustainable" energy. The politics of ecology had become as complex as ecology itself.

Hunter did not appear visibly shaken by the fact that control of Greenpeace had shifted to the Europeans and that they did not immediately embrace his ideas. "They'll do it their own way," he said. "I would expect nothing less."

On November 18, after a campaigns committee session, Hunter pulled Moore and Gannon off to the pub for a beer. I stayed in the office for the publication committee meeting, led by Campbell Plowden and Kay Treakle from Seattle. Treakle planned a story on the Trident nuclear submarines, and I gave her the phone numbers for Anna Gyorgy and the Natural Guard researchers. We discussed stories on acid rain, oil drilling in the Beaufort Sea, toxic dumps, and the irradiated islanders on Rongelap. I summarized the carbon dioxide and uranium cartel stories. However, I realized our newspaper, like the council, would go its own way. Kay Treakle wanted no advertising, a popular opinion, but this meant we would have to submit a budget to Greenpeace. I floated the idea that we might maintain a more objective voice if we had independent income, but sensed that my logic failed to sway. "It wouldn't hurt to skip an issue and get a consensus," Treakle said. "Everyone wants to have input into what goes in the publication." Perhaps I could have held McTaggart to his word and forced the January issue as planned, but I would have to go over the heads of these people and I didn't have the political will. The opportunity to give it away presented itself, and I handed Campbell Plowden a collection of the twenty-one past issues of the *Greenpeace Chronicles*, dating from the fall of 1975. After half an hour of discussion, I slipped out to find my old comrades.

In fact, our private fears about letting go would prove trifling. The ecologists in Europe and North America fully appreciated the powerful concept that Greenpeace had stumbled upon. Over the ensuing decades, the mystical spirit and radical theatrics would survive a burgeoning bureaucracy required to operate the global organization. The icons of the past — the Vega hove-to before the nuclear bomb, Zodiacs in front of harpoons or under the barrels of nuclear waste, rainbows appearing at auspicious moments — would inspire ever more creative demonstrations of public concern about ecology.

GAIA'S ADVOCATES

I strode Kalverstraat in the light rain, past the bronze street urchin reflecting colours in Spui Plaza, and into the Hoppe Bar to find Hunter, Moore, Gannon, Newborn, and David Moodie. After Newborn and Moodie had departed, and as we drank and talked, I noticed among the patrons a young girl, perhaps ten years old, tumbling blonde curls, a red sweater, blue jeans, and shoes with tiny leather straps and buckles, sitting at a table with her handsome father and his friends, writing peacefully in her notebook. She whispered something to her father and went back to her private thoughts and journal. The light through a window and lace curtains lit only her face in the dark corner of the foggy beer parlour, just like the painter had highlighted the face of the bold maid in the huge painting over the bar, as if nature intended to remind us that there is a higher purpose and that all our talk and designs will pale before innocence and beauty. Struck by this vision, I wanted to go to her and explain, "It was for you. Everything we did was for you. The whales. The seals." Even at thirty-two, after a decade of public activism, I felt like a naïve Holden Caulfield, longing to stand at the cliff edge in the rye field, safeguarding the children.

"I think I'll go be a farmer," said Hunter. He turned to Moore. "Is that my left hemisphere taking over?"

"No, your right."

"It's all one. Doesn't it all come down to that, what's it …"

"Well, yeah, left, sort of."

"… The *corpus callosum*, that bridge thing."

"Yer always trying to unify dualisms, Hunter."

"You're always so argumentative, Patrick," Gannon said.

"No, I'm not."

I looked around at my friends. We *had* overestimated ourselves. We *were* mindpunks, and the world would prove far more complex and mysterious than our simple dream of natural justice, as it had proven more complex and more merciless than the dreams of the civil rights marchers or the Chipko people holding hands around their trees.

"We did it, brother Bill," said Hunter, clinking Gannon's glass. "Do you remember," he said, "what Captain John used to say — did I ever tell you this? — he said," Hunter puffed out his chest like Cormack, proud and self-assured, " 'Yar the only guys I know who ever-time ya fall down a shithole, you come up smellin' like a *rose*.' "

"To Captain John." We raised our glasses and drank under the painting that rested above the bar, where bottles sat in ancient, private places: Janvere, Hoppe, Bols, Advocaat, Brandywine, and one smudged, labelless relic, which the bar master lifted without looking and poured into the empty glass of a white-haired gentleman with a brushy moustache and wool tie. Beyond him, the blond child wrote her secret notes.

Moore went up for more beer, and Hunter said, "I didn't think he had it in him." Gannon's ruddy cheeks glowed. Moore returned and set out four glasses. "There's lots for us to do in Canada," he said.

"The important outcome of the last decade," proclaimed Hunter, "is that ecology took root in industrial culture."

Greenpeace had been both a product and cause of the change. Although humanity would have embraced ecology without Greenpeace, the change would not have been as quick or as decisive. Whereas pioneers like Henry David Thoreau and Alice Hamilton spoke out as lonely voices, Greenpeace had endowed ecology with a public mythology. Statistics and polemics could not have achieved this. Peaceful insurgents in rainbow ships: that was news. Saving the environment had become heroic. If we overstated our case, such an error paled — in our minds — against decades, centuries, of fraud and extortion for the sake of extracting personal wealth from nature's bounty.

In the footsteps of Thoreau, Hamilton, Carson, and John Muir, Greenpeace helped give their insights a global constituency. Ecology simply arose as a rational and emotional human response to events such as strontium-90 in breast milk, leukemia victims on Rongelap Island, sick children at Love Canal, and deformed fish in the Elbe.

"When the Atomic Energy Commission or Japanese whalers called us crazy," said Hunter, "they were, essentially, right. We acted out like insane teenagers, exposing the family lie. It's not surprising the French reacted like an alcoholic father, beating up David. In a dysfunctional family, the culprit always ridicules the whistle-blower."

We believed that in the face of society's psychotic behaviour — slavery, death camps, random murder, the fouling of rivers, decimation of whales, and so forth, all common occurrences in our age — *someone* must stand outside the system, and perhaps break a rule to convey the unorthodox idea that might nudge society from its habitual course.

Over these earnest deliberations I heard the child's voice and turned to see her pinch her fingers together to animate a point, as her father leaned toward her and held up his hand to quiet his friends. The happy voice of the young girl, impeccably enunciating this exigency to her father, cut through the beer-loud laughter of the Hoppe Bar with the high resonance of a golden chime.

CAST OF CHARACTERS

Hundreds of ordinary citizens contributed to the founding of Greenpeace. This list, necessarily incomplete, is roughly chronological. The central characters in our present story are listed first and annotated.

IRVING AND DOROTHY STOWE: Jewish-American Quaker pacifists, arrived in Vancouver in 1966, and founded the Don't Make A Wave Committee. Their children, **Robert** and **Barbara**, organized students during early Greenpeace campaigns. Irving passed away October, 1974; Dorothy lives in the home on Courtenay Street where meetings were held in 1971.

BEN AND DOROTHY METCALFE: Journalists from Winnipeg, Manitoba, arrived in Vancouver in 1956. Ben worked for *The Province* newspaper and the CBC. The Metcalfes managed the media during the first two Greenpeace expeditions. Ben became the first Chairman of the Greenpeace Foundation; he passed away on October 14, 2003.

BOB HUNTER: Writer and journalist from St. Boniface, Manitoba, popular *Vancouver Sun* columnist in the 1960s, wrote *The Storming of the Mind* (McClelland and Stewart) in 1971, on media and social action. He coined "Don't Make a Wave," joined the first Greenpeace campaign, became president of the Greenpeace Foundation in 1973, and lead Greenpeace through its transformation into an international ecological navy. He is now the environment specialist for CityTV in Toronto.

JIM AND MARIE BOHLEN: American Quaker pacifists, moved to Canada in 1967 and co-founded the Don't Make A Wave Committee. Marie conceived the idea to sail a boat into the test zone at Amchitka. They live in Courtenay, BC.

DR. PATRICK MOORE: From Winter Harbour, BC; earned a Ph.D. in ecology from UBC, sailed on the first Greenpeace voyage, drafted the Greenpeace Declaration of Interdependence with Hunter in 1975, and became president of the Greenpeace Foundation in 1977. Moore left Greenpeace in 1985 over policy disputes and is currently an environmental consultant.

JOHN CORMACK: Skipper of the seiner *Phyllis Cormack* on the first Greenpeace voyage in 1971, the first whaling campaign in 1975, and subsequent campaigns in 1976 and 1977. He passed away on November 17, 1988.

LYLE THURSTON: Medical doctor, sailed on the first Greenpeace voyage and subsequent campaigns, and served on the board of the Greenpeace Foundation throughout the 1970s.

ZOE HUNTER (RAHIM): A pacifist in London, where she met Bob Hunter and introduced him to the disarmament movement; she lives in Vancouver and remains active with Amnesty International.

HAMISH BRUCE: Vancouver lawyer, envisioned the "Green Panthers" in 1969; President of Greenpeace in 1973 and intermittently through 1975.

BILL DARNELL: Said "Make it a *green* peace," at the close of a Don't Make a Wave Committee meeting in 1971, thereby coining the term "Greenpeace."

TERRY SIMMONS: Co-founder of BC Sierra Club, sailed on first Greenpeace voyage to Amchitka.

BOB KEZIERE: Photographer on the first voyage and author of a Greenpeace scientific report on the dangers of nuclear testing, 1971.

ROD MARINING: Vancouver street-theatre artist, saved the entrance to Vancouver's Stanley Park in 1970, joined the first Greenpeace voyage in Kodiak, coined the term "Green" as a political constituency, and served on the Greenpeace Foundation board throughout the 1970s.

WALRUS (DAVID GARRICK): Anthropologist, historian, writer, and close ally of Native American activists; cook on the first Greenpeace whale campaign, led mission to Japan with Taeko Miwa, and first harp seal campaign with Watson.

DAVID MCTAGGART: Canadian real-estate developer, retired to the South

Pacific and volunteered to sail his ketch into the French bomb-test zone in 1972; rammed and beaten by French sailors, won a court case against the French government, and became the first Chairman of Greenpeace International in 1979. McTaggart passed away in March 2001.

PAUL WATSON: Radical among the radicals, sailed on *Greenpeace II* to Amchitka, went on whale campaigns, and launched the Greenpeace harp seal campaign. Watson's tactics lead to conflict, and he left Greenpeace in 1977, founded the Sea Shepherd Society, and rammed the pirate whaler *Sierra* in 1979.

DR. PAUL SPONG: New Zealand scientist, who trained the first captive *Orcinus orca*, Skana, at the Vancouver Aquarium, studied wild whales in northern BC, and proposed the first Greenpeace campaign to save the whales. He continues to study whales around Hanson Island, BC.

LINDA SPONG: Launched the first whale campaign with husband Paul; served on subsequent campaigns, on the Greenpeace board, and in fundraising throughout the 1970s.

BOB CUMMINGS: Underground newspaper correspondent, sailed on the Amchitka campaign in 1971 and served Greenpeace until just before his death in 1987.

BOBBI INNES: From Port Moody, BC; a workflow manager for a cable company, moved in with Bob Hunter in 1974 and organized the first Greenpeace office and fundraising projects.

BILL GANNON: A Dubliner, raised in Winnipeg, became chief accountant for an international developer, served as Greenpeace accountant, 1975-1980, and played bass in the Greenpeace band.

MEL GREGORY: Street musician, joined the 1975 whale campaign, wrote songs chronicling the movement, kept the "Dream Book," and led the Greenpeace band in the 1970s.

GEORGE KOROTVA: Czechoslovakian, arrested by Soviets in Prague, held in a work camp, escaped, and came to Canada in 1968. Russian translator on 1975 whale campaign, skipper of *James Bay* in 1976 and *Ohana Kai*, 1977.

TAEKO MIWA: Japanese translator during early whale campaigns, led whale mission to Japan in 1976, and initiated Greenpeace campaigns to halt mercury poisoning in Japan and Canada.

DON FRANKS: Actor, musician, participant in whale and seal campaigns, 1975-1979.

CARLIE TRUEMAN: Diver, deckhand, and responsible for Zodiac maintenance during 1975 whale campaign; later served on first Greenpeace International interim board, 1977-1978.

EILEEN CHIVERS (MOORE): Greenpeace whale campaigns, 1974-77, Greenpeace board member and fund-raiser, 1975-1979.

DAVIE GIBBONS: Lawyer for Greenpeace in Canada 1972-79, founded a Greenpeace Group in Ontario, served as legal counsel during seal and whale campaigns, presided over October 1979 meeting to resolve internal conflicts and set terms for a permanent Greenpeace International.

REX WEYLER: Journalist, Greenpeace photographer, correspondent, editor of the *Greenpeace Chronicles*, and board member 1974-1979.

Some others who contributed to the founding and early success of Greenpeace, or opposed Greenpeace, are listed below. The author appologizes for omissions of participants. To correct errors or add information, see the author's website.

DON'T MAKE A WAVE COMMITTEE and **AMCHITKA CAMPAIGN:** Paul Cote, Deeno and Dave Birmingham, Paul Nonnast, Lou Hogan, Peter Fraser, Charles Lew, Michael Harcourt, Richard Fineberg, Doug McGinnis, Joni Mitchell, James Taylor, Phil Ochs, Bill Henderson, Chilliwack, Tony Dunbar, Ron Jones, Gordon Sutter, Dan McLeod, Gwen and Derrick Mallard, Dr. Alfred Turnbull, Thomas Perry, Ken Farquharson, Lille d'Easum, Dr. John Gofman, Dan Wilcher, Palo Alto and Oregon American Friends Service Committees, Sierra Club, Katy Madsen, Louis Boyce, Stuarte Keate, Jack Webster, Pierre Berton, Charles Templeton, US Senator Mike Gravel, Mark Burns, Kimiko Bruce, Elizabeth Dunn, Ann Jones, Jason & Katerina Halm, Burrard Chief Dan George, Bill Moore, Richard Lahn, Lilly Jaffe, and Mark Rose MP.

CREW OF THE *GREENPEACE I, PHYLLIS CORMACK*, 1971: Captain John Cormack, Dave Birmingham, Jim Bohlen, Robert Hunter, Bob Keziere, Ben Metcalfe, Bob Cummings, Bill Darnell, Patrick Moore, Lyle Thurston, Terry Simmons, Richard Fineberg, Rod Marining (replaced Fineberg in Kodiak, October, 1971).

***GREENPEACE II*, AMCHITKA:** Captain Hank Johansen, Willard Jones, Joe Breton, Dr. Joe Stipec, Chris Bergthorson, Jim McCandlish, Gerry

Deiter, William Smith, Ken Berge, Gerald Bickerton, Robert Whyte, Donald Maclean, Leroy Jensen, Kurt Horn, Gundar Lipbergs, Ivar Skog, Kim Whale, Gerald King, Doug Collins, David Price, James Hunt, William Stewart, Douglas Sagi, Paul Watson, and joined by Birminham, Cummings and Marining.

CANADIAN AND US GOVERNMENTS, 1971: Pierre Trudeau, Prime Minister of Canada; Richard Nixon, President of the United States; Russell Train, US environment advisor; Jack Davis, Canadian Environment Minister; Mitchell Sharp, Foreign Affairs, Canada; Paul St. Pierre, Member of Parliament; Arthur Schlesinger, US Atomic Energy Commission.

CREW OF THE *GREENPEACE III, VEGA*, 1973: Captain David McTaggart, Ben Metcalfe, Nigel Ingram, Grant Davidson, and Roger Haddleton; and in **1974,** Ann-Marie Horne and Mary Lornie.

MURUROA CAMPAIGN: Janine Bensasson, Gene Horne, Mabel Hetherington, Richard Northey, David Moodie, Thierry Garby-Lacrouts, Brice Lalonde, Linus Pauling, Jean-Paul Sartre, Albert Beale, Herbert Marcuse, Nicholas Desplats, Jean-Jacques Servan-Schreiber, Stewart Savard, Gordon Edwards, Jim Boyack, Francis Sanford, Peter Hayes, Naomi Petersen, Paul Hovan, and Robert Lett in Peru.

FRENCH GOVERNMENT AND MILITARY: President Charles De Gaulle, President Georges Pompidou, Valéry Giscard d'Estaing, François Mitterand, Admiral Christian Claverie, Captain Patrick de la Rochebrochard, and Henri Messiah at Commissariat a l'Energie Atomique.

CREW OF THE *GREENPEACE IV, LA FLOR*, 1974: Captain Rolf Heimann, Richard Hudson, Rien Achterberg.

GREENPEACE, 1973-1975: George Dyson, Leo and Audrey Fox, Neil Hunter, John Keating, Brian Kendrick, Teresa McDowell, Andre Morin, Karen Perry, Mike Reese, Maureen Sugrue, Jenny Stark, Peter Thomas, Ron Wilson, David Waugh, Blanche Bucsis, Findlay Clark, Michael Angel, Sue Hynd, Peter Heiburg, Bree Drummond, Dave Johnson, Sonny Lewis, Leigh Wilks, Bill Harvey, Gary Barclay, Murray Armstrong, Wilf Chipman, Glenn Jonathans-Weyler, Brian Anderson, Gordy Gobel, Dave Gobel, Jerry Duncan, Katey Walker, Dave Campbell, Al Clapp, Kurt Musgrove, Cam Scott, Eric Ellington, Daniel Koffman, Bob Wingen, John Lilly, Joan McIntyre, Maya Koizumi,

Michiko Sakata, Paul Horn, Ann Mortifee, Paul Winter, Farley Mowat, Joan McIntyre, Allen Ginsberg, Tamar Griggs, Bill Harvey, Brian Anderson, John Moelaert, Leroy Jensen, Virginia Pollock, Gail Anthony, Blair Halse, John Beveridge, Peter Chataway, Jim Land, Yola Childs, Janet Cook, Jerry Priestly, Ian Irving, Bruce Logan, and Dr. Peter Beamish.

CREW OF THE *GREENPEACE V, PHYLLIS CORMACK*, 1975: Captain John Cormack, Bob Hunter, David Garrik (Walrus), Hamish Bruce, Rex Weyler, Carlie Truman, Paul Watson, Patrick Moore, Leigh Wilks, Paul Winter, Myron MacDonald, George Korotva, Carol Brian, Al Hewitt, Will Jackson, Taeko Miwa, Gary Zimmerman, Nicholas Desplats, Ron Precious, Fred Easton, Michael Chechik, Don Franks, and Melville Gregory.

CREW OF THE *GREENPEACE VI, VEGA*, 1975: Captain Jacques Longini, Matt Herron, Ramon Falkowski, and Dr. John Cotter.

GREENPEACE, 1975-6: Marylin Kaga, Henry Payne, Gary Gallon, Phyllis Cormack, Marvin Storrow, Peter Speck, Al Clapp, Kurt Musgrove, John and Toni Lilly, Brian Davies, Sandy and Jackie Innes, Bill and Julie McMaster, Starlet Lum, Barry Lavender, Druid, Ron Orieux.

SEAL CAMPAIGN, 1976: Laurent Trudel, Paul Watson, David Garrick, Henrietta Nielsen, Dan Willens, Bonnie MacLeod, Paul Morse, Marilyn Kaga, Al Johnson, Ron Precious, Pat Moore, Eileen Chivers, Bob Hunter, Marvin and Colette Storrow, Michael Chechik, Carl Rising-Moore, Jack Wallace, Bernd Firnung, Art and Emily Decker, Art Elliot, and Doug Pilgrim.

By 1976, so many people actively worked for Greenpeace, they could no longer know each other personally, and a global structure of operations thereby ensued. The following were among thousands who served on campaigns or otherwise helped create Greenpeace International: Ted Haggarty, Lance Cowan, Bruce Kerr, Kazumi Tanaka, Chris Aikenhead, Michael Manolson, Bob Thomas, Mary-Lee Brassard, Susi Leger, Michael Bailey, David Weiss, Norm Seaton, Don Webb, Hal Ward, Ross Thornwood, Bonnie Thorne, Rita Outlaw, Leslie MacDonald, Sam Stewart, Fiona McLeod, Shivon and Lee Robinsong, Bruce Weyler, Kaye Weyler, Marian Yesinski, Paul Krassner, David Tussman, Hank Harrison, Jeannie McNaughton, Peter Fruchtman, Virginia Handley, Stan Minasian, John

Frizell, Cindy Baker, Dino Pignataro, Robert Taunt, Dick Dillman, Mickey Pflager, Michael Shandrick, Byrd Baker, Gary Young, Franz Weber, Brigitte Bardot, Leo Ryan, Jackie Speier, Pamela Sue Martin, James Jeffords, Monique van der Ven, Lorene Vickberg, Alan Wade, Margaret Tilbury, Liz Tilbury, Jim Taylor, Judy Drake, Steve Bowerman, Peter Fruchtman, Cleveland Amory, Alan Thronton, Julliette Williamson, Yasha Spong, Daisy & Lucy Sewid, Fred Mosquito, Country Joe McDonald, Graham Nash, Tom Campbell, Jackson Browne, Bonnie Raitt, Gordon Lightfoot, Elton John, Rusty Frank, Jean-Paul Fortom-Gouin, Jack and Patsy Davis, Peter Ballem, Don Ayres, Vibeke Arviddsson, Erol Baykal, John Hinck, Susi Newborn, Denise Bell, Rémi Parmentier, Jon Castle, Tony Mariner, Alan Thornton, Charles Hutchinson, Athel von Koettlitz, Nick Hill, Peter Bouquette, Hilari Anderson, Sally Austin, Pete Wilkinson, Jerry Garcia, Supertramp, Valdy, Pied Pumkin, Lawrence Ferlinghetti, Ann Dingwall, Nick Wilson, Elizabeth Rasmussen, Kirstin Aarflot, Ingrid Lustig, Bruce Bunting, Dexter Cate, Nancy Jacks, Don and Sue White, Michael Sergeant, Gary Zimmerman, Eddie Chavies, Dan Ebberts, Kay Treakle, Steve Sawyer, Charlotte Funston, Mike Studney, David Cohen, Wayne Christensen, Campbell Plowden, Kelley Dobbs, Keith Krueger, Oliver Clifton, Dennis Feroce, and many more during the course of our present story, through 1979, and thousands thereafter.

NOTES & SOURCES

"No one lies like an eyewitness." Peter Tabuns, former Greenpeace Canada Executive Director, divulged this morsel of Russian folk wisdom over coffee as we discussed Greenpeace history. An eyewitness has the evidence — "I was there" — but memories are fallible. Witnesses exaggerate their roles, expunge what they abhor, and often believe their own remakes of history. Some of the past written Greenpeace record is accurate, some is dubious, and some is outright fabrication.

Such is the nature of history from Gilgamesh to John Kennedy. The best a journalist or historian can do is talk to witnesses and compare the versions against the verifiable public record. For the Greenpeace record, Irving Stowe kept impeccable documentation of the first years, 1969-71. Ben Metcalfe kept tapes and detailed notebooks, 1970-73. From 1974-1979, Michael Chechik's film team documented crucial events. Robert Hunter's newspaper columns, 1969-75, document portions of the story. Hunter, David Garrick, Susi Newborn and others kept daily journals. Bobbi Hunter and Bill Gannon kept financial records, 1975-80. John Cormack, David McTaggart, George Korotva, and other sea captains kept logs. I kept daily records, 1973-80. I interviewed or corresponded with all living participants in the founding of Greenpeace.

Through five drafts, my sources made corrections. Frank Zelko, who completed his doctoral dissertation on Greenpeace history in 2003, reviewed the manuscript, refined historical points, and provided additional interviews. If historical errors persist, fault rests with the author, although I have attempted to provide an accurate record, in spirit and in fact, of the first decade of Greenpeace as it emerged from a loosely knit band of pacifists and ecologists into a global voice.

A WORD ON DIALOGUE:

The dialogue is truncated, not verbatim. Sources include Metcalfe and Hunter tapes, the film recordings, and journal notes. After 1975, I transcribed conversations during formal and informal meetings. My original notes are condensed from conversations replete with digressions, non-sequiturs, and redundancies. The versions reproduced here are adapted from those notes, emphasizing the relevant comments and omitting the extraneous. In some cases, conversations from more than one session — for example, sessions around the galley table during a campaign — have been joined together for brevity. Live readings from the *I Ching* are generally paraphrased in the speaker's voice, such as altering gender-specific language or skipping across the text; I kept the paraphrased versions, without internal quotes.

A NOTE ABOUT NOTES:

The text eschews footnotes, in deference to the narrative. General Sources below are followed by Chapter Notes. Rather than Latin abbreviations, *Op. cit.* or *ibid*, I use a shortened form: Hunter, *Warriors*; Spong, orcalab, and so forth. I use abbrev. where obvious, drop "Press" from University publishing houses, drop www. from websites, and use short form or homepage. For full, updated links, see the author's website. Sources fall into four categories: (1) printed and recorded public record: books, articles, news, audio, film, and so forth, including unsourced news clippings in notebooks; (2) Internet records; (3) primary interviews, journals, meeting minutes; and (4) author's journals, reporter notebooks, 1973-1980.

For extended and annotated sources, additional history of Greenpeace, data and interviews not in the book, and updated links, see: rexweyler.com.

GENERAL SOURCES IN PRINT: BOOKS AND DISSERTATIONS

Warriors of the Rainbow, Robert Hunter, (Hold, Rinehart and Winston, 1979); not to be confused with *Warriors of the Rainbow: Strange and Prophetic Dreams of the Indian Peoples*, William Willoya and Vinson Brown (Naturegraph, 1962); "Make it a Green Peace: The History of an International

Environmental Organization," Frank Zelko (Ph.D. dissertation, U. of Kansas, 2003); *Greenpeace III: Journey Into the Bomb*, David McTaggart with Robert Hunter (Collins, 1978); *Outrage!*, David McTaggart (J.J. Douglas, 1973); *Sea Shepherd*, Paul Watson with Warren Rogers (Norton, 1982); *The Greenpeace Story*, Michael Brown and John May (Dorling Kindersly, 1989); *Witness: Twenty-Five Years on the Environmental Front Line*, Kieran Mulvaney and Mark Warford (André Deutsch, 1996); *McLuhan's Children: The Greenpeace Message and the Media*, Stephen Dale (Between the Lines, 1996); *Greenpeace: Changing the World*, ed. Conny Boettger, Fouad Hamdan (Rasch & Röhring, 2001); *The Greenpeace Book*, Karl and Dona Sturmanis, (Orca Sound Publications, 1978); and "Mind Bombs and Whale Songs: Greenpeace and the News," Sean Cassidy (Ph.D. dissertation, U. of Oregon, 1992).

The Georgia Straight: *What the Hell Happened?*, ed. Naomi Pauls, Charles Campbell (Douglas & McIntyre, 1997); *The Last Great Sea*, Terry Glavin, (Greystone, Douglas & McIntyre, 2000); *The Whale War*, David Day (Douglas and McIntyre, 1987); *Mind in the Waters*, ed. Joan McIntyre, (Charles Scribner & Sons, 1974); *International Regulation of Whaling*, P.W. Bimie (Oceana, 1985).

The Power of the People, ed. Robert Cooney and Helen Michalowski (New Society, 1987); *Political Protest and Cultural Revolution: Nonviolent Direct Action in the 1970s and 1980s*, Barbara Epstein, (U. of California, 1991); *Killing Our Own: The Disaster of America's Experience with Atomic Radiation*, Harvey Wasserman & Norman Solomon (Delta, Dell, 1982).

NEWSPAPERS & JOURNALS:

The Georgia Straight, ed. Dan McLeod (Vancouver Free Press, Issue 1, May 1967 — Issue 600, May 1979); *The Vancouver Sun* and *The Province* (Pacific Press, 1967-1979); *Greenpeace Chronicles*, ed. Watson, Garrick, Weyler, Hunter (Greenpeace Foundation, issues 1-22, September 1975 to December 1979); news clippings, some unsourced, in journals of author, Hunter, Moore, and Garrick.

GENERAL SOURCES, INTERNET:

Environmental History Timeline, William Kovarik, runet.edu/~wkovarik/hist1; *Environmental Ethics*, Marius Necsoiu, U. of North Texas, cep.unt.edu/

default; *Environment and History*, erica.demon.co.uk; *Environmental History Journal*, American Soc. for Environ. Hist. and European SEH, h-net.org.

Bulletin of Atomic Scientists, "Known Nuclear Tests Worldwide, 1945-98," Robert Norris, and "Poisoned Pacific: The legacy of French nuclear testing," Bengt Danielsson, thebulletin.org; *Nuclear Files*, timeline, nuclearfiles.org; *Atomic Archive*, original papers, atomicarchive.com; *Nuclear Explosions*, map and list of events, seismo.ethz.ch/bsv.

Whaling History, Claire Johnson, helios.bto.ed.ac.uk; *Captured Orcas*, data from Erich Hoyt, members.aol.com/orcainfo/page3; *Order Cetacea*, Eric Ellis, animaldiversity.ummz.umich.edu; and *Orcinus orca* family structures, orcalab.org, Dr. Paul Spong.

GENERAL SOURCES, INTERVIEWS AND JOURNALS:

Primary interviews used throughout: Bob Hunter, Ben Metcalfe (deceased, October 2003), Pat and Eileen Moore, Dorothy Stowe, Paul Watson, Rod Marining, Lyle Thurston, David Gibbons, Myron MacDonald, Paul Spong, Linda Spong, David McTaggart (deceased, March 2001), John Cormack (deceased, November 1988), and Bob Cummings (deceased, 1987). Copied records from David Garrick. Financial records, Don't Make a Wave and Greenpeace, 1971-79. Bob Hunter's journals,1969-79, portions copied in author archive.

Crucial to the early chapters, 1966-73: Interviews with Barbara Stowe, Robert Stowe, Bill Darnell, Dorothy Metcalfe, Zoe Hunter, Terry Simmons, Hamish Bruce, Jim and Marie Bohlen, Ken Farquarson, Tom Perry, Katerina Halm, Irene McAllister, and Gary Gallon (deceased July 2003). Interviews and correspondence, 1973-1979: Fred Easton, Ron Precious, Bree Marining (deceased 1997), George Korotva, Michael Bailey, Paul Hovan, Kaye Moss, Steve Sawyer, and Dick Dillman. For Europe: Pete Wilkinson, Rémi Parmentier, Susi Newborn, David Moodie, Martini Gotjé, Geert Drieman, Gijs Thieme, Peter Bouquet, Harald Zindler, Gerhard Wallmeyer, and Christian Krüger. For Greenpeace International: Steve Erwood, Brian Fitzgerald, Sara Holden, Elaine Lawrence, and Peter Tabuns. Frank Zelko provided additional interviews with McTaggart, Metcalfe, Hunter, and David Tussman. Author's journals, notebooks, photographs, and records, 1973-1980.

CHAPTER ZERO: WHO GOES THERE

1. Dialogue is adapted from author's journals, interviews, and records of Hunter, Moore, and Gannon.

2. Provos: "Dutch Provos," Teun Voeten, *High Times*, January 1990, online at pdxnorml.org; "Provos Provoke Police," *Georgia Straight*, May 5, 1967; "Provos & Kabouters," Rudolf de Jong, communitybike.org. Most print sources are in Dutch, such as *De boodschap van een wijze kabouter*, Roel Van Duyn (Kritiese Biblioteek, 1969). The author interviewed Albert Hendrix, Francine Jonathans, Kerst Das, and Geert Drieman in Amsterdam.

CHAPTER 1: THE BOMB STOPS HERE

1. Einstein's 1939 letter: Nuclearfiles.org and dannen.com.

2. Marie Curie's 1910 *Treatise On Radioactivity* could be considered the beginning of the nuclear era. Einstein worked out the famous formula, and Austrians Otto Hahn and Lise Meitner first split a uranium atom in 1938: Nuclearfiles.org and atomicarchive.com; *The Nuclear Age Reader*, ed. Jeffrey Porro (McGraw Hill, 1988); *Man and Atom*, Glenn Seaborg (Dutton, 1971); *The Curve of Binding Energy*, John McPhee (Ballentine, 1973; Farrar, Straus and Giroux, 1974); and Wasserman, *Killing Our Own*.

3. Trinity test: eyewitness accounts at dannen.com and Nuclearfiles.org. *Day of Trinity*, Lansing Lamont (Atheneum, 1965); *The Day the Sun Rose Twice*, Ferenc M. Szasz (U. of New Mexico, 1984).

4. Hiroshima: *The Decision to Drop the Bomb*, Len Giovannitti and Fred Freed (Coward-McCann, 1965); *Hiroshima*, John Hersey (Vintage Books, 1985); and eyewitness account *Nagasaki 1945*, Tatsuichiro Akizuki (Quartet Books, 1981).

5. Nuclear Guinea pigs: 628 soldiers were irradiated at Trinity. By 1954, the US military had exposed 132,000 soldiers, initiating leukemia, myeloma, lymphoma, liver cancer, and so forth. A similar fate befell the Pacific islanders and citizens of the Soviet Union, China, and Britain. See the Human Radiation Experiments Information System (HREX), declassified US documents, at hrex.dis.anl.gov; *American Ground Zero*, Carole Gallagher (MIT Press, 1993); *The Myths of August*, Stewart Udall (Rutgers U. Press, 1994); *Eyes of Fire*, David Robie (Lindon Publishing, 1986); Wasserman, *Killing Our Own*; and "American Nuclear Guinea Pigs," from Edward Markey, House Subcommittee on Energy Conservation,

to US Secretary of Energy, October 24, 1986, at epwijnants-lectures.com. For Soviet experiments on citizens, "The Nuclear Guinea Pigs," Rosemary Righter, *The Times* (London, July 31, 2002).

6. Castle-Bravo test: *Dark Sun,* Richard Rhodes (Simon & Schuster, 1996); "A Bomb's Legacy of sickness on Rongelap," Beverly Deepe Keever, *Honolulu Weekly*, Feb., 25, 2004; Robie, *Eyes of Fire*; *The Voyage of the Lucky Dragon*, Ralph Eugene Lapp (Harper, 1958); "The Lucky Dragon" Bruce Kennedy, cnn.com; "Race for the Superbomb," PBS, January, 1999, pbs.org; Nuclearfiles.org; and bikiniatoll.com.

7. Irving and Dorothy Stowe: Interviews with Dorothy, Barbara, and Robert Stowe; Zelko, *Make It A Green Peace*.

8. Ben and Dorothy Metcalfe: Interviews with Ben and Dorothy Metcalfe; Zelko interviews; "Protest in Paradise," Phyllis Webb (*Maclean's*, June 1973); Ben Metcalfe's reporter notebooks, 1956-1973. Metcalfe passed away during the preparation of this manuscript, October 14, 2003.

9. Bob Hunter: Interviews with Hunter; Zelko, *Make It A Green Peace*; *Red Blood*, Robert Hunter (McClelland & Stewart, 1999). *Erebus*, Robert Hunter, (McClelland & Stewart, 1968); and Hunter's childhood writings and journals.

10. Disarmament, 1950s: Cooney, *Power of the People*; *The Campaign for Nuclear Disarmament*, Paul Byrne (Croom Helm, 1988); *By Little and by Little: The Selected Writings of Dorothy Day*, ed. Robert Ellsberg (Knopf, 1983); *Resisting the Bomb: 1954-1970*, Lawrence Wittner (Stanford U., 1997); *Peace Agitator: The Story of A.J. Muste*, Nat Hentoff (MacMillan, 1963); and *The Power of Nonviolence: Writings by Advocates of Peace*, Howard Zinn (Beacon Press, 2002). Peace Symbol origins are at nonukesnorth.net/peacesymbol and scientium.com. UK CND, cnduk.org.

11. Quakers: *The Beginnings of Quakerism*, William Braithwaite (Macmillan, 1923);

The Quiet Rebels, Margaret Bacon (New Society, 1985); "Speak Truth to Power," pamphlet (American Friends Service Committee, 1955).

12: The *Golden Rule*: *The Voyage of the Golden Rule*, Albert Bigalow (Doubleday, 1959); and Cooney, *Power of the People*, includes voyages of *Phoenix* and *Everyman*. These three boats were precursors of the first Greenpeace boat.

13. Polaris, Groton, Connecticut, 1960: D. Stowe interview; *Peace, Civil Rights, and the Search for Community*, Robert Swann, schumachersociety.org;

Chicago '68, David Farber (U. of Chicago, 1988); *Tales of Beatnik Glory*, Ed Sanders (Stonehill, 1975); and Cooney, *Power of the People*.

14. Jim and Marie Bohlen: *Making Waves*, Jim Bohlen (Black Rose, 2001); correspondence with the Bohlens; *The New Pioneer's Handbook*, Jim Bohlen (Schocken Books, 1978); Zelko, *Make It A Green Peace*.

15. Vancouver counterculture 1966-1969: Interviews, Hunter, Metcalfe, Dorothy Stowe, Pat Moore, Marining, Paul and Linda Spong, Paul Hovan, Fred Easton; Pauls & Campbell, *The Georgia Straight: What the Hell Happened?*; *The West Beyond the West*, Jean Barman (U. of Toronto, 1996); *The Vancouver Sun*, *The Province*, and *The Georgia Straight*; Hunter's columns, *V. Sun*, 1969; Ben Metcalfe, CBC radio transcripts, notes.

16. Skagit River Campaign: *A Citizen's guide to the Skagit Valley*, Thomas L. Perry Jr. (Run Out Skagit Spoilers Committee, 1981); "The Damnation of a Dam: The High Ross Dam Controversy," Terry Simmons (M.A. thesis, Department of Geography, Simon Fraser U., 1974); interviews with Thomas Perry, Ken Farquarson, Simmons, and Metcalfe. For the highway campaign, see *Freeway Planning and Protests in Vancouver 1954-1972*, Kenneth MacKenzie (Simon Fraser U., 1985).

17. Vietnam War: Edwin O. Reischauer — future US Ambassador to Japan — warned in *Wanted: an Asian Policy* (Knopf, 1955) of unfavourable terrain and "a veritable quagmire" of civilian resentment. Reischauer's *Beyond Vietnam* (Knopf, 1967) remains a vivid critique of US policy. *Vietnam*, Stanley Karnow (Viking Press, 1983), the definitive history; *A Bright Shining Lie*, Neil Sheehan (Random House, 1988); *The Uncensored War*, Daniel Hallin (U. of California, 1989); *Dispatches*, Michael Herr (Knopf, 1977); *Everything We Had*, ed. Al Santoli (Random House, 1981); a comprehensive chronology, 1945-1975, is available at historyplace.com; and Bob Hunter's *Storming of the Mind* (McClelland and Stewart, 1971), articulates the war's significance to our story.

FURTHER READING, 1950S AND 1960S: *The Technological Society*, Jacques Ellul (Knopf, 1964); *Dr. Strangelove's America*, Margot Henriksen (U. of Calif., 1997); *Pillar of Fire*, Taylor Branch (Simon & Schuster, 1998); *The Kennedy Tapes*, ed. Ernest May, Philip Zelikow (Belknap, 1997); *Heretic's Heart*, Margot Adler (Beacon Press, 1997); *On the Trail of the Assassins: My Investigation and Prosecution of the Murder of President Kennedy*, Jim Garrison (Sheridan Square Press, 1988);

Beneath the Diamond Sky: Haight-Ashbury 1965-1970, Barney Hoskyns (Simon & Schuster, 1997); *The Sixties*, Todd Gitlin (Bantam, 1993); *The Making of a Counter Culture*, Theodore Roszak (Faber, 1970; U. Calif., 1995); and *The Population Bomb*, Paul Ehrlich (Buccaneer Books, 1968, 1997). Two anthologies of ecological thinking prior to Greenpeace: *The Subversive Science*, ed. Paul Shepard (Houghton Mifflin, 1969); and *Thinking Green*, ed. Michael Allaby (Barrie & Jenkins, 1989).

CHAPTER 2: DON'T MAKE A WAVE

1. Amchitka Island: *Amchitka and the Bomb*, Dean Kohlhoff, (U. of Washington Press, 2002); *U.S. Nuclear Weapons: The Secret History*, Chuck Hansen (Orion, 1988); *Nuclear Flashback,* Pam Miller and Norman Buskin (Greenpeace, 1996, greenpeaceusa.org); *Aleuts,* William Laughlin (Holt, Rinehart and Winston, 1980); *The Thousand Mile War*, Brian Garfield (U. of Alaska, 1995); Glavin, *The Last Great Sea*; "Nuclear Testing in the Aleutians," Lillie D'Easum (Don't Make A Wave Committee, 1970); interviews: Moore, Simmons.

2. SPEC: Now called "The Society Promoting Environmental Conservation," spec.bc.ca. A history of the organization appears in "Spectrum," Volume 27, Number 1, Spring 1999; interviews, Hunter and Gary Gallon.

3. Green Panthers: Interviews with Hunter and Hamish Bruce; Hunter, *Storming of the Mind*.

4. Ecology symbol designed by Ron Cobb, first published in the *L.A. Free Press*, October 25, 1969 and imparted to the public domain. Hunter reproduced the symbol in his *V. Sun* column, December 11, 1969. Metcalf's symbol and sign, photograph of billboards, in author's archive.

5. Don't Make A Wave Committee: Interviews, D. Stowe, B. Stowe, Hunter, Marining, Metcalfe; "Greenpeace is Beautiful" columns, Irving Stowe (*Georgia Straight*, August 1970 to June 1971); Bohlen, *Making Waves*; correspondence with Bohlen; Vancouver Archives, Greenpeace Foundation Fonds, Volume I, file 13; V. II, files 1-7; and V. III-VIII.

6. "Sierra Club Plans N-Blast Blockade," *The Vancouver Sun*, February 9, 1970.

7: "Make it a Green Peace": This moment passed undocumented, except in memory. Some accounts place this event at the Stowes' home, but the majority recall the Fireside Room at the Unitarian Church, 49th and Oak, Vancouver. Interviews with Bill Darnell, Dorothy Stowe, Hunter, Simmons, and Marining; Bohlen, *Making Waves*; Hunter, *Warriors*.

8. Sierra Club: Interviews and correspondence with Terry Simmons; *History of the Sierra Club*, Michael Cohen (Random House, 1988). Michael McCloskey's comment is from *A Fierce Green Fire*, Philip Shabecoff (Hill and Wang, 1993), cited by Chris Kuykendall in "Remaking a Modern Conservationist" (Endnote 8, 31 August 2002, csf.colorado.edu). Shabecoff recalls that the established environmental groups — Sierra Club, the National Wildlife Federation — played almost no role during the inaugural Earth Day, April 22, 1970.

9. LSD: Metcalfe and Thurston were clinical trial subjects when LSD was considered a promising therapeutic tool; Cholden, Kurland & Savage, 1955; Dr. Albert Kurland through 1971; *The Use of LSD in Psychotherapy and Alcoholism*, ed. H.A. Abramson (Bobbs Merril, 1967); and Metcalfe's account in *The Province* (September 2, 1959). Thereafter, prominent publishers, celebrities, and church ministers attended sessions at Vancouver's Hollywood Hospital. Clinic financier "Captain" Al Hubbard drove a Rolls Royce, carried a briefcase of exotic drugs, and dosed Timothy Leary in Cambridge in 1963. "B.C.'s Acid Flashback," Ross Crockford (*Vancouver Sun* December 8, 2001); "The Original Captain Trips," Todd Fahey (fargonebooks.com/high); *Acid Dreams: The Complete Social History of LSD*, Martin Lee and Bruce Shlain (Grove Press, 1986); and the ensuing cultural conflict documented in *The Drugtakers*, Jock Young (Paladin, 1971).

9.All Season's Park: Interviews with Marining, Hunter, and Metcalfe; *Vancouver Sun*, *Georgia Straight*, undated clippings; Marining notebook.

10. Mindbombs: Bob Hunter develops his idea of using electronic media to speed up social change in *The Enemies of Anarchy* (McClelland and Stewart, 1970) and *The Storming of the Mind* (McClelland & Stewart, 1971).

11. Patrick Moore: Moore interviews and letter to Greenpeace, March 16, 1971.

12. *Wall Street Journal*, "Blasting the Blast," June 24, 1971.

13. AEC hearings: Moore interview; Bohlen, *Making Waves*; Irving Stowe in the *Georgia Straight*, June 4 and 11, 1971; "The Cannikin Test," Robert Keziere (Don't Make a Wave Comm., 1971).

14. Jack Davis, boat insurance: letters from Jack Davis, Canada Minister of Fisheries, May 19, June 8 and 24, 1971; letter from Patrick

Moore to Davis, June 4 1971; Vancouver Archive, Greenpeace, V. VI, File 13; interviews, Moore, Hunter, and Metcalfe; Irving Stowe in the *Georgia Straight*, June 4, 1971.

15. US Coast Guard "Restricted Area" around Amchitka: Richard Fineberg phone conversations with Capt. Warren Mitchell, US Coast Guard, and Dixon Stewart, AEC, Anchorage, quoted in letter, Fineberg to Moore, September 2, 1971, author's archive.

16. Last crew position: Interviews, Ben and Dorothy Metcalfe, Lou Hogan, Marining, Hunter, Thurston and Jim Bohlen. Bohlen's dissenting view is that "Marie's not going had nothing to do with it." He recalls "no struggle for women's rights." For a treatment of gender-bias in progressive organizations of the era, see *Gendering War Talk*, ed. Miriam Cooke (Princeton U., 1993); *The Remasculinization of America*, Susan Jeffords (Indiana U., 1989); "Masculinity and the Anti-War Movement of the Vietnam Era," Hanna Roman (Department of History, U. of British Columbia, 2002).

FURTHER READING, RELEVANT POPULAR BOOKS, 1967 72: *The Greening of America*, Charles Reich (Random House, 1970); *Understanding Media*, Marshall McLuhan (Bantam, 1967); *Operating Manual for Spaceship Earth*, Buckminster Fuller (Simon and Schuster, 1969); *Custer Died for Your Sins*, Vine Deloria, Jr. (Scribner, 1969); *Sexual Politics*, Kate Millett (Doubleday, 1970); *The Female Eunuch*, Germaine Greer (McGraw-Hill, 1970); *Be Here Now*, Baba Ram Dass (Three Rivers, 1971); *Gestalt Therapy Verbatim*, Frederick Perls (Real People Press, 1969); *A Sand County Almanac*, Aldo Leopold (Oxford U. Press, 1949); and *Silent Spring*, Rachel Carson (Houghton Mifflin, 1962).

CHAPTER 3: ON AN OCEAN NAMED FOR PEACE

1. Amchitka voyage: Interviews, Ben and Dorothy Metcalfe, Hunter, Thurston, Dorothy Stowe, Simmons, Cormack and Cummings (1975-82); correspondence with Jim Bohlen; Hunter columns, *V. Sun*, September, October 1971; Hunter and Metcalfe notebooks; *Greenpeace*, Robert Keziere and Robert Hunter (McClelland & Stewart, 1972); Hunter, *Warriors*; Bohlen, *Making Waves*; newspaper clippings, Vancouver Archive, Greenpeace, Volumes VI, VII, and VIII; and news accounts, *Vancouver Sun*, *Winnipeg Free Press*, *Winnipeg Tribune*, *Toronto Daily*

Star, *New York Times*. Dialogue on board is adapted from the sources, with addition of Metcalfe tapes, "Between Ourselves," Metcalfe, CBC, 1971; radio clip of Metcalfe transmitting from the *Phyllis Cormack*, archives.cbc.ca (life, society/greenpeace).

2. Metcalfe broadcast, "The Greenpeacing of America," (Canadian Broadcasting Corporation "Morning Commentary" text, September 16, 1971).

3. Passages from *Warriors of the Rainbow*, Willoya and Brown (Naturegraph, 1969).

4. Motions in Canadian Parliament: House of Commons, Routine Proceedings; September 10, 1971, and thereafter.

5. US lawsuit: *The Committee for Nuclear Responsibility, Inc, et al, v. Glen T. Seaborg, et al*, July 9, 1971, US National Archives. Other plaintiffs: Sierra Club, Friends of the Earth, Wilderness Society, Society Against Nuclear Explosions, and the Federation of American Scientists; "The Coming Atomic Blast in Alaska," Paul Jacobs, *New York Review*, July 22, 1971; *New York Times*, October 6 and 28, 1971; "Judge Upholds Amchitka Test," *Winnipeg Free Press*, November 2, 1971; Kohllhoff, *Amchitka*.

6. Nixon/Kissinger tapes: US National Archive, segment provided by Barbara Stowe; Kissinger notes that the Amchitka decision will appear to come from the Supreme Court. See "Revelations and gaps on Nixon tapes," Kevin Anderson, BBC, 2002 , bbc.co.uk.

7. Media and science: Terry Simmons, in correspondence with the author, wrote, "Metcalfe was prone to outrageous exaggeration." Metcalfe respected good science but attributed more influence to a good headline. The debate becomes a motif in our story and endures in Greenpeace three decades later.

8. Walk up Akutan: Interviews with Hunter, Moore, and Thurston; Keziere and Hunter, *Greenpeace*; Hunter, *Warriors*;

9. Coastguard seizure, *Confidence*: US Bureau of Customs, Case 72-3126-10064, October 8, 1971; Hunter columns *V. Sun*, October 13, 14, 15, 1971; interviews, Hunter, Metcalfe, Thurston, Cormack, Cummings; the note signed by 18 crew members of the *US Confidence* is in the Vancouver Archive, Greenpeace, V. 3, File 6; a photograph appears in *Greenpeace*, Keziere and Hunter. Signatories include: Richard Barrich, Steven Todd, David Bayer, James Pratt, R.V. Sanford, Eric Anderson, Joe Grimes, Kenny Wilcox, Bobby Bryce, J.M. Smith, Don Harrison, and six illegible.

10. Robert Stowe: Interview, handwritten notes, "Press Release," Student Action Committee Against Nuclear Testing, November 3, 1971; letter from Office of the Prime Minister to Robert Stowe, December 17, 1971, copies in author's archives.

11. Union Protests: *Vancouver Sun*, *Winnipeg Free Press*, *Toronto Daily Star*, Nov. 3, 4, 1971; Hunter column, *V. Sun*, November 4, 1971.

12. James Schlesinger on Amchitka: *Vancouver Sun*, November 5, 1971; Kohllhoff, *Amchitka.*

13. US Supreme Court and Amchitka: *The New York Times, The Vancouver Sun*, *Winnipeg Free Press*, *Toronto Daily Star*, Nov. 3-7, 1971; Kohlhoff, *Amchitka.*

14. *Edgewater Fortune*, *Greenpeace II* (Also "*Greenpeace Too*"): Interviews Marining, Cummings, Simmons; Zelko interview with Paul Watson, *Make it a Green Peace*. Jim Bohlen's "Report on the *Greenpeace Too* Voyage," December 5, 1971, claims Johansen did not make a "best effort" to reach the test site and therefore the Don't Make a Wave Committee didn't owe him the $12,000 charter fee. The money was paid, but animosity lingered. Watson argues that the second crew was more serious about reaching Amchitka than the *Phyllis Cormack* crew (see Zelko, n. 419).

17. *Time* magazine: "Amchitka's Flawed Success," quoted from Hunter, *Warriors.*

FURTHER READING, ALEUTIANS: *Aleuts: Survivors of the Bering Land Bridge*, William Laughlin (Rinehart and Winston, 1980); *The Environment of Amchitka Island, Alaska*, Melvin Merritt and R.Glen Fuller (US Energy Res. Devel. Admin., 1977); *Island Between*, Margaret Murie (U. of Alaska, 1977).

CHAPTER 4: LAW OF THE SEA

1. Hunter, *V. Sun* column, October 23, 1971: "[We] had been defeated. We did not make it to the bomb. The only hope left was that the voyage of *Greenpeace* — the idea, not the boat — had just begun."

2. Ole Holsti letter, *Vancouver Sun*, Dec. 15, 1971. Bohlen replied to Holsti that Greenpeace had petitioned the French and Chinese governments, letter (Vanc. Archive, Greenpeace, V.2, f.10.)

3. French nuclear testing: *Moruroa, mon amour*, Bengt and Marie Danielsson (Penguin, 1977); *Poisoned Reign: French Nuclear Colonialism in the Pacific*, Danielsson (Penguin, 1986); Danielsson online at thebulletin.org; *French nuclear testing, 1960-1988*, Andrew Burrows (Natural Defense Resources Council, 1989); *Chronology: The French Presence in the South Pacific, 1838-1990*, Julie Miles (Greenpeace NZ, 1990).

4. Moruroa and Mururoa: The French misspelling, "Mururoa," common in 1972, is retained in direct quotes and quotes from printed material.

5. November 1, 1971 Don't Make a Wave meeting notes: Vanc. Archive, Greenpeace, V.1.

6. Greenpeace Foundation: Disputes about founders have endured since Greenpeace became well known. Bohlen names the directors of the Don't Make A Wave Committee; Metcalf names attendees of the first Greenpeace Foundation meeting. Hunter quipped in 2001, "You can go into any pub in British Columbia and meet a founder of Greenpeace." Most lists to date are gender-biased at least. Frank Zelko said in correspondence: "Unlike Friends of the Earth, for example, which sprung fully formed from the forehead of David Brower, Greenpeace developed in a more evolutionary manner." Stories about the name "Greenpeace" being independently coined in other places, such as New Zealand and London, are apocryphal. For a discussion of this, see author's website, rexweyler.com.

7. Metcalfe's story in New Zealand: *New Zealand Herald*, page 1, April 4, 1972.

8. Copy of McTaggart's letter to Metcalfe in author's archives.

9. McTaggart: McTaggart interview, *Greenpeace III*, and *Outrage!*; *Shadow Warrior*, McTaggart, with Helen Slinger (Orion, 2002); "Greenpeace, IWC, & Money," Leslie Spencer, Jan Bollwerk, Richard Morais, *Forbes Magazine*, November 11, 1991; "The McTaggart Myth," Leslie Spencer, suanews.com; obituary by Bruce and Roma Orvis, *Alpine Enterprise*, April 11, 2001. McTaggart's proclivity for spinning history left him vulnerable to journalists such as Spencer.

10. Hunter's "Whole Earth Church" manifesto and Minister Certificate in archives of the author.

11. The radio breakdown story relies on contradictory versions by McTaggart and Metcalfe. Grant Davidson confirms Metcalfe's version, letter to Metcalfe, September 5, 1972, and in correspondence with the author.

12. *Greenpeace III* voyage: *Greenpeace III* and *Outrage!*; interviews, McTaggart and Metcalfe; correspondence Grant Davidson; Zelko interviews with Nigel Ingram, *Make it a Green Peace*.

13. Admiral Claverie's discussions with officers: McTaggart interviews; McTaggart's account of two meetings with a French Navy radio technician and an officer, who claimed to have been privy to these discussions and involved in the surveillance of the *Vega* (*Greenpeace III*, pp. 360, 361).

14. The Greenpeace missions in Paris, Rome, and Stockholm, 1972: interviews with Marining, Thurston, Moore, and Ben and Dorothy Metcalfe.

15. Stockholm Environment Conference 72: Proceedings at unep.org/Documents; *New Zealand Herald*, June 15, 1972, story on the NZ nuclear resolution; *Only One Earth*, commissioned by the Secretary General, Barbara Ward and René Dubos (W.W. Norton, 1972). The Swedish government initiated the Conference in response to acid rain from industrial Europe. It marked the dawn of global environmental governance. "Environment" and "sustainable development" entered the public lexicon after this meeting. See *Reclaiming Paradise*: *The Global Environmental Movement*, John McCormick (Indiana U. Press, 1989).

16. Debates of the House of Commons of Canada (Hansard), quoted from McTaggart/Hunter, *Greenpeace III*.

17. Correspondence between McTaggart and the Canadian government is published in *Outrage!*, Appendix D.

18. Journalist in Rarotonga: Grant Davidson letter to Metcalfe, September 5, 1972; *Greenpeace III*; interviews and correspondence, Davidson, Metcalfe; McTaggart told the author in conversation: "The guy was a drunk and he was out to do a hatchet job on us regardless of what I did."

FURTHER READING: *Boy Roel: Voyage to Nowhere*, Barry Mitcalfe, Boshier, others (Alister Taylor, 1972); *The Great Uranium Cartel*, Earle Gray (McLelland & Stewart, 1982); *Fri Alert*, ed. Elsa Claron (Caveman Press, 1974); *Nuclear Playground*, Stewart Firth (Allen & Unwin, 1987).

CHAPTER 5: STOP AHAB

1. McTaggart in Vancouver, Prime Minister: *Greenpeace III*; interviews, McTaggart, Metcalfe, Hunter, D. Stowe.

2. *Jeanne d'Arc*: Interviews, Bob and Zoe Hunter, Marining, Watson,

Thurston; undated clippings in Marining papers, *Vancouver Sun*, *The Province*.

3. Spong: Interviews, Paul and Linda Spong; *Song of the Whale*, Weyler (Doubleday, 1986); Hunter, *Warriors*; Pauls and Campbell, *The Georgia Straight*.

4. Cetacean intelligence, influences on Spong: Dr. John Lilly, *Man and Dolphin* (Doubleday, 1961) and *The Mind of the Dolphin* (1967); *Whales, Dolphins and Porpoises*, ed. by Kenneth Norris (U. of Calif., 1966), includes Gregory Bateson's "Problems in Cetacean and Other Mammalian Communication." Bateson foreshadows the Spong/Skana encounter, suggesting that during future research, cetaceans may "make characteristic attempts to modify the context (i.e. manipulate the humans)."

5. Dr. James Tyhurst: Spong interviews; *Abuse of Trust: The Career of Dr. James Tyhurst*, Christopher Hyde (Douglas & McIntyre, 1991).

6. Orca captures: "Live capture statistics for the killer whale (Orcinus orca) 1961-1976," E. Asper, *Aquatic Mammals* (5)1, 1988; *The Performing Orca — Why the Show Must Stop*, Erich Hoyt, (Whale and Dolphin Conserv. Soc., 1992); *Orca: A Family Story*, Peter Hamilton (Lifeforce Foundation, 1993); "Orcas in Captivity," members.aol.com/orcainfo; animaldiversity.ummz.umich.edu; and orcalab.org.

7. Whale Dialects: Spong interview; "Call traditions and dialects of killer whales (Orcinus orca) in British Columbia," John Ford (Ph.D. dissertation, UBC, 1984); "Acoustic traditions of killer whales," Ford, *Whalewatcher* (American Cetacean Society, 1985).

8. Orca census: Spong interview; orcalab.com; *Orca: The Whale Called Killer*, Erich Hoyt (Camdon House, 1990); *Killer Whales*, Michael Bigg, G. Ellis, J. Ford and K. Balcomb (Phantom Press, 1987); genealogy and natural history.

9. *I Ching*: Quotes from the 1967 edition of the Richard Wilhelm and Cary Baynes translation (Princeton U.); the "Foreword" by Carl Jung is a useful introduction, online at iging.com.

10. South Pacific flotilla, 1973: Interviews, David Moodie, Rein Achterberg; "Blast echoed around world: The Mururoa Vigil," *New Zealand Sunday Star-Times*, July 19, 1998; Caron, *Fri Alert*; Szabo, *Making Waves*; McTaggart/Hunter, *Greenpeace III*; Brown and May, *The Greenpeace Story*.

11. McTaggart beating: McTaggart interview; *Greenpeace III*; Brown and May, *The Greenpeace Story*; Zelko, *Make it a Green Peace*;

McTaggart interview with Peter Gzowski, CBC radio, September 14, 1973, clip at archives.cbc.ca.

12. Hoa Atoll, where France held the captured crews from the *Fri* and *Vega*, is colonial headquarters in the Tuamotu Archipelago, staffed by legionnaires. In 1985, Major Alain Mafart and Captain Dominique Prieur — French Sécurité Extérieure agents responsible for bombing the *Rainbow Warrior* and killing photographer Fernando Pereira — were held in this garrison. See "The French Secret Service Agents: Where are they Now?" at archive.greenpeace.org; *The French Secret Services*, Douglas Porch (Farrar, Straus and Giroux, 1995); and Robie, *Eyes of Fire*.

13. Hunter/Weyler dialogue: author's notebooks.

14. French minister Galley quoted in *Vancouver Sun*, August 31, 1973.

FURTHER READING, CETACEANS AND HUMANS: *Behind the Dolphin Smile*, Richard O'Barry and Keith Coulbourne (Algonquin, 1988); *Dolphin Societies*, ed. Karen Pryor and Kenneth Norris (U. of Calif., 1991); *Whale Nation*, Heathcote Williams (Harmony, Crown, 1988); *In the Company of Whales*, Alexander Morton (Orca Books, 1993); and *A Whale for the Killing*, Farley Mowat (McClelland & Stewart, 1972).

CHAPTER 6: THE GREAT WHALE CONSPIRACY

1. Greenpeace 1974: Interviews with Bob and Bobbi Hunter, Pat and Eileen Moore, Marining, McTaggart, Bruce, Paul and Linda Spong, MacDonald, Thurston; author's notebooks and journals; Hunter, *Warriors*; McTaggart/Hunter, *Greenpeace III*.

2. Giorgio Pilleri: *Investigations on Cetacea*, ed. by Pilleri, 25 volumes and 5 supplements (Institute of Brain Anatomy, University of Bern, 1969 to 1995).

3. McTaggart in Paris: Interviews and discussion with McTaggart; *Greenpeace III*.

4. Voyage of *La Flor*: *Knocking on Heaven's Door*, Rolf Heimann (Friends of the Earth, 1979); correspondence with Heimann; interview, Rien Achterberg.

5. Greenpeace NZ: *Making Waves: The Greenpeace New Zealand Story*, Michael Szabo (Reed Books, 1991); *Peace People: A History of Peace Activities in New Zealand*, Elsie Locke (Hazard, 1992); Claron, *Fri Alert*; and McCormick, *Reclaiming Paradise*.

6. Spong's espionage in Norway: Interviews Paul and Linda Spong; Weyler, *Song of the Whale*; Hunter, *Warriors*.

7. For Captain Ahab on the quarterdeck of the *Pequod*, see Herman Melville's *Moby Dick*, Chapter 36, "The Quarter-Deck," (Harper Bros., 1851).

FURTHER READING, VARIETIES OF ECOLOGY: *The Rights of Nature: A History of Environmental Ethics*, Roderick Nash (U. of Wisconsin, 1988); *Philosophers of the Earth: Conversations with Ecologists*, Anne Chisholm (Dutton/Plume, 1972); *Sustaining the Earth: The Story of the Environmental Movement*, John Young (Harvard, 1990); and Zelko summary in *Make it a Green Peace*.

CHAPTER 7: MENDOCINO RIDGE

1. Whale voyage, 1975: Author's journal, notebooks, and photographs; interviews, the Hunters, Spongs, Pat and Eileen Moore, Thurston, Marining, Watson, MacDonald, Precious, Easton, Chechik, and Korotva; written accounts, David Garrick; Hunter, *Warriors*; film *Voyages to Save the Whales*; newspaper reports in *The Vancouver Sun*, *San Francisco Chronicle*, *The Daily Yomiuri*, and others; "Between the Harpoon and the Whale," Charles Flowers, *The New York Times Magazine*, August 24, 1975; and Hunter interview with Adrienne Clarkson, CBC television, *The Fifth Estate*, March 16, 1976 (clip at archives.cbc.ca).

2. Dall's porpoises, gray whales and blue whales: Author's notes; *Mind in the Waters*; "Order Cetacea," animaldiversity.ummz.umich.edu.

3. Haida Gwaii: *A Guide to the Queen Charlotte Islands*, Neil Carey (Raincoast Books, 11th edition, 1995); *The Raven Steals the Light*, Bill Reid and Robert Bringhurst (Douglas and McIntyre, 1984); and *Haida Gwaii*, Ian Gill and David Nunuk (Raincoast Books, 1997).

4. Whaling history and population data: "Whale Catch Hisotories," 1910-1989, Whaling Library, luna.pos.to/whale; "The Politics of Whaling," Table of Catches 1965-1976, (Project Jonah, 1977); *Men and Whales*, Richard Ellis (Knopf. 1993); Glavin, *Last Great Sea*; Day, *Whale War*; Bimie, *International Regulation of Whaling*; Whale and Dolphin Conserv. Soc., wdcs.org; and "The Best Scientific Evidence Available: The Whaling Moratorium and Divergent Interpretations of Science," A. W. Harris, Humboldt State University, 2001, isanet.org/archive/harris.

5. Amy Ephron in New York: from her version, told to us in San Francisco, 1975.

FURTHER READING, ECOLOGY IN THE 1970S: *Man in the Landscape: A Historical View of the Esthetics of Nature*, Paul Shepard (Knopf, 1967); "Conscious Purpose versus Nature" Gregory Bateson in *Dialectics of Liberation* (Penquin, 1968); The *Closing Circle*, Barry Commoner (Knopf, 1971); "Should Trees Have Standing? Toward Legal Rights for Natural Objects," Christopher Stone, (*So. Calif. Law Review*, 450, 1972); *Exploring New Ethics for Survival*: Garrett Hardin (Viking, 1972); *The Comedy of Survival*, Joseph Meeker (Guild of Tutors Press, 1972); *Steps to an Ecology of Mind*, Gregory Bateson essays from 1948-72 (Jason Aronson, 1972); *Earth Wisdom*, Delores LaChapelle (Guild of Tutors Press, 1972); *The Tender Carnivore and the Sacred Game*, Paul Shepherd (Charles Scribner's Sons, 1973); "The Shallow and the Deep, Long-Range Ecology Movement," Arne Naess (*Inquiry*, vol. 16, 1973); *Pilgrim at Tinker Creek*, Annie Dillard (Harper & Row, 1974); *The Monkey Wrench Gang*, Edward Abbey, (J.B. Lippincott, 1975); *Animal Liberation*, Peter Singer (Cape, 1976); and *Woman and Nature*, Susan Griffin (Harper & Row, 1978). For more influences on ecology, see author's website.

CHAPTER 8: YEAR OF THE DRAGON

1. Dialogue with Jack Richardson adapted from author's notebooks.

2. Erik Nielson: Interview by Paul Watson in *Greenpeace Chronicles* #1, October 1975, author's archives.

3. McTaggart in Paris: Interviews, McTaggart and Rémi Parmentier; McTaggart/Hunter, *Greenpeace III*; *May '68 and Its Afterlives*, Kristin Ross (U. of Chicago, 2002); *Intellectuals and the Left in France Since 1968*, Keith Reader (Macmillan, 1987).

4. Seal campaign, 1976: Interviews, Watson, Hunter, Al Johnson, Pat and Eileen Moore; Hunter journal, *Warriors*; *Sea Shepherd* and *Seal Wars*, Patrick Watson (Key Porter, 2002); *Sea of Slaughter*, Farley Mowat (McClelland and Stewart, 1984); *Of Men and Seals: A History of the Newfoundland Seal Hunt*, James Candow (Environment Canada, 1989); "Shepherds of the Labrador Front," Watson, *Greenpeace Chronicles* #3, Spring 1977; and *Bitter Harvest* (Northern Lights Film, 1983).

5. Rex Murphy, "The Noxious Twit is also endangered," *Vancouver Sun*, November 25, 1975.

6. Seal Populations: Peak population in the eighteenth century unknown, but estimated to be 20-30 million; records show 34 million harp seal pelts harvested, 1821 to 1900. In 1972, Dr. R. L. Allen revealed that the population had declined by 50 percent since the first rigorous population study in 1950, from 3 to 1.5 million ("Recommendation to Canadian Dept. of Fisheries," 1972). Thus, the remnant herd in 1976 represented approximately 5 percent of the peak population. Data from "The Present Status of Western Atlantic Harp Seals," Dr. David Lavigne, *G. Chronicles* #4, Spring 1977; *Harps & Hoods: ice-breeding seals of the Northwest Atlantic*, Lavigne, (U. of Waterloo, 1988).

7. Pat Moore on seal herds, 1976-1981: "The Slaughter of Seals Must Stop," *G. Chronicles* #4, Spring 1977; and "The Management of Marine Mammals in the Context of a Total Ecosystem Approach to Fisheries Policy," from Moore to the Canadian Commission on Pacific Fisheries Policy, 1981.

FURTHER READING, SEALS: *Red Ice,* Davies Brian (Methuen, 1989); *The War Against the Seals: A History of the North American Seal Fishery*, Briton Busch (McGill-Queen's University Press, 1985); a Newfoundlander's view: *Season of the Seal,* E. Calvin Coish (Breakwater, 1979); *Seals*, Sheila Anderson (Whittet Books, 1990); and *Man Kind?* Cleveland Amory (Harper & Row, 1974).

CHAPTER 9: HOTEL PAPA

1. Canadian Bay Class minesweepers: The first four, 1953 and 1954, went to France; two from 1954, the *Fortune* and the *James Bay*, became *Greenpeace II* and *VII*; "Canadian Navy," Haze Gray "Naval History," hazegray.org.

2. The first "Memo from Fido," April 11, 1976 — typed on Greenpeace letterhead, mimeographed; subsequent issues photocopied, in author's archive.

3. Saul Alinsky and Joseph Meegan founded the Back-of-the-Yards Neighborhood Council in 1939 and exposed Chicago's worst slum landlords with flamboyant boycotts: *Reveille for Radicals* (Random House, 1946); *The Professional Radical* (1970); and his "pragmatic primer,"

Rules for Radicals (1972). Biography: *The Radical Vision of Saul Alinsky*, David Finks (Paulist Press, 1984).

4. Thomas Banyacya: Address to the UN Human Settlements Conference, June 6, 1976, reprint, American Friends Service Committee; author's notes; Weyler, *Bood of the Land* (New Society, 1992).

5. Plutonium black market: *The Province*, June 9, 10, 1976; "2 Tons of Nuclear Materials Missing," *The New York Times*, reprinted in *Honolulu Star-Bulletin*, July 23, 1976; Hunter interviews, notebooks, and media release, June 1976.

6. "Declaration of Interdependence," *Greenpeace Chronicles* #3, Winter 1976-77; unattributed manifesto written by Bob Hunter and Patrick Moore, typed copy in author's archive. Watson's claim in *Sea Shepherd*, p. 154, that he wrote the "Laws of Ecology," is not accurate. Hunter solicited Moore to help draft the Laws after ideas borrowed from the "Three Laws of Ecology," by Barry Commoner in *The Closing Circle*, 1971. See a detailed history of the slogan on author's website.

7. *Greenpeace VII*: Interviews with crew, author's journal and photographs; Hunter notebooks, *Warriors*; Greenpeace Foundation financial records; interviews with the Hunters, Moores, Spongs, Gannon, Marining, Precious, Easton, Korotva; film, *Voyages to Save the Whales*; newspaper accounts, *The Vancouver Sun*, *The Province*, *Georgia Straight*, *The New York Times*, *SF Chronicle*, *Examiner*, *Honolulu Star-Bulletin*, *North Shore News*; and *G. Chronicles* # 3, December 1976.

8. Ted Haggarty's "Friendly note from the Chief Engineer" in author's archives.

9. Whale quotas, 1976: Day, *The Whale Wars*; "Whale Catch Hisotories," luna.pos.to.

10. Ed Daly: Radio transmission copied in author's notebook, July 20, 1976. The real story of the last flight out of Da Nang in 1975 was told by UPI reporter Paul Vogle, on front pages and in network leads worldwide: "DA NANG, MARCH 29 (UPI) — Only the fastest, the strongest, and the meanest of a huge mob got a ride on the last plane from Da Nang Saturday." Daly's "not one person got hurt," is spin; many died. See colleague Glenn MacDonald's tribute to Vogle, "The Last Goodbye," militarycorruption.com /paulvogle.

11. Hunter's shipboard "James Bay Bulletin" became the "James Bay Daley Bulletin" on August 8, 1976, and the last "Daley Bulletin" appeared

on August 24; copies in author's archive. Hunter wrote "Daley;" I've used "Daly" throughout..

12. Nikolai Makarov in Vancouver: "Goodwill mission of Soviets marred by demonstrators," and "Whale season in doubt," *The Vancouver Sun*, August 30, 1976; tape transcripts, Dr. Peter Beter and General George S. Brown, Chairman of the US Joint Chiefs of Staff, 1976; text at peterbeter.host.sk.

FURTHER READING: *Ecotopia*, Ernest Callenbach (Banyen Tree, 1975); *Ecology and Consciousness*, ed. Richard Grossinger (North Atlantic, 1978); *Toward a Transpersonal Ecology*, Warwick Fox (Shambhala, 1990); *A Chorus of Stones*, Susan Griffin (Doubleday, 1993).

CHAPTER 10: A NAME FOR WHAT IS NATURAL

1. Schism 1976: "Minutes: Meeting of the Greenpeace Board of Directors," September 13, 1976, and attached resolutions and letters to Mark Lavell, Howard Arfin, and Paul Watson; copies in author's archive.

2. McTaggart letters to Hunter, August 27 and 31, 1976; author's archive. McTaggart's "ecology fad" appears in *Greenpeace III*, p. 9; his "hippie element" spoken to Hunter.

3. Greenpeace Foundation: "Minutes: Board of Directors," January 4, 1977; Greenpeace Foundation financial records: Gannon archives and B.C. Registrar of Companies.

4. Seal Campaign, 1977: "Minutes, Seal Policy Committee," January 10, 1977; interviews, Watson, Hunter, Easton, Moore, Ballem, Al Johnson, Mike Bailey, Erol Baykal; Hunter's Journal, 1977; Hunter, *Warriors*; Watson, *Sea Shepherd* and *Seal Wars*; Coish, *Seasons of the Seal*; Candow, *Of Men and Seals*; *A Bonfire in My Mouth*, Susi Newborn (HarperCollins, 2003), and correspondence; news accounts.

7. Franz Weber: "Toy business offered Newfoundlanders," February 1, 1977; Watson, *Sea Shepherd*; and Coish, *Seasons of the Seal*.

8. Brigitte Bardot: copies of her handwritten journals and English translation, "Victory for the cause of the baby seals," from Sygma/Paris, March 14-19, 1977. Watson writes: "I was not opposed to bringing Brigitte Bardot to the ice floes ... She met me at the airport and kissed me. I did not like Moore trying to dictate to me — that was the problem. Moore never pulled rank on me because I never let him, and this was

the root of his anger on this campaign."

8. Hunter's newspaper interview upon resignation: "Story of the Greenpeace-makers," *The Province*, March 5, 1977.

9. Douglas Channel: Interviews, Marining, Gannon, Linda Spong, Melville Gregory; "Ambush at Douglas Channel," Hunter, *G. Chronicles* #5, July 1977; "Greenpeace," Roger Rapoport, *Outside*, 1979; Jack Davis quoted in "Super Spills," Rod Marining, *Chronicles* #5.

10. Watson dismissal: "Minutes of the Board of Directors Meeting," Greenpeace Foundation, July 7, 1977; author's meeting notes; interviews: Watson, Moore, Hunter, Marining, and Gannon; In *Sea Shepherd*, pp. 152-154, Watson faults the Greenpeace bureaucracy, Moore's ambitions, and their mutual antipathy.

11. *Island Transport*: Don White announced the *Island Transport* would confront the whalers in November 1976, as a "Save the Whales Hawaii," campaign, before the ship was purchased. In correspondence with the author, he recalls, "Save the Whales Hawaii and Greenpeace began to be used interchangeably: 'Greenpeace' did have a succinct ring to it." Groups adopting the name "Greenpeace" date from *Peace News* in 1971. In New Zealand in 1973, "Peace Media" renamed themselves "Greenpeace." Naomi Petersen, cook aboard the *Fri*, told Michael Szabo, quoted in *Making Waves*, "Greenpeace was such a good name — it summed up what we were about."

12. ABC News: Don White received, as Greenpeace, the $60,000 from ABC. Bill Gannon later accounted for the money.

13. The voyage of the *Ohana Kai*: interviews, conversation, and accounts from Korotva, Spong, Kazumi Tanaka, Nancy Jack, Gary Zimmerman, Dino Pignataro, Dexter Cate, and Dick Dillman; Hunter, *Warriors*; Brown and May, *The Greenpeace Story*; and newspaper accounts, *Honolulu Advertiser* and *Star-Bulletin*, November 1976 — August 1977.

14. Australia campaign: Interviews, Bob and Bobbi Hunter, and Hunter notebooks; Hunter, *Warriors*; *Greenpeace Chronicles* #6, October 1977, and #8, September 1978; *The Whaling Question: The Inquiry*, Sir Sidney Frost of Australia (Friends of the Earth, 1979).

15: Greenpeace in Europe, 1977: Interviews, McTaggart, Peter Bouquet; correspondence with Newborn, Parmentier, Peter Wilkinson; Newborn, *Bonfire*; Robie, *Eyes of Fire*; Brown and May, *The Greenpeace*

Story; Mulvaney and Warford, *Witness*; Boettger and Hamdan, *Greenpeace*; and newspaper accounts.

16. *Sir William Hardy*: "Bill of Sale," UK Department of Trade, January 26, 1978, for £32,500 plus the deposit of £4,372, sold to Greenpeace UK Ltd. This price, renegotiated by Hutchinson, is £6,000 below their original bid.

17. Naming the *Rainbow Warrior*: Newborn, *Bonfire*, and correspondence with the author. David Robie's account in *Eyes of Fire*, a generally accurate history, is incorrect. Robie cites a translation of "Le Combattant de l'Arc-en-ciel," from French novelist Hugo Verlomme's *Mer-mere*, through Rémi Parmentier. He points out the source could not be Hunter's *Warriors of the Rainbow*, published a year later in 1978. However, Hunter had inculcated the myth since 1971, Newborn had been exposed to it in March 1977, and the Willoya/Brown *Warriors of the Rainbow*, the actual source, had circulated among the London group.

18. Boarding a whaler: During the last encounter with the *Vladivostock* in the summer of 1977, Pat Moore, American Robert Taunt, Russian translator Rusty Frank, and I boarded harpoon ship ЛК-2027. Sailors told Frank they had found few whales, were bored, and wanted to go home.

19. Ferlinghetti's dream: *Northwest Ecolog*, Lawrence Ferlinghetti (City Lights Books, 1978); and *Greenpeace Chronicles* #8, September 1978; the dreambook has likely perished in the Gregory fire.

20. The first global Greenpeace meeting: author's journal, October 1977; Hunter interview and journal; Moore interview and archives.

FURTHER READING, POETS: Most poets are naturalists, some particularly so: Basho, Li Po, William Blake, Mary Oliver, Denise Levertov, Gary Snyder, Wendell Berry, Susan Griffin, Nanao Sakaki, Diane di Prima, Antler, and Walt Whitman; two good anthologies are *News of the Universe*, Robert Bly (Sierra Club, 1980) and *Poems for the Wild Earth*, Gary Lawless (Blackberry Press, 1994); *Imagining the Earth*, John Elder (U. of Georgia, 1996), is a critical survey.

CHAPTER 11: LAWYERS OF THE RAINBOW

1. John Frizell, in correspondence, recalls the schism of 1978 differently: "The fact that I was a board member but representing new blood, not drawn from the original group, was what caused representatives

of new groups, the 'dissidents', to approach me," he writes. "There was no snub ... saying I was not elected is incorrect." Frizell served on the Greenpeace Foundation board in 1977, but not in 1978 (Annual Reports, BC Reg. of Companies). He recalls that "Most or all of the 'splinter groups' wanted to unite under a single Greenpeace," but not one controlled by the Greenpeace Foundation. See Zelko, *Make it a Greenpeace*, on this schism.

2. Seal Campaign, 1978: Author's notebooks; interviews, Hunter, Moore, Ryan, Martin, Taunt; "The Laws of Nature vs. the Laws of Canada," Hunter, *G. Chronicles* #7, June, 1978; news reports; John Baker, filmed interviews with Leo Ryan, James Jeffords, Pamela Sue Martin, Charles Friend, and John Lundrigan, and our arrest at the fisheries office, CBC television, "Take 30," April 24, 1978; film clip at archives.cbc.ca/300c.asp?id=1-69-867.

3. Greenpeace in Europe, *Rainbow Warrior*: Interviews and correspondence with McTaggart, Parmentier, Newborn, Wilkinson, Bouquet, Harald Zindler, Gerhard Wallmeyer, Christian Krüger; Hunter notebooks; "Why?: The story of Greenpeace," Peter Wilkinson, *Hemisphere* Magazine, 1979; *Greenpeace Chronicles*, #s 7-10, 15, and 21, June 1978 to November 1979; Newborn, *Bonfire*; Brown & May, *The Greenpeace Story*; Robie, *Eyes of Fire*; Zelko, "Make it a Green Peace." Sources conflict over the *Rainbow Warrior* launch date, April 29 or May 2, 1978; this account adheres to Newborn's, May 2.

4. Nuclear industry, 1970s: "Nuclear Power Costs," Leo Ryan, Chairman, US House Subcommittee, Environment, Energy, and Natural Resources, April 26, 1978; *No Nukes,* Anna Gyorgy (South End Press, 1979); Wasserman, *Killing Our Own.*

5. Seal Trials: Author's notebooks, interviews with Gibbons, Ballem, and Moore; "Corelli vs. Duplaise," Canadian legal precedent restricting a public official's discretionary authority.

6. Ryan assassination: Complex and creepy, far beyond the scope of this book; see, *Guyana Massacre: The Eyewitness Account*, Charles Krause (Berkley Books, 1978); *A Sympathetic History of Jonestown*, Rebecca Moore (Edwin Mellon, 1985); for a view skeptical of CIA involvement, see *Raven: The Untold Story of the Reverend Jim Jones and His People*, Tim Reiterman (Dutton, 1982); "Jonestown Massacre," by

Fiona Steel at crimelibrary.com; and "Alternative Considerations of Jonestown" at jonestown.sdsu.edu.

7. Campbell Plowden in Chile: "No Whale Too Sacred," and "On Board a Whaling Boat," Plowden, *G. Chronicles*, #s 14 and 15, March, April 1979.

8. Orkney Islands Seal cull: *Let the Seals Live!*, by Sue Flint (Thule Press, 1979); *The Grey Seal*, by Sheila Anderson, (Shire Publications, 1988); Wilkinson's "Why?" *Hemisphere* 1979, an account of the *Rainbow Warrior* involvement.

FURTHER READING, ENVIRONMENTAL LAW AFTER STOCKHOLM 1972, RADIOACTIVE FALLOUT, WHALES, THE LAW OF THE SEA CONFERENCE, AND 200-MILE FISHERY JURISDICTIONS: *International Law and the Environment*, Patricia Birnie (Clarendon, 1992); "The Most Creative Moments in the History of Environmental Law," by William H. Rodgers, Jr. (*University of Illinois Law Review*, 1, 2000); *International Environmental Law and Policy*, Edith Brown Weiss (Aspen Law & Business, 1998); "The International Whaling Commission and the Future of Cetaceans," William Burns (*Colorado J. of Intern. Environ. Law & Policy*, 1997); and see elaw.org, the Environmental Law Alliance Worldwide.

CHAPTER 12: THE SCEPTRE

1. 1979 seal protests: author's journals; interviews, Moore, Cummings, Bruce Weyler, Steve Sawyer; "To Save a Species," *Greenpeace Chronicles* # 15, April 1979; Watson, *Sea Shepherd* and *Seal Wars*; Brown and May, *Greenpeace Story*; and news accounts.

2. Three Mile Island: *Tales from the Heart of the Beast*, Randall and Marian Thompson (Izzat Publications, 1980), privately published timeline account by a health physics technician who worked at TMI April 1979; *Crisis Contained*, Philip Cantelon (DOE 1982); "Report Of The President's Commission On The Accident At Three Mile Island," at stellar-one.com; "Zirconium Connection," Dr. Daniel Pisello, *Greenpeace Chronicles* #19, September 1979; "Post-Harrisburg," accounts by Gofman, Caldicott, and others, *Chronicles* #16, May 1979; Gyorgy, *No Nukes*; Wasserman, *Killing Our Own*; *Three Mile Island*, Daniel Ford (Penguin, 1982); and *The Warning*, Michael Gray and Ira Rosen (W.W. Norton, 1982)

3. Pirate whaler, *Sierra*: Day, *Whale War*; "The Pirate Whalers," Craig van Note, *Greenpeace Chronicles*, # 11, December 1978; "Pirate Whalers Rammed," Watson, *G. Chronicles* # 19, September 1979; Watson, *Sea Shepherd*; correspondence.

4. "Agreement," between Greenpeace Foundation and Greenpeace Foundation of America, Fund For Greenpeace, and Greenpeace USA, May 1979, unsigned; author's archive.

8. Rocky Flats: interviews, Dr. Anthony Robbins, Colorado Health Dept. and Dr. Carl Johnson, Jefferson County Health Dept, 1977-79; *G. Chronicles*, Weyler, July 1977, June 1978; Kristen Haag case in Wasserman, *Killing Our Own,* Chapter 8; "Health hazards of plutonium release from the Rocky Flats Plant," J.V. Sutherland in *Health Effects of Low Level Radiation*, ed. William Hendee (Appleton-Century-Crofts, 1984); DOA Rocky Flats Citizens Advisory Board at rfcab.org.

7. Greenpeace International: "Terms of Settlement," October 14, 1979, signed by Moore, Weyler, Hunter, Marining, Ballem, Watson, Michael McGonigle, David Garrick (Walrus), Gibbons, and McTaggart; copy, author's archivc.

8. Zelko, *Make it a Green Peace*, examines the forces that engendered the particular shape of Greenpeace International. Thereafter, Zelko points out, in the 1980s, Greenpeace International helped pioneer what Paul Wapner called a new "world civic politics" in *Environmental Activism and World Civic Politics* (State U. of NY, 1996).

FURTHER READING: By 1979, ecological acumen flourished worldwide and any short bibliography would be highly subjective. The following are a selected few of the author's favorites, cited chronologically: *Mind and Nature,* Gregory Bateson (Dutton, 1979); *Gaia. A New Look at Life on the Earth*, James Lovelock (Oxford U., 1979); *The Death of Nature,* Carolyn Merchant (Harper & Row, 1980); *The Reenchantment of the World*, Morris Berman (Cornell U., 1981); *The Politics of the Solar Age*, Hazel Henderson (Bootstrap, 1981); *The Gift of Good Land*, Wendell Berry (North Point, 1981); *The Ecology of Freedom*, Murray Bookchin (Cheshire, 1982); *Deep Ecology*, William Devall and George Sessions (Peregrine Smith, 1985); *The Redesigned Forest*, Chris Maser (R. & E. Miles, 1988); *The Coming of the Cosmic Christ*, Matthew Fox (Harper, 1988); *Ecology, Community and Lifestyle*, Arne Naess (Cambridge U.,

1989); *For the Common Good*, Herman Daly, John Cobb (Beacon, 1989); *In Praise of Nature*, Stephanie Mills (Island Press, 1990); *The End of Nature*, Bill McKibben (Viking, 1990); *The Rebirth of Nature*, Rupert Sheldrake (Bantum, 1991); *The Spell of the Sensuous,* David Abram (Pantheon, 1996); *Darwin Among the Machines*, George Dyson (Penguin, 1997); *The Life of the Cosmos*, Lee Smolin (Oxford U., 1997); *Guns, Germs, and Steel*, Jared Diamond (Norton, 1999); *Widening Circles*, Joanna Macy (New Society, 2000); *Thermageddon*, Robert Hunter (Arcade, 2003); and *The Devil and the Disappearing Sea*, Rob Ferguson (Raincoast, 2003).

CHAPTER ETERNITY: WERELDRAAD

1. Brown, Kistiakowski meeting: author's journal, 1979.

2. Greenpeace International Council and committee meetings: author's journal, 1979; minutes; interviews, Moore, Hunter, McTaggart.

3. Conversation, Hoppe Bar: adapted from author's journal, 1979.

4. A moratorium on pelagic whaling passed at the 1982 International Whaling Commission. French saboteurs bombed the *Rainbow Warrior* in Auckland Harbour, July 10, 1985, killing Fernando Pereira, the first Greenpeace volunteer to perish in the service of ecology. Greenpeace went on to stop nuclear dumping at sea and the transboundary trade in hazardous waste; they stared down Shell Oil over the dumping of petroleum installations and cajoled Coca-cola into abandoning climate-wrecking refrigerants; they changed logging practices from the Canadian boreal forest to the Amazon basin. Brian Fitzgerald, with Greenpeace since 1982, wrote in 2004 that the magic never abandoned Greenpeace: "Ask anyone who sails aboard any of the ships these days, works in the offices, or volunteers in the campaigns, and you'll hear similar stories of the right people turning up at the impossibly right time, with the same passionate sense of ownership of the organization, warts and all, that drives ordinary people to do extraordinary things, then and now."

FURTHER INVESTIGATIONS: For complete and updated links to the sites mentioned, extended and annotated bibliography, Greenpeace and environmental links, other sources, and to correct or contribute information, see author's website: rexweyler.com.

ACKNOWLEDGEMENTS

This story could not have been compiled and told without substantial help. It is with great pleasure that I thank the following contributors:

Lynn Henry, my editor at Raincoast Books, guided the manuscript from beginning to end, through six drafts, with astonishing patience, compassion, expertise, and narrative vision.

Norm Gibbons and Monte Paulsen provided strident assessments of the text, without regard to the author's self-esteem, and the story could not have taken shape without them. Andrew Blauner's faith, in the face of discouraging evidence over several years, proved heartening.

Allan MacDougall at Raincoast Books took the risk to support the protracted research and writing and made the magnanimous decision to print this and other books on post-consumer, recycled paper. The integrity and professionalism of the team at Raincoast Books — Michelle Benjamin, Kevin Williams, Jesse Finkelstein, Genevieve Nicholson, David Leonard, Jamie Broadhurst, Simone Doust, Paul Hodgson, Scott Steedman, Monique Trottier, Tom Best, Cindy Connor, Teresa Bubela and many others — inspired the author throughout. Copyeditor Barbara Kuhne caught numerous glitches while improving the text.

Rodale Press provided critical support in publishing the English language edition of this book worldwide. The author thanks Stephanie Tade, Jennifer Kushnier, Cathy Gruhn, Tom Mulderick, Jane Tappuni, Anne Lawrance, the team at Rodale US, Rodale UK, Pan Macmillan Australia, and Pan Macmillan New Zealand.

I am deeply indebted to the authors whose books comprise the Greenpeace cannon, as detailed in the Chapter Notes. Notably, Robert Hunter's writings, daily journals from 1969 through 1979, and many hours of interviews comprise a primary source. Frank Zelko's "Make it a Green Peace: The History of an International Environmental Organization" (Ph.D. dissertation, University of Kansas, 2003), is the first objective, broadly sourced history of Greenpeace; Zelko provided the author with indispensable interviews, critique, and assistance.

Ben Metcalfe's keen grasp of history added depth to this story. Dorothy Metcalfe, Dorothy Stowe, Barbara and Robert Stowe, Pat and Eileen Moore, Zoe Hunter, Hamish Bruce, Lyle Thurson, Myron MacDonald, Bobbi Hunter, Davie Gibbons, Rod Marining, Jim and Marie Bohlen, Paul Watson, David Garrick, Terry Simmons, Paul Spong, Linda Spong, Fred Easton, Ron Precious, and Bill Gannon supplied essential perspectives on the early years of Greenpeace. Pete Wilkinson, Rémi Parmentier, Susi Newborn, and David McTaggart helped with the European history. Francine and Glenn Jonathans, Albert Hendrix, and Kerst Das provided background history and hospitality in Amsterdam.

Steve Erwood at Greenpeace International served as a hub for critical communications over three years. Erwood, Brian Fitzgerald, Rémi Parmentier, Sara Holden, Steve Sawyer, Elaine Lawrence, and Peter Tabuns reviewed the manuscript and provided important insights. The author thanks Alison Cox, Natasha van Bentum, Gerd Leipold, Elkie Jordans, Geert Drieman, Gijs Thieme, Kerstin Eitner, Conny Böttger, Fouad Hamdan, Peter Bouquet, Harald Zindler, Gerhard Wallmeyer, Christian Krüger, Peter Küster, Regine Frerichs, Martini Gotjé, John Passacantando, Dick Dillman, John Frizell, Laura Lombardi, Kieran Mulvaney, Joanne Dufay, Rob Milling, Kim Kerridge, Rebecca Moershel, Jen Stefferahn, Carol Gregory, Melanie Hill, Bunny McDiarmid, Sonia Zavesky, Steve Smith, and other Greenpeace volunteers and staff for support, ideas, and goodwill.

Although I relied on the help of others, any historical errors that persist in the text remain the responsibility of the author alone.

Danielle LaPorte, Ian Weir, Tom Campbell, Leigh Badgley, Chris Aikenhead, John and Leslie Izzo, Jeremy Eynon, Lew and Jilly Carlino, David Wimbury, Arthur Evrensel, David Shipway, George Sirk, and David

Abram provided feedback, tips, and professional guidance. *The Vancouver Sun*, *Shared Vision* magazine, and Dragonfly Media published portions of this book, 2001-2004.

Special thanks to Joel Solomon, Carol Newell, Renewal Partners, Nicole Rycroft and Markets Initiative, Gregor Robertson and Happy Planet, Dana Bass Solomon, the team at Hollyhock and Hollyhock Leadership Institute, the Social Venture Institute, Tides Canada Foundation, Shivon Robinsong, Bill Weaver and Media That Matters, Jason Mogus and Communicopia, and Ron Williams and Dragonfly Media.

To Pat Skidmore, my wife Lisa Gibbons and my boys — Liam, Jonah, and Jack: I thank them for their patience and support.

Many acts of courage and commitment by Greenpeace volunteers and other citizens during the era of this story are not recounted in this tale, and I owe them all a special acknowledgement. Many others — and I was not able to mention them all by name — contributed immeasurably to this telling. Thank you all.

INDEX

ABC TV, 461, 466
Achterberg, Rien, 217–18
Akutan, Aleutian Islands, 108–9
Alert Bay, 97, 126, 336
Alinsky, Saul, 389
All Seasons Park protest, 75–78
Amchitka Island US Federal Wildlife Refuge, 81
Amchitka nuclear bomb tests, 55–56, 58–59, 130–31, 132; *Greenpeace* (boat) and, 78–80, 87–88, 90, 94; protests against, 55–60, 64–68, 69–70, 72, 74, 81–82, 86–87, 96–96, 103–4, 110–11, 115–16, 122–23, 129–30
American nuclear bomb tests, 18–21, 22-27. *See also* Amchitka nuclear bomb tests
Amory, Cleveland, 347, 531
Animal Bill of Rights, 252
Atomic Energy Commission, 81
Australian whaling protest, 471–75, 483
Bailey, Mike, 423, 424
Baker, Bobby, 467
Ballem, Peter, 446–47, 495, 496–99, 517–18
Banyacya, Thomas, 391
Bardot, Brigitte, 448–50
Barrett, Dave, 232, 344
Beale, Albert, 475–76
Bell, Denise, 475–76, 478–79
Belle Isle, seal campaign in, 365, 367–68, 371–73, 446
benefit concerts, 267, 344, 468–71, 556–57
Bensasson, Janine, 152, 167–68
Berry, Wendell, 550–51
Bigalow, Albert, 36–37
Bigg, Michael, 214
Blanc Sablon, seal campaign in, 445–46, 448, 449, 450
blue whale, 284, 542
Bohlen, Jim, 43–45, 65–66
Bohlen, Marie (née Nonnast), 43–44, 65, 86, 88
boycott, French wine, 201
Brown, Jerry, 565–66
Bruce, Hamish, 61, 62–63, 278–79
Byrde's whales, 542

Campaign for Nonviolent Action, 40–41
Campaign for Nuclear Disarmament, 36, 146
Campbell, Tom, 469–71
Canadian government harassment of protesters, 82–83, 84, 179, 244, 398–99, 364, 376, 493, 495–98
Canadian uranium, 173, 244, 563
Cannikin nuclear bomb test (Amchitka 1971), 59, 130–31
Carter, Nick, 512, 541, 543
Cashin, Richard, 362, 363, 448
Castle-Bravo nuclear bomb test (Bikini Atoll 1954), 22–27
Cates, J. A., 293
Chechik, Michael, 466, 476
Cheynes Beach whaling station, 472–75, 483–84
Chivers, Eileen, 354, 374
Clapp, Alan, 264–65, 390
Claverie, Christian, 181–83
Clifton, Oliver, 454, 455
Cobb, Ron, 62
Cobb seamounts, 300
Codpeace, 361, 516
Commoner, Barry, 520
coral atolls, 157
Cormack, John, 78–80, 86, 254–55, 441, 462. *See also* Phyllis Cormack
Cormack, Phyllis, 86
Coté, Paul, 60, 78–79
Cotter, John, 280
Cree First Nation, 396–97
Cuban missile crisis, 38
Cummings, Bob, 47, 48
Cunningham, Jack, 219
d'Easum, Lille, 69
Dalnyi Vostok whaling factory ship, 314–16, 409, 412, 433, 467; Greenpeace disruption of hunt by, 414–15, 426–27, 428–30, 432
Daly, Ed, 417–18, 420, 432
Darlington Nuclear Generating Station, 545
Darnell, Bill, 53, 67, 86
Davidson, Grant, 156
Davies, Brian, 347, 450
Davis, Charles, 462
Davis, Jack, 82–83, 453
Davis, Patsy, 462
Day, Dorothy, 34
Decker's Boarding House, 358, 494–95
Deep Throat (whaling informant), 398, 407
de Gaulle, Charles, 134
Dellwood Knolls, 289
Desplats, Nicholas, 280
Dillon, Janice, 514
dioxins, 352
dolphins, Risso's, 401
Don't Make a Wave Committee, 57, 60, 65, 66–67, 70–71, 72, 74, 87, 135–36, 137
Doran, Jerry, 543–44
Douglas Channel, 453–56
Douglas Point nuclear plant, 511
Drummond, Bree, 226
Dworkin, Larry, 527–28
Dyson, George, 214
Earl, Randy, 514
Earth First!, 521
Earthforce, 457
Easton, Fred, 287, 297, 311, 314, 317, 318–22
ecology symbol, 62

Ecotactics handbook, 69
"ecotage," 402, 521
Edgewater Fortune (*Greenpeace II*), 111, 127–29
Einstein, Albert, 18, 34
Ephron, Amy, 333–34, 462
extinction, 522–23
factory ships, whaling, 293, 311–25
factory trawlers, 307–8
Falkowski, Ramon, 280
Farquarson, Ken, 53–54
Ferlinghetti, Lawrence, 482–83
Fermi, Enrico, 18, 20–21
Feroce, Dennis, 269, 454–55
film offer, Paramount, 333–34, 462
fin whales, 306, 504
Fineberg, Richard, 88–89, 105
Firnung, Bernd, 363
fish stocks, decline of, 97
fishing limit, 200-mile, 278, 363, 435
Flowers, Charles, 277–78
Fortom-Gouin, Jean-Paul, 471–74
Four Seasons Hotel protest, 75–78
Francolon, Jean-Claude, 366, 374–75
Franks, Don, 529, 530
French government, and Moruroa protests, 149, 176, 178, 183, 223–24
French Navy, 162–63, harassment of *Vega*, 170, 172, 178, 180, 218, 221; in Vancouver, 201–2
French nuclear bomb tests, 133–35, 146, 157, 180, 216–17, 224–25, 246
Fri, 217–18
Friend, Charles, 495, 496–97, 498, 514–15
Frizell, John, 490
Fruchtman, Peter, 390, 398
Gallot, Jean, 338
Gannon, Bill, 341–43, 487
Garby-Lacrouts, Thierry, 243, 337–39
Garcia, Jerry, 469
Garrick, David (Walrus Oakenbough), 76, 259–60, 297, 340, 357–58, 549–50
Georgia Straight, The, 46
Germany, Greenpeace, 501, 539–40, 568
Gibbons, Davie, 514–15
Ginsberg, Allen, 47, 228
Gitga't First Nation, 453, 454
Gofman, John, 81
Golden Rule, 36–37
Gotje, Martin, 217–18
gray whales, 283–84, 285
Great Whale Conspiracy, 247, 265, 266, 267–68, 269–71. *See also* whale campaign
Greek monk seal hunt, 538–39
Green Panthers, 61
Green Party, 501, 512, 540
Greenpeace (boat), 67–68. *See also* Phyllis Cormack
Greenpeace: administration, 346, 442, 458–59, 546, 558, 569–71; ecology manifesto, 393; factional disagreements, 226–27, 229–32; finances, 341–43, 349–50, 388, 394–95, 397, 425, 433, 434, 442–44, 459, 462–63, 486–87; lawsuit, 549; Vancouver office, 256, 350; trademark, 394, 439
Greenpeace Annual General Meeting (1977), 442
Greenpeace Chronicles, 345, 393, 441, 510, 512, 545
Greenpeace V. See Phyllis Cormack
Greenpeace Foundation, 135–36, 137, 558

Greenpeace IV (*La Flor*), 245–46
Greenpeace global offices, 252, 347, 404, 443–44, 481, 485–87, 501, 540; administration, 485–86, 490–93; Germany, 501, 539–40, 568; Hawaii, 444, 460–62, 486–87; San Francisco, 433, 434, 546, 548–49 UK, 476–80, 481; unification of, 546–64, 558–63, 569–71
Greenpeace VI. See Vega
Greenpeace VII. See James Bay
Greenpeace III. See Vega
Greenpeace III, Journey into the Bomb (book), 440
Greenpeace II (*Edgewater Fortune*), 111, 127–29
Green Robes, 149
Gregory, Mel, 297, 248, 300–301, 402, 441–42, 455
Griefahn, Monika, 539–40
Groot, Huig de (Hugo Grotius), 158
Gyorgy, Anna, 520–21, 536
Gypsy moths, 545
Haddleton, Roger, 146, 161
Hagwilget First Nation, 557
Haida Gwaii (Queen Charlotte Islands), 292–96
harpoon boats, 316–17, 318–21
harp seal campaign, 340, 345–46, 347, 352–76, 387, 438–39, 444–51, 493–501, 514–19, 527, 531
Harrison, Hank, 330–31
Hawaii, whale campaign in, 419–26. *See also* Ohana Kai
Heimann, Rolf, 245–46
Heintzman, Tom, 514
helicopters, 363, 364, 376
Herron, Matt, 280, 285–86
Hewitt, Al, 260, 297
Hiroshima, 21
Hogan, Lou, 88–89
Holtom, Gerald, 36
Hopi Nation, 391–92, 555, 556
Horn, Paul, 210, 211
Horne, Ann-Marie, 221, 222–23
Horne, Gene, 146, 156
Hudson, Richard, 246
Hunter, Bob, 31–33, 37–40, 48–51, 212, 233–35, 340, 351, 442, 451–52, 479, 502; at Amchitka protests, 56–58; and Australian whale hunt, 471–75; and Greenpeace Foundation, 135–36; health, 203, 403–5; and International Board, 491–93; and David McTaggart, 200–201, 440; in seal campaign, 354, 357, 358–59, 374–75, 444–45; and Whole Earth Church, 150. *See also* whale campaign
Hunter, Bobbi (née Innes), 451–52, 471–75
Hunter, Zoe (née Rahim), 39, 200–201
hunting protest, trophy, 557–58
Hyak, 207, 208
Icelandic whalers, 475, 504–5
Ingram, Nigel, 145, 221–22, 223
Innes, Bobbi, 240–41. *See also* Hunter, Bobbi
International Whaling Commission, 211, 215–16, 259, 307, 435, 542; 1975 meeting, 304–5, 323; 1976 meeting, 407; 1977 meeting, 472; 1979 meeting, 540–41
Jack, Nancy, 467

Jackson, Will, 288–89, 297, 318
James Bay (*Greenpeace VII*), 388–89, 399, 402, 403, 408, 419–26; whaling protests, 397–433, 463, 464–65
Japan, whale campaign in, 241–42, 389, 439
Japanese whalers, 407, 419, 421, 542
Jeanne d'Arc protest, 201–3
Jerry Garcia Band, 468–71
Johnson, Al "Jet," 353, 369
Johnson, William, 538
Joliot, Jean Frédéric, 151
Jones, Will, 126–27
Juneau, *Phyllis Cormack* in, 125
Kaga, Marilyn, 353
Kannon, 257–58
Keddy, Caroline, 468–70
Keziere, Robert, 86
killer whale. *See* orca
Killer Whale (*Orcinus Orca*) Foundation (KWOOF), 209
Kistiakowsky, George, 565–66
Kitimat Pipeline Company protest, 453–56
Klemtu, *Phyllis Cormack* in, 98
Kodiak, *Phyllis Cormack* in, 124
Korotva, George, 260, 297, 460
Kunz, Jeff, 530
Kwakiutl First Nation, 97
La Flor (*Greenpeace IV*), 245–46
La Paimpolaise, 180–81
Lakota Nation, 556
Lalonde, Brice, 477, 501–2
Lavender, Barry, 345
Law of the Sea, 158
Law of the Sea Conference, 278
LeBlanc, Romeo, 276, 376, 448, 450, 493
Lett, Roberto, 49, 160, 162
Lewis, John, 507
Lightfoot, Gordon, 233
Linton, Annie, 530–31
Loftsson, Kristján, 504
Longini, Jacques, 264, 280, 286
Lornie, Mary, 221–22
Lundrigan, John, 496, 516, 517
MacDonald, Myron, 261, 278, 279
MacLeod, Bonnie, 353
Maddy, 63–64
Makarov, Nikolai, 435–36
Mallard, Derrick, 56
Mallard, Gwen, 56
Marining, Rod, 75–78, 150–52, 168–69, 257, 455
McFadyen, Joanna, 530
McIntyre, Joan, 332
McLeod, Dan, 46
McTaggart, David, 366, 479–80; assaulted by French Navy, 221–23, 224; –Ben Metcalfe friction, 153, 155, 156–57, 158–59, 161; Bob Hunter's book about, 440; and global Greenpeace offices, 476–78, 486, 547–48, 550, 551–53, 559–60; and Greenpeace Europe, 353, 503, 537, 538, 552; lawsuits against French government by, 157–58, 197, 199, 219–20, 230, 243–44, 337–39; and Moruroa campaign, 142–48, 152–62, 183–85; and smuggling charges, 147–48, 153–54
McTaggart, Drew, 223–24
Meander, 454–55
media: and seal campaign, 365–66, 375, 498, 500; and whale campaign, 272, 276, 277–78, 322–23, 328–30, 406, 407, 420–21, 466.

See also Francolon, Jean-Claude
Mendocino Ridge, whaling protests at, 298–325
Mendocino Whale War, 441
Metcalfe, Ben, 29–31, 46–47, 53–54, 83, 95–96; –David McTaggart friction, 153, 155, 156–57, 158–59, 161; Moruroa campaign, 136–37, 139–41, 149, 152–62, 163–65
Metcalfe, Dorothy (née Harris), 31, 104, 140, 163–65
M'Gonigle, Michael, 552
Midway Islands, 422–23
Milrow nuclear bomb test (Amchitka Island 1969), 55–59, 81
"mindbombs," 73, 76, 332
Mitchell, Joni, 70, 151
Miwa, Taeko, 260
Moby Dick (German protest boat), 539
Moby Doll, 204, 249–50
Moodie, David, 217–18
Moodie, Emma, 217–18
Moore, Patrick, 79–82, 236, 297, 442, 452, 547, 548–49; –Paul Watson friction, 284, 351; and seal hunt protests, 354, 499–500, 530
Morse, Paul "Pablo," 353
Moruroa campaigns, 139–42, 144–85, 245–46
Mosquito, Fred, 396–97
Mowat, Farley, 210–12
Mumford, Lewis, 34
Murphy, Rex, 355
Musgrove, Kurt, 266
Musicians United for Safe Energy (MUSE), 556–57
Muste, A. J., 34, 40
Myers, Norman, 522
Nagasaki, 21
"Natural Guard" news network, 521
Navajo Nation, 556
New Zealand government, harassment of David McTaggart by, 147–48, 153–54, 155
Newborn, Susi, 475–77, 478–79, 480, 481, 537–39, 552
Newfoundland Fishermen, Food, and Allied Workers Union (NFFAW), 363
Newfoundland Law Society, 514, 517
Newman, Murray, 204, 208
Nielson, Henrietta, 353
Nielson, Stolt, 484
Nixon, Richard, 110
No Nukes, 510
non-violence, 457, 521
Northey, Richard, 146
Norwegian whalers, 262
Notre Dame protests, 167
nuclear accident, Chelyabinsk, 100
nuclear bomb, opposition to, 19, 21, 34, 35–36
nuclear bomb testing: American, 18–21, 22–27, 55–59; ban, 175; French, 133–35, 180, 225, 340. *See also* Amchitka nuclear bomb tests; nuclear weapons
nuclear reactors, 392, 503, 509–11, 520
nuclear waste, 392, 505–7, 555
nuclear weapons, 436, 451, 531–32, 565–66
Oakenbough, Walrus (David Garrick), 76, 259–60, 297, 340, 357–58, 549–50
Ohana Kai, 460–61, 463, 464, 465–68, 487
orca capture, 62, 344–45, 388
orca studies, 203–210, 214–15

Orkney Islands, gray seal hunt in, 508, 520
papal audience, Greenpeace, 165–67
Parmentier, Rémi, 477–78, 551–52
Payne, Henry, 253–54, 258–59
Peace News, 475–76
peace symbol, origin of, 36
Persky, Stan, 47
Peruvian boat in Moruroa campaign, 149, 160
Peter Principle, The, 458
Phyllis Cormack, 441; (*Greenpeace*), 78–80, 87–88, 90, 94; (*Greenpeace V*), 254, 255, 264, 351. *See also* Amchitka nuclear bomb tests; whale campaign
Pignataro, Dino, 467
Pilgrim, Doug, 494–95
Pilgrim, Roy, 357, 358–59
pirate whalers, 521–22, 541, 542
Plowden, Campbell, 524
plutonium, 392, 441, 555–56, 557
Polaris submarine protests (Groton CT), 40–41
porpoises, Dall's, 283
Portland, *James Bay* in, 400
Precious, Ron, 260–61, 297, 354
Project Jonah, 211
protest boats, 36–37, 61, 62–64, 67–68, 70, 141, 217, 454–55, 539. *See also* James Bay; La Flor; Ohana Kai; Phyllis Cormack; Vega; Zodiacs
Quakers, 28
Quebec, seal campaign in, 445–46
Queen Charlotte Islands (Haida Gwaii), 292–96
radiation sickness, 21, 22–23, 26–27, 81, 134–35, 201, 511–12, 534–35, 536
Rainbow Warrior, 479–80, 502–3, 505–7, 552, and seal hunt, 508, 527; and whaling protest, 504–5, 507–8. *See also* Sir William Hardy
Raines, Mark, 531
Rarotonga, *Vega* in, 160
Reggane nuclear tests, 134
Reid, Madeleine, 163–65
Richardson, Jack, 334–36
Rippey, Betty, 459
Rising-Moore, Carl, 361–62
Rochebrochard, Patrick de la, 181–82
Rocky Flats plutonium trigger plant, 555–56
Rotblatt, Joseph, 19
Roys, Thomas, 293
Rubin, Jerry, 47
Russell, Bertrand, 35–36
Russian trawler, in Vancouver, 343–44
Russian whalers, 401, 407, 508. *See also* Dalnyi Vostok; Vladivostok
Ryan, Leo, 523–24
St. Anthony, Newfoundland, 356–68, 494–500
San Francisco Greenpeace office, 347–48, 433, 434, 461
San Francisco, whale campaign in, 401–3, 468–71
Sand Point, *Greenpeace* at, 117–18
Schlesinger, James, 130
Scott, Peter, 211
Scottish nuclear protest, 503
Seabright, Gordon, 515, 517–19
seal hunt: campaign against Canadian harp, 340, 345–46, 347, 352–76, 387, 438–39, 444–51, 493–501, 514–19, 527, 531; Greek monk, 538–39; Orkney Islands, 508, 520; Pribilof Islands, 544, 545–46

Seal Protection Act, 493, 496
Sea Shepherd, 521, 543–44
Servan-Schreiber, Jean-Jacques, 243
Sierra (pirate whaling ship), 542–44
Sierra Club, 59–60, 68
Silkwood, Karen, 520, 545
Simmons, Terry, 59, 86
Sir William Hardy (*Rainbow Warrior*), 478–79
Skana, 205–8, 234–35, 266–67
Soviet warships, in Vancouver, 435–36
Soviet whalers, 401, 407, 508. *See also* Dalnyi Vostok; Vladivostok
Spanish whalers, 507–8
Spatsizi Plateau, 557–58
SPEC, 56
Speier, Jacqueline, 523
sperm whale, 259, 312, 317, 318, 418–19, 483–84, 541
Spong, Paul, 62, 203–4, 205–16, 261–63, 304–6, 403
spruce budworms, 456
squid, giant, 405–6
Stowe, Dorothy, 41–42, 64–65. *See also* Strasmich, Dorothy
Stowe, Irving, 41–42, 52–53, 64–65, 240, 251–52; and Amchitka benefit concert, 70, 73–74. *See also* Strasmich, Irving
Strasmich, Dorothy Anne (Rabinowitz), 27–28, 41–42. *See also* Stowe, Dorothy
Strasmich, Irving, 27–28, 33–34, 35, 41–42. *See also* Stowe, Irving
Supertramp, 390
synchronicity, 248
Szilard, Leo, 18, 21
Tasu, *Phyllis Cormack* in, 295
Teller, Edward, 25
Test Ban Treaty, 55, 176
Thornton, Allan, 475–76
Three Mile Island nuclear reactor, 532–35
Thurston, Lyle, 86, 278, 279
Tofino, *Phyllis Cormack* in, 274
Trinity nuclear bomb test (New Mexico, 1945), 18–21
Trudeau, Pierre, 199
Trueman, Carlie, 260, 280, 297
Turner, Ron, 330
Tussman, David, 547, 548–49
United Fishermen and Allied Workers Union, 276–77
United Nations Conference on Human Habitat (Vancouver), 390–91
United Nations Conference on the Human Environment (Stockholm), 172–73, 174–75
Universal Life Church, 63, 155
uranium, Canadian, 173, 244, 563
Vancouver Aquarium, 204, 344
Vancouver highway protest, 53
Vega, 244; (*Greenpeace III*), 144, 145, 169–72, 176–78, 179–83, 220; (*Greenpeace VI*), 264, 266, 271, 285–86. *See also* Moruroa campaigns
Vietnam war, Canadian military research for, 52
Vladivostok, 464, 482
Vostok. *See* Dalnyi Vostok
Wade, Alan, 403
Wallace, Jack, 363
Ward, Hal, 427, 428
Warriors of the Rainbow, 97–98, 396–97
water pollution, 539, 545

Watson, Paul, 71, 76–78, 241, 279, 297, 340, 438, 457; –Patrick Moore friction, 284, 351; and pirate whalers, 521–22, 543–44; and seal hunt, 369–70, 374–75, 444–47, 528, 531
Weber, Franz, 448, 449
Weiss, David, 425–26
Wells, Bob, 514
Wells, Clyde, 517
Weyler, Bruce, 530
Weyler, Rex, 137–39, 499, 500, 514–16, 521, 548
whale campaign, 233–35, 253–337, 346–47, 395–436, 460–75; benefit concerts, 267, 395–96; film and photos, 311, 318–21, 328, 411; international, 241–42, 389, 439, 444, 471–75, 483–84; US informant, 398, 407; Whale Shows, 227, 232–33, 241–42, 294, 295, 296, 305
whale hunt, 293–94, 316–17, 331–32, 541. *See also* whaling
whales, 203–210, 212–15, 249–51, 542; fin, 306, 504; gray, 238–39, 283–84, 285; sperm, 259, 312, 317, 318, 418–19, 483–84, 541
whaling, 262, 401, 407, 409, 475, 519; moratorium, 174, 215; pirate, 389, 512, 521–22, 541, 542; records, 261–63. *See also* Dalnyi Vostok; Vladivostok
Whaling Commission. *See* International Whaling Commission
White, Don, 460
Whole Earth Church, 150. *See also* Universal Life Church
Wickaninnish Bay, 283–85
Wilde, James, 233
Wilkes, Leigh, 261, 287
Wilkinson, Peter, 480, 505
Willens, Dan, 353
Winter Harbour, protest boats in, 275–80, 297
Winter, Paul, 284–85, 344, 524–25
Woof, Peter, 543–44
World Greenpeace Foundation. *See* Greenpeace Foundation
World Wildlife Fund, 479
Wright, Bob, 344
Zimmerman, Gary, 283, 467
Zindler, Harald, 539
Zodiacs, 225–26, 282, 292, 298–99, 455; and nuclear waste protest, 507; photography from, 260, 306, 320, 411–12; and whaling protest, 317–21, 410, 411–12, 413–14, 415, 432, 464–65, 473–75

PHOTO CREDITS

PAGES 186–194:

1. Courtesy of Dorothy Stowe; 2. Courtesy of Dorothy Metcalfe; 3. Courtesy of Ben Metcalfe; 4. Ron Cobb's ecology symbol is in the public domain; 5. Courtesy of Dorothy Stowe; 6. Courtesy of Jim Bohlen; 7. Courtesy of Robert Stowe; 8. Photo by Robert Keziere; 9. Photo by Robert Keziere; 10. Photo by Rex Weyler; 11. Courtesy of Rod Marining; 12. Photo by Gerry Deiter; 13–14. Photos by Grant Davidson; 15. Photo by Gerry Deiter, Courtesy of Paul Spong; 16–25. Photos by Rex Weyler; 26. Courtesy of Rex Weyler

PAGES 377–384:

1. Courtesy of Rex Weyler; 2. Photo by Patrick Moore; 3. Photo by Rex Weyler; 4. Photo by Pat Moore 5. Courtesy of Susi Newborn; 6–12. Photos by Rex Weyler; 13. Photo by Matt Heron; 14. Photo by Nick Wilson; 15–16. Photos by Rex Weyler; 17. Courtesy of Bob Hunter; 18. Photo by Hilari Anderson; 19. Photo by Robert Godfrey; 20. Photo by Rex Weyler; 21. Courtesy of Greenpeace; 22. Photo by Rex Weyler

PHOTO CREDIT: KEN VILLENEUVE

REX WEYLER is a journalist, writer, and ecologist. He was born in Denver, Colorado in 1947, went to high school in Midland, Texas, and attended Occidental College in Los Angeles. Weyler worked as an apprentice engineer for Lockheed in 1967, but left engineering to pursue a career in journalism. In 1969, he published his first book, a pacifist discourse with photographs from a winter in California's Yosemite Valley.

Weyler immigrated to Canada in 1972, worked at the *North Shore News* in North Vancouver, and with Greenpeace since 1973. He sailed on the first Greenpeace whale campaign, was editor of the *Greenpeace Chronicles*, the organization's first monthly news magazine, and was a cofounder of Greenpeace International in 1979. His photographs and news stories helped make Greenpeace a household name around the world.

Weyler received a Pulitzer Prize nomination for his Native American history, *Blood of the Land*, and he co-authored the self-help classic *Chop Wood, Carry Water*. He co-founded Hollyhock Educational Centre on Cortes Island in British Columbia, dedicated to environmental, personal, and professional studies. It remains Canada's leading educational retreat centre.

Weyler is editor-at-large for Dragonfly Media in the US and Canada, writes for magazines and newspapers, and is widely reprinted in print and on the Internet. He lives in Vancouver, BC, is married, and has three sons.